Charles Carroll Fulton

Europe Viewed through American Spectacles

Charles Carroll Fulton

Europe Viewed through American Spectacles

ISBN/EAN: 9783337213053

Printed in Europe, USA, Canada, Australia, Japan

Cover: Foto ©Andreas Hilbeck / pixelio.de

More available books at **www.hansebooks.com**

EUROPE

VIEWED THROUGH

AMERICAN SPECTACLES.

BY

CHARLES CARROLL FULTON,

EDITOR OF THE BALTIMORE AMERICAN.

"C. C. F."

PHILADELPHIA:
J. B. LIPPINCOTT & CO.
1874.

Entered according to Act of Congress, in the year 1873, by
CHARLES C. FULTON,
In the Office of the Librarian of Congress at Washington.

Lippincott's Press,
Philadelphia.

PREFACE AND DEDICATION.

"EUROPE VIEWED THROUGH AMERICAN SPECTACLES"—the title chosen for this book of travels—will be found to express its distinctive characteristics. It contains precisely such facts about Europe, and the social life and peculiarities of the people of most of the Continental nations, as all Americans ought to know, which they desire to know, and which are usually ignored in similar books of travel.

The author visited Europe to inform himself as to the difference between life abroad and life at home, and to study the social questions of different nations. He has endeavored to describe what came under his observation with fairness and candor, so that the reader may see exactly what he saw, and travel hand in hand with him. The contents of this volume were published in the columns of THE BALTIMORE AMERICAN mostly during the past year, as familiar letters, written in the haste of travel. They are now placed in book-form in compliance with what seems to be a very general demand, and in the hope that their extensive dissemination may lead all Americans to hold in higher estimation their own free institutions, and to cherish and love the land where freedom of speech and of the press exists,—where the youth of the country are not reared in military barracks or slaughtered on battle-fields to uphold the "divine right" of kings,—where religion is not hampered by state interference,—where marriage is not obstructed by laws which render immorality and vice the necessary fate of a large class of the people,—and where women are regarded as the helpmates and bosom companions of men, and neither bartered off in marriage for a money consideration, nor used by hundreds of thousands as common laborers in field-work and among bricks and mortar,—where they are not required to do scavenger-work, be the bearers of the heaviest burdens, or draw carts and wagons yoked by the side of mangy curs.

By those who have visited Europe this volume will be found especially interesting, entertaining, and amusing; to those who intend to visit Europe, the author thinks it will be more valuable than most of the guide-books; and to those who do not expect to make a European tour, it will furnish much practical information that cannot be found in any other volume extant.

To the Press of the country generally, which has so largely published fragmentary extracts from this tour of Europe, it is respectfully dedicated, in the hope that it will still further aid in enabling all Americans to see Europe through "American Spectacles." To our friend and fellow-traveler of ante-bellum times, that prince of good fellows, Murat Halstead, Esq., Editor of the *Cincinnati Commercial*, and our excellent friends, Colonel George W. Childs, Editor of the *Philadelphia Ledger*, and Hugh J. Hastings, Esq., of the *New York Commercial*, all of whom have given to their readers such copious extracts, we especially tender our thanks for a generous appreciation of our labors.

C. C. F.

TABLE OF CONTENTS.

	PAGE
OCEAN EXPERIENCES	9
Monotony of Ocean Travel	9
Experiences of the Sea	9
Amusements at Sea	10
Charms of the Sea	11
First Impressions of the Sea	301
Miseries of the Sea	302
Intimacies of the Sea	302
Jollities of the Sea	303
Sunday on Shipboard	304
Icebergs on the Ocean	305
Among the Icebergs	305
Homeward Bound	308
The Ocean Highway	309
CITY OF BREMEN	12
Sunday at Bremen	13
Emigration to America	13
A Beautiful City	13
Undecayed Mummies	14
CITY OF BERLIN	14
Trials of Travel	14
The Royal Museum	15
Impressions of Berlin	15
Working Women	15
Working Dogs	16
Cost of Royalty	16
Berlin and its People	17
Military Display	17
The Berlin Opera	17
Berlin Hotels	18
CITY OF DRESDEN	19
First-class Travel	19
Masculine Kisses	19
Beer-Drinking	19
Impressions of Dresden	20
Dresden by Gas-light	21
The Green Vault	21
Dress of the People	22
Old Churches	22
Sunday in Dresden	22
The Zwinger Palace	23
Sunday on the Elbe	23
Dresden Houses	23
Market-Places	24
Pet Sparrows	24
CITY OF VIENNA	25
Vienna the Beautiful	25
Working Women	26
Café Life in Vienna	26, 63

	PAGE
CITY OF VIENNA—Continued.	
Drinking-Water	27
Shopping in Vienna	27
Ladies of Vienna	28
Religious Freedom	28
The Volksgarten	28
Vienna Hotels	29
Twelve Hours a Day's Work	29
The Ringstrasse	30
The Grand Opera	30, 43, 53
A Paper-money Country	31
The Esterhazy Keller	32
The Vienna Exposition	32, 38, 48, 71, 76
The "Dutch Treat"	34
Emperor's Summer Palace	35
Scenes on the Präter	36, 50
Experience of German Life	37
Strauss and his Music	39
Street Scenes in Vienna	39
Funerals by Contract	40, 67
Wedding Peculiarities	41
The Royal Jewels	41
Virtue of the Empire	41
Life among the People	41
American Drinks	42
Vienna Building Associations	44
Austrian Germany	46
"Nix Deutsch"	47
A Musical People	47, 68
Grand Military Review	53
Vienna Fire Department	55
The Beauty of Vienna	56
Kissing Hands	57, 77
Austrian Politeness	57
Beer and Coffee	58
Vienna General Hospital	58
Vienna Extortion	60
Morals and Marriage	60
Marriage among the Well-born	61
German Life—Beer-Drinking	63
Absence of Intoxicating Liquors	64
Scarcity of Drinking-Water	64
The Vienna Bourse	65
Austrian Women	65
The Military Adonis	66
Want to go to America	67
Respect for the Law	68
The German Birthday	71
The Catholic Shrines	72
Poodle Dogs	73
The Austrian Ladies	74
The Workingwomen	75
Gentlemen of Vienna	75
Foreign and Home Food	77

TABLE OF CONTENTS.

	PAGE
PESTH AND TRIESTE	78
From Pesth to Trieste	78
Down the Danube	78
City of Trieste	79–82
Pesth and Ofen	80
The Blue Adriatic	81
The Women of Trieste	83
Railroad Experiences	83–84
The City of Steyer	85
GERMAN WATERING-PLACES	85
Hall, and how we got there	86
A Chapter of Mishaps	86
Advice to Travelers	87
Attractions of Hall	88–90
The Austrian Women	89
Strong-minded Women	89
The Austrian German	92
Vice in the Cities	93
Virtue in the Rural Districts	93
German Temperance	94
Extreme Politeness	94
German Summer Resorts	95
Use of Tobacco	95
Baden-Baden on Sunday	96
The Gambling Scene	97–100
Rouge-et-Noir	97–101
The Springs,—"Hell"	99
The Conversationshaus	99
The Temple of Silence	102
Temptations to Play	103
BAVARIA—MUNICH	103, 109
Our "Horrible Language"	105
The "Königs-See"	106
The Berchtesgaden Salt-mines	106
City of Munich	109
Soldiering in Bavaria	110
The King of Bavaria	110
Bavarian Beer-Drinking	112
The Royal Brewery	113
The Innkeeper's Commandments	114
More about Beer	115
Matrimonial Customs	116
The Yankee School-Teachers	117
The Royal Palace	118
The Munich Park	118
Statue of Bavaria	119
Academy of Fine Arts	120
Beer! Beer! Beer!	120
Munich Bronze Foundry	121
Studying English	122
Hotel Greetings	123
WURTEMBERG	123
Notes by the Way	123
Sunday in Stuttgart	124
Visitors to the Fatherland	125
The Marriage Question	126
DUCHY OF BADEN	126
Castle of Heidelberg	128
The German Tourist	129
Student-Life at Heidelberg	130
Heidelberg Dueling	111, 133
DARMSTADT	133
City of Darmstadt	134
These Old Towns	134

	PAGE
DARMSTADT—Continued.	
Religious Toleration	135
Provision Stores	135
Female Clerks	136
German Babies	136
FRANKFORT-ON-THE-MAIN	136
City of Frankfort	137
Jewish Quarter	137
Ariadne on the Panther	138
Emigration and Military Service	138
DOWN THE RHINE	139
Rhine Tourists	140
Mayence to Bingen	140
Bingen to Coblentz	140
English Tourists	142
Rhine Dinner	143
Rhine Exaggerations	143
CITY OF COLOGNE	143
View of the City	144
Cathedral of Cologne	144
Relics of St. Ursula	145
CITY OF PARIS	145
Gayety of Paris	145
Paris and Vienna	145
Paris by Gas-light	146
Social Statistics of Paris	147
Dead of Paris	147
Parisian Foundlings	148
Love of Dogs	148
Yankee Doodle in Paris	149
Paris Boulevards	150
Paris Underground	151
Beautiful Paris	151
Abattoirs of Paris	152
Wages in Paris	152
Paris Hotels	154
Cleanliness of Paris	154
Bois de Boulogne	155
Jardin d'Acclimatation	156
Markets of Paris	156
Market for Old Clothes	157
"Château Rouge"	158
The Grisette	160
"It's Naughty, but it's Nice"	160
The Mabille Audience	161
The Mabille Dancers	161
The Champs Elysées on Sunday	163
Place de la Concorde	164
Business Women	164
Social Questions	165
Matrimonial Agencies	165
French Marriage-Laws	166
Omitting the Ceremony	166
Social Degradation	167
English and American Travelers	168
Amenities of Travel	168
Horse Butchers	168
Duval's Boucherie	169
Exemption from Fines	170
Mysterious Work of Art	171
How Paris is painted	172
Fête of St. Cloud	173
Sunday Amusements	175
Americans Europeanized	175
Boarding-School French	176
American Food Troubles	176

	PAGE		PAGE
CITY OF PARIS—*Continued.*		THE CITY OF VENICE—*Continued.*	
Mending their Manners	177	A Gondola Ride	231
No "Rings" in Paris	178	Venetian Newsboys	232
The Mont de Piété	179	The Venice Bourse	232
Etiquette of the Streets	179	Venice as it is	233
Construction of Houses	180	The Gay Gondolier	233
Shop-keepers of Paris	181	History of Venice	234
"Au Bon Marché"	183	Islands and Canals	234
Scarcity of Water	183	Piazza of St. Mark	235
Hot Bread	183	St. Mark's on Sunday	236
		The Cries of Venice	236
CITY OF MARSEILLES	184	Stores of Venice	237
Sunday in Marseilles	185	Feeding Pet Pigeons	237
Public Gardens	185	Surroundings of Venice	238
Scenes on the Streets	186	St. Mark's Cathedral	239
Law and Order	186	Female Water-Carriers	240
Scene at the Bourse	186	The Jews' Quarter	240
Table-d'Hôte	187	Bridge of Sighs	240
		Churches of Venice	241
ITALY, NAPLES, ROME, ETC	188	Venetian Palaces	242
On the Mediterranean	188	Rialto Bridge	242
City of Genoa	188	Venice by Gas-light	243
Leghorn and Pisa	190	Ladies of Venice	243
The Leaning Tower	191	Theatres of Venice	243
Civita Vecchia	191	Venice Fictions	243
Fleas and Beggars	192	Love of Music	244
Italian Cooking	192		
City of Naples	192	THE CITY OF VERONA	244
Naples on Sunday	193	Romeo and Juliet	244
A Walk on the Toledo	194	The City of Verona	245
Neapolitan Ladies	194	Roman Amphitheatre	245
Happiness of the People	195	Churches and Cathedrals	245
How the Babies are nursed	197		
The Faithful Donkey	197	CITY OF MILAN	246
Pompeii—its Ruins	198	Railroading in Italy	246
Ascent of Vesuvius	202	Milan on Sunday	246
The Craters—a Night Scene	204	Cathedral of Milan	247
Lava and Ashes	205	Streets of Milan	247
Vesuvius in Eruption	205	Ladies of Milan	248
A Fiery Experience	207	Shopping in Milan	248
Exaggerations of Italy	208		
Liquefaction of the Blood of San Gennaro	209	VOYAGE ON LAKE COMO	248
		Farewell to Italy	248
The Dead of Naples	210	From Milan to Como	249
Italian Scenery	211	The Lake of Como	249
Ruins of Pæstum	212	Beauties of the Lake	250
Temples of Pæstum	213		
Street Scenes in Naples	213	SWITZERLAND	250
City of Rome	214	Crossing the Alps	250
Italians and Priests	215	The Splügen Pass	251
Visit to St. Peter's	217	The Via Mala	251
Miraculous Relics	218	Haps and Mishaps	252
Down among the Ancients	218	Head of the Rhine	252
Mendicant Priests	219	Attractions of Switzerland	252
The Roman Palaces	220	Town of Coire	253
Down among the Dead Men	221	Springs of Pfaffers	253
"Brother, we must all Die"	221	Swiss Railroads	254
Churches of Rome	222	Fair Zurich's Waters	254
Sunday in Rome	223	City of Zurich	255
Garibaldi and Savonarola	224	People of Zurich	256
City of Florence	224	Europe and America	256
Burial of the Poor	227	Sunday in Zurich	257
		Houses of Zurich	257
THE CITY OF VENICE	228	The Black Virgin	258
Across the Adriatic	228	Lake Lucerne	260
Gondolas and Gondoliers	229	Town of Fluelen	260
A Stroll through the City	229	Honors to Tell	261
The Streets of Venice	230	Ascent of Mount Righi	262
Churches and Bells	230	A Night on Righi	262
Public Garden	230	The Bernese Alps	264

TABLE OF CONTENTS.

SWITZERLAND—*Continued.*
Berne and its Bears............... 264
Bernese Women................... 265
Interlaken......................... 265
Lake of Brienz.................... 266
Giesbach Cascades................ 267
Ascent of the Giesbach........... 267
Blue-beard's Castle................ 268
The Jungfrau..................... 269
City of Geneva.................... 269
City of Lausanne.................. 270
Lake of Geneva................... 270
Mont Blanc........................ 270
Burdens for the Back............. 271
Hotel Mistakes.................... 272
Gastronomy in Europe............ 272

CITY OF LONDON.................... 273
Crossing the Channel............. 273
An Agreeable Sensation........... 274
Up to "Lunnen" Town............. 274
London and Paris................. 275
Drunkards and Beggars........... 275
How to See a City................ 275
Stores of London.................. 276
Public Parks...................... 276
Service at Westminster........... 277
Underground Railways............ 277
Rambles in London................ 278
Tower of London.................. 278
Crystal Palace.................... 279
Zoological Gardens............... 279
The American Abroad............ 279
Street Experiences................ 280
Westminster Abbey............... 280
Spurgeon in the Pulpit............ 281
Spurgeon's Peculiarities.......... 282
Excursion on the Thames......... 284
Houses of Parliament............. 285
English Ladies' Peculiarities..... 286
Peculiarities of Englishmen...... 286
English Oddities.................. 287

SCOTLAND........................... 287
City of Edinburgh................ 287
Rapid Traveling.................. 287

SCOTLAND—*Continued.*
Monument to Scott............... 288
Nelson's Monument............... 288
Edinburgh Notables.............. 289
Palace of Holyrood............... 289

CITY OF GLASGOW................... 290
Down the Clyde................... 291
City of Greenock................. 291

IRELAND............................. 291
City of Belfast................... 291
Trip to Galway................... 292
City of Dublin.................... 292
Scenes on the Route.............. 293
Dublin Beauties.................. 293
Capital of Ireland................ 293
Trinity College................... 294
Phœnix Park...................... 294
Tomb of O'Connell............... 295
The Irish Jingle.................. 295
Police of Ireland................. 295
City of Cork...................... 296
Cove of Cork..................... 296
Irish Jaunting Cars.............. 297
Blarney Castle................... 297
The Blarney Stone................ 298
Groves of Blarney................ 298
An Irish Race.................... 298
Round Towers of Ireland........ 298

CITY OF LIVERPOOL................. 299
Aspect of Liverpool.............. 299
Street Scenes..................... 299
Liverpool Docks.................. 299
St. George's Organ............... 300

LIFE AT SEA...................301–310

HINTS TO EUROPEAN TOURISTS...... 311
Patience and Good Temper....... 311
Firearms.......................... 311
Clothing and Money.............. 311
Guides and Guide-Books......... 311
Passports......................... 311
Railroad Travel.................. 312
Hotels, etc....................... 312
Cost of Travel................... 312

EUROPE

VIEWED THROUGH AMERICAN SPECTACLES.

STEAMSHIP BALTIMORE,
OFF SOUTHAMPTON, 1873.

THE sight of land, after thirteen days of ocean travel with its monotonous water scenery, is most cheering and invigorating, even when, as in the present case, we have yet five hundred miles farther to journey to Bremen through the waters of the treacherous North Sea. We here bid adieu to a portion of the companions of our voyage, who have just landed at Southampton, but expect again to meet them a month hence at Vienna, which is the Mecca of Americans during the present season. Those, however, who desire to visit Northern Germany, and make a brief sojourn in Berlin on their route to Vienna, continue with us on our sea journey.

MONOTONY OF OCEAN TRAVEL.

Two weeks on the ocean, with but little more than the dull daily routine of gazing on the "waste of waters," and responding four times per day to the bell for meals, is almost as irksome as being shut up in a sick-room. The days seem as long as weeks, and half the nights are spent in vain efforts to drop off into forgetfulness of the discomforts of the surroundings. Reading is next to impossible, the motion of the vessel affecting the eye so as to make the effort anything but agreeable. The first three days of our voyage were as calm and quiet as the run down the Chesapeake, and everybody imagined that there was nothing to dread for the balance of the voyage, and all was becoming as monotonous as a long drive to a funeral. A party of a half-dozen young Americans, who kept up a perpetual round of fun and frolic, were the only persons on board who seemed able to make a break in the solemn aspect of the passengers.

FARE ON A GERMAN STEAMER.

The passenger on a German steamer commences his experience in foreign life the moment the hawsers are cast off. He finds the table served and the food prepared precisely as he will find it on shore when he arrives at Bremerhafen. The *table-d'hôte*, which ultimately makes the American long for a square home dinner, begins so soon as the engine is in motion, and from that hour forward he commences his foreign experience. Perhaps it is as well that he should have this preparatory training, as there is much to learn, and it takes time to accustom the palate to foreign cooking and the tastes and smells of unknown dishes. Our specimens of Young America have much sport over the bill of fare, and bring out their German dictionaries to translate what they term "conundrums." It requires wine or beer to secure good digestion, and our German companions, with this addition, enjoy it amazingly. The table is just such as is suitable to healthy people, and not so tempting as to induce dyspeptics to overload their stomachs.

EXPERIENCE OF THE SEA.

Some men are regarded as Jonahs when on the sea, storm and disaster keeping pace with their movements. The sailor regards the presence of a priest or preacher as premonitory of a rough and stormy passage, and is to that extent prejudiced against the cloth. We have had a pretty extensive sea experience in various wanderings, and it has always been our fortune to encounter favorable weather. Even Cape Hatteras has not been able to get up a storm for our benefit on any of the numerous occasions of our rounding it. The British Channel, generally the terror of tourists, has always become as calm as the Chesapeake during our crossings, and the dreaded Mediterranean is bright, blue, and beautiful. We have encountered storms on land, but never on the water, old Neptune having invariably been kind and considerate. The first three days of our present journey on the broad Atlantic were marked by a bright sky, a warm sun, and a light rolling sea. Some of the passengers were a little nauseated, but our merry little party, male and female, continued to enjoy the games and promenades on deck without the slightest evidence of seasickness. The chambermaid had evidently marked the ladies of our party for her most careful nursing, and seemed astonished that they did not succumb with the other ladies on board. If they happened to roll themselves in their shawls for an afternoon *siesta* on deck, she rushed for a cup of gruel, and was astonished at their perverseness in not requiring her services.

A CHANGE OF WEATHER.

On the morning of the fourth day we rose to find our state-rooms in commotion, and the wash-stand and looking-glass making an apparent effort to come in violent collision, whilst our satchels and brushes were chasing one another around the floor. The effort to dress amid such commotion was a strong test on the capacity of the stomach to resist the demands of the troubled waters, but it was finally accomplished, with some misgivings as to a continuance of the power of resistance. On reaching the deck we found a fine rolling sea, with a strong but favorable wind, making locomotion very difficult. The response to the breakfast-bell showed the effect of the change of weather upon the passengers. Out of twenty-six cabin passengers but ten appeared at the table, including the nine Americans on board, and one German. There was not a lady present except the two from Baltimore, who during the next five days were almost the only representatives of the sex at the table. Of the Marylanders among the passengers but two succumbed to the prevailing epidemic, one of them representing Baltimore, and the other a worthy legal gentleman hailing from the head-waters of canoe navigation. The Germans, on the contrary, with one exception, male and female, if they attempted to venture to resume their seats at the table were compelled to beat a rapid retreat, greatly to the amusement of those whose stomachs were proof against the moving dishes and oscillating motion of the table and the vessel. Persons suffering from sea-sickness receive but little commiseration, and must expect to be laughed at. When they recover it is amusing to listen to the descriptions they give of their sufferings and the misery of mind and body through which they have passed. A young friend from Baltimore, who was very anxious to be seasick, now thinks he will be compelled to spend the balance of his days in Europe, having serious doubts if he will ever have the nerve to run the risk of a second attack by venturing on shipboard again. After five days of rough weather we passed the Banks of Newfoundland, and were again in a rolling but quiet sea, approaching the coast of Ireland. To those of us who have been exempt, the voyage has been as pleasant as sea travel can be expected to be to the landsman, but the extent of sea-sickness on board has been more than the average. During the last four days all have been well, and though we have been plowing along at the rate of three hundred miles per day, through a high rolling sea, with a fair wind, the ship vibrating all the time like a pendulum, it no longer has any disagreeable effect on the convalescents. Their brains and legs are attuned to the motion, and they can now enjoy all that is enjoyable on the sea. The fifty-six steerage passengers were all sick, and for a time two Baltimore ladies were the only females on the vessel, except the chambermaids, who were able to appear at table or promenade the deck. We were advised by our German friends to drink wine and beer, as they did, as a preventive, but having stuck to cold water, we claim it as a better specific.

AMUSEMENTS AT SEA.

The amusements of the voyage depend a great deal upon the weather, and upon the character and disposition of the passengers. During most of the present trip the weather has been too cold and the sea running too high for amusements on deck. There was also too much seasickness for the passengers to muster in sufficient force until the tenth day out, when, all having recovered, we had quite a spirited dance on deck, a youth from the steerage with an accordeon furnishing the music. Although the ship was rolling at an angle of twenty degrees, the dancers managed, with an occasional fall and roll, to enjoy themselves until nine o'clock in the evening under a bright moonlight. All had their sea-legs fully under control, though so great was the rolling motion of the vessel that none of those who participated in the dance could have even maintained their footing on the deck a week ago. The Baltimore proved to be an excellent roller, especially when encountering the groundswell from the Irish coast.

The only other amusement during the voyage has been an occasional game of shuffle-board; but there has been too much wind and rain for this, except at occasional intervals. The weather has also been decidedly cold, and the cabin amusements have been very limited.

THE COAST OF ENGLAND.

Our voyage around the southern coast of England, passing the great naval station of Plymouth, and also the fortifications off Dartmouth, was through a sea as calm as the Chesapeake. There was scarcely a ripple on the ocean, and not a perceptible motion of the steamer. This run on the coast continued for nearly twenty hours before reaching Southampton, and the quiet of the scene was very acceptable after the rolling and rocking we had gone through during the preceding ten days. The sun was bright, and the day was enjoyed on deck. Those who were to land at Southampton, having cast aside their sea clothing, and being hailed as they appeared on deck as new-comers. We had dreaded this coasting as likely to be rough and unpleasant, but it proved to be the most agreeable portion of our journey. All the passengers were well and in high spirits at the sight of land, and thankful that they were so rapidly approaching the end of their journey. We left Southampton about seven o'clock on Friday evening, and had a fine view of the fortifications near Portsmouth, which are very formidable, but in this age of ironclads would prove of very little service.

The entrance to Southampton, through the Solent, affords a fine view of the shores of the Isle of Wight, which are very beautiful, dotted with villas of the nobility, watering-places, and a very elegant seaside palace of the Queen. The trees were in full foliage, and the fields clothed in the brightest green. At seven o'clock on Saturday morning we passed through the Straits of Dover, having a fine view of Folkestone and Dover, with its ancient castle on the hill, this being the point where William the Conqueror landed. In the dim distance, the morning being bright and beautiful, Calais, on the coast of France, was visible, and we soon passed into the open North Sea, and were again out of sight of land and steaming towards Germany.

THE NORTH SEA.

The North Sea, which has a very bad name in the nautical calendar, was in its most lovely mood when we entered upon its waters. A bright and warm sun drew every one to the deck, and so quiet was the ocean that there was scarcely a perceptible motion of the vessel as we steamed along towards the mouth of the river Weser. During the whole of the thirty hours consumed in crossing the North Sea, a distance of nearly three hundred miles, there was scarcely a ripple on its surface. It was more like a steamboat excursion on the Chesapeake than ocean travel. The weather was, however, decidedly cool as we approached the coast of Germany.

CHARMS OF THE SEA.

Novelists and poets have succeeded in producing a very general impression among the uninitiated that there is something delightful in life on the sea. Depend upon it, there never was a greater delusion. The novelty wears off very rapidly, and time drags slowly, until the days seem like weeks and the weeks like months. Some time must elapse before one gets accustomed to being rolled up and packed away on a rocking and pitching shelf all night, to the perpetual jingle of the machinery, and to the stifling atmosphere of a close state-room. Even when tolerably accustomed to it, the hours are counted and the log watched with anxiety to note the number of miles yet to be passed before reaching the desired haven. During two-thirds of an ordinary passage one must of necessity keep below deck, even in day-time. Rainstorms and wind-squalls are equally prohibitory of deck enjoyment. It is next to impossible to read, and cabin amusements soon become tiresome. Among the passengers there are always to be found some who have crossed the ocean a dozen times, and they are no more happy or contented than is the novice. So also with the officers of vessels: they are always looking forward to some distant prospect of securing land employment. When to all these sources of discomfort are added constant seasickness and nausea to the great majority, some idea may be formed of the amount of human suffering to be endured by the twenty thousand Americans who are now moving or preparing to move towards Vienna. Of course, nothing can be more delightful than to pay a visit to Europe, but the sea-going must not be counted among the attractions of the trip. Depend upon it, the most romantic of your readers will, with their first experience, wonder whether it is not possible that the poets and romancers of the sea were paid puffers in the interest of ship-owners, or were laboring to secure free tickets for a trip across the ocean.

CHANGE OF TIME.

In crossing the ocean the gradual change of time amounts to about twenty minutes every two hundred and fifty miles on the route. In approaching Europe from America, to keep your watch up to ship time you must move the hands forward daily from twenty to thirty-five minutes. Many jokes are told of the youngsters who get out of all conceit of their timekeepers whilst on an ocean journey. Having kept up Baltimore time throughout the trip, we find just five hours and five minutes difference at Southampton. In other words, we arrived here at six minutes past six o'clock this evening, whilst our watches record precisely one o'clock P.M. as Baltimore time, having made the journey in one hour less than thirteen days.

BREMEN.

BREMEN, May 12, 1873.

We entered the Fatherland at Bremerhafen at five o'clock last evening, and in two hours were at our present location, by a special train of cars in waiting for our arrival. Two weeks ago we were in Baltimore, and now we are in Germany, almost as quickly as we could reach some of our summer resorts by slow stages of travel. We intend to have a good summer run through Northern Europe, and propose to have a good time of it, Providence and weather permitting, though at the present time we scarcely know whither we shall go or where we shall cease our peregrinations.

CITY OF BREMERHAFEN.

We had only a bird's-eye view of Bremerhafen, which is the commercial *entrepôt* of Bremen, thirty miles distant, at the head of ship navigation on the Weser River. It is a purely commercial city, of about twenty thousand population, with some fine docks, similar to those at Liverpool, and an abundance of large and extensive warehouses. It will ultimately become to Germany what Liverpool is to England, and large numbers of new buildings are now being erected in all directions.

The country between Bremerhafen and Bremen is almost like one of our Illinois prairies, and is nearly as barren of trees. The cultivation of some points on the route is very fine, but the most of it exhibits rather careless husbandry compared with the fields of England. One of our traveling companions, from Prince George's County, remarked that he could almost imagine that he was traveling through that section of Maryland, if it were not for the absence of worm-fences. There was an abundance of the Holstein cattle, so highly prized in America, grazing in the fields, reminding us of a commission we have from an estimable lady of Baltimore to send her three choice heifers.

CITY OF BREMEN.

The city of Bremen being out of the usual route of German tourists, little is known of it, and we had always imagined it to be one of those cities in which trade, business, and commerce are the principal attractions. A walk before breakfast satisfied us that there are few handsomer cities for its size in Europe, and for cleanliness it will compare with the most attractive portions of Paris. In ancient times it was a walled city, but the ramparts which separated the old town from the suburbs have been removed and turned into promenades, which almost make a circle through the heart of the present city, constituting one of its principal ornaments. The picturesque groups of trees, the broad surface of the moats, which have been retained, forming small lakes, and the rich vegetation of the opposite bank, upon which a line of magnificent residences extends through the heart of the city, present a succession of striking pictures. Extensive pleasure-grounds, with cafés, etc., are interspersed on the Weser at the upper extremity of the promenades.

The private residences nearly all have broad gardens in front, each rivaling its neighbor in the display of flowers. Whole miles of these elegant buildings, in every variety of architecture, can be seen along the promenade, indicating great wealth and an appreciation of the comforts and pleasures of a bright and beautiful home. The fronts are all decorated with lace curtains, and flowers in full bloom are abundant at the parlor windows.

THE PEOPLE OF BREMEN.

Bremen has a population of about one hundred thousand, and, next to Hamburg, it is the most important commercial place in North Germany. It is chiefly indebted for its present prosperity to the foundation of Bremerhafen, or the harbor of Bremen, which, although thirty miles distant, is regarded as a suburb of the city. It is visited annually by about four thousand vessels, of which four hundred, including about thirty-five sea-going steamers, are owned in Bremen.

SUNDAY AT BREMEN.

We landed in a hail-storm, which has followed us on to Bremen, but it did not prevent us from viewing the city by gaslight on the only Sunday evening we shall spend here. After partaking of a most delicious supper at the Hôtel du Nord, our entire party started out under the guidance of H. Raster, Esq., editor of the Chicago *Staats Zeitung*, who, with his family, was one of our passengers, to see how the people in this ancient city spend their Sunday evenings. We found the stores generally closed, except those for the sale of tobacco and cigars, though many of them were lit up for the display of goods. The rain doubtless occasioned more dullness than usual out-of-doors, but the resorts for eating and drinking were all crowded to excess.

We visited the great wine-cellar under the City Hall, which is a government establishment, with its butts of wine, the heads of which are twelve feet in diameter. It is an immense restaurant, and here were gathered fully one thousand gentlemen and ladies, eating their suppers and partaking of wine and beer. They have wine here of the vintage of 1624, which is, however, only partaken of by strangers as a matter of curiosity. We found present many of the leading merchants of the city, with their wives and daughters, each of the numerous tables being occupied by a party of personal friends, all enjoying themselves, amid a cloud of smoke that was almost stifling on entering. This cellar has been the favorite resort of the people of Bremen for several generations, many families taking their meals here most of the time. There were at the tables young men with their sweethearts, and old men with their wives, and it was pleasing to observe the marked order and decorum which prevailed among such a large gathering. The oldest of the immense casks in this cellar are called "The Rose" and the "Twelve Apostles," the head of each being elaborately gilded and covered with inscriptions. The magistrates are said, in ancient times, to have held their most important sessions near the spigot of the former, such deliberations having been kept profoundly secret.

Some of the young American portion of our party, at a later hour on Sunday night, visited the theatre, admission to see the last act costing ten cents, including a glass of beer, and at twelve o'clock stopped in at a billiard-saloon, which was in full operation. The rain having ceased about ten o'clock, the streets soon became thronged with promenaders, and up to midnight presented a lively appearance.

EMIGRATION TO AMERICA.

Bremen is the principal point for the concentration of emigrants going to America. Throngs of them, consisting of men, women and children, such as congregate weekly at Castle Garden or Locust Point, can be seen at all hours of the day in groups around the shipping-offices, or wending their way to the depot, bound for Bremerhafen, preparatory to embarkation. They come here from all parts of Germany, and are an entirely different class of people from the inhabitants of Bremen, being mostly agriculturists. We remember on visiting Dublin some years since to have remarked that but few specimens of the American idea of the personal appearance and characteristics of an Irishman could be seen in that city. The same may be said of Bremen. With the exception of the emigrants, there are few persons to be seen in this city who would be recognized at a glance as German, either in dress, manners, or facial expression. Indeed, it would be difficult to find a finer-looking class of people anywhere than the inhabitants of Bremen, or any that are more kind, courteous, and agreeable in their manners. The ladies have a healthy appearance and ruddy countenances, are handsome and graceful, and dress with excellent taste and freedom from gaudy colors. Their kindness to Americans is most marked and general. On our making inquiry of persons on the street as to the location of different objects of interest, they not only took great pains to give the proper direction, but on more than one occasion accompanied us several squares to make sure that we did not get astray.

UNDECAYED MUMMIES.

The Cathedral, erected in the twelfth century, is the only interesting church of which Bremen can boast. It is now a Protestant church, and contains the finest organ in Germany. Its greatest attraction to strangers is the exhibition of several mummies, the oldest having been for four hundred years, and the most recent for sixty years, in an undecayed condition. The vault in which they repose possesses the property of preventing decomposition, in proof of which poultry is frequently suspended in it, a venerable turkey, one hundred years old, being at the present time hanging on the wall. The corpses bear no evidence of decay as in the case of the Egyptian mummies, but carry on their countenances the appearance of recent death, except that the dust of ages has somewhat discolored them. There are about a dozen bodies laid out in their coffins. The flesh feels like parchment, and the cheeks of an old countess, who has lain here four hundred years, look and feel quite plump. One is the remains of an English officer, shot in a duel ninety years ago, with a bullet-hole in his breast and a shattered shoulder. A corpulent old general is still corpulent, and a dozen chickens hung up ninety years ago have their feathers all intact. The vault in which they lie is about thirty feet long and fifteen wide, and is above-ground, in one of the crypts of the church. There is nothing peculiar about it, and there seems no reason why it should preserve bodies from decay more than any other room in Bremen. The exhibition of these curiosities gives an income to the church of about twenty dollars per day, and is quite a valuable source of revenue. It is not everybody who can expect to be so remunerative after he has given up the ghost.

NEWSPAPERS AT BREMEN.

There are two newspapers printed here, but nobody seems to care anything about them. There is not a newsboy to be seen on the street, and the newspaper files in the hotels are seldom disturbed. Visitors sit and drink their beer and wine, but seldom read. The citizens of Bremen are decidedly a talking people, and seem to take no time for reading or studying the current of events as recorded in the public prints.

BERLIN.

BERLIN, May 14, 1873.

We reached Berlin, the capital of Prussia, at breakfast-time on Tuesday morning, after a long night ride from Bremen, passing through Hanover about two o'clock in the morning. Railroad travel in Europe is accompanied by many trials and annoyances that are not experienced in the United States, the detention and trouble with baggage not being the least of them. At Bremen our luggage was all examined on leaving the city, and then weighed, and, although nothing was found strictly contraband, the officer was in great doubt about the propriety of passing a small bundle of paper on which we propose to write the notes of our journey. On our explaining to him the purpose for which it was intended, it was allowed to pass. A box of fifty choice cigars was not allowed to remain in a trunk, but we were permitted to carry it in our hands, the result of which was that before reaching our destination it was lost. At Hanover we were compelled to change trains, having to wait over an hour in a reception-room crowded with men, women, and children, on emerging from which the ladies of our party discovered that they had made acquaintance with a goodly number of those pests of Europe that are only to be found in dog-kennels on our side of the Atlantic.

TRIALS OF TRAVEL.

We arrived at Berlin at seven o'clock in the morning, the time from Bremen being nine hours. Quite a storm was in progress as we reached the depot in Berlin, when, with our baskets, bundles, shawls, and valises, we were seized upon by a Commissionnaire and a military-looking official with a spiked helmet. The said Commissionnaire assured us that there was no Hôtel de Russie in Berlin, and that the best hotel was the Hôtel de l'Europe. Being anxious to get located, we were packed in a carriage and sent off. On entering the hotel we came to the conclusion that if "de l'Europe" was the best house in Berlin it had a shocking bad exterior appearance. We were shown up to chambers on the second floor, carpetless, and almost furnitureless, whereupon we came to the conclusion that the Kaiser's depot regulations are calculated to allow strangers to be swindled. Being in a strange city, and our carriage having departed, we concluded to make the best of a bad bargain, and called for breakfast, which we will do the proprietor the credit to say was palatable and well served. Leaving the ladies for a short time, we strolled out, and soon found the Hôtel de Russie, and also the Hôtel du Nord, two first-class houses, in the latter of which we secured quarters. The swindle cost us about five dollars, which we charged to "experience," hoping to profit by it before we leave Germany. The complaint we have to make to the Kaiser is, that one of his spiked-helmet officials, when appealed to as to the truth of the Commissionnaire's story, assured us that it was all right.

IMPRESSIONS OF BERLIN.

Our first impressions of Berlin were decidedly unfavorable, though the cold and dismal rain-storm which has followed us thus far is not calculated to make any place look very bright and attractive. But Berlin is a sombre, massive city, lacking the bright and brilliant aspect of Paris. Its public buildings, although equal to those of any other city in Europe in imposing grandeur, are more solid than beautiful. There is no section of the city that is exclusively devoted to elegant stores, they being scattered about in every direction, intermingled with warehouses and junk-shops. It is said to be the determination of the Emperor to make Berlin rival Paris as the most attractive city of Europe, but we rather think that it will require rebuilding, almost, to accomplish the undertaking. A grand arcade has just been completed, running diagonally through two squares, similar to the magnificent establishment at Milan, which is quite Parisian in its beauty and proportions.

THE ROYAL MUSEUM.

We spent several hours to-day in the Royal Museum, which is a vast structure, to which there is no charge for admittance. The painting-gallery is very extensive, but not very attractive. The pictures are decidedly ancient, and consequently not appreciated by the average American. There are some few paintings here that all can admire, though the vast majority are graceless and unnatural in their presentation of the human figure. The coloring is, however, very rich and natural, for which they are mostly admired. Most of them, if seen anywhere else than in a royal gallery, would be regarded as the daubs of amateur artists. Around the few good paintings there were generally two or three artists busily engaged in making copies.

Another portion of the Museum is devoted to plaster casts of ancient sculpture, including copies of nearly all the great masterpieces to be found at Rome and Florence. As we had seen the originals of these, the copies commanded but little of our attention, except such as could be given during a leisurely stroll through the extensive galleries.

THE ZOOLOGICAL GARDENS.

We next proceeded to the Zoological Gardens, which are outside of the walls of Berlin, adjoining the grand Park. Here we found a collection of beasts and birds equal in number and extent to the menageries of Forepaugh, Barnum, and all the other traveling institutions of the United States combined and multiplied by six. The grounds are very extensive, and the buildings in which the animals are kept have been erected regardless of expense. Quite a number of small but beautiful lakes are filled with an extensive variety of aquatic birds, many of them of the most brilliant plumage, and each species in great number. The aviaries are also large and fine, and the lions, tigers, leopards, and panthers embrace many fine and rare specimens. Take the gardens altogether, they are superior to those of London or Paris; but in the latter city many of the animals were eaten during the siege.

WORKING WOMEN.

German women are undoubtedly able to do a man's work, and some of them do more in that line than most men are willing to do. The very hardest species of manual labor is spading ground and turning over the sod. In the Park to-day we passed nearly fifty women, all strong and muscular, busily driving their spades into the earth. They worked in gangs of five, side by side, apparently as contented as if they had been piercing a cambric handkerchief with a needle. When women can perform this kind of labor, they are certainly on an equality with men in some things if not in all, and need no protectors. Only think of marrying a woman who can dig all day with a spade! It would not do for most of the lords of creation to have such wives, or at least to provoke them to a trial of strength.

LOCOMOTION IN BERLIN.

There are no street passenger railways in Berlin, and there are comparatively few omnibuses. The population is now said to be nine hundred thousand, or nearly three times that of Baltimore. The carriages, however, are very cheap and numerous, being of three classes, and at three grades of prices, first, second, and third class. A second-class carriage, with one horse, carrying four passengers, charges about sixty cents per hour in our money, the first class eighty cents, and the third class forty cents. The first class has two horses, and the other classes have one horse.

WORKING DOGS.

In all parts of Germany the dog is a beast of burden, and works with as earnest a will as the horse or the mule. Hundreds of hand-carts can be seen moving through the streets, with one or two dogs harnessed, and they never allow their traces to slacken. The size of the wagons, and the loads they pull, are truly surprising to those who only know the dog as a lazy, sleeping animal. The man or boy accompanying the dog merely keeps his hand upon the tongue of the wagon to steady or guide it, whilst the faithful animal does all the work. These dogs are all muzzled, as they are apt to bite any stranger who approaches the wagon, especially during the absence of the master. Whilst resting anywhere, they lie down in their traces and sleep, but at a word are up again, and intent upon their work. They are of no especial breed, but all kinds, including the Newfoundland and the bulldog, are to be seen in harness. All that is required is strength and muscle and proper training. There are very few idle dogs to be seen in Berlin.

THE COST OF ROYALTY.

The American traveling in Europe is astonished at the vast expenditure and waste of money that is required to maintain royalty. There cannot be in Germany less than fifty palaces for the accommodation of the royal family, each one of which is ten times larger than the President's house. None of them have less than one hundred rooms, and some of them from two hundred to three hundred, all decorated and furnished in the highest style of art, with picture-galleries and halls of statuary, whilst temples, fountains, monuments, and every manner of ornament adorn the surrounding grounds. At Potsdam, about ten miles from Berlin, there are five magnificent palaces, and there are quite a number in this city. They are all in charge of hosts of retainers, ready for the reception of royal visitors at a moment's notice, and each guarded by garrisons of soldiers larger than those in charge of all the fortifications in the United States. However, the people seem to take pride in all this as evidence of the greatness and glory of their country, and if they are satisfied there is no reason why any one else should grumble about it. Everybody here wonders how it is possible that the United States is so steadily and persistently paying off its national debt. It is no matter of wonder to us why the nations of Europe are so persistently increasing theirs. There must, however, be an end of all this some day.

A STROLL THROUGH BERLIN.

We took a long walk to-day, to the distance of six or seven miles, away from the centre of Berlin, winding around through all sections of the business portions of the city. We found it all alike everywhere, fine buildings intermixed with ancient structures, and no one section much superior to another in its attractiveness. Stores of every variety and character are intermixed, and military barracks with bristling bayonets interspersed through all sections of the city. We came across an extensive market, occupying a whole square, upon which were hundreds of booths, the principal articles on sale being wooden ware, baskets, and brushes, with a few cake and toy stands. It was thronged with purchasers, and presented quite a stirring scene. These baskets and wooden-ware booths also extended down all the neighboring streets, and it seemed strange that there should be a demand to warrant such an immense exposure of such goods.

The streets generally are broad and well paved, but the houses and stores by no means attractive, though many very fine buildings are in the course of erection all over the city. But when one has walked two hours through the streets of Berlin he may conclude that he has seen the whole city, the characteristics of all sections are so similar. In most respects it is so like an American city that it is difficult to note anything in the habits or ways, or even in the appearance, of the people, that would prove of interest to your readers.

MONUMENT TO FREDERICK THE GREAT.

Near the eastern extremity of the Linden, opposite the palace of the Crown Prince, stands the statue or monument of Frederick the Great. It is in bronze, by Rauch, and is said to be the grandest monument of its kind in Europe. The pedestal is divided into three sections. At the corners of the upper are represented Moderation, Justice, Wisdom, Strength. On the sides of the monument are eight reliefs,—representing the birth of the King, his education, Minerva presenting him with a sword, Frederick after the battle of Kolin, his love of art, his taste for music, his promotion of commerce, and his apotheosis. At the corners of the central section are four equestrian figures, on the east the Princes Henry of Prussia and Ferdinand of Brunswick, and on the west Generals Ziethen and Seydlitz. Around the monument are grouped lifesized figures of distinguished officers. The lower section contains names of other prominent men, especially soldiers of the time of Frederick. The monuments in Berlin, are not numerous, but they are of a superior character.

BERLIN, May 15, 1873.

BERLIN AND ITS PEOPLE.

Berlin improves with acquaintance, and the more we see of it the better we like it. It is, however, by no means a gay city. The people are neither gay nor merry, except on the occasion of some commemoration of victories in war, or in honor of the Kaiser and "Our Fritz." They are even silent over their beer and Schweitzer cheese, and there are no jolly gatherings of an evening such as can be nightly witnessed in the gardens and saloons of Baltimore. We walked several miles the other evening in pursuit of such an establishment as that of Franz Gardiner on High Street, and were content to finally drop into a quiet resort in a basement on the Poststrasse, where there were a number of visitors, all as silent as possible, with no singing or music or jollity of any kind. Germans in America are an entirely different class of people from those in the great cities of the Fatherland. The most enthusiastic Americans I have met with here are the German-Americans on a visit to their old homes. They find fault with everything, and complain that the people are too slow and lack energy and enterprise. Mr. Raster, the editor of the Chicago Staats Zeitung, was out of patience even in the lively little city of Bremen. How he has gotten along in the more staid and solemn cities of the interior, it is not easy to imagine.

THE MILITARY DISPLAY.

The fact that Prussia is a military government is apparent all over Berlin.

Almost one-fourth of the men to be met on the streets are in military dress, with epaulets and swords, and the "man with a military walk" is no curiosity here. Soldiers on guard are in and around all the public buildings, the police are in military dress, with spiked helmets and swords, the railroad officials wear uniforms, and the telegraph operators and boys are all arrayed in a semi-military costume. So also with the post-office officials and the custodians of the public buildings. Regiments of soldiers march through the streets with brass bands, and the relief-guard parties seem to be always in motion. The store-windows are filled with prints of the Kaiser Wilhelm and his staff, in full feather, and the minor military dignitaries are presented in the photograph establishments as the greatest attraction. They, however, did well for their country in the late war, and are deserving of all the honor they receive. Every man in Germany must serve in the army from one to three years. If he has passed a good examination at a military academy, his term of service is but one year, but otherwise he must serve for three years. Thus it was that there were no raw recruits in the immense army brought so suddenly into the field to resist and drive back Napoleon. Every man was a soldier, trained and accustomed to the life of a soldier, under the greatest soldier of the age, and the most strict disciplinarian even in times of peace. Fortunately, we can do without such expensive ornaments as a standing army, and this is the reason why so many Germans are thronging the steamers for America. The number would be still greater if they were all possessed of the means to carry out their desire to escape from military service. Regiments of cavalry, infantry, and artillery are parading the streets to-day, but they attract no attention from the people. The sight is evidently too common.

THE BERLIN OPERA.

The operatic spectacle, with an intermixture of what is known in America as the "leg opera," called "The Lady in White," has been attracting the attention of the Berlinese for the past one hundred and fifteen nights at the Grand Opera House, and thither we wended our way last evening. Reserved seats for our party of four cost seven thalers and ten groschen, which is about one dollar and thirty-four cents per head. We went early, for the purpose of seeing the audience assemble, and to notice whatever else might seem to us of interest. The ladies will be interested in knowing that an entirely new mode of dressing the hair is in vogue here, and that there seems to be very little false hair used. The hair is frizzed all over, and the back hair confined in an invisible net, whilst the front stands out in crimped confusion. On the top of the head a bow of ribbon is worn similar to a gentleman's neck-tie, with short fringed ends. All ear-rings are infinitesimally small, and mostly of diamonds or pearls.

The ladies were largely in excess of the gentlemen, and, singular as it may seem, they came in without male escort, sometimes singly, sometimes in groups of four or five. These independent ladies were mostly young, and among the best dressed in the house, and were without bonnets, as were nearly all except strangers. The inevitable brass buttons and shoulder-straps predominated among the gentlemen, and a glance in any direction was sure to encounter a bevy of handsome young patriots.

As to the theatre itself, the interior or auditorium is about twice as large as Ford's Opera House, though it would not seat double as many, as the single seats are each fully four inches wider. One-half the Berlinese ladies and gentlemen could not wedge themselves into a narrower space. The seats are automatic, and if you rise they fly back, so that there is no difficulty in persons passing to interior seats, the rule being to rise. You are almost required to leave your hats, coats, canes, etc., outside with the custodians. Most Americans object to this, however, having a vivid recollection of ball-room scenes at home, and of missing coats, hats, bonnets, and furs. People here wonder why they refuse. Perhaps it would not be well to inform them.

The Opera House is a very grand affair, elaborately decorated with statuary, paintings, and rich carving. Next to the stage come what we would call the stage-boxes, only, instead of there being but three on each side, there are, including the top boxes, twelve on each side, or twenty-four stage boxes in all. The remainder of the house is divided into five tiers, including the parquet. The royal box is circular, very elegant, and elaborately decorated, and is capable of seating at royal ease about twenty-five persons. The height of the box is that of the three lower tiers, and the canopy at the top is surmounted by the crown and other royal insignia. No one enters this box without the royal sanction, and, with the exception of a lady sitting alone throughout the performance, it was entirely empty. The parquet was full, most of the seats in the five tiers of stalls occupied, and the stage-boxes about one-third full. The upper tier, or what in American parlance is styled "the peanut-gallery," was thronged with very respectable people, mostly ladies. The performance was very good, and the piece was presented on the stage in grand style. The orchestra consisted of forty-four performers, and the chorus and villagers on the stage numbered fully one hundred. The scenery was perfect, and was evidently gotten up by the hand of a master. Instead of flies, the side scenes were solid, giving the sides of the room or castle chamber to be represented; so also with the ceiling, presenting the appearance of a closed room on all sides except that towards the auditorium. The rural scenery was equally artistic and natural in its perfection.

THE BERLIN HOTELS.

The best hotels in Berlin are about equal to those of the second and third class in Paris. Indeed, they are not so good here as at Bremen, nor are the accommodations or the table so good, whilst prices are considerably higher. Such a thing as an elevator is not known, nor are there any public parlors for the accommodation of guests. Hence it is that strangers, and especially Americans, make but a brief stay in Berlin and hurry on to Dresden, where the accommodations and attractions are said to be much better. The table-d'hôte comprises a variety of inexplicable dishes, potatoes being about the only thing that is recognizable. One hour and a half is the shortest time required for this daily nuisance, and we have come to the conclusion that life is entirely too short to be thus wasted on unsatisfactory dinners. The Germans and the English seem, however, to enjoy them, and remain at the table a half-hour after the Americans have retired, smoking, and munching raisins and nuts. The ladies like it as an opportunity for the display of rich toilettes and diamonds, and a means of killing time. Gentlemen who are traveling with ladies are usually compelled to submit to the infliction rather than to forage among the restaurants.

The principal street in Berlin, on which most of the public buildings and hotels are located, is *Unter den Linden*,—a double row of lime-trees and a promenade adorning the centre of it. The number of fine stores upon it is, however, extremely limited; and it possesses but little more attraction for the stranger than any other street.

Immediately outside the Brandenburg Gate is the Thiergarten, a magnificent park, shaded by fine old trees, two miles in length and half a mile in breadth. For two miles on each side of the park there is an array of the most magnificent palatial residences, the extensive gardens around which are adorned with statuary and fountains and brilliant with flowers and ornamental trees.

DRESDEN.

DRESDEN, May 16, 1873.

We left Berlin at noon to-day, and at five o'clock this afternoon were driving through the city of Dresden, the favorite city of Saxony for American residents. There are said to be a large number of American families permanently located here, the object being the education of their children, though English is so generally spoken that it is beginning to be difficult for them to learn German. Some families who came here to teach their boys and girls to speak German have been compelled to change their location to the interior on that account.

SCENES ON THE ROUTE.

The country through which we passed on our route from Berlin was mostly rough and poorly cultivated, the land being thin and sandy, and at times the road was lined with pine forests, similar to those in North Carolina, the trees bearing marks of having been tapped for turpentine. At other points the country was as rough and barren as the worst portions of that on the railroad between Baltimore and Washington. We saw no one working in the fields except women, who were handling the hoe and spade. Scarcely a fence was to be seen for the whole hundred miles, this being an expense that is not known to European farmers. When they let their cattle out to graze, they have a man or boy to watch them, which is much cheaper than the labor and expense of keeping up fences.

MASCULINE KISSES.

We were much amused at many of the stations on the road to see great, rough-bearded men kissing each other at parting or meeting. They would first salute each other on the cheeks, and then bring their lips together. It seemed to the gentlemen spectators a burlesque on kissing, whilst the ladies declined to express any opinion on the subject, but it may be presumed that they regarded it as about on the same level as a matter of enjoyment with the practice of kissing each other whenever they meet or part.

FIRST-CLASS TRAVEL.

In Germany nobody but "princes, fools, and Americans" travels in first-class cars, the principal difference between the first- and the second-class car being that one is upholstered with velvet and the other with cloth. Any one who gets in a first-class car is regarded by the people on the platform as an object of curiosity, and so at all the stopping-places on the road; no one looks at second-class passengers, whilst the first-class are stared at as being either "princes, fools, or Americans." One of our party, being a novice in European travel, desired to test the difference in the cars, so we to-day traveled first-class to Dresden. We had scarcely got seated before we heard ourselves spoken of as "rich Americans," and the attendant who came to examine our tickets saluted us with, "Will your honors please show me your tickets?" When traveling second-class, an official jerks open the door and exclaims, "Tickets!" without even adding the American salutation of "gentlemen" to it. There is, however, an advantage in traveling "first-class" that is sometimes worth the additional cost, especially at night. There are so very few who take first-class cars, that a party of three or four are sure to have the entire section to themselves, and not be annoyed by strangers intruding and crowding upon them at every station. The ladies of the party can then lie down and sleep as comfortably as if in a sleeping-car. The additional cost is about one-fourth more than second-class fare. The fare from Berlin to Dresden is, in American money, as follows: first-class, $4.00; second-class, $2.64; third-class, $1.75, the latter being plain board seats without any kind of upholstering. The distance is about one hundred and thirty miles, so that "first-class" is only about the same as the American rate of travel.

BEER-DRINKING.

Everybody in Germany drinks beer, it being part of the daily food, as much so as coffee is in America. Mothers wean their infants on beer, and they are brought up accustomed to drink it as freely as water. At all the stations on the road an opportunity is given to the passengers to secure a supply, and it is more easily obtained than water, and almost as cheap. The Germans attribute the absence of dyspepsia to beer, and point to the rosy cheeks of their daughters as the result of this wholesome beverage. Our party are all giving it a fair trial, and hope to return home with a new lease of life and health. With all due respect to our American brewers, we do not think that any of them come up to the quality of the German article, which is of a bright and clear amber color and sparkles under a heavy froth. The taste for it is an acquired one, and we are all getting quite accustomed to its use. It seems to be free from all intoxicating effects, and if it proves a cure for dyspepsia, as is claimed by our German friends, it will do much more than the doctors have been able to accomplish in most cases of the kind.

FIRST IMPRESSIONS OF DRESDEN.

We had no sooner secured our rooms at the Victoria Hotel than we started out for a promenade through the main thoroughfares of Dresden. We found it to be a much more lively and stirring city than Berlin, the streets being so densely thronged that it was difficult to make our way through them. The population is nearly two hundred thousand, and the city is divided by the river Elbe, one side being called the *old* town, and the side upon which we are located the *new* town. The houses of the new town are generally five stories high, and are very similar in their appearance and construction to those on the boulevards of Paris. The streets are mostly broad, and beautiful little squares with fountains are thickly interspersed. The stores are quite elegant, and make a fine display of all kinds of rich and rare goods. A city passenger railway, the first, we believe, in Germany, has just been completed, and the cars are running through the city. They are of the large double-deck species,—the top seats being for the accommodation of smokers.

The number of English and Americans we encountered on the streets was truly surprising. We could hear boys calling to each other, girls chatting on the street-corners, and misses simpering along with their beaux, all speaking good and plain English.

PRUSSIAN MONEY.

An American traveling in Germany longs for a return to his native greenbacks and paper currency. The confusion of money growing out of the union of Germany is almost inexplicable, and when making a purchase you are tempted at times to hold out a handful of ragged coin and let the seller help himself. Another mode is to commence dropping the smallest coin into the outstretched hand, and stop as soon as the countenance of the receiver indicates satisfaction. The silver and copper coins are innumerable, commencing with a thaler and going down to a pfennige, one hundred and sixty of which are equal to an American dollar. They are also of a dozen different styles of coinage, all, probably, as plain as a pike-staff to a native, but a monstrous puzzle to strangers. Prussian money is, however, good all over Europe, and we learn that Prussian paper money commands a heavy premium in Austria. In Europe, nothing more clearly proves the power of a government than the value of its money across the border; and Prussia is to-day the recognized master of Europe, both in strength and brains.

IMPRESSIONS OF DRESDEN.

Our first impressions of Dresden have been more than realized by a five-hour drive through all its thoroughfares and suburbs, and we do not wonder at its being selected as the favorite resort for Americans residing in Europe. It is very much like beautiful little Bremen, though on a larger scale and more magnificent in its attractions. The ancient city of Dresden was inclosed by a wall and moat, the site of which now forms a magnificent promenade, extending through the heart of the present city. Extensive palatial residences, surrounded by flower-gardens, statuary, and fountains, border this grand public square, which, to-day being bright and beautiful, is now thronged with people and blooming with flowers. The whole city has a gay and lively appearance, and the display of the stores far exceeds that of Berlin. The hotels are also better, and that in which we are stopping, the Victoria, as well as the Bellevue and the Saxe, would do credit to Paris. We are in what is called the English quarter of the city, the houses in all directions being occupied by English and American families. Each floor has its separate family, like the houses in Paris. The houses are very large, being five and six stories high. A family can live here in good style for almost one-half what it would cost either in London or the United States.

THE GREEN VAULT.

One of the greatest curiosities here is the "Green Vault," consisting of eight rooms in the palace, so named from the color of their original decorations. It contains one of the most valuable collections of curiosities, rare works of art, jewels, etc., in the world, the contents of one of the rooms alone being valued at fifteen million dollars. The immense wealth accumulated in the Green Vaults is attributed to the fact that the Saxon princes were formerly the richest monarchs in Europe. Most of their wealth was derived from the Friedburg silver-mines, which, previous to the discovery of America, were the richest in the world. Much of the proceeds of the mines they expended in the ornamentation of jewels and works of art. It is impossible for me to mention in detail the numerous works of art which fill up these eight large chambers. As to the value of the contents of the different rooms, it may safely be set at eighty million dollars. The first room is filled with magnificent bronzes, the second with works and ornaments of all kinds carved in ivory, the third with mosaics principally, in which diamonds and precious stones are inserted in the most lavish profusion; in the fourth room is all the Court plate, in which are also diamonds and precious stones; in the fifth room are various articles of ornament, including a number of jewel-boxes ornamented with rubies and diamonds; in the sixth room are magnificent jewels, carved ivory and ebony, curious caricatures, etc. In the seventh room are the regalia of Augustus II., King of Poland, carvings in wood, of the Resurrection, Descent from the Cross, the Archangel Michael's contest with Satan, also two little pieces in wax. The eighth room greatly surpasses all the others in the costly splendor of its contents, consisting of diamonds, crowns, sceptres, chains, and collars, Orders of the Garter, the Golden Fleece, and the Poland Eagle; coat-buttons, all diamonds of the purest water, weighing from forty to fifty carats. All the gala ornaments of the Elector of Saxony, consisting of his coat-buttons, vest-buttons, sword-belt, scabbard, and collar, are set with diamonds. There are also several magnificent rings, two of which belonged to Martin Luther.

There are thousands of rare and curious articles in these rooms, every one of which is worthy of close and critical examination. The cost of admission for from one to four persons is one thaler and ten groschen, or about ninety-six cents in our money. There were about fifty visitors at the time of our visit.

DRESDEN BY GAS-LIGHT.

In a European city, there is no night in the week like Saturday night to take a general survey of gas-light scenes. We accordingly, after supper last evening, took an extended stroll over the city, finding ourselves at ten o'clock in the suburbs, amidst a tangle of streets through which we wended our way, hoping soon to strike upon some thoroughfare that we would recognize. We were finally compelled to employ an expressman to guide us back to our hotel, which we reached in good order and condition, though rather tired, considering that we had been roaming and riding, and perambulating palaces and vaults and gardens, all day long.

Dresden at night is almost as lively as Paris. The streets everywhere were thronged with men, women, and children, and the restaurants well filled with customers, sipping their beer and eating their Schweitzer cheese in as merry a mood as possible. There was no music, however, as in our beer-gardens; indeed, we have not heard a band of music in Germany, unless in attendance on a company or regiment of military. At the great restaurant near the bridge, on the banks of the Elbe, there were hundreds of visitors, all enjoying themselves in comparative quiet. The stores were nearly all closed at dusk, and the work of cleaning the streets everywhere progressing, which appears to be done principally by the people in front of their own doors. The students, with their red caps, were promenading with the girls and studying German as well as German character and habits at the same time, under most agreeable circumstances.

The Brühl Terrace, rising on the bank of the Elbe, approached by a broad and handsome flight of stone steps near the old bridge, is the most popular promenade, and presents a fine view of the river and the city. This was crowded with promenaders, and, being brilliantly illuminated with gas-jets, presented quite an interesting scene. The boats on the river and the lights on the long stone bridge, with its ceaseless throng of travel, presented a stirring scene from the Terrace.

DRESS OF THE PEOPLE.

If the prediction of General Grant that the English language is likely to become the language of the world is rather problematical, there is no doubt of the fact that the English and American style of dress is already universal throughout Christendom. On this bright Sunday morning, as we look out upon the thronged streets of Dresden, so far as the dress and manner of the people are concerned, were it not for the fine and cleanly Belgian pavements, we might imagine ourselves gazing on the streets of Baltimore or any other American city. The people are dressed precisely in every respect as they are with us, excepting, perhaps, that the gentlemen, or at least some of them, sport broader brims to their hats. The ladies are all attired precisely as those of Baltimore are, and the array of bright and light spring bonnets would do credit to Charles Street or Broadway. At the Dresden Cathedral this morning there was as fine an array of handsomely-dressed ladies as was doubtless to be seen at the Baltimore Cathedral, or at Mount Vernon or St. Luke's. The only difference to be observed here is the vast number of men in military dress, who are swarming all over the city, generally fine-looking youths, dragged from the walks of private life to learn the art of soldiering.

SUNDAY IN DRESDEN.

Precisely at eight o'clock this morning all the church-bells in the city sent forth their sonorous announcements, and on looking out we found the people in commotion, in their best Sunday attire, moving towards the churches, whilst all the carriages in the city appeared to be in procession, filled with men, women, and children, heading towards the country, evidently on picnic enjoyment intent. The stores were all closed, and all out-of-doors presented as quiet a Sabbath aspect as it doubtless did in Baltimore. A Sabbath morning in Germany is as quiet and impressive as in more strait-laced sections of the world, but after two o'clock the devotions of the day cease, and pleasure and enjoyment assume full sway. It is the day in Dresden for social calls, friendly reunions, family entertainment, and not only a day of rest, but of freedom for both the mind and body from the labors of the week. The streets soon became thronged with husbands, wives, and children, beaux and belles, the old and the young, all in commotion. The grand promenade is packed with people, the bridges are crowded with citizens passing from one side of the city to the other, and the "Restaurations" attract and refresh the weary, or furnish the usual evening meal of Schweitzer cheese, bread, and beer. Very few Germans take any regular meal after dinner, depending entirely on this evening lunch.

The stores, with the exception of those for the sale of cigars, cakes, and eatables, were closed, and the day was generally observed as one of rest and devotion, the amusements and recreations being of the most innocent character. The churches were all largely attended in the morning, and the immense cathedral was literally packed with people. High mass was celebrated at eleven o'clock, accompanied by grand music, both vocal and instrumental. In addition to the immense organ, there was a band of forty performers on brass and string instruments, and a large choir of singers, including some fine solo voices, both male and female. All the strangers in the city appeared to have congregated here, to listen to the music, and most of them had to stand throughout the entire ceremony. The cathedral is nearly as large as that of Baltimore, and the music sounded grand throughout its vaulted ceilings.

On Sunday afternoon and evening the favorite place of resort appeared to be the Zoological Garden, which was thronged with visitors. Many brought their lunch with them, whilst others took their evening meal at the restaurant in the Garden. Whole families seemed to move together, and were joyous and happy, doubtless having attended their churches in the morning.

OLD CHURCHES.

It is a notable fact that in Italy there is scarcely a church to be seen that does not bear evidence of having been built at least two hundred years ago, and very few which those who came after the builders have thought it worth while to keep in decent repair. We were not prepared to look for a similar state of affairs in Germany, but we have yet to see a church, either in Berlin or Dresden, that does not bear the impress of centuries. Even the churches and chapels along the road in the rural districts have the same mark of antiquity. Fortunately, or unfortunately, our ancestors did not build churches, or we might not have taken so much interest as we have in this and other kindred improvements.

THE ZWINGER PALACE.

We put off until to-day our visit to the famous picture-gallery of the Zwinger Palace, as a place, to us, of minor attraction. Those who have traveled much in Europe get heartily tired of picture-galleries, though it is regarded as fashionable to gaze and admire, and pretend to appreciate them, whether you can heartily do so or not. We decidedly object to straining our necks in staring up at frescoed ceilings and endeavoring to unravel the meaning of the painter in grouping together hundreds of allegorical figures of men and angels. Mark Twain expressed the honest convictions of two-thirds of those who pretend to admire and enjoy ancient paintings, with their allegorical figures and uncertain meaning.

The picture-gallery of the Zwinger Palace, and the museums contained in this immense structure, are great attractions. The collection of paintings is the finest on this side of the Alps, consisting of two thousand three hundred pictures, filling the walls of forty-five separate rooms. There are quite a number of the exquisite works of Raphael in the collection, the most important of which is the Sistine Madonna, around which there are always several artists busily employed making copies. It represents the Virgin and Child in clouds, with St. Sixtus and St. Barbara and two cherubs beneath. It was purchased in 1753 for forty-five thousand dollars.

The Museum of Engravings and Casts in the same palace is also very interesting, but the Historical Museum, contained in the western wing of the palace, is the most instructive, far exceeding in extent and attraction the museum in the Tower of London. The first hall contains a collection of curious antique furniture, with Luther's cabinet, beer-goblet, and sword. The second room is filled with ancient apparatus, spears, cross-bows, and other implements of the chase in use a thousand years ago, with the hunting-horn of Henry IV. of France. The third room is the Tournament Hall, in which are an immense number of richly decorated suits of armor arranged on horseback, with elaborately decorated shields and helmets. The fourth is the Battle Saloon, containing the armor and weapons used by the distinguished kings and generals in famous battles three hundred years ago, and numerous trophies of the battles with the Turks and Saracens. There are five other rooms, containing embroidered and ornamented trappings for horses, decorated with a great variety of precious stones, and some literally covered with diamonds and sapphires; also an immense number of Turkish swords, the scabbards and hilts of which are covered with precious stones, together with the elaborately worked Turkish tent of Kara Mustapha, captured at the siege of Vienna, and a vast collection of Turkish and Oriental weapons.

SUNDAY ON THE ELBE.

Sunday, when the weather is clear and bright, as it was yesterday, is a great day on the river Elbe. The steamboats leave every hour during the morning, thronged with men, women, and children, for the various gardens on the river a few miles above the city. Many carry with them baskets of refreshments, and make family picnics in the woods, getting their supply of beer from the restaurants. Between seven and eight o'clock in the evening the boats commence to return, loaded down with the excursionists, and during the hour we spent on the promenade last evening, not less than from eight to ten thousand were landed on the banks of the river just below us. They were joyful and happy, and we did not see one that appeared the least intoxicated. We have yet to see the first drunken man in Germany, or one that was even boisterous or noisy from the effect of liquor. Indeed, the people are singularly taciturn and quiet, much more so than are the Germans in America. Everybody appears to be comfortable, well fed, clothed, and contented, but a loud voice or a hearty laugh is seldom heard on the street. Neither have we met with any beggars in Germany, nor any one who bore the slightest appearance of destitution.

EUROPEAN HOUSES.

As many of those who build houses, as well as those who live in them, do not understand the style of dwelling-houses now in general vogue in all large European cities, we will endeavor to describe one of them now in course of erection directly in front of our hotel window. In this case the builder has a front on the main street of about one hundred and forty feet, sufficient to accommodate seven houses on the ordinary Baltimore style. He, however, builds but one house, with a court entrance in the centre, and eight stores below. The upper portion of the house, to the height of five stories, is completed with all the requirements for two or more families on each floor, and each story will have from four to eight good rooms, four of which will front on this street. The upper story is generally completed so as to accommodate four families, each being given smaller accommodations. In the rear of the centre stores on the first floor two sets of staircases pass up, one for servants and the other for tenants and visitors. An old woman or man is also provided with quarters on this floor, who is called the porter, and is always on hand to answer all questions as to who live there, whether they are in or out, what floor they live on, and also to do little chores of various kinds for the tenants. Each suite of rooms is complete and independent in its accommodations of all kinds, and we have been assured that the families are just as much separated from each other as if they lived in separate houses. There are elevators for the hoisting of wood and coal to the different stories, which must of course be obtained in small quantities. We have had occasion to enter several of these houses at times, and always found the general staircase clean and in good order, finely carpeted and cared for at the expense of all the inmates. They are preferred to the old style of separate houses, as affording better accommodations and an opportunity to make a better appearance for a small outlay.

All the houses now building inside the city of Dresden are in this style, and they are occupied as fast as built. The one to which we allude, opposite our hotel window, is not yet completed, but most of the stores, and the three upper stories, are occupied, the windows being handsomely decorated with lace curtains and every evidence of comfort and refined taste.

THE JEHUS OF DRESDEN.

The carriage fare in Dresden is exceedingly moderate, and any attempt on the part of drivers to impose upon strangers by overcharging is a penal offense. If you do not understand the currency, you can hold out a handful of coin to the driver, with the assurance that he will not take more than the law allows. He will even watch to see that no one else cheats you if you should stop to purchase anything. Give him an occasional glass of beer, and he is intensely happy. The legal charge for a horse and carriage per hour is two marcs, or forty-eight cents. They carry four passengers, being twelve cents each per hour. For a two-horse carriage the charge is one thaler, or seventy-two cents, per hour.

PET SPARROWS.

The birds in Germany, especially in the cities, are the pets of the people. The little sparrows are to be met with everywhere, and so gentle and tame that they will almost eat out of your hand. In the promenades and parks they hop around your feet and eat crumbs thrown to them. They protect the trees and shrubbery from worms, and in the public grounds afford so much enjoyment to the people that they are treated with special favor. Even the children never disturb them, but are taught to carry crumbs in their pockets to feed them; and in winter they are not allowed to suffer for food. In building a house, provision is made for the nests of the sparrows, little boxes being inserted at intervals among the tiles on the roof.

THE PARK OF DRESDEN.

We discovered during our extensive drive in the suburbs of Dresden that the city has a very beautiful park on its eastern boundary, near the Zoological Garden. It is laid out very handsomely, and is adorned with quite a number of pieces of fine statuary, lakes, etc., and has in it the Museum of Natural History and other public institutions. We passed a number of family parties spending the day in the woods. Beyond the park are a large number of elegant private residences, located in a beautiful region of country, and surrounded by gardens and every evidence of luxury and cultivated taste.

MARKET-PLACES.

There are no market-houses either in Berlin or Dresden. The market-place is invariably a well-paved square in a central location, upon which the vendors have tables, or have erected small booths, from which they sell their wares. There appear to be no regular meat-markets, meat being sold from provision stores which are scattered all over the city. Indeed, most of the booths at the market-places are for the sale of fruits, vegetables, toys, candies, cakes, and notions of various kinds. As about two-thirds of the people take their meals at restaurants, the amount of family marketing is comparatively small. At the hotels half a hundred persons are fed, through the *table-d'hôte* system, on what would be cooked in America for a family of ten persons, and when dinner is over there is nothing left but the bones. They count their guests, and cook just enough to go around sparingly.

THE CITY PASSENGER RAILWAY.

After leaving the Historical Museum this morning, our party took seats on the top of a two-story railway car, and paid our passage, equal to six cents, to the end of the route, which we found to be the village of Blasewitz, about six miles from the city, on the banks of the Elbe. Steamers to and from the city stop there every hour, as at numerous stopping-places on both banks of the Elbe, which, for beauty of scenery and magnificence of country residences on its banks, rivals the famous Rhine. The suburban residences on our route were truly beautiful, and scores of new and extensive villas were being erected along the line of the road, which is a new institution in Dresden, having recently commenced running. It has but one track, and inside the city limits does not stop for passengers except at the turning-out places, where the cars pass each other. Men with flags and whistles are stationed at all the corners, and at other points on the route, to warn off carriages, and the speed at which they run cannot be less than six miles per hour. There is a conductor, besides the driver, on each car, who takes up the money and gives the passengers tickets, and detectives jump on occasionally to see that each passenger has a ticket.

The village of Blasewitz, at which we stopped, is a congregation of beer-gardens, being one of the numerous places of a similar kind on the banks of the Elbe, from which we noticed the return of so many thousands of people on the boats on Sunday evening.

AUSTRIA.

THE CITY OF VIENNA.

VIENNA, May 20, 1873.

ENTRY INTO AUSTRIA.

We entered the dominions of Francis Joseph, Emperor of Austria, at midnight, and found his officials on the border, in the matter of examining luggage, very gentlemanly fellows, who, on being assured that we were on a pleasure-trip, did not require us to open our trunks. At daybreak we were passing through a most desolate region of country, abounding in pine forests, with very little cultivation. As we sped on towards Vienna there was a marked improvement in the land, and for the next two hundred miles the agricultural display was very fine, the principal crops being wheat, rye, and timothy. The houses of the tillers of the land are generally grouped together, forming small towns, which are scattered along the road, some very pretty, from each of which the steeple of a church is visible. Along the turnpike, which passes near the railroad, the marks of a Roman Catholic country were everywhere visible, at about every mile there being a shrine erected, with numerous crosses, having on them a representation of the crucifixion. As we approached Vienna some splendid country villas lined the road, and at twenty minutes past nine o'clock we crossed the Danube and reached the depot on time, having come through from Dresden, a distance of three hundred and seventy-five miles, in thirteen hours. We were fortunate in having friends to meet us at the depot, Dr. S. L. Franck, of Baltimore, and his estimable lady, daughter of Wm. S. Rayner, Esq., who have been residing in Vienna for the past year. They relieved us from all the annoyances that befall strangers on entering a city where the people are all stark mad with the Exposition fever. We found the same kind friends had secured rooms for us at the Hotel Austria, in which we were soon comfortably domiciled.

VIENNA, THE BEAUTIFUL.

This is the only city of Europe which attempts to rival Paris; and our first glance at its attractions, and at the vast improvements that are in progress, warrants the belief that it will soon be nearly its equal. Everything is on a grand scale, and the vast array of new buildings which have been erected in anticipation of the Exposition makes a grand architectural display through the heart of the city. Sites have also been selected for a new Parliament House, a Museum of Art, and a Historical Museum, in the vicinity of the palaces. The hotels are also on an extensive scale, several of which, including the Hotel Austria, in which we have taken quarters, are entirely new, and are on the style of the Grand Hotel at Paris. The new buildings on the Ringstrasse are all from five to six stories in height, and are magnificent in their architectural finish. They each occupy a whole block, and are superior to any of the private buildings in Paris. In every direction other buildings of the same class are in course of erection, crowded with workmen and workwomen. The palaces of the numerous Grand Dukes, of whom Austria has a host, are all as large and more ornamental than the President's house, and display their architectural beauties in all portions of the fashionable sections of the city. In fact, Vienna already exceeds Paris in the variety and superiority of its architectural decorations, every style of art being adopted here, whilst there is a painful sameness observable in Paris. We yesterday passed a new beer-saloon, larger and more elegant and elaborate in its architectural display than the Peabody Institute. They are, however, of plastic, in imitation of stone, but present a solid and massive front.

WORKING WOMEN.

We have before alluded to the fact that women perform the hardest kind of laboring-work in Germany, but were not prepared for the sights we have witnessed to-day in Vienna. In America mixing mortar and carrying the hod is considered such hard work that few white men can be found willing to undertake it. An immense building near our hotel, occupying a whole block, is in course of erection, on which not less than four hundred persons are employed, fully three hundred of whom are women. All the hard laboring work is done by women, such as making and carrying mortar in buckets on their heads to the workmen, and handling the brick. They are not allowed a moment's leisure, several overseers being on guard to keep them constantly in motion. We found the same proportion of women at work on all the new buildings, and there must be many thousands of them to-day doing this species of laboring work in Vienna. They comprise young, middle-aged, and old, but all seem to be strong and healthy. At dinner-time they swarm into the shops to purchase a piece of brown bread and fat bacon and a mug of beer, and eat their dinners sitting on the curb-stones. Their wages are one florin, or forty-eight cents, per day, and we are assured by a gentleman resident here that most of them sleep about the buildings on shavings, or in barns or sheds, having no homes. Amidst all the splendor and wealth of this great city, with its million of inhabitants, there is, perhaps, more destitution, want, and suffering than in all the cities of America. Still, we frequently hear some of our countrymen praising and preferring the governments of Europe. Whilst viewing this scene, the Emperor and Empress, with his staff and outriders, glittering in gold and precious stones, dashed along the Ringstrasse, on the way to the palace, whilst a short distance off stand the royal stables, an extensive establishment, covering at least four blocks of ground, each; the meanest animal in which is better cared for than these women. It is not to be wondered that of the many thousand births annually in the lying-in hospital of Vienna, less than five hundred are of children born in wedlock.

CAFÉ LIFE IN VIENNA.

The restaurants and coffee-rooms of Vienna are greatly superior to those of Paris, while at the same time the rates are much more moderate. Having friends here, we have preferred to take our meals at the cafés with them, and can truly say that we enjoy life in Vienna better than has been our experience in any other European city. The custom here is to take a cup of coffee at the usual breakfast hour, with a roll, a lunch at eleven o'clock, dinner at three o'clock, and supper, or ices and cake, between eight and nine o'clock in the evening,—or to drop any of them as the appetite may dictate. We have thus far provided ourselves outside of the hotels, and it is more like home life than the execrable *table d'hôte* of the hotels. Vienna bread is famous for its sweetness, and the coffee served to thousands every morning at a coffee-room in close proximity to our hotel is delicious. Our dinners are taken in a magnificent restaurant, of which the main hall is larger than the Assembly Rooms in Baltimore, and where hundreds of ladies and gentlemen are dining or supping, at all hours. The cooking and service are admirable; the bill of fare embracing everything that the market affords. When moving about in other sections of the city, we dine or take refreshments wherever we may happen to be, as there are numbers of these eating establishments to be found in every direction. Our friends, speaking German fluently, and having resided here for nearly a year, know the established prices for everything, and protect us from the usual fate of strangers in this city. An instance of this occurred at the depot on our arrival, when the expressmen wanted five florins to convey our trunks to the hotel. The price was a florin and a half, and a few words in German satisfied them that this was all that they were to receive. So it is with everything; and it is very comfortable to feel under safe protection especially during the prevalence of the Exposition fever.

HONESTY OF CAFÉ LIFE.

The manner in which the payments are made in these large Vienna restaurants is very peculiar. In the one in which we dine there are four collectors, each having a section of the hall. Parties sit down to the tables and order whatever they may desire from the waiters, and, when they are done, signal for the collector to come to them. They then tell him what they have had, and he sets each item down on a card with the charge, hands it to the customer, and receives the money. They keep no account as to what is furnished to any person, but depend entirely on the honesty of the customer to make a correct statement of what he has consumed. An account, however, is kept in the kitchen of each dish that is furnished to the tables under the charge of each of the four collectors, and they are required to pay to the cashier the full amount charged to their tables. If they have been cheated it is their loss; but experience has proven that there is no loss from dishonesty. These collectors not only receive no salary from the proprietor, but each of them pays two florins per day (equal to one dollar) for his position. They receive their pay from the visitors, it being a settled custom to give them a few small coins on the payment of the bill. Under the system in vogue in France the waiter receives no pay except what he gets from the customers. Here the waiter handles no money, and obtains his pay from the landlord.

DRINKING-WATER.

There is no doubt about the fact that the drinking-water of Vienna is not palatable, whatever it may be in the matter of health. It has a most insipid taste, as if impregnated with alum, and, as it is always lukewarm in summer, cannot be considered as desirable for the slaking of thirst. Very few persons in Vienna drink simple and pure water, even among the poor, as they all continue to put something in it to give it a taste. It is what we would call excessively hard water, soap instantly curdling on the top of it. On questioning people here, it will be found that nine out of ten will say, "I never drink water." If you call for it in a hotel, the waiter looks at you in wonder, starts off, and, after staying long enough to go to the top of the house, brings you a decanter filled, and then stands off and stares in apparent wonder at you gulping it down. If ice is called for, at least half an hour's further delay is necessary. In short, nobody drinks water or uses ice, and all demands for either are extraordinary and out of the regular order of events. The water here does not seem to slake thirst, although it is pure and sparkling to the eye. We do not, however, believe it to be unhealthy. Most of our party are great water-drinkers, and use it freely notwithstanding its bad name, and are all in the enjoyment of extraordinary health. With water so little tempting to the palate, it is not to be wondered at that people prefer wine or beer when they can get it, and give water the go-by. There is no beer in the world equal in quality to that of Vienna, and the quantity consumed in a day must be immense. The city is surrounded by breweries, and if they should happen to all burn down, it would be as bad as the water famine in Baltimore last year.

SHOPPING IN VIENNA.

The ladies find a great many articles cheaper here than in Paris. Kid gloves of the very best quality, with three buttons, cost but sixty cents per pair, such as would cost six francs, or a dollar and twenty cents, in Paris. Silks are also cheaper here, but velvets and laces much higher. Ladies' boots of the most elegant material and elaborate workmanship cost but five dollars. Narrow laces made here, such as are suitable for ordinary trimming, are very cheap, costing only from twenty to forty cents per yard. Linen handkerchiefs, with worked corners, can be purchased for but little more than the cost of the linen, and very elegant ones for one florin, or fifty cents. Women's work, such as embroidery, or trimming and working of dresses, is exceedingly cheap. A lady's dress, embroidered all over with silk cord, that would have required ten days' close application, was shown us today, the work upon which cost but seven dollars. The fashionable dressmakers, however, charge Paris prices, and run up very heavy bills on the strangers who visit here.

The display of goods in the stores and the windows is not, of course, equal to that in Paris, but there are great numbers of fine stores on all the leading streets, as well as in the old sections of the city. Indeed, the city has a bright and gay appearance everywhere. Even when one finds himself in a labyrinth of winding and narrow streets he sees much to admire; whilst the cleanliness is proverbial.

RELIGIOUS FREEDOM.

Vienna is an intensely Catholic city, but the largest liberty is now given to all denominations of Christians. We have, during to-day, passed on the streets at least a dozen processions of priests, with attendants carrying banners and crucifixes, and throngs of men and women following, chanting a monotonous prayer. But this is an every-day, and almost an every-hour, incident. We stopped in at the cathedral last evening, and there was quite a large attendance of laboring people at one of the altars, joining in the service, which is progressing at all hours of the day. The Protestants now have their churches, and no restraint of any kind is placed upon the freedom of worship, as was formerly the case.

THIRD DAY IN VIENNA.

The rainy weather which set in with the Exposition on the 1st of May still holds full sway, and the showers have been almost unremitting during the past twenty-four hours. We have seen much of the city, and have come to the conclusion that it is almost as beautiful and attractive as Paris, and equally gay and charming to the stranger. When the new Parliament House, the University Building, the new City Hall, and the Academy of Arts and Sciences, and other public buildings contemplated, and some of them commenced, on the Ringstrasse, are completed, it will have no rival in the world for solid grandeur as well as architectural beauty. Our view of it has been under great disadvantage of weather, but its attractions are too apparent to be clouded by an atmosphere that would render most cities gloomy. We are still assured by our kind friends here that we have as yet seen but little of its beauties, and that there is much in store for us independent of the Exposition.

THE LADIES OF VIENNA.

The ladies of Vienna do not keep themselves housed up, and out of sight, as is the practice of those of Paris. In Paris a really finely-dressed lady is seldom to be seen upon the streets, unless she be a stranger. If those who do dress well in parlors, or in their carriages, venture out for a promenade, they put on plain black dresses, and assimilate themselves to the masses. In Vienna, however, fine dressing is the rule of the street, and you frequently see ladies in complete velvet or satin suits, with trails sweeping the pavements. The weather has been bad for spring dresses and bonnets, cold and raw, with intermittent rains, but a gleam of sunshine brings them on the street, and they make a grand display on all the thoroughfares. They are also decidedly handsome, and some of them remarkably beautiful. A lady of youth and personal attractions must, however, never walk alone on the streets, or she is liable to be joined, and probably insulted, by the crowds of smart-looking Austrian officers who are always ogling the ladies. Two ladies together can go anywhere with impunity, even enter the cafés or gardens, and take their refreshments as safely as if they had a male attendant, but singly ladies must not venture anywhere.

The Ringstrasse, and the grounds and gardens of the Emperor's palace, are the favorite promenades, and here the ladies of Vienna hold their grand dress carnivals on bright and clear days. The display of laces and diamonds, and of all manner of rich attire, is not to be excelled in any city in the world. There are, however, many other localities for the display of the beauty and wealth of Vienna still to be seen, so soon as a bright sunshine shall warrant the resumption of their usual gayety.

THE VOLKSGARTEN.

At five o'clock yesterday afternoon we repaired to the Volksgarten, or the People's Garden, an immense music-saloon in the grounds in front of the Emperor's palace. Here the famous Baron Hess Band, alternating with other bands, gives a concert every afternoon, from five to eight o'clock, admission one florin, or about fifty cents. These bands consist of sixty performers, on string and wind instruments, and are fully equal to the Theodore Thomas orchestra now giving concerts in our cities. Two evenings of the week the famous Strauss Band, led by a brother of the Johann Strauss who attended the Boston Carnival, gives concerts in the same hall, for which, during the Exposition, two florins admission is demanded. The hall is filled with tables, and during the progress of the concert the audience drink coffee or sip their beer, and the gentlemen, and some of the ladies, take a quiet smoke. Among the audience were Turks, Greeks, and Russian ladies and gentlemen, many Englishmen, and a good attendance of Americans. The music was very fine, including several solos, and the novel scene by which we were surrounded added zest to our enjoyment of the music. Near us sat some Italian ladies smoking cigarettes, and on all sides were ladies drinking wine or beer, or sipping coffee. This is the case in all the concert-saloons and places of amusement in Vienna, and is regarded as right and proper by all classes. The evening meal is taken by nearly every one in some of the saloons, and when they can avail themselves of a concert, and can afford the extra expense, the Germans always seek its enjoyment.

THE VIENNA HOTELS.

The new hotels built in Vienna during the past year and opened on the 1st of May are very numerous, and four of them would be regarded as first-class houses even in New York. The Hôtel de France, the Austria, the Métropole, and the Imperial are all larger than the Carrollton or Barnum's, in Baltimore, and have imposing architectural fronts on the Ringstrasse. The Métropole and the Imperial are larger than the Fifth Avenue Hotel in New York. They are furnished throughout in the most costly manner, and are each provided with elevators, the first, with the exception of that at the Grand Hotel, ever used in Vienna. Their proprietors anticipated that in six months they would make fortunes, and commenced by charging five dollars per day for single rooms without board. The result was that the moment the opening ceremonies of the Exposition were over every stranger packed up and left. Ten dollars per day was the lowest cost at which any one could live at a hotel, and few were willing to stand this extortion. At this time, although prices have been reduced to about one-fourth of the amount at first charged, there is none of them more than one-third full. The Austria, in which we are stopping, though capable of accommodating fully three hundred, had but sixty guests in the house this morning; and some of the other houses are still more bare. Those who intended to remain here for a month now limit themselves to a week, and it is evident that this rapacity of the hotel-keepers and of the caterers for strangers has greatly damaged the reputation of the city. Vienna has always been famous for its greed in plucking strangers, having been regarded as the most costly city in the world; and it will now have a worldwide reputation. The city authorities did their best to establish moderate prices by the enactment of laws, but the dozen leading hotels defied all control, and have now, when it is too late, learned to regret their folly. Nearly a dozen new second- and third-class hotels were opened at the same time, and, as these paid some respect to the law, they have fared better than the larger houses.

The extortions upon strangers are, however, not confined to hotel-keepers. The German can live as cheaply in Vienna as in any other European city, but in the coffee-rooms and cafés the stranger is regarded as lawful plunder. One-third more is charged him for everything he may order, and if he happens not to understand the language a heavier tariff than this is imposed upon him. If he is so fortunate as to have a German friend to settle for him, he is astounded at the cheapness of everything as compared with any other city in Europe. If, therefore, the people of Vienna ever learn to treat strangers even as fairly as they are treated in Paris, it will become one of the favorite cities of the Continent. If a commissionnaire is employed, he only assists in plundering, and divides with the plunderers.

TWELVE HOURS A DAY'S WORK.

It is just six o'clock in the morning at the time we close this letter. The myriads of workmen and workwomen on the grand new building of the Stock Exchange, in course of erection opposite our hotel, have all been at work for the past half-hour, and thus they will continue, with the exception of an hour for dinner, until seven o'clock this evening. Twelve hours is a day's work here for the laborer and mechanic, whilst the bank and business clerk and all lighter labor is content with six to eight hours. Those who are so sweeping in their denunciation of trades' unions should witness the condition of the laborer in countries like Austria, where prices are regulated by the will of the employer, and just enough pay is given to prevent actual starvation. It is the abuse of power by trades' unions, and the manner of enforcing their decrees, that can alone be objected to: but that they should in America be awarded the right to combine for the regulation of prices, is justified by the condition of the workingman in some portions of Europe. The laborer here is more a slave than ever our colored "chattels" of the South were, and the three years that he is cared for and fed by the government as a soldier are very often the happiest of his life. If he were to strike for higher wages he would be driven back to his work at the point of the bayonet. There has been lately the first strike ever known in Austria, that of the cab- and carriage-drivers. The employers were notified that if they did not arrange to resume their business immediately the government would seize and run the carriages. This frightened the drivers more than the employers, and they made haste to make their peace and resume work.

VIENNA, May 24, 1873.
WHAT IS TO BE SEEN IN VIENNA.

Baedeker says that all that is worth seeing in Vienna can be seen in ten days. He is good authority on most subjects; but, as our party profess to be pretty active explorers, we must express a doubt on this point. We have spent four days, and have as yet seen literally nothing of what we desire and expect to see. Those who find nothing of interest in a city but old palaces and bad paintings may get through with Vienna in ten days, but if they take any interest in the active, moving scenes of the present they will find much to interest them for a month, independent of the great Exposition.

THE RINGSTRASSE.

It becomes so frequently necessary to mention the Ringstrasse, that we must endeavor to give some account or description of it. It is a broad avenue, part promenade and part street, extending around the entire city, with double lines of lindentrees down the centre, something like "Unter den Linden" at Berlin, but much more extensive and imposing. This broad avenue is the site upon which the old walls of Vienna were located, and, with the Quaistrasse on the Danube, encircles the whole interior of the city, or rather is the boundary line between Old Vienna and most of New Vienna. On this broad avenue are being located, nearly throughout its entire length, the most elegant and imposing structures. Those of private individuals and companies vie in elegance with the government structures. Although nearly double the width of our Broadway or the New York Broadway, it is hardly wide enough now for the concourse of people and vehicles that constantly crowd upon it. Several lines of passenger railways run over it, and branch off to other sections of the city. It at all times presents a gay and festive scene, even in such weather as we have been enduring during the past week.

There are lines of seats under the trees for pedestrians to rest upon. Property fronting upon this great thoroughfare commands fabulous prices, it being sold at so much per square foot. Outside of the Ringstrasse the city is extending in every direction, and the population is now estimated at one million. The new part of the city consists entirely of five-and sixstory houses, all erected on the "flat" system, and remarkable for their fine architectural appearance. All the new hotels are on the Ringstrasse, as well as the Emperor's palace and gardens, the city park, and nearly all the palatial residences of Austria's Grand Dukes.

THE GRAND OPERA HOUSE.

Our first visit to the Grand Opera House of Vienna was made last evening. It is the largest and most magnificent establishment of the kind in the world, excepting the new Paris Opera House, which is not yet finished, having been some twelve years in the course of erection. You cannot secure reserved seats, and unless application is made two or three days in advance it is difficult to obtain seats of any kind. When application is made for tickets they hand the number required, and you are compelled to take them without any certain knowledge as to their location. The house is immense, with four tiers of boxes, and a gallery above. The boxes or stalls are all rented by families at five thousand florins, or two thousand five hundred dollars, per annum, with the exception of the Emperor's box and the stage-boxes for the royal family and the Grand Dukes. The only portions of the house in which seats can be obtained by the public and strangers are the third and fourth galleries and the parquet. When imperial performances are given, no one is admitted without a ticket from the Emperor. The cost of a seat in the parquet at ordinary performances is about four florins, and in the third gallery three florins.

The performance last evening was a grand scenic and ballet spectacle, gotten up for the visitors to the Exposition. It exceeded in magnificence the Black Crook and all the other pieces of that character ever produced at Niblo's. The ballet corps consisted of at least two hundred dancers, and the scene presented at times on the immense stage was startling in its effect. During the progress of the piece each of the three hundred performers who took part in it appeared in at least six different dresses, and at one time the ballet-dancers gave the national dances of nearly all countries, including America, the air to which they danced being Yankee Doodle. They were arrayed in this dance in the costumes of the several countries, including Chinese and Japanese. The carnival scene at Naples was actually grand, and at times fully three hundred were dancing together and moving with wonderful precision. It would be impossible to attempt to describe the innumerable grand scenic spectacles presented, but they were most of them of a character we had never before witnessed, during a pretty extensive theatrical experience. It was a pantomime, with a well-developed love-story in it, and the most wonderful optical illusions produced by the free use of calcium lights from the scenes above. The ballet-dancers seemed to be all of the first class, both male and female, and the principal artist is an Italian danseuse, who is permanently engaged at twenty-four thousand florins per annum. This piece has been a long time in preparation, and will be presented twice a week during the progress of the Exposition. During the evening the Emperor's brother and some of the Grand Dukes were occasionally in their boxes; but the Emperor's box was empty all the evening.

THE CITY RAILWAYS.

Vienna has an abundance of city passenger railways permeating through every prominent avenue of the city. The cars are divided off into three sections, the first section being a coupé, holding three passengers, in which no smoking is permitted; the second or middle section holds twelve passengers; and the third section, which is open, and forms a portion of the platform, holds three seats, and standing-room for a dozen. They are often packed as closely as our own cars. They never stop to take on passengers or let them off except at the stations, which are about two squares apart, marked by a sign-board. The cost of a ride is just five cents in our money, extending from one end of the city to the other, a distance of about seven miles. They all strike into the Ringstrasse, and here the different lines occupy the same track, as they do on Baltimore Street. The conductor gives each passenger a ticket on the payment of his fare, the ticket being numbered, at the same time tearing a corner off it. A detective occasionally jumps on a car and takes the ticket out of the hands of each passenger and tears another corner off, and makes note of the number of it. Each morning the conductor is given a package of tickets, all numbered, and he must return the money for all the tickets that he does not return to the office. By this means there can be no dishonesty practiced by the conductors. It seems a simple system, and is said to work very satisfactorily. The companies are all very wealthy, and the stock is said to be one hundred per cent. above par. These railways all connect with suburban roads extending out to the villas and towns surrounding the city. The conductor never knows when the detective will appear, but always expects him, and is always honest. If any passenger is found without a ticket, the conductor is suspended on the spot.

A PAPER MONEY COUNTRY.

Austria is at the present time, like the United States, a paper money country, or, in other words, gold is at a premium of about eleven per cent. Strangers here who have letters of credit on the bankers, of course, have the advantage of this premium. Thus, in drawing twenty-five pounds yesterday, which would represent one hundred and twenty-five dollars in our money, or two hundred and fifty florins in Austrian gold, we received two hundred and seventy-five florins in Austrian paper money. The Austrian money is very easily understood by an American. A florin is equal to fifty cents, and a hundred kreutzers represent one florin. A kreutzer is just equal to a half-cent, American. A ten-kreutzer piece represents our five-cent piece, and a twenty-kreutzer piece, our dime. So, also, a fifty-kreutzer piece represents our quarter of a dollar. Thus, if we are asked ten florins for anything we desire to purchase, we at once know the cost to be five dollars; and so on with all other sums.

There was an expectation here among the banks and brokers that the Exposition would bring paper money back to par. The calculation was that from two to three millions of gold would be spent here daily by strangers; but the result has thus far been a great disappointment. It is presumed that matters will improve, and the receipts greatly increase next month; but as one-half of the strangers here are State or Government Commissioners, they expect free admission to the Fair. It is said that out of thirty thousand visitors last Sunday, less than fourteen thousand paid their admission fee.

They are, however, spending a great deal of money in the city, and the hotels are grinding everything out of them that is possible. At the restaurants a much better dinner can be had for one florin than can be had at the hotels for four, and a better breakfast for about thirty cents than can be had for a dollar.

THE ESTERHAZY KELLER.

Among the singular places to visit is the wine-cellar known as the Esterhazy Keller. It appears that Prince Esterhazy, a great Bohemian wine-grower, decreed in his will, many years ago, the establishment of this wine-cellar, his object being that the poor people of Vienna should always be enabled to obtain good and pure wine at the cost of production. It is only kept open from eleven o'clock to a quarter-past one, and from five to half-past seven o'clock in the evening. We passed down from the street two flights of stone steps to the depth of about thirty feet, when we entered an irregular-shaped cellar, which appeared to extend under the foundations of several of the neighboring houses. Around the walls were arranged a number of large casks of wine, with which the recesses of the cellar were well stored. There were in the cellar no less than two hundred persons, most of them of the poorer classes, though there were some well-dressed men sipping their wine. All were standing around against the walls, there being no seats, and the most remarkable quiet prevailed. Many women and children came with bottles and flasks, and for about six cents received a pint of very good wine. We took a glass, and found it very good and palatable. It is furnished from the extensive estates of Prince Esterhazy by his family in compliance with the order in his will. In a country where wine is considered a part of the daily food of a family, the value of this bequest is undoubted, as good wine cannot be purchased elsewhere for three times the money. It is a dark and gloomy place, and when we entered from the daylight the silent people standing around reminded us of the mummy vault at Bremen.

VIENNA, May 25, 1873.

FIRST VISIT TO THE EXPOSITION.

We yesterday paid our first visit to the Exposition, and were really astounded, both at its extent and wonderful magnificence. From ten o'clock in the morning until five P. M. we roamed through its vast halls, taking time only for a brief and hasty glance at the articles on exhibition, and when the time for leaving arrived we had barely accomplished one-half of the main building, leaving the painting-gallery, the machine department, and the horticultural exhibition, which were in separate buildings, unvisited. That the enterprise is a grand success, beyond anything that could have been anticipated, even by the Austrian authorities, is beyond dispute.

THE GRAND HALL.

When we get up fairs and mechanical exhibitions in America, a temporary board building is constructed, whitewashed, and the rough places covered with calico. The Vienna Exposition building itself is a great curiosity, being constructed as if it were to stand for ages, mainly of brick, stone, and iron, and grand in its architectural proportions and finish, both inside and out. The entrance and exit doorways are ornamented with statuary, and its dome is surmounted by a gilded crown, standing some twenty feet higher than the ball on the dome of St. Peter's. The hall of the Paris Exposition was twice as large as that of London, and the main building of the Vienna Exposition is computed to be more than five times as large as that of Paris. Besides this, there are two separate buildings, the machinery hall, which is about six times as long and twice as wide as the hall of our Maryland Institute, and the painting-gallery, which is three times as long and twice as broad as that of the Institute. The floor of the main building, with its sixteen transepts, is about one mile long and one hundred feet broad. The rotunda in the centre of the building is immense, and is itself larger than any hall in the United States; whilst the ceiling towers up more than three hundred feet to the crown of the dome, which is twice as large in circumference as the dome of St. Peter's. The grounds around these immense buildings have been laid out in vast gardens, with fountains, gravel-walks, and flower-beds, and hundreds of restaurants and cafés are erected within the inclosure, representing all the nations in Christendom, and even the heathen Chinee, the Turk, and the Japanese. Two of these restaurants are under the American flag; and some of them are as large and almost as fine in their appearance as the Mansion House at the Park. Near the centre of the main hall is a very fine building, erected for the Emperor, in which he is to receive and entertain his royal guests. Although merely for temporary use, it is a very elegant structure, about one hundred feet in length, and is ornamented with statuary and bas-reliefs, and the walls inside elegantly frescoed. Fine gardens and grounds have been extemporized around it, and it might be regarded as a very elegant country villa. But we find it impossible to convey any adequate idea of the magnificence of the Exposition buildings and their surroundings. They are vast and wonderful, far exceeding our expectations; and if Philadelphia hopes to rival or excel Vienna at its Centennial Exposition, it must be up and doing. Even with the cheap labor of Austria, the construction of these buildings and the preparation of the grounds have cost the Austrian government over forty millions of guilders, or about twenty million dollars in our money.

Large as this vast building is, it has been found entirely too small for the display of the goods brought for exhibition. The United States, England, France, Prussia, Russia, and several other countries have found the space allotted to them entirely inadequate, and have been allowed to construct additional wings between the transepts. The United States has enlarged its space by roofing over the ground between it and England, thus adding a hall about two hundred feet long and one hundred feet wide, with doors opening to it from the main hall; so also have the other countries named. Between some of the transepts private exhibitors have constructed large halls for their own exclusive display of goods, and, although the buildings are now full, train after train of additional goods is hourly arriving. Just imagine the Vienna Exposition to be the great wonder of the present century, and you will not fall much short of the mark.

WHAT IS TO BE SEEN.

There are some things that can be described, but we admit at the outset that the interior of the Exposition building is something beyond our ability to convey any idea of its wonderful and gorgeous display. There is here to be seen everything that is rich, rare, and beautiful, from all the four corners of the earth. The manner in which the goods have been placed upon exhibition has astonished us as much as their richness and character. The exhibitors have endeavored to excel each other in the magnificence of the thousands of beautiful and costly cases in which they display their goods, nearly all of these being elegantly constructed and ornamented and inclosed with plate glass. Millions of dollars must have been expended by exhibitors in fitting up the spaces allotted to them, and they have in reality opened business establishments for the sale of their goods, with clerks and salesmen in attendance. The rotunda has an immense fountain, with statues in the centre, and its vast interior is being fitted up with mammoth cases, many of them twenty feet in height, stored with valuable goods. Austria has furnished a magnificent temple for the use of the depositors, and they are sparing no expense in ornamenting its interior in a manner worthy of its grandeur.

THE DISPLAY OF GOODS.

Whilst all the nations have made a grand display, the most attractive department, and that which draws the largest throng of visitors, is that of Italy. The display of statuary and mosaic tables, and the rich and rare jewelry of Naples, Genoa, Venice, Florence, and Rome, attract throngs of ladies. The silks, satins, and velvets of France, the shawls of India, the laces of Brussels, and the diamonds of all the world, are here in glittering array. It is estimated that the diamonds alone on exhibition are worth ten millions of dollars, among which is one necklace for which one hundred and seventy-five thousand dollars is asked. Her Majesty the Empress was much pleased with this trifle, and the owner of it hopes to effect a sale before the Fair closes. The most elegant diamond cross on exhibition, valued at six thousand dollars, is marked as having been already sold to Johann Strauss, the leader of the great band which visited America. A beautiful piece of statuary in the Italian department, regarded as the gem of the collection, has been purchased by an American gentleman. It represents a boy sitting on a gate, blowing bubbles, and a little girl climbing up and reaching to catch the bubble, which is represented by a glass ball on the mouth of the pipe. The fun of the thing is so clearly depicted in the countenance and action of the children that it draws forth an involuntary smile from every spectator.

There are, probably, several hundred pieces of modern statuary in the Exposition, from all the best living sculptors, and to our uncultivated taste they are better worth seeing than all the mutilated remains of marble antiquities that have been unearthed at Rome. In addition to their beauty, they represent bright, living ideas and thoughts, and not the mere corrupting ideas of heathen mythology and impure scenes from Bible history. So also with the gallery of paintings, in which we spent a few moments before leaving. There is not a painting on the walls that needs any explanation. They all speak the thoughts of the artist from the canvas, and, as specimens of the skill of living painters from all quarters of the globe, give proof that high art, combined with sensible ideas, still exists.

We were rather disappointed in our expectation of seeing people dressed in the costumes of all nations among the exhibitors and spectators. On the contrary, there was nothing in the dress of any one to indicate that we were on this side of the Atlantic, except the long gowns of two greasy and dirty-looking Syrians whom we passed in the grounds. All, even Turks, wore the European dress, except that the latter retained their red skull-caps, with a long black tassel hanging down. Even the Chinese have cut off their tails, donned coats, pantaloons, vest, necktie, and felt hat, and no longer attract attention except by their almond-shaped eyes.

SUNDAY IN VIENNA.

There is evidently no law for the observance of the Sabbath in Vienna, every one being permitted to follow the dictates of his own conscience in this matter. The out-door mechanic, who has to keep all rainy days, is very apt to take advantage of a clear Sunday to put in a good day's work, and the storekeeper, if he can sell anything, has no scruples of conscience on the subject. A large proportion of the stores were, however, religiously closed all day, whilst others were kept open until noon. Those for the sale of provisions of any kind, tobacco, confectionery, etc., were open all day, as to them it is the principal business day of the week. The bricklayers were at work on all the new buildings on the Ringstrasse, and the women were mixing and carrying the mortar, until noon, when they stopped, in order to participate in the sports and merry-making of German Sunday evening. The churches were well attended during the morning, and the streets presented a holiday aspect, the people being arrayed in their best apparel, and all seeming intent upon personal enjoyment. The Opera House and the Music Halls were in full blast during the evening, and were all more thronged than on any other evening of the week.

The great Austrian bands gave concerts at the principal gardens, and the thousands of coffee-saloons and restaurants in which the whole population appear to eat all their meals on Sunday were crowded to excess. We entered one of the finest of these, to take supper, last evening. In it there are two hundred tables, each holding from six to eight persons, and we had to wait for a vacant table. This we learned was always the case on Sunday evening from six to ten o'clock, and that this particular café frequently furnished ten thousand meals during the day. But there was no drunkenness to be seen anywhere; and in this one saloon, although the party around each table were all in pleasant converse, it was in a tone that did not disturb their nearest neighbor. An American gentleman who has resided here for the past year assures me that he has as yet seen but one drunken man in Vienna, and he had, for the first time in his life, been testing the merits of American whisky.

The Exposition building was, of course, opened on Sunday, the price of admission on that day being reduced to about a quarter of a dollar. The number of visitors is said to have exceeded one hundred thousand yesterday, being mostly of the poorer class. If they could not have an opportunity of seeing it on Sunday, few of them could see it at all; for they could not spare any other day in the week for the purpose.

THE "DUTCH TREAT."

The Germans in the United States, and those Americans who affect a fondness for lager-beer, don't drink it as it is drunk in Germany. They rush into a restaurant and gulp down two or three glasses, and move on. Here a German never thinks of finishing his glass of beer in less than ten minutes, or of drinking it without eating something at the same time, even if it is only a crust of brown bread. In fact, a German in the Fatherland is constitutionally opposed to doing anything in a hurry, and especially to drinking beer with "rapid speed." The consequence is, that we do not see men here with great, huge paunches, as at home, capable of swallowing a keg of beer after supper. They never treat one another, but sit down to the tables, and, though they drink together, each man pays for what he consumes, whether it be beer or food. This of itself is a great preventive of excess, as if a half-dozen or dozen were to sit down to drink, as with us, each man must treat in turn, and thus six or a dozen glasses would be guzzled, whether they wanted it or not. If our temperance friends could institute what is called the "Dutch treat" into our saloons, each man paying his own reckoning, it would be a long step towards reform in drinking. In short, beer in Germany is a part of each man's food. He takes it as a sustenance, and not as a stimulant.

THE EMPEROR'S SUMMER PALACE.

We proceeded on Sunday afternoon to one of the most popular resorts of the people of Vienna,—the garden and park of the Emperor's summer palace, called Schönbrunn, located on an eminence about one mile west of the city. We were not prepared to find so beautiful and attractive a place, or one that so richly repaid the trouble of a visit. The palace is a very large one, and although completed under Maria Theresa, one hundred years ago, is kept bright and beautiful with paint. The front of it, with the wings for servants and attendants, is about half a mile in length, and with the Gloriette, a fine colonnade on an eminence in the rear of it, presents a most imposing appearance. It was in this palace that Napoleon the First established his headquarters in 1804 and 1809 and at the cannon's mouth dictated terms for the surrender of Vienna.

The most attractive and interesting part of the palace is the gardens, which are nearly as extensive as Druid Hill Park; and, as the royal family are to take up their residence there to-day, everything was probably in extraordinarily good order and condition. The view through the long avenues of trees, broken by statues and fountains, looks more like a theatrical scene than like reality. These avenues resemble those at Versailles, but are far more extensive: every tree appears to have been cut and trimmed for ages, so that they present for a half-mile at a stretch a solid wall of green, perpendicular to the height of fifty feet, and as smooth and regular as if constructed by hand, instead of being the growth of nature. Indeed, nature has evidently, for half a century, been nothing but an adjunct to art in the arrangement of these avenues, and they form an admirable background of solid green for the numerous statues which adorn the gardens. On an eminence in the rear of the gardens is the Gloriette, a colonnaded temple, erected by Maria Theresa whilst residing here, from which to have a fine view of Vienna stretched out before her. On the side of the eminence is a splendid and very elaborate fountain and cascade, with a large number of marble mermaids, and Neptune sporting in the spray. We, of course, ascended to the Gloriette, and found everything being put in good order in anticipation of the visit of the Emperor of Germany. We were not permitted to ascend to the balcony, but every part of Vienna, including the dome of the Exposition building in the far distance, was distinctly visible.

This park is open at all times to the people of Vienna, and in one portion of it is quite an extensive Zoological Garden, the menagerie containing a fine collection of animals. On Sunday the view of the animals is also free, and, as a matter of course, thousands avail themselves of the opportunity of breathing the pure atmosphere and strolling over the grounds, when the weather will permit. The cars run from the city to the palace, and it can be reached from most parts of the city for five cents.

THE PRINCE IMPERIAL.

When we reached the Gloriette, we found one of the royal carriages, with footmen in silver livery, and an officer gayly dressed, waiting near a gate which led into the thicket beyond. The crowd were all standing watching for some one, and we naturally joined them. Finally an officer in undress uniform, and a boy wearing a slouched hat and having a shot-pouch over his shoulder, emerged from the thicket, which was the signal for all the attendants to take off their hats, and for two or three flunkeys to run with coats and wraps towards the approaching couple. We were in supreme ignorance as to what it all meant, and as to which of the approaching pair was the one to whom all were so obsequious, but naturally thought it was the man, and had hardly noticed his companion until they approached the carriage, when the youth, a sprightly boy about twelve or thirteen years of age, jumped into the carriage and gracefully raised his hat to the assembled spectators, and the officer, who was his tutor, took his seat beside him. As they drove off, most of the spectators uncovered, and he gracefully saluted them by raising his hat. This boy, we were then told, was the Crown Prince; but, as his father is only forty-five years of age, he will evidently be a man before he is called upon to be an Emperor.

As we were about returning from the palace, another royal carriage drove up, containing the Empress and a female attendant. She had evidently come out to see that everything was in order preparatory for the arrival of the Emperor and the rest of the family to-day, though it is said that she and the Emperor are on such bad terms that they only appear together on great state occasions, he living in one end of the palace and she in the other. They had a mother-in-law, who died recently, and who, gossip says, kept the whole brood in hot water. There is now said to be peace in the family, but it is only a kind of armed neutrality. Wagon-loads of trunks were arriving at the palace, and the servants were moving about, appearing to have full possession.

We have also had two or three glimpses of the Emperor as he flies about the city in his carriage. He has with him, generally, no attendants, except an officer riding with the driver.

SCENES AT THE PRATER.

The Prater is an immense park in the northwestern section of the city, on the outer portion of which is erected the Exposition building, and through which all the visitors must pass, either in the cars, carriages, or on foot. It has fine, broad avenues leading through it; that on the left, the Würstelpräter, being the favorite haunt of the lower classes. Along this, for nearly a mile, are a succession of cafés and beer-gardens, theatres, circuses, wax figures, Punch and Judy shows, fat women, and all manner of attractions, and crowds of people. The Hauptallee, the farthest avenue to the right, about two hundred feet in width, is the favorite promenade and drive of the higher classes, and the Emperor and Empress (never together) are to be seen here every fine afternoon. It presented a gay and pleasing scene yesterday, the carriages with their bright equipages being so numerous that it was difficult for them to progress more rapidly than at a walk. Near the extremity of their drives, and bordering the Exposition inclosure, there are a vast number of gardens and restaurants, many of them being gotten up for the occasion. Two of these are American restaurants, and innumerable others are German establishments. It would be difficult to find anywhere a more gay scene than the Prater presented throughout its broad bounds, and it is truly a popular resort equally for all classes of the people. The occupants of the carriages generally stopped at some of the gardens, and partook of refreshments, listening for a time to the fine bands of music stationed at the largest of them, and met and joined with friends in social converse. We could not but contrast it with the stiff formality of the scene on the plateau in front of the Mansion at Druid Hill Park, where a formal bow is all that passes between friends as they meet or pass each other.

THE ROYAL STABLES.

Having procured tickets of admission, we proceeded this morning to the royal stables, which are located in the heart of the city, and were astounded at their dimensions. We found upon entering them that they cover about twenty acres of ground. The number of blooded horses in the stalls is four hundred, and they are all, with a few exceptions, English horses. Here were the Emperor's riding horses, the Emperor's riding and hunting horses, the Empress's ponies, the Prince Imperial's riding and carriage horses and ponies; white horses, to the number of over one hundred, for the royal carriages on state occasions; over a hundred brown and sorrel horses for light carriages; about fifty coal-black horses to be used for funerals and when the royal family is in mourning; and about twenty mules, together with several pet jacks and jennies belonging to the Empress. There are seventy royal coachmen, forty postilions, and two hundred grooms for the horses, with about fifty stable-boys and laborers. The Emperor and Empress are both passionately fond of horses, and could "talk horse" to the entire satisfaction of President Grant. It is evident that they do not intend this to be regarded as a "one-horse country." There is a hospital for horses, with a professor and students, and a large horse apothecary-shop, among the buildings.

We were next taken into the carriage loft, and here we saw two hundred carriages, about one-third of which were immense and ponderous vehicles covered all over with gilt, some of them especially for grand state occasions, and others for daily use, all as bright and beautiful as if just from the factory. There was also the grand gilt chariot built for Maria Theresa, the panels of which were painted by Rubens. Then there were the gilded sleighs and the smaller chariot of the sainted Maria, with a dozen little pony phaetons, used in their day by the Emperor and the Empress and a host of other great folks when they were little boys and girls. There was also in this loft the mourning hearse upon which the remains of Maximilian were conveyed to the tomb, and the mourning carriage in which the Emperor and Empress rode on that occasion. In another building we were shown an immense array of gilded harness, hundreds of sets, all ready for use, with the suits of livery to be worn by the coachmen and postilions with each set of harness. Then there were a vast number of sets of harness for funeral and mourning occasions, light harness, saddles, etc. The saddle used by Maximilian in Mexico was also shown us, with other matters pertaining to the horse, too numerous to mention.

We also visited, in a large building, the royal riding-school for use in winter, where the boys and girls of royal blood are taught to ride on horseback. It is an immense hall, two hundred and forty feet in length by one hundred and twenty in width, with a canopied box for the Emperor and Empress to sit and witness the performance. It has a carefully prepared turf floor, and the walls and ceilings are elegantly ornamented. This being only for winter use, furnaces are placed under the floor, with flues for heating it. The whole establishment is almost as elegant as the palace, and everything is clean and in fine order. The horses are all kept in broad stalls, which have cushioned sides to them, swinging from a bar. The main building is about a third of a mile long, and there are a half-dozen immense buildings in the rear. Carriages with the royal coachmen and postilions can be seen flying about the city at all hours, and the Emperor and the Empress and the father of the Emperor appear almost every day either on the streets or at the Präter.

EXPERIENCE OF GERMAN LIFE.

We have had one week's experience of life in a German restaurant, and it has been a very pleasant episode in the routine of travel. With our friends here, all Baltimoreans, our party numbers seven. The saloon in which we usually dine has nearly two hundred tables, and when we enter at half-past two o'clock each of these tables has from six to eight persons seated at it, partaking of their dinner. Being regular customers, a special table is reserved for us, and as we march through the hall there is a general buzz of curiosity at the sight of so many live Yankees, nearly half the party being ladies. We are thus living as the people of Vienna live, and find the life has its charms and is quite a merry one, and a happy escape from the nauseous *table d'hôte* dinners of the hotels. We are as jolly as the rest of them, and have taken a decided liking to the famous beer of Vienna. Everything is served up fresh and hot, and the variety is equal to that furnished at the tables of the best of our American hotels. The interesting sights and scenes around us also give a zest to the dinner-hour, and we are so happy and contented in Vienna that we shall probably remain for three or four weeks longer. At supper the hall is still more densely thronged, and, with appetites sharpened by the active life we are leading, we do not mind the clouds of tobacco-smoke, and some of us soon join in increasing its volume. Surrounded by those who are jovial and happy, we have come to the conclusion that properly to enjoy foreign travel it is necessary to live as the people live—when "you go to Turkey, to do as the Turkeys do." The coffee furnished at the coffee-rooms is excellent, and breakfast, consisting of bread and butter, coffee, and eggs, can be had for about thirty cents. These cafés are immense, and are always crowded with customers from seven to ten o'clock in the morning, and also in the evening. Most of them furnish their guests with all the European and some American papers.

LETTING ROOMS.

American readers will scarcely be able fully to comprehend the system of living in Vienna, without further explanation. There are very few houses in this city in which from ten to twenty families do not reside, nor are there any houses, in the new sections of the city especially, which cover less than the half of a square: most of them, indeed, take in the whole front, from corner to corner. The lower story, and very frequently the two lower stories, are taken for business, and the three or four upper stories are let out to families. Many of these families take more rooms than they require, which they furnish and let out to students and others, at so much per month. Thus it is that almost every housekeeper has furnished rooms to rent. Many of the occupants of these rooms contract with the landlady to furnish them with the usual German breakfast, consisting of a cup of coffee and a roll of bread. The rest of their meals are taken at the restaurants and cafés. Among the poorer classes there are some houses containing from eight hundred to three thousand people.

KEEPING OF PUBLIC SQUARES.

The Councils of Baltimore and New York, it is gratifying to see, have ordered the removal of the iron railings from around some of the public squares. These unsightly and unnecessary contrivances are generally ignored in all parts of Europe. The parks are the property of the people, and under the protection of the people, and need no iron railings to guard them. The removal of these fences will also, it is to be hoped, lend to the adoption of another European idea, that of placing the squares in charge of active and industrious young gardeners, who will employ their time in planting and cultivating beds of flowers, and otherwise ornamenting the grounds under their charge, instead of giving them into the hands of old broken-down politicians. The numerous "Rings" scattered through Vienna are not only breathing spots, but beauty spots, during spring and summer. The most beautiful beds of flowers are placed wherever they will add to the attractions of the promenade, and for any one to disturb them would be regarded by the people as an offense akin to burglary.

VIENNA, May 31, 1873.

THE EXPOSITION.

We spent most of yesterday at the Exposition, and have seriously come to the conclusion that it has been overdone,— that there is too much of it to be properly seen by any one before being satiated and exhausted in the effort to see even that in which he may take the most interest. We found that independent of the great Exposition Hall, and the separate Machinery Building, the latter being fully a third of a mile in length, and the Hall of Paintings, nearly as long, each separate government has a distinct building for the exhibition of agricultural implements, every one of which is filled to its utmost capacity.

THE EXPOSITION GROUNDS.

Whilst the interiors of the buildings of the Exposition are so vast and wonderful, the grounds are equally startling in their extent, and the scenes they present. The inclosure in which the Exposition is held covers nearly four hundred acres of ground, and the number of elegant buildings upon it is really wonderful. In addition to the spacious structure for the Emperor and his guests, nearly every government has constructed very ornamental buildings for its Commissioners. That of England is in the form of a country villa, inclosed by a paling fence, with flowers and shrubs in profusion. The grounds around the Emperor's villa, to the extent of three or four acres, are also laid out in grass-plots, with gravel-walks and fountains, evergreens, and even statuary. No one would suppose, to look at these structures, which are built with heavy walls and strewn with elaborate ornaments, that they are merely for temporary use, to be removed some months hence. But of all the nations the heathen bid fair to excel in the erection of these structures. Turkey is just finishing a splendid mosque directly in front of the main entrance to the painting-gallery, which is to be a fac-simile in all its appointments of the genuine article. Turkish mechanics are doing the work, and the decorations are all here, ready and waiting for the carpenters to finish the interior. Even the three drinking-fountains usual on the sides of these buildings are here, with their running streams and cups. But Turkey will eclipse Persia in the fac-simile it is erecting of the favorite country palace of the Sultan. It is nearly completed, and with its dome and minarets would outshine all the country villas on Charles Street avenue in its picturesque beauty. It is to be decorated and finished similarly to the Sultan's palace, and in the stables attached is to be a specimen of each of the domestic animals used in Turkey.

But even this rambling notice can give the reader no idea of the magnificence of the grounds of the inclosure. From a rough field it has everywhere been laid out with gravel-walks, beautifully sodded, and interspersed with fountains; hundreds of men and women being still at work keeping in order what has been finished, or completing the ornamentation of other sections.

The exterior buildings thus connected with the Exposition form a complete cordon around the whole immense structure, and still outside of these is the circle of restaurants and cafés, all the proprietors having been required to put up handsome buildings, which present a very picturesque appearance. Excellent meals are served at them, but pretty stiff prices are charged.

THE AGRICULTURAL BUILDINGS.

The farmers of America would be startled if they could wander through the immense agricultural buildings of the different countries. In the French department they would see a steam plow, built for one of the Archdukes of Austria, which could not have cost less than fifty thousand dollars. Only think of paying such a price for a plow! It is a mammoth piece of machinery for agricultural purposes. The plow and steam-engine are separate, and a practical farmer would be inclined to regard the man that conceived either of them to be an imbecile. In the first place, the engine is nearly as large and fully as heavy as a small locomotive. Its wheels, which are cogged, so as to retain a hold on the ground, are twelve inches wide, and the whole engine cannot weigh less than six tons. The plow is another immense iron apparatus, with two gangs of six plows each, one gang to be used in crossing a field, and the other in returning, so as not to require the unwieldy machine to be turned around. The apparatus to which the plows are attached, which is on wheels also, is fully thirty feet long, made entirely of cast and wrought iron, and the plows are each nearly twice the size of those in ordinary use. Each is ranged about one foot in advance of its next neighbor.

The apparatus looks strong enough and powerful enough to plow up Captain Jack's lava beds; but we have never seen any ground fit for agricultural purposes that could carry such a weight as is here massed, without taking it in at least to the hubs.

England presents a great mass of agricultural machinery, some of it of mammoth proportions, intended doubtless as playthings for its aristocratic farmers. There is one threshing and cleaning machine considerably larger than many of the cabins in which the agricultural laborers and their families live. Both France and England, however, present much that is useful and valuable, and are evidently finding it necessary to economize human labor.

There will be a test of plows and reapers about the end of June, when America expects to win the prize. Both the English and French machines are pirated from ours, and are of course inferior. The whole world seems to have gone to work to steal the American sewing-machine, as every nation except the heathen has a large number of machines on deposit. But we do not intend to attempt to give any idea of the Exposition. It is too vast even for a general notice, and any serious attempt to describe it would be regarded by the outside world as an exaggeration.

STRAUSS'S MUSIC.

We spent last evening in the Volksgarten, sipping our coffee, and listening to the great Strauss Band, of sixty professors, led by Edmund Strauss himself. Such music is never heard in our concert-rooms, not even from Theodore Thomas and his excellent orchestra. They lack the fire and enthusiasm which Strauss imparts to his whole band. Whilst leading, every member of his body is in motion, arms, legs, hands, feet, and head are swinging to and fro, and in the more stirring parts even the performers join in the motions. It is certainly live music, and lacks the funeral tone in which we are accustomed to hear scientific music rendered. Most of the pieces performed were either his own or those of his brother, interspersed with some selections from Mendelssohn. "Ein Stück Wien," the "Music of the Spheres," and other of the Strausses' compositions were produced; and by request of some American ladies he gave the "Beautiful Blue Danube," as only this great band could render it. An amusing incident occurred in connection with the request of the ladies. One of the waiters being requested to carry the card to the great leader and composer, positively declined to do so, as he had taken such a request to him on a former occasion, and had been told that "none but crowned heads could have such requests complied with." The ladies, having assured the waiter that we are all sovereigns in America, deputed one of the gentlemen to carry up the request, and in due time we had the "Blue Danube," and it was repeated in an encore. In this and all his own pieces, Strauss led with the violin, occasionally joining in the most difficult parts. He is a very fine-looking man, in the prime of life, and dresses with great taste and elegance. He affects the aristocrat by having a servant always following at his heels, in livery, carrying his umbrella, extra coats, and mufflings.

STREET SCENES IN VIENNA.

Yesterday being the first clear day for a month, the streets in all parts of the city were thronged with people, and among the stores, on shopping intent, the display of finely-dressed ladies was larger than we have ever seen in a European city. They trailed their dresses in the dust with all the freedom of our Baltimore belles, and, what seems to be peculiar here, the white underskirts were of the same length, and were trailed on the streets in company with their silks, satins, and velvets. They were suggestive of not very nice reflections as to the probable condition of the ankles of their wearers on returning from their promenade.

In the old portions of the city the streets are as narrow and crooked as those of the old parts of Naples, and the houses from four to five and sometimes six stories in height. The streets are all paved with the Belgian square blocks, and are kept scrupulously clean, mostly by voluntary scavengers, who are always at hand to gather up any dirt that may be found. They make their living by the sale of the manure they thus forage for. These narrow streets are lined with elegant stores of all descriptions, including dry goods, fancy goods, jewelry, and laces. They generally lead into squares occupied as markets and ornamented with fountains and statues.

There are no beggars to be seen on the streets, except blind ones, and these mostly perform on some instrument. We passed this morning a company of five blind musicians, playing together on the violin and accordeon with considerable skill. A box before them received the deposits of the charitable, and they stood against the wall and played without knowing what success they were meeting with pecuniarily.

The only men or women to be seen in the streets of Vienna who do not look and dress very much as we look and dress at home are the Bohemians and Polish Jews. The latter wear the long, closely-buttoned black coat, trailing upon the ground, which their ancestors wore, a black skull-cap, and a long, curled sidelock protruding. The Bohemians are an Italian-looking set of people. The women wear dresses made of old white blankets, whilst the men wear coats made of sheep-skins with the wool on. They seem to be poor outcasts, for whom no one cares.

The finest-looking class of men in Vienna are the Hungarians. There are a great many Hungarian regiments here, and the men average fully five inches more in height than the Austrians. The Hungarian officers are proud of their personal appearance, and walk the streets or stroll through the gardens with the air of men who know that they are the objects of personal admiration. Their uniforms are also gay and attractive.

THE VIENNA JEHUS.

The carriage-drivers of Vienna are all great scamps, and pay no regard to the law unless they happen to fall into the hands of a German, who gives the legal charge and walks quietly off, paying no attention to their abusive language. To a stranger they are such ruffians that most foreigners escape their clutches by riding in the street cars, which carry passengers to all sections of the city for about five cents. Fast and reckless driving is the rule in Vienna, and pedestrians must get out of their way or be run over. They dash along at a furious speed, even through the narrow streets, let them be ever so crowded, and never hold up or check their horses for old or young. Police-officers are stationed at some of the most crowded points, but they appear to think that their duty consists only in picking up those who have been run over. The drivers are the only people in Vienna who drink intoxicating liquors, and they are just the same kind of people as drunkards in America.

Courts and arcades, running through the middle of squares, from street to street, many of them lined with stores, are to be found in all sections of the city. By passing through these the throng of carriages can be escaped by pedestrians, and when one becomes acquainted with the labyrinth of by-ways the facility of passing from one point to another is very great.

FUNERALS BY CONTRACT.

The system of conducting funerals in Vienna is quite novel. There are funeral companies, which, for a fixed price, attend to all the details and deposit the coffin in the ground. They take charge of the body, prepare it for the grave, furnish the hearse and carriages, and act themselves as pall-bearers. The hearse is black, with dead-black horses, and driver clothed in the blackest of black, whilst at its four corners are immense bunches of black ostrich feathers. Alongside the hearse the burial society march, all clothed in black, with black cocked hats, and swords at their sides. The carriages that follow are only used for funerals, and are gloomy-looking vehicles, with black horses and solemn-looking drivers, arrayed in the same color. The cost is graded according to the number of black knights in attendance, the number of carriages, and the display of plumes. This system is universal in Vienna, and it has the advantage of fixing the price and steering clear of all extra charges. So, also, people can provide during life for their funerals by paying the amount required to one of these associations.

WEDDING PECULIARITIES.

There is a peculiarity not only in funerals, but also in weddings, in Vienna. Among the middle classes a wedding-party, in going to church, instead of securing closed carriages, employ open barouches. The bride and bridesmaid, with the groom and groomsmen and relatives, all seated in these open carriages, the ladies with white dresses and veils, without bonnets, fully intent on being seen, and carrying immense bouquets, pass through the crowded streets. If the weather is fine, after the ceremony is over they proceed to the Präter and join in the fashionable afternoon drive. Whether this is the only bridal tour they take, we are not yet well enough versed in Austrian habits to say. It is, however, a very pretty sight, and adds considerable zest to the enjoyment of a drive on the Präter. There is no more pleasing spectacle than a bride fresh from the altar, being suggestive to the younger portion of the spectators, and a reminder to the old folks of their own happy experiences in the long-flown past.

THE ROYAL JEWELS.

Among the curiosities of Vienna are the royal jewels, deposited in the Treasury Department. These halls are always thronged with strangers gazing upon the diamonds of the Empress and the jewels of the Emperor, which are kept in glass cases when not required for use. The crowns are also here, each a mass of diamonds and sapphires, also the celebrated diamond weighing one hundred and thirty-three carats, valued at one hundred and twenty-five thousand dollars, with the diamond buttons of the royal coat and vest, and the glittering orders of the Emperor, one of which contains one hundred and fifty diamonds. The necklaces, brooches, and other jeweled ornaments of the Empress are very numerous and extremely brilliant, though a great many of them have been just removed to be worn at the reception of the visiting Emperors of Russia and Germany. Among the curiosities here deposited are the gold and jeweled cradle presented to the First Napoleon for the use of his son the Duke of Reichstadt, the royal robe and sceptre of Napoleon, and the regalia of Charlemagne. There is also in one of the cases, set in a gold and jeweled frame, a piece of the tablecloth on which Christ is said to have communed with his disciples; and another contains a piece of the towel with which he wiped their feet, the lance which pierced the Saviour, fragments of the cross, etc. Of course they are all genuine.

THE VIRTUE OF THE EMPIRE.

Public gossip in Vienna represents the Emperor and Empress as by no means very happy in their conjugal relations. Her photographs in the windows show her to be a very handsome woman, about thirty-five years of age. She is said to be of remarkable intelligence and sprightliness of manner. The royal palace is in the heart of the city, and the Emperor resides in one wing of it and she in another, living entirely apart except when they meet on state occasions. He lives a very loose life, and, like the kings of the olden times, has an abundance of female favorites. Corruption and lack of virtue are the predominant traits of the court of the Empire, though the Empress is regarded as a pure and exemplary woman. This, at least, is the general conviction of the people; and, judging from the fact that there are annually born in the general hospital from ten to twelve thousand illegitimate children, Vienna may fairly be set down as a city of very loose virtue in all grades of life. The Viennese are quite a different class of people from the staid and solid population of Prussia and Northern Germany, resembling more the French and Italians in their habits and modes of life.

LIFE AMONG THE PEOPLE.

The youth and flower of the young men being forced into the army, there are not many youthful marriages in Austria, and among the working classes the excess of females over males is perhaps greater than in any other civilized country. This of itself causes great demoralization, and is one cause of so many females being compelled to resort to manual labor. The soldier cannot marry unless he has means of support independent of his pay, and even the officers receive barely sufficient to keep themselves in decent appearance. When a young Austrian of the lower classes does really marry, he regards himself as having made a great personal sacrifice, and as having conferred a prodigious honor upon the girl he has taken to himself. From that moment she is to be his humble slave, to work and toil and strive for his comfort. Even if she brings in by her own labor as much money to the joint stock as he does, all must pass through his hands, and be used first for his comfort and enjoyment. The wife must scrape together what she eats at home, whilst he spends his evenings eating and drinking in the restaurants. If they happen to be traveling, the husband walks from the depot with his cigar in his mouth and his hands in his pockets, whilst the wife trudges on behind with the valise and bundles, and, as in a case we witnessed last Saturday, also actually carrying the hat-box of her husband. If they happen to have children they trudge by the side of the mother also, or, if too small, are piled up somewhere among the bundles. The young Austrian is a peg above carrying bundles.

A TRADE NOTION.

The leading dry-goods, jewelry, and fancy stores of Vienna are each known by some fancy name. If a lady has bought a piece of jewelry she does not say, I bought it at Canfield's, at Warner's, at Larmour's, or at Webb's, as with us, but at the White Swan, the Black Bird, the White Dove, or the Humming-Bird; or if silks or satins have been the article purchased, she does not say, I bought them at Kos Parker's, at Easter's, or at Fugle's, but at the Red Lion, the Spotted Leopard, or the Gazelle. The proprietors are never known or mentioned, and the receipt for any purchase made is to the Lion, or the Swan, as the case may be. This is a good idea, as the death of the propr'etor would not damage the business, and the bereaved widow could sell out the establishment to much greater advantage, or carry it on herself.

TELEGRAPH POLES.

The telegraph poles through the streets of Vienna are immense cast-iron affairs. Indeed, it would be impossible for wooden poles to carry such a mass of wires. The poles on the Ringstrasse each carry eighty-four wires, and on the line of the river sixty-four. This indicates the extent to which the telegraph is made use of by the government. The telegraph is under government control, and the cost of dispatches is much cheaper than with us.

AMERICAN DRINKS.

The warm weather had its effect on one branch of Americanism on exhibition here. A month ago the impression was v ry general that the American bars would do a very poor business, on account of the high cost of their drinks, as well as from the fact that a half-gallon of beer could be had for the cost of one of their fancy glasses. They were then occasionally drunk as a matter of curiosity, and several Germans could be now and then seen at one of the tables with a solitary "cobbler" or "cocktail," each taking an occasional suck through the straw, and discussing its merits. It was a mere testing process, each, according to German custom, paying his share of the expense. Yesterday, however, the American bars were thronged with visitors, and the colored waiters, who are decided objects of curiosity, were kept busy filling their orders. These waiters are a sharp set of fellows, most of them from New York, and are of all shades, from the coal-black to the yellow pine. The former tell many amusing stories of their experience, and they seem to enjoy the inspection that they are constantly subject to. They have picked up a little German, but are each provided with a price-list, which they hand to the customer, who points out the article he desires. The following is a list of the plain American drinks that our German friends are beginning to learn to like, which are served up, smothered in crushed ice, at thirty, fifty, sixty, and eighty kreutzers each, or at fifteen, twenty-five, thirty, and forty cents in American currency, under the title of "American Mixed Drinks:"

Apple jack and cocktail-Jersey, brandy and soda (English), brandy champarelle, brandy crusta, brandy fix, brandy julep, brandy punch, brandy sangaree, brandy sling, brandy smash, brandy sour, brandy toddy, Baltimore egg-nogg, Boehm & Wiehl's favorite, claret cup, claret cobbler, claret punch, claret sangaree, Catawba cobbler, Catawba punch, champagne punch, champagne cobbler, champagne cocktail, egg flip, eye-opener, French cocktail, gin cocktail, gin julep, gin crusta, gin punch, gin sling, gin smash, gin sour, gin toddy, hock cobbler, John Collins (English), Indian wigwam punch, Jamaica rum punch, Jamaica rum sour, Knickerbocker, lemonade (plain), lemonade (with a stick), lemonade (fancy), milk punch, Metropolitan punch (U.S.A.), pousse café (New York style), pousse café (New Orleans), pectoral (Cuban), port wine sangaree, pine-apple punch, port wine flip, porteree, phlegmcutter, sherry and bitters (plain), sherry and egg, sherry cobbler, Shanghai Saratoga, soda cocktail, St. Croix fix, St. Croix sour, St. Croix punch, whisky cocktail, whisky punch, whisky julep, and old Kentucky, whisky sling, whisky smash, whisky sour.

The champagne punches and cobblers

are a florin and a half each, or seventy-five cents in our money. The plain drinks, which are equally numerous, range from twenty to forty cents each, or forty kreutzers and upwards. Fifteen per cent. of all the receipts, however, go to the Exposition fund.

HOTEL AUSTRIA, VIENNA, June 2, 1873.

THE WEATHER AGAIN.

We expected to see Vienna yesterday enjoying one of its most strictly observed holidays, it being Whitsunday, but from daylight in the morning until ten o'clock at night there was an incessant rainstorm, and so cold and disagreeable that we were glad to spend most of the day in-doors. To-day is Whitmonday, a general holiday; and, as the day dawned bright and beautiful, we started out early to see something of the mode in which the Austrians observe this annual festival.

WHITMONDAY IN VIENNA.

This is one of the most universally observed holidays in Austria, and before nine o'clock in the morning the whole population appeared to be in motion on the streets, arrayed in their best attire, whilst business was entirely suspended, which is far from being the case on Sundays. The cars and omnibuses were crowded, and carriages laden with women and children were moving in every direction. On the Ringstrasse, in the vicinity of the Imperial Palace, and along the road extending out towards Schönbrunn, or the Summer Palace, where the Emperor of Russia is quartered, three thousand policemen were stationed, in their handsome uniform, with swords at their sides, keeping the road clear for the royal cortége, which was momentarily expected to come into the city with the royal guests. From nine o'clock until eleven the streets for miles were lined with an immense mass of men, women, and children, waiting to get a glimpse at royalty. It reminded us of crowds that sometimes congregate on Baltimore Street to witness the parade of the Fifth Regiment, or the entrance of Dan Rice's circus, and the people appeared to be equally patient, standing in the first warm sun of the season. Our patience was not equal to the task of waiting for the royal pleasure, and at eleven o'clock we proceeded to the Exposition. How long the people were kept waiting we did not ascertain.

VIENNA THEATRICALS.

In addition to the Opera House, there are a large number of theatres in Vienna, of all grades. Those of the better class all have private boxes, occupying more than half of the house, rented by the year to families. In front of all the theatres, for two hours before the doors are open, there are throngs of men and women ready to rush in and secure the best of the seats that have not been taken. Then there are what are called "standing seats," and the rush to secure a good position to stand in is equally great. There are no reserved seats, and no choice is allowed. You ask for as many seats as you may desire in the parquet or upper tier, and you are given numbered tickets, but are not allowed to select them. The speculators, by collusion with the ticket-clerks, generally secure the best seats, and sell them at an advance to strangers and others who may desire to attend. Sometimes they get "stuck," as the newsboys say, and then tickets can be obtained very cheap after the curtain rises. At the Grand Opera all the seats are taken two days in advance, either by bona fide purchasers or by the speculators. On Wednesday evening there is to be a grand performance at the Opera House in honor of the Emperor of Russia, and all grades of royalty will be present. The ticket-office on Monday morning opened at nine o'clock for the sale of tickets for Wednesday night, and has been besieged for three hours by a struggling and excited throng of people. Those who wanted tickets had to employ strong and rough men to "wade in," and in a half-hour every seat was sold. We were on hand in good time, with an experienced friend, but were told when we reached the ticket-office that the tickets were all gone. There is no doubt that the speculators secured them all, and that there is collusion between them and the sellers, as the first twenty-five who reached the window seemed to have taken the whole, and we, with many others, were disappointed. But this, we are told, is a daily scene at the Opera House, all the tickets being sold two days in advance. The few boxes that are for sale could not be had before Wednesday, and we shall be compelled to forego the opportunity of witnessing this performance of "Faust" before the crowned heads of Russia and Austria, and all the scions of royalty of greater or less degree. The audience are requested to appear in full dress as far as practicable, which means that the ladies must appear without bonnets, and in light dresses, and the gentlemen with yellow or white kids, and white neckties.

EARLY TO BED.

There is a city ordinance which requires the front doors of all dwelling-houses to be locked by the porters at ten o'clock at night. Those returning home after that hour, and rousing the porter, are required to pay him ten groschen (about five cents), and if after twelve o'clock, twenty groschen. As there are few dwellings in which there are not from ten to twenty families, this ordinance has almost universal application; consequently, at a quarter of ten o'clock there is a general getting home, and the cafés and restaurants are soon vacated. It seems singular that there should be such a law in a city with a population, of nearly one million. The streets are usually very quiet after ten o'clock.

BUILDING ASSOCIATIONS.

The building associations of Vienna are on an entirely different basis from those in the United States. They consist of combinations of capitalists, who purchase land and build houses and hotels, and either sell them or rent and hold them. They have in their employ architects, engineers, and superintendents for every department of construction, and even contract to put up public buildings as well as private structures. They own their brick-yards and saw-mills, and have almost entirely displaced what is known among us as the master-builder. The new hotels that have sprung up so rapidly are all the property of building associations, and these have secured possession of every lot of vacant ground on the Ringstrasse but one. They also purchase every piece of private property that is offered for sale, and run up the rents upon the tenants at a fearful rate. The population of the city increases so rapidly that the demand for rooms is always in excess of the supply, which is one reason why it has always been more costly to live in Vienna than in any other European city.

These building associations have also in their employ all the best artistic talent required in finishing and ornamenting the fronts of buildings. This has become a necessity of the style of building, and it would almost puzzle our friends Hugh Sisson and Samuel Bevans to say at a glance whether these elaborately ornamented fronts are of stone or of its counterfeit presentment. Indeed, the cornices, lintels, architraves, balustrades, and statues of Cupids, fairies, athletes, and military figures, holding up or hovering over balconies and doorways, are much more artistic in design and execution than similar devices cut out of the solid stone to be seen elsewhere. These fronts, being backed by brick walls, commencing with a thickness of four to five feet, and taking on the cornice, with a solid backing of not less than two feet, seem to be as durable as stone. The walls are all laid in cement; and a crack in the plaster, a broken wing of a Cupid, a damaged nose to a statue, a limping fawn, or any evidence of the action of the weather, is never seen. The fronts, extending generally from eighty to three hundred feet, are among the finest specimens of architectural skill and beauty of design, and a stranger first viewing them is likely to suppose himself to be in a city of grand hotels, but looks in vain for a sign to indicate their character. They often occupy a whole block, and are built without shutters, but all have double sets of glazed sashes, and between these sashes there is generally a Venetian blind, by which the rooms can be darkened when necessary. The double sashes are regarded as keeping the heat out in summer and the cold out in winter, and even the smaller houses are all supplied with them. The distance between the two sets of folding sashes is about seven inches, and in the hotels and the better class of dwelling-houses there is always a cushion, just fitting between the sashes, encased in white linen, to lean upon when looking out of the window. The law requires the stairways of all buildings to be entirely of stone, and they are invariably so constructed in half-circular form, with iron balusters from the cellar to the roof. This is intended to be, and is, a great security from fire, which is very important, in view of the large number of families living in each house.

THE VIENNA BOURSE.

The Stock Exchange, or Bourse, of Vienna, increases so rapidly that it cannot furnish accommodations for its members. It vacated its old building some years since for a new one on the Ringstrasse, which occupies two-thirds of a square. It has long since outgrown this, and during 'Change hours even the streets around it are thronged. The board is

AMERICAN SPECTACLES. 45

now, however, erecting an immense structure on the Ringstrasse, nearly opposite our hotel, which has just reached its first story. I should judge its size to be about four times that of the Baltimore Custom-House, Post-office and Merchants' Bank building combined. It will be of nearly double the size of the Paris Bourse, and will add another to the many beautiful structures now rising along this great thoroughfare.

VIENNA LOCALS.

The bricks used for building-purposes in Vienna are twelve inches long, six inches in breadth, and three and a half inches thick. Immense quantities of them are used in the construction of a house, as all division-walls of rooms are of brick, and the outer walls generally are double as thick as they are with us.

All the most menial work in Vienna is done by women, such as cleaning and sweeping the streets, gathering up garbage, carrying water and pumping it from the cisterns to the reservoirs in the upper stories, sawing wood, etc. Woman has the "right" to do a man's work in Austria, and, as the "lords of creation" have no rights of their own, she is on full equality here. They are also the carriers for all the newspapers.

There are plenty of fleas in Vienna, notwithstanding the cold weather. The natives never feel them, however, nor do any other Europeans except the English. They seem to have a special fondness for American ladies, but do not approach them in such hordes as in Italy. Still, there are sufficient to keep up a pretty continual irritation.

No one in Vienna chews tobacco, and there is none on sale anywhere. Cigars are manufactured by the government, and are sold only at stores where nothing else is sold except postage stamps. They are at fixed prices, the lowest costing four kreutzers and the highest eight, or about four cents in our currency. The latter are about equal in quality to American domestic cigars that bring three dollars per hundred. A single cigar is sold here at the same rate as if one thousand were purchased.

The lottery system is in full blast in Austria, under the sanction and authority of the government, and flaming posters on the street-corners promise immense prizes, as was the case in Baltimore during the palmy days of France, Broadbent & Co.

OBJECTS OF PLUNDER.

The people of Vienna seem determined to impress the whole world with the conviction that whenever a stranger stops here he must expect to be regarded as an object of lawful plunder by all with whom he is liable to come in contact. The government has done all in its power to attract the whole world to Vienna, and has gotten up an Exposition that all the world ought to see, but the world doesn't come, and won't come. Although there are more strangers here this week than there were last week, there are scarcely as many as will be attracted to Baltimore during the Jockey Club races. Three days is the limit they give themselves for remaining in a city almost as beautiful and attractive as Paris, and where most of them would be glad to remain for a month if they could expect fair and honest treatment. Even when they visit the cafés and gardens, if they are not under German protection the waiters will charge them double prices for everything. To attempt to employ a commissioner is to have two rascals to pay instead of one. The city may be beautiful, and its attractions multiplied, but it will never rival Paris until some protection is extended to strangers and they are not so persistently "taken in and done for."

LIVING IN VIENNA.

The better class of people deplore this condition of affairs, and some of the papers denounce and ridicule the extortionists, but it has no effect. They have all built great expectations of fortune from the Exposition, and persist in grasping at every florin that can be reached. An American gentleman, from Baltimore, told me that he employed a commissionnaire to go to a store with him to make some purchases, and, on leaving, observed the storekeeper drop two ten-florin gold pieces into the hand of the commissionnaire. This was his pay for bringing such good fish to his net. Hence it is that travelers who spend so much money in European cities seldom purchase anything in Vienna.

Notwithstanding all this, both shopping and living in Vienna, to those who speak the language and are sharp enough to protect themselves from fraud, are nearly as cheap as in any other European city. An American gentleman who has been residing here for a year and a half assured me that it did not cost him more than fifty dollars, or one hundred florins, per month to live as satisfactorily as he would in a hotel. He has his furnished room and attendance for thirty florins per month, and lives at the cafés and restaurants for two florins, or a dollar, per day. A stranger, not understanding the language, would fare but little better at six dollars per day.

SHOPPING IN VIENNA.

In all the large shops of Vienna prices are enormously high, as compared with the charges in neighboring cities. There are seldom fixed prices marked on the goods here, as is almost universally the case in Paris, and the price is fixed after you enter the store, according to the judgment of the storekeeper as to the verdancy of the purchaser. The smaller stores are more honorable in their dealing, and those who know where to find them can make purchases as cheap here as at Berlin or Dresden, though not so cheap as in Paris or London. English and French goods are much higher here than anywhere else in Europe.

The residents of Vienna are, however, able to buy everything they desire at very fair prices, and Americans, after they are here long enough to learn " the ropes" and the language, say that they have but little cause to complain. What they may pay additional for the material is more than balanced by the cheapness of making it up as compared even with Paris prices; though the fashionable modistes charge fashionable prices also, and pay their sewing girls about twenty-five cents per day.

AUSTRIAN GERMANS.

The Austrian Germans are an entirely different class of people from the American Germans, or at least those Germans who usually come to America. They are more like the Italians or French in their dispositions and modes of life, as well as in their vivacity and impetuosity. They are neither frugal nor careful of their earnings, but will spend the proceeds of a week's work in a half-day's enjoyment. The better classes are given to speculation and money ventures of all kinds, and are lavish in their personal expenditure when they are in funds. Even those who prey upon the sojourner in their midst seem to regard it rather as shrewdness and smartness in business than as practical dishonesty. If anything is bought at a store, when it is sent to the hotel with the bill, two or three florins are added to the price originally agreed upon, under the plea that it was a mistake. If you refuse to pay it, the dealer will shrug his shoulders like a Frenchman, and exclaim, "Well, I will have to lose it!" He will relate to his friends all these small specimens of rascality as a practical joke, and draw out others of a similar character from his hearers in return. The same man will probably at the next moment throw all the amount he has thus gained to the waiter-boys at the café-table.

But the most marked difference between the Austrians and the Prussians is the lack of virtue among a large class of the women, and the fact that a husbandless mother stands as fair in public estimation as the mother of a child born in wedlock. Her reputation among her friends and associates is as bright as before her fall, and these little irregularities are no bar against her subsequent marriage. Italy is supposed to be the most immoral country in the world, but we have seen and heard enough here to convince us that Austria is close on her heels. The fact that about ten thousand illegitimate children are born in the general hospital in this city every year is proof positive of the laxity of the public morals. Notwithstanding all this, there is but little to be seen, on the streets or in the public places, of licentious women. There is no place here for these professionals, as it is mainly the working girls who are thus led astray, who are victims rather of the affections, and of this loose public sentiment, and can scarcely be classed among those who sell themselves for the greed of gain and a life of gilded vice. The common soldier in Austria cannot marry during his time of service, but he invariably forms a temporary female alliance wherever he may be stationed, and neither party is degraded by the connection. The mothers of the children born at the hospital return to their work, and the children are sent to the Foundling Hospital, where three-fifths of them die. Such a condition of society and public sentiment has its effect, more or less, upon all grades of life, and virtue is regarded pretty generally as at a discount. Even the pictorial papers here constantly publish cartoons illustrative of the state of morals. One, the other day, was the figure of a stranger just arriving in front of a hotel with his wife, and two young girls pointing and laughing at them. To a question as to "What are you laughing at?" the answer was, "We are laughing at the idea of a man being fool enough to bring a wife to Vienna." Everybody understood it, and everybody laughed.

"NIX DEUTSCH."

There is another peculiarity about the Austrians that indicates how different they are from the North Germans. If you stop on the street, or before a window, any one that may be standing near is almost sure to address you, and your next neighbor in a passenger-car invariably persists in commencing a conversation. Having endeavored in vain to make one of these talkative gentlemen comprehend that we did not understand a word he was saying, he finally looked puzzled, and exclaimed, "Nix Deutsch," to which we responded, "Yaw! nix Deutsch;" and thus we took our first lesson in German. We were subsequently taught on all such occasions to exclaim, "Ich kann kein Deutsch sprechen," which, we suppose, is the same thing in more polished language.

CONFIRMATIONS.

During the whole of the past week, being Whitsuntide, throngs of children, with their parents, have been proceeding from all parts of the city to St. Stephen's Cathedral, which is the oldest and finest church structure in Vienna, having been built nearly seven hundred years ago. Here all the children of the city of proper age gather to be confirmed. Yesterday afternoon we dropped in, and found lines of children, boys and girls, extending up and down both sides of the broad aisles, dressed mostly in white, with a white ribbon tied around their foreheads. The number present could not have been less than six hundred, and the venerable bishop was administering the rite of confirmation, assisted by a number of priests. Three times a day, every day during the week, a similar number presented themselves for confirmation.

NEWSPAPERS OF VIENNA.

There are quite a number of daily newspapers in Vienna, all of which publish both morning and evening editions. They are not very famous as newspapers, except in recording the movements of royalty, but are teeming with advertisements. Most of them are owned by bankers and wealthy capitalists, and are used to bull and bear the stock markets. Some have the reputation of being regular blackmailing concerns, and extort money from banks, insurance companies, brokers, opera singers, performers, musical leaders, etc., who pay them for puffing up or for keeping silent with regard to the financial standing or capacity of such men and establishments. Two editors were recently arrested and imprisoned for demanding ten thousand florins from a banker as the condition upon which they would withhold the publication of an article damaging to his financial standing. He pretended to agree to their demand, and, when they came to close the agreement, had two officers concealed in his room, who, on hearing their proposal, arrested them.

The principal subscribers to the papers are the restaurants and cafés, most of which take a half-dozen copies of each paper for the use of their customers. As there are many thousands of these establishments in the city, most of those who read the papers do so whilst eating their suppers or sipping their coffee. They are all sixteen-page papers, considerably smaller than *Harper's Weekly*, and badly printed on very inferior paper. The size is small, that they may be convenient for handling at the restaurant tables.

A MUSICAL PEOPLE.

During a week's sojourn in Berlin we never heard a band of music, except it was in attendance on a regiment of soldiers. On more than one occasion we made an extended search to find a music hall or garden, such as we expected to find everywhere in a German city, but did not succeed in the effort. In Vienna, however, music appears to be a part of the sustenance of the people. We visited last night what is known as Vauxhall, a large garden on the Pråter, the admission to which was equal to about thirty cents in American money. Here we found three large orchestral bands stationed in different parts of the garden, performing the choicest operatic airs. There were in the three orchestras over one hundred and fifty performers. Here the people sat, from four o'clock in the afternoon, many of them taking their supper, sipping their coffee, or drinking their beer. At nine o'clock quite a large music hall, with a stage, was thrown open, and a performance, consisting of comic dances, pantomimes, and juggling, commenced, one of the bands on the outside taking position in the orchestra. This continued until after ten o'clock, and was very amusing, after which dancing commenced in the garden, and we left them at eleven o'clock apparently intent upon making a night of it. But there are similar concerts in the Präter, and in all the Präter gardens, every afternoon and evening in the week, and the bands here, from Strauss's down, are admitted to have no superiors and few equals in the world.

VIENNA, June 7, 1873.

THE EXPOSITION.

We spent yesterday at the Exposition, and it may seem strange to your readers when we assure them that, although this was the fourth day of our exploration, we scarcely visited any part of it that we had before examined.

THE MACHINERY DEPARTMENT.

This vast building is a museum of wonders in mechanism, every nation being largely represented. The only machinery that was yesterday in operation was the woolen and cotton-spinning and weaving machinery of the different countries. This structure is nearly as long as the main building of the Exposition, and when the many thousand specimens of mechanism it contains are in operation, it will become the greatest attraction. At present it is very difficult to ascertain what many of these silent machines are expected to accomplish, so strange and incomprehensible do many of them appear. The American department has in it about fifty pieces of machinery, to which belting is being applied, and will, it is thought, be very creditable. There are none of those immense and ponderous machines which England and France have on exhibition, our deposits being all small labor-saving contrivances, which we expect to do their work and explain themselves when in motion. None of our locomotives or stationary engines are exhibited, whilst all the nations on this side of the Atlantic have abundance of them. The locomotive engineers of America will be pleased to learn that the European practice of keeping the engineer exposed to storm and heat has been abandoned, and that among the numerous locomotives on exhibition there is not one that has not complete protection for the engineer, with windows through which to sight the road, to keep off the pelting of the storm, and break the cutting force of the wind. One year ago on the English roads the engineer was entirely without shelter; and it is pleasing to see that the English locomotive manufacturers have adopted this American innovation.

There are at least fifty different varieties of the printing-press on exhibition, most of them being constructed on principles entirely different from the American press, but all of them stealing what is known as the "Hoe fly," without which no power-press can be a success. The majority of these presses are from Austria, France, and Prussia, and are very elegant pieces of mechanism. None of them are yet ready for the steam, though the work of attaching belting is in progress.

THE AGRICULTURAL MACHINERY.

Each nation has a separate building for the display of its agricultural machinery. They are very finely constructed wooden buildings, that of England being more than three times as large as the Maryland Institute, whilst France, Austria, and Prussia have structures equally large. Their agricultural buildings have in them hundreds of engines for farm work, constructed like locomotives on wheels. There are also steam-plows in great number, and thousands upon thousands of articles the inventors of which would have to "rise and explain" before the spectator could conceive what they are intended for. It is impossible to convey to the reader any idea of the extent of these vast collections. Even Italy, which ten years ago did all her plowing with a sharpened log of wood, has quite a respectable display; and although labor is so cheap in Europe, it is evident that the necessity of adopting labor-saving machinery is being universally recognized.

We yesterday measured the length of the engine and steam-plow on exhibition in the English department, built for the Grand Duke Albrecht of Austria, and found the plow-carriage to be twenty-one feet long, and the engine which is to propel it fifteen feet long, making the whole apparatus when in motion forty-six feet in length. The Grand Duke, it appears, has immense landed possessions in Hungary, and is going to farm them on high-pressure principles. The practical farmers here look upon it as a huge joke. It cost the moderate sum of fifty thousand florins, or twenty-five thousand dollars.

THE REFECTORIES, ETC.

The refectories, cafés, and soda establishments on the Exposition grounds, independently of their being a necessity, are all well worth visiting as a matter of curiosity. Each nation has two or three, and most of them are very extensive establishments, both in-doors and out-of-doors. It is no unusual thing to see five hundred persons in and around one of these establishments taking refreshments at one time. The condition upon which they are permitted to sell is that fifteen per cent. of all their receipts be paid to the Austrian government; consequently it is not to be wondered at that they charge tolerably high prices. The American bar, behind the music-stand, does a good business in American drinks during the afternoons, in good weather. Half a florin, or twenty-five cents, is charged for a sherry cobbler, and seventy krentzers for a mint julep. The same party, hailing from New York City, run all the American establishments, inside as well as outside, and, if they paid five thousand dollars for the privilege, as is alleged, will make a very poor business out of it. People taste the cobblers and juleps out of curiosity, but the German will never indulge much in such strong or costly drinks. As to the American cafés, there are too few English-speaking people here to support them, and, whilst the German establishments are so crowded that it is at all times difficult to get a table, everything looks bare and desolate at the American café. We took dinner there yesterday, in company with perhaps a dozen, whilst fully a thousand were at the two German restaurants in close proximity. Those who cannot speak English naturally shun an establishment where they will not be understood. As almost ninety-nine-hundredths of the visitors to the Exposition are German-speaking, there is every probability that the American eating and drinking establishments will not be very profitable speculations, unless the cobblers and juleps save them.

[During the excessively hot weather, which was very brief, the American bars did a good business; but later in the season they were totally abandoned. All went into bankruptcy, and were sold out and closed up. Beer triumphed in the contest, and continued to the close, even with the Americans and English, the favorite beverage of the Exposition ground. C. C. F.]

ARTICLES SOLD.

A great many persons have purchased articles on exhibition, with the expectation of being able to remove them immediately. This was the case with a fashionable lady on her way to the springs, who was charmed with a magnificent fan, which she intended to sport with during her summer tour. She paid down one hundred florins for it, and when she expected to receive the coveted treasure saw the seller appending a card to it, "Purchased by Mdme. von Smith for one hundred florins," and placing it back in the case. When she remonstrated, the lady was shown the rule, which forbids the removal of anything until the close of the Exposition, on the 1st of November next,—after the end of the season for fans. A large number of pieces of statuary and machinery are thus marked as sold.

EXPENSE OF THE EXPOSITION.

Philadelphia will have an expensive affair on her hands if she expects to rival Austria in the Exposition of 1876. The cost of erecting the buildings and preparing the grounds, even with the cheap labor of this country, has been forty-two millions of florins, or twenty millions of American dollars. The daily current expenses since it has been open have been fifteen thousand florins per day, or about seven thousand five hundred dollars. The receipts thus far have fallen short of the expenses; though that is not likely to be the case in Philadelphia, as the visitors from any one of our large States will exceed the entire number of even German-speaking foreigners from all the surrounding nations that will visit Vienna. The great mass of the people in this part of the world never travel, for the reason that they have not the means to do so. The number of Englishmen who travel in Europe is hardly equal to those from the United States, whilst Frenchmen are at the present time too severely pressed financially to indulge in any sight-seeing expenditures. Russians are here in goodly numbers, and there is a sprinkling of Italians and Swiss; but it is evident that the authorities and people of Vienna have largely over-estimated the anticipated visitors. Then the great mass of the people of Vienna are poor, and will only visit the Exposition on the fifty-groschen days. Baron Schwartz, who has had supreme control in the management of everything in connection with the Exposition, is a man of great energy. He has gone on regardless of expense, having expended more than double the sum originally estimated. But it has grown in magnitude so rapidly that the first estimates as to space were found entirely inadequate. The buildings since constructed for agriculture alone are almost equal to the original designs, and there are still piles of goods here that can find no space for exhibition. All Europe will, of course, be represented at Philadelphia, but it is doubtful whether any nation, except England, will make as good a show there as the United States does at this Exposition. Whatever may be the cost, it will not do for Philadelphia to make any backward step in its competition with Vienna, for as Vienna has outstripped France at the rate of five to one, so Philadelphia will be expected at least to equal, if not indeed to exceed, Vienna.

THE PRATER THRONGED.

On the evening of Whitmonday the scene on the Prater, as we came in from the Exposition, was one that would have astonished the inhabitants of a quiet little city like Baltimore, or even New York. Five avenues branch off at different parts of the Exposition inclosure, and come to a point at the "Präter Stein." Each of them is over one hundred feet in length, and bordering on them are circuses, exhibitions of various kinds, and restaurants and cafés innumerable. It being a general holiday, all Vienna, men, women, and children, seemed to be here congregated, eating, drinking, and making themselves merry. As we passed through this merry scene, one hundred thousand visitors to the Exposition were wending their way homeward, the cars and omnibuses not being sufficient to accommodate one in twenty of them. At the "Präter Stein" all the avenues were literally massed with people, and those who have not been in Vienna can form no idea of the number this vast space can accommodate. As our car moved along the Präterstrasse the broad pavements and parts of the street were filled with a throng of men, women, and children, who had given up all hope of finding room in the cars, and were making their way homeward as rapidly as possible. The Präter is the favorite resort of the working classes, and most of it has been given up for their enjoyment, one only of the five avenues having been kept clear of the resorts at which they congregate in such vast numbers on Sundays and holidays.

SCENES ON THE PRATER.

We spent the afternoon of yesterday on the Präter, and wandered about for several hours viewing the novel spectacle there presented. When there is a cattle-show at home there are generally half a dozen outside shows of giants, fat women, woolly horses, etc.; but at the Vienna Exposition the outside shows number several hundred. All the monstrosities of the world have been collected, and for a mile the Präter is filled with them. Many of them have gone the rounds of the United States. There are half a dozen fat women, monkey shows, wax works, Punch and Judy, hippodromes, rotary swings, fortune-telling, tableaux vivants, dwarfs, and other attractions too numerous to mention, the admission to each of which is ten kreutzers, or about five cents, or twenty kreutzers for reserved seats. They have all constructed attractive houses, as they propose to remain here and shout forth the wonders they have on exhibition daily and nightly for the next five months. After strolling for a couple of hours among the wonders of creation, we proceeded to the promenade avenue, where, securing chairs, we remained until eight o'clock in the evening, viewing the fashion and beauty of Vienna taking its evening airing. From five to eight o'clock all the fine turn-outs of the city were on these avenues, passing and repassing, whilst the sidewalks were thronged with gentlemen and ladies. Several military bands are stationed also at the large and fashionable restaurants bordering the Präter; and many of those in carriages alight, join friends in a cup of coffee or mug of beer, and resume their drive. The Emperor and the Empress frequently enliven the scene by their presence, with a throng of courtiers, and there was some expectation that the Czar of Russia might have honored it with a visit yesterday, but royalty did not put in an appearance. The drive is about two miles long, extending beyond the Exposition grounds, and with the pavements, and the trotting road, is fully two hundred feet wide. Fine rows of trees are on both sides of it, and here, either riding or walking, the fashion of Vienna daily assemble in good weather. The portion of the Präter in which the shows, amusements, and circuses are, is fully a half-mile from the Exposition, and bordering on the edge of the city. They are located everywhere in and around the numerous beer-gardens, and all seemed to be doing a thriving business.

SCENE ON THE GROUNDS.

Wonderful as are the buildings proper of the Exposition, and magnificent as is the display of goods, the grounds of the Exposition are equally attractive.

Many exhibitors who could not get as much space as they desired inside of the buildings have erected separate structures on the grounds, and make a special display of their own. There are at least fifty of these structures in course of erection, and it may safely be said that everything will not be complete before the middle of July. The whole of these three hundred acres of grounds presented the appearance, during the afternoon, of about forty of our ordinary Schützenfests combined in one, and when we passed out of the gates at seven o'clock in the evening, the halls having been just closed, the grounds, as far as the eye could reach, were almost massed with people. Seven large fountains, located in the beautifully laid-out garden in the rear of the dome, were throwing their streams high in the air, and numerous swans were gliding about in the large circular basins. The palace erected for the Emperor, with the elegant covered walks, had been finished and magnificently furnished, and carpets were being laid on the steps leading to the gravel-walks, in anticipation of the visit of the Emperor of Russia to-morrow. The flower-beds in the rear of the palace were all in full bloom, whilst the vestibule was adorned with all manner of rich and rare plants.

The Turkish palace, with its minaret rising nearly two hundred feet in the air, and its beautiful dome, will not be fully completed for a month to come; but the building for the reception of the Sultan is finished, and furnished with great elegance. The Emperor of Russia has also a very elegant building constructed for his accommodation, furnished in royal style. There are Chinese, and Japanese, and Turkish shops for the sale of curiosities, constructed and ornamented just as such establishments are in those countries, and doing a brisk business.

THE AMERICAN DEPARTMENT.

The American department has at last been thrown open to the public, and has been pretty harshly criticised by the Vienna press, which, from the long delay, professes to have expected greater attractions. This harsh criticism has had the effect of drawing more general attention to the American department, and we found it well thronged with visitors, and their close inspection of the articles indicated that they found much there to interest and instruct. Paris and London have emptied their glittering shop-windows into the Exposition, which are well enough to look at and admire, but there is nothing in the American department of this character. Everything here pertains to the useful rather than the ornamental, and, whatever may be the opinion expressed as to its character by other members of the American press, we predict that it will command more steady attention than some of the more glittering portions of the Exhibition, and take as many of the premiums. The extra wing erected by our Commissioners is largely occupied by the different American sewing-machines, and they have each attempted to excel the other in the brilliancy and elegance of the temples which they have erected for the display of their machines and the exhibition of specimens of workmanship. They have all the variety of their machines in operation, and they are constantly surrounded by spectators. The knitting-machines are especial objects of curiosity to the German ladies, who imagined that this work, in which they are all proficient, could never be better done by machinery. The display of American shoes, which is very fine, charms the ladies; and the extensive exhibitions of American dentistry, in which we beat the world, are thronged by that portion of humanity who have outlived their teeth. Indeed, if the character of any department is to be judged by the manifest interest of the visitors, no American will have occasion to be ashamed of the display. That there has been great bungling and neglect in getting the department in order is evident.

The American division of the machinery department is not extensive, but there are about sixty different compact little labor-saving machines in motion, which always attract eager crowds of spectators. All the different machines used by the manufacturers of shoes are entirely new in this country, and are in practical operation. So also with the American agricultural building. It is well filled with labor-saving machinery, and, although not so extensive as that of England, has the advantage of being acknowledged as the source from which England has pirated most of its machinery of this character.

As to the extent of the three departments of the American division, your readers can form some idea of it when they are assured that it occupies a combined space equal to three times the size of the Maryland Institute Hall, and that it is much larger and more attractive than the exhibition of the Mechanics' Institute at New York last year. That was mainly an exhibition of shop goods, its machinery department being the only real attraction. This is entirely composed of American productions, manufactures, machinery, and other evidences of our progress and devotion to the useful rather than the ornamental. We encountered a great many Americans yesterday, and most of them had come expecting to be mortified at our meagre display, but they were all well satisfied, and, considering the distance and expense to individual depositors, were rather surprised at the extent and number of the articles on deposit. There was general dissatisfaction, however, at the shabby quality of the American flags with which our department is decorated. They are all of muslin, with a brick-dust red, a yellow white, and a black blue. Some of the individual depositors have good specimens of the starry banner, but the Commissioners have used almost a burlesque of the flag.

THE AMERICAN SCHOOL-HOUSE.

The American school-house, which has just been finished, and opened for the inspection of visitors, is an object of great curiosity, especially to the more intelligent portion of the people. It is located in front of the English transept, and represents a rural school-house, such as can be found in all the school districts of New England and most of the Middle and Western States, but would be almost as much of a curiosity in Maryland, outside of Baltimore, and in the Southern States, as it is here in Austria. It is a one-story frame building, painted a light blue, with white sashes and green shutters, about fifty feet in length and thirty-five in breadth, one-half of which is the school-room proper, and the other half the recitation-rooms. There are the teacher's platform, chair, and desk, and the desks and seats for all the scholars, each desk with slates and books on it, whilst the walls are decorated with the usual maps and charts found in our public schools. There are two entrances, one labeled "boys' entrance," and the other "girls' entrance," and the inevitable water-cooler, with cups, on each side of the school-room. The desks somewhat resemble those made by Mr. Charles P. Stevens, of Baltimore, and used in most of our public schools. The recitation-rooms are also supplied with maps, globes, and all the furniture and appliances of education usually found in our rural school-houses. This building, together with the educational division of the American department, is very creditable, and helps greatly to refute the attempt made by the Vienna papers to belittle the American display.

BALTIMORE IN THE EXPOSITION.

Baltimore has not done much to bring itself to the notice of the world at Vienna. A diligent search yesterday brought to view the following articles: A very handsomely coopered barrel of lard, with a specimen glass jar of the same article, deposited by "Cassard Brothers, Baltimore, Maryland," and one of the patent iron-framed school desks and seats of our enterprising citizen Charles P. Stevens.

In the educational department, the Baltimore Public School Chart, giving the number of our schools, teachers, scholars, attendance, etc., is suspended in a very prominent position, and is flanked on either side by two specimens of crayon drawing, one by "Miss Maggie J. Ryan, aged seventeen, fourth-year class, Western Female High School, Baltimore, Maryland," and the other "drawn from a plaster bust, by Miss Alice J. Hank, aged seventeen years, third-year class, Western Female High School." There are also in a glass case, immediately under the chart, specimens of crayon drawing by the following scholars in our different public schools: Harry Stuhman, Bessie G. Thomas, C. M. Hiss, M. E. Shorte, B. T. Hanck, Carrie A. Summers, Annie Van Daniker, Laura M. Smith, Nellie B. Small, and Lillie W. Miller. There are also in the same case specimens of penmanship from Sophie Digges, Lizzie Williams, and Henry Weber. The educational chart is signed by John T. Morris, President, H. M. Cowles, Secretary, and William R. Creery, Superintendent, and is itself a very elegant specimen of penmanship. They are all in a very prominent position, which will be a source of satisfaction to those who have made these deposits.

The public schools of Washington City are nearly all represented by photographic plates of their several buildings, and the Franklin School-house, one of the largest of the Washington structures, has a large model of its building on exhibition, which gives a partial idea of our large city public schools. There are also specimens of writing and drawing from the scholars of the Washington schools.

New York, Philadelphia, Boston, and Cincinnati have also charts and specimens in abundance, and the school-book publishers of those cities have all their various editions on deposit. The South is largely represented by specimens of cotton, sugar, molasses, and tobacco.

VIENNA, June 3, 1873.

ARRIVAL OF VISITORS.

The month of June set in with the stormiest day of the season, but, as it has been succeeded by two bright and beautiful days, we are in hopes that it was the clearing-up storm. The change has already caused quite a number of tourists who were in the neighboring cities to come to Vienna, and yesterday the hotels commenced to show some evidences of life, and they are now resuming their high prices. Sleeping-accommodations have advanced to from three to five dollars per day, and they imagine that the long-expected harvest is about to commence. There will undoubtedly be a great crowd here in a few weeks; but we shall not be surprised if the extortionists compel them to disperse again very rapidly.

THE CZAR OF RUSSIA.

The Czar and Prince Imperial of Russia do not seem inclined to show themselves very freely to the people of Vienna. Wherever they go they are accompanied and guarded by two or three hundred policemen, and there is an impression abroad that they fear an attempt at assassination from some of the Polish refugees who have made their home in Austria. The Crown Prince visited the Exposition yesterday almost *incog.*, and passed only through the Russian section, which was closed to the public during his visit. He also attended one of the theatres last night, but his coming was not known a half-hour before his arrival, and a thousand policemen preceded him in and around the theatre.

THE EMPEROR AT THE OPERA.

We did our very best to secure seats at the Grand Opera House last night, to witness the display of royalty and fashion, the performance being given in honor of the Czar of Russia. We offered double prices for a box, but failed to get any, and finally gave up the effort. Not being able to get an inside, we took an outside view of the Opera House, to witness the illumination of the building and to see the grand array of aristocratic toilets, as well as the entrance of the royal family and guests; but, as their carriages dashed into the building through a waiting throng of people, but little could be seen of them. Whilst waiting, one of the speculators offered us three seats on the fourth bench in the fifth gallery for fifty florins, or over eight dollars apiece, but, concluding that we could see nothing worth seeing from this position, in what we would call the "peanut gallery" at home, we respectfully declined the proposal. The first act was then over, from which some idea may be formed of the difficulty of obtaining tickets when anything of real importance is to take place. Indeed, to secure tickets for almost any night requires a large stock of both patience and perseverance. The approach to the ticket-office has a kind of wall-of-Troy railing, in which the purchasers can only enter one abreast, extending through a long passage for about fifty feet. To have a chance for securing tickets it is necessary to be on hand at six o'clock in the morning, and the sale commences at half-past nine. This passage-way is crowded with several hundred excited people, who have to work their way gradually through this railing, and nine times out of ten all the tickets are gone before their turn comes. They profess to be very fair about it, but it always happens that the best seats are in the hands of speculators. On a royal night it seems to be necessary to have a card from some member of the court to have any chance. The Opera House is a government affair, all its deficiencies being made up out of the royal treasury. The number of singers, ballet-dancers, choruses, and attachés of the establishment is over six hundred, some of them receiving as high as from twenty to thirty thousand florins per year, with four months' leave of absence. The prima donnas, who receive these high prices, stipulate only to sing four times per month.

THE GRAND MILITARY REVIEW.

A military review in Europe is a very grand and wonderfully extensive affair, and royal in its magnificence. But by a civilian it is regarded as a matter with which he has nothing to do, and he is kept at such a respectful distance that nothing but a powerful field-glass will render him any satisfaction. Thus it was yesterday morning. The field upon which the review was held was about a mile in breadth by about a mile and a half in length. It was nearly level, without a tree to obstruct the view, and the infantry to the number of twenty-five thousand extended nearly its whole length, in two lines, whilst the artillery and cavalry were to the rear, about the centre of the line, numbering probably five thousand, with nearly one hundred guns. The people were massed around this field on every side, and were kept back by the military-looking police-officers, most of whom were splendidly mounted, and all carried swords. We managed to secure a position in the front line, and hence had a good view, at the distance of half a mile, of all that passed, a friend at our elbow explaining all that could not be clearly understood, and pointing out in the regal pageant the distinguished and prominent figures, who were recognized by their attire and the aid of our glasses. Two ambulances, with a squad of the ambulance corps, were on hand with stretchers to carry off any poor fellow who should not be able to stand the exposure to a hot sun; and, sure enough, at the first movement of the troops, one man was observed to fall out of line exhausted, when a stretcher was brought and he was carried off the field.

ARRIVAL OF THE ROYAL PARTY.

At nine o'clock the Crown Prince of Austria, a lad about fifteen years of age, dressed in the uniform of a general, arrived on the grounds in a carriage drawn by two sorrel ponies, accompanied by several military officers, footmen, postilions and others, and was greeted with cheers by the populace, in response to which he quite gracefully bowed.

At a quarter-past nine o'clock the Empress arrived in a carriage drawn by four roan horses, the footmen and coachmen being arrayed in yellow livery, with white plumes. Immediately following her were four other carriages, containing the ladies of the court. The Empress was arrayed in a pink satin dress, and carried on her a superabundance of diamonds and jewels. The carriages moved along about three hundred yards in front of the line of troops to the centre of the line, and there halted, with her son, the Crown Prince, to await the arrival of the Emperor.

At half-past nine o'clock a long line of royal carriages, which could be distinguished by the livery, was observed entering the farthest corner of the field, fully a mile from the position we occupied. They contained the Emperor of Austria and his suite, with the Emperor of Russia and the Crown Prince and their suites. There were also a large number of officers on horseback with them. They came to the ground by the roads leading from Schönbrunn to the summer palace, where the guests of the Emperor are stopping.

The whole royal party were now upon the ground; but there was no salute fired, nor any other demonstration, except that the nearest military band struck up a beautiful air, and the flashing of bright steel in the sun indicated that there was a presentation of arms along the whole line. We expected to see an abundance of powder burned, but the cannon were mute.

ROYALTY IN MOTION.

The royal party, headed by the two Emperors, and followed by the two Crown Princes and the Empress, with her ladies, in carriages, now started on the tour of review along the front of all the lines. There could not have been in this party of brilliantly-dressed nobles, all splendidly mounted, comprising the cortège of the two monarchs, less than three hundred persons, besides the Empress and her ladies, and they were followed by a detachment of the Emperor's body-guard. They moved slowly along the front column of infantry, and then turned, passing through the second line; then, again turning, they passed in review the artillery. Returning again, they passed the cavalry; and then the whole party moved to a prominence near the western extremity of the line, and took position whilst the troops passed them in marching order.

The fact that the Emperors of both Russia and Austria appeared in similar attire—that of generals of the Austrian army—was explained to me as according to custom on all these royal visits. It appears that these Emperors, who every few years drag their people into bloody wars, profess to be brothers when at peace, and honor each other by naming crack regiments after their "beloved" kinsmen. Thus, in the Austrian army there is a regiment named after the Czar of Russia and one named after the Crown Prince. Hence, military etiquette requires that they should appear in the uniform of these regiments when attending a military review; and they were thus arrayed yesterday. The sight was truly a magnificent one, and the royal party showed to great advantage in all the trappings and gilded glory that pertain to royalty.

A MARCHING REVIEW.

As soon as the sovereigns had taken their position, surrounded by their military families, the infantry commenced to move off towards the western extremity of the field, and in a few minutes the head of the column, in platoons of one hundred men each, marching thirty-three in a line and three deep, in tolerably close order, commenced to file past for inspection. It was a very beautiful sight, the white Austrian uniform giving to the platoons the appearance of white lines on the green sward. The time required for the whole force to pass in review before the royal party was one hour and thirty minutes. After passing, they deployed off to the border of the field nearest to their respective barracks, passing through different sections of the city, with bands playing.

The number of people assembled on the border of the field to witness this military spectacle was very great, consisting of men, women, and children of almost all classes. Without a field-glass but little could be seen by any one; and not one in a thousand was provided with this requisite. But even to see the glimmer of royalty and military display at this distance has a charm for the people which they seldom forego. From the palace to the Opera-House last evening the streets were lined with people to see the royal carriages pass; and when they did come the crowd was so great that but few saw anything but the hats and feathers of the flunkeys on the boxes at the back of the vehicles. No doubt the same crowd was in attendance at the close of the performance, to see them pass back to the palace.

VIENNA, June 9, 1873.

A BRIGHT SUNDAY.

Yesterday was the third Sunday we have passed in Vienna. On the immense building in the course of construction near our hotel, there was not more than one-fourth of the usual force of bricklayers and female laborers working, and these all stopped at noon, making a half-day's work. It seems to be at their option whether they work or not, and most of them avail themselves of the day of rest. The churches were well attended in the morning, and in the evening the gardens and cafés were thronged to excess. The concert halls were all in full blast, and the attendance at the Exposition exceeded that of any day of the past week. The admission on Sunday is only a half-florin, and the poorer classes avail themselves of the holiday and the low charges to take their families.

THE AMERICAN CHAPEL.

The American Chapel was attended yesterday morning by what was probably the largest foreign Protestant congregation that has ever assembled in Vienna. The chapel is one built by the government for the use of the Protestant soldiers of the adjoining barracks, and the use of it, at half-past eleven o'clock on Sunday mornings, has been secured for the accommodation of Americans during the time of the Exposition. There were nearly two hundred present yesterday morning, and quite an excellent volunteer choir of ladies and gentlemen accompanied the organ. There is no stationed minister, but as there are usually one or two Episcopal ministers among the visitors, their services are secured. Quite an excellent sermon was preached by a New York clergyman, from the fourth and fifth verses of the second chapter of Acts. Among the congregation we had the pleasure of meeting Minister Jay, Professor Blake, of Washington, and Mr. McElrath, of New York.

THE VIENNA FIRE DEPARTMENT.

There was an alarm of fire on Saturday, and the whole fire department of Vienna was out; but, as we could neither see smoke nor hear of any damage, it was probably a trifling affair. The fire-brigade are government officers, and some of them are mounted, and appear in very fine uniforms. The small hand-engines, about half the size of our old hand-machines, with side levers, and drawn by horses, were driven rapidly through the streets, a shrill brass horn being blown to warn all vehicles to move out of the way. The firemen are carried to the fire in a species of omnibus, that they may be fresh for work on reaching the ground. The amount of property destroyed here by fire per annum is said to be extremely small, a gentleman who has spent a year in Vienna informing me that he has not heard of a house having been burnt out during that time, though there has been slight damage to houses. The houses are so nearly fire-proof that fire is not likely to extend from one room to another, all division-walls of rooms being of brick, not less than twelve to sixteen inches thick, and all the stairways, from the cellar to the roof, solid stone. The consequence is that the flames spread slowly, and the firemen, reaching the ground very rapidly, are soon able to subdue them. The steam fire-engine is not known here.

We visited one of the fire-engine stations yesterday, of which there are seven in the city, and the officer in charge took great pains to explain the whole system, and to show us the apparatus, which he seemed to regard as perfection. There are three classes of engines, one for large fires, one for small, and the other for chimneys; and three sets of officers, who are called out when their apparatus is ordered out, by means of telegraph-wires to their houses. When the fire is on the first floor, they take with them hogsheads of water, on wheels; to be used with buckets, the city being but poorly supplied with water. The engines closely resemble the small side-lever machines used in New York thirty years ago, but are considerably smaller, being roughly built, without a particle of ornament, and painted a solemn black. They had twelve horses in the stable, all harnessed ready for use, the men all living in the building. They are required each to spend an hour per day in gymnastic exercises. Their ladders and fire-escapes are very good, but the whole establishment looked to us exceedingly primitive. The telegraph system is very complicated, and they use no alarm-bells, as the men are always on hand. We explained to them our system of districts, and of alarm-boxes on the telegraph poles, but they require the police officers to run to the nearest station and give the alarm. The elaborate iron telegraph poles, of which we have already spoken, carrying eighty-four wires, are for the exclusive use of the fire department.

THE BEAUTY OF VIENNA.

The more we see of Vienna, the more thorough is our conviction that it is one of the most beautiful and attractive cities in the world. It has also the advantage of being an unfinished city, especially in its most prominent parts, the finest possible locations having been reserved for the four most important of its public buildings, the erection of which is now being commenced. When its magnificent House of Parliament is finished, and its new City Hall, the cornerstone of which is to be laid by the Emperor on Saturday next, rears its beautiful proportions in the Schiller Platz, flanked by the Academy of Science and Art, and the Museum of Natural History, surrounded by the fountains and gardens of Parade Platz, it will present a combination of ornamentation, centrally located, that will eclipse the beauties of the Louvre and the Tuileries. We perceive that Bayard Taylor agrees with us that Vienna will soon eclipse Paris, if it has not done so already, and that there is no thoroughfare in the civilized world combining so many attractions as the Ringstrasse and its diverging streets. The removal of the old walls, parade-grounds, and fortifications of the city furnished the site for this great improvement, and it has been availed of to the fullest extent, whilst the sale of building lots has furnished to the government a mine of wealth with which to make Vienna the gem of cities. Such a noble thoroughfare, winding its way around the old sections of the city for the distance of nearly five miles, demanded handsome structures, and they have been erected with a lavish expenditure, and the employment of the best architectural skill that Europe could furnish. These tall and stately structures, following each other in endless succession, rich in ornamentation, each endeavoring to excel its neighbor in artistic skill and architectural taste, present the appearance of a series of massive public buildings or palaces, rather than private residences and places of business. The much-admired buildings on the Boulevards of Paris dwindle into commonplace structures in comparison with those of the Ringstrasse, as throughout its borders everything that is beautiful clusters. Nearly opposite the new Bourse, which will be double the size of the Paris Bourse, there is approaching completion the New Théâtre Comique, which will be nearly three times as large as Ford's Opera House, whilst block after block of the same class of buildings as those on the Ringstrasse are being erected on all the adjoining streets. The seven or eight new hotels just finished, and opened for the first time last month, are each as large as the Fifth Avenue Hotel, and much more handsome and elaborate in their architectural ornamentation. In short, everything here is on a grand scale, and if the people would only learn to treat strangers fairly and honorably, Vienna would soon become the favorite city of Europe.

PECULIARITIES OF CLIMATE.

The climate of Vienna very much resembles that of San Francisco. If the sun shines out bright and clear at early dawn, it is deemed prudent to take an umbrella along, as a sudden shower or a succession of showers is inevitable. If, on the contrary, the morning is dull and cloudy, it is regarded as indicative of a clear day. If the weather is warm and oppressive at midday, the evening will surely be cold and chilly: hence summer dresses are but little worn by the ladies, and both ladies and gentlemen carry overcoats and wraps with them, confident that they will be required for comfort after sunset. Home is regarded by most people only as a place to sleep at; hence those who are on the street seldom expect to reach their sleeping-quarters until it is time to make use of them. It therefore becomes necessary to provide in advance for a change of weather, and those experienced in the variableness of the climate are seldom caught unprepared. It also resembles San Francisco in the fact that the wind blows in currents through certain streets, and the turning of a corner brings you into a chilly and searching atmosphere, whilst on a second turn it becomes warm and mild. Thus, on a decidedly warm day, gentlemen almost invariably carry a thin overcoat, thrown over the arm, even while wearing white waistcoats and drilling pantaloons. The evenings and nights are generally cool through the summer.

KISSING HANDS.

Among the Viennese children and maidens there is a singular mode of returning thanks for a favor or a present, which is very startling to a stranger. Your hand is immediately seized, kindly and reverently, and kissed, the only words uttered being, "I kiss your hand." If anything is given to a little beggar-girl on the street, you must submit to having your hand kissed. At the cathedral on Saturday afternoon, whilst the ceremony of confirmation was progressing, this was almost a momentary occurrence. It is customary for the friends and sponsors of those being confirmed to present them with ribbons, cakes, and other mementoes, which are sold around the door of the cathedral. Consequently, the ceremony of kissing hands was in constant progress throughout the week. The number of persons confirmed is said to have exceeded twenty thousand, most of them children.

A SINGULAR MONUMENT.

Among the monuments in the squares or plazas of Vienna is one in the Graben that is so peculiar as to command even the attention of the European traveler who has been surfeited with the sight of those pillars of stones to the memory of men and women, most of whose lives were infamous, and their death a blessing. This is called the "Trinity Column." It represents a dense volume of smoke or cloud rising from an altar to the height of about thirty feet, and has figures of angels, to the number of not less than thirty, hovering around it, their heads and wings protruding. It was erected, as an inscription upon its base informs us, by order of Emperor Leopold 1., in 1683, as a token of thanksgiving on the cessation of the plague. The idea of the artist is remarkably well executed, and if the dust and smoke of one hundred and eighty years were removed, the monument would command marked attention.

DEPARTURE OF THE CZAR.

The Emperor of Russia and the Crown Prince, with their attendants, have all gone home, and the Vienna press details many incidents of the fear of assassination entertained by the royal visitor while here. Before his arrival at the palace, a Russian detective examined the apartments, to see that no one was concealed, and familiarized himself with the voices and features of all the servants and attendants who were to be permitted to enter that part of the palace during the royal sojourn. There was a fear that some Polish refugee might smuggle himself in, arrayed in the palace garb. Besides this precaution, the immediate attendants were all brought with them from Russia. This was the reason it was so difficult to get a glimpse of the Emperor, and that he visited only the Russian department at the Exposition, all visitors being excluded whilst he was passing through. When he visited the opera, no one whose character was unknown was allowed to have a ticket, and whenever he drove through the city thousands of policemen and detectives hovered around him. The nearest we got to him was at the review, when we saw him about a half-mile distant, through a field-glass. Who would care to be an Emperor, and be compelled to be thus guarded from assassination? Perhaps the fear of French vengeance is the cause of the alleged illness of the Emperor of Germany.

AUSTRIAN POLITENESS.

The Viennese are as polite and courteous as the Frenchmen. No one thinks of entering a store, an office, or a place of business without taking off his hat, and keeping it off, as well as exchanging a polite bow on leaving. To keep the head covered is deemed extremely rude and offensive. If you happen to make inquiry on the street, either of a man or a boy, the greatest pains is not only taken to give the right direction, but he will even follow you to see that you make no mistake, and when you stop to look around in perplexity you will generally find the same kindly stranger at your elbow to point the way again. Even on entering a café or restaurant all the waiters bow to you; and on entering or leaving a store the proprietor follows you to the door, and the clerks make their obeisance to you with all the grace of dancing-masters. It is singular that such a people, apparently so kind and courteous, are so given to deception and downright knavery in all their dealings. The ladies of our party, in their little shopping excursions, have invariably found an attempt to increase charges from their first agreement, under some plea of error or mistake. There is an attempt to overcharge in everything, unless the agreement is in writing. In conversation to-day with the proprietor of the American restaurant on the Exposition grounds, he aptly remarked that "the people of Vienna were the most courteous and agreeable he had ever met with, and as lavish with their money as Americans; but," he added, "they seem to take pleasure in cheating everybody they deal with."

STOCK GAMBLING.

The people of Vienna have a general mania for dealing in all manner of fancy stocks, lottery tickets, policies, etc., and the recent failures have affected all classes of people, but especially those of the middle strata, who had their all invested. Small storekeepers, seamstresses, actresses, and those who had accumulated a few hundreds or thousands of florins, had everything swept away. At the Bourse, among the throngs of excited men called curb-stone brokers, at least a thousand of whom surround the building every morning, can always be seen large numbers of equally excited women, who fall easy victims to the more experienced sex. Indeed, we find everything in Austria so contrary to our previously conceived notions of German character that were it not for the language we might suppose ourselves among a population of vivacious and excitable Frenchmen. Hundreds of boys are always on hand at the Bourse, who rapidly copy the bulletins of prices, and rush off through the Ringstrasse, offering them for sale to every passer-by, and finding more purchasers among the women than among the men. The females are also the principal purchasers of the lottery tickets, being easily deceived by the flaming announcements of fortunes gained by the investment of a few florins. How contrary to the American idea of the German character is all this!

BEER AND COFFEE.

We have found the most healthy and palatable drinks in Germany to be beer and coffee. The water is certainly not palatable, especially without ice, and ice is scarcely a marketable commodity here. Nobody uses it, and hence it is very difficult to find. The water is as hard as a dissolved paving-stone, and it is impossible to make a lather with soap when washing one's hands. It appears to curdle the soap, and makes it adhere to the flesh. All the washing is done on the creeks outside the city, it being impossible to wash with the city water. It may or may not be healthy, but, as nobody drinks it, the question is yet to be settled. Most excellent coffee is made of it, however, as can be decided at any one of the thousand coffee-houses spread over the city. Beer and coffee are the only drinks used in Vienna, with some wine, and they are invariably good.

THE VIENNA GENERAL HOSPITAL.

A few mornings since we visited the Vienna Hospital, which is one of the largest in the world, having over two thousand beds, and sometimes they are increased to three thousand. Being accompanied by our friend Dr. Franck, of Baltimore, who is attending the lectures on the eye and ear, intending to make this a specialty in his practice on his return, we had unusual opportunities to view the whole interior of the establishment, which would make an excellent study for the gentlemen having charge of the construction of the Johns Hopkins Hospital, of Baltimore. Each different class of disease to which the human system is liable has separate wards and a separate professor, as well as separate lecture-rooms. The first lecture-room we entered had over two hundred students awaiting the coming of the professor. They were of all nationalities, including a dozen or more Americans, and we were pleased to learn that the latter are the most studious and attentive to the lectures of any who attend. The professors all admit this, and hold them up as examples to the German students, most of whom come here merely to enjoy Vienna life. The patients are brought into the lecture-room, and operations are performed in the presence of the students. We passed through another department where a lecture on skin disease was in progress and a number of students were attentive listeners, and then through the wards, where an average of ten thousand children, only two hundred of them legitimate, are annually born. Several little Viennese were just making themselves heard in the world for the first time. The most interesting, however, was the department for diseases of the eye, where the eminent Professor Von Ault was operating on several cases, surrounded by a throng of attentive students. We afterwards visited him in his lecture-room, where he receives out-door patients for one hour every day, and operates upon them without charge. There were at least fifty of these awaiting their turn, each having been given a number stamped upon a piece of tin on making application, and they must be in daily attendance until their number is called. On the same afternoon we called upon him at his house in the city, and found not less than fifty private patients, similarly waiting their turn. He is renowned all over Europe as the greatest oculist living, and has accumulated an immense fortune from his practice.

THE DISSECTING-ROOMS.

In the course of our rounds we dropped in at the dissecting-house, one of the peculiarities of this great hospital being that all who die within its walls must be subjected to a post-mortem examination. With so many patients, the number of deaths daily ranges from thirty to fifty, and every morning the professors with crowds of students are present to witness the opening of this hecatomb of dead, and to decide upon the cause of death in each case. Relatives or friends of the dead are allowed to take them away when the professors are done with them, and provide for their burial; but if they are friendless, as is generally the case, they are cut up and quartered off among the students, one taking a leg, another an arm, another a head, as the case may be. Each body is brought into the rooms with a tin token tied to the right great toe, numbered and telling the ward in which he died, whilst around the ankle is tied a piece of paper, upon which is the opinion of the physician attending as to the cause of death. In one of the basement rooms was a row of twenty-six bodies just from the dissecting-room, the breast of each of which was split open, presenting a most ghastly spectacle. In another room were those who had recently died, they being kept there for twelve hours, with strings leading to a spring clock tied to their hands, so that an alarm would be given in case of reanimation. The student who spends a year in this extensive hospital ought certainly to learn something about the internal structure of the "human form divine."

THE JOLLY STUDENTS.

Many of the thousands of young gentlemen who are sent here to finish their medical education live a jolly life, and pay more attention to the enjoyments of this gay metropolis than to the pursuit of their studies. They all soon learn to like the life, and to like the city, and when their time of attendance expires, leave it with regret. They can be found of an evening scattered around among the cafés and restaurants, or studying German by intimacy with the German girls. They can generally talk German like a native before they have been here a year, as they mix among the people, and never lose an opportunity for an argument.

There were upwards of fifty American physicians here the past winter, many of them from New York and Massachusetts, a number of them being professors of some of our medical schools. Among the number, we mention Drs. Pomeroy, Merrill, Sinclair, Morgan, and Lefferts, of New York; Drs. Jorne, Green, Ring, Sprague, and Hunt, of Boston; Franck and Seldner, of Baltimore; and a great many from other States.

[We were absent from Vienna about two weeks, at the Iodine Springs of Hall, about two hundred miles from Vienna. Our letters from this place will be found in another part of this volume, under the heading "Life at the German Springs."]

HOTEL HAMARAND, VIENNA, June 25, 1873.

RETURN TO VIENNA.

After a few days of inactivity at Hall, we have returned to Vienna. Hall is a very healthy place, and a very pleasant place in which to while away the lazy hours of summer, but does not abound in such matters of interest as are calculated to amuse or instruct.

A FENCELESS COUNTRY.

From Hall to Vienna the distance is about one hundred and fifty miles, the road passing its entire length through the broad and magnificent valley of the river Ems. The land in this part of Austria is decidedly rich, and on the whole route the cottages of the farmers were bright and beautiful, bearing evidence of being inhabited by a prosperous and happy people. The fenceless fields, with scarcely a hedge except at the roadside, were waving with heavy crops of wheat, rye, and barley, indicative of the most careful cultivation. To an American, accustomed to the perpetual network of rail- and worm-fences, the sight of a country without fences is quite a novelty; and when the hundreds of millions of dollars spent by our farmers in this really useless luxury are considered, the wonder is that the European practice is not adopted, especially in the far West. They have fences around their stable-yards to keep the cattle in, but none even on the turnpike or roadsides. In all this distance not a single cow could be seen running loose, though occasionally a cow or a horse could be observed, led by halter, and allowed to nibble the grass along the roadside. The turnpike, visible from the cars, was marked by rows of tall poplar-trees, as it swept along through fields of grain or grass, without a fence or a hedge to divide it from the tilled lands. There is evidently no necessity here for self-opening or any other description of patent gates, which are so abundant in America.

The barns along the route of our journey were generally immense structures, forming squares, with a court-yard for the cattle in the centre of the square. They are built of brick, and very massive, nearly all having thatched roofs. Some of the longest of them were about two hundred feet on each of the four sides of the square, and in many of them one of the corners is occupied by the family of the farmer. Thus all his interests are under one roof, and the cattle are confined to the limits of the court-yard. We were assured that the whole establishment is kept scrupulously clean, and that the family section usually abounds in rural comforts.

THE VIENNESE EXTORTIONS.

Having reached Vienna again, we will sweep off in the present letter such notes on general subjects as are upon our notebook.

The Vienna papers contain a list of over eight hundred hack- and carriage-drivers who were arrested and fined during the past month, charged with imposing upon and taking advantage of strangers. There are very few Englishmen in Vienna, fewer than were here at this time last year. The London *Times* continues to urge them to keep away on account of the extortions, and an Englishman never goes where the *Times* advises him not to go. At the Anglo-Austrian Bank the number of Americans recorded daily is fully twenty to one Englishman.

A gentleman and his wife from Roumania, who stopped two days at the Grand Hotel last month, informed me that they were charged thirty florins, or fifteen dollars, per day for sleeping accommodations alone. The charges now are not so excessive. Good single rooms can be had at most of the hotels for from two to three florins per day, and none of them are more than half full at these reduced rates. The immense increase in the number of hotels, there having been more than a dozen large houses opened on the 1st of May, has completely overthrown the combination for excessive charges, and they now get as much as they can, but are also inclined to take what they can get.

The cost of living at the restaurants has come down to the old standard, and is extremely moderate, compared even with Baltimore prices. Coffee of the very best quality, with butter and bread, costs but fifty kreutzers, or twenty-five cents. A good dinner, of three or four dishes, including beer, costs about one florin, and supper, with beefsteak or other meat, less than a florin. Everything is fresh cooked and well cooked, and no one need desire better living than can be had at one dollar and a quarter per day.

MORALS AND MARRIAGE.

In our former letters allusions have been made to the condition of morals which pervades Vienna and is rapidly spreading among all classes. In order that no unjust impression may be given the reader as to the character of the people of Austria, who are so different in every respect from the Germans of Prussia, we have made special efforts to obtain authentic information as to the causes which are leading to this extensive demoralization. That there are many good and virtuous people here, there is no manner of doubt, but that the next generation will greatly deteriorate is equally certain. Ten years ago it was regarded as somewhat degrading to a woman to live with a man without marriage. Now no woman is considered as having lowered herself much in the esteem of her neighbors unless she becomes a brazen courtesan. Of this class it is but proper to say that Vienna, with its million of population, has fewer than the smallest of the principal cities of the United States. There are, however, more people living together without marriage than with marriage, and this condition of life, with the privilege of separating at pleasure, which often takes place at the birth of the first child, is becoming daily more popular.

The laws regulating marriage are, we have ascertained, different from those of any other civilized nation. The Church is forbidden to marry any man or woman without the consent of his or her parents. The parties proposing marriage must also have the written consent of the burgomaster and authorities of the place of their nativity, which will not be given unless they can prove that they have means sufficient to support a family and will not become a charge upon the community. During the three years which every able-bodied man is required to serve in the army, he is not permitted to marry except he has also the consent of the Secretary of War, or of the general under whose command he is serving. Some of these laws can be evaded by going to some other section of the country; but the bars to marriage are so great, and the difficulties to be overcome so numerous, that vast numbers prefer to do without the ceremony, and start off in life just as so many of their neighbors and friends have done before them. There is a recent law which is intended to protect the female in these left-handed marriages. If she ascertains that her " man," by whom she has children, is about to contract marriage, she can enter protest and put a stop to the ceremony. It does not, however, prevent him from abandoning the mother of his children and taking up with his new love, just as he in days long past took up with her. The novels daily published here all recognize this new phase of life, and the most popular are those which represent the heroes and heroines falling in love with and eloping with wives and husbands. Matrimony is ignored entirely in most of them. The marriage ceremony is daily growing more unpopular, and bids fair soon to come, in Vienna at least, to be regarded as one of the follies of the past generation.

MARRIAGE AMONG THE WELL-BORN.

The ladies of America, as well as the gentlemen, would be apt to enter an earnest protest against the system of marriage prevalent all over the Continent of Europe, but especially in Austria. Young ladies here, among the well-to-do and wealthier classes, are seldom allowed to go into company until they are engaged to be married. They are not allowed, in going to or coming from school, to have young gallants to trot along by their side and carry their books and whisper complimentary nothings in their ears. They are mostly sent to boarding-schools, and kept in such rigid seclusion that the sight of a man is almost a novelty to them. If allowed to come home during vacation, it is under strict family guard, but most of them remain until their education is finished and they have budded into early womanhood. Both father and mother then put their heads together and fix upon the amount of dower which they are willing and able to give her on her wedding-day. The next move is to look for a suitable husband, who will be able to bring to the common stock a similar amount of hard cash. If they cannot find one among their acquaintances to suit them in all respects, they call in the services of a professional matrimonial agent, who is well posted as to all the marriageable young men in the market. He, or she, as it may be, keeps a journal of the marriageables, not only in Vienna, but in the provinces, and proceeds to negotiate with the parents of some young man to receive the applicant as their daughter-in-law, and draws up the agreements and bonds necessary for the security of the money part of the transaction. Sometimes the young lady is allowed to see the youthful Adonis selected for her life-partner, before the agreement is closed, but in most cases she must accept the choice of her parents. Love comes after marriage in many cases, but is by no means a general result. If the money part of the contract is fulfilled, nothing is allowed to prevent the marriage, as this seems to be the main consideration. There are constantly cases occurring here in Vienna where the expected marriage is either postponed until the dower is paid up, or broken off entirely on account of failure to put up the money at the appointed time. The recent money crisis has led to many cases of abandonment, and there are no broken hearts to be mended. Thus, marriage has nothing to do with love, but is a purely business transaction,—a question of dollars and cents. Children are often pledged to each other by their parents before they enter their teens, and are then allowed to associate and form attachments, but this is not often the case. The parents of the daughter, who must pay down the money agreed upon, in hard cash, are somewhat at the mercy of the parents of the groom, who may put up their share of the money as a mere matter of form, and receive it back from the affectionate son the day after the wedding is consummated, with a good share of the bride's dower. But in matrimonial alliances everywhere the woman and her kindred are at the mercy of the husband.

We met, during our sojourn at Hall, a very handsome and intelligent lady from Roumania, who was sojourning there with her husband. She was undoubtedly most happily married; indeed, it would be difficult to find anywhere a more devoted couple. They had been married ten years, and she showed us a family photograph of herself and husband, with four bright and beautiful nestlings around them. In reply to our Yankee curiosity on this marriage question, she assured us that she had never seen her husband before she was engaged to him, and was married six weeks after they first met. She was educated at Paris, at a boarding-school, where she had been for seven years without seeing her parents. When she had nearly finished her education, and was preparing to start for home, her mother sent her the names of seven gentlemen who had proposed for her hand, with their photographs. She duly examined them, and finally selected the last on the list, her present husband. She then purchased her wedding trousseau, and started home to get married. On her return she met him, and learned to love him during the six weeks that intervened before the marriage. In looking at the subsequent career of her other six proposers, she assured me that she had never any cause to regret her choice. Glancing over the Vienna papers to-day, we find that they are at Schönbrunn Palace, the guests of the Emperor, in company with the Prince of Roumania, in whose suite the husband holds a high position.

VIENNA, June 26, 1873.

THE WEATHER.

The Baltimore papers of the 11th of this month have reached us, and record the commencement of "the heated term." We have had two or three warm days in Vienna, but on the morning of this 26th day of June we found an overcoat quite comfortable, the wind being cold and piercing. The "weather," as a rain is called here, was pouring down, as it has been almost daily for the past two months. Let the sun be shining ever so brightly, it is always unsafe to venture out without an umbrella, and this "weather" bids fair to hold out during the entire season.

THE NEUE WELT.

To visit all the places of recreation and amusement in and around Vienna would require a month of successive evenings, and each one appears to be more attractive than the last. The gardens, especially, present scenes that would be astounding to the denizens of Baltimore. Schneider's Neue Welt, a garden at Hitzing, in the suburbs of Vienna, which we visited a few evenings since, presented a scene that was truly surprising. It is about three times the size of the Baltimore Schützen Park, and every portion of it was almost as brilliant with gas-jets as the famous Mabille Garden of Paris. Three bands of music, each of not less than sixty performers, occupied elaborately-decorated and illuminated music-stands in different portions of the garden, the central one, called the Alhambra, being, with its wings, not less than three hundred feet in length, brilliantly illuminated with thousands of gas-jets. The central portion of the garden was filled with tables, sufficient to seat comfortably five thousand persons, and they are usually all filled, whilst an army of waiters are rushing to and fro to supply the calls for refreshments. Near the farther end of the garden is the dancing-circle, with another music-stand, whilst beyond it is the open-air theatre, with boxes and parquet, where there are nightly performances: one of the attractions, at present, being a band of Ethiopian singers, with tight-rope and slack-rope dancing. The price of admission to the garden is about thirty cents, and the number of visitors on all clear evenings is from five to ten thousand. On holidays and Sunday evenings everything is in full blast, and it would be impossible to convey to your readers any adequate idea of the immensity and brilliancy of the scene presented. The festivities are kept up until after midnight. On last Friday evening, in addition to all the musical attractions, the singing associations of Vienna, to the number of over one thousand trained voices, gave a grand open-air concert from the celebrated wings of the Alhambra, the central portion being occupied by the combined orchestras of the Neue Welt, numbering over two hundred string-instruments alone. The illuminated grounds in front of the Alhambra afford seats at tables, with rooms left for the free access of the visitors, for eight to ten thousand spectators.

The character of the orchestral music on ordinary nights, from each of the several bands, is of the highest order, being mostly by the great military bands, all the members of which are required to be proficient performers on string-instruments also. Every member of Strauss's Band can perform on two or more instruments; and so it is with all the great bands of Vienna. But the people of Vienna are critical judges of music, and do not applaud indiscriminately, no hired claquers being allowed. If the pieces are well rendered, there is applause; if not, a dead silence ensues. Hence, whenever there is even moderate applause, the leader comes with apparent delight to the front, bows, and repeats a portion of the air. Whenever any great success is achieved by an orchestra, the applause is renewed until the entire orchestra rise and bow to the audience. There is a constant demand for new musical productions, and Johann Strauss devotes his whole time to the labor.

MORE ABOUT CAFÉ LIFE.

Not desiring to be shut up to the monotony of hotel life, we have invariably, whenever it was possible, mixed with the people, as affording better opportunities for obtaining correct information in regard to national peculiarities and modes of life. To-day we dine, breakfast, or sup in one restaurant or café, and to-morrow in a similar establishment in another section of the city; and they are so numerous that they can be found at every turn. They are all excellent, and are invariably crowded with customers, including ladies, many of whom drop in unattended, partake of their meals, and depart. It would almost seem that three-fourths of the population live entirely in these establishments, as there are many hundreds of them which are also visited by the poorer classes. We took supper last evening at the Riedhof, where there could not have been fewer than twelve hundred ladies and gentlemen partaking of their evening repast. At the table on one side of us were four Turks, on the other side were four officers of the Austrian army, and in front of us four elegantly dressed ladies. No sooner was a table vacated than others waiting rushed to secure it. This establishment, with hundreds of others, is similarly crowded from seven to ten o'clock in the morning, from twelve to three in the afternoon, and from seven to eleven o'clock in the evening, but at all hours of the day there is a good attendance. They were mostly eating in the court-yard, under the trees, an abundance of gas-lights being interspersed. To eat out-of-doors is the delight of the Viennese, and those establishments that can furnish this luxury do the largest business in summer. In Paris the restaurants are chiefly up-stairs, whilst in Vienna they take the ground floor, and occupy the most valuable property and locations in the city. The food is also superior, in cooking and quality, to any that can be found in Paris, except in the fashionable and high-priced restaurants. Everything is cooked to order, and served up fresh and hot from the kitchen. In the cafés, where coffee, bread, and eggs alone are served, the coffee is made fresh every half-hour, and in quality it is equal to the best that can be found at some of our old Maryland family tables. If all visitors to Vienna would do only their sleeping in the hotels, they would find it to be the most delightful city in Europe for a prolonged sojourn.

THE MODES OF GERMAN LIFE.

Having heard much of the modes of social life of the German in the Fatherland, both in approval and in condemnation, one of the purposes of this visit to Germany has been to give the readers of *The American* the opportunity of forming a fair judgment on what we hope they will deem unprejudiced and impartial testimony. If the love of music, and a high appreciation of its charms, are commendable, then no one can find fault with these assemblages, which are as quiet and orderly, and as free from all manner of excesses, as one of Theodore Thomas's concerts. Whilst listening to music they like to eat, drink beer, and smoke in the open air, the eating being, to the great mass of them, their usual evening repast. Many take coffee instead of beer, whilst the ladies are eating cakes or ices; but even the children partake of beer. It is part of the food of every household, and there is nobody of any class of the community too high or too exclusive to join in these nightly gatherings, which are to be found in all parts of Vienna. They are places of relaxation after the labors of the day, and are so regarded and enjoyed by the best people of the city. The good order that prevails is remarkable, and any unseemly noise or excess would cause the prompt removal of the offender.

ABSENCE OF INTOXICATING LIQUORS.

There is not in the whole city of Vienna a place to obtain strong, intoxicating liquors, in which any one of the visitors to Levell's or Geekie's could be coaxed to enter. It can only be found here, in any of its varieties, in what we would call low "rum-mills," frequented by hack-drivers, who are, in fact, the only class of people in Germany who have come down to the American level of making beasts of themselves. They are the only drunkards in this immense city, and, in fact, the only men who show in their countenances any evidence that their beverage is other than cold water. We have seen Germans at home whom we regarded as swollen up and bloated with lager-beer, but now we are rather inclined to suspect them of producing this result by mixing whisky with their beer. The women here drink nearly as much beer as the men, and more healthy and finely developed specimens of feminine humanity cannot be found anywhere than are to be met in the restaurants of an evening, with their parents, husbands, brothers, or lovers, partaking of their evening repast, washed down with one or two goblets of the national beverage, which most of them were reared upon and weaned with from the cradle.

An American gentleman who has several times visited Vienna, and has traveled extensively in Europe, remarked to me to-day that he was satisfied that there is no other people living who understand how to enjoy life so well as do the Viennese. Husbands, wives, and children all move about together, and enjoy themselves in company. There are no anxious wives waiting and watching for the coming home of husbands from convivial gatherings, and no occasions for "Caudle lectures" among the family men of Vienna. If nothing more could be alleged against them than their mode of eating and the quantity of beer they drink, they would be a very exemplary people. This mode of out-door life certainly has the merit of relieving the wife from that greatest of all vexations of the present day, the management of the culinary department. The old axiom, "As to to-morrow, it will be time enough to consider it when it becomes to-day," is the favorite sentiment of the people, and, under the conviction that "a fresh mind keeps the body fresh," they have adopted as their practice and rule "to take in the ideas of to-day, and drain off those of yesterday." They hold to the idea that by the enjoyment of life themselves they are contributing to the enjoyment of others. As to their Christian duties and the observance of the Sabbath, no man has the right to judge them. They attend church on Sunday morning, doff their hats and cross themselves before each of the numerous shrines erected along the thoroughfares as they pass, and spend the afternoon and evenings on Sunday in listening to music and engaging in social converse in the gardens, or attending the theatres or the opera. They consider life too short to lose any opportunity for its full enjoyment.

SCARCITY OF WATER.

In connection with this subject of beer-drinking, the fact ought to be mentioned that drinking-water is not only scarce, and is a merchantable commodity, but that it is very unpalatable, and if drunk exclusively it is apt to lead to chronic affections of the bowels. It is so hard that it is difficult to wash the hands in it with any hope of their purification, the soap curdling and forming a sticky substance on the surface of the water. The only supply is from slow-running hydrants on the public streets, the water for other household purposes being obtained from cisterns, and being meted out in small quantities to the residents of the houses. The hydrants on the streets are thronged night and day by crowds of girls and women waiting for their turn to fill their buckets and tubs, many of whom make a business of carrying supplies to families. Arrangements for a more extensive supply of better water are being made, but it will be two or three years before the work is completed.

THE BELVEDERE.

Among the curiosities of Vienna is its Belvedere, an imperial château, erected by Prince Eugene of Savoy in 1722, which consists of two separate buildings, the Upper and the Lower Belvedere. They are located on the eastern suburbs of the city, and are surrounded by grounds about a mile in length, laid out in gardens, and brilliant with flowers. Indeed, the flowers, fountains, and gardens had more interest to us than the old paintings, by the great masters of the Italian, Netherland, and German schools, with which the walls of these extensive palaces are covered. We spent about two hours in passing through these galleries, viewing some of the masterpieces of Paul Veronese, Rembrandt, Rubens, and others of the great masters. They were undoubtedly very fine, but the wing devoted to modern paintings suited our taste much better, and we regretted that we did not enter this side of the palace first, as before we got through with it one of the custodians gently hinted to us, by silently closing the blinds, that the hour for "shutting up the shop" had arrived.

It is always necessary to go to these old galleries, and it is always fashionable to go into ecstasies over the great productions of the "masters," if one wishes to be regarded as capable of appreciating high art; but we would not give a view of the productions of the modern masters, as displayed in the gallery at the Exposition, for all the old paintings in Europe. We have spent a full day viewing these great productions, as well as the statuary and other works of art, and regretted that we could not give them more time; but these musty old galleries, the Belvedere being about the one hundred and fiftieth we have entered during our travels, have long since lost all their attractions. The structure itself, which was built just one hundred and fifty years ago, is very elegant, and the Marble Saloon is a fine specimen of the good taste of its builder. There are two or three other painting galleries, but, as we can find matters of considerably greater interest in and about Vienna, both to ourselves and the readers of *The American*, we have concluded to imagine that they are very fine, and all who read these letters will please to consider them wonderful specimens of ancient art.

THE VIENNA BOURSE.

After several unsuccessful attempts, on Friday we succeeded in getting admission to the hall of the Vienna Bourse. We fortunately had in our company Mr. A. G. Hutzler, of the firm of Hutzler Brothers, of Baltimore. His fluent German secured us from the Director a ticket of admission, and we were soon in the midst of this extensive hall, surrounded by a seething mass of humanity, all in the highest state of excitement. Old and young were mingled together, occasionally rushing about with as much fury as if they had suddenly discovered that the house was on fire. Some were yelling out offers of stock, and others bidding, and violently gesticulating. A stranger might suppose that it was a revolutionary gathering, and that the rush and crowd around some of the bidders meant personal violence. One of the most excited men in the room was an old fellow who had lost his eyesight, and was rushing hither and thither, literally "going it blind," in his anxiety to buy or sell stock. He seemed to distinguish persons by the sound of their voice, and addressed them by name. None of the members are allowed to enter the room with either a cane or umbrella, as they often come to blows on what are called "field days," and it is considered unsafe to allow the presence of anything that might be used to punch out each other's eyes.

The hall is nearly as long as the House of Representatives at Washington, and has a small gallery on one side for spectators, no one being permitted to go on the floor except members, unless with a special permit. We pleaded the privilege of the pass to go everywhere, and, after the exercise of considerable Yankee pertinacity, the doors were opened to us. There are forty-six pillars around the hall, which are all numbered, and are the standing places of various prominent brokers, who are always to be found at their base whenever they have any stocks to dispose of. There are also numerous stands throughout the room on which the names of different brokers are lettered. The "curb-stone brokers" gathered in front of the Bourse, who are not permitted to enter, were quite as numerous, and almost as much excited, though it was represented to us as an extraordinarily quiet day.

AUSTRIAN WOMEN.

Whilst it would not do for any one to assert that Austria, and especially Vienna, is distinguished for the beauty of its women, it may be safely said that there are more really handsome women in Vienna than in any other city in Europe. To be sure, the great mass of the women of Austria are neither handsome of feature nor graceful in person, but whenever you find one of these prerequisites they seem to be all combined to a greater extent than is seen elsewhere. A woman here is either homely and ungraceful, or else she has all the graces and attractions of the sex to perfection, with a bright and animated countenance, sparkling eyes, and rosy cheeks, which are the essentials to female loveliness. The more elegant of them promenade the streets, with their robes trailing after them in the dirt and mud, with all the dignity of queens, and as erect and graceful in their movements as if they had been under military training. Their blonde tresses, which appear to be the accompaniment of beauty here, are luxurious, and they have the more solid quality, generally, of being colored by nature as well as genuine. As in all blondes, the complexion corresponds; and a young Baltimorean whispered in my ear last night, whilst gazing at one of these admirable specimens of female beauty, "She is as sweet as a peach." They dress, too, with the greatest taste, avoiding all mixture of colors, the tight-fitting velvet coat or jacket, trimmed with lace, being in great favor.

But elderly Austrian ladies may be classed as among the decidedly homely and ungraceful. They do not seem to retain the beauty of youth long, but gradually develop into obesity, a waddle taking the place of the graceful step, and a saffron hue that of the peach-bloom which in early life graced their cheeks. They sparkle for a time, are gay, vivacious, and abound in animal spirits, but with matrimony and maternity they disappear like stars gone into an eclipse, and, as they age rapidly, the widow has but little opportunity of recuperating and reappearing to reassert her claims to the admiration and devotion of the other sex. However, money, not love, governs everything here, and whoever will bring the most wealth to lay at her feet, and is willing to accept her from her parents with the smallest dower, can command beauty; and if the widow happens to have been left well provided for by "the late lamented," she often becomes a formidable rival to youthful charms. The laboring women, who are exposed to all weather from early youth, are very coarse, and have but little of the grace or attractions of ordinary womanhood. Indeed, they appear more like men dressed in female attire, and most of them are strong and muscular enough to fell an ox with their fists. There are no tapering waists or ethereal forms among them, even in youth, and their blonde tresses become of a brick-dust hue from exposure, whilst the carrying of burdens on the head thins out the hair, and often before they reach the age of twenty-five a bald spot asserts itself on the top of the cranium.

THE MILITARY ADONIS.

His Majesty Francis Joseph is by no means a handsome or graceful man. Although of good height, he has a puny and effeminate appearance, and has the general aspect of a man who might, by sheer accident, break in two in the middle. He sits a saddle gracefully, however, and when mounted and arrayed in soldierly trappings, makes a very respectable appearance. He evidently thinks that good-looking youths make the best officers, as it would be difficult to find a more presentable-looking body of men than the thousands of colonels, majors, captains, and lieutenants who are strutting through the thoroughfares at all hours of the day and night, in their bright and elegant uniforms. They are all of good size, faultless in form and carriage, and walk along with the apparent conviction that they are objects of admiration. These men are seldom so indiscreet as to marry, unless they should be proposed for by some youthful beauty with a large dower, but spend their days in scheming and their nights in executing all manner of lascivious designs against female virtue. The whole sex, whether married or single, are preyed upon, and the wife or daughter of their bosom friend is neither shielded nor protected from their wiles. They are so bold and unblushing in their lustful pursuits, that a lady without male company, having any personal attractions, would be accosted twenty times in passing a few squares along the Ringstrasse. This practice has been so long in vogue that it creates none of that indignation that it would in an American community, and even the ladies no longer take offence at it. When thus accosted, a virtuous lady will exclaim, "You are mistaken, sir," but feels no more aggrieved than if she had been asked the simplest and most innocent question. Indeed, they seem, many of them, to regard such a salutation as a compliment to their personal attractions. When it is taken into consideration that these youthful and middle-aged Adonises, glittering with tinsel and brass buttons, number several thousand, that they are all elegant specimens of humanity, with all the airs and graces and seductive wiles of the professed libertine, and that they are known to be always on the war-path for new victims, the present state of morals in Vienna is not at all surprising. A striking instance of the boldness of these officers was given a few weeks since. A respectable gentleman was sitting with his wife in one of the concert-gardens, when a waiter was handed a card to deliver to the wife by one of these officers, sitting at an adjoining table. The lady quietly passed the card to her husband, who immediately called the officers to account, and struck one of them in the face. Swords were immediately drawn, and the spectators took sides with the insulted citizen. The swords were seized and wrested from the officers' hands, and one of them broken in pieces. The police rushed in and arrested all the parties, and charges were made against the officers. A court-martial was promised, but in a few days they were transferred to one of the provinces. They were afterwards tried, and, it is reported, were acquitted. Besides, there are thirty thousand men in their commands who emulate their officers and are ambitious to excel them in the number of their triumphs.

EXCESS OF MILITARY.

The number of military in and about Vienna is over thirty thousand, mostly youth under twenty years of age. They are serving the three years required by law, and have a pretty rough time of it. Youths are constantly arriving to take the place of those who have served out their terms. These boys are put under the severest training, and during the first year are exposed to all manner of hardships. Before six o'clock in the morning they march out for company drill, and during most of the rest of the day are drilling in squads on all the parade-grounds in the city. The regimental parades pass and repass through the city without attracting the slightest attention, unless they should have with them a good band of music. They are thus inured to all the exposure and hardships of a soldier's life, and their faces are almost burnt black in the sun. If there are any of our people still so stark mad as to express a preference for monarchial government, let them come here and see the youth and flower of the land drawn away from their homes and crowded into these barrack prisons for three long years, all to aid in keeping in subjection their fathers and brothers. Thus the people are used to rivet their own chains, or to go out and be slaughtered by the thousand, to assist some neighboring potentate to carry out his ambitious designs or capricious whims.

WANT TO GO TO AMERICA.

There is no doubt that, large as the emigration from Germany to the United States is, there are thousands here who are only waiting money and opportunity to join in it. In looking at the mammoth press at the Exposition grounds a few days since, the pressman, on being informed of the nature of our calling, begged us to take him and his wife to America. Car-drivers and all manner of mechanics express a desire to go, but have not the means. Almost every one of them to whom we speak is looking forward to emigration, or expresses the hope that he may be able to join friends and relatives there before many years. The laboring and agricultural women seem to regard America as the haven of all their hopes, and if there were three thousand miles of desert instead of water rolling between them there would be a general rush. In short, there is a great deal of military pride, but there does not appear to be much love for the "Fatherland" on this side of the water. Among our Germans at home it is possibly distance that lends enchantment to the view. Those who have wealth or have got into a money-making groove can live as well and happily here as in any other country in the world; but as the poor man is by no means a curiosity, and the poor woman can be found without a very diligent search, and as the sons of these poor men and women think they can do without learning the art and mystery of war, the tendency of almost everybody is decidedly Westward.

A FIRST-CLASS FUNERAL.

All funerals here are very much alike, but we to-day witnessed what is regarded as a first-class funeral. First came two mounted outriders, on black horses, with black cloth swallow-tailed coats, trimmed with silver lace, epaulettes on their shoulders, and swords at their sides. They each carried in their hands black poles, about six feet in length, on the tops of which were large silver lanterns, with a light burning within. They wore black chapeaus, also trimmed with silver lace. The trappings of the horses were heavily covered with black trimmings, presenting a very sombre aspect. Next came the hearse, not much different from the most elegant of our city hearses, but more ponderous, and drawn by six solemn black horses, arrayed similarly to those of the outriders, they being almost covered with mourning harness. The two foremost horses of the six drawing the hearse also had postilions mounted upon them, wearing the same funeral uniform as the outriders. Two men, similarly arrayed, occupied the driver's seat, and on the sides of the hearse twelve more of these grave-looking gentlemen marched along, with large silver-gilt candlesticks in their hands, with candles burning. Eight carriages followed, horses and everything else of the blackest black, and a driver and footman upon each, wearing the funeral garb. These men make a business of burials, and take charge of everything, keeping carriages and horses that are not used for any other purpose. The extent of the display they make is governed entirely by the amount paid. Sometimes the body is carried to the grave on the shoulders of the same men, in the same uniform, with the same candles and other paraphernalia of death.

POSTAL CARDS.

The "postal cards," which have just been introduced in the United States, are a European notion, and if they should prove as popular at home as they are here, will yield a large revenue to the Department. Everybody seems to use them here, both for mail and local delivery. It is said that not less than fifty thousand pass through the Vienna post-office daily, and sometimes the number is even larger. The letter-carriers are kept constantly in motion delivering them, they being largely used for local business purposes. We have had occasion to use over a dozen of them during our sojourn here, and have found them very convenient, as a sharp lead-pencil answers the purpose of ink. We frequently see a gentleman lay one on top of a letter-box in the streets, write a note, direct it, and drop it in. The post delivery, both here and in Prussia, is very prompt, and notes thus sent from one part of the city to another are generally delivered in about two hours. Instead of having the letters in the boxes collected by carriers, they are taken to the post-office in wagons, boxes and all, a new box being left in place of the old one. The letter-box is an oblong iron box, with a hole in it, which is locked up inside of a larger iron box, with a corresponding hole. The empty boxes are brought in the carriage and exchanged for the full ones. The arrangement is very simple and expeditious, the wagon flying around on its route with great rapidity.

RESPECT FOR THE LAW.

The Austrian has great respect for the law and its officers. Such a thing as an attempt to escape from a police-officer is never known in Vienna. It is not necessary for a policeman to arrest and drag an offender to the station-house. All he has to do is to say to a man, "You are under arrest," and the man will stand stock still until the officer has time to attend to him. The certainty of punishment if he should do otherwise may have much to do with this. The resistance of an officer of the law would, however, bring every bystander to his assistance, as it is not the officer, but the representative of the law, that they would regard as being outraged. In the public squares, if a citizen should witness any violation of the rules and regulations he would feel it his duty to arrest the offender at once and hand him over to an officer. There is no class of people who disregard the law except the carriage-drivers, and they are brought up by the fifties every day. As their offenses are mostly against strangers, who do not wish to be at the trouble of informing upon them, they can afford to pay the fines in a few cases for the profits they make from the many. A citizen pays what the law allows, and if the driver demurs he jumps back in the carriage and tells him to drive to the station-house. This has the desired effect, and the growling ceases.

But in all other respects the law in Vienna is supreme. Punishment of the severest character is sure to follow its slightest violation. Noise or improper conduct on the streets is never heard; but as men here never get drunk, that may be one of the causes of this difference from other large cities.

LOVE OF MUSIC.

In no other city of Europe are there so many large bands of skilled musicians as there are in Vienna. They each number between fifty and sixty performers, and there are at least sixty orchestral bands each of which is as perfect as that of Theodore Thomas. On Sunday afternoons every garden around the city, even those where the working classes resort, has one or more of these bands in attendance, the price of admission being from thirty to fifty kreutzers, or from fifteen to twenty-five cents. They perform operatic music, or some of the lively productions of Strauss, and all classes seem to be equally critical in their judgment of the character of their performance. Yesterday (Sunday) evening we visited a number of the gardens, and found whole families, including the children, taking their evening meal or indulging in beer and cigars, and listening to the music. In most of them there were as many ladies as gentlemen present, and they all presented scenes of innocent recreation and enjoyment. At the Volksgarten the celebrated band of Strauss, led by himself, was in attendance, and there was here assembled as fashionable an audience as could be found at any of the great two-dollar concerts in America, the price of admission being only thirty cents. At the Neue Welt there were five bands in attendance, and an audience of several thousand around each of them. Music is both good and cheap, and a poor or inefficient band would be nowhere tolerated for a moment. We took our suppers at a garden in the southern suburbs of the city, which is principally visited by mechanics, and here found one of the great bands that was performing on the grounds of the Exposition at our last visit, discoursing most delightful music, the pieces performed being successively announced by placard. The same quiet and good order prevailed as at the more fashionable resorts. On Saturday night we visited the Blumensaal, or Floral Hall, being an immense hall with two wings, in the shape of the letter T. Here the orchestra consisted of sixty females, a portion of them being the same orchestra that visited the United States a few years since. There was an immense audience, and their performance elicited great applause. The military are, of course, the organizers of the best of these bands; but still there are a number of independent organizations of great merit. The great Baden-Baden Band, which performs every afternoon from four to nine o'clock at the principal stand at the Exposition grounds, is an independent organization, and is believed to have no superior in the world. Gambling having been stopped at Baden-Baden, their occupation was at an end, and they are under engagement for the entire duration of the Exposition.

THE POLICE OF VIENNA.

The police of Vienna wear a semi-military dress of green cloth, with a jacket-coat closely buttoned up to the throat with brass buttons. Each policeman carries a sword at his side, and presents quite a military aspect. Around his neck, suspended close under his chin, is a brass plate, crescent-shaped, upon which, in large black figures, is engraved his number. What is the extent of the force, we have not ascertained; but the highest numbers we have yet seen upon these plates was three thousand four hundred and twenty-seven. These policemen are to be seen everywhere, in all sections of the city, but seem to have little or nothing to do. The city is so orderly that they merely walk their rounds, their presence, apparently, being all that is necessary for the preservation of the peace. There are a few of them mounted; but perhaps these are merely for the Ringstrasse during the time of the Exposition. They wear their swords gracefully, having all served their three years in the army. Most of them are not over thirty years of age, and they are selected with great care as to their private standing in the community.

DOGS AND HORSES.

The dog is not so generally used for work in Vienna as in Berlin and Dresden, though dogs can occasionally be seen drawing small wagons. Those that work are, however, the happiest of dogs, as they tug at the harness with all their strength, and the greatest good will. We saw a man pulling a wagon for a short distance the other day, he having unharnessed his dog, which was yelping at him, and taking hold of the shaft with his teeth, being apparently unwilling that the wagon should move without his having a share of the burden. Nearly all the hauling here is done by horses, and they are mostly large and elegant-looking animals, of great strength. A carriage never moves along the street at a slow pace, but is driven with great speed, regardless of the people who may be crossing the streets. A few evenings since, in returning from the Neue Welt, the speed was so great that we feared every moment we should be run over by the passing vehicles, or be overturned at some of the corners.

[We again left Vienna for a trip down the Danube and through Hungary to Trieste and Venice, the letters describing which will be found in another portion of this volume. We returned to Vienna again on the 17th of July.]

VIENNA, July 18, 1873.
RETURN TO VIENNA.

We are back again in Vienna, intending to bid it a final adieu one week hence. We have become so familiar with the city, and are so charmed with its attractions, that it seems almost like going home to get back here again from our wanderings. We know exactly where to go to find good quarters, good music, and good eating. We know all the multiplicity of signs on the various street-cars which crowd the Ringstrasse, and we jointly know sufficient German to make ourselves understood in an emergency.

STRANGERS BETTER TREATED.

We are pleased to find that the caterers of Vienna have at last come to their senses, and are more kind, courteous, and liberal to the strangers visiting the Exposition. There is now little or no complaint anywhere, and visitors are not hurrying away after a hasty view of the Exposition. The hotels are not, however, so crowded as those of Paris are reported to be, and it is becoming the settled opinion that there will be no such rush of strangers here as was anticipated. There is an intense feeling among the better class of people against those whose grasping propensities have so greatly damaged the character of the city, and upon them is laid the blame of having rendered the Exposition a comparative failure in a financial point of view. Good rooms can now be had at the best hotels at from two to four florins per day, and the restaurants have all come down to ante-Exposition prices.

MISFORTUNES IN VIENNA.

The cholera is making its appearance in the suburbs of Vienna, and there are a dozen or more cases reported daily. There have been some cases in the hotels, but they were parties who came from Turkey, where it is prevailing to a considerable extent. The financial losses to Vienna from the Exposition, which was looked forward to with such confidence as a means of placing it at the pinnacle of prosperity, have already been immense. A good crop in Hungary was looked to as a sure means of resuscitating business and saving Vienna, but from all parts of that grain-growing country come accounts of serious damage to the wheat crop from rust. The fates seem to be arrayed against her. Three months ago everybody thought that the people would be rolling in wealth by this time, and that the whole world would be pouring in its tribute. Then the Exposition was regarded as the "goose that was to lay the golden egg." Now it is viewed as having been the cause of all their woes, no one being willing to acknowledge that their own folly has brought upon them most of their troubles. All now are anxious that the time should come for killing and cooking the goose that has brought disaster instead of prosperity to Vienna.

RESPECT FOR THE LAW.

We have already alluded to the universal respect for the law, and for the officers of the law, which is maintained throughout Austria. To resist an officer of the law, as we before stated, is regarded as a most heinous offense, not against the man, but against the majesty of the law. Such an offense as that of attacking a member of the City Council as he came from the Council Chamber, as recently occurred in Baltimore, would have given the offender imprisonment for life at hard labor. A case has recently occurred here in Vienna illustrative of this sentiment, which we will relate for the benefit of Judge Gilmor and all other judges who may have in charge the trial and sentence of parties guilty of such offenses.

Since the commencement of the Exposition, several mounted policemen have been stationed at the head of the Präterstrasse to carry out the published regulations with regard to carriages coming from and going to the Präter. A few weeks ago, the young Baron von Heine dashed along with his team of spirited horses, and was halted by the police and directed to proceed on the other side of the street. He was indignant at the interruption, gave the whip to his horses, and drove on, but was soon interrupted by two other policemen, when he again applied his whip to both the horses and the officers. He was immediately dragged from his seat and sent to the station, where he presented his card and was allowed to depart. A trial was, however, ordered, and he was sentenced to fifteen months' imprisonment at hard labor, and to forfeit his title of Baron, with all its rights and privileges. He is now in jail, waiting the result of an appeal to the Supreme Court, which has the power to modify the punishment, but cannot restore to him his title. This can only be done by the Emperor, and not even by him until the expiration of five years. Thus it will be seen that neither money nor station is an exemption to those who violate law or resist an officer in the performance of his duty. Baron von Heine is a nephew of the celebrated German poet Heinrich Heine, and his father is a millionaire, being also the editor and proprietor of the *Fremden Blatt*, one of the leading papers of Vienna. It is thought that the court will reduce the time of imprisonment to six months, but that the general verdict will be approved.

THE GERMAN BIRTHDAY.

The celebration of the anniversary of the birthday is observed in Germany to a much greater extent than in any other country. We Americans, who allow our birthdays to come and go almost without remembering or noting their occurrence, cannot but admire the kindly feeling evinced by relations and friends, especially towards ladies and children, on these occasions. During our stay at the springs at Hall, a number of the lady guests celebrated their anniversaries. All their friends and acquaintances at Hall sent them immense bouquets, one lady receiving as many as twenty, whilst boxes from home were at hand, with cakes and presents and letters with loving greetings. We had the pleasure of participating in one of these anniversaries, the lady being a native of Baltimore, of German parents, temporarily residing in Germany. At least ten immense bouquets decorated the room, whilst the presents from friends and relatives were spread out upon a table like bridal offerings. Her acquaintances called during the day to congratulate her and partake of cake and wine, and all went on as merry as a marriage bell. Her parents were too distant to participate in the festivities at Hall, but she assured us that the day was being similarly celebrated at a certain mansion on Madison Avenue, and that cake and wine would be partaken of by a band of little orphan children in whom she felt a deep interest. Although far from home and relatives, many presents and kind greetings reached her from friends in Vienna, where she has made her home for the past year. These observances at a summer resort were, of course, but tame affairs compared to the day celebrated at home, surrounded by parents, sisters, and brothers, but were sufficient to give us some idea of this beautiful custom of the Fatherland. Everything is done, however, to make it a merry festival, even the servants dressing the dinner-table with flowers, whilst the health of the absent ones is toasted, and the whole day is devoted to innocent festivities.

PROGRESS OF THE EXPOSITION.

The main building of the Exposition, in which all the shop-goods of England, France, and the other European nations are exhibited, has become the least interesting portion of the display. To the rural visitor the attraction still holds good, but to those who come from large cities it soon becomes like gazing in at the shop-windows of their own stores, on displays of rich goods and fancy novelties. The machinery department, the agricultural buildings, and the galleries of paintings and statuary, are the great attractions. These will interest the visitor after a dozen visits; but the main structure is now little more than a promenade hall, through which the people stroll to see each other, giving little more than a glance at the goods on exhibition. They view it rather as a whole, presenting a grand scene to the vision in every direction, scarcely ever stopping to examine anything, unless it be to take a glance at some of the cases in which there is a magnificent display of diamonds, which have a never-failing interest to the ladies.

THE AMERICAN DEPARTMENT.

The goods on exhibition in the American department continue to command as much attention as those of any other country in the Exposition, if not more. They have the merit of being nearly all novelties, and the only articles of their kind to be found in the Exposition. There are no fancy goods, and very few of the ornamental, but they partake rather of the necessary and the useful. The appreciation of visitors is shown by the fact that, comparatively small as the display is, there are more articles marked "sold" than in the department of any other country. It is, in fact, the only department in the main building where visitors closely examine everything, for the reason that they are mostly articles which have never been seen before in Europe, and have been brought here because they are new. The American division of the machinery department attracts great attention, and nearly every piece of machinery has upon it a card with the word "sold" printed in large letters. This of itself is a mark of appreciation that is unmistakable. So also in the American agricultural building nearly all the reapers and mowers are marked "sold," as well as many of the drills, horse-rakes, and plows. Indeed, it is evident that there will be very little of what has been brought here from the United States to be taken back again; and when at Trieste last week our consul told us that one of the vessels which brought the goods over was about to be sent home. The American machinery for the manufacture of shoes, of which there is a good display, attracts great attention. It was in motion to-day, and so great was the throng of spectators that we could not get within ten feet of the rail that surrounds it. It is also all marked "sold," and many orders have been received for similar machines.

In photography the American display not only exceeds that of every other country in the way of execution, but the ladies whose likenesses are presented are regarded as wonderful specimens of female beauty. Many of them are of life size, and are presented in rich and tasteful attire, with none of that exposure of the person by low-necked dresses which distinguishes the European photographs.

THE CATHOLIC SHRINES.

Austria exceeds Italy in the number of its roadside and street-side shrines. They are also more elaborate and costly, and most of them are kept constantly decorated with fresh flowers, especially during the season of flowers. On the road between Hall and Steyer, a distance of less than ten miles, there are more than a dozen, and in the town of Steyer they stand sentry on the bridges and are to be seen at every turn in the streets. Most of them are life-size images of the Saviour on the cross, whilst others are paintings of the Virgin and Child. During our extensive journeyings on the railroads in Austria similar representations of the Crucifixion were to be seen in the fields, on the roadside, and along the turnpikes. There are thousands of them in every direction, and they are all kept bright and attractive. The field-hands in passing them invariably cross themselves, and many of the women and children kneel and say a brief prayer. Our carriage-driver on the way from Hall raised his hat to every shrine; and in the streets of Steyer a similar token of prayerful recognition was observed on the part of every man and woman who passed them. They are not so numerous in Vienna, but they are seldom passed by any one who does not either cross himself or raise his hat. That the largest religious freedom is enjoyed in Austria, however, is evident everywhere. A weekly illustrated paper, called *Der Floh* ("The Flea"), something like the London *Punch*, but far more amusing in its wit, striking right and left at men and things, and unsparing in its sarcasm, has a full-page illustration every week that might be regarded as most offensive to the Catholics. The Pope is lampooned more freely than Nast presents him and the Catholics in *Harper's Weekly*. Crowds of people can be seen at the paper-stands laughing at the bites of "the flea," and apparently enjoying the fun of the thing. In a country so intensely Catholic this would never have been allowed before the days of "infallibility," which has loosened the power of the Church over the people throughout Europe. The shrine, however, is undoubtedly an hourly reminder to the people of their religious duties, and no Christian of any denomination can fail to recognize its utility.

LOVE OF FLOWERS.

The Austrians are passionately fond of flowers in all grades of life. Every little cottage or hovel has its flower-garden, whilst the windows are always decorated with flowers in full bloom. The dwellings of the wealthier classes also abound in flowers, and the demand for bouquets in town and country is immense. A birthday celebration brings a bouquet from every friend and acquaintance,—not a little bunch of flowers, but a huge collection of all the flowers in bloom, arranged with artistic taste. The ladies of our party, when they left Hall yesterday for Vienna, found themselves literally covered with huge bouquets, as we sat in the carriage about taking our departure. Every friend sent a floral offering; and thus it is invariably at the parting of friends. Another birthday was being celebrated when we left, and, after a serenade at seven o'clock by a full band of music, the floral offerings commenced to flow in. When we left, at nine o'clock, the room of the lady whose birthday was being celebrated was decorated with flowers, and in the centre of the room a large circular table, with a floral wreath around the edge, contained a display of the more substantial and enduring presents that friends and relatives had sent her.

The display of flowers in the public squares of Vienna is truly grand. The artistic arrangement of floral colors is sometimes attempted in Paris and in London, but never reaches the perfection attained in Vienna. Indeed, flowers are universally cultivated here so as to variegate the colors of both leaves and flowers, different plants being intermixed and grown in the same bed, so as to present distinctly-marked lines, circles, parallelograms, and even figures and lettering. These floral displays are not protected by fences, but are in most cases open to the street, and any one attempting to disturb them would be arrested by any citizen who happened to witness the act. Cows are not allowed to run at large in this country, and cattle are never driven through the streets. If a cow should make its appearance, it would be made beef of on the spot. If the freedom of Vienna were given to cows, they would make sad havoc in twenty-four hours; and if it is intended to make an attractive city of Baltimore, they must either be kept up or kept out of its limits.

POODLE DOGS.

Whilst the large dogs in Austria are taught to work, and make themselves useful in various ways, the little fellows are taken to the bosoms of the ladies and treated as if they were veritable angels. It is not uncommon when traveling to see almost every lady with a dog in her arms, occasionally accompanied by a footman or maid, whose duty in traveling with the mistress is to take care of the dog and see that it has water and food on the route. The doctors tell many amusing anecdotes of being called up at midnight and finding that their services are needed for a poodle that has been overfed in the effort to kill it with kindness. They could make heavier charges with the assurance of prompt payment in such cases than if the patient were a child or a husband. "Love me, love my dog," seems to be the sentiment of these ladies: on one occasion we saw a finely dressed lady who had her dog in her arms take off her gloves whilst standing in a depot, and diligently pursue and kill a flea which she had discovered depredating among the fleece of her favorite. It is quite common to see dogs led tenderly along with ribbons, and in some cases to see a gold chain attached to a lady's belt, and at the other end of the chain a poodle dog traveling by her side or reposing in her arms. Signs in the shop-windows tell you that "Dog soap is sold here," and that various patent compounds that will induce canine health and longevity are on sale. A lady walking in any of the public grounds without a dog is sure to be accosted by a number of seedy-looking individuals who will draw out of their pockets pups, which they offer for sale. The offering for sale of anything in the public grounds being prohibited by law, they keep them concealed in their pockets. In the upper grades of life a mother trusts her children to servants and governesses, but her poodle dog she keeps under her own eye, and a scream from the nursery might pass unheeded, but a yelp from the drawing-room or the boudoir would startle madam from the soundest sleep. Of course these are exceptional cases; but the passion for pet dogs is shared by most of those who aspire to fashionable life. We see dogs caressed much more than children are, and their comfort studied with jealous care.

SCARCITY OF APOTHECARIES.

An hour's walk this morning through the most populous parts of Vienna, in search of a Seidlitz powder, was a failure, so far as the object of the search was concerned. We could not find an apothecary-shop in all this long walk and diligent search. In the same space we could have found fifty in Baltimore, or in any other American city. Being in pursuit of knowledge, we made inquiry as to the cause of this scarcity, desiring to know whether the sages of Vienna had discovered that Shakspeare was right when he consigned "physic to the dogs." The physicians of whom we inquired assured us that, although the people did not physic themselves much in Vienna, an average amount of medicine was consumed. The scarcity of apothecaries grew out of the fact that the law was very strict as to the qualifications of all aspirants, and that they must obtain a certificate from an examining board, all of whom are apothecaries, and interested in restricting the number. Thus it is that the business is kept in certain families, and that very few, except such of their children as take a fancy to the business, are inducted into its mysteries. The difficulty that a stranger experienced in finding them was partly owing to the fact that they had no competition in their several neighborhoods, made very little display, and very often had their establishments in back streets or courts, where convenience or cheap rent induced the location. They charge high prices, and are generally quite wealthy.

VIENNA, July 21, 1873.

AMERICAN CHURCH-GOING.

Yesterday was Sunday, and we attended the American Chapel, which has been opened during the Exposition, expecting to find a large attendance of Americans, as there must be over a thousand of them now in the city. On the contrary, when the minister came to the desk there were precisely eleven persons in the church, including Minister Jay. Before the sermon commenced they had increased to sixteen. From this it is evident that when Americans are traveling in Europe they are more disposed to join in the merry out-door life of the people than to attend to their religious duties. We dropped in during the afternoon at the Volksgarten, where a concert by one of the great military bands was in progress, and found at least one hundred Americans among the audience, sipping their coffee and ices. There was a large and fashionable audience in attendance, including a large number of Viennese ladies. Many of the latter had gentlemen accompanying them, but a still larger number came unattended, took their seats at the tables, and called for refreshments and coffee with as free and easy a manner as those of the sterner sex. The rule is that a woman has the right to go wherever a man can properly go, and thus far woman has obtained and maintains her rights in Vienna. These concerts commence at five o'clock and continue until eleven o'clock, admission thirty cents, and during that time the audience changes two or three times, people being always coming and going.

THE AUSTRIAN LADIES.

A young lady writes to us from Baltimore, urging us to let her know "how the Vienna ladies dress," "how they wear their hair," "whether they are pretty," or "whether they are only youthful prototypes of the stout, red-faced German women who arrive in the emigrant-steamers." As there are probably many others of our lady readers desirous of categorical answers to these important questions, we will endeavor, to the best of our ability, to give them the required information. If by beauty our correspondent means that description of prettiness termed ethereal, with slightness of form and delicacy of feature and expression, there are no beauties in Austria. If, on the other hand, a well-developed form, with a bust such as is only at times attained by matrons of other countries, but not so great as to prevent a slender waist and expanding hips, needing neither bustles nor distending contrivances to make up a good figure, is her estimate of one of the requisites of beauty, then the young women of Austria are nearly all beautiful. If to these qualities are added a bright countenance and lively expression, then we would consider all reared in gentle life as having some claims to the beautiful. So far as features and complexion are concerned, the number of beautiful women is rather limited, but still there are enough to charm the eye at every turn on the Ringstrasse or on the promenade at the Präter. They nearly all have good forms and erect carriage, rather graceful than otherwise; and when these are accompanied by a beautiful complexion, regular features, and flowing ringlets, which is very often the case, it would be difficult for even Baltimore to excel the beauties of Vienna. The Hungarian women, of whom there are a large number always in Vienna, are famous for personal beauty, having all the form, feature, and complexion required to charm the eye. We may also add that a Viennese lady is always full of animation and vivacity, and has been reared to the enjoyment of life regardless of many of the constraints that are put upon her sex in other countries.

HOW THEY DRESS.

"How do the Vienna ladies dress?" Well, the ladies of Vienna wear no bustles, and we may as well speak plainly, and add that it is because most of them need none. In all other respects they follow the same fashions that the ladies of America adopt. Their dresses and overskirts have all the folds, frills, plaits, points, ruffles, laces, and trimmings that are to be found in Paris, and their skirts drag in the dirt of the pavement just as long, and gather up as much filth, as those of the sisterhood of the rest of the civilized nations. The only difference that we have observed in this respect is that they wear all their underskirts with trails also, and when the pavements are wet and dirty they let them drag much more recklessly than the ladies of Baltimore do. They seldom raise them to avoid a puddle, but move on as unconcernedly as if their skirts were trailing over a velvet carpet.

HOW THEY WEAR THEIR HAIR.

"How do the Vienna ladies wear their hair?" In answer to this query we must inform our querist that most of the ladies wear *their own hair*. Being compelled to dress it in simple plaits whilst children and until they enter society, it is not prematurely destroyed by crimping-irons and frizzing and twisting into tight knots, but obtains its full natural growth. Thus, most young ladies have a splendid head of hair, "all their own," which costs nothing. Perhaps for this latter reason they do not value it as much as they would if it depended upon purchase, and hence they do not evince much skill or good taste in dressing it. It is generally gathered into a loose and careless-looking knot on the back and top of the head, or carelessly packed into a net, and looks as if it had been tossed about in a windstorm. Sometimes there is a flower stuck on the side of the head, without regard to size or quality, so that it is red. The practice of "banging" the front hair and allowing it to straggle over the forehead is almost universal among the young ladies, and detracts much from their personal beauty. They do not wear the hat down over the eyes, but place it on the back of the head, leaving the front hair and the "bangs" exposed in reckless and careless *abandon*, which seems now to be the ruling fashion. But, notwithstanding this neglect of the greatest ornament of the sex, they look beautiful as they promenade the streets, and, if in conversation, the countenance is always beaming with animation and the eyes are sparkling with fun. Some, however, wear ringlets hanging down their backs. The Viennese, whether male or female, are intent on the present enjoyment of life, and are always in a merry mood. They never think of to-morrow, "nor meet troubles half-way." They are not censorious or proud, but treat every one who behaves like a lady or a gentleman in public as if his or her record were untarnished. They all live a free and easy life, and if any of them choose to carry their freedom to extremes they regard it as their own business and nobody else's.

LADIES' BONNETS.

Having given this summary of the personal appearance of the ladies of Vienna, in response to our fair correspondent, the picture will not be complete without describing their head-gear. As to bonnets, they have been entirely discarded by both the young and the old, and hats are now universally worn. They are precisely the same description of hats as are worn by the ladies of Baltimore, being of every conceivable shape and material. They are profusely trimmed with artificial flowers, with streamers of lace and flowering vines trailing down the back. In short, they are precisely the same "loves of bonnets" that the ladies of Baltimore aspire to, but, being worn on the back of the head, instead of close down on the forehead, look much prettier in the bandbox than they do on the promenade. If a dozen of these Viennese ladies were to stroll out Charles Street, they would not, by any peculiarity of dress or personal appearance, except the way they wear their bonnets, be suspected of being foreigners. Many of them are as pretty and graceful as the handsomest of our Baltimore ladies, and they all seem to be in the enjoyment of excellent health. A delicate-looking young lady is seldom seen among the belles of Vienna.

THE WORKING-WOMEN.

The "stout, red-faced German women who arrive in the emigrant-steamers" come from the rural districts, and have been raised to a life of toil which has hardened their muscles and made them short and shapeless specimens of humanity. Most of their mothers for several generations back have lived in the same daily routine of masculine labor until the female has lost all her traces of graceful form and feature. They are, however, sober and industrious people, simple in their tastes and wants, and are free from the vanity which is attributed to the sex of most other countries. There are very few of these to be seen in Vienna, except at the markets. The laboring women of the cities are of an entirely different class, and, though strong and muscular, have none of the healthy complexion that the countrywomen carry with them. Men who do coarse laboring work at home become rough and coarse, and these women, from constant exposure to the sun and the hard lives they live, become even coarser in their features than men. Before they are "out of their teens" they look like rough and dirty boys in female attire, though they all wear long boots, and many of them old and ragged coats. They climb up ladders to the tops of five-story buildings, with buckets of mortar or brick balanced on their heads, wheel wheelbarrows, and handle the shovel and pick with all the muscular agility of men. They are arrayed in a mixed attire, with long boots, old coats, pantaloons; and the skirt or petticoat is about the only feminine garment that is distinguishable. They eat their meals on the curb-stone, and sleep in cellars and sheds. They have never known any better life, and seem to be contented. The rest of the community pays no attention to them, regarding them rather as beasts of burden than specimens of humanity. "What's the odds, so we are happy?" is the Viennese motto; and the general impression is that these people are as happy in their way as those in the higher grades of life.

THE GENTLEMEN OF VIENNA.

The gentlemen among the wealthier class of Vienna are remarkably fine-looking, being generally tall, well formed, and graceful in their movements. They also dress with excellent taste and elegance, and are wholly different in appearance from the American idea of German characteristics. Not one of your fair readers would be able to decide from their appearance whether they were Germans or Boston Yankees, except that they have more ruddy complexions and are generally more robust in their physical development than the latter. The officers of the army, of whom there are thousands in Vienna, are seldom less than six feet in height, and are, as a body, the finest-formed men to be found in any part of the globe. They dress in tight-fitting uniforms, and, as we once before remarked, move along the streets with the air of men who know themselves to be objects of admiration. At the Reidhof to-night about thirty of them were taking their supper, and every one of them would be classed in New York or Baltimore as a handsome man, of more than ordinary good physical development, fine form and feature, and all the other requisites of perfect manhood. The men in the lower strata of life are, however, neither handsome, well formed, nor graceful in their motions. A considerable portion of them are, on the contrary, short and ungainly in appearance, with the exception of those who come from Hungary, from which country come the brains, muscles, and sinews of Austria, as well as most of the food consumed by the people of Vienna.

VIENNA, July 22, 1873.

As we propose to take a final adieu of Vienna to-morrow, we have spent our last day at the Exposition, and ran rapidly through all the departments. In the vast machinery departments everything was in motion, and the throng of people among the revolving machinery was very great. This large attendance has given renewed hope that the last days of the Exposition will be more prosperous than its commencement.

In taking our farewell of the Exposition, we cannot but repeat that it is wonderful in its immensity and glorious in its varied attractions. It is too large for any one to see in a dozen visits, and we do not believe that one in a thousand of the visitors sees one-half that is on exhibition, whilst many get wearied and exhausted before they have entered one-half of the buildings. We have spent about twenty days in exploring its wonders, and we yesterday got into several buildings, by mere accident, that we had never before entered. That there are still others that have escaped our vigilance, we have not the slightest doubt.

THE AMERICAN DEPARTMENT.

In the American machinery department there are one hundred and forty-nine depositors, some of them having several machines on deposit. In one of my recent letters I noticed the fact that nearly all the machinery in motion, and many of the agricultural implements, had upon them cards with the word "sold." I learn upon inquiry that not only have all these machines been sold, but that orders have been received for large numbers of duplicates, which have been sent home to be filled. In fact, there are no depositors here in better humor than those from America, and they find that they have done a good stroke of business in coming to Vienna.

We close our notice of the Exposition with the expression of the belief that, though it may prove a pecuniary failure to the government, its effect upon Austrian agriculture and machinery will more than recompense for all the pecuniary loss. It will tend to the development of the resources of the country, and to the promotion of all the great interests that go to making up a great nation. The agricultural implements on exhibition have been heard of, but never seen before, by Austrian and Hungarian farmers, and our plows will take the place of the primitive wooden instruments that are so extensively used. Mowers, drills, horse-rakes, and the thousands of articles in use in other countries were wholly unknown in Austria; and it is curious to see the old farmers roving about in the extensive agricultural buildings among steam-plows and pieces of machinery as large as some of the houses in which they have been accustomed to live.

THE EXPOSITION BUILDINGS.

We have frequently alluded to the number of buildings on the grounds, independent of the grand hall, the three art-galleries, and the machinery department. An official list just published shows the number of these outside buildings to be one hundred and sixty-eight, and others are still building. The following structures are very interesting: English workmen's dwellings, Hungarian peasant huts, Saxon huts, Guydalerhouse hut, Roumanian hut, cotter's cottage of Borkowsky, Alpine hut, Lapland hut, Hungarian shepherd's cottage, Alsatian farm-house, and Russian dwelling-house,—all of which had escaped our attention until our last visit. The palace of the Sultan of Turkey is now completed and finished, as well as the Persian villa.

Most of these outside buildings are large, and very elegant in their structure. There is nothing on the grounds of the Exposition that has the appearance of being merely intended for temporary use. The Turkish palace is as large as the Peabody Institute, and has two tall towers and two domes. The Persian villa is a gem of sparkling beauty, both inside and outside, and will be the reception-house of the Shah when he visits the Exposition.

FOREIGN AND HOME FOOD.

We are living well in Vienna, notwithstanding the great luxuries of the season in America are almost unknown here. Good meat, well cooked, sweet and crisp bread, the best-made coffee in the world, sweet butter, and good beer, can always be had in Vienna. Of course, any one can live well upon these solids and substantials, and to those who know no better they are the summing up of human happiness. That anything else should be wanting is regarded as ridiculous; and when an American undertakes to describe the variety of human food that tempts the palate in his favored land, he is listened to with a shrug of the shoulders, expressive partly of doubt, and partly of disgust that any one should want to eat such things. The Viennese regard fruits as unhealthy, and most of them will never venture further than to eat a half-dozen cherries. There are peaches here, but they are very poor, and sold merely from the fruit-stands. There are also plenty of apricots, which no one seems to care about. Last evening, at the Reidhof, whilst the merits of the food of different countries were being discussed, and the several Americans present were describing a number of our special luxuries, a Cuban gentleman, who has been roaming over the world for the past eight years, and has resided much of his time in America, was appealed to, when he delivered himself in substance about as follows: "If you want good beef and mutton, with good ale, go to London for them; if you desire the best pastry and fancy dishes, go to Paris for them; if you prefer the substantials, well cooked and served, and the best-made coffee, and excellent beer, come to Vienna for them; but if you desire all these essentials to good living combined, together with soft crabs, oysters, terrapins, canvas-back ducks, and an endless supply of the most luscious fruit, you must go to America for them." There are several American Germans now here, among them Mr. Raster, editor of the Chicago *Staats Zeitung*, who are more enthusiastic on the subject of American living than the Americans are, declaring that the real enjoyment of life is unknown in Europe.

"I KISS YOUR HAND."

Kissing the hand is a national custom in Austria. A gentleman on meeting a lady with whom he is acquainted, especially if she be young and handsome, kisses her hand. On parting from her he again kisses her hand. At the Reidhof last evening a young man who is paying his addresses to a young lady, on taking his seat at the supper-table around which the family were seated, kissed the mother's hand, and also the hand of his affianced. It is very common to see a gentleman kiss a lady's hand on the street, on meeting or parting with her. If you give a beggar-woman in the street a few coppers, she either kisses your hand or says, "I kiss your hand." We have had our hand kissed twenty times since we have been in Austria, by chambermaids and beggars, and on one occasion by an old man. The words "kiss your hand" appear to be the same in German as in English, or at least sound the same. The gentlemen kiss the hands of married women as well as the single, and it is taken as an ordinary salutation and a token of respect. American ladies are startled when they first experience the application of this custom, but soon submit to it with a good grace. Children also, when presented to a stranger, take his hand and kiss it, showing that it is a custom to which they are educated from their cradles.

BLONDES AND BRUNETTES.

We ought to have stated in our last letter, in reference to the Austrian ladies, that there are very few blondes in this section of Germany. The ladies are mostly brunettes, with dark hair and eyes. There are, however, some blondes, with light complexions and blue eyes, and they are as much admired here as they are in America. They take much more care of their hair than the brunettes do, glorying in ringlets and curls, and dress it with great taste and skill. There are no artificial blondes here, however, with dyed hair, that being a fashion which has not yet reached Austria. The German blondes all come from Northern Germany, and they are probably more numerous in Baltimore than they are in Vienna.

AUSTRIAN FUEL.

Throughout Austria, along all the lines of railway there are piled up large masses of a species of lignite, which is used as a substitute for coal in generating steam. It is in the form of flakes rather than of lumps, and is of a brownish black, resembling rotten or decayed wood more than it does coal. It is broken up into small pieces, and piled in baskets, from whence it is supplied to the tenders of passing locomotives. It emits a strong black smoke, but it does not annoy the passengers with dust or soot. Judging from the immense quantities to be seen, the supply must be as extensive as coal is with us, and it must be very easily mined. There is an abundant supply of wood, mostly pine, in Austria, her mountain regions being dense pine forests; but this fuel is used even on the Crown-Prince Rudolph Road, which passes through pine forests and over mountains clad with heavy timber. The fuel used for domestic purposes in Vienna is wood and charcoal, and, as most of the people do their eating in the restaurants, there are many houses in which a fire is never lighted for six or eight months of the year, except a spirit-lamp or a pan of charcoal.

PESTH AND TRIESTE—DOWN THE DANUBE.

On the 2d of July we proceeded from Vienna to Pesth, taking one of the steamers on the Danube, a distance of nearly two hundred miles. Our letter describing this interesting trip, which was mailed at Pesth, the capital of Hungary, failed to come to hand, as well as a letter describing Pesth.. We find it impossible to supply either at this late day. We found the Danube almost as interesting as the Rhine, though not so romantic. It passes through the rich agricultural regions of Hungary, and is a broad, rushing stream, our boat going down the current at the rate of almost twenty miles an hour. From Pesth we took the railroad to Trieste, a long and wearisome ride, which is described in the following letters.

HOTEL DE LA VILLE,
TRIESTE, July 5, 1873.

We spent the anniversary of American Independence in the very unpatriotic way of traveling some four hundred miles over the dominions of Francis Joseph, Emperor of Austria, and eating our meals as we could gather them on the roadside. We did not hear a cracker explode, nor smell gunpowder, until we reached Trieste at nine o'clock last evening, when the United States vessels in port were closing the observance of the day by the firing off of rockets and the burning of Costar's signals in full view of the thousands of people assembled in front of the cafés and ice-cream saloons along the quay. It was a very pretty sight, and stirred within us those patriotic emotions which had lain dormant all day under clouds of railroad dust and the scorching rays of a semi-Italian sun. We gave three cheers internally, and called for a lemonade.

FROM PESTH TO TRIESTE.

We left Pesth, the capital of Hungary, at nine o'clock in the evening, and at daylight this morning found ourselves in the midst of the garden spot of Europe, the great grain-growing region of Hungary, from which England draws her supplies during seasons of scarcity. The wheat stood very heavy in the fields, but it is said to be badly damaged by rust on account of the protracted season of rain, there having been until recently scarcely a clear day for the past two months. A great deal of Indian corn is also grown here, which looked promising, though it was not so far advanced as with us at this season of the year. The fields were well filled with women, either hoeing corn or reaping the rye-fields. There were some men, but the women predominated. Thence we passed through the regions known as Galicia, Styria, Croatin, the Tyrol, and Carniola, the land becoming thinner and less productive as we approached the Italian coast. For fully one hundred miles through Carniola the road wound its way through a region that was probably never inhabited before the road was constructed, as nearly all those now living there seem to be connected with the road. It is the military frontier of Austria, and we should regard it as difficult for even a scouting-party intent on destroying the road to reach it either on foot or horseback. It reminded us of a legend applied to the dominion of one of the Northern princes. It is to the purport that the angels of the Lord, after the world was made, had a large lot of loose stone left, which they hurriedly dropped, and thus his territory was formed. The whole face of the earth is nearly covered with loose stone of all shapes and sizes, with bushes and grass interspersed. The residents had contrived to clear small spots for the cultivation of their vegetable-gardens, but this seemed to be a herculean task, judging by the mountains of loose stone that were piled up around their claims, which ranged from a twenty-foot square lot to the fourth of an acre, according to the energy of the explorer after mother earth. At one point it had been necessary, in this inhospitable country, to erect immense stone walls, twenty feet high, and a quarter of a mile long, to protect the trains from tornadoes, to which the district is frequently liable, from northeast winds. So great is their violence that loaded wagons have been overthrown; and these stone walls are used as a sort of breakwater, behind which the trains can run for protection if a storm should be imminent or prevailing.

The only interesting points of the route were those through the Tyrol and Hungary. In Hungary the road ran along the shore of the Plattensee, which is fifty miles in length and abounds in fish. The great summer resorts of the nobility of Hungary are here, and resorts for amateur fishermen abound along its banks. After passing Pragerhof, the mineral baths for which this portion of the world is famous were frequently encountered as we sped on our journey. Whilst steaming along the banks of the river Laibach, in Tyrol, with an atmosphere in the cars ranging about ninety degrees, in the near distance could be seen the Julian and Carnic Alps, with their snow-clad summits glittering in the sun.

THE ADRIATIC SEA.

About twenty miles before reaching Trieste the road breaks away from its mountainous and rugged tracks and boldly strikes on to the shore of the Adriatic, which presented quite a reviving scene as the closing one of our long journey. The sun had just sunk below the horizon, and its lingering rays were reflected from the bosom of the deep-blue waters. In the distance could be seen the domes and spires of Venice, the Queen of the Adriatic, and at the head of the Bay the city of Trieste was soon spread out before us like a map. A few miles before we reached Trieste, we saw Punta Grignano, a rocky prominence extending out into the sea, upon which stands the château of Miramar, the favorite residence of Maximilian and Carlotta before ambition lured them to seek the crown of Mexico. It is truly a magnificent structure, being built of white marble, and surrounded by a fine park and gardens, with the blue Adriatic spread out before it. It is a princely home, and will always have a mournful interest connected with it as the former residence of "poor Carlotta," whose sad fate as a confirmed maniac has won for her the heartfelt sympathy of the whole world. It is open on Sundays and holidays for public enjoyment. In a few minutes after passing Miramar, we dashed into a tunnel, from which we emerged into the streets of Trieste.

THE CITY OF TRIESTE.

The city of Trieste is the only seaport of the Austrian dominions. It contains a population of about one hundred and twenty thousand, composed of all nationalities, the Italians predominating, and it has all the characteristics of an Italian city. After reaching our hotel last evening we started out for a stroll through the city, and found the streets literally thronged with men, women, and children, whilst thousands were taking creams and refreshments in front of the large cafés on the Piazza Grande. The main streets are broad, and are paved with large oblong blocks of granite, kept very clean, and the promenaders filled up the whole street, walking indiscriminately everywhere. Turks and Greeks and Armenians mingled with the Italians and Germans, whilst there were also abundance of English and Americans. The peasants of the surrounding districts, with their picturesque costumes, are Sclavonians, whilst the sailors and fishermen are principally Dalmatians and Istrians. There is on the streets of Trieste the greatest commingling of tongues that can be found anywhere in Europe except at Marseilles. Trieste holds the same commercial relation to South Germany that Hamburg and Bremen do to North Germany.

So strictly Italian are the habits of the people that it was very easy in the gaslight, as we strolled along the Corso, the principal street of Trieste, and through the Piazza Grande and the Piazza della Borsa, to imagine ourselves in the city of Naples, or in the Piazza of St. Mark, in Venice. There was the same indiscriminate mingling of the sexes, the same free and easy manners, whilst loud conversation and the humming of popular airs were to be heard in every direction. The streets of the old town, which are too narrow and steep for vehicles, were similarly crowded with the lower classes, and in some of them pandemonium seemed to be let loose. If any other evidence were required of Trieste being a genuine Italian city, it would be found in the fact that we have caught two black Italian fleas on our hand since commencing to write this letter, and that this morning we were aroused from our first morning nap at early dawn by the shrill scream of a native Italian donkey directly under our chamber window.

HUNGARY.

PESTH AND OFEN.

Our sojourn in Pesth satisfied us that Baedeker has not done justice to this thriving capital of Hungary. We spent the day in walking through the city, or riding on its passenger railway cars, by which we accidentally struck upon many places of interest which are not mentioned in this usually correct guide-book. One of these is a large and very fine park, called Varosliget, which we found thronged with people, whilst the fashion of the city were driving around the main drives in their fine equipages. Like all the public parks in Southern Germany, it is given up entirely to the enjoyment of the people, and numerous refreshment-gardens are to be found in all sections of the grounds, in and around which men, women, and children were listening to the strains of music, though not such as we have become accustomed to in Vienna. Hungarian music may be very good, but we do not think it would be much admired far away from its native soil. Nor is there any but the briefest mention by Baedeker of Margaretta Island, which is one of the greatest attractions of this thriving and enterprising commercial city of the Danube.

THE CITY OF OFEN.

The city of Ofen, or as it is more generally called, Buda, which is connected with Pesth by a magnificent suspension bridge, also abounds in interest. Ofen and Pesth are so closely connected as to seem but one city, the Danube merely dividing them. The royal palace, the base of which is at least three hundred feet above the roofs of the houses along the line of the river, presents from Pesth one of the most picturesque views imaginable, it being, with its gardens and out-buildings, fully one thousand yards in length. The rock upon which it stands rises almost perpendicularly, and the upper level can be reached by cars drawn up an inclined railway by a stationary engine, similar to that at Pittsburg. In order to give expeditious access to that portion of the city beyond this rock, a tunnel for carriages, about a half-mile long, has been excavated through it, being a continuation of the bridge. This bridge, by the way. is not a wire suspension bridge, but is a succession of immense steel plates, with swinging bolts, hanging from towers one hundred and fifty feet high, like a wire bridge, but much stronger and more massive. It was built by an Englishman named Clark, and, being four hundred yards in length, is considered one of the finest specimens of bridge architecture in Europe. The bed of it is laid with the Nicholson pavement, and, although it is always thronged with carriages and pedestrians, there is not felt the least vibration. A second bridge, for passengers, and one for railroad purposes, are being constructed. On a still higher rock, to the left of the city, not less than six hundred feet above the water-level, is an immense fortress, with winding carriage-way, by which it is approached. The weather was too hot, and the rays of the sun were too powerful, for us to venture the ascent.

Among other interesting matters in Ofen (Buda) are the remnants of Turkish architecture, this city having been in past ages, for one hundred and fifty years, in possession of the Turks. Like Pesth, it is also ambitious, and all the new buildings in course of erection are of a very elegant and elaborate architecture.

THE CITY OF PESTH.

The city of Pesth is, however, the great attraction, and its commercial importance is evidenced by the number of steamers constantly arriving and departing, many of them carrying on trade with Constantinople and the various ports on the Adriatic, the Mediterranean, and the Black Sea. Its domestic commerce is also immense, and the scene along the wharves would do credit to Baltimore, whilst the attractions of the city front have no superior in any of our commercial cities. It is earnestly contending with Vienna in its ornamentation, and a Ringstrasse running through the heart of the city and terminating at the Park is in course of construction. Central avenues are being laid out and trees planted, whilst the buildings going up along the line of this broad thoroughfare are equal to the tall and graceful structures of Vienna.

The Grand Hotel of Pesth is also another evidence of the ambition of the people. It seems strange to find in this comparatively remote city the largest and most elegant hotel in Europe. It is more truly "grand" than any other hotel we have entered bearing this high-sounding name, not even excepting its namesake of Paris. Both the exterior and interior are finished in the most elaborate style of art, and it is furnished with equal elegance and taste. Among its other peculiarities, it has in its upper story a handsome chapel for religious worship. There are also a Grand Assembly saloon, a large glass-covered and lighted court-yard, dining-saloon and cafés, and three hundred and two chambers, with over five hundred beds. For a good room with two beds, facing the Danube, we were charged but three florins per day, or one dollar and a half in our money, for two persons. This elegant building is, however, only one of an extended line along the greater portion of the river front, on a level with the grand promenade.

There is also in Pesth a Zoological Garden, with a large collection of wild beasts; and the same care is taken in everything to furnish amusements for the people. The large boats, crowded with passengers to Margaretta Island and the bathing establishments in the upper part of Ofen, were arriving and departing during our sojourn at all hours of the day, and tug-boats towing lighters and barges laden with merchandise were always puffing up the river against the heavy tide, many of them doubtless bound for Vienna.

FOR VENICE.

Desiring to spend Sunday in Venice, which is but six hours' run across the bay, we will go this Saturday evening and spend a few days with the Queen of the Adriatic, returning to Trieste on Tuesday.

[The account of our trip to Venice, and a full description of this most interesting city, will be found in another portion of this volume.]

TRIESTE (AUSTRIA), July 12, 1873.

We returned from our very pleasant and interesting trip to Venice yesterday morning, having left that city on the steamer Milano at midnight, in the midst of an outpouring of rain which was peculiarly Italian. We, however, had a pleasant trip, the weather clearing shortly after we took our departure. There was an abundance of passengers, among whom were several Americans. They are on their way to Vienna, the length of their stay depending entirely on the question as to whether they can get accommodations at fair prices. They say they expect to be plucked everywhere whilst traveling, but they decidedly object to staying long where the people have hung out the sign of roguery so distinctly as they have in Vienna. However, prices are now much lower, but they are still fifty per cent. higher than anywhere else in Europe.

The American flag greeted our vision this morning as we entered the harbor of Trieste, flying from the peak of the frigate Wabash, which was also flying the broad pennant of Admiral Case. She arrived during our absence at Venice.

THE BLUE ADRIATIC.

Trieste is situated at the head of the Adriatic, the harbor being formed by a sea-wall, or breakwater, which protects the shipping from the turbulence of the sea during storms. The scene from our hotel windows at sunset is very beautiful; and of an evening, when the moon is casting its rays over the deep blue of this beautiful sea, a more picturesque view can scarcely be imagined. No matter how oppressive may be the rays of the sun during the day, the evenings are always cool and pleasant, and yachts and boats are moving about on the water till a late hour. During the afternoon the fishing-boats can be seen coming in well laden with the products of the net and the line, and steamers are always coming from or departing to the neighboring islands and towns on the coast. Next to Naples, the harbor of Trieste is the most beautiful in Europe. On a clear day the steeples of Polo can be seen in the distance on the opposite coast. A fine turnpike runs along the coast for many miles close to the seashore, and affords a pleasant evening drive in summer. The steamer to Venice runs three times a week, making the passage across in six hours.

THE GREEK CHURCH.

There are a great number of Greeks in Trieste, some of whom retain their turbans and flowing robes, though most of them are in European attire, save the red skull-cap and black tassel. One of the most elegant churches in the city is that of the Greek Catholics on the quay. We were allowed by a fee to the sexton to enter and examine it yesterday, and found its arrangements and ornamentation of the altar quite different from those of the Roman Catholic churches. There are a number of very elegant scriptural paintings on its walls, and the silver figures of the apostles in bas-relief are not only fine specimens of art, but show that the congregation must be a very wealthy one. The whole interior of the church, which is comparatively new, is magnificently painted, gilded, and decorated, and, though not excessively large, is sufficient to accommodate about eight hundred worshipers.

PLENTY OF FRUIT.

The city of Trieste is famous for its fruit, and a visit to the market yesterday morning was quite refreshing to an American who is used to an abundance of this healthy summer sustenance. Apricots, peaches, plums, pears, and cherries were displayed in great profusion and at very moderate prices. There were also figs, larger than a peach, both ripe and luscious. The cherries are much larger than those in our colder climate, and are very fine' to the taste. The tour of Europe during summer subjects the American lover of fruit to great deprivation. There is but little fruit, and that of an inferior quality and of high price, in Central Europe, until the grape crop is gathered, with the exception of the apricot, which, from its insipid taste, soon wearies the appetite. For the sake of good fruit and plenty of it we are willing, for a few days at least, to stand the heat and tolerate the company of the fleas.

THE PEOPLE OF TRIESTE.

The people of Trieste seem to live more at home than those of Vienna. There is scarcely a restaurant in the whole city where a good meal can be had. Indeed, they are so few that it is difficult to find any of them of any description. Beer-houses are also very scarce, and it is evident that beer-drinking is not much in vogue. There is a good demand for coffee, lemonade, and ices, the saloons being very abundant, but there is little drinking done here, with the exception of wines. It seems that America is almost the only country where intoxicating liquors are drunk as a beverage, and where a large proportion of the people think it manly to make beasts of themselves. There are some dirty shops where the lazzaroni obtain an intoxicating beverage, somewhat resembling our whisky, but there is no place in Trieste where even a glass of brandy can be had, and of course there are no first-class drinking-saloons. If there was any demand for such drinks there would be plenty of them; and, as there are none, it may be taken for granted there is no demand.

THE CITY OF TRIESTE.

The city of Trieste is peculiarly a commercial mart, and has but few attractions for the stranger. The wharves along the city front, for more than a mile, are lined with vessels stern foremost to the shore, over which they discharge and take on their cargoes. There are, so far as we have been able to discover, but few private residences in the city, all of the better class of citizens residing in beautiful villas high up on the mountainside to the north of the city. Nearly all the houses seem to be devoted to some species of trade, except those occupied as hovels for the poorer classes, and as hotels, eating- and beer-houses. It seems strange at night where all the well-dressed people who throng the streets and the cafés come from, but they may be supposed to be, in a great measure, the wives and daughters of the shop-keepers, who reside over their respective places of business.

A STROLL THROUGH THE CITY.

We took an extended stroll after dinner yesterday through all sections of the city, and find that, with the exception of the fine buildings and hotels fronting the bay, it has all the characteristics of an old Italian town. The Italian women from the country were moving off with their piles of baskets on the backs of their donkeys, and hundreds of lazzaroni were lying about on the pavements, asleep. In the narrow streets, varying from eight to twelve feet in width, the women and children were sitting on the pavements, and sailors of all nations wandering about among them. On Via del Torrento, a broad thoroughfare, for several squares the street was lined with booths for the sale of old clothes, most of which appeared to be so old, dirty, and ragged as to be only fit for the paper-mill. Everybody appeared intent upon selling something, including articles which in almost any other part of the world would be considered unsalable.

In the middle of Via del Torrento a large wooden shanty is erected, labeled Teatro, which must be a jolly place at night.

In the lower section of the city, along the water-front, the buildings are very large and ornamental, and the theatre, which is also in this section, is a large and elegant structure, but is now closed for the season. In one or two of the adjoining streets are some very fine stores and numerous coffee and ice-cream saloons, which at certain hours of the day are all well attended. The city puts its best foot foremost, and will not bear an inspection of its interior.

During the middle of the day the heat is more intense than we have ever felt it. An hour's exposure in such heat as we had yesterday would be death to almost any one: even in crossing the street its effect was most oppressive. All out-of-door labor ceases during this heated term, and does not commence again until three o'clock.

THE WOMEN OF TRIESTE.

The ladies of Trieste are of all complexions and all nationalities, and speak so many different languages that it is difficult to describe them. They dress well, and the better classes have all the grace of carriage which distinguishes the Italian woman in all grades of life. Dark hair and dark eyes predominate, but the countenance is sallow, and harsh rather than pleasing. Occasionally a German blonde is seen among them ; but, although this is an Austrian city, the language most spoken is Italian, and the number of Germans is comparatively small. Among the lower classes there is but little female beauty to be seen. They appear to commence to age before they are out of their teens, and are sallow and sunken about the eyes, with but little vestige of the sprightliness of youth left. They live a terrible life of exposure, and toil for their living from the time that other children are but just commencing their education. Children of this class have no youth, and are early inured to all the sufferings and responsibilities of mature life in other countries.

HALL, NEAR STEYER, July 15, 1873.

We arrived at Steyer on Saturday last, from Trieste, after a journey of precisely twenty-four hours, and soon reached this cool resting-place in the mountains. Steyer is about one hundred and twenty miles from Vienna, and about five hundred miles from Trieste, and is in the centre of the iron region of Lower Austria. It has about fifteen thousand inhabitants, and, being situated at the confluence of the river Enns with the river Steyer, does a very extensive business in lumber, which is floated down the Enns from the pine-clad mountains through which it passes. But before taking a glance at Steyer we must give the reader some account of our journey from Trieste, with the incidents and sights of travel.

A RAILROAD EXPERIENCE.

There are no sleeping-cars in Europe, and, as a general thing, those who travel at night must sit bolt upright, with merely a head-rest. We left Trieste at seven o'clock on Wednesday evening, having before us a twenty-four hours' ride. Myself and companion were placed in a section with six other passengers, filling it up to its utmost capacity, some smoking pipes, and others cigarettes and cigars, but all puffing away to the fullest extent of their smoke-generating abilities. To make the matter worse, a heavy rain-storm was in progress, which compelled the closing of the windows, and we determined to see if we could not do better at the first stopping-place. Here we intimated to the conductor that if he could give us a separate section to ourselves we would make it all right. In a few moments he made a sign to us to come out, which we did with our valises, and, following in his wake, we were soon ushered into a section which was entirely empty. Whether he had removed the passengers or had reserved an empty car for such an emergency, we were not informed, but upon our placing in his hands a couple of florins he smiled blandly, took out his key, and not only fastened, but, with a wink, locked both doors, as much as to say, "You are alone for the night." In a few minutes two other gentlemen, who had doubtless followed our example, were brought forward and locked in the other section, the bell was sounded, the conductor blew his little brass horn, the locomotive whistled, and we were off. Each having a long seat, extending all the way across the car, we stretched ourselves out, and were soon sleeping as soundly as if reposing in a Pullman Palace car. It will thus be seen that with a little management sleeping-cars can be had on European railroads much cheaper than upon our roads at home. The conductor was as good as his word, and we were alone until after we changed conductors at Grütz at ten o'clock the next morning.

AGRICULTURAL NOTES.

We passed through the rocky fields of Carniola during the night, which is a region of country strongly resembling Captain Jack's lava beds, especially if they should ever be plowed up. The whole country is a heap of loose stones, from the size of a piece of chalk to a grindstone, from the interstices of which cedars and green bushes are sprouting up. At daylight we were approaching Grätz, in the heart of the rich agricultural region of Styria, where everything was green, bright, and beautiful, and the farmers were busily at work harvesting their rye crops and making hay. We did not observe, nor have we anywhere in Austria seen, a single agricultural implement of any kind except the plow and the hoe, nor have we seen any wheat that appears to have been planted with the drill. Crowds of women and girls were working in the fields with the hoe, or reaping with the sickle. The proportion was about ten women to one man engaged in farm-work.

There was, however, evidence of good husbandry everywhere. There being no fences, the division of land is marked by small square stones with the initials of the owner carved upon them. Small farms appeared to be the rule, as scarcely more than an acre of one species of grain could be seen in one plot. The mode of planting is generally in lands,—one of wheat, one of oats, another of potatoes, and another of corn, the latter planted so thick as to indicate that it was raised for fodder.

But little ground is anywhere spared for clover or timothy, and in sowing it the greatest care is taken for its preservation. Instead of raking it up in the field in cocks, as our farmers do, a number of poles are stuck up in the field, having pegs interspersed so as to hold up the hay which is piled up around them. By this means it is kept almost entirely off the ground, and in case of rain is not damaged. This is a universal practice, and a larger class of poles are used for wheat and rye. Many of the poles are made of young cedar-trees, the limbs being cut off so as to leave protrusions of five or six inches, which answer instead of pegs. The poles stand about eight feet out of the ground, and when clothed with the hay present a very strange aspect, being entirely concealed from view. The hay barely touches the ground, and there is no doubt that its sweetness is better preserved than by our process. They have but little ground to devote to this purpose, and they desire to make the most of the yield.

The farm-houses are generally small, of but one story, but their surroundings bore evidence of cleanliness and thrift. Their little flower-gardens were in full bloom, and the whiteness of the walls of their dwellings indicated that the whitewashing season arrived at least once a year. No cattle could be seen unless tied to a stake or in charge of boys. The farm-buildings were generally sufficiently large for small farms, but none so extensive as the barns in Lower Austria, where the farms are evidently very extensive.

AUSTRIAN RAILROADS.

The railroads of Austria are constructed and managed with a greater regard to safety than those of any other country on the Continent. Accidents are almost unheard of, and next to impossible. They all have double tracks, and, although they mostly pass through very mountainous country, especial effort seems to have been made to give assurance to the mind of the passenger that, though he may be gliding along the edge of a precipice, he can admire the scenery with no dread of accident. A heavy stone wall, six feet thick, covers all embankments, whilst a similar impediment guards the track at all dangerous points. A telegraphic bell at the road-crossings announces an approaching train five minutes before it dashes along, and at every mile-stone on the road a guard in the livery of the company, with his rolled-up flag in hand, gives a military salute to the engineer as he passes, that being the assurance that all is right on his division of the road. All the stations on the road are neat and elegant structures, with fine floral displays, and everything clean and in order around them. A train arrives, the officer in attendance, with three strokes of the depot-bell, announces all ready to depart, the conductor sounds a half-note on the little brass horn suspended around his neck, the locomotive responds with a whistle, and we are off again.

A WILD COUNTRY.

The Austrian roads, though under no supervision of the government, being owned and run by companies, are all named after royal personages, as, for instance, the "Kaiser Franz Josef Bahn," the "Kaiserin Elisabeth Bahn," and the "Kronprinz Rudolph Bahn." Desiring to strike across the country from Brück, so as to reach Steyer without going to Vienna, we took passage at that place on the Kronprinz Bahn, a new road, which has been many years in construction, passing through the Wienerwald Mountains, a portion of the Swabian Alps. The road follows a mountain torrent, the Ernsthal, and the scenery eclipses all that is to be seen on the Alleghany or even the Rocky Mountains. At times the precipitous rocks towered over our heads to the height of five thousand feet, and again we were flying along with a precipice of many hundred feet under the car-window. We passed over innumerable viaducts, and through interminable tunnels, hewn out of the solid rock, so solid and immovable that arching would be altogether unnecessary. Many of the tallest mountains were clad with snow, whilst those of less altitude were covered with pines. For about a hundred miles there was presented a succession of surprises, which rendered the journey quite interesting. The country through which the greater portion of this road passes is the great iron region of Austria. The great Erzberg mines are in this vicinity, which are worked by the government. The "ore mountain" is so productive that the ore is quarried in summer without the aid of mining operations, whilst in winter the subterranean mode of operations is more convenient. The mines and furnaces, some of which have been in operation for a thousand years, employ about five thousand hands, and yield twenty thousand tons of iron annually. The river Ernsthal is a rushing torrent, somewhat resembling the Rhine at its mountain source, and the roar of its waters added to the picturesque aspect of the country through which we were passing.

At seven o'clock in the evening, after precisely twenty-four hours' run from Trieste, we landed at the brisk little city of Steyer, the last fifty miles of the journey being through the beautiful valley of the river Enns; our destination being the Springs of Hall, ten miles distant by carriage, which we reached at ten o'clock in the evening. Having had a few days' rest, we concluded to make an excursion to-day to Steyer, to view some of its attractions as enumerated by the faithful Baedeker.

THE CITY OF STEYER.

Steyer is a purely manufacturing town, iron being the basis of its wealth, and wool from the mountains a source of increasing importance. Here is the manufactory of all the arms for the Austrian army, which is now being supplied with the famous needle-gun. We visited most of its establishments, clambered up to the eminence upon which stands the Castle of Steyer, and were assured by the custodian that Prince Lamberg, who makes his residence here, would be pleased to see us, but was not at home at present. He hoped we would call again; but, as we came to see the castle, and not the prince, we left our cards, and expressed our regrets that our stay would be so short that it would not be possible for us to avail ourselves of the pleasure of meeting his excellency. We also visited the old churches of the place, one of which was consecrated in 1443 and has some very fine old paintings. Indeed, we found but little in Steyer worthy of note in this correspondence, though we spent a very pleasant day in roaming through its ancient streets and viewing the rushing waters of the Steyer and the Enns as they come together and mingle and then move on to swell the waters of the Danube. The only thing we brought away from Steyer to remember it by is a pair of well-made calf-skin boots, for which we paid six florins, or precisely three American dollars.

THE GERMAN WATERING-PLACES.

HALL SPRINGS, AUSTRIA, June 13, 1873.

"WHAT IS THE MATTER WITH YOU?"

We are now, as will be seen by the date of this letter, nearly two hundred miles northwest of Vienna, at one of the German springs, known by the simple name of "Hall," but famous for its curative properties for a variety of "the ills that flesh is heir to." The fact is that there are very few people who visit the springs of Germany unless they suffer from disease of some kind, and they are consequently not places of fashionable resort, as with us in America. "What is the matter with you?" is the question asked of all new-comers; and most of them place themselves in the hands of the doctor, who prescribes the number and temperature of the baths, and the amount of the water to be taken internally. The arrival of a party of Americans at a place like Hall is of course a novelty, and is regarded by the people as an indication that the fame of their little town up here in the mountains has spread across the Atlantic. Certain it is that we never heard of "Hall" before, or of the virtues of its waters, but are here to see life at a German watering-place, and to enjoy the company of some kind friends who are visitors at the springs.

HALL, AND HOW WE GOT THERE.

We reached Hall at a very untimely hour, about two o'clock in the morning, tumbling into one of its hotels after a carriage-drive of over two hours, preceded by some five hours in the cars. Such a thing as the arrival of guests in the night was itself a novelty, and that they should be Americans was still more curious. Sick people never travel at night, and everybody who comes to Hall is either sick or accompanying sick friends. Then Germans never do anything in a hurry, and to travel in a carriage at night to reach a summer resort would be considered contrary to all precedent, a thing unheard of before in the quiet village of Hall, where everybody goes to bed early and is sound asleep before ten o'clock. We were acting contrary to all precedent, and by way of explanation to the worthy people of Hall, not one of whom it is probable ever heard of the English language, and who are not likely soon to aid in verifying the prediction of President Grant, we will detail how it all happened, as well as some of the mishaps which rendered it necessary for us to come posthaste, in the small hours of the night, to this retired and retiring village.

A CHAPTER OF MISHAPS.

Before proceeding further, let me advise all your readers whose education has been so far neglected as not to have acquired a knowledge of the German tongue, never to enter the dominions of the Emperor of Austria unless they have some one to take charge of them who is thus qualified. We have never spent a month in Europe so pleasantly as the past month in Austria, but have been in charge of good friends, who not only understand the language, but understand the people and all their peculiarities. To make a long story short, it may as well be acknowledged that, as on a memorable occasion in the wilds of San Domingo, *we got lost*, and were in pursuit of our friends, being both anxious to rejoin them, and to relieve their minds as early as practicable of the uneasiness which we knew they felt on our account.

HOW IT ALL HAPPENED.

On Wednesday morning we settled our bill at the Hotel Austria in Vienna, and requested our baggage to be sent to the railroad depot, stating that our destination was Steyer. We had previously made arrangements to join our friends at the depot and travel with them to this summer resort. The hotel official procured us carriages and dispatched our baggage, and at the appointed time we were at the depot, and, not finding our friends, soon became convinced that the stupid porter had sent us to the wrong depot, to the Ostbahn instead of the Westbahn, the depots being about five miles apart. Here we were with a pile of trunks, two ladies, and all their satchels, shawls, baskets, etc., and a half-dozen porters and depot bummers, each seizing hold of a trunk or a basket, and all talking to us at once in an unknown tongue, desiring, we suppose, to know where we were going, not one word of which was understandable. None of them had apparently ever heard of the English language before, and French was as much Greek to them as their German was to us. If we had been at the right depot we could have dispatched our business easily enough; but it was impossible to explain to them that we did not want to go anywhere,—in fact, that we were lost innocents, and perplexed as to what we should do and where we should go. After about an hour of vexation we discovered an official who actually understood English, and to him we explained our difficulty and the stupid blunder of the hotel porter. It was eleven o'clock—and our train started at nine—when we succeeded, after much tribulation, in getting ourselves and baggage transferred to the Westbahnhof, and there we learned that another train would start for Steyer at half-past four o'clock in the afternoon. It being impossible for us to communicate with our friends by telegraph, or for them to communicate with us, until after their arrival at their destination, we determined to start off as rapidly as possible in pursuit; and it was thus that we broke in upon the quiet village of Hall in the small hours of the night, and brought joy to the hearts of our friends by arousing them at early dawn with the information of our safe arrival. Their dispatches had not reached us, and we had a jolly time over the incidents of our mishap. We had reached Steyer about ten o'clock at night, and, after an hour's renewal of our linguistic difficulties with railroad-officials and carriage-drivers, started, with ourselves in one carriage and our baggage in another, for a two hours' night drive into an unknown region, over hills and plains, through villages, but along a smooth road, and with rapidly-traveling horses. The distance, about ten miles, was accomplished in two hours, and at one o'clock the clanging bell of the Hôtel Karl summoned master and mistress and several half-dressed servants to receive us and care for our baggage. After a refreshing sleep we joined our friends in the morning at the Hôtel Kaiserin Elisabeth, and determined never again during our sojourn in Austria to trust ourselves out of leading-strings. The English language we found to be just about as useful to the traveler in Austria as Greek would be among the Choctaws.

ADVICE TO TRAVELERS.

When any one speaks to you, especially in or about a German hotel, and you do not wish to show your ignorance, it is safe to pull out your wallet and hand your questioner a piece of money. The answer will seldom fail to be the right one.

If you know the legal charge for anything, hand the precise amount and walk quietly away. It is very convenient on such occasions not to understand the language, and to be uncertain whether it is blessings or curses that are being showered upon you.

If you happen to be sent to the wrong depot, keep your pocket-book closed, as no one will do anything for you or with your baggage or your bundles without being paid for it, and consequently they will not be sent off in the wrong direction.

If you want to purchase anything, never get any one about a hotel to show you the way to a store. The rule is for the storekeeper to pay all such persons a heavy commission on the amount of sales. Of course the purchaser has the commission added to the price of the goods he buys.

If you want to go to the opera or a theatre, always employ some one about the hotel to get tickets for you. It is impossible to get them without paying a heavy price to the speculators, and by yielding gracefully there will be a saving of both time and patience, and no loss of money.

Never enter a bank, a store, or a place of business, in Austria, without taking off your hat and bowing to the proprietors. Never leave any such establishment without making your obeisance to all present. A neglect of these observances is considered downright rudeness, and on a second visit you will be treated coolly, even by a shopkeeper.

When you are dealing with any one who has anything to do with horses, be on your guard for deception and plunder. Our horse gentry are so proverbial for their honesty, probity, and fair dealing, and so seldom take advantage of any one, that this distinguishing trait of the Vienna horse-dealers will be the more remarkable.

THE ATTRACTIONS OF VIENNA.

We have left the city of Vienna, which, with all its faults, is one which few who have enjoyed its gay and merry life for any length of time are anxious to leave. The young students, who spend a year or more here to finish their medical education, carry with them a bright memory of the happy season of enjoyment, and long for a renewal of their visit. The free and easy life that is led by those who mingle with the people is a glorious relief from the monotony of social existence in hotels, which many strangers who visit Vienna fail to enjoy. The last evening of our sojourn will dwell long in our memory, and may induce us to pay Vienna another visit before our return to America. There were nine in our party who sat down to supper in a "restauration" with fully one thousand Viennese ladies and gentlemen, all enjoying themselves in groups around the two hundred tables, as few could do even in the brightest home-circle. Everything that could be called for by the most fastidious appetite was served up in excellent style, and the clatter of a thousand tongues in social converse, with the moving panorama around us, added to the pleasure of the occasion. Most of the people, in family or friendly parties, thus spend the evening, nothing stronger than beer being partaken of, and continue at the tables talking and smoking up to a quarter of ten o'clock, when they all disperse to their homes. Drunkenness or excessive drinking of beer is almost unknown, the latter being a beverage that is used by the mass of the people as we use coffee and tea, and having very little more exhilarating effect when taken in moderation. Among this mass of people scarcely a loud word could be heard, and thus it is everywhere among the thousands of cafés and "restaurations" that are to be found on every street throughout this immense city. Whisky, brandy, or any strong drink, is used only for medicinal purposes, except by the hack- and carriage-drivers, who are nearly all bloated drunkards, and care no more for beer than the more respectable portion of the Viennese do for water.

One of our party, on this memorable evening, called for a goblet of milk, which is regarded as among the unhealthy fluids. Its passage through the hall in the hands of the waiter excited general remark, and a German friend from the interior, who was supping with us, expressed his surprise that any one should drink milk, as well as that it could be had on call at an eating-saloon. It is rated, like water, as unhealthy, and probably with about as much cause.

SOMETHING ABOUT HALL.

Hall is regarded as the most costly summer resort in Germany, except Baden-Baden, and consequently very few come here, unless ordered to bathe in and drink its waters by their physicians, and we learn that the whole number of visitors last year did not exceed two thousand eight hundred. For two of the best rooms in the best hotel, with three beds, we pay four florins, or about two dollars, per day. We take our meals in the restaurant attached to the hotel, at a cost of less than nine florins per day, or four and a half dollars, making the entire expense about six dollars and a half per day for three persons, or two dollars and sixteen cents each. Our rooms are far better than the best of those at Cape May, are on the first floor, and we call for whatever we desire at the table, all of which is well cooked and palatable. Still, these Springs are regarded as very expensive.

ATTRACTIONS OF HALL.

There are five hotels in Hall, all of them rather small in American estimation, but every house in the village has furnished rooms to let, and there are several furnished cottages in the vicinity for rent to families. The iodine water, it being more strongly impregnated than any similar water in the world, is pumped from a well by water-power, and forced to the tanks that supply the bath-house, which is an immense building with two wings, and is now being enlarged. On each side of the long halls are rows of bath-rooms, some of them fitted up very elegantly, with marble tubs, and all supplied with hot and cold water, the attendants arranging the temperature according to the written order of the physician, as well as the time which is to be spent in the bath. In other rooms there are wooden bath-tubs, like everything else in Europe, first and second class, and first and second prices. The marble-tubbed rooms cost seventy-five cents per bath, and the wooden-tubbed thirty-five cents. In the second story of the bath-house there are a reading-room, a coffee-room, and a ball-room. In the rotunda the drinkers of the water assemble at seven o'clock in the morning and take their draughts from a fountain, and walk around the beautifully-arranged grounds between the glasses, whilst a fine brass band discourses most excellent music from a canopied music-stand in the midst of the lawn. It would be difficult to find a more beautiful and attractive spot than the Park, with its finely arranged gravel-walks, extending through the shaded groves for a mile or more to the west of the building. There is also a cold-water douche-bath, in a thickly shaded vale, which is for gentlemen at certain hours of the day, and for ladies at specified hours. It has all the attractions for a popular resort, and will probably become fashionable when the railroad reaches it, which is expected very shortly, in anticipation of which arrangements are making for new and larger hotels by the company which owns and manages the place. They will then, it is presumed, abandon the plan now adopted of putting everybody who arrives here on the sick-list, and taxing him, if he remains more than five days, for the use of the water, whether it is drunk or not, and for the privilege of strolling occasionally through the promenades which they have prepared for visitors.

FESTIVAL OF "CORPUS CHRISTI."

When we entered Hall on Wednesday night, we could see by the bright moonlight that all the houses were festooned with evergreens and hung with wreaths of flowers, whilst in the centre of the town a floral arch was erected across the broad thoroughfare, under which we were probably the first to pass. We observed that numerous shrines were illuminated as we drove along the road from Steyer, and that pictures of the Virgin and Child were displayed in some of the windows, with candles burning before them, although, it being past midnight, the people were evidently all sound asleep. Knowing that we were in a country intensely Roman Catholic, we supposed that they indicated some Church festival that had passed, but were not well enough posted to know that these were all preparations for the festival of Corpus

Christi, which was observed as a general holiday throughout Austria on the day of our arrival.

At early dawn we were aroused by the sharp rattling of a drum under our window, which passed through the town, being intended to arouse the people for the early morning services. Soon after, a company of volunteer militia, finely uniformed, with a full band, marched past to the church in close proximity to our hotel, to which the people were all moving, with numbers of children dressed in white and wearing on their heads wreaths of flowers. At about eight o'clock, as soon as the services were over, the military, the firemen, children and nuns, and the clergymen in their vestments, a scarlet canopy being carried over the head of the officiating priest, moved in procession, followed by the whole population, the men and women marching in separate bodies. They passed through all parts of the town, the streets on the whole line of the procession being thickly strewn with fresh-mown hay. Along the fronts of all the houses, limbs of trees were stuck in the ground, and an altar under a canopy of evergreens was erected in close proximity to the floral arch. On the return of the procession, the clergymen stopped at this altar, and the people knelt whilst mass was said, a choir of singers being present, who took part in the ceremonies. Immediately at the conclusion of the services, the crowd scrambled to get possession of pieces of the evergreens that formed the canopy under which the altar was erected. Several volleys of musketry were fired by the soldiers, and the assemblage dispersed. During the march, the throng of men and women following the procession were chanting prayers in a loud voice.

THE AUSTRIAN WOMEN.

The ceremonies being over, the balance of the day was spent in merry-making, the farmers and their wives and daughters from the country for many miles around having come to town to spend the day. During the afternoon the streets were literally massed with people, the women being all dressed very nearly alike. They had their heads tied up in heavy black silk scarfs or handkerchiefs, the two stiff ends floating like black wings behind them. The hair was entirely concealed, and the only ornaments worn were heavy gold ear-rings and breastpins. They all wore either black silk, satin, or velvet coats, some of which were either braided or trimmed with lace. This is the national costume, and it is strictly adhered to throughout this section of Austria. It seemed singular to see youthful and handsome faces peering out from this gloomy head-gear, and bright laughing eyes sparkling between the solemn black wings. The young men were all dressed like their fathers, black velvet vests with silver buttons being a distinguishing feature of their costume. This annual gathering in the streets of Hall on the festival of Corpus Christi is one upon which fathers and mothers arrange for the marriage of their sons and daughters, and there is a great deal of match-making perfected under the groves lining the main streets of the town. There was no evidence of poverty among them, all seeming to be well-conditioned people. It is also an occasion for the sale and exchange of horses, the purchase of lands, etc., as well as for friendly intercourse. In number the women largely exceeded the men, and they seemed to be the ruling power in whatever business transactions were in progress. They were all stout and strong in appearance, looking, indeed, as if they had more muscle and strength than the men, and were generally more energetic in their appearance and manner than the sterner sex. Their quilted skirts were largely distended by immense hoops, and some of the younger ones allowed a glimpse of the color and texture of their hair by a rippling wave on their foreheads peeping from under the solemn black scarf that bound their heads, whilst others showed the edge of a white collar and light-colored scarf between their chins and the closely-buttoned coats. It was evident that vanity is commencing to make inroads on the solemn and funeral garb that has come down to them from their mothers and grandmothers. There could not have been less than two thousand of these highly respectable and substantial-looking females, assemble l as if in mass-meeting under the linden-trees that form a grove near the centre of the town. Not a loud voice could be heard, and, with the exception of some of the younger lasses chatting with their beaux, the countenances of all seemed as solemn and serious as the outer garb.

STRONG-MINDED WOMEN.

The women of Austria, in the agricultural regions, are, like those of Switzerland, the master-minds of the family. They are strong-handed and strong-minded, and can take care of themselves, and of their husbands also when necessary. They are evidently the "lords of creation" outside of the cities, and need no one to take care of them. There is no labor too hard for them to undertake and perform a full day's work at. Whilst I write, my eye is upon twenty or more of them engaged in the construction of the new Trinkhalls in the rear of the hotel. The whole business of mixing and preparing the mortar is in the hands of stalwart women; the carrying of brick and mortar up the ladders, in tubs balanced on their heads, is being gracefully, and with apparent ease, performed by brighteyed lassies and their more grave-looking mothers. They work as if they were used to it and liked their vocation, and would scorn to be pitied by what we call the sterner sex. For all that we know, they may be the wives and daughters of the dozen or more automatical-looking men on the scaffolds who are slowly laying the brick and spreading the mortar which are brought to them on the top of the blonde locks or auburn curls of the "gentler" sex. That these women should be allowed to vote, and will have the franchise whenever it is given to their husbands, there is no manner of doubt, and they will then virtually have two votes, as no husband in the rural districts of Austria or Switzerland would dare to vote against the sentiments of his wife. In the cities of Austria, such as Vienna, the woman, and especially the wife, is the abject slave of the man. The wife works and toils, and carries on her shoulders all the burdens of the household, whilst the husband spends his leisure hours jovially in the restaurants and cafés. Husbands are scarce in Vienna, and the poor woman who can claim a legal father for her children thinks she has reached the summit of earthly happiness and is blessed beyond her deserts, let the man to whom she is bound be ever so brutal or worthless.

HALL, AUSTRIA, June 16, 1873.

SUNSHINE.

One day of warm sunshine and bright weather has enabled us to come to the conclusion that the Springs of Hall are located in the midst of the most charming mountain scenery, and that its natural advantages have been availed of to the greatest possible extent to add to its rural beauty. To the south, the lofty mountains of the Tyrol, with their peaks clad in perpetual snow, are distinctly visible, although fifty miles distant, whilst range after range of lesser mountains intervene, bright with forest foliage. It is the close proximity of these mountains that keeps the climate of Hall always cool during the summer months, and makes a blanket comfortable for covering at night, and a shawl or overcoat in the evening a necessity even in the month of August.

THE WATER CURE.

The iodine springs of Hall are famous throughout Germany, and even in Russia and France, for cleansing the blood from all impurities. Some both drink and bathe in it, whilst others bathe in it but drink the waters of other springs, which are to be had here in great purity and variety. Most of those who come here do so under orders from their physicians, and are provided with written instructions as to the quantity of water to be drunk, the time of drinking it, and the temperature, time, and duration of the bath. There seems to be a systematic course of treatment as to mineral spring waters in Germany, some having instructions to remain at Hall for a certain time and then proceed to some other spring to follow up a similar course with a different character of water. Thus one water is used to prepare the system for the action of another, just as a physician will frequently use different kinds of medicines.

HALL AND ITS SURROUNDINGS.

The village of Hall and its surroundings contain a population of about two thousand five hundred, most of them being engaged in the keeping of stores and lodgings, and in providing the other usual necessities of a summer resort. During nine months of the year they are preparing for their summer harvest; and the latter three of these nine seem to have been spent in painting and whitewashing and otherwise rendering their habitations bright and cheerful. The village consists principally of one main street, about a half-mile in length, upon which are located all the hotels, the city hall, and the finest of the houses in which furnished lodgings are provided for the summer season. The main street is about two hundred feet wide, having three rows of broad-leaved horse-chestnut trees down the centre, under the shade of which there are multitudes of seats, and about the centre of the village a music-stand is erected, on which every morning, from eleven to half-past twelve o'clock, an excellent band of string and wind instruments, numbering about twenty performers, discourses most admirable music. This is located directly in front of our hotel, and whilst we are writing the band is performing the overture to Der Freischütz. This band also performs in the promenade at seven o'clock in the morning, and from six to eight o'clock in the evening. There are also on the main thoroughfare three handsome fountains. The shady groves around the village are laid out as promenades in every direction, and there are other villages scattered around, within twenty minutes' walk, to which fine gravel-paths lead, where refreshments, fresh milk, cream, honey, and fruit can be had in abundance.

THE GAME TRUMBULO.

In the rear of our hotel there is a small shady grove, which in clear weather is used as a place for serving up meals to the guests of the hotel, no one in this country eating or drinking in-doors when the weather permits doing it in so pleasant a retreat as this. Here, also, in the afternoons, a variety of amusements are gotten up for the enjoyment of the guests. On Sunday and Thursday afternoons, after dinner, the game of Trumbulo is played here, better known as the game of "Lotto." The tickets are sold at about ten cents each in our money, and the bag containing the numbers is carried around so that the ladies may draw them. The record of the numbers drawn is kept on a large movable blackboard, and some two hours of amusement is afforded. There are fifteen prizes, in three different grades, consisting of a variety of fancy articles, ladies' fans, etc., all of which are displayed upon a table. It is a game of chance, costing but little and affording a fund of amusement. The numbers are called out successively in German, French, and Hungarian.

"THE GERMAN" BY GERMANS.

There was quite a fine hop on Saturday evening in the saloon over the bathing-hall, which was attended by nearly all the visitors here, consisting mainly of Germans, with some Russians, Hungarians, and French, and our party of six Americans. The reading and coffee-rooms were also filled by those who did not take part in the dance, showing a larger number of guests than we had supposed to be here. The German was danced as only Germans can dance it, and is much more intricate and tortuous than is attempted on our side of the Atlantic. The ladies and gentlemen who took part in it, to the number of nearly one hundred, seemed at times to be wound up into an inextricable knot, but all unraveled in the most easy and graceful manner. The American ladies who participated in the dance returned to their seats almost exhausted by the intricate and rapid lesson which they had taken in the "poetry of motion." The etiquette of the ball-room at the German springs is somewhat peculiar. A gentleman does not wait for an introduction to ask a lady to dance with him, but merely steps up and asks the pleasure of her hand. He is forbidden by etiquette to enter into any conversation with the lady whilst dancing, unless she invites it. At the conclusion of the dance he conducts her to a seat, politely bows, and leaves her. Acquaintances thus made end with the ball, unless invited and encouraged by the lady. Thus much of the difficulty in making up cotillions and quadrilles and furnishing partners is avoided.

SUNDAY AT HALL.

The only difference between Sunday and other days at this summer resort is, that from six to eight o'clock in the morning the residents are out in their best Sunday attire, going to or coming from church, and a good many people from the country around, having come to the village church, spend the rest of the day viewing the visitors in their promenades, among whom there are a prince, several young barons, and two counts and countesses. The sight of one of these has charms unspeakable to the simple peasant. The women have their heads all decked out in their sombre black handkerchiefs, with the ends flying, completely hiding their hair, and all but the lower tips of their ears, from which most of them have quite handsome ear-rings pendent. This has been for centuries the universal head-dress among these people, with whom the bonnet, in all its varied shapes, has never been known. They all wear immense hoops, widely distending their skirts, which was also the fashion here ages before the Empress Eugénie adopted them for the sisterhood of all creation. They have evidently no idea of discarding them, now that they have disappeared from the skirts of the fashionable guests at the hotels, and waddle about with them with the air of peacocks. With such immense busts as the peasant ladies have, the hoops seem a very suitable appendage for the continuation of the figure. The short dresses and distending hoops tend to the display of substantial continuations and ankles that are more stout than graceful and more useful than ornamental. The more youthful of them all have rosy cheeks, and are pictures of comfort and good health.

The orchestral band performed as usual on Sunday at noon, in the centre of the village, and both morning and evening on the promenade. At five in the afternoon the game of Trumbulo was played in the grove, at which there were about two hundred ticket-holders, and the prizes were contended for and distributed. The stores were all open, but the working-people generally suspended labor, and were strolling about and gazing at the fashionably-attired strangers, who, as usual at the summer resorts at home, were promenading in the finest dresses their trunks could furnish. The observance of Sunday ends always in most European countries with the close of the morning services, and the rest of the day is devoted to all manner of innocent recreation. There is, however, the most perfect order and quiet, and no excesses of any kind are indulged in, social converse being the main feature of the Sabbath recreation of the Germans. Their fondness for out-door life, which they consider eminently conducive to health, attracts them to every shady retreat where refreshments can be had, and thus the Sunday is spent. One of the never-failing injunctions of the German physicians to their patients here is, "Never eat in-doors when the weather will permit the taking of your meals in the open air."

THE VISITORS.

The visitors now here exceed three hundred, a goodly number of whom are Hungarians, Bavarians, Tyrolese, Russians, and French. There are many who are lame, others with diseases of the throat or swellings of the glands, and not a few who are drawn about in chairs on wheels. The larger portion, however, exhibit no outward evidence of ill-health; but there are few who do not take the baths or drink the waters. All are supposed to be here for special ailments, and all who remain longer than five days are taxed for their share of the water-expenses, which are collected by the village authorities. The continuous cold weather has caused the number of visitors thus far to be unusually small, but to-day has been warm and pleasant, and we are expecting a rapid increase. The money panic at Vienna, whence most of the guests usually come, has also had its effect in rendering the season thus far very unprofitable to the hotel-keepers.

THE PROMENADE.

The scene on the promenade in front of the bathing-house last evening whilst the band was performing was very interesting. All the visitors were here assembled, either strolling through the avenues or sitting around at the tables sipping their coffee, whilst the country-folks were gathered at the outskirts, viewing the scene. All nations were here represented, and the variety of tongues, and the varied toilets of the ladies, added to the novelty of the scene. It was probably the first time when America had been so strongly represented, we at present numbering eight, having two new recruits in the persons of Mr. and Mrs. Kahler, from San Francisco. As we moved around on the promenade, it was evident that we excited something of a sensation, and we were consequently all on our good behavior, feeling that we had the national reputation to sustain. The country-people especially seemed to be greatly interested in us, as coming from a part of the world where so many of their friends and countrymen have settled, and to which many of them are contemplating an early emigration.

THE AUSTRIAN-GERMAN.

Among our guests are quite a number of the business-men of Vienna. The Austrian-German, as developed in Vienna, is as essentially different in his habits of life from the Prussian-German as the French are from the English. It is from Northern Germany that most of the emigrants to the United States come, and with the economical and thrifty habits of these we are all familiar. They, as we know, are industrious, prudent, economical, and careful of their earnings, and are not given to speculation or the running of dangerous risks. The Viennese Austrian, on the contrary, thinks only of "the day, and takes no heed for the morrow." Life to him is a game of chance, and he takes the prizes or the blanks as a part of the lottery. He works and schemes and speculates with all the energy of a Wall-Street broker, and spends his gains as freely as if they had come to him without effort on his part. When adversity comes, he struggles manfully against it, and dreads more the loss of position, which wealth gives him, than the loss of money. The numerous suicides which accompanied the recent financial troubles in Vienna were of those whose reputed wealth gave them the entrée to the palaces of royalty. The thousands who lost all merely shrugged their shoulders and have gone to work, scheming and speculating, and confident that the next turn of the wheel will bring them to the top again. A Vienna banker now here, whose fortune was swept away, remarked to me to-day that he had a few thousand guilders left, and would resume business in the fall, confident of recovering his losses during the winter.

But these characteristics pervade all grades of life in the cities. All are given to speculation and a desire to accumulate money rapidly, and take but little care of it when they are successful. The purchase of lottery-tickets and lottery-policies sweeps off the earnings of the working-people, while the traffic in fancy stocks is indulged in by all who have accumulated a few hundred guilders. Where so much money is lost, a great deal must be won, and there are consequently numbers of millionaires in Vienna whose equipages and villas compare favorably with those of royalty, and there are always enough at the top of the ladder to make up for those who lose their hold and fall to the ground. Those who have money, however, spend it freely, and live a life of reckless jollity. A man's wealth is often estimated in Vienna by the number of mistresses he keeps, and by the magnificence of their equipages, diamonds, and dresses.

VICE IN THE CITIES.

There is no other city in the world, not even Paris, that can rival the metropolis of Austria in sensuality and immorality, and in these respects there is a universality of sentiment that is quite remarkable. There are no establishments in Vienna, however, like those which have proved such a nuisance to the citizens of the Eastern School District of Baltimore, for the reason that professionals of that class do not exist there. There are, in short, no flaunting courtesans in Vienna, as are to be seen on the streets of Paris, or even in New York or Baltimore. Where virtue is such a rarity there is no opportunity for making a specialty of vice, and it has no special locality. In this respect Vienna would appear to the casual visitor more free from this species of social evil than any other large city in the world; but a visit to the foundling hospital, where upon an average about forty infants are received daily, or to the general hospital, where the illegitimate births average thirty a day, shows the pre-eminence of Vienna over all other cities in the world. There are twenty thousand soldiers always in the city, mostly young men from the provinces, who could not marry if they would, and would not if they could. They have no means to support a wife, and seldom have money sufficient to pay the Church charges for the performance of the marriage ceremony. They can be seen in crowds with the young girls on the Ringstrasse and the Präter. They form attachments, but are never expected to marry. Their example is followed by the young men in other walks of life, and we are told that there are fewer marriages in Vienna than in almost any other city of one-third the population. There seems to be no attempt made by the authorities or by the Church to remedy this evil, which has become so universal that, among the laboring classes especially, there are few mothers who have husbands.

VIRTUE IN THE RURAL DISTRICTS.

Whilst this is the condition of affairs in all the large cities of Austria, virtue is the rule and vice the exception in the rural districts. There are no more virtuous people in the world than the agriculturists of Austria. They are industrious, cleanly, and temperate, and it would be difficult to find a people anywhere, male and female, whose personal appearance gives more complete assurance of the possession of all these virtues. They are all robust in health, physically strong, comfortably but plainly attired, remarkable for cleanliness, and seem both happy and contented. They come to town in good carriages, drawn by strong and well-fed horses, and no country can present a finer peasantry. To expect lewdness among such a people would be like looking for it in a Shaker settlement. The farmers' daughters dress precisely as their mothers do, nothing but solemn black being allowed. Indeed, if there is any difference it is in the quality of the silk, satin, or velvet, and the mother is always clad in the more costly raiment. The young men are also dressed like their fathers, and their strong limbs and ruddy faces indicate that they have been brought up to work. They are never seen about the towns except on Church holidays, and they participate in the ceremonies with an earnestness and enthusiasm that are not to be seen among the young men of the cities. They are all given a limited education; they are at least taught to read and write, and occasionally the most precocious of them are sent to college. They are compelled to serve three years in the army, and whatever vices they may have contracted during their service must be abandoned on their return to the family homestead.

BIRDS OF GERMANY.

The birds of Germany, like the crows of Ireland, are the pets of the people, both in the city and the country. They are protected by law; but no law is needed for their protection. They are so tame that many of them build their nests inside of the houses, and are never disturbed by old or young. Throw down a few crumbs, and they will come down from the trees and almost eat out of your hand. The consequence is that fruit-growers never suffer from the invasion of worms, and the plum and damson, which have almost disappeared from our markets, grow here to the greatest perfection. The holidays are not distinguished, as they are with us, by a throng of boys and men with shot-guns pouring into the country and slaying out of mere wantonness the feathery tribe, which are regarded here as the most efficient co-laborers to the agriculturist.

GERMAN TEMPERANCE.

Horace Maynard, in his address before the managers of the Harlem Inebriate Asylum of Baltimore, alluded, I see, to the baneful effect of that social sentiment in America which regards a refusal to accept an invitation to drink as a cause of personal offense, whilst a refusal to take a cigar or to eat is not so regarded. This is undoubtedly the foundation of intemperance; but it has no existence in Germany. No one here invites or urges another man to drink with him or at his expense. Men sit down and drink together, as a general rule; but no man pays for what the other drinks unless that other is too poor to pay for it himself. Each drinks as many glasses as he may desire, and when the waiter comes for the money each pays for what he has drunk. According to our system, if a half-dozen men sit down to drink, each one must treat in his turn, and thus each must drink six times, whether he desires it or not. It is thus that drunkards are made and fortunes are acquired by tavern-keepers. If it were not for our system of "treating," excessive drinking would not be so common, and inebriate asylums would be as unnecessary as they are here. Nothing stronger than beer or wine finds any sale, and even this is drunk in moderation. It is not gulped down, but drunk slowly, or rather sipped, whilst eating. If you desired to offend a German you could not accomplish it more successfully than by insisting on paying for what he has drunk or eaten at the same table with you. "Do you wish to insult me?" would be the exclamation that would greet you on the introduction of such an American idea at the social board in Germany.

WEALTH OF THE CHURCH.

The Catholic Church in Austria is almost the only Church, except in the Hungarian portion of the empire, although full liberty in religion is granted to every one of late years. Hungary is Protestant, and Hungary is the heart of the present Austrian Empire, and to satisfy Hungary all the barriers against religious freedom have been swept away. The Catholic Church is, however, the great land- and property-holder of the nation, and from its income could pay the interest on the national debt without seriously feeling it financially. A fine property is seldom offered for sale that the Church is not the purchaser, even to dwelling-houses in Vienna. We have been surprised very often, whilst passing through the country, to find such immense possessions pointed out to us as belonging to the Church, and in Vienna we have been assured that nearly one-tenth of the population reside in houses which are the property of the Church. Among these Church houses in Vienna are several covering entire blocks, in which the number of people who are residents ranges from twelve to twenty-eight hundred, all occupying separate suites of rooms or renting furnished apartments.

EXTREME POLITENESS.

We have before noticed the extreme politeness of the Austrians, which we find to be as general in the country as among the Viennese. A nod of recognition is not sufficient, but you are deemed rude and unmannerly if the hat is not raised clear from the head every time you pass any one to whom you have been introduced. The people of the village are equally persistent in the exchange of bows; whilst the waiters, chambermaids, and everybody about the hotels make a set bow to their guests every time they pass them. "To do as the Germans do," every one must constantly be on the *qui vive* to return a salutation with the same measure of politeness with which it is given. Even at the store of the village apothecary you are expected to uncover on entering, return the polite bow of the proprietor and his clerks, and keep your hat off until you make your bow on retiring.

GERMAN SUMMER RESORTS.

We have during our journeying had some experience at German watering-places, and especially at the Iodine Springs of Hall, which we have made a resting-place, as a point where we could always find a cool atmosphere, and some kind friends who are availing themselves of the use of its waters. Whilst Baden-Baden had the attractions of its gambling-saloons, people went there who were not sick. It was a place for frolic and fun and gambling; but it has now, like all the rest of the German springs, become almost exclusively the resort of those who are suffering from some of the ailments that "flesh is heir to." European tourists always stopped to see life at the German springs, but life has suddenly gone out of those resorts. At Hall we have hops, music on the promenade, theatricals, Hellman the magician, etc. The lame and the halt are the spectators at the balls, and those whose ailments do not interfere with their locomotion help to make up the quadrilles. But one-half of the visitors have their jaws tied up, a goodly portion are wheeled about in chairs, and some hobble along with crutches and canes. This is the case at most of the summer resorts of Germany, and those who profess to have come for the "fun of the thing" are laughed at. The first question of a new acquaintance is, "What is the matter with you?" The presence of Americans who profess to be sound is a marvel to the ailing visitors. A young Baltimorean who asserted that he came for the "fun of the thing" was caught drinking the waters the other morning, and, in response to a query of doubt, replied that he wished to see if it would not make his moustache grow. However, a visit to these resorts of the suffering and afflicted is apt to cause a feeling of thankfulness among those who are enjoying good health and who have the full use of their limbs and faculties. Is is sad to see the number of children here who have been sufferers from their cradles, many of them prostrate and helpless at an age when all should be life, joy, and activity. No one is allowed to drink the "iodine water," or to take a bath, without a prescription from the physician. This, of itself, will show how few visit these springs who are not compelled to do so under the direction of their physicians. Singular as it may seem, most of those who are here for medical treatment are in the spring-tide of life, and the place is not without gayety and amusement. Hall being ten thousand feet above the level of the sea, with snow-clad mountains glittering in the sun in the distance, the summer solstice is disarmed of its powers, and whilst the heat of Vienna, a hundred miles distant, is reported as almost unbearable, we are only comfortable in woolen clothing.

THE ENGLISH LANGUAGE.

Among the guests at Hall are quite a number of Russian and Austrian children, nearly all of whom can speak the English language. This is the case especially with the Russian and North German children. They are in charge of governesses, and their general conversation is in English, though they speak French and their native tongues also. A little Russian here, not five years of age, speaks very correctly in English, French, and Russian. We were astonished a day or two since at hearing a voice under our window exclaiming, "William, if you do not come here this minute I will tell your mother." The children are taught to speak English, although their parents have no knowledge of the language. This would indicate that the next generation will at least speak our language more extensively than the present does. So much for President Grant's prediction.

THE USE OF TOBACCO.

We have been rather surprised to find so few persons smoking pipes in Austria. Indeed, a pipe is very seldom seen except among the laboring classes. The favorite mode of using the weed here is in cigarettes, almost every gentleman being provided with a silver box, which contains Turkish tobacco and small slips of paper with mucilage on them, ready for rolling. They make them as they use them, and are very expert in the handling of the tobacco. The chewing of tobacco is universally repudiated, being regarded as the height of vulgarity. The Turkish tobacco is of fine flavor, and commands high prices. It is very much in appearance like the fine-cut chewing-tobacco so extensively used at home. The cigars made by the Austrian government, which are the only description to be had, are very inferior, and it is not to be wondered at that the cigarette is so generally used in preference. The smoking of cigarettes by ladies is quite common, especially among the higher classes.

[The following letters were written a short time before the famous gambling-saloons were closed. These saloons must have been the main attraction of Baden, as its numerous hotels are now nearly empty, and many of them closed.]

BADEN-BADEN.

GAMBLING AS A SCIENCE.

HÔTEL D'ANGLETERRE.
BADEN-BADEN, August 18, 1872.

We left Geneva at noon on Saturday, after four days very pleasantly spent in that beautiful city, *en route* for the great German springs of Baden-Baden. The distance being rather great for one day's journey, we divided it by stopping overnight at the beautiful town of Neufchâtel, on the Lake of Neufchâtel, where we arrived about six o'clock in the evening. Like all Swiss towns, it is famous for its hotels, and the Mont Blanc, at which we spent the night, is one of the most elegant houses we have seen in Switzerland. It appears to have been constructed regardless of expense, and in all its appointments and furniture is equal to the finest of the New York hotels.

Neufchâtel is beautifully situated on the slope of the Jura mountain, and is immediately on the lake, rendering it a delightful place for a few days' sojourn. The excursions into the mountains are very fine.

TO BADEN-BADEN.

Being desirous always to spend Sunday, or at least as much as possible of it, in an important place, we determined to push on with our journey, so as to reach the famous watering-place of Baden-Baden as early as possible on Sunday. Leaving Neufchâtel at seven o'clock in the morning, we hoped to reach our destination early in the afternoon, but it was six o'clock in the evening before we arrived. It was the most difficult day's travel we have yet encountered, having had to change cars six times during the journey, and, the orders being given in German, we were constantly upon the alert lest we should find ourselves off the route. At Basle, on passing from Switzerland to Germany, we not only had our luggage examined, but were transported from one depot to another, about three miles across the city, in omnibuses. We came to the conclusion that it would be a blessing to travelers if a Tom Scott should turn up here who would contrive to consolidate their roads and run through trains. It was a long and tedious journey, but nothing of interest occurred on the route. On the Swiss side of the line musical societies, with their bands and banners, were arriving and departing from the different stations.

BADEN-BADEN ON SUNDAY.

It was almost dark in the evening by the time we had secured quarters, which was only done after application at three different hotels. We made our first movement on the streets of Baden-Baden just as the lamps were being lit, leisurely strolling along in front of the principal hotels. We were musing upon the similarity of the scene to that presented at Saratoga on a summer evening, when, turning a bend on the street, there suddenly appeared to our vision one of the most brilliant gas-light scenes we have ever witnessed. It had become quite dark by this time, and the lights were all ablaze in every direction, but immediately before us the profusion of gas was almost dazzling, and was shining upon an assemblage of not less than ten thousand people, male and female, who were congregated around an immense palatial building with Corinthian columns, from every door and window of which were streaming rays of light. Directly in front of the centre of this building stood a temple or pagoda, somewhat similar in shape to the music pagoda at Druid Hill, but made of iron, and light and graceful in its proportions. In the centre of this pagoda hung a single chandelier, with nearly one hundred lights, and between every two pillars was a very large glass globe, containing several gas-jets. A band of fully sixty performers was stationed in the pagoda, playing, as we approached, the concert being interspersed with occasional solo performances by distinguished artists. The front of this structure is fully three times the breadth of the mansion at Druid Hill, and both inside and outside, to the extent of several hundred yards each way, was a mass of people, either seated or walking, through which it was difficult to make one's way. Immediately in front of the building thousands of ladies and gentlemen were taking refreshments, furnished from an elegant restaurant located in the further end of the building, whilst an extensive array of ladies, flashing with diamonds, were seated under the porticoes, and conversing with groups of gentlemen congregated around them.

This of course proved to be the famous *Conversationshaus*, or more properly speaking, the great gambling-house of Baden-Baden, the most splendid establishment of the kind in the world. Immediately to the right of the grand promenade in front of the building were two rows of stores, probably numbering a hundred, all of which, notwithstanding it was Sunday evening, were open, and their goods displayed under a full blaze of gas-light. They consisted of such fancy and jewelry stores as we usually find at watering-places, and people were strolling around and making purchases. The outdoor scene was undoubtedly very brilliant, the grounds and gardens in front being also interspersed with numerous gas-lights and thronged with promenaders.

THE GAMBLING SCENE.

We finally made our way into the building, and found the immense assembly-room in the centre thronged with most respectable and decorous people, and a large number of men in showy livery, with breeches and knee-buckles, running about. The gentlemen were all required to take off their hats upon entering, and if they failed to do so one of the attendants would politely jog them on the elbow with an invitation to remove their chapeau. Profound silence was maintained, and groups of ladies and gentlemen were reclining on ottomans near the windows, listening to the exquisite music of what is said to be the finest band in the world. We had no thought of finding gambling in progress on Sunday evening, but observing at the upper end of the room a table about thirty feet long, with a throng of men and women around it, three or four deep, we made our way towards it. Here we found four elegantly-dressed gentlemen sitting on either side of the centre of the table. One was turning the roulette-wheel, and the other three were paying the losses or hauling in the winnings of the bank, from piles of gold and silver heaped up before them. They each had a stick with a wooden block upon the end, with which they pushed the losses to the throngs of players, or hauled in their winnings. Numerous similar sticks were lying around the table, which the players used in pushing their money to the figure or color on which they desired to bet,

7

or in hauling in their winnings. The inner line of players around the table, among whom were seven females, were seated in chairs. The outside players would occasionally lay down a five-franc piece, which is the smallest sum allowed to be bet. Some of those on the inner circle at times bet quite heavily, as high as five or ten napoleons on a figure or color, and, so far as our observation went, the bank was largely the winner. The female players all showed their feelings in their countenances, but most of the men reminded one of the automaton chess-player; their countenances were immovable and stolid to a degree that was most remarkable. Whether winning or losing, they made no sign of feeling. After viewing this novel scene for some time, we passed into an adjoining room, and here found a second table, thronged with players at roulette in full blast, some betting gold and others silver. In the rear, to the right of this room, was a third roulette-table, similar to the other two, surrounded with players and spectators. The women betting at these tables were more numerous than the men, and most of them invariably bet gold. They were nearly all elderly women, elegantly dressed, with a profusion of diamonds. I observed one young man, with his bride at his side, betting very heavily, and invariably losing. When his purse was empty she drew forth hers and placed a pile of gold in his hand. He played on, and this was soon gone also, when, taking his wife's arm, they both walked off as cheerful, apparently, as if their losings had been so many grains of corn. But many have left these tables at night, making no sign of feeling or remorse, to blow their brains out before morning.

ROUGE-ET-NOIR.

Observing a fourth one of these elegant apartments to be pretty well thronged, we entered there also, and found the game of *rouge-et-noir* progressing. This is played by the dealing out of seven cards, the players betting on certain numbers on the table on either side of the dealers. The same throng of players, male and female, were here also, and the same surrounding of spectators, some of whom would occasionally make a bet. Our attention was attracted to a young man who was standing next to the inner line of players, with the most immovable countenance. He was not over twenty-five years of age, and whilst the others seemed to be playing and betting at hap-hazard, his whole mind was upon the game. He alone seemed to be playing upon system, and, whilst others were nearly always losing, he was continually drawing in his winnings. His whole mind was so intent upon the game that he noticed nothing that was going on around him. He had no eyes for anything but the table or the player. An old lady who was sitting near him had lost everything, when her attention was attracted by his success. She had risen up to retire, when she borrowed a five-franc piece from a woman behind her, and, resuming her seat, pushed the coin towards the young man, asking him to bet for her. He pushed it back to her without a word or a gesture, and went on with his playing. The woman behind whispered to her, and she then commenced to bet just as he bet, and to win just as he won. An hour afterwards, as we passed through this room, the silent man was betting and winning, and the woman availing herself of his luck, or his skill in playing, we were unable to decide which. Certainly he must have won many thousands of francs during the evening, unless his luck deserted him at a later hour. The other players were so intent on their own bettings that they did not note this little side-game that was in progress. Our impression was that he had discovered that the best plan was to place his money where no one else was betting, and where the bank would lose the least by allowing him to win. Sometimes, at the last moment, he would push his money from one point to another, and the woman would imitate him, always with success.

FIRST IMPRESSIONS.

Whilst all this gambling was progressing inside the hall, it attracted no attention from the great mass of people assembled who were sitting around the balconies in conversation, or promenading. Those who were looking on seemed, like ourselves, mostly strangers, and the betters may possibly also have been the greenhorns of the same class. It was altogether a novel scene, and a most brilliant one in all its surroundings. Meantime the band was performing the most artistic music, and occasionally round after round of applause would greet its rendering of favorite airs. The whole mass of visitors to Baden-Baden undoubtedly were here assembled to spend the evening, and there could not have been less than ten thousand.

BADEN-BADEN, August 19, 1872.

Baden-Baden is described in the guide-books as the greatest and most famous watering-place in the world. It may possibly be the greatest in Europe, but it cannot in any respect be compared with Saratoga. It is beautifully located in a mountain valley, and is at all times cool and pleasant, with a temperature seldom exceeding eighty degrees. It has all the accessories of fine drives and walks and shady retreats, but its waters are nothing better than can be obtained at home from the spout of a tea-kettle with a little fire under it. A drink of hot water upon an empty stomach has been discovered by the German doctors to have the same good effects as one drawn from the springs of Baden. We went up this morning at seven o'clock to the Trinkhalle, where the water is conducted from the springs in pipes, and where the people go to drink it. We did not find a dozen persons there, and those were mostly old people who are endeavoring to cheat old Time out of his dues. We tasted the water, and it was hot, decidedly hot, and the steam was ascending from the stone basin into which it was running. Most of those who were drinking stirred something in it from a paper which they brought with them, and others mixed it with liquid from a bottle. Whether they were making hot whisky punches or merely endeavoring to make the hot water more palatable we do not know; but very few drank it simple and pure as we tasted it.

THE BADEN HOTELS.

We expected to find the hotels here something superior to anything in Europe, but in size and appearance, and all their appointments, the best of them are scarcely up to the second-class hotels to be found all over Switzerland. There cannot be said to be more than three first-class houses here, and they are not, all combined, as large as the Métropole in Geneva. Congress Hall and the Union, at Saratoga, can accommodate more than all the hotels, large and small, in Baden. The number of visitors here this season, up to this seventeenth day of August, is just forty thousand. None of the hotels here are more than three or four stories high, and there is not an elevator in the place. There is a stream of water running down from the springs through a walled-up sluice passing through the city, which borders the grand thoroughfare on which the Trinkhalle, the Conversationshaus, and the principal hotels are located.

This street, with its dense foliage of shade-trees and vines, is very beautiful; but the back streets, upon which no hotels are located, have very few attractions. They are narrow and winding, and plentifully supplied with small stores and restaurants. The local population is about six thousand, and, including the boarding-houses, there is accommodation at any one time for more than a thousand strangers.

THE SPRINGS—"HELL."

That portion of the city in which the springs are located is called by the people "Hell." The hot springs are thirteen in number, the principal one being of a temperature of 153° Fahr. The water is very clear and tasteless, but has rather a disagreeable smell when it first issues from the springs. It is said by some to taste like weak broth; but we could discover nothing but the ordinary taste of hot water, though we all imbibed it very sparingly. The chemists say that its quality is saline, with a mixture of muriatic and carbonic acid and small portions of silex and oxide of iron. A building is erected over the principal spring, but we could not see that any one was troubling the waters. It is conveyed from the springs in pipes to numerous bath-houses, which are very complete in all their arrangements. Hot baths could be had, heated from the fires below, in either Turkish or Christian style. They do not seem to be much attended, the whole rush of the town being to the Conversationshaus, where from two to eleven o'clock P.M. all the visitors to Baden seem to have congregated in and about it, old and young, grave and gay. Those who don't play seem to like to look on, whilst others are attracted by the music, or come to see the throng who congregate here daily. It is a beautiful spot, and would, with its accessories, prove an endless attraction anywhere. Its broad portico, lofty ceilings, splendidly decorated walls, its brilliant chandeliers, the main one with over three hundred lights; its abundance of chairs, sofas, and ottomans, and every appliance of comfort; its free open-air concerts, its shady walks and promenades, all combine to make it the most perfect temple for the pleasures of life that could be devised. Here idlers, pleasure-seekers, and invalids from all parts of the world are congregated, and the fools with more money than brains come to Baden to try their luck. Last week the Prussian Minister was here, and lost seventeen thousand dollars at one sitting.

THE GAMBLING-HOUSE.

The Conversationshaus or gambling-house of Baden is undoubtedly the great attraction of this place. Without it, —and the law for its abolishment will go into force at the close of the present season,—Baden will no longer attract visitors from all parts of the world. There is nothing in its waters to attract, and nothing in its mountain scenery that is not far excelled at Interlaken and other places in Switzerland. But it is not alone the gambling that attracts, but the adjuncts of the establishment,—its extensive reading-room, supplied with all the papers of Europe, its fine music, its spacious and elegantly furnished halls for conversation and social intercourse, its shady walks, its theatre, concert-hall, and ball-room, all of which are part and parcel of this great gambling establishment, out of the profits of which these attractions are furnished, and are free to the visitors of Baden. This banking-house is the property of one man, and all the elegantly-attired operators at the tables are his employed clerks. For the exclusive privilege of keeping a gambling-house in Baden he contracted to furnish all these adjuncts to his establishment, and he has faithfully adhered to his contract. The band performs three times a day, from seven to eight o'clock in the morning, from three to four in the afternoon, and a regular concert at night, commencing at eight o'clock and closing at half-past ten. The performers are all solo artists, and many of them are at high salary. The players and cashiers at the tables number over fifty, there being two sets for each table, and the liveried attendants are at least fifty more. It is their duty to furnish seats and cards for the players, take charge of their coats, shawls, and parasols, and to preserve order and decorum in and around the building and grounds. Over the Corinthian columns in front of the main entrance is the word "Conversation" carved in stone, but it should be "the hall of silence." With more than a hundred persons sitting and standing around each of the four tables in the four largest rooms, everything is so profoundly quiet that, were it not for the lowly-uttered announcement of the game, a person blindfolded might suppose the rooms to be empty. All conversation is conducted in the lowest whisper, and the players never exchange words with each other. The playing commences at eleven o'clock in the morning, and closes promptly at eleven o'clock at night, the game going on without the slightest interruption for twelve hours.

GAMBLING SCENES.

We spent several hours yesterday in the vicinity of the gaming-tables, and watched the game and the players very closely. Our conclusions were that the profits of each of these four tables were not less than five thousand dollars for the day, or twenty thousand dollars for the whole. The constant change that is going on among the players indicates that the losses of each are comparatively light, and that the number of players at each table during the day is probably several hundred. Every moment some one draws off and leaves, with his money all gone, endeavoring to conceal the chagrin which is too apparent to one who closely watches his countenance. His place is immediately taken by another, who in his turn is cleaned out and departs. Some of the players bring large amounts of gold with them and play heavily, betting from fifty to one hundred dollars on each deal of the cards or turn of the wheel. These we closely watched, and saw the last gold coin depart. Some, as their stock became low, would send for more; but most of them withdrew, assuming a careless and nonchalant air. As we passed around among the tables it frequently happened that scarcely any who had been playing a half-hour previous remained, their places being filled by new aspirants for fortune's favors.

At some of the tables mothers and their daughters were playing side by side; at others, husband and wife, and lover and betrothed. It was curious to watch their rising and falling fortunes. In numerous instances we witnessed wives endeavoring to draw their husbands away from the table; but the etiquette of the gambling-saloon required that it should be done by signs rather than by words. In one case the wife stood by with trembling lips and watched her infatuated husband lose a handful of gold coin, until the last one had slipped through his fingers. He then rose, and they walked quietly away arm in arm. In about ten minutes they returned, and the husband took his seat at the table with about thirty gold coins in his hand. He played wildly, laying down from three to five coins at each bet, and when he won he would leave the whole amount on the number. Finally they were all gone but three, and both seemed in great distress.

The wife leaned over her husband's shoulder and whispered something in his ear, when he handed her the three coins and left, she taking his seat. She played cautiously, and gradually won, having, when we last saw her, about forty napoleons in her hand. The sign of sorrow on her countenance had departed, and she was looking around for the return of her husband. Whether she withdrew before her luck changed we do not know, but an hour after, when we returned to the table, neither husband nor wife was there.

The young man whom we left at the table on the previous night with his pockets full of gold that he had won, was not to be seen about the saloons to-day. Whether he continued to play and lost, or whether he retired with his winnings, we do not know; but, as it was near the closing hour, the latter is most likely. The woman who retrieved her fortune by following and imitating his bets was, however, early on hand yesterday morning, and was very flush. We passed the table several times during the afternoon, and she was still playing; but on our return after tea she was sitting on one of the sofas, her countenance too plainly indicating the result of her day's venture. Several times she held up her fan before her face to conceal the act of wiping away her tears; and this was but one of several similar instances that passed under our observation. Several old men, bent and decrepit with age, maintained their seats nearly all day. They never bet more than one dollar, and their losses were consequently light, but we saw them frequently hand in notes to be changed. Independently of those who would sit down regularly to play, there was a constant throng of men and women, standing two or three deep, who would occasionally venture a dollar, and, losing two or three, would depart, wiser if not wealthier.

In a game of chance those who are looking on can generally see more of the game than the players. Those who were playing and losing doubtless thought that others around them were winning; but we feel confident that not a man or a woman of the thousands venturing on these tables did not leave with less money than they brought with them. Men who win money at gambling never stop playing; those who lose all must stop. Several times we picked out a player who had a large sum of money piled up before him, and watched his varying fortunes and his pile. Invariably the pile decreased, and invariably the player retired. The women seemed to be the most persistent, and several times we observed them return with more money, to endeavor to recover their losses. Still, all was quiet as death in the hall and around the tables, not a word being uttered, except the announcements of the games.

AN HOUR IN THE TEMPLE OF SILENCE—THE ATTRACTIONS OF BADEN.

BADEN-BADEN, August 21, 1872.

Everybody has heard of Baden-Baden and its attractions and peculiarities, though but few have any idea of the singular scenes hourly presented. There are not many Americans here, and of these very few approach the gaming-tables otherwise than as spectators. Some of them occasionally throw down a dollar, lose it, and depart; but among the persistent players we have not yet seen either an American or an Englishman. The mass of players, male and female, are Germans, with a few French; and, from the fact that fathers frequently have their sons by their sides trying their luck, and mothers their daughters, it is evident that they do not regard gambling in the same light that American mothers and fathers generally do. They may possibly be "showing them the folly of it," but their manner would seem to indicate a desire to inculcate a love for "the little joker."

The temptation to take a chance is undoubtedly very great, especially when the players happen to be winning freely, as of course sometimes is the case. We saw a young man to-day, who had been looking on for some time, lay down a five-hundred-franc note. In an instant it was doubled. He still left the whole amount on the table, and in a half-minute more his five hundred francs were increased to two thousand. He deliberately put the money in his pocket and left, having in two minutes won three hundred dollars. Had he remained ten minutes longer, ten chances to one he would have been penniless.

"ROUGE-ET-NOIR."

This is the favorite game of all the heavy players. At these tables the principal betting is with gold. It often happens that several thousand francs are on the table at one time. The heavy players are generally elderly men, who go on playing as if it were the business of their life, and, so far as the countenance or manner would indicate, show not the slightest interest as to whether they win or lose. We saw an old gentleman to-day, who had played heavily and lost his last napoleon, get up from the table, quietly draw out his box and take a pinch of snuff, then, taking up his hat and smoothing it with his silk handkerchief, move off towards the door. He had evidently lost more than a thousand dollars; but there was not the slightest indication in his manner that it troubled him in the least.

The elderly female players also prefer rouge-et-noir, and seldom approach the roulette-tables, where the younger ladies generally congregate and bet their five-franc pieces. The latter play very cautiously, and are not generally so successful in concealing their emotions as the elderly ladies. They are compelled by the rules to maintain absolute silence; but their countenances are apt to betray their feelings.

Rouge-et-noir is played with cards, which are handled only by the dealer. He has four packs of cards carefully shuffled together, and cut by the players. The betting is made upon squares and diamonds on the green baize tables, and when he deals out nine, and sometimes ten or twelve, cards, the result of the bets is in some instances very decided, most of the betters either losing all or doubling their money. It does not require a half-minute to settle each game, and the board is swept by either the bank or the player at least sixty times per hour. As the game continues without the slightest intermission from eleven o'clock in the morning until eleven at night, there must be over seven hundred games played at each table during the twelve hours.

There are seats for eighteen players, one dealer, and three bankers, at each of the rouge-et-noir tables, whilst there are rows of spectators and occasional betters surrounding the table three or four deep. The occasional betters are tempted by degrees to venture more deeply, and when those that are seated retire they take their places. There is never any scarcity of players, as a crowd is always on hand waiting for the bank to open at eleven o'clock. This morning, ten minutes after the opening all the tables were in full blast, the seats filled, and a circle three or four deep formed around them.

THE ROULETTE-TABLES.

The roulette-tables have four bankers, one of whom turns the wheel, and two men seated at each end of the table, who see that the bets are all properly laid and generally superintend the game.

These tables seat about eighteen players, whilst those among the spectators who occasionally make a venture are much more numerous than at the rouge-et-noir tables. Whilst the betting is not so heavy, the number who play is considerably larger.

The bankers each have before them long rolls of silver five-franc pieces, and rolls of gold in sealed packages,—twenty-five napoleons in each. We should judge there are not less than twenty thousand dollars on each table, and although they are constantly changing notes for the players, which go into boxes, their stock of coin never appears to diminish. The bankers are relieved every two hours, others taking their places, and the game goes steadily on without the slightest intermission. In this game, by placing the money in certain ways the winner receives several times as much as he lays down, but most of the bets are merely to duplicate the sum mentioned. No one is allowed to play who is not of mature age, unless accompanied by his or her parents, which, singular to say, is very often the case. Husband and wife sitting side by side and playing, he with gold, and she with silver, can be seen at all times at all the tables.

Last evening the tables were more densely crowded than at any time during our visit. A grand concert was in progress on the lawn in front, which drew an immense assemblage, but the players heeded not the outdoor attraction, contenting themselves with listening to it at a distance. The betting, as usual at night, was heavier, and we could not discover that any one was winning. Not one of those whom we left at the tables before supper was there on our return.

THE TEMPLE OF SILENCE.

What strikes the stranger as most singular is the extreme order that is preserved in every part of the building. On entering the outer colonnade a notice meets his eye to the effect that gentlemen must not smoke. If he fails to regard the notice one of the liveried attendants politely calls his attention to it. On entering the door he finds a large assemblage of ladies and gentlemen, the latter with their hats off, either sitting on the sofas or moving about as quietly as if they were in the house of death. A little stretch of the imagination might conceive that the silent throng bending over the long table at the other end of the room were surrounding and paying the last tribute to the lamented dead. No one for a moment, unaware of the fact, could possibly conceive that he was in a gambling-saloon, and that these silent people were all intent upon winning money at a game of chance. Passing into the next room, and the next, and the next, a repetition of this scene is presented, amid the most solemn silence. People appear to walk upon their tiptoes, as not the slightest shuffling is to be heard, and when conversing, do so in the lowest possible whisper. Order and quiet are here more strictly observed than in the churches, and were it not for the gay scene by which one is surrounded, the strains of music from the band outside, the frescoed walls, lace curtains, gilded ceilings, and brilliant chandeliers, the voice of Brother Slicer, "Brethren, let us pray," might not sound altogether out of place.

The reading-room at the upper end of the grand saloon is fitted up in the most elegant style, and is always thronged with both gentlemen and ladies. On the long table which passes through the centre of the room are to be found files of all the principal papers of the continent of Europe, carefully arranged, as well as those of London and New York. The table is surrounded by elegant easy-chairs, and along the walls sofas and divans are arranged for the ease and comfort of visitors. The reading-room is brilliantly lit up at night, and, enter it when you will, there is always a full attendance of visitors poring over the papers. The café at the opposite end of the building is very extensive and finely conducted, and a great number of the boarders at the hotels take their meals here in preference. There is also a coat and shawl and umbrella room, where the players leave any articles that would otherwise incumber them, and receive checks from the attendant. Retiring-rooms for both ladies and gentlemen are also provided, and everything arranged that is calculated to make gambling appear respectable and reputable.

The theatre is a separate building, about the size of the Holliday Street Theatre, but is not open at present. There are two arcades of stores between the theatre and the grand promenade, which are stocked with rich and rare goods. All these combine to make the Conversationhaus the grand focus of attraction at Baden, and the afternoon and evening are spent here even by those who could never be induced to gamble.

THE TEMPTATION TO PLAY.

The casual observer, seeing parties occasionally win, takes but little notice of their losses, and is strongly tempted to try his or her luck. Those who lose say nothing as to their losses, and the few who win boast and magnify their gains. A young American was about to test his fortune this evening, when we prevailed upon him to watch any one player for a half-hour, and he would see that every player lost. At this moment an elderly gentleman stepped up and changed three napoleons for twelve five-franc pieces. He commenced betting two of the silver coins at a time. At his third investment he won eight five-franc pieces, and became more free in his ventures. In ten minutes his money was all gone. He then got three more napoleons changed, and in ten minutes more the last of these was gone, and he left the table with a loss of one hundred and twenty francs in less than twenty minutes. Others were watched with similar results, and we came to the conclusion that all who played lost, except the few who made a lucky venture and immediately stopped playing.

ATTRACTIONS OF BADEN.

The drives, promenades, and shady retreats in and around Baden-Baden are undoubtedly very fine, and you can step into them in a few moments' walk from almost any part of the city. The mountain-sides are beautifully terraced, and can be ascended with ease by gradual approaches. The valley in which the town and springs are located extends back many miles in the country, affording beautiful drives through the most romantic scenery. Many wealthy Germans have cottages here, and spend the whole summer, whilst others bring their horses and carriages. There are some very fine turn-outs, including ladies' pony phaetons.

BAVARIA.

THE SALT-MINES.—THE KÖNIGS-SEE.

REICHENHALL, BAVARIA, July 24, 1873.

We yesterday morning left delightful Vienna and the dominions of Francis Joseph, and after seven hours' run arrived at five o'clock in the afternoon in Salzburg, which is close on the borders of the kingdom of Bavaria. Our baggage was formally examined; that is to say, they looked at the inside of one trunk out of five, and passed the rest, which gave us a decidedly favorable impression of Bavarian intelligence, as the officer accepted our assurance that we had nothing which we had not brought from America with us, except a meerschaum pipe.

THE CITY OF SALZBURG.

This is a very quaint old city, situated on both banks of the river Salza, and has a population of almost twenty thousand. It is quite remarkable for the beauty of its situation, being, with its environs, hemmed in by mountains towering to the height of from three to five thousand feet, covered to their summits with dense pine forests. An old castle and fort stand on a high hill to the left of the town, and the Kapuzinerberge Mountain rises on the right bank of the river. Two bridges and a railway bridge connect the two parts of the town, the gray glacier water of the river rushing rapidly on towards the plains of Bavaria. Salzburg is a very old town, and has been alternately, amid the fortunes of war, Bavarian and Austrian, it now belonging to Austria. The houses, with their flat roofs, the immense fountains, and the elegant structures in white marble, remind the traveler of Italy, whence the architects were usually brought by the archbishops prior to 1803, up to which time it was a spiritual principality. It has a fine old palace, erected in 1592, and the Government buildings, which contain a public exhibition of art of considerable merit. The principal attraction of Salzburg to the tourist, however, is that it was here Mozart, the great composer, was born. His house on the Hannibal-platz, and the house where he was born, are indicated by inscriptions, whilst a fine statue in bronze, by Schwanthaler, erected in 1842, adorns the adjacent Platz. In the centre of the Platz is a very elegant ancient fountain, erected more than two hundred years ago, with four hippopotami at the corners, and a figure of Atlas in the centre, whilst the water is spouted out of a horn by a Triton at the summit.

A RAILWAY ACCIDENT.

We left Salzburg about half-past seven o'clock in the evening for our present stopping-place, the town of Reichenhall, expecting to reach there in an hour, but were detained on the road by an accident to our train. We had just left the first station, and were moving on through a splendid mountain panorama, the slopes and little hillocks being finely cultivated, when a sharp, hissing explosion, which echoed through the mountains, together with the gradual stopping of the train, notified us that something was wrong with the engine. We soon found that its steam-chest had exploded, the rushing steam hiding that portion of the train from view. Fortunately, however, no one was hurt; though the fact that the train was on the top of a high embankment at the time was suggestive of what might have occurred. The passengers, to the number of about two hundred, so soon as they could get the conductors to unlock the doors of the cars, turned out *en masse*, and were soon back at the little town from which we had just started, and all quaffing immense mugs of Bavarian beer.

THE TOWN OF REICHENHALL.

A new locomotive was telegraphed for, and we finally got in motion again about nine o'clock, and reached our destination at the beautiful little town of Reichenhall about ten o'clock at night, but not too late to get a good supper. The frontier line between Austria and Bavaria was passed upon the road, which winds through a narrow defile along the base of the lofty Untersberg Mountain.

Reichenhall cannot have a population of less than fifteen thousand inhabitants, and is quite a solid and substantial town, being the central point of union of the four principal Bavarian salt-works, which are connected by pipes and conduits of an aggregate length of forty-five miles. The surplus brine from the Berchtesgaden mine is conducted to Reichenhall, and pipes lead from here to two other towns in which salt-works have been erected, each of which becomes, like Reichenhall, a summer resort for salt-water bathing and the "whey cure." This salt water is so strong that over a quarter of a pound of salt is obtained from a pound of water, and bathing in it must be like taking a bath in strong pickle. There are saline springs here also, the waters from which are at once conducted to the salt-pans.

It is very evident that the Germans are losing their faith in the curative properties of medicine, and are resorting to various other means of restoring health. In walking through Reichenhall between six and eight o'clock in the morning, especially at the grounds of the bathing-houses, where bands of music are in attendance, one encounters many hundreds of persons imbibing wine-whey, from goat's milk, and walking so many rounds of the promenade between each glass. The whey is brought in from the surrounding country in wooden churns, on the backs of those never-failing carriers of heavy burdens, women, each of whom has her regular customers, depending in a great measure on the quality of her commodity. Thus, between the wine-whey and the salt baths, Reichenhall has become a great summer resort, with its hotels and boarding-houses, and plenty of people to fill them. There are "wine-cure" doctors here who give prescriptions as to the number of glasses and the strength of the brine to be used in bathing. The greater number of the visitors to Reichenhall come, however, for a few days' sojourn, during which they make excursions to the Königs-See and Berchtesgaden, to visit which every traveler between Munich and Vienna stops here on his route. To pass on without stopping here would be regarded as gross neglect of all that is grand, wonderful, and beautiful. It is thus that we are here to see these great German wonders.

The town of Reichenhall is, however, a very interesting place, being very picturesquely bounded upon three sides by a fine amphitheatre of mountains,—the Untersberg, six thousand feet high, the Lutherberg, of five thousand five hundred and fifty-three feet, and the Müllnerhorn, of four thousand seven hundred and thirty-seven feet; whilst the Ost, five thousand seven hundred and eighteen feet, stands sentry at the outlet of the salt regions.

THE SALT-WORKS.

These salt-works are all the property of the Bavarian government, which makes a monopoly of the manufacture, as does also the Austrian government. Extensive works for the evaporation of the brine and for boiling it are erected here to manufacture into salt the surplus brine from the great Berchtesgaden mine, which we will visit to-day and endeavor in a subsequent letter to describe to your readers. There are also a number of saline springs here, the water of one of them being impregnated to the extent of twenty-three and a half per cent., and being at once conducted to the salt-pans, whilst that of the others is first evaporated in the graduating houses, which generally consist of twigs of blackthorn closely stacked under long roofs or sheds. The brine is conducted to the upper part of these sheds, and allowed to trickle slowly through the twigs, by which process it loses a large portion of the watery particles before it is collected into the reservoirs below. The great practical value of the process consists in the fact that, whilst the water is thus evaporated, and the other ingredients of the brine, carbonate of lime, etc., form a gradual incrustation on the thorns, the salt remains, almost without loss, in a state of solution. The twigs remain in use from three to six years, when they are burned, and their ashes form excellent manure. We, of course, visited the works, and examined the subterranean brine conduit and the vaulted channel, but imagine that a description of them would be rather dry reading, as well as very difficult.

OUR "HORRIBLE LANGUAGE."

We find that Bavaria knows as little of English as Austria does. A few evenings since, whilst we were sitting at one of the tables in the Volksgarten, in Vienna, enjoying the delightful music of Strauss, as rendered by Edward Strauss and his excellent orchestral band, two strange but evidently respectable German ladies were seated at the same table, so close that the conversation of one party could be distinctly heard by the other. A discussion arose between two of the American party as to the relative merits of the music of Wagner and Strauss, and at one time the conversation continued for a few moments after the music had commenced. One of the ladies looked around quite indignantly, and remarked to the other, in German, "You cannot expect people with such a horrible language as that to be able to appreciate or enjoy music." To this the other responded, "Yes, it is almost as bad as the jargon of the Hungarians." Of course, they had no idea that any of us knew what they said, or had any better knowledge of their jargon than they had of ours. Now, it happens to be the invariable custom in Vienna when parties are thus sitting at the same table for the first that leaves to bow politely and say to whoever may be left at the table, whether it be a gentleman or a lady, "*Ich habe die Ehre,*" which, in plain English, means, "I have the honor." Two of our party, being thoroughly versed in the German tongue, thus politely commended themselves to the ladies, who at once became considerably confused at learning that their harsh criticism of us and our pet language had been distinctly understood. However, we quote this incident to show what a hard time President Grant will have in persuading these stiff-necked people that they should teach their children the English language and blot out their mother tongue. Notwithstanding, it is beyond doubt that the English language is being very extensively taught to the rising generation here, as it is more common to find German children who speak English than it is to find native grown persons who can do so. English governesses are in great demand among the educated and wealthy classes, and it will be remembered that the Emperor of Russia, who is about to marry his only daughter to one of the English princes, issued an order that "the American" language be taught in all the government institutions of learning in his empire.

REICHENHALL, BAVARIA, June 25, 1873.

A MOUNTAIN RIDE.

We started out at an early hour this morning for a carriage-drive among the Bavarian mountains, and a visit to the famous Königs-See, or King's Sea, as well as to the equally wonderful salt-mines at Berchtesgaden, which are about fifteen miles from Reichenhall. The whole day, until nine o'clock in the evening, was consumed in this excursion, which abounded in interest. The journey was through a series of lofty mountains, many of them six thousand feet high, and some of them attaining the altitude of nine thousand feet, the summits of the latter being covered with snow, which was glittering in the bright sunshine. The reader will please to understand that these mountains, through which our excursion carried us, average one mile in height, and one of them a mile and a half, or that they are from sixty to ninety times higher than the Washington Monument, many of them being bold precipices, and also that the turnpike traverses a narrow gorge, occasionally spreading out into little valleys, dotted with the cottages and gardens of the Bavarian mountaineers. The scenery at all points is bold and picturesque, most of the mountains being covered on the slopes with dense forests of pine. The day was bright and beautiful, and the fresh mountain breeze tempered the rays of the sun, so that the heat was very seldom oppressive. By the side of the turnpike rushed the swift and clear waters of the river Alm, which flows from the Königs-See, dashing over their white, pebbly bed, and occasionally forced through rocky gorges reminding one of the Via Mala on a small scale. There were also on our route small villages, and numerous saw-mills, at which the pine forests are converted into lumber,—all calculated to render more picturesque the beauties of nature by which our eyes were regaled.

THE "KONIGS-SEE."

We reached the Königs-See (King's Sea), or Lake of Bartholomew, about one o'clock, and were astonished to find from sixty to seventy carriage-loads of people had preceded us on a visit to this famous mountain sea, which is said to be at times as turbulent as the Atlantic Ocean. A small village, with restaurants, is located at its western end, and here are the boats for excursions on the lake, rowed by Tyrolese peasant girls dressed in their national costume, who ply the oar with great expertness. As the lake, although six miles long, winds around the bases of the lofty mountains, its surface is visible for only a short distance from the point of embarkation, and every one who desires to see the whole of this most beautiful sheet of water in Germany, vying in grandeur with the lakes of Switzerland and Italy, must take a sail on it. We were not many minutes out of the carriage before we found ourselves seated in a long bateau, with three rowers, all of whom were seated in the stern of the boat. Like all bateaux, it was a shaky concern, and the slightest deviation of any of its passengers caused it to dip, which was anything but pleasant, in view of the fact that the water on which we were sailing was from three to six hundred feet deep, and that its mountain-sides were so precipitous that it would have been difficult for passengers from a capsized boat to find a landing anywhere.

When fairly out in the middle of the lake, which is about a mile and a half wide and six miles long, the scene is one of awful grandeur. In this respect it has scarcely its equal among the Italian and Swiss lakes. The mountains, which rise precipitously from its depths, some of them almost perpendicularly from the water's edge, to the height of nine thousand feet, seem almost to inspire a dread that some of their huge cliffs might come sliding down on your frail vessel. This feeling was increased when some parties in a boat just ahead of us fired a shot-gun, the report from which was not an echo, but was like a deep, long, rolling clap of thunder, just such as sometimes startles our citizens during a spring thunderstorm. It seemed to rattle around among all the mountains which towered up over our heads, and could not be distinguished from a sharp crashing thunder-bolt. Immediately following this experiment, three more shots were fired in quick succession, and the echo was really terrific. It would be a curious experiment to fire a ten-pounder and listen to its reverberation. There is but one point on the whole lake where this curious phenomenon occurs. A gun fired anywhere else awakens but a moderate echo, but here all tourists generally explode their pistols, and some of the enthusiastic sight-seeing Germans often bring their shot-guns all the way from home to use them thus on the König-See. To us the reverberation was unexpected, having never heard it described, and we assure the reader that we have not experienced any crash of thunder for years that was more startling and terrific than the echo of this puny shot-gun. It seemed almost as if the mountains were cracking over our heads, and as if we might momentarily expect an avalanche of rocks.

The promontory of St. Bartholomew, about the middle of the sea, has a restaurant and shady retreat, on which there are also a royal hunting château, and an ancient chapel, to which pilgrimages are made on St. Bartholomew's day. At the eastern end of the sea, on a small island, a prominent rock, surmounted by a cross, commemorates the wreck of a boat containing a large party of pilgrims, and the loss of many lives. There are also caverns and other attractions at which the boats stop, but they are of minor interest, and not worthy of more than a mention. Many tourists spend an entire week exploring the surroundings of the sea, and to those who are fond of mountain-climbing it well repays them for the fatigue. Artists and naturalists are especially delighted with a week's sojourn at St. Bartholomew.

The sea was dotted with boats containing tourists of various nationalities; and this is the case throughout the traveling season. Every train that arrives at Reichenhall brings a new supply of sightseers, independently of those who come to enjoy the salt baths and drink the wine-whey. What with the salt business, the baths, and the mountain sights, it has grown to be a most beautiful and attractive town.

THE BERCHTESGADEN SALT-MINES.

On our way back from the Königs-See we proceeded to Berchtesgaden to explore the famous salt-mines, or rather salt mountain, of the Bavarian government, and reached there about four o'clock in the afternoon, after a very pleasant drive. As a regular business is made of exhibiting this mine by the government, from which a large revenue accrues, we experienced no difficulty or delay in entering it.

Twice a day, at eleven o'clock in the morning and at five o'clock in the afternoon, general excursions are made into the mines, at which time there are a large number who present themselves, generally not less than fifty, the price then being but forty kreutzers. Special parties in charge of guides are, however, entering at all hours, the charge for them being about forty kreutzers each, which in Bavarian currency is about equal to fifty-five cents of our money. We entered about four o'clock in the afternoon, there being but six in the party, including three ladies, and we had an excellent opportunity to view its wonders.

In order that the reader may have some idea of these mines, we will state that they are situated in the bowels of a mountain some three thousand feet high, and their existence was first surmised from the springs of brine that flowed from its sides. A shaft was then opened, which ran on an inclined plane for several hundred feet through the rock before the salt rock appears to have been struck; and, judging from appearances, although over one hundred miners have been working in it for several hundred years, the supply is inexhaustible. From the lowest depth to which it has been mined a shaft has been dug, which now penetrates down one hundred and twenty-five feet farther, and is still being pushed deeper to ascertain to what depth the salt exists. There is just such a mountain of salt in San Domingo, but the product appears to be much richer than this, whilst it crops out of all sides of the mountain in pure crystal salt. The San Domingo mountain is also three times as large, and could be made to supply the world with salt. The yield of salt from the Berchtesgaden mine is now five hundred thousand barrels per annum, each containing one hundred pounds.

DRESSING FOR THE TRIP.

The entrance to the mines is on a level with a slight ascent through a granite arch about five feet wide, and is perfectly dry, with a tramway down the centre, the floor being smoothly boarded. Before entering, however, we were all provided with coarse woolen miners' dresses, the ladies having to remove their outer skirts and don the pantaloons, over which a half-skirt woolen coat, extending to the knees, was furnished them to wear, the funny little woolen caps, with white bands, which completed the outfit, giving the appearance of the bloomer costume worn by Mrs. Dr. Walker. The men were transformed into miners, with rough felt hats, and a strap buckled around the waist, with miners' lamps hung on in front, and a leathern apron behind, the object of which we found was to prevent our setting fire to each other's clothing as we marched in single file through the narrow passages. The arrangements were so formidable that two of the ladies of our party declined to join us, only the youngest one having the required pluck for the occasion. Apartments in a building adjoining the mine were provided as dressing-rooms for the visitors, and when they emerged they were so thoroughly transformed as to be scarcely able to recognize each other.

ENTRANCE TO THE MINES.

We started immediately, following three guides, and passed through the long, narrow passages, which for the first five hundred feet were elegantly walled with granite, before we came to any signs of salt. When the granite walls ceased the same passage continued on through the crystal salt, which is so solid as to, need no walling. Sometimes we passed up granite steps, and again down, there being no evidence of dampness or water. Each one of the party, and the three miners, having wax candles, we had abundance of light whilst passing through these passages, and, although quite chilly on entering, we soon became pleasantly warm. We stopped occasionally to examine the salt deposits, and traveled on for fully twenty minutes, passing various passages, branching off from the one through which we moved, and leading to other parts of the mine in which the actual work of mining is in progress, the part which is opened to visitors being evidently one in which active operations have been suspended for the visiting season.

THE SALT LAKE.

Whilst following our leaders through the narrow passages we suddenly emerged into an immense chamber, and were startled by the scene presented. We scarcely know how to describe the salt lake, or reservoir, hewn out in the centre of this mountain. It was brilliantly illuminated by over two hundred lamps arranged around the gallery which surrounds the lake, and, as each lamp was reflected in the water, there appeared to be double the number. The cave itself is about three hundred feet long by one hundred in width, and a gallery with a railing surrounds the entire excavation for the lake. The ceiling is of solid rock salt, about twenty feet above the level of the lake, and has no supports, and, of course, needs none; but when we reflected that some thousand feet of mountain, clothed with pines, were suspended over our heads, we felt as if it was not a very desirable place to remain in for any length of time. A boat was moored to the shore of the lake, and in this we were invited by our guides to take seats, and were soon being rowed towards the opposite end, where we were landed on a platform and shown the manner in which the fresh water is percolated through masses of crystal salt and collected in this lake, and then allowed, as it rises beyond a certain level, to flow off through iron pipes to the several boiling-houses, some of which are near the mine, and others many miles off, as are those at Reichenhall. The water in the lake is ten feet deep, and is always kept at this level. We tasted the water as we passed over in the boat, and it was so sharp with salt as to seem like the pure article itself. This lake has been formed in one of the old excavations of the mine, which, being above the level of the surrounding country, gives a natural flow for the brine through the pipes, though it has to be forced over the mountains from the first outside reservoir by hydraulic process. We were informed that the yield of salt from this water was twenty-seven per cent.,—in other words, that over one-fourth of the contents of this vast reservoir was pure salt.

RIDING ON A RAIL.

After passing up a flight of stairs from the head of the lake, we came to a point where it was necessary for us all to take seats on a board slide at an angle of forty-five degrees, and make a descent of about eighty feet, sliding down with a miner in front of each party of three, who regulated our speed by a guide-rope, which he allowed to pass rapidly through a heavily-gloved hand. It then became apparent why we were furnished with miners' clothing, as well as for what purpose the pantaloons and bloomer dresses with which the ladies were provided were intended. It was a rapid journey, but the skill of the miner landed us on our feet at the bottom without a perceptible jar. After going through a long passage we were then led on to the gallery of another immense cave, perfectly dry. The gallery which surrounded it was hewn out of the rock, and provided with a railing. The ceiling above the point at which we were standing was about twenty feet high, whilst looking down from the gallery the bottom of the excavation was about one hundred feet below us. The cave was about one hundred feet wide on each side of us, and was feebly lighted by miners' lamps stationed at various points on the bottom and along the galleries. As we passed around the gallery we entered a side chamber, about as large as the counting-room of *The American* office, in which some miners were busily at work cutting out the rock salt with picks and chisels and drilling for the insertion of blasts, each having a miner's lamp to light him at his work. The temperature was very pleasant, and the air very pure; though it appeared to be a gloomy spot in which a human being should be required to spend the daylight of his life, only emerging from it when night is approaching. These workmen were doubtless here merely to show visitors the process of excavation, as we did not enter those portions of the mine in which the hundred and twenty-five miners were said to be at work.

On returning to the cave we followed our guides around the gallery until we came to another point where a sliding-board was erected, down which we all slid the hundred feet intervening between us and the bottom of the cave. It was a pretty strong test of the nerves, of the ladies especially, but, as there was no escaping the ordeal, they all submitted quietly. We reached the bottom as safely and smoothly as on our previous descent, and, after walking around and examining the crystal walls, reascended by an inclined plane used for hauling the rock salt out of the cave. Another party were about making the descent on the sliding-board, with whom were several ladies, and, as they were merry and noisy, their laughter and loud exclamations echoed throughout the cave with a ringing sound. I must not forget to mention here that we were shown a shaft for ventilation through the bottom of this cave, which we were assured passed down one hundred and forty-five feet through the salt rock, and the bottom of the deposit had not yet been reached.

THE MOUNTAIN MUSEUM.

After reaching the gallery our guides led us through a long passage, hewn out of the rock salt, until we came to the small illuminated chamber, in which was displayed a collection of minerals dug out of the mines at different times. They were so arranged as to be illuminated by the lamps, and the specimens of pure crystal salt were similarly illuminated. At the extremity of the chamber was a broad slab of salt, on which were carved the insignia of the king, and which was brilliantly illuminated by lamps suspended behind it. In front of this tablet there was a little basin, with a fountain in the centre of it, throwing up sprays of salt water, which we all tasted, and it seemed almost like liquid salt. After admiring the minerals and the peculiar novelty of this scene in the very bowels of the earth, we were invited to take seats on small cars, which were waiting at the entrance to the chamber, each of which was in charge of one of our guides, who had control of the brakes. We moved along on the tramway at first slowly, but as we progressed through the narrow passages it was evident that we were going down grade, as the speed gradually increased, until we dashed along and turned curves at railroad speed, and, considering that the salt wall on either side of us was but about a foot distant, the prospect of getting off the track was not very promising for whole bones. All our lamps, with the exception of the one in charge of the guide, were soon extinguished by the "rapid speed," and when we could perceive a long way ahead of us a glimmering of daylight, giving the assurance that there were no more curves to turn, the sensation became rather pleasing. On we dashed, however, until we suddenly flew out into the open air and were safely landed in front of the retiring-rooms, where a crowd of some fifty visitors, arrayed in miners' garb, including a number of ladies, were in readiness to enter.

As we had no conception of what was to be seen on the inside, Baedeker being very brief on the subject, the visit was altogether a very satisfactory one. We hope the reader will be able, from our description of what we saw, to see something of it also; but should he ever travel between Munich and Vienna, we would advise him to switch off at Salzburg and take a run down, or rather up, to the Königs-See and Berchtesgaden.

MUNICH.

Munich, July 27, 1873.

We have now been in Munich, the capital of Bavaria, for two days, and have commenced our exploration of this beautiful and attractive city. It has a population of about two hundred thousand, and is chiefly Catholic, the Protestants numbering about twenty thousand. To those who delight in works of art, both ancient and modern, Munich will always present great attractions, though the climate is said to be unhealthy to strangers, on account of the sudden changes of temperature. It is the cheapest city in Europe in which to live, and in many respects is one of the most pleasant.

THE CITY OF MUNICH.

Munich is a very beautiful city, and one in which Americans greatly delight to linger. Like all the German cities, it had in the olden times walls and moats and fortifications on its suburbs. These ancient necessities for protection being no longer required, and the city having outgrown its granite restrictions, they have been all removed, leaving a broad space, something like the Ringstrasse of Vienna, between the old and the new Munich, but too wide and irregular for any extensive ornamentation. This space has been laid out in public squares and promenades and broad avenues, which form fine breathing-places for the people close to their own doors. Munich has not yet, however, become sufficiently modernized to permit the construction of city railways, and the old lumbering omnibus is the only mode of conveyance from one section of the city to another for the mass of the people. The new sections of the city are laid out in broad, straight avenues, and the buildings are large, and many of them elegant in architectural design. There is a greater variety of architectural display in the public buildings of Munich than in those of Vienna, but the private and business structures are not so elegant and elaborate.

THE PEOPLE OF MUNICH.

There is little or no similarity between the habits and temperament of the people of Munich and those of the Viennese. The former are more of the North German type, and are less volatile and visionary than their neighbors of Vienna. The streets of Munich, from daylight in the morning, show that the people of all classes are stirring, and the coffee-houses are crowded with visitors an hour before they are thoroughly opened in Vienna. The coffee-houses in the latter city are filled with loungers all day, who sit and sip their coffee and talk and read the papers. It is a matter of wonder to even the old Viennese who and what all these people are, where they come from, and, above all, where they obtain the means to secure good clothing and pay their reckoning. Here in Munich there are comparatively no coffee-house loungers. They come at an early hour for their coffee, and move off as soon as it is disposed of. Except at the regular German hours for coffee, there are but few visitors at the cafés. In short, Munich is a city noted for the active, stirring business-habits of its people. They deal but little in lotteries and stock-gambling, and when they grow rich, they do so by the slow old-fashioned process, which is more stable and enduring. The paper money of Bavaria means gold and silver, whilst that of Austria is very much in the same condition as our own. Whilst there is so much vice and immorality in Vienna, only two hundred miles distant, Munich is distinguished for its comparative freedom from such excesses. The ladies here are much more delicate and refined in their appearance and manner, and, although they dress with as much elegance, do not go into such extremes as those of Vienna. They do not trail their skirts through the streets; indeed, their dresses are seldom to be seen even touching the pavements; nor do they startle the eye with low-necked dresses, or follow any of the other extremes of their Austrian sisters.

SOLDIERING IN BAVARIA.

Bavaria is as much afflicted by the soldier as the more pretentious governments of Europe. A standing army of one hundred thousand men is kept by this little kingdom, which does not comprise ten thousand square miles, a considerable portion of which is mountainous and unproductive land. Although still independent, it is controlled by Prussia, and the northern part is intensely antagonistic to Austria. It joined Prussia in the war against Austria, and it is said to have declared war against France some half-hour before Bismark had placed Prussia in a hostile attitude. On the streets of Munich the soldier is to be seen at every turn, though most of the army, by the direction of Bismark, is kept close to the Austrian border. The officers are dressed with great elegance, and wear on their breasts the orders with which they have been decorated for bravery in the late war. The privates are short, thick, broad-shouldered men, and are charged with having been the most brave, as well as vindictive and oppressive, of all the invading army within the borders of France. The young men are compelled to serve three years in the regular army, and thus the drilling of new recruits is in constant progress, and the tap of the drum or military music, accompanying squads and regiments to and from the parade-ground, is hourly heard on the streets. The American, whose children are free from the necessity of this military service and training, cannot witness the scene without a feeling of commiseration, and of gratitude that his lot is cast far away from the dominion of kings and emperors and queens and nobles.

THE KING OF BAVARIA.

Bavaria has an oddity for a king, who spends most of his time in seclusion at one of his palaces in the mountains. He is the grandson of the old King of Bavaria, who, it will be remembered, ran crazy after the danseuse Lola Montez, took her into his palace, allowed her to control the destinies of the country, and finally made her Countess of Lansfeld. The people stood it until forbearance ceased to be a virtue, and then drove her out of the country. The present King Ludwig ascended the throne when he was only sixteen years of age, and is now but twenty-four; and if all the stories about him are true, he is as queer a specimen of royalty as has existed during the present generation. He is still single, and has the reputation of being scrupulously virtuous, having a dislike for the whole female sex. He does not allow any one to see him when he can help it; and, though he seeks amusements of various kinds, he endeavors to enjoy them in solitude, expressing anger and dissatisfaction if anybody intrudes upon him. The only man who ever had any influence over him was Wagner, the great musical composer, who at one time so completely controlled all his actions that he was compelled by the people to leave. The king's engagement to marry a princess is said to have been suddenly broken off because she persisted in refusing to express admiration for Wagner's music. Among his freaks was the construction of a lake on the top of his palace, in which he sails about in a boat for recreation, and catches fish. A few years since he took a notion that he wanted to see a representation of an eruption of Mount Vesuvius, and immediately ordered the court pyrotechnist to proceed, regardless of cost, to produce such a spectacle on a mountain, near his secluded palace. He complied with the order, but the representation was not satisfactory. The court pyrotechnist at Vienna was then sent for, and he made extensive preparations, and gave entire satisfaction, and had an order for its repetition, the king thinking that he had been and would be the only spectator. He, however, heard that the villagers had assembled at the foot of the mountain, and had witnessed the spectacle also. On hearing this he countermanded the order for its repetition, sent the pyrotechnist home, and, summoning the burgomaster of the village before him, severely rated him for allowing the people to approach the mountain. During the reign of Wagner he ordered a new opera he had written to be produced at the opera-house regardless of expense, and on the night of its production took a seat in the royal box, and directed all the doors to be closed and locked, and the performance to proceed, with only himself as the audience.

King Ludwig is, however, harmless in his vagaries, and, as the country is prosperous, and he has proved himself a thorough German, the people rather laugh than frown at his peculiarities. Although professing to be a Catholic, he utterly refuses to join in the Corpus Christi and other Church celebrations and processions, as his predecessors have done for hundreds of years, and as is now done by the Emperor of Austria. He, however, took the lead for German unity, proclaimed war against France before Prussia took decided action, and has a strong hold on the hearts of the people. He is regarded by some as a misanthrope, and by others as somewhat of an imbecile. The Bavarian army is by treaty under the command of the Emperor William during times of war, and in peace it is the plaything of the king.

King Ludwig I., the grandfather of the present king, and who died in 1868, was greatly beloved by his people, and it is the respect they bear his memory which makes them patient with the follies of his grandson. The latter came to the throne before he had completed his education, and was at first a mere willful, headstrong boy, but has since developed into his present condition. It will be remembered that the Bavarian troops were led in the Franco-Prussian war by the Crown Prince of Prussia, and to their bravery and dash many of the decisive strokes of the war were attributed. Recently, when the Crown Prince visited Munich, he was received by the people and the military with great enthusiasm and honors. At the opera-house when he appeared the performance was suspended, and so demonstrative were the people that it was impossible to resume it. The king became indignant, and, refusing to see the prince, retired to his mountain château, and remained for some time in strict retirement, scolding every one who came near him for having extended such honors to the Prince of Prussia. As the whole destiny of the country is in the hands of Bismark, it matters little who or what the king may be, as he is merely a gilded puppet, with no power to do much harm even if he had the will. King Ludwig is regarded as devoted to the honor and glory of Germany, and, being the grandson of the much-beloved King Ludwig I.,—to whom Munich is indebted for her great progress in science and art, he having made it, in the treasures of painting, sculpture, and architecture, one of the richest cities in Germany,—he is, notwithstanding his peculiarities, a great favorite with the people. Before his accession to the throne, Ludwig I. was a munificent patron of art, and during his reign he almost created the present Munich; and his grandson is also a munificent patron of modern art.

HEIDELBERG DUELING.

There are always to be seen in Munich parties of German students from Heidelberg, especially on Saturdays, when they come here to spend their Sundays, though there are more here now than usual, on account of the vacation. They are a frolicsome set of fellows, always seeking a quarrel, especially with those who they think will fall easy victims to their prowess. They wear dark cloth caps, with a white, red, or yellow band, and swagger about as if they were a superior class of human beings. The young Hotspurs of the South, of the Rhett school, who are always thirsting for human blood, ought to be sent to Heidelberg, where they could have full opportunity for studying and practically learning the rules of the duello. A Heidelberg student of three years' standing who has not his face slashed and scarred with sword-cuts is regarded as a poltroon, unless he has the proud record of having done his share in slashing and cutting the faces of one or more of his fellow-students. The proudest man at the Munich Park last evening was a young student who wore three long strips of court-plaster on his face, one of them extending from the left eye down across the nose to the right side of his mouth. A throng of students were following him, and two, whom we judged to have been his seconds in the encounter, were hanging on his arms. He was evidently the lion of a recent conflict; and later in the evening he came in, similarly attended, to a restaurant where we were taking supper and listening to a fine military band. They doubtless paid similar visits to all the public resorts in the city, to show off their gallant companion.

GOVERNMENT PAWNBROKERAGE.

In Munich, as well as throughout Austria and Prussia, and also in Paris, the business of the pawnbroker is carried on by the government. We passed this morning an immense structure, with iron-grated windows, the sign over the principal entrance giving information as to the character of the business transacted within. A throng of females with bundles were passing in and out, either to place articles in pawn, or having redeemed those previously pledged for small sums of money. There is no doubt that this establishment is a great protection to the poor, who are constantly compelled, in their struggles for bread, to obtain temporary loans on their household goods. Government officers are in charge of all its departments, and printed rules and regulations are given to the applicants for relief, so that they know exactly how long their goods will remain, and when they will be sold at public auction if not redeemed. If they sell for more than the amount advanced upon them, they are notified to come forward and receive their money. No bid lower than the amount advanced to the owner is taken for anything that is put up for sale. About one-half of the value of the article is advanced upon it, and, as in all other establishments of the kind, much that is deposited is never redeemed. Whatever profits may arise from the business are devoted to the maintenance of hospitals for the poor.

MUNICH, July 28, 1873.

We are still enjoying our German life in Munich as we did in Vienna, living as the people live, and like it much better than hotel life. We have, just at eleven o'clock P.M., returned from supper, having taken it in a garden, where for nine kreutzers' admission (six cents) we were enabled to listen while eating to an excellent concert by a band of Tyrolese vocalists. Last night, whilst taking the same meal, we enjoyed a concert in another garden by a full military band; and this evening we propose to visit still another garden, where another of the great military bands of Munich will be in attendance. All of these are within five minutes' walk of our hotel. At least one thousand persons take their evening meal at each of these gardens every evening, and there are dozens of them in all sections of the city similarly attended. The admission is a trifle, merely sufficient to pay for the music.

Tourists who live in hotels know nothing of the people among whom they are journeying, and return home from their travels fully posted about painting-galleries and old churches, and castles, and monuments, and palaces, but know very little about the habits and customs of the people.

BAVARIAN BEER-DRINKING.

We intend this letter to be about nothing but beer,—Bavarian beer,—and the manner in which it is drunk by a people who would, as soon submit to be deprived or circumscribed in the use of the air they breathe as to be dictated to respecting the amount of beer they shall consume. This is a subject which is greatly misunderstood in the United States, and we have therefore paid more than ordinary attention to it in all the parts of Germany in which we have spent the past three months. Although not accustomed to drink either malt or spirituous liquors at home, we have seldom drunk water since we landed in Germany. We at home have the best and most palatable drinking-water in the world. Here it is all limestone water, excessively hard and unpalatable, and, to the stranger unaccustomed to it, is calculated to produce diseases of the bowels. Everywhere the physicians say that it ought not to be drunk without either wine or sugar in it. Hence we have drunk beer, and drunk it freely, and are free to admit that, without having been accustomed to it from our cradle, as the Germans are, if we were to spend the balance of our lives in Germany we should continue to drink beer, and drink it to the almost total exclusion of the unpalatable and iceless drinking-water. Whether the beer in

AMERICAN SPECTACLES.

America is as good and pure and healthy as it is here is another question. Here its quality is regulated by the government breweries, or by the high standard maintained by the Pillsen breweries. An article under these standards would meet with no sale, and hence it is not made. The people, too, are all good judges of a good article, and the slightest deterioration in quality would be instantly detected.

THE ROYAL BREWERY.

We visited yesterday afternoon the royal brewery, an establishment managed for several hundred years back by the government, where a mug of beer, containing nearly three pints, or at least two pints and a half, equal to five mugs of the size sold in Baltimore, is furnished for eight kreutzers, or about five and a half cents. The government retails beer here at very little over the cost of manufacture, and furnishes a better article than can be had from any of the private breweries about Munich. The size of the mug and its price are thus made universal by the government, as any innovation on the standard as to price and quantity as furnished by the government would cause a cessation of sale. All attempts made by the government to advance the price or reduce the size of the mug have produced such mutterings among the people that they have of necessity been abandoned. The Bavarian loves his beer, must have it good and pure, and is unwilling to pay more for a given quantity than his father and grandfather paid before him. A recent attempt at Frankfort to reduce the size of the glass caused a most serious revolt; the troops were called out, men and women were shot down in the streets, and those arrested have been sentenced to penal servitude for a term of years. Any suggestion here to meddle with size or price has met with such demonstrations that it has been abandoned, and although the demand constantly increases at the royal brewery they do not increase the quantity manufactured. That which was being sold to-day, as indicated by a notice in the tap-room, was purchased from private breweries, government stock having thus early in the season become exhausted. Almost any species of tyranny will be submitted to by the Bavarian, but if you touch his beer all the ferocity of his nature is aroused.

THE COURT-YARD.

In order that your readers may understand the scene we witnessed, it will be first necessary to give them some idea of the premises of the brewery. It is a long steep-roofed building with wings, apparently two or three centuries old, located in the heart of the city, and covering three or four acres of ground. The beer-drinkers enter it through the same paved court-yard that the beer wagons and malt carts enter, passing under an arch in the main building. On getting inside of the court-yard, a number of tables and seats, sufficient to accommodate about two hundred, are seen to be ranged along the wall to the right side of the entrance, under a long shed built against the wall of that wing of the brewery. Here, on the day of our visit, were seated all classes of people, including many ladies, if elegance of dress and refinement of manners form any criterion. Most of these were with their husbands, and they drank their beer just as they would when hungry eat their bread and meat. Most of those who had their wives with them, it is but proper to add, obtained but one of these large mugs, from which man and wife drank alternately until it was empty, and then left.

We sat here about an hour, noticing the moving scene before us, desirous of giving as accurate and correct a description as possible of what occurred. We also plead guilty of having during that hour consumed one of these immense mugs of beer, and, although unaccustomed to drinking inebriating fluids, we felt no more effect from it than we would had the fluid we imbibed been milk or water. If a person were to sit down and empty two or three of these mugs in succession, he might be intoxicated, and probably would be, but among the thousands here assembled there was not one that was even "merry over his cups," nor did we see any one who had on him any of the outward signs of a drunkard. Neither old nor young looked like men addicted to drinking. There were no bloated faces or besotted countenances, and if we except two or three old men and women with the tips of their noses rather highly colored, there was nothing among them to denote that they did not all belong to the cold-water army.

THE TAP-ROOM.

A door to the left of the court-yard led to the tap-room. Here was a plain board counter across the room, and behind it two barrels of beer mounted on skids, with two men to attend to the spigots, which, when once turned, are seldom stopped until the barrel is empty. At the other end of the room was a trough with running water, and a row of shelves with empty beer-mugs upon them, just as they had been brought in from the tables, without being washed or cleaned. Any one who desires a mug of beer must enter this room, take one of these mugs and wash and clean it himself, carry it to the counter, and hand it to one of the men at the spigots. On its being filled, it is handed back to him, when he pays his eight kreutzers and hunts a seat and table where he can sit down and enjoy it. There are no waiters of any kind about the place, except a few old women, who, in return for the privilege of selling radishes in the court-yard, are required to bring in the empty mugs and place them on the shelf in the tap-room. Here we saw well-dressed gentlemen and laboring people all on an equality, the officer and the private soldier, the lady and the sewing-girl, not only sitting side by side and drinking their beer, but rinsing and washing their own mugs at the same trough. The prince and the beggar are here on an equal footing, and good beer, better than can be had elsewhere, is served out to all alike; pride or position can claim no special privileges after entering the court-yard of the royal brewery. There are also rooms on the lower floor of the left wing of the brewery building, provided with benches and tables sufficient for four or five hundred persons, which are used in winter or during rainy weather.

A CASE IN POINT.

Immediately in front of us we noticed a young couple, whom we supposed to be man and wife. The man was as well dressed as either of us who were noting his movements, and his companion bore all the outward indications of refinement, and her countenance indicated extreme delicacy and modesty. They walked into the court-yard with the air of persons who had been there hundreds of times before. Having reached the tap-room door, he entered, and she waited outside until he had washed his mug, had it filled, and paid for it. On coming out she again took his arm, and they walked over the cobble-stone pavement in search of a vacant seat. Having secured seats, they alternately sipped out of the same mug until it was empty, when they retired arm-in-arm, as graceful and as pleasing to the eye as any young couple that may promenade on Charles Street this bright summer evening. The probability is that this young couple were reared on beer,—that it has been part of their daily nourishment from their cradles down to the present day. We frequently see whole families dining in the "restaurations," and the beer-mug is handed around to the youngest of the children. Even nursing infants are accustomed to drink it, and will stretch out their little hands in entreaty before their tongues have been taught to lisp the word "beer."

THE INNKEEPER'S COMMANDMENTS.

Whilst traveling through the mountains of Bavaria we stopped to rest our horses at a wayside inn, and on the top of one of the immense beer-jugs was engraved on the china the following modest inscription, from which it will be seen that the innkeeper holds himself in high esteem, whatever may be the opinion of others.

"Ten Commandments of the Innkeeper:
"1. Du sollst täglich bei mir einkehren. (Thou shalt visit me daily.)
"2. Du sollst mich nur rufen um zu zahlen. (Thou shalt only call me to pay.)
"3. Du sollst keinen Hund mitbringen. (Thou shalt bring no dog here.)
"4. Du sollst mich ehren dass es dir gut gehe. (Thou shalt honor me that thou mayst prosper.)
"5. Mache aus den Gläsern keine Scherben. (Make no fragments of my glasses.)
"6. Vergreif dich nicht an Frauen und Kellnerinnen. (Keep your hands off my wife and waitresses.)
"7. Nimm nichts mit als einen Rausch. (Take nothing with thee but tipsiness.)
"8. Du sollst eher mehr als zu wenig zahlen. (Thou shalt rather pay too much than too little.)
"9. Du sollst nur begehren was zu haben. (Thou shalt demand only what is to be had.)
"10. Du sollst nie mit der Rechnung durchbrechen. (Thou shalt never abscond without paying.)"

Another mug had the following inscription over a mug of beer, with pipes crossed, surrounded by playing-cards: "Bei Spiel und Bier schmeckt Pfeifchen mir." (When I play and drink beer the pipe tastes best.)

MUNICH (BAVARIA), July 29, 1873.

We have had several hot days, probably as hot as you have them at home, but the evenings and nights in Germany are always cool and pleasant. We sleep under covering, with our windows closed, although the thermometer at noon is among the nineties. For sight-seeing, and wandering through galleries of paintings and sculpture and museums of antiquities, which are open only during the heat of the day, the weather is, however, decidedly unpropitious. These abound in Munich, and we find them all thronged with strangers, who have stopped here for a few days, going to or coming from Vienna. A party of some sixty Americans (Cook's excursionists) are stopping at our hotel and roaming among the galleries to-day. About half of them are ladies, and most of them are school-teachers, spending their vacation in a hasty tour of the Continent and a visit to the Exposition. The German papers express their surprise at school-teachers being able to make a tour of Europe, as they are a class who are so poorly paid in this country as to be almost dependent on the charity of their scholars for their daily bread.

MORE ABOUT BEER.

It is difficult to pass a day in Munich without striking upon a new phase of the beer question, and it is equally difficult to write a letter without taking it as a text for at least one of the chapters. There is probably not a human being, from the infant in the cradle to the old man or woman tottering to the grave, who does not drink at least one litre of beer per diem, which is equal to four full glasses such as are sold in the beer-saloons of Baltimore. Most men and women drink two litres per diem, and some four, five, or six, and it must be understood that each litre, independently of the froth, represents a full solid quart of beer. There are, besides the saloons and "restaurations," forty-three "kellers," or breweries, in Munich, where the people assemble as in mass-meeting, and drink these huge litres of beer. At these places there are no waiters, everybody being compelled to wash his mug and wait upon himself.

Let the reader imagine forty-three Schützenfests, similar to those we sometimes have in Baltimore, all in daily progress, and some idea can be formed of everyday life in Munich. At these kellers all classes of people, with their wives, daughters, and sons, young men with their sweethearts, and children in arms, are among the visitors. Beer is part of the daily food of every one, and is drunk at the breweries and gardens because it is always cold and fresh there. At every one of these places a barrel is emptied every few minutes from sunrise to sunset, and stale beer is consequently an impossibility. When the Germans drink it at home they send their servants with their glasses to the kellers, and have it always fresh and good.

Whisky, brandy, gin, or any other intoxicating liquor, is not known in Munich. Brandy can only be had at the apothecary-shops on a physician's prescription. If brandy or whisky were called for at any of the restaurants, there would be as much surprise as if laudanum had been demanded. Beer is part of the daily food, and it is called for and drunk with as much innocence of any idea of intoxication as if a cup of tea or coffee was being partaken of. Sometimes a man who has drunk too much beer will fall asleep, but intoxication is entirely unknown. The workingmen drink a litre of beer at dinner-time, and another at supper, but seldom go beyond this, except on Sunday, when they have nothing else to do. Being accustomed to it, the effect on them may produce drowsiness, but never drunkenness.

We were called upon last evening by Professor Rothmund, of Munich, who desired us to accompany him to one of the kellers in the western section of the city, to see Munich life as it really is. We reached there about eight o'clock, and, although there were seats and tables for fully two thousand persons, it was with difficulty we could find room in any part of the grounds. It was in a section of the city where the laboring people reside almost exclusively. Nothing could be had here but beer, bread, cheese, and radishes, and all that vast mass of people were sitting together, with their wives and children, partaking of this simple food, to the great majority of whom it was their only supper. We remained until nearly ten o'clock, at which time the company had thinned down more than one-half, and during the two hours we heard not a loud word spoken, nor anything said at one table so loud as to be heard at another. Everybody had to wait upon himself and wash his own mug, and sometimes the throng at the windows of the tap-room was five or six deep. The tables were closely packed together, each being about sixteen feet long, with plain wooden benches of the same length, and just room left between them to pass in or out. All classes of people were here mingled together, and we observed at some of the tables people who bore all the outward evidences of being of the very best class in Munich. There were a number of carriages waiting to take home parties who had come here to spend the evening. We got into conversation with a German lady at the table at which we were sitting, who we found could speak some English. She was surprised—almost shocked—at one of the ladies of our party refusing to drink beer, and laughed heartily as she saw her drinking water from a brown beer-mug, the only drinking-vessel we could find. She told us that she and her husband made a practice of visiting this keller every clear evening, and that it was always precisely as we found it, and equally thronged. The only question ever asked as to a place was as to the quality of its beer. All were served alike and treated alike, whether prince or peasant, laborer or mendicant, and all were expected to behave themselves alike. There were no police-officers in attendance, and none were required. Both this lady and her husband (he proved to be a clergyman, and she the sister of the Chief Justice of Bavaria) made many inquiries as to the beer question in America, both of them persisting in regarding beer as an essential and necessary article of food. They contended that it was also healthy, much more so than coffee; and, although they admitted that some persons injured themselves by drinking too much of it, they insisted that they should be classed among the gluttons, who were still more numerous, and injured their health by eating too much. To drink beer to personal injury they regarded as a long and arduous undertaking, requiring so much time and so much beer that few ever succeeded in it.

MATRIMONIAL CUSTOMS.

It may be an interesting item of news to some of your lady readers to notice the fact that on every Monday morning a list of all the engagements for marriage that have taken place during the preceding week is published in the morning papers. They proceed to state that "John Schmidt, son of Tomas and Marie Schmidt, has entered into a contract for marriage to Fräulein Katherine Von Jones, second daughter of Josef and Emile Von Jones, and that all the papers have been signed and approved by the parents of both contracting parties." How would our ladies like this formality of proceeding, which virtually cuts them off from the society of all gentlemen except that of the affianced one? He is allowed to spend only one evening a week with her, in the company of father and mother until the ceremony is performed. How would our youthful Benedicts like this, especially as they are not expected to give much time to their lady friends after the publication of this formal announcement?

THE CHURCHES OF MUNICH.

There are no old Gothic cathedrals in Munich to compare with those of Vienna, Strasburg, and Cologne, but yet there are several whose external peculiarity of style, and internal magnificence of proportions and dazzling pomp of ornament, are well calculated to interest and attract the lover of art and things that are ancient. The Church of Our Lady is an immense structure, being three hundred and forty-six feet long, one hundred and twenty-eight wide, and in height to the top of the roof two hundred and thirty feet. The two towers are three hundred and eighty-six feet high. It was built in 1468, over four hundred years ago, and is constructed of hard-burned brick, with but little interior or exterior ornament. It has twenty different altars, all ornamented with statuary, carving, and paintings. Most of the churches, of which there are about a dozen, were erected during the present or towards the close of the last century, and, although all are worthy of a visit, we imagine that a description of them would not prove of much interest to the reader. The churches built by King Ludwig the First surpass in completeness of execution any others built in Europe during this century. The magnificent Basilica of St. Boniface, the beautiful Gothic church of Our Lady of Succor, with its exquisite stained-glass windows, the Church of All Saints, which is wonderfully and richly decorated, and the Church of St. Louis, with the splendid picture of the Last Judgment, by Cornelius, are, however, more to our taste, and have the merit of having been built by those who worship in them.

THE ART-GALLERIES.

We have visited nearly all the great art-galleries of Munich, which are very numerous and rich in their collections of paintings, statuary, and antiquities. These structures are themselves among the finest specimens in Europe of the leading styles of architecture, which are represented by perfect examples with their appropriate decorations, thus materially facilitating the study of the art. The city is indebted for these advantages to

King Ludwig I., who died in 1868, who even previous to his accession to the throne was a munificent patron of art. We have visited the Old Pinakothek and the New Pinakothek, the former a repository of pictures by the old masters, and the latter exclusively for the productions of modern artists. They are both very large and grand collections, and it is needless to say to the readers of these letters that the modern gallery commanded most of our attention. We visited them both on the same day, and there were ten visitors enjoying the modern paintings for one who was roaming among the ancients. We liked them better than the pictures of Rubens, Vandyke, Murillo, Titian, Guercino, Raphael, and Correggio, and the other great masters of past ages which adorn the walls of the Old Pinakothek. They are very interesting as specimens of what the ancients could do. The Glyptothek, with its fine collection of ancient and modern sculpture, is another of these great art-galleries erected during the past twenty years by King Ludwig I., as well as the gallery for the exhibition of modern works of art, and the magnificent Gate of the Propylæon, which rears its massive columns between them. These are, however, matters for the eye, and cannot be described. If any of your readers desire to know what they are, and what they contain, they must come and see them; only we would advise that they take a cooler season of the year for the laborious task than we have selected.

MUNICH, July 30, 1873.

THE YANKEE SCHOOL-TEACHERS.

Quite a sensation was created in Munich yesterday by the arrival of Cook, the great European traveling-agent, with a party of American tourists, consisting of thirty-three Yankee school-teachers, about one-third of them ladies. They took quarters at our hotel, "The Bellevue," and the first intimation we had of their presence was the appearance of a large number of people in the corridors who really seemed to be enjoying themselves, and laughed and talked like a parcel of children going on a picnic-party. A little observation discovered them to be Americans, and on inquiry we learned that they were the veritable school-"marms" and school-masters on their vacation-frolic. They assured us that they had enjoyed themselves hugely, and had just come through Switzerland from Paris, having on account of the heat agreed not to go to Italy. It seems that there were a hundred and fifty in the party originally, and that they divided off in London, in three sections, on three separate routes. Of course the whole party were not school-teachers, but a large majority were. They express themselves as highly delighted with Mr. Cook, who accompanies them, and declare that he has done all and more than he promised, and that they have been shielded from all the annoyances that befall travelers in Europe. The hotel-porters and waiters, whose whole salary consists of what they can bleed out of the guests, don't like to see Cook coming along, and it would not be surprising to hear of a strike among them to prevent his being received in the hotels. His people are told to give "nothing to nobody" unless they feel charitably inclined, as he pays all their traveling- and hotel-expenses. He says, and I give his words for the satisfaction of the fraternity at home, that he never traveled with a party of ladies and gentlemen who gave him so little trouble or who seemed so thoroughly to enjoy themselves. They were always "up to time" when the depot- or the excursion-carriage was at the door, and always, in his own language, "jolly."

As many persons will doubtless like to know what the expenses of this party are, we will state that they are to be back at New York in eight weeks from the day they sailed, and that the whole cost for traveling and hotels, including their meal-tickets, to each of the party, is four hundred dollars in gold, or about seven dollars per day. They crossed the ocean in nine days, and have thus far had not a single mishap of any kind. They landed in England, visited Glasgow and Edinburgh, spent five days each in London and Paris, passed through a large part of Switzerland, have spent two days in Munich, and are off to-day for Vienna, where they will arrive to-night, and revel in the Exposition to-morrow. They, of course, pay their own sight-seeing expenses, and generally separate in parties of four or five for this purpose. Fifty-six days is undoubtedly a short time in which to see Europe, but still, to those who cannot spare more, it is much better than seeing none of it. It is a jolly summer frolic, much better than being cooped up at a summer's resort, and not much more expensive, especially to the ladies. They can wear out their old clothes in Europe, and have no anxious toilet-preparations for the trip.

THE MUNICH PARK.

Munich, although well provided with squares and plazas, has one of the grandest parks in Europe, called the English Gardens, on the northern environs of the city. It is five miles long by one and a half broad, and was formerly a marshy woodland, but has been made into a grand drive and promenade. The trees are all of virgin growth, and some of them are really immense. Count Rumford was the projector and improver of this fine park, for which all Munich is now truly thankful. Some branches of the river Isar have been carried through the park by canals, and, being bright, running streams, add greatly to its attractiveness. At various points in the park are houses of refreshment, where beer and coffee, and even a good dinner, can be had at a moment's notice. Thus in Europe all these breathing-places are utilized for the enjoyment of the people. Two afternoons in the week the best bands of Munich give open-air concerts in the vicinity of the pagoda, and here, on the occasion of our visit, thousands of people were listening to the music, and eating and drinking. Carriages, with citizens and strangers, were moving around or halting near the band. There are also several asylums for old soldiers, and other institutions, within the limits of the park.

RAILROAD PRECAUTIONS.

In the *American* of the 10th of July, just received, there is an account of an attempt to throw a train of cars off the track by placing timbers on it. In Austria this species of villainy is guarded against by a system that renders it next to an impossibility. On every mile of road there is a watchman, who is provided with a cottage and a small tract of land, and a part of whose duty is to walk over and examine the track between his post and that of the next watchman, and to be constantly on the look-out for any obstructions. The cottage of each of these watchmen is also clearly in sight of the similar cottages to the right and to the left of him. He is bound to present himself to every passing train in front of his cottage, with his red flag rolled up in his hand, and make a military salute to the engineer, as much as to say, "Go ahead, all is right," or, if "all is not right," to unroll and raise his flag for the train to stop. But this is not all. At every one of these stations a tall pole is erected, having two arms at the top of it, one pointing towards the road, and the other from it. The moment a train passes to his right, the inner arm is lowered, and if to his left, the outer arm is similarly lowered, which says to the next watchman on either side of him, "The train has passed my station all right." These watchmen also have control of all the gates of roads crossing the track, and are enabled to lock and unlock a gate even a half-mile distant, and ring a bell the moment they ascertain that a train is approaching. This is done by means of a strong wire carried along the ground on short posts attached to a lever at the station. The telegraph is also used from the main station; but this system of watchmen and signal telegraphing is for the intermediate stations. At night, instead of the arms on the post, red and green lights are hoisted and lowered as signals. With such arrangements, obstructions of the track or accidents by landslides or loose rails are next to impossible. It is costly, but the saving in damages is believed to be greater than the cost, whilst the security to life and property adds greatly to the business of the companies. The watchmen are generally old soldiers, who know the necessity of watchfulness, and are disciplined to the faithful performance of their duties.

THE ROYAL PALACE.

We put off to our last day in Munich a visit to the royal palace, which we found to be a very capacious establishment, full of faded royal gilt and crimson splendor. The walls are frescoed with war scenes and peace scenes in the history of Bavaria. We passed through from forty to fifty spacious halls and rooms, consisting of ball-rooms, concert-rooms, and chambers, the ceilings of which were fully thirty feet high, paneled, and ornamented with gilt and frescoes. War scenes figured everywhere, most of them seeming like a mass of horses, men, banners, cannon, and warlike accoutrements, thrown together in inextricable confusion, each warrior with sword, battle-axe, or dagger, just about to plunge it into the bowels of his next-door neighbor. Indeed, in most cases, if the fight should have gone on as it was in progress when the painter caught a glimpse of the scene, in a very few moments there would have been no one left to tell the tale. There were two large rooms, however, which contain a collection of paintings of Bavarian beauties. Old King Ludwig had a passion for ordering a painting of every very handsome woman that he met, and there are about sixty of as beautiful specimens of humanity in these two large halls as the world can produce. The two handsomest of the collection were from the lower strata, one of them being the wife of a circus-rider, and the other a cobbler's daughter. The famous Lola Montez, who bewitched the old king, had a place here once, but she has been removed. The throne-room is very large and elegant, the ceiling being forty feet high, and paneled in gilt, whilst along the walls of the room are stationed statues of the sixteen kings of Bavaria, more than life-size, cast in bronze and richly gilded. The present king is quite a fine-looking fellow, but he keeps himself shut up in his country palace, and will seldom see any one. He is only a king by name, as Bismark is the master of Bavaria, and he is probably disgusted with the empty bauble he holds by divine right.

STATUE OF BAVARIA.

Among the various wonders of art in Munich are the Hall of Fame and the colossal female figure, in bronze, called the Bavaria. This statue is on a marble base, and is reached by forty-eight broad steps leading to the level on which the pedestal stands. The figure is fifty-four feet high, and from the feet to the top of the wreath held by the uplifted hand the height is sixty feet. The pedestal is thirty-six feet high, thus making the whole height ninety-six feet. Sixty steps lead up through the pedestal to the feet of the figure, and from the knee an iron staircase of sixty feet enables the curious to ascend inside of the figure to the head, within which two seats, capable of holding six persons, are placed. From here, by looking through the eyes of the figure, a view of the beautiful environs and mountains can be obtained. The Hall of Fame, surrounding the statue on three sides, is a temple built in the form of a triple hall, supported by Doric columns, which was erected by King Ludwig the First to receive the busts of celebrated Bavarians. It was built in 1853, and is two hundred and thirty feet long, with two advancing wings, each one hundred and five feet long, and is sixty feet in height. The relievos on the two pediments, in each of which are two female figures, with the symbols representing the different races of Bavaria, and various statues, adorn the frieze over the architrave. Forty-eight representations referring to the social history of Bavaria are placed between forty-four statues of victory. The ceiling of the temple is adorned with lions and sphinxes, and the inner compartments with stars. The interior walls are divided into compartments, on which the busts of celebrated Bavarians are placed on consoles, according to the order of time. At the present time there are seventy-five busts in position.

This is undoubtedly the grandest of all modern architectural displays in Europe, and is on a scale that has never been attempted since the palmy days of Greece and Rome. It is not a building, but an open temple, of the same description as the famous Grecian temples at Pæstum. The view of this immense statue from the base of the hill on which it stands, with this grand temple in the background, is undoubtedly the most imposing to be found in Europe.

This wonderful statue is still more wonderful on a close inspection. We drove out in the cool of the morning yesterday, before the sun had concentrated its rays on the burnished metal, and thoroughly explored it. A winding iron staircase passes up through the white marble pedestal, and continues on through the body of the statue, the whole number of the steps being about one hundred and thirty, one-half of which are through the pedestal, and the remainder through the internal portion of the statue. The stairs are narrow, only large enough for one person to go up, but until the waist of the figure is reached the baluster on each side is fully four feet from the outer metal. A gentleman and lady had passed up before us, and when we reached the head they were seated side by side in one of the cheeks, leaving room enough for four more inside of the capacious head. We looked out of her eyes on Munich and the mountains, and also, by standing erect, through a hole, about as large as a man's hand, at the base of her waterfall, or twist of hair. To do this, the reader will please to understand that we had to stand erect inside of the head and rise on tiptoe. It was too hot at this early hour to remain long, and, hearing some more visitors coming up, we concluded to beat a hasty retreat. At the foot of Bavaria a lion is sitting, and on the inside both the lion and the dress of the figure form one cavity. The appearance of this statue as it is approached across a broad meadow, with a large white marble colonnade to the rear and on each side of it, is that of a magnificently-formed giantess, with her right arm extended over her head, holding a wreath. The idea that the figure itself is sixty feet high from the heel to the top of the wreath seems preposterous, and that it is possible for six persons to enter the cavity of the head at one time you feel disposed to doubt. However, we thoroughly tested it, and although there were four of us in it at one time, we assure the reader that there was abundant room for two more ordinary-sized mortals to be comfortably seated. It stands on the summit of a hill, and forty-eight broad marble steps have to be mounted to reach the level on which the pedestal and the marble temple stand. The wreath in the hand of Bavaria is, therefore, nearly two hundred feet above the level of the surrounding country.

ACADEMY OF FINE ARTS.

In company with Mr. Keyser, of Baltimore, who is studying sculpture in the Munich Academy of Fine Arts, we to-day visited that establishment, where we found about thirty of the students busily at work moulding groups of statuary. Most of the work was very fine, particularly several groups by a young Greek, who is regarded as the most promising of the class. There are about seventy aspirants for fame at work in this institution, including a goodly number of Americans. Instruction in painting is also given here, and Munich is beginning to rival Florence as the home of the artist. An immense old monastery, so large as to have four court-yards within its domains, is used for the Academy, and we regretted that most of it was closed and the students absent, enjoying the summer vacation. Mr. Keyser is engaged on several busts, one of them a member of his own family, working it out from a photograph, and evinces considerable skill in his chosen profession.

RETURN OF BAVARIAN TROOPS.

A regiment of Bavarian troops which has been quartered in France since the war, holding one of the provinces as security for the French indemnity, returned home last night. They were received at the depot by a large throng of citizens, and feebly cheered as they passed through the streets on their way to their barracks. Some flags were suspended from the houses near the depot, but there was no such enthusiasm evinced as we had expected on the return home of the veterans. There has been so much of this, however, during the past two years, that the enthusiasm has probably exhausted itself. The peculiarity of the cheer of these phlegmatic Germans struck us as very strange, and different from anything we had ever heard. It sounded like "Ho! ho! ho!" each long drawn out, and had not the hearty and cordial sound of the American hurrah.

BEER! BEER!! BEER!!!

We continue to be astounded with the beer question as it is presented in this Bavarian city. Just imagine our water-tanks spouting beer, and all the hydrants running with the essence of hops and malt, and you will have some idea of the amount of beer consumed here. Indeed, we have some doubt whether the dogs and horses do not turn up their noses at water. The number of breweries is increased annually, but they fail to keep up a supply of the winter-brewed article, and before the summer is gone the stock on hand is consumed. The summer-brewed beer is already being dispensed at most of the establishments, and notices are posted informing the beer-loving community that on a certain given day the stock will be exhausted, and their establishments will probably close. It is, perhaps, on this account that so much is now being sold, as everybody is looking forward with dread to the coming famine. There are certain famous breweries that make good beer, and others that make a very inferior article. So long as the former have any stock on hand the latter can do no business, but when the royal brewery is closed, and the stock of the good breweries is exhausted, these second-rate establishments commence to monopolize the business. The people must have beer of some kind, and if they cannot get the good they take the inferior article.

A visit to the breweries and beer-establishments of Munich would astonish the most inveterate of the beer-drinkers of Baltimore. We dropped in last night at a garden near the depot, where the lower and laboring classes mostly resort. The beer was being dispensed from five different points, and there were no waiters in attendance. All who wanted beer had to wash their own mugs, carry them to the windows of the tap-room, wait their turn, pay their money, and then search for a table. Some were eating bread with it, others radishes, and a very few meat and cheese.

There could not have been less than one thousand persons at the tables, though we were assured that it was a dull evening. All were quiet and orderly, but in earnest conversation around the tables, as is usual with the Germans. Occasionally some one would strike up an operatic air, in which others would join, and although there was occasionally loud laughter, it never became boisterous, or annoying to others.

ART IN MUNICH.

We have not alluded to one-half of the grand artistical and architectural structures which adorn different sections of Munich, nor to the numerous elaborate buildings, monuments, and statues erected in the various public squares. Beyond the handsome bridge over the Isar, on an elevation, stands the Maximilianeum, an institution for students about to enter the service of the government, and destined for the reception of a gallery of modern historical paintings. The Felderhalle, or Hall of the Generals, a successful copy of Orcagna's Loggia dei Lanzi, at Florence, at present contains the statues only of Tille and Wrede. Then there are the arcades of the Polar Garden, with their fine frescoes; the Library Building, the Ethnographical Museum, the Hofgarten and its arcades, and the several palaces; the new City Hall, and the new bronze historical monuments and fountains, are all modern, though an imitation of the ancients, and are correspondingly more handsome than the dilapidated structures of a similar character. The Siegesthor, or Gate of Victory, erected in 1850 to the Bavarian army, in imitation of the Triumphal Arch of Constantine at Rome, is surmounted by a figure of Bavaria in a chariot drawn by four bronze colossal lions, and is one of the grandest works in Europe. The bronze monument to Max Joseph, erected by the city in 1825, is very elegant and elaborate. But bronze statues are distributed about in every direction, and are executed with all the artistical skill in this branch of art for which Munich is so famous.

MUNICH BRONZE FOUNDRY.

We drove out yesterday afternoon to the famous bronze foundry of Munich, where most of the bronze statues erected throughout the world have been cast. The United States has been a liberal patron of this foundry, as is fully evidenced by the models which are now standing in the museum connected with the foundry. The largest of these models is that of the colossal equestrian statue of General Washington, erected at Richmond, together with the figures of Jefferson, Mason, Nelson, Lewis, and Henry, which stand at the foot of the pedestal. The monument ordered by the Legislature of Maryland for Chief-Justice Taney was cast here, and a model of the female figure by Reinhart which adorns the lot of Wm. T. Walters, Esq., at Greenmount Cemetery, is in the museum. A monument for Spring Grove Cemetery, Ohio, commemorative of the bravery of the Ohio troops, is in progress; also one of a similar character for Massachusetts, on the main shaft of which is to be the Goddess of Liberty, with four soldiers, representing the cavalry, infantry, artillery, and engineer corps, on the base. Two tablets for the latter, one having President Lincoln on it, and the other Governor Andrew, are already completed. We also observed a statue of President Lincoln, but could not understand where it was to be erected. There are statues of Henry Clay, Thomas Hart Benton, George Peabody, and Horace Mann, of Boston, also one of Beethoven, which has been erected at Boston. All the models for the great Davidson fountain at Cincinnati are here, where the work was executed from models by Rodgers. The government has sold out this foundry, and it is now carried on by the old superintendent, Ferdinand Müller, who purchased it. An immense amount of work is now in progress, and the monument of Stonewall Jackson, by Reinhart, had, we were informed, just been forwarded to Virginia.

SCARCITY OF WATER.

Water—that is to say, pure drinking-water—is scarcer in Munich than in any other part of Europe. Nobody seems to want it or care about it. Unless it happens to rain, the gutters are always as dry as dust, indicating that very little water is used, even for household purposes. At the hotels it is necessary to ask for it a half-dozen times before it is brought to you, and when it comes it is sufficiently warm to indicate that the vessel from which it was taken has been standing in the hot sun for several hours. It is too troublesome to get for any one to rely upon it as a beverage, and too unpalatable to have any serious longing for it. As much beer as a person can drink, cold and sparkling, can be had for four kreutzers, or about two and a half cents, from fresh-tapped barrels, at every turn of the streets, and it is not to be wondered at that everybody relies upon it. One of the ladies of our party persists in demanding water, and it is obtained only by bribing the servants and feeing the kellner. There is no sprinkling of the streets here with water, as in Vienna, and when the wind blows the clouds of dust are almost impenetrable. A wind-storm last evening brought such clouds of dust from those portions of the city that are macadamized that the vehicles passing our hotel were completely hidden from view. We could hear the rolling of the wheels and the tramping and snorting of the horses, but not the slightest sign of them was visible. The people ran into the houses on the right and the left, as if fleeing from a sirocco on the desert. Before it commenced they seemed to know what was coming, and began to run. Those who were caught out riding returned to the hotel almost suffocated with dust. A shower of rain that followed soon cleared the atmosphere, and the city became as bright and charming as ever.

A CHEAP CITY.

Munich is undoubtedly a very cheap city. Even the rates at the hotels are lower than we have found them anywhere else in Europe. The expense for rooms is about seventy cents per day, and although the hotel restaurants charge nearly double the price for meals that is charged elsewhere, it is difficult to make the entire living expense exceed two dollars and a half per day. Carriage-hire is very cheap, and cigars are better and cheaper in Munich than anywhere else in Europe. English goods of all descriptions are sold as cheap as they are in London. There is abundance of fruit here, such as cherries, peaches, apricots, plums, greengages, and some very good peaches, all of which are sold at moderate rates. Cherries are to be had throughout the summer, they being brought to the city from so many different surrounding climates that so soon as they are over in one section the supply comes in from another. We have been eating cherries for two months, and obtained this morning some of the largest and finest whitehearts that we have yet tasted, for about twelve cents per pound. A gentleman's well-made calf-skin Congress boots cost less than three dollars. They are as soft as buckskin, and most admirable to travel in. I see English razors in the windows for twenty-six kreutzers (about eighteen cents), and three-bladed penknives for about forty cents. Full business suits of cassimere are marked at about ten dollars, and everything else is at correspondingly low rates. Thus, beer is not the only thing that is cheap, and we expect labor is correspondingly cheap. Many of the laboring men and women who flock to the breweries at noon seem to make their dinner off a mug of beer, with a big radish and salt, and a roll of bread and sausage, all of which costs but thirteen kreutzers, equal to about eight cents in our money. They are, however, strong, stout, and muscular, and look as if they were well fed. Our party, numbering six, have just taken dinner at one of the best restaurants. We had soup, beefsteak, roast beef, roast duck, potatoes, and pie, with a full supply of beer, and good appetites, each calling for what he or she wanted, and the whole cost was less than six florins, or about forty cents apiece. The inferior qualities of meat are obtainable at the restaurants at much lower rates than the better qualities, and a good dinner is served to the carriage-drivers, who eat in a separate apartment, for less than twenty cents in our currency.

MUNICH NEWSPAPERS.

With all its art treasures, and its other evidences of high civilization, the city of Munich has not within its limits a decent newspaper. Indeed, there appear to be but two small affairs published here, and they are records of amusements rather than newspapers. To-morrow morning's paper is published at one o'clock to-day, and sold upon the streets by a few old women, who also have with them some Frankfort papers, and occasionally one from Cologne or Vienna. All the newspaper-reading is done in the cafés, where the journals of other cities are kept on file, and handed around to the customers while sipping their coffee. This seems singular, with a population of two hundred thousand, amid the evidences on every hand of active business energy, and with a people all of whom are at least so far educated as to be able to read and write. They contain no advertisements, except of amusements and banks, and although not much larger than a half-sheet of the *American*, about half the space is occupied by stories, sketches, etc.

STUDYING ENGLISH.

The German lady to whom we have alluded as the sister of the Chief Justice of Bavaria, assured us that she had been studying English for two years, and added "that everybody in Munich is studying English." There are so many English and

Americans constantly visiting Munich, and so many students and others permanently residing here, that all people in business find it to their advantage to have some knowledge of the language, whilst others are picking it up by coming in contact with American and English families. English is also taught in the schools. A few evenings since, as we were taking supper at the garden of the Maximilian Restauration, a large family of Germans were sitting at the adjoining table, including eight grown persons and three children. The children were playing around the table, and although the conversation among the elders was entirely in German, the children talked together in English, and whenever the mother addressed them it was always in broken English. The children would occasionally come up and take a sip of beer out of the father's or mother's glass, at the same time exchanging kisses, and slip off to their play again.

HOTEL-GREETINGS.

Munich is decidedly an interesting city, a very interesting city, and if it were not for the heat we should probably remain here some days longer. We do not expect to get into a cooler climate, but we have studied the poetry of motion so thoroughly that we are never so well content as when on the move, "strange sights for to see." We shall, therefore, hasten to finish up Munich, pack our trunks, pay our bill, and run the gauntlet of chambermaids, waiters, porters, etc., which the European tourist always finds so delightful an experience. To have a string of them bowing at you all the way from your room-door to the carriage-steps, and looking beggary without exactly soliciting alms, gives the traveler some idea of his importance, and he tries to persuade himself that "it is always pleasanter to give than to receive." However, beggary is the business of their lives, as they receive little or nothing for their services but what is gathered up from the guests.

The Cook tourists, who left our hotel a few days since, had printed instructions from Cook not to give a farthing to any one, unless they did so as charity; that their tickets embraced all manner of service. When they left for Vienna, the whole household was bobbing and smiling around them, and they persisted in not understanding what it all meant, and quietly shook hands, bidding them all an affectionate adieu. Most of them were Yankee school-teachers who had no florins to spare, and, traveling hastily as they do, it would require a heavy outlay every day to meet all their demands. They had no sooner left than the smiles changed to frowns, and all hands were abusing Cook and his people. Fifty Americans passing through a hotel and leaving no money with the servants was not to be borne, and it would not be surprising if the servants on the Continent were to strike against allowing Cook's people to enter the hotels.

WÜRTEMBERG.

STUTTGART, WURTEMBERG, August 3, 1873.

We left Munich yesterday morning, and shortly after noon took up our quarters in the city of Stuttgart, the capital of the kingdom of Würtemberg. Thus we fly over these little kingdoms, none of which are as large as the State of Pennsylvania, and some of them scarcely as large as "My Maryland." Two hours' more of travel will carry us to Heidelberg, the heart of the grand duchy of Baden, and a few hours more to Frankfort, which now belongs to Prussia.

NOTES BY THE WAY.

Four hours' run from Munich brought us to Ulm, which is on the boundary of Bavaria, and is a very ancient city, containing about twenty-five thousand inhabitants, largely engaged in iron manufactures of all kinds, and said to be the most wealthy and prosperous city in the kingdom. We were surprised to find along the route so much barren land, overgrown with pines, whilst thousands of acres were bogs, from which peat was being dug in immense quantities and carried off by rail. After passing Ulm the country became quite mountainous, and the scenery very fine, the foot-hills being carefully cultivated, whilst the cottages of the farmers looked more cheerful. Little villages and towns occurred nearly every mile, and large factories for the manufacture of linen were quite numerous. The harvest-fields were thronged with men and women, busily at work reaping and gathering in a fine crop of oats. We passed also two quite large cities, Esslingen and Cannstadt, both of which, from the cars, presented a prosperous appearance. Indeed, everywhere throughout Prussia and its vast dependencies great improvements are in progress, the war with France having been a very remunerative speculation to the people. The supplies required by the government were immense, and fortunately it got the money to meet promptly all claims upon it.

We reached Stuttgart about noon, and were rather surprised at our first glimpse of the city. The depot into which we were ushered was so magnificent and immense that we turned to Baedeker, and found that he had credited Stuttgart with the finest depot in Europe, which is saying a great deal, as the poorest of them are very much finer than those of either the Baltimore and Ohio or the Northern Central Railway at Baltimore. As to the Philadelphia depot, those of the country way-stations are more elegant and imposing.

THE CITY OF STUTTGART.

As we proposed but a short stay in Stuttgart, we started out after dinner to get a view of the city. Stuttgart is the capital of the lively little kingdom of Würtemberg, and has recently improved so vastly that the old town can scarcely be discovered. It has a population of one hundred thousand, and there are evidences everywhere of great business activity. The retail stores are very numerous, and make a much finer display than those of Munich, whilst the private residences in the new portions of the city will compare with the finest we have seen in Europe. As a general rule, people live here in separate houses, if they are able, though there are a goodly number of the Vienna flats in all sections of the city. Some of the private residences, all of which are built of a light-blue stone, are of the most elaborate architecture, and are richly ornamented with statues and carving. Hundreds of new mansions were also going up in all directions, and, depend upon it, Stuttgart is on the high-road to prosperity.

The king's palace and gardens are very elegant, and are extensively ornamented with statues, monuments, and two of the most elegant fountains in Europe. The public gardens are very large, but *have no fences*, and the grass is everywhere interspersed with beds of flowers arranged with artistic skill. The new palace is very extensive, having in it three hundred and sixty-five rooms, and is quite an elegant structure. The main street of the city, called Königsstrasse, is equal in attractions to the Rue Rivoli at Paris, especially along the front of the palace gardens.

The principal trade of Stuttgart is in wine, it being located in the heart of a wine-growing district. The city is surrounded by mountains on every side, which are cultivated to their summits with the vine, and thus is like the centre of an amphitheatre, presenting a very picturesque view. It has the reputation of being excessively warm in summer, though we found it so cool last evening whilst listening to the music in the Stadt Gardens as to compel us to retire before the close of the concert. The public buildings are all new, and very elegant, and there is a Polytechnic Institute here, said to be the very best in Europe.

SUNDAY IN STUTTGART.

We spent Sunday in this rejuvenated ancient city, and found it quite different from Sunday in Austria. This is a Protestant country, there being but ten thousand Catholics in this city to ninety thousand Protestants. As usual, we started out in search of fruit, but found everything closed up, as if hermetically sealed. The market-house was not only empty, but cleaned and washed, so that you could scarcely tell whether it was a market-hall or a ball-room. The bells all over the city were announcing the Sabbath day, and the people were out in their best attire for early morning worship. The beershops were all closed, and all manner of business was suspended. A more staid observance of the day could scarcely be found in Old England, though in the evening the strictness was somewhat relaxed so far as all kinds of eating and drinking were concerned. The beer of Stuttgart is not inviting, and tastes very much as if it were the rinsings of the Munich breweries. It is not, therefore, drunk to any great extent, except by those who cannot afford wine, which is so cheap and abundant here. In fact, we are grateful to be able to record the fact that we are again in a city where water is used for some other purpose than squirting it through fountains. There are plenty of fountains here, and the water is good and palatable. We record it to the honor of Stuttgart, that it is the only city on the Continent where drinking-cups are suspended at the fountains, giving an opportunity for man to slake his thirst in passing, without being compelled to lap up the water like a brute.

But Sunday in Stuttgart is so anticontinental that we do not wonder that it is becoming a favorite place of residence for both English and Americans. A large number of American and English families have located here to educate their children. At the hotel-table this morning a majority of those present were using the English language. On the corners all over the city posters were up with a representation of the American flag, under which was a notice to Americans to attend the Fourth of July celebration. At all the hotels the waiters speak English, as the clerks do in most of the stores, which fact please report to President Grant, in proof of the approaching millennium of language, when all the world will say its prayers and ask for its beer in good plain English. Although we liked the opportunity of returning again to good water and finding the English language spoken, we felt a longing this morning for the rich and luscious coffee of Vienna, where no one knows how to make bad coffee. We could stand the bad beer of Stuttgart by doing without it, but we think we have seldom tasted worse coffee, even when brewed in a hut in San Domingo, than that placed before us at the most fashionable hotel in Stuttgart this morning.

VISITORS TO THE FATHERLAND.

We met to-day in the cars on our way to Stuttgart a German who has for many years resided in California, and who is now returning from a visit to the home of his childhood. He had his youthful remembrances of its attractions, and of the joyful days when all seemed bright and beautiful. For many years he had longed for the time to come when he could revisit the Fatherland. He even imagined that the fruits of Germany were more luscious and sweet than those of California, and had often boasted that such was the case. He had finally come to spend a few months amid the scenes of his youth, and was now returning disgusted with everything. Most of his old acquaintances were either dead or gone to America. Many of them had been killed in battle. The fruits which had tasted so sweet were insipid as compared with the fruits of California. None of the comforts of life were known here, except to the titled and wealthy. Hotel life, as compared with hotel life in San Francisco, was worse than living in a hovel at the mines. He had found it a constant struggle to get anything fit to eat since he landed at Liverpool. The table-d'hôte he regarded as a burlesque on good living. He had found everybody he came in contact with planning some mode to swindle him, or begging for money for services that had not been rendered, or for which he had already paid. A more thoroughly disgusted individual we had never met with, unless it was Mr. Raster, editor of the Chicago *Staats Zeitung*, who is also on a visit to the Fatherland. When we last met him he was more in love with his adopted country than ever, and longed for the comforts of his home. This is the case with nearly all the American Germans whom we have met with. They have been thoroughly cured of their longing for home, and will return better Americans than ever. They can no longer see any pleasure in the glitter of royalty, or admire the costly palaces and monuments to the memory of dead tyrants, whose whole glory consisted in leading to slaughter hecatombs of their countrymen to maintain kingly prerogatives or avenge personal grievances. The young men of Europe, cooped up in barracks, and marched and drilled in the scorching sun, that they may be ready to lay down their lives at the bidding of their masters, are to them a sad sight, when they remember the freedom of their own children from military service. It would do good to many of our naturalized citizens to pay a visit to the Fatherland. Many of them are like the grumbling husband who imagines that nothing tastes so good as that which his mother cooked, forgetting that he then had a youthful appetite that sweetened his food and helped his digestion.

PREPARING FOR WAR.

Although Prussia, Bavaria, and Würtemberg have just come out of a successful contest with France, there is no cessation of warlike preparation for any emergency that may arise. Regiments and brigades are marching and countermarching, or holding camps for instruction, new recruits are being drilled, and to the eye of an American it looks as if the country might be on the eve of another war. At Ulm, on the boundary of Bavaria, extensive fortifications are being built, and are swarming with workmen. They are of the most formidable character, and are being constructed of brick and granite. This place has always been extensively fortified, but new works that are deemed necessary to make it impregnable are being rapidly constructed. We also passed a great number of immense barracks, covering acres of ground, swarming with soldiers, whilst others were in course of erection. The Bavarian troops who had been holding several of the provinces of France as security for the indemnity to Prussia, after resting a few days at Ulm and getting new uniforms, were in the cars on their way to Munich. The cars were dressed with evergreens, as were also the depots, whilst the Bavarian and Prussian flags were suspended in great profusion. At Munich, not only during the day, but in the middle of the night, regiments of infantry and troops of cavalry passed our hotel, generally with full bands of music. What they were doing, or where they were going, we could not ascertain, but presume they were on their way to the camp of instruction, as they were generally accompanied by baggage- and ammunition-wagons.

Prussia is gradually overshadowing all these petty kingdoms, and will soon get rid of the kingly incumbrances attached to them. Their military system is under the supreme control of Prussia, and the Prussian uniform is being gradually made to take the place of their own pet colors. Here, in Würtemberg, the spiked hat and dark-green coat of Prussia have already been substituted; but Bavaria resists, and still holds to her national colors of blue and white. The Prussian fatigue-cap and other peculiarities of trimming have been accepted by the artillery of Bavaria; and it will not be long before the whole national suit will disappear.

THE MARRIAGE QUESTION.

Whilst driving around and viewing the sights of Stuttgart, yesterday afternoon, a conversation with the carriage-driver was thoroughly corroborative of a statement made in a former letter as to the difficulty a poor man had to encounter before he could get married in any of these German countries. It will be remembered that, as one of the reasons for the great disregard of the marriage relation in Austria, we stated that men and women were driven to lives of shame by the obstructions of the law to marriage; that unless a man could prove to the Mayor and Council of the town in which he was born that he was able to support a family, and that his children, if he should have any, would not become a charge on the town, no priest or clergyman was allowed to marry him. It seems that this law prevails throughout all German-speaking countries, and is rigidly enforced, for the protection of each other from pauperism. The carriage-driver inquired whether there was any law to prevent a man from marrying in America, and, on being assured there was not, proceeded to state his own case. He was a man but little under forty years of age, of more than ordinary intelligence, having all the appearance of a sober, industrious, and honest man. He said he had been driving a carriage for a great number of years here in Stuttgart, and had saved sufficient money to enable him, on the death of his employer, seven months since, to purchase from his widow not only the carriage and horses which he was driving, but the license and number, which it seems are also marketable commodities. Being now fully convinced in his own mind of being able to support a wife and family, he had applied to the authorities of his native town for a permit, forwarding them also proof of his present prosperous condition. Several months had elapsed, and no permit had yet been given, though he was not without hope that recent efforts which he had made would be successful in procuring it. But unless it was given he could not be lawfully married. He might go on, as we rather expect was the case, and have a family without marriage, but they would not, if illegitimate, in case of his leaving them destitute, become a charge on his native town. Is it any wonder that the poor are fleeing from such a country, where a man is born a slave to military service in the prime of his life, and forbidden all the rights of manhood in his maturity? This carriage-driver had spent the best portion of his life in military service. Thus it is that the fact of a man and woman living together without marriage in Austria does not lower them in the estimation of their neighbors, even if they should change their "partners" annually. We were not prepared to find such obstacles to marriage in this more staid and solid portion of Germany. Human nature revolts at such laws, which are unworthy of a civilized community in any part of the world.

DUCHY OF BADEN.

HEIDELBERG.

HEIDELBERG, August 4, 1873.

We left Stuttgart at noon yesterday, and reached the ancient and romantic town of Heidelberg for early dinner. The country through which we passed was very beautiful, and in a high state of cultivation, the mountains and hill-sides being clothed with the vine, and the valleys devoted largely to the growth of tobacco and hops. In two hours we passed the boundary of the kingdom of Würtemberg and entered the duchy of Baden, to which Heidelberg belongs. There was no work going on in the fields, the roads being lined with the agriculturists going to and from their churches, the steeples of which indicated that they were mostly modern structures, built by those who worship in them. Wherever the old churches are most numerous, Sunday is seldom observed, except to say an extra prayer in the morning before breakfast.

As we approached Heidelberg the country became more hilly and mountainous, the foot-hills being cultivated with the grape, and the sides of the mountains ledged and walled and green with the running vine. At length the famous Castle of Heidelberg, looming on the mountain-side over the town, could be seen in the distance, and in a few minutes we were in the depot, where from three to four hundred tourists daily arrive during the summer season to visit these historical scenes.

THE TOWN OF HEIDELBERG.

Heidelberg has a population of seventeen thousand, about two-fifths Catholics and three-fifths Protestants, with five hundred Israelites. It was a Roman town, with castles and towers for the protection of their frontiers, in the first century. For the next seventeen centuries there was perhaps no other spot on earth that was so severely afflicted by the ravages of war as this little town, it being the key to the valley of the Neckar. It has been totally destroyed a half-dozen times by contending armies in the intervening centuries, and twice destroyed by fire. The castle, which was first built at the end of the thirteenth century, was several times blown up and burnt, and again rebuilt, only to meet the same fate again in succeeding years. When partly rebuilt by King Theodore, in 1764, it was struck by lightning, and the whole of the interior destroyed, leaving it a blackened ruin, as it now stands. The walls are of vast extent, and form the most magnificent ruin in Germany. Its towers, turrets, buttresses, balconies, lofty gateways, fine old statues, and extensive courts and grounds, render it the Alhambra of the Germans, who flock here annually by thousands. The ivy-clad ruins are connected with innumerable historical associations, and the striking contrast here presented between the eternal rejuvenescence of nature and the instability of the proudest monuments of men has called forth many a poetic effusion. The main street of Heidelberg is over a mile long, and is devoted principally to business and a superabundance of beer-saloons and refectories. The two back streets between the mountain and the river are very beautiful, consisting principally of hotels and boarding-houses, interspersed with gardens, groves of trees, and several fine promenades. A majority of the visitors are Americans and English, and on that side of the city the English language is very extensively spoken. The number of Americans here, either stopping for a few days or making a prolonged stay for excursions into the mountains, is quite surprising. The atmosphere is very cool, and in the evenings and at night cloaks and overcoats and blankets are in demand. As in all German towns, the "whey cure" is extensively practiced, and no more cool and pleasant retreat could be desired than Heidelberg. Last evening we found overcoats and water-proof cloaks quite comfortable while strolling along the river. The city lies between the mountain on one side and the river Neckar on the other, and is necessarily long and narrow, the villas and cottages on the mountain-side being built high up among the rocks.

ASCENT TO THE CASTLE.

Several hundred enthusiastic tourists present themselves every day at the foot of the mountain, intent upon visiting these extensive ruins, perched three hundred and thirty feet above the level of the river Neckar, which winds around its base and flows on to swell the waters of the Rhine at Mannheim, near the head-waters of steamboat navigation on that historical river, only about six miles distant from Heidelberg. The mountain is ascended to the level of the ruins of the old castle, either by a winding carriage-way or by a bridle-path, on the backs of mules, which are always waiting customers at the corn market, though the majority of the inveterate mountain-climbing Germans who come here ascend on foot, with alpenstock in hand.

We joined the explorers at an early hour this afternoon, proceeding in a carriage from our hotel by the winding road that leads to the ruins of the castle. Quite a number of tourists were proceeding up a shorter but steeper bridle-path, mounted on mules, whilst the enthusiastic German, who scorns to ascend a mountain otherwise than on foot, was climbing up the ascent. It was a bright and clear day, with a warm sun, and a cool breeze blowing from the surface of the river Neckar. It required about a half-hour to make the ascent to the old embattled gate, and we were astonished at the extent of the ruins, as well as at the excellent state of preservation in which they are kept, the government having for the past fifty years taken the greatest care to protect them from further decay.

THE CASTLE OF HEIDELBERG.

Looking up at the castle from the east end of Heidelberg, it appears to hang directly over the town. From this point no conception can be formed of its extent, as only the front walls of the main building and the towers are visible; but on reaching the summit it is found to extend over at least ten acres of land, including a large garden without the walls, which has been restored to the condition it was in when the castle was in all its glory and the home of the rulers of the Roman Empire. On entering the garden, immediately to the left is seen the Elizabeth gate, built by the Elector Frederick the Fifth, in 1615, as the inscription says, "To his dearly beloved wife, Elizabeth of England." Each side of the stone gateway represents four trunks of trees, entwined with ivy, and above the archway are two female figures holding cornucopias, whilst the frieze of the arch is decorated with the lions of England and the Palatinate. This gate is the entrance to the Common Garden, which at one time was part of the ramparts, but is now a beautiful grove of lime-trees, from which a splendid view of the town and the fertile valley of the Rhine is obtained. On the north side of the Common Garden are the walls of the Thick Tower, a colossal building which closes the north side of the castle. It is ninety feet in diameter, and in it was the banqueting-hall, sufficiently capacious to contain a hundred tables and dine four hundred guests. In the niches in the wall, partly concealed by ivy, are the statues of two of the Electors, and a Latin inscription giving a history of the building. At the destruction of the castle by the French in 1689, the tower was blown up, and half of it fell in the town. The English building, likewise blown up at the same time, adjoins the Thick Tower. Beyond the castle ditch are Rupert's Hall, Rudolph's Building, and Rupert's Building, underneath all of which, as well as the gardens, are subterranean passages, extending to the large watch-tower, and communicating with other parts of the fortifications. Inside of the gardens stand the bridge-house and the large watch-tower. Over the gate to the bridge are the statues of two clumsy-looking squires. Over the Gothic doorway of Rupert's Building are two angels bearing a wreath of roses, in the midst of which is a pair of half-open compasses, which are supposed to have had a Masonic signification. Farther to the left of the entrance is a stone tablet with the following inscription:

"One thousand four hundred years were counted when Palsgrave Rupert was elected King of the Roman Empire, and governed and inhabited this castle, which Palsgrave Louis restored. He was ever gay, and in his 44th year, the year 1500, he departed this life. May Jesus Christ keep them both in his blessed care. Amen."

In this hall, which is in a tolerable state of preservation, a museum of antiquities found in the vicinity of the castle is exhibited. Under an effigy of Christian II. of Denmark, exhibited here, is the following inscription:

"His spouse of royal ancestry, Dame Dorothea is her name, born Princess of Denmark, Norway, and Sweden, three mighty kingdoms."

From these inscriptions it would seem that these old-fogy kings thought more of their wives than some of their successors of the present day do. The Rupert Building has been roofed, and is now used for festivities of various kinds.

The most richly decorated of these old palaces within the walls of the castle is Frederick's Building, built in 1601. It is of three stories. On the front, facing the court-yard, are four rows of statues, sixteen in all, some of them partially dilapidated during the various wars, and from the conflagration of the castle. Over the doorway is the following inscription: "Frederick, Count Palatine of the Rhine, Elector of the Holy Roman Empire, and Duke of Bavaria, caused this palace to be constructed for divine service and commodious habitation, and ornamented it with statues of his ancestors, in the year of our Lord 1669."

This building has been also roofed, and in the second story are a picture-gallery and a collection of antiquities which particularly refer to the history of the castle.

Connected with this building is the balcony of the castle, from which a fine view is to be had of the surrounding country. The decorated vestibule leading to the balcony, with Doric pillars and vaulted roof, is very imposing. We next viewed the ruins of the arsenal, which has been partly restored, and passed on to the building which holds the great tun or wine-barrel of the castle, built in 1751, to replace the old one which was built in 1591, but had become decayed. It is thirty-two feet long, and from the middle of the barrel twenty-three feet high. It is bound with eighteen wooden hoops eight inches thick and fifteen inches broad. In 1752 it was filled for the first time, holding equal to two hundred and eighty-three thousand bottles, but it is now empty and unused. Near the tun is a little statue of Clemens Perko, the court-fool, who, like other fools, drank from fifteen to eighteen bottles of strong wine daily.

The Octagon Towers and Otto Henry's building, the latter of which was the palace of the castle, are especially interesting. The court-façade is decorated with masterpieces of statuary and sculpture, representing the figures of men struggling with lions. The statues on the front are Joshua, Samson, Hercules, David, Strength, Faith, Hope, Charity, Justice, Saturn, Mars, Venus, Mercury, Diana, Sol, and Jupiter. On the gable ends are eight medallion heads, representing distinguished Romans.

There is nothing special about the Lewis Building, the Towers, or the Fountains, worthy of description, except to show the extent and perfection of this vast mountain-ruin. Over the door of the Fountain-house is this curious inscription, showing that water was once deemed a healthy drink in Germany:

"New and very wholesome spring of Charles Theodore, the father of his country, and of Elizabeth Augusta, the mother of her country, is also recommended as a new source of health."

As we passed through the old chapel, the sound of a piano was distinctly heard, and on inquiry of our guide we were informed that an English family had rented a suite of rooms in that part of the castle for three years, and were educating their children in Heidelberg. We also passed high up on the mountain, fully five hundred feet above the castle, a beautiful little villa, which, we were informed, was owned and occupied by Dr. Sprague, an American gentleman.

MOUNTAIN RAMBLES.

Higher up in the mountain are the ruins of the old castle, which was the residence of the old Roman Palsgraves, before the large castle was built, as far back as the year 1200. It was afterwards used as a magazine, and in 1537 it was struck by lightning, and the whole castle was scattered around the mountain by the explosion. Here is now located the Molkenkur, or Whey-cure establishment, at which there is a large throng of guests, resorting to this mode of curing all variety of diseases, and taking exercise by exploring the castle and the mountains. From thence we proceeded to the cave of Enchantress Gheta, commanding a fine view of the ruins of the castle, the town, and the surrounding mountains, and the Rhine can be seen winding along in the far distance. We are now one thousand seven hundred and fifty-two feet in the upper air, and have pointed out two rocks, named respectively Königsstuhl (King's seat) and Kanzel (the Pulpit). A tower is erected on the former, and from thence we passed to the Riesenstein Inn and to the Pavilion, there being, in addition to the restaurant in the castle garden, an abundance of provisions for the inner man during the trip, beer being the principal commodity consumed. The castle is kept in excellent condition, and the garden is very beautiful, a good band of music being in attendance every afternoon at the restaurant.

THE GERMAN TOURIST.

The German tourist is generally a man of sedentary habits, whose idea of sight-seeing has combined with it the recovery of health and good digestion, and he goes into it with a vim that is not exhibited by other nationalities. He generally takes with him his wife or daughters, and they, being of the sisterhood not afflicted with "weak backs," accompany him in all his excursions. They are never satisfied with looking up at the snow on a mountain, but have an ambition to look down on mother earth with their feet imbedded in the snow. The sight of a waterfall rushing over from rock to rock, and taking long leaps over precipices, is tame to them compared with tracking it up the ascent, reveling in the spray, and finally examining the source whence it comes. They carry neither trunks nor bandboxes with them, but with a blanket shawl strapped over one shoulder, and a field-glass suspended from the other, and alpenstock in hand, they climb over the mountain and make a circuit of the country, taking to the rail only when they desire to reach some distant point from whence more pedestrian researches are undertaken. The men wear loose jackets with belts, and sometimes a small knapsack on their backs, and the ladies are attired in traveling-dresses, with broad-brimmed straw hats. At six o'clock this morning, thus equipped, they could be seen plodding along towards the ascent to the Heidelberg Castle, and were doubtless among the ruins long before the tourists of other nationalities took their seats in the carriages before their hotels. The latter will spend a few hours among the ruins, and return in time for the evening train to carry them to Munich or Stuttgart, whilst the former will spend several days in their wanderings over these historical heights, the history of which they had well conned before leaving their homes. They generally spend the whole day at the castle, ruminating among the ruins, reading the guide-books and scraps of history in relation to the different wings of the castle, and staring the old statues out of countenance. It is their greatest remnant of antiquity, and as a visit to Heidelberg had been the longing desire of their previous lives, they make the most of it. There are numerous other historical points in the surrounding mountains, all of which must be visited, and they plod along, male and female, with unwearied enthusiasm that no historical stone may escape their inspection. The site of this castle was selected by the Romans in the first century as the key to the valley of the river Neckar, which flows at its base, and the fact that in succeeding ages it was so often destroyed by contending armies shows that the "flanking" process was not practiced in those days.

HEIDELBERG, August 5, 1873.

STUDENT-LIFE AT HEIDELBERG.

During our sojourn at Heidelberg we have paid considerable attention to a subject with which the whole world is somewhat familiar, though generally only in the form of incidents and anecdotes illustrative of student-life in this ancient University city. We all know that a goodly number of the students here live a rollicking life, and that some of them are occasionally killed in duels, whilst others carry home with their diplomas scarred faces, and sometimes broken constitutions, from the effects of the wild and reckless course of living into which they fall here when freed from parental restraint. Of the thousand students who annually attend the Heidelberg University, there are, of course, a large proportion who are no worse than other young men attending similar institutions in all parts of the world, but Heidelberg is renowned for the lack of restraint, the practical approval which seems to be extended to those who choose to pursue vicious courses. In all these military countries the duello is regarded as chivalric and honorable, and if anything would tend to render it ridiculous, it seems to us that the way in which it is practiced by these beardless youths ought to have that effect. That the reader may be correctly informed as to what student-life in Heidelberg really is, what is the character of the associations which lead to this condition of affairs, we have collected from authentic sources such facts as could be obtained during a brief visit.

THE GERMAN STUDENT.

We took a stroll yesterday afternoon along the main street of Heidelberg, which is about a mile and a half in length, passing the various buildings of the University, and were much amused with our first sight of the Heidelberg student in full feather, making his Sunday rounds. It appears that they are divided up into a dozen or more societies, each having a combination of colors to distinguish it. These colors are displayed in the color of the cap and of the band around it, as well as by a broad tri-colored ribbon worn across the bosom of the shirt. Two or more members of different societies are seldom seen together, as the whole object of the societies seems to be the generation of feuds and quarrels and the resort to the duello. One party of five, walking arm in arm, particularly attracted our attention from the fact that each of them had scars across his face, indicating recent wounds, and one of them still wore strips of adhesive plaster. We passed a good many going singly or in couples similarly marked, and regretted that the close of the lecture season a few weeks since had taken so many of these chivalric youths to their homes. So universal is this dueling practice that a scarred face among professional men in Germany is regarded as signifying the possession of a Heidelberg diploma. They are, however, a fine-looking set of young fellows, all strong and athletic, with a rakish devil-may-care air about them. It is one of the peculiarities of German universities, that no student can gain admission unless he has not only previously graduated in a college, but has also graduated from a gymnasium, and has all his muscles strong and well developed. Hence there are no sickly students here, and none appear to be much under twenty-one years of age.

Any youth of a wealthy family coming here and going earnestly to study, and refusing to join any of these roistering and beer-drinking societies, at once incurs the animosity of all of them, and particular members are appointed by each society to seek an opportunity for a quarrel with him. They have thus frequently stumbled upon adversaries who were not to be trifled with, and who paid no attention to the code, which regards a scratch drawing blood as sufficient for the satisfaction of an intended insult. In times past, some students have thus been killed, especially such as had been universally successful in carving the faces of fellow-students, and imagined themselves sufficiently skillful to make it safe for them to insult and encounter army officers.

A HEIDELBERG DUEL.

Less than a year since, a student of quiet and gentlemanly demeanor had been frequently insulted by these Hotspurs with the view of a fight, but refused to be thus dragged into personal conflict. All their efforts having proved unavailing, they imagined that it was cowardice that induced him to refuse to take offense. The matter was taken up at the meeting of one of these societies, and a young student, who was very expert in the use of his sword, named Ruelling, was selected to dog his steps and seek every opportunity of insulting him. His efforts were unavailing, until one morning he met him at the depot, whither he had gone to see a lady friend off in the cars. Here Ruelling so grossly insulted him in the presence of the lady that forbearance ceased to be a virtue, and he was forthwith challenged. To the surprise of all who had doubted his courage, the quiet youth indignantly declined to recognize the Heidelberg code, but demanded that the encounter should be with broadswords and to the death. The matter was taken up by the society which had appointed Ruelling to insult him, and, under the belief that their expert champion would be able to disarm and overpower him, if not slay him, the terms of the challenge were accepted, and a place of meeting selected. The matter was kept secret from the authorities, and at the appointed time they met, with their seconds and medical attendants. So confident were all in the triumph of Ruelling that bets of ten to one were offered on the result, with no takers. Their swords were, however, scarcely crossed before it became evident that the youth whom they regarded as a poltroon was not only dreadfully in earnest, but that he was thoroughly master of his weapon. The fight had not lasted very long when Ruelling fell mortally wounded, and none of his valiant backers and instigators were found willing to take up the quarrel. This ought to have put an end to these duels; but the fresh-scarred faces to be seen on the streets show that it has only had the effect of causing more care in the selection of their intended victims.

THE DUELING CODE.

The term for studying in the University is five years, and these young bloods of wealthy parents seldom attend a lecture during the first four years of their residence in Heidelberg. The fifth year they usually abandon the societies and commence to study, and it is a singular fact that many of them have subsequently become eminent in their several professions. The majority of them are turned out upon the world professors of nothing but roistering and beer-swilling. After four years of such life as they have led at Heidelberg, it is not all of them that can recover their manhood, and devote themselves to study and subsequently to a career of usefulness.

The occasional fatal results that have ensued from these duels have led to government interference, so far as to require them when they fight to wear a peculiar style of spectacles for the protection of the eyes, long padded gauntlet buckskin gloves, extending to the shoulder, for the protection of the hands and arms, and a similar padded buckskin apron for the protection of the breast and body. A peculiar broad-bladed sword, sharp only at the point, was also established as the regulation weapon, with which a stunning blow may be struck on the head, and the face gashed, which are the only parts left unprotected, a thrust or blow anywhere else being deemed a violation of the code. It is thus arrayed, and thus they fight, a cut across the countenance leaving a scar being deemed a mark of honor. As we seldom see these caps and ribbons unless they are accompanied by a scarred face, some idea may be formed by our Southern chivalry what a glorious time they would have at Heidelberg to satisfy their cutting and slashing propensities. So dearly are these scarred faces valued, that when the wound is not deep they keep it festering with nitrate of silver, and it is not allowed to heal until there is an assurance that it will leave its mark. Of course there are plenty of students here who come to study, and live very exemplary lives, having neither the money nor the inclination to join these roistering and fighting societies, which are composed mostly of the sons of wealthy parents. They have their club-rooms, and generally spend largely in excess of the allowances sent them from home. The better class of students have all gone for the vacation, and it is only some of these young bloods who are still here finishing their line of dissipation, and probably waiting for remittances to enable them also to leave for home.

THE SOCIETY HONORS.

The fighting proclivities of these societies are the main features of the organizations. They have their teachers of sword-exercise, and when they walk the streets they occasionally swing their canes over their heads, or twirl them in the air, as if conning over the lessons they had received, and aiming to become dexterous in the execution of certain movements with the weapon. They have, in connection with their club-rooms, apartments for practice, in which the clashing of swords is constantly to be heard. When they cannot get up any personal quarrels six or a dozen of their members are named, and a challenge sent to some antagonistical society to name a similar number, to meet them at the dueling-house opposite the castle, and fight out the point of difficulty. So soon as blood is drawn the fight ceases, and the victorious student is required to encounter another of the selected champions. Thus the fight progresses from day to day, and whichever society has the fewest scarred faces at the end of the contest is proclaimed the victor. Thus it is that so few escape with whole faces, and that the scar is the insignia of personal prowess and bravery. In selecting the officers of these societies the man who can prove that he has done the most cutting, and has thus maintained the credit of the organization, is usually chosen as President, and the other officers are graded in accordance with the number of scalps they carry at their belts. Another grade of honor is awarded to the member who can drink, at one sitting, the largest number of glasses of beer. To attain this honor, they have sometimes been known to secretly swallow an emetic when their capacity to take down more was about to cease, go out and empty their stomachs, and return ready to carry on the contest indefinitely. They swagger along the streets with the air of princes, and appear to expect everybody to get out of their way, and as a general thing the town-people appear to have a wholesome dread of coming in contact with them.

UNIVERSITY FENCING-SCHOOL.

Close to the main University buildings we observed a sign with the following inscription: "University Fencing-School." As a means of self-protection, every new student is expected to take lessons at this academy. He cannot, if insulted, knock down the man who insulted him, and fight it out on the green, but must be in readiness with his sword to encounter those who have been for a long time under instruction and practice. Fist-fighting is voted vulgar and unchivalric, and not such a mode of settling disputes as gentlemen should resort to. Hence the necessity of this department for study, which is regarded as under the patronage of the Professors. A young man who comes here and declines to take lessons is looked upon with suspicion, as he is supposed to have perfected himself in the "manly art" before leaving home. He is suspected of being an expert, which of itself is a sort of protection, almost equal to that obtained by the student who has proved himself superior to all his fellows in the handling of the weapon. No one being desirous to be the first to test his ability, gives him an immunity from insult. Many come thus prepared, and they are seldom troubled until the extent of their proficiency is known. It might be supposed that parents would keep their sons from such associations, but it must be remembered that there are few who come here under twenty-one years of age, and that many of them are their own masters. Then the University has a high reputation, and many parents think that the "rough and tumble" life which they lead here will best prepare them to encounter the trials and cares of the life upon which they are about to enter.

THE STUDENTS' PARTING.

This afternoon three or four of the members of these societies started for their homes, and they were accompanied to the depot by all the members still remaining here of the two prominent societies which are on good terms. They filled about twenty open barouches, and each had on the cap which they wear on important occasions, some with crimson worked all over with silver, and others of blue and silver. These caps are not much larger than an old-fashioned tea-cup, and seem to be fastened on the tops of their heads with strings, as they are all too small to stay there without some fastening. They were all in great glee, and brimming full of wine drunk at the parting dinner from which they had just arisen. At the depot they kissed each other in the most affectionate way, and parted with all manner of cordial greetings.

THE HEIDELBERG BRAND.

Whilst returning yesterday from our visit to the Castle of Heidelberg, we passed on the mountain-road six carriages filled with students, lying back in their seats and smoking, with their little skull-caps perched jockey-like on the sides of their heads. Having met them at a bend in the narrow road, they all had to stop whilst we passed, giving a good opportunity to scrutinize their countenances. Of the twenty-five, four had both broken noses and scars, three had their faces patched with strips of adhesive plaster, one had a black silk handkerchief tied around the upper portion of his forehead, and the faces of all the others but one had scars or cuts. They were, as usual, in a merry mood, and evidently intent upon a jollification at the restaurant in the castle-garden, which is kept open and the band playing until ten o'clock at night. They were all dressed elegantly, and were evidently aware of the aggregate good looks of the party. A few minutes after, as we reached the mountain-road overlooking the Neckar, our driver pointed out to us the restaurant on the other side of the river, beyond the bridge, a large white house, which he informed us was the place in which the students had rooms in which they fought all their duels. It is a restaurant, whither they also repair on the occasion of any extraordinary jollification. On our way to the depot we passed a restaurant where some fifty of them were assembled, arrayed in their silver-braided coats and caps, with a band of music, all hands accompanying the instruments with a merry bacchanalian song.

NOTE.—The following incident, which occurred at Heidelberg a few weeks after our visit, will satisfy the reader that there is no exaggeration in our statement of "Life at Heidelberg."

A game of cards, in which a human life was at stake, was played on the 9th of September, at the Ritter Hotel, Heidelberg, by four young students, one of whom, Silfred Meyer, was an American from Chicago. It appears that the four men had formerly been intimate friends, and they met, it seems, on the above day at the Swan Tavern, where they drank a good deal, and finally began to quarrel. One of them, Count Ottendorf, called Meyer a cowardly Jew, whereupon the latter promptly challenged him. Ottendorf accepted the challenge immediately. Meyer, in a tone of great excitement, proposed that all four should repair to the Ritter Hotel and there play a game of "sixty-six." The loser should shoot himself with a pistol. This proposition was accepted, and the four students repaired to the hotel. They ordered wine and cards to be brought up to a private room, and Ludeken, one of the four, procured two loaded pistols from a neighboring armorer. The four students dealt the cards, and Ottendorf and Meyer seated themselves, a pistol lying by the side of each. The first few minutes the game remained almost even. But when Meyer obtained a single advantage, Ottendorf, seeing that he was lost, suddenly jumped up, and exclaiming, "Adieu, my friends," seized his pistol and shot himself through the right temple. He fell a corpse to the floor, while his companions stood as if petrified for a moment, then hurried from the room. When the proprietor of the hotel hastened into the room, he found the dead count lying on the floor. He gave an alarm, and the police started in pursuit of the fugitive students. Late in the afternoon they succeeded in arresting Immich, who made the above statement. Meyer and Ludeken escaped across the French frontier. Ottendorf was the son of a wealthy landed proprietor in Westphalia. At the time of his death he was only nineteen.

DARMSTADT.

DARMSTADT, August 9, 1873.

We left Heidelberg, in the duchy of Baden, at noon yesterday, and in two hours were at Darmstadt, at the capital of the dukedom of Darmstadt, another of those petty principalities that still bar the way to a united Germany. The Duchess of Darmstadt is a sister of the Emperor of Russia, and the wife of the heir to the dukedom is the Princess Alice of England. These two influences alone prevented Prussia from wiping out this little dukedom and incorporating it in the kingdom of Prussia. England and Russia would have been offended, and hence Bismark contented himself with the control of the military power of Darmstadt, all of the soldiers of which are now clad in the full uniform of the Prussian service. Although still a dukedom, all the power and control of the diplomatic and military relations of the country are in the hands of Prussia.

THE CITY OF DARMSTADT.

This is a bright little city, more modern in its appearance than most of these old German cities. It was remodeled by the Grand Duke Ludwig in 1830, and has broad and well-paved streets running through it in all directions, and the buildings generally have a modern aspect. It has a population of thirty-nine thousand, and, with the exception of two thousand five hundred Catholics, it is a Protestant city. On the Louisenplatz, in the centre of the city, a very elegant monument of red sandstone, about one hundred and fifty feet high, has on it a statue of the Grand Duke Ludwig, erected "by his grateful people." It has several fine palaces, that of Prince Charles being handsomer and finer than that of the Grand Duke or of the Princess Alice, who is a great favorite with the people. But these palaces are tiresome to look at, and would be much more tiresome to the reader if we were to attempt to describe them. In the Schloss Palace there is a very fine collection of paintings, some seven hundred in number. In the first saloon there is a good collection of modern paintings, from the middle of the last century to the present day, which plainly shows that those of the present day are better even than those of the last century. The rest of the gallery is of the old Dutch and Italian schools, which are very fine in the eyes of those who can see nothing good or perfect in the present, and have no hopes for the future.

In the steeple of the Schloss Palace there is a very remarkable musical clock. About two minutes preceding the close of every hour the bells, of which there are about forty in the steeple, of all sizes, play an air, which is distinctly heard at night at our hotel, about two squares distant. It resembles the Swiss bell-ringers, and is very perfect in its performance.

THESE OLD TOWNS.

We have roamed over Darmstadt, as we have during the past week over Stuttgart and Heidelberg, and, with the exception of the palaces and the public squares, one looks as much like the other as two peas. The people, too, look and dress just as the people of Baltimore look and dress, and the ladies are pretty, in our eyes, everywhere. They are mostly blondes in this section of Germany, and are finely formed, with delicate expression of countenance and bright eyes. They dress with great neatness, and do not take to the gaudy colors to which the ladies in Austria are so partial.

In roaming through these old cities, eating breakfast in one and dinner in another, we feel at times a singular sensation of surprise that one is thus able "to hop, skip and jump" over the Old World. Sometimes we have to stop and think where we were yesterday, and the day before, and, waking up almost every morning in a strange hotel, we are puzzled at times to remember where we are to-day. Where we will be to-morrow, or next day, or next week, is always uncertain. The cholera having thrown us off of our track of travel, we are wandering about, without aim or destination. We may go to Frankfort, or we may go down the Rhine, to-morrow, just as the whim or notion may take us at the time of starting.

But to be walking on the streets and among the people of one country in the morning, and elbowing those of another in the afternoon, is an odd sensation, even to those accustomed to roam around the world. If the people would only dress different and look different, or build their houses in a different style, the novelty of travel would be much greater. But there, right around the square from our hotel, stands a building that looks very much like Guy's Hotel, though it lacks those modern steps of that popular establishment. The palace of the Princess Alice, at the opposite corner, with a sentry-box on either side of the front door, somewhat resembles the residence of Enoch Pratt, Esq., but it is not so handsome. The monument to the Grand Duke Ludwig, in the centre of the square, is like the

Washington Monument, only not so large or high, and of red sandstone instead of white marble. The palace of the Grand Duke, on the other side of the square, is too plain a building to compare with even our court-house, and the Post-Office, at the other corner, looks very much like that ancient structure which, in the olden days, stood on the corner of Baltimore and Liberty Streets, in which the Congress of the early days of the republic is said to have assembled. The large public building in the centre of the north side of the square looks very much as the old Fountain Inn on Light Street did in its palmy days; and the hotel in which we are taking our ease, although surrounded by such brilliant company, is an extremely plain three-story white stuccoed building, with a long row of garret-windows peeping out from its steep slate roof. These old cities not only resemble each other, but look just like a good many of our American cities, and the people who walk the streets might be transferred *en masse* into the streets of any of our large cities, and no one would suspect that there were any strangers in town, unless there should happen to be a few stray Turks among them. There is one thing, however, in which the meanest German city excels Baltimore, and that is in its street pavements, and the universal cleanliness in which the streets are kept. In this respect Darmstadt is worthy of a visit from our City Fathers.

RELIGIOUS TOLERATION.

South of the river Main, all Germany is devoutly Catholic, whilst north of that river the Protestants predominate, eleven-twelfths of the people of Darmstadt being anti-Catholic. Everywhere, however, we are happy to be able to state, the largest liberty in all spiritual matters is enjoyed. We entered an immense brown-stone church in Heidelberg the other day, with imposing steeple, and statues in the niches on the walls, which we supposed to be a Catholic cathedral. On entering we observed that it was divided in two parts by a wall in the centre, and actually discovered that one end of the church was Catholic and the other end Lutheran, both worshiping under the same roof. We remember last year at Interlaken, in Switzerland, to have met with something similar,—a Catholic and an Episcopal congregation assembling at one time under the same roof, within the walls of an old monastery. This is all so different from what was the case ten or twelve years ago, that it may be hailed as the commencement of a new era.

PROVISION STORES.

There is no regular meat-market in any of the German cities, and, with the exception of Stuttgart, we have not met with a market-house of any description. There is usually a public square set apart for a market, well paved with stone, but without even a shed or permanent stall upon it. The market-people merely set their baskets down and stand alongside of them, though some bring stalls with them, and have large umbrellas. All kinds of meat are obtained from the provision stores, which are very numerous, and are fitted up with great elegance. To look in at an American provision store on a warm day is enough to spoil one's appetite, but the German provision store makes a man hungry to look at it. The meat is displayed on white marble slabs, the windows are ornamented with specimens of meat, sausages, and other articles, with a little fountain playing over an urn full of gold-fish. There is an air of cleanliness and sweetness about the whole establishment, and the duty of salesman is usually performed by a bright, rosy-cheeked lass, who handles the weapons of her profession with all the skill of a professor. We always make it a rule to stop and look in at these neat little establishments, and wonder why it is that we, with our superabundance of ice, cannot present similar stores. Fruits and vegetables are not eaten here as with us. With the exception of pears, plums, and cherries, there is nothing in the markets, and these are in such limited quantities that one of our fruit-dealers at the Lexington or Marsh Market would monopolize the whole stock offered this morning to a population of forty thousand people. A pound of plums was an extensive sale to any one purchaser, and most satisfied themselves with a half-pound. Peaches are a curiosity, and are hard and sour. They are always sold at so many kreutzers apiece, and never by the measure. Truly, the American tourist deprives himself of many of the joys of life by spending his summer in Europe. Only think of the loss of cantaloupes, watermelons, peaches, and hot corn, and having to put up with a spoonful of strawberries or raspberries without cream.

TOBACCO AND CIGARS.

During the Southern rebellion, when tobacco got to a very high figure, all the

German States commenced experimenting on raising tobacco for themselves, and, although the quality is very inferior, an immense quantity is now raised, and every farmer grows sufficient for the consumption of himself and family. Between this city and Stuttgart we passed hundreds of acres of it, and it looks well on the field. The cheapness of cigars has almost driven the pipe out of use, as one is seldom seen now, except in the hands of some octogenarian who persists that the old mode of doing things is best. The cigars offered for sale in the stores, made of German tobacco, look well, and are of all shades of color, but no one need fear having his nerves troubled by smoking them. Their flavor is not bad, for the simple reason that they are nearly flavorless. The prices range from a half-kreutzer (about one-third of a cent) to ten kreutzers, and a person lighting one of them blindfolded could not tell whether it was the higher or lower article that he was smoking. A call for some of their best cigars last evening at a restaurant brought two on a plate for three kreutzers, and we came to the conclusion that they were among the best we had yet smoked. The probability is that they furnish all prices out of the same box, giving the purchaser the choice as to the price he may desire to pay. However, they are not bad cigars, and are pretty nearly equal to our American cigars at four dollars per hundred.

FEMALE CLERKS.

Throughout Germany, wherever females can be employed to advantage, they are taken in preference to young men. At Munich the clerks and bookkeepers in the banks are nearly all young and handsome girls. Like the female clerks in the Departments at Washington, beauty seems to be one of the requirements to secure an appointment. At the depots many of those who attend the windows for the sale of tickets are girls, and the cashiers in all the cafés and restaurants are of the same sex. They are generally very expert at figures, and in mental arithmetic have no superiors. In view of the fact that so many females are employed in the rougher and hardest descriptions of laboring work, it speaks well for the sex that they are seeking and securing more desirable and lucrative employment. It may possibly arise from the fact that the young men are generally of the "fast" order, and are not to be relied upon in positions of trust. We are under the impression in America that our young men are not as steady and staid as they ought to be, but they are miracles of steadiness compared to the average young men of Germany. The students at Heidelberg can give them a start of half a day and beat them before bedtime. They don't drink strong liquor; coffee, beer, or wine being the extent of their libations; but they devote the best part of the day to the café or the beer-saloon, reading the papers, playing billiards, chatting or studying the plates in the numerous satirical illustrated papers. How the many thousands of young men in Vienna obtain a living and good clothing, who are always to be found in the coffeehouses, is a mystery "that no fellow can find out." It is equally a wonder to the people of Vienna as it is to the stranger.

GERMAN BABIES.

The babies of Germany are not allowed as large a liberty as those of America. They are, for the better part of the first year of their earthly pilgrimage, tightly wound up in swaddling clothes, with both arms and legs pinioned, and carried about on a pillow especially made for the purpose. After they escape from their wrappings a bag of feathers is tied on their backs, so that when they tumble over they have something to fall upon. Those of the poorer classes are laid in a basket with a little bag of sugar in their mouths, and are expected to behave themselves without much further attention from mother or nurse. The nurses on the streets generally carry the babies in their arms on a pillow, and they are tied to it with pink ribbons, lying as still and as motionless as if they were little mummies. They cannot kick or use their arms, and evidently they are not allowed to know during their puling days what their legs and arms are intended for. We don't think that our babies would stand it, as we observe that German ladies when they come to America don't attempt to practice any such tyranny on their babies.

FRANKFORT-ON-THE-MAIN.

FRANKFORT-ON-THE-MAIN, August 9, 1873.

Being within but thirty minutes' travel of this enterprising and prosperous city, we could not withstand the temptation, notwithstanding the excessive heat, of taking a run down this morning from

Darmstadt, for a rapid view of its many attractions. The heat must have been away up among the nineties, as it was undoubtedly the hottest day we have yet experienced during our three months' tour through Germany. Securing a carriage at the depot, and a very intelligent driver, he took us on a round through the various attractive parts of the city and suburbs.

THE CITY OF FRANKFORT.

Frankfort-on-the-Main has a population of over eighty thousand, which Baedeker sets down at sixty thousand Protestants, eleven thousand Catholics, and eight thousand Jews. It was until 1866 one of the free towns of the German Confederation, but it is now under the Prussian government. Old watch-towers indicate the extent of the ancient city in which the Emperors were elected and crowned. It is situated in a spacious plain, bounded by mountains, on the river Main, which is navigable for vessels of considerable size, and a source of great commercial advantage. The public grounds and promenades encircle the old city on three sides, and are splendidly laid out and adorned with flowers and shade-trees. Like all the German cities in modern times, the space formerly occupied by fortifications, walls, moats, and parade-grounds has been used to ornament the city, which has largely outgrown its former dimensions. Bordering these public grounds a succession of magnificent private villas and mansions have been erected, surrounded by gardens and the finest floral display, which gives to the city an air of wealth, indicative of the success and extent of its commercial relations.

The business sections of the city are very fine, the streets being broad, and the houses generally constructed of a light pink or red sandstone. The retail stores are elegant and attractive, one of the surest signs of the wealth of a city.

The old portions of the city are full of quaint and antiquated houses, many of them doubtless several centuries old. Some of the streets are so narrow that two vehicles cannot pass, whilst the houses tower up to the height of four or five stories. The spirit of improvement is gradually invading these antiquated places, and new and spacious streets are being opened, and fine modern buildings erected.

THE MONUMENTS.

The most famous monument in Frankfort, which all strangers are sure to visit, is that of Gutenberg, the inventor of printing. On the pedestal, which is about twenty feet high, stand three bronze figures. The central one, with types in the left hand, is Gutenberg, with Faust on his right and Schöffer on his left. On the frieze are thirteen likenesses of celebrated printers, Caxton among them. In four niches beneath are the arms of the four towns where printing with types was first introduced: Mentz, Frankfort, Venice, and Strasburg. On four separate pedestals are figures representing Theology, Poetry, Natural History, and Industry. The heads of four animals, which serve as water-spouts, indicate the four quarters of the globe and the universal diffusion of the invention.

Near this monument in the Goetheplatz is Schwanthaler's monument of Goethe, this being the city in which he was born. The poet holds a wreath of laurels in his left hand. The pedestal is covered with bas-reliefs, emblematic of his literary productions, Faust and Mephistopheles, etc. We were also shown the house in which Goethe was born, which bears an inscription recording the birth of the poet on the 28th of August, 1749. It is open for public inspection, and the rooms facing the court are pointed out as those in which he wrote his Götz and Werther, and as the scene of the adventures which render his biography so interesting.

We also visited the monument to Schiller, which is a plain pedestal, with his statue surmounting it in bronze. The Hessian monument, erected by Frederick William II. of Prussia "to the brave Hessians who fell victorious on the spot in December, 1792, fighting for the Fatherland," is very peculiar. It consists of masses of rocks, on which a pillar stands, surmounted by a helmet, sword, and ram's head, the latter emblematical of the attack made upon Frankfort by the Hessians, then occupied by the French under Custine. Their remains rest here, and on the pillar their names are all recorded in letters of gold.

THE JEWISH QUARTER.

Frankfort is famed for its old Jewish Quarter, and the carriage-drivers take all strangers through it as one of the curiosities of the city. As early as the twelfth century many Jews settled here, and founded this street in 1642, which, until 1806, had a gate at each end of it, which was closed and locked at nights, after which no Jew could venture into any part of the town, under a heavy penalty. The house in which the senior Rothschild lived, and in which the present generation of this opulent family was born, was pointed out to us, as well as the dwelling and birthplace of the great Baring family, who now rule kings and princes by the power of their wealth. The houses of this quarter are very peculiar in their construction, being a combination of stone and wood, four stories high, and generally not more than eight or ten feet in width. Many of them are in such a dilapidated condition that they are closed up, the authorities having compelled the removal of the tenants, for fear they would be crushed in the ruins. The houses on the opposite side of the street have all recently been removed for the same reason, most of them having fallen down, and as many as twenty-three were killed in one house. In a short time this old quarter will entirely disappear, though the locality is permanently marked by a fine Jewish synagogue and the Jewish Hospital, founded in 1830 by the Rothschild family, who have also built recently a magnificent hospital for all creeds in Vienna, which is regarded as the model hospital for the world.

ARIADNE ON THE PANTHER.

We have not viewed anything in the way of art, during our tour, which gave so much satisfaction as on the occasion of a visit made this morning to Bethmann's Museum, a circular building erected for the purpose of exhibiting Dannecker's exquisite groupe of Ariadne on the Panther, a work regarded as the youthful sculptor's masterpiece, which would add to the laurels of any living or dead artist. It is the property of a wealthy banker of Frankfort, who has put up this building for its exhibition, there being no charge for admission, except a trifling donation to the custodian. In order that the visitor may be able to compare this modern masterpiece with the works of the ancients, its owner has procured casts of Achilles, Silenus with the young Bacchus, Germanicus, the Gladiator, Laocoön, Apollo Belvedere, Venus de Medici, and Diana of Versailles,—all taken from the originals.

The Ariadne is exhibited under a pink canopy, through which the light from above penetrates, and, as it is slowly turned on its pedestal, the perfection and beauty of the figure are truly marvelous. The reflection makes it almost seem like flesh and blood. The position and ease of the figure have given it a world-wide renown, and the building was surrounded by carriages of visitors, among whom were many Americans.

EMIGRATION AND MILITARY SERVICE.

In the little province or dukedom of Darmstadt, in which we have sojourned for a few days, the military is, as elsewhere in Germany, an important part of the population. The territory of Darmstadt is about equal to that of the State of Maryland, or somewhere between Delaware and Maryland, but it is required to keep, always ready for the field, thirty thousand well-drilled troops of the different branches of the service. The standing army of Darmstadt is, to-day, on the peace-footing, nearly equal to all the Federal troops of the United States, even with the Modoc war on hand, and an extensive boundary to protect from Indian incursions. The officers are all very fine-looking men, most of them of good stature, and are dressed with great elegance in bright new Prussian uniforms. They nearly all wear the iron cross, as do many of the men, indicative of personal bravery in the recent war with France.

The military law in Darmstadt requires every man to serve three years in the army, from eighteen, if of sufficient stature, to twenty-one. For the next nine years he is in the reserve, required to report for monthly drill and inspection, and in case of war to hasten at once to the standard of his regiment. Each man knows where to find his place and his officer and who stands next to him in the ranks. Thus it was that the landwehr, as it was called, followed the regulars in solid phalanx, and enabled Prussia to overpower France. They were better drilled and more experienced soldiers than the regular army, each man having served three years and been regularly held under military supervision. The only escape from this military service is emigration; and as most men are too young to emigrate before they are eighteen, and have no means to emigrate when they are twenty-one, having received literally nothing but food and clothing for their three years' service, they are compelled to become mere military chattels. Many remain permanently in the army, as the only pursuit they have any knowledge of. Whilst emigration to America is the great earthly heaven of all the poorer classes of Germany, it is only the few who are ever able to accumulate sufficient money to enable them to leave. When you see on the street an emigrant followed by his wife and children, you see a brave and determined man, who has overcome more difficulties to get where he is than most of us are required to encounter in our earthly pilgrimage. In the cities there are young men's associations for emigration, and also in the country towns. They each contribute to the funds of the association a few kreutzers per week, and when the treasury is sufficiently replenished to pay the passage of one or more the ticket is purchased, and lots are cast among the members as to who shall have it. Thus it is that some of the young men reach America; but most of them come through the aid of funds sent to them from America by friends who have gone before them.

PUBLIC GARDENS.

From the Römer we proceeded to the Zoological Gardens, which are very extensive, but the collection of large animals is not equal to some we have viewed in other cities. It is a beautiful resort, and the evening concerts and a good restaurant attract throngs of people, who assemble here to take their suppers and listen to the music. Nobody in Germany will eat without a musical accompaniment, if they can help it.

The Garden of Palms, about a mile from the city limits, is another great attraction, where music and good eating add to its charms. It takes its name from having an immense crystal palace in its centre, in which are growing all the varieties of tropical palm-trees, just as they can be seen in Cuba. It was formerly the private property of the Duke of Nassau, but has been purchased by the city as a public resort. In all the German cities a resort of this kind is gotten up by the authorities, and the expense borne by charging a small admission-fee. A city passenger railway traverses the city, and passes out the road upon which both of these gardens are located.

BEET SUGAR.

It is not generally known by the rest of the world that the people of the Old World depend upon the sugar-beet for the manufacture of nearly all the sugar they use. This is the case on the Continent, and even in France, every farmer raising as part of his crop the sugar-beet, which meets with ready sale at the sugar-houses; though most of the farmers raise their own sugar. It would be difficult to produce a more pure article from the sugar-cane than that furnished at the hotels and for sale in the stores. It is generally in small, square cakes, though it is also manufactured in long, cone-shaped loaves, like our best sugar, and sold at about the same price as in America. Along the road between Darmstadt and Munich fully one-third of the growing crop was the sugar-beet.

DOWN THE RHINE.

We start down the Rhine from Mayence this morning, and will be in Paris to-morrow, having sojourned for precisely three months on German soil and among German-speaking people.

DOWN THE RHINE.

ON THE RHINE, August 9, 1873.

We left Darmstadt at half-past seven o'clock this morning, after an early breakfast, for Mayence, and within an hour we were on board the steamer Humboldt on the Rhine, awaiting our departure down the Rhine to Cologne, with between two and three hundred other tourists. The boat, which is built like our ordinary American river boats, and about two hundred feet in length, was literally crowded. The promenade-deck, which extends the whole length of the vessel, is covered with awnings; and here were the choice positions for which every one was struggling. To give some idea of the number of tourists now swarming over Europe, it is only necessary to state that three boats leave Mayence for Cologne every morning, one having started an hour before our arrival, and another was to start one hour after our departure. These are what are called first-class boats; but there are others of a smaller class that start higher up the river, and stop for passengers at all the small places on the route. In addition to all this flood of travel, the two lines of railway, one on each side of the river, flying along at the water's edge, carry as many passengers as they can accommodate. The railroad time from Mayence to Cologne is six hours, while the fastest boats take nine hours. They must necessarily have powerful engines to enable them to make the up trip against the current, and consequently they go down stream with great rapidity.

OUR FELLOW-PASSENGERS.

This is the second time within a twelve-month that it has been our fortune to pass down the Rhine, and we have not been able on either occasion to go into an ecstasy of enthusiasm over its great wonders. We this time fortified our imagination by reading Kiefer's Legends of the Rhine, but found them to be a collection of impossible and improbable stories, in which an effort is made to people the walls and ramparts of the old castles with spirits and fairies, gnomes and devils. Being exceedingly matter-of-fact in our temperament, we threw Kiefer overboard, and with Baedeker in one hand, and an opera-glass in the other, we stood on the watch for something that would startle us. But, gentle reader, we were not startled, and of all the throng of passengers going down stream with us, we do really believe that we were more deeply interested than any one of them. About one-third of the whole number were eating and drinking all the way from Mayence to Cologne. The German rule is, "when you have nothing else to do, always eat," and, as three-fourths of all on board were Germans, the waiters had a busy time of it. We noticed every bend in the river, every change in the conformation of its towering rocks, the ledging of the mountain-sides to form shelves for the growth of the vine, and the remnants of towers and castles. But the great mass of our passengers were apparently as little interested in the moving panorama as if they had been born on the Rhine and its beauties had lost their attractions. A little knot of enthusiasts, mostly English and Americans, had fixed themselves near the bow of the boat, where they could see either side of the river at a glance.

FROM MAYENCE TO BINGEN.

We left the wharf at Mayence at nine o'clock, and for the first two hours, until we reached Bingen, the Rhine is about as plain and unpretending a river as the Ohio. It has a few venerable-looking old towns, whilst those on the Ohio are bright and beautiful, and for the first two hours the Ohio has decided advantage. The river-banks are hidden from view either by bushes or marshes, and may be very beautiful if the deck was only high enough to see over them. Thus it is that when taking to the Rhine, even as low down as Mayence, a feeling of disappointment comes over the tourist. He had heard of the wonders of the Rhine, and imagined that it was all wonderful, all startling, and that he was to encounter a succession of such grand and ecstatic scenery as can be found nowhere else in the wide world. For two hours after leaving Mayence, there is but little to admire, excepting a few fine villas, built close to the water's edge, and surrounded by gardens and shrubbery. Small towns with their steeples can occasionally be seen on the high grounds in the distance, but the banks of the river are generally low and flat.

At eleven o'clock, after two hours' run, we approached Bingen, which the poets have described as "Sweet Bingen on the Rhine." It is a very small town, of six thousand inhabitants, and, as viewed from the river, has a very ancient appearance. It is at the mouth of the river Nahe, which forms the boundary between the dominions of the Duke of Darmstadt and Prussia. The scenery around it is very fine, and perhaps the poet had this in her mind when she went into ecstasies over Bingen. On a mountain-side, directly over it, are the ruins of the old castle of Klopp, and on the other side the mountains of Rochusberg and Elisenhöhe, on the latter of which is a very fine Gothic château. Here, however, at Bingen, commences the beautiful scenery of the Rhine, with its vine-clad mountains, and old towers, fortresses, and castles. It is that portion of the Rhine between Bingen and Coblentz, where the river forces its way through the mountains on either side, the passage of which in the olden time was controlled by the robber nobles, who lived in these old castles, and exacted toll from all vessels passing them, amusing themselves with occasionally cutting each other's throats and storming and taking possession of the castles of their enemies. In our day they would be called pirates or freebooters, but history proclaims them noble, some of them saints, and monuments to some of them are still standing in the towns in the vicinity.

FROM BINGEN TO COBLENTZ.

This is the only portion of the river that can be called attractive. We passed Bingen at eleven o'clock, and at one o'clock the majestic fortress of Ehrenbreitstein, which is justly termed the Gibraltar of the Rhine, directly opposite the city of Coblentz, loomed up before us. Thus the beauties of the Rhine are all viewed in two hours' travel, as below

Coblentz the river widens to the extent of about one mile, and with the exception of the seven mountains, as we approach Cologne, its shores are generally low and flat. Most of the German tourists stop a few days at each of the prominent points on this portion of the river, changing their location after pedestrian tours among the ruins of the old castles and the surrounding mountains.

Opposite the castle of Klopp, near Bingen, on a rock in the middle of the Rhine, is the Mouse-Tower, which derives its name from the well-known legend of Bishop Hatto, who built this tower as a sort of custom-house, where tolls were forcibly levied on all passing vessels. He was a great tyrant, and during a famine which prevailed bought up all the food in the district and sold it at such exorbitant prices that the people soon had no more money, and were in a starving condition. They sent to the bishop a large delegation, begging for bread, hinting that they would take it by force if he did not give it to them. He received them very affably, and told them to go to a barn, where they would be supplied, but no sooner were they in the doors, than he closed and locked them, and set fire to the barn. On hearing their howling cries of pain, he exclaimed, "Hear how the corn-mice squeak. I treat rebels as I do mice; when I catch them I burn them." The legend goes on to say that out of the ashes of the barn came legions of mice, which swarmed through the castle, compelling his retainers all to fly, and finally to escape them the bishop proceeded to his tower in the river, but the insatiable mice followed him, and finally gnawed the flesh off his bones. This is a sample of the legends of these old Rhine castles; but there stand the ruins of the castle and of the tower, and, if the story be true, the old fellow deserved to be eaten up, even if he was not.

The next tower is Ehrenfels, which was erected in 1210. The steep slopes of the neighboring mountains form one of the finest wine-districts of the Rhine. These mountain-sides look from the river as if planted almost to their summits with pea-vines. Concerning this castle of Ehrenfels there is a love-legend, in which a horse is the hero. His mistress was being taken to church by her cruel father to marry her to a wicked knight. Just as they reached the church-door, the horse, instigated by the saints, to whom the girl had prayed, ran away, and carried her to the castle of her true love, both the father and the bad knight having fallen and broken their necks in the effort to overtake her.

The castle of Falkenburg comes next, an immense ruin, which was built by one of the boldest robbers of the Rhine; then follows the tall tower of Sonneck, which commanded the entrance to a ravine. Sonneck belongs to the Prussian royal family, and has recently been entirely restored, as one of a number of the finest of these old ruins.

Near the village of Lorchhausen, six hundred feet above it, on the mountain-side, are the ruins of the castle of Nollingen, of which the legend records that a knight of the Lord, with the assistance of certain mountain-spirits, once scaled the Devil's Ladder, leading up to it, on horseback, and thus gained the hand of his lady-love. On a rocky eminence below this rise the picturesque ruins of the castle of Fürstenburg, which was several times rebuilt and destroyed during the last eight hundred years. In 1700, the French blew it up for the last time. These ruins, as well as those of the great castle of Stahleck, which next come to view, belong to the royal family of Prussia, and it is the intention to rebuild and restore them all as nearly as practicable to their ancient condition.

Above the town of Caub, rising in the middle of the Rhine, appears the castle of Pfalz, reminding one of the Château d'If, on the Mediterranean. It was erected in the beginning of the thirteenth century, as a toll-house for exacting tribute from passing vessels. This castle has also a love-legend connected with it.

The stately castle of Gutenfels, which must have been one of the largest on the Rhine, rises behind the town of Caub. History says that it was there, in 1269, that the English Earl of Cornwall, then Emperor of Germany, became enamored of the beautiful Countess Beatrix of Falkenstein, and married her. Next come the picturesque ruins of the castle of Schönberg, the birthplace of Marshal Schönberg, who fell in the battle of the Boyne, and whose remains are buried in Westminster Abbey. The imposing rocks of the Lurley were next pointed out to us, connected with which is the well-known legend of the siren who had her dwelling in the rock, and, like the sirens of old, enticed sailors and fishermen to their destruction in the rapids at the foot of the precipice. This has long been a favorite theme for the poet and the painter. Next comes the castle of Katz, but it is insignificant as compared with the ruins of Rheinfels, three hundred and ninety-three feet above the Rhine, rising back of the town of St. Goar, which in 1692 successfully withstood a siege of fifteen months by an army of twenty-four thousand men. Thurmberg and Deuzenberg, near the town of Welmich, erected in 1363, is also an extensive ruin, and must have been a most formidable castle.

The next point of interest is the town of Bornhofen, on a rocky eminence, above which are the castles of Sonnenberg and Liebenstein, better known as the Brothers, connected by a short chine of rock. The legend of these castles is that Conrad and Heinrich, sons of the Knight Bayer von Boffard, owner of Liebenstein, were both enamored of their foster-sister, the beautiful Hildegarde. With rare generosity, Heinrich tore himself away and joined the crusades, leaving his brother Conrad to win the prize. The old knight built the castle of Sonnenberg for their reception, but, his death occurring before its completion, the nuptials were postponed. Meanwhile, Conrad's heart grew cold towards Hildegarde, and, hearing of the valiant deeds of his absent brother, he joined the crusades. Hildegarde, brooding over her sad lot, but not doubting the love and return of Conrad, passed her days in the lonely castle of Liebenstein. Suddenly Conrad returned with a Grecian wife, and Hildegarde, stunned by the blow, shut herself up in her castle, refusing to see any one. Late one night, Heinrich, hearing of the perfidy of his brother, returned to avenge his foster-sister's wrongs. He challenged Conrad to single combat; but, just as the brothers' swords crossed, Hildegarde's figure interposed between them and insisted on a reconciliation, to which they reluctantly consented. Hildegarde then retired to the convent at the base of the rocks. Conrad's Grecian wife soon proved unfaithful, and he, overcome with shame and remorse, threw himself on his generous brother's breast, and abandoned his castle, after which they lived together in harmony and retirement at Liebenstein.

The castle of Marksburg next looms up, near Braubach, and is a very imposing ruin. Konigsstuhl, which was the castle where emperors were elected, treaties concluded, etc., near Kapellan, has been partly rebuilt. The castle of Lahneck, behind Oberlahnstein, is owned by an Irish gentleman, Mr. Moriarty, who has rebuilt it, and occupies it as his country villa. The next and the last of the old castles of the Rhine is Stolzenfels, near Kapellan, which has been completely restored, at an expense of a quarter of a million of dollars, and attracts numerous visitors. Next we approach Coblentz, where the narrow and beautiful portion of the Rhine terminates, the river spreading out to more than a mile in width, with low and level shores, dotted here and there by cities and towns. The grandest and most imposing view on the river, however, is that of Coblentz and the immense castle and fortress of Ehrenbreitstein. The Rhine is here spanned by two bridges, one of boats, and the other an iron railroad-bridge. Ehrenbreitstein is an immense affair: it was first built in 1018, but has since been enlarged and strengthened and rebuilt, at the cost of many millions of dollars. It is on a precipitous rock four hundred feet above the Rhine, and is unapproachable on three sides, whilst the exposed side is defended by double lines of bastions. It has stood many a siege, and was once captured by the French and blown up, but they were afterwards compelled to pay three millions of dollars to the Prussian government for its restoration.

BRIDGES OF BOATS.

On our trip to Cologne we have passed half a dozen of these bridges, which are similar to those used by our army during the war, though of much larger proportions. They are opened for the passage of vessels by floating out a section of the boats, and require a large force of men to be in constant attendance to draw them back into their places against the rapid current. They are, however, very cheap in their construction, and where labor is so low and abundant as it is in Germany, the attendance of the draw may not be so very costly.

The vessels used upon the river are very much like canal-boats, except that they are about three hundred feet long. They float down stream with the tide, and occasionally use their sails, but in ascending the river have to be towed by steamers, which are very powerful, and draw after them a half-dozen of these vessels laden with coal or merchandise.

ENGLISH TOURISTS.

Among our passengers were a large number of young Englishmen, returning from the tour of Switzerland. They were all gotten up in approved Alpine outfit,—shoes with heavy nails, pants to the knees, and blue woolen stockings, short shooting-jacket, round-top felt hat, with a white scarf or a blue veil around the crown, hanging down behind, and alpenstock in hand. They had spent their time at the public resorts, but all admitted that they had climbed no mountains. "It's such denced hard work, you know," was their response to our inquiry. They had looked at the Jungfrau from Interlaken, got a glimpse of Mont Blanc from Geneva, and sailed upon the lakes.

A RHINE DINNER.

Having reached Coblentz at one o'clock, the bell summoned us to dinner, and a meaner dinner no civilized company was ever before asked to partake of. They have American boats on the Rhine, but no dinner that an American can eat. The roast beef had done previous duty in the soup-pot, and the juice of the decayed stewed plums was served up as sauce for a brown-bread pudding. There were eight courses, and when the plates were removed the knife and fork was left to do duty throughout the meal. Up and down the table every man and woman could be seen between every course scouring knife and fork on their napkins, which, when the meal was over, all resembled greasy dishcloths. We would advise all who go down the Rhine to carry some crackers and cheese with them, and with a bottle of Rhine wine they can make a much better dinner than the boat can afford. The Germans were generally thus provided, and kept clear of *table-d'hôte* dinner. By the time dinner was over, we were within an hour's run of Cologne, where we are now about to land, at half-past four o'clock in the afternoon.

THE RHINE EXAGGERATIONS.

It is the historical events connected with these old castles that give to the Rhine most of the interest with which it is viewed. The mountain scenery, the vine-clad hills, and the old castles between Bingen and Coblentz are well worth seeing, but they lack the natural grandeur and ornamentation of the mountains of Lake Como, or the rural and scenic beauty of Lake Lucerne and Lake Zurich. In order to appreciate the beauties of the Rhine we were assured that we ought to have seen it before going to Switzerland, and, we might have added, before seeing the Hudson, Lake George, and Lake Ontario. To view the Rhine you must go down stream on a rapid steamer, fourteen hours; and were it not for the historical associations of the ruins and the castles, and the poetical fancies of Byron and Southey, we think that the Rhine would never have obtained the fame it has for unrivaled attractions. It has become the custom, the world over, to speak of the Rhine as the most beautiful of all rivers, but we think there are few Americans who will admit that it is superior to the Hudson, or few honest travelers who will claim for it any equality with the lake scenery of Italy and Switzerland. The Königs-See, which we visited a few weeks since, with its precipitous mountains seven thousand feet high, and its wonderful mountain echo, swelling the explosion of a pistol to clap after clap of rolling and reverberating crashes of thunder, caused a feeling of ecstasy as something above and beyond our expectations; but we have been unable to get up any ecstatic feeling of surprise at the scenes and sights of the Rhine. It is fine, but not grand, and does not come up to the high expectations of the tourist, who has been reading such startling and poetic descriptions of it from his school-days. The greater portion of the trip is rather tiresome on a crowded boat, six of the eight hours being little more than ordinary river sailing, with little to claim the attention but a wearisome waste of water.

CITY OF COLOGNE.

COLOGNE, August 11, 1873.

We arrived at Cologne at dusk last evening, and never in all our travels were we beset by such a horde of ravenous porters, commissioners, and hack-drivers. They seized hold of and endeavored to drag our valises out of our hands, and succeeded in so thoroughly separating our party that it was ten or fifteen minutes before we got together again. When that was accomplished, our luggage was scattered we knew not whither, and, what seemed most strange, the finely uniformed and accoutred police seemed to encourage them in their rascality. After much tribulation, we finally got into a carriage, and paid the gang of meddlers all the small change we had, when we discovered that one of the trunks was not in the carriage. We called to the driver to put it up, when it was seized by another porter and put upon the top of the carriage, who came to the door and demanded pay for doing so. We gave him two small

German coins, all that we had left, when he demanded more, and his tongue clattered like a wild man's, as he jerked open the carriage-door and made motions and gestures as if he was about to attempt to drag us out of the vehicle. One of the military police came up and sustained the porter, when we pulled the carriage-door to and called to the driver to go on. We finally got off; and when we arrived at the hotel the driver demanded the pay for the porter, and we settled with him with the aid of the hotel-keeper, giving him much less than the coin we had in hand ready to pay him for his service alone.

VIEW OF THE CITY.

We succeeded in getting excellent quarters at the Hotel Disch, and started out early this morning to view the city. We found the streets very narrow, and the pavements in front of the houses seldom more than two feet in width, the pedestrians taking to the streets along with the horses. The stores on these narrow streets are very fine, and the display of goods equal to that found in almost any European city. But the streets proved such a labyrinth, winding to the right and left every hundred yards, that it was with difficulty we could find our way. At no time can the eye command the prospect half a square in advance, and the stranger must roam about at random amid the almost inextricable maze. The houses are well built, and the city very clean, although Coleridge many years ago wrote of it:

"Ye nymphs who reign over sewers and sinks,
The river Rhine, it is well known,
Doth wash your city of Cologne;
But tell me, nymphs, what power divine
Shall henceforth wash the river Rhine?"

Since Coleridge wrote these lines, a great change has taken place, and we can bear witness that the Cologne of to-day is a sweet-smelling city, and worthy of its fame as the great depot for the manufacture of *eau de Cologne*, the liquid of all Christendom. This article is here manufactured in all its purity, and is exported in very large quantities. We looked in vain in the windows of the different establishments for the "Grand Duchess," which we presume is manufactured exclusively for the Baltimore market.

The population of Cologne is about one hundred and thirty thousand, including that of its suburb Deutz, with which it is connected by a bridge of boats. It is the third city in importance in the kingdom of Prussia, and is built in the form of a crescent, which may account for its crooked streets. The walls of the city form a circuit of nearly seven miles, and are strongly fortified.

CATHEDRAL OF COLOGNE.

This immense structure, which looms up so high over the surrounding buildings, is the only guide-post which the stranger has to assist him in threading his way through its labyrinth of streets. It is the glory of Cologne, and when completed will almost rival the great Cathedral of Milan as a specimen of Gothic architecture, although its spires will reach a much greater altitude. It was commenced over six hundred years ago, but is still unfinished. The work is now rapidly progressing, nearly two million dollars having been expended upon it during the past forty years by the kings of Prussia, and we could see that much work has been done since we visited it last year. The face of the marble of that portion first constructed is crumbling with age, whilst the rest of the building seems entirely new. The body of the structure is completed, and the work is now progressing upon the towers. The two main ones, when completed, will be five hundred and seven feet high. The length of the building is five hundred feet, its breadth two hundred and thirty, and the height of the choir one hundred and sixty one. There is a society formed, with branches all over Europe, for the purpose of soliciting money for the completion of this cathedral, it being estimated that about one million dollars more will be required for that purpose.

Behind the high altar is the Chapel of the Magi, or the three Kings of Cologne. We were assured by the custodian that the silver case contains the bones of the three wise men who came from the East to Bethlehem to offer their presents to the infant Christ, and that the case, which is ornamented with precious stones, and the surrounding valuables in the chapel, are worth six million dollars. The remains of the wise men are said to have been presented to the Archbishop of Cologne by the Emperor Barbarossa, when he captured the city of Milan, which at that time possessed these wonderful relics. The skulls of the Magi, crowned with diamonds, with their names written in rubies, are shown to the curious on the payment of six francs by a party, and charges are made for admission to the choir and gallery. Among the numerous relics exhibited in the sacristy is a bone of St. Matthew, whose bones seem to be scattered all over Europe. In the Chapel of St. Agnes there are some very fine paintings, including one of St. Ursula, with her seven thousand virgins.

RELICS OF ST. URSULA.

Cologne abounds in sacred relics, and those in the Church of St. Ursula present one of the most remarkable sights in Christendom. The tradition of St. Ursula is this: She was the daughter of the King of Brittany, who sailed up the Rhine as far as Basle, and then, accompanied by eleven thousand virgins, made a pilgrimage to Rome. From Basle she traveled on foot, and was received with great honors at the holy city by the Pope. On her return the whole party was barbarously murdered by the Huns because they refused to break their vows of chastity. St. Ursula was accompanied by her lover, Conan, and an escort of knights. St. Ursula and Conan suffered death in the camp of the Emperor Maximin. Ursula was placed in the Calendar as the patron saint of chastity, and the bones of all the attendant virgins were gathered together, and the present church erected to contain the sacred relics. On every side you turn, skulls and arm- and leg-bones meet your eye, piled on shelves built in the wall. In every direction these hideous relics stare you in the face. Hood says it is the chastest kind of architecture. St. Ursula herself is exhibited in a coffin which is surrounded by the skulls of a few of her favorite attendants. The room in which she is laid contains numerous other relics; among these are the chains with which St. Peter was bound, and one of the clay vessels used by the Saviour at the marriage in Cana. We saw two other chains with which St. Peter was bound in Rome.

HO! FOR PARIS.

We start this evening for Paris, and expect to spend a few weeks in that beautiful city.

FRANCE.

THE CITY OF PARIS.

HOTEL DE L'ATHÉNÉE, PARIS, Aug. 12, 1873.

We left Cologne at half-past ten o'clock at night, and reached the Paris depot at ten o'clock on Sunday morning. On our way to the hotel we observed that many of the stores were open and their goods displayed, whilst workmen were busily pursuing their avocations, such as house-building, street-paving, etc., though the great mass of the population were on the streets, moving about in their Sunday attire.

GAYETY OF PARIS.

Paris never appeared more "gay and happy" than it is at present. The people are rejoicing over the departure of the German troops from the provinces, and the payment of the last installment of the indemnity to Prussia. The days of their humiliation, which they have borne with commendable fortitude, have passed, and they now look forward to revenge and retribution. They are justly proud of the bravery they have exhibited under adversity, as well as of the recuperative power of the nation which has been so strongly displayed. Whilst engaged in paying this enormous indemnity, the work of restoring and beautifying Paris has gone steadily on, with a determination that every outward mark of her humiliation shall be removed as rapidly as possible. The rebuilding of the Tuileries has not been checked, but the mansard roofs are now to have frameworks of iron instead of wood.

The great and crowning work of restoration has been commenced in the Place Vendôme. The base left of the Vendôme column has now erected around it, and towering above it, a massive scaffolding to the altitude of two hundred feet, and a throng of men were yesterday at work putting up the tackling and guy-ropes necessary for the commencement of its erection. The large open space around the column has been inclosed with a high fence, and inside of this inclosure the stone and plates, many of the latter having been recast, are being piled up preparatory to the work of reconstruction. One year more, and the Vendôme column will be restored, and the question will in the mean time be decided whether it will be again surmounted by a statue of Napoleon or the Goddess of Liberty. The work on the Academy of Music has also steadily progressed, and it is thought that in one year more the ornamental work of the interior will be completed.

PARIS AND VIENNA.

The hotels of Paris are doing a much more extensive business than those of Vienna, notwithstanding the great Exposition. To secure rooms in any of the large hotels here, it is necessary to telegraph in advance of your arrival. Visitors to Paris come to make a prolonged stay, whilst those going to Vienna rush through the Exposition and immediately pack their trunks for departure. The Exposition, instead of benefiting Vienna, will be a permanent injury to it, and Paris will be more popular than ever. It is the only city in Europe that could have rivaled Paris, but it has lost its opportunity. There are hundreds of Americans here who have given up all idea of going to Vienna, mainly on account of the bad reputation it has secured for itself in the matter of plundering strangers. Paris has profited by the fate of Vienna, and is more fair and liberal than ever in its treatment of tourists. There are no complaints in any quarter, and the cost of living is less here than it was last year.

PARIS BY GAS-LIGHT.

The boulevards of Paris, extending for miles through almost all sections of the city, present a gay scene at night. The thousands of cafés, brilliant with gas-jets, have their tables out on the broad pavements, and from eight to ten o'clock in the evening it is difficult to obtain a seat at any of them. Ice-cream and coffee is the extent of the Parisian's indulgence, though a few add a little cognac to their coffee. They spend their summer evenings in promenading the boulevards and occasionally stopping for a cup of their favorite beverage. The sidewalks of the boulevards are at least thirty-five feet wide, and in many prominent places women are stationed along the curb-stones with chairs to rent, on which those who are tired may for a few centimes rest themselves and view the promenaders as they pass. The broad streets are also filled with carriages, so that it is difficult to effect a crossing. They are required by law to have their lamps burning. Strangers in the city who wish to view these gas-light scenes generally engage carriages and drive slowly through the different boulevards, and vast numbers of carriages are constantly passing to and from the various places of amusement. Everybody seems happy and intent upon enjoyment. The people of Vienna are equally fond of this out-door life, but prefer to assemble in the gardens and listen to the music of their unrivaled bands. Eating, and drinking beer and coffee, seem to employ all the leisure hours of the Viennese. They seldom care to walk, the streets of Vienna being comparatively deserted at night, and most of the stores closed. The very reverse is the case in Paris. The stores are not only brilliantly lighted, but nearly all of them have rows of gas-lights on the outside, making the streets almost as light as day. The display of the stores last night on the Boulevard des Capucines exceeded anything we had ever before seen even in Paris. It seemed as if all the goods in the grand central building of the Vienna Exposition were spread among these magnificent establishments. The tasteful arrangement of the goods, the disposition of the lights, and the reflection in the side-glasses with which the shop-windows are always provided, presented a continuous spectacle of surpassing beauty. Ten years ago the Palais Royal was the great central attraction of Paris, but the boulevard stores have so greatly excelled these small establishments that it is now comparatively deserted at night. The hundreds of jewelers' windows were sparkling with diamonds and precious stones, and even the fancy and dry-goods stores tried to excel one another in the effort to attract the attention of the throngs of promenaders.

We walked through some of these central boulevards for nearly two hours, and everywhere the pavements were so filled that it was difficult for three to walk abreast without being continually jostled by the promenaders. This was also the case in the arcades running through the interior of the squares, where the display was equally attractive. The best possible order was everywhere preserved, and the gensdarmes, with their huge cavalry-swords, stood like statues on the corners of the streets, having no occasion to do more than remain quietly at their posts. There being no cobble-stone pavements in Paris, the carriages and omnibuses make little or no noise as they glide along on the smooth asphaltum, nor is there any dust for them to stir up to vex the eyes and lungs of the people. The sweeping-machines are going all night and until ten o'clock in the morning, making the streets as clean as they could be swept with a corn-broom by hand, and lest any dust should be left in the crevices they are washed off with hose. In short, Paris is grand. She has passed through her tribulations, and has again presented herself to the world more beautiful and attractive than ever. That the world is pleased is evident from the many thousands of strangers now lingering here to enjoy the brilliant spectacle.

SOCIAL STATISTICS OF PARIS.

The population of Paris at the last census, taken this year, was one million eight hundred and fifty-one thousand seven hundred and ninety-two souls, or about six times as many as the city of Baltimore, and double that of New York. This number is exclusive of strangers, so that the whole population must average nearly two millions. The number of deaths of males in Paris always exceeds that of females by several thousand, although the females are most numerous. This is such a marked feature of Parisian life that families constantly residing in Paris soon become extinct; that is to say, the name disappears on account of the death of the male children. The statistics, notwithstanding, show a considerable excess of male children born in the city annually. The vital statistics of the city show these facts, which may probably be owing to the loose life led by so many of the young men of the rising generation. The philosophers can give no satisfactory reason for this anomaly, as the health of the city is undoubtedly good.

Of the population of Paris nearly one-half are reported as working-people. There are about eighty thousand servants and one hundred and fifteen thousand paupers. Nearly twenty-one thousand patients are always in the hospitals, and four times that number pass through them in the course of the year. The cost of maintaining the hospitals and other establishments for the relief of the poor during the past year is set down at the enormous sum of twenty-two million three hundred and forty-six thousand francs. All public places of amusement pay a tax of eight per cent. on their receipts towards the support of the hospitals, and a heavy tax for their support is levied upon every piece of ground purchased for the purpose of burial in the cemeteries. Private munificence also contributes largely towards their maintenance. During the past year the tax on theatres and places of amusement amounted to one million seven hundred thousand francs. With a population so large, a proportion of which is merely able to make a living whilst in health, it is necessary to have an abundance of hospitals for them when sick.

THE DEAD OF PARIS.

The whole arrangements for burying the dead, and furnishing coffins, carriages, and all the requisites for funerals, are in the hands of an incorporated company, no one else having the right to interfere with the business. In fact, it is, like the tobacco business, a source of large revenue to the government. The monopoly is granted to this incorporated company under the title of *Entreprise des Pompes Funèbres*, whose principal office is at 10 Rue Alibert, whilst it has branch-offices in each of the arrondissements into which the city is divided. The officers of this company take charge of the body, and prepare for the funeral upon just such a scale and at such expense as the family may desire. Their schedule of prices is such as to suit the purses of all parties, and they are required to bury the very poor gratuitously. A "first-class funeral" is set down on the schedule as costing seven thousand one hundred and eighty-one francs (about one thousand five hundred dollars), the cost of each item of expense being enumerated. There are nine other classes, the lowest costing eighteen francs and seventy-five centimes, including the religious ceremonies. There are, however, no limits to the cost of first-class funerals, as it depends altogether upon the means of the family and its desire for funeral pomp. The horses, hearses, carriages, and drivers are all of a different character for each of these ten classes, the difference being in the age and spirit of the horses, the good looks of the drivers, the quality of their clothing, the harness of the horses, the ancient or modern build of the carriages, etc. The hearse is graded from a splendid structure down to a hand-cart, and the extremely poor are merely furnished with a hand-barrow to enable the friends to carry the body on their shoulders to the grave. The quality of the grave-clothes, of the coffin, and of everything else, is graded to the price, as they may be ordered, from class No. 1 to class No. 10. Besides getting the dead poor buried without cost, the government receives from the company thirty-three and a third per cent. on the produce of funeral ornaments, and fifteen per cent. on that of all other articles furnished. The revenue from these sources is quite large, and, as the cemeteries are also the property of the city government, the dead, as well as the living, contribute their quota to beautifying Paris. The dead poor are allowed to occupy the ground for only five years, when their bones are carted off, probably for agricultural purposes, and the space they occupied is given to some new claimant for the privileges of the soil. There are three kinds of graves in the cemeteries, even for those who pay for the right of sepulture. Some persons purchase the perpetual right for their friends to occupy the soil, but it is generally conceded for five years or more, subject to renewal. If not renewed, the bones are taken up, and the ground is prepared for lease to some new-comer. In the common graves, or, as they are called, *fosses communes*, the poor are gratuitously buried four and a half feet deep in coffins placed close to, but not on top of, each other. This economizes space, as well as saves labor in their removal when the five years have expired.

Among the items of city receipts last year in Paris are the following: Dues on burials, 696,000 francs ($120,000); sale of lands in cemeteries, 1,546,000 francs ($255,000). We do not, however, find any return for the sale of human bones, which is probably a perquisite of the grave-digger.

PARISIAN FOUNDLINGS.

The official returns of the hospitals of Paris show that of the fifty-five thousand births in the city during the past year, fifteen thousand three hundred and sixty-six were illegitimate. The proportion of illegitimates to the number of inhabitants is not quite up to that of Vienna, which has ten thousand for one million inhabitants, whilst the population of Paris is nearly two millions. In various parts of Paris boxes called *tours* are established, each of which revolves upon a pivot, and, on a bell being rung, is turned around by the person inside to receive the child that may have been deposited in it, without attempting to ascertain who the parents are. The child is taken to a hospital and cared for, and so soon as a nurse from the country can be procured, it is given into her charge. Nurses from the country, of good character, are always applying for these infants. The nurses are paid by the city from four francs to eight francs per month, according to the age of the child, care being taken to assign the children to nurses living as far as possible from their birthplaces. After the second year, the nurse may give the child up, when, if no other nurse can be found for it, it is transferred to the Orphan Department. Sometimes the nurses become so attached to the children that they retain them. The number of children thus placed out in the country to nurse is about four thousand annually. The abolition, in some of the departments, of this humane custom of receiving these little waifs and asking no questions has caused infanticide to become very frequent. As for infanticide before birth, the number is said to have doubled and trebled in some districts, and to have risen to four and five times the usual amount in others. The average number of foundlings maintained at the Paris Hospital is four thousand four hundred. At the age of twelve the boys are bound apprentice to some trade at the expense of the city. A portion of one hundred and forty-eight francs is awarded by the city to female foundlings when they marry, provided their conduct has been unexceptionable throughout.

The *Hospice des Enfants Assistés*, founded in 1640 by St. Vincent of Paul, is for the reception of foundlings. For a child to be received at this hospital, however, it is necessary that a certificate of abandonment be produced, signed by a Commissary of Police. The Commissary is bound to admonish the mother or party abandoning the child, and to procure for them assistance from the hospital fund in case of their consenting to retain and support the child. Every encouragement is thus given to those who relinquish the idea of abandoning their offspring and consent to support them at home. Of the children received at this hospital, those that are healthy are put out in the country to nurse, whilst those that are sickly are retained at the hospital until they die or recover. The number of beds in this hospital is about six hundred, and the children annually sent from it to the country are about three thousand four hundred. The children are first placed in a general reception-room, called *La Crèche*, where they are visited in the morning by the physicians and assigned to the different infirmaries. In each of these infirmaries, as well as in *La Crèche*, cradles are placed around the walls in rows, and several nurses are constantly employed in attending to them. An inclined bed is placed in front of the fire, on which the children who require it are laid, and chairs are ranged in a warm corner, in which those of sufficient age and strength sit part of the day. Everything is admirably conducted, and to all outward appearances they are kindly and humanely cared for.

THE LOVE OF DOGS.

All over Europe the love of dogs among both sexes is remarkable, although they are made to work in Switzerland and some parts of Germany. Here in Paris it is quite common to see a mother dragging her almost infant child by the hand, weary and fretful, and carrying a dog in her arms, which she will occasionally stop to kiss, or dispose of so as to make it more comfortable. This trait is peculiar to no one class, but all seem to have a strong affection for the dog. To see a lady at her door or window without a lap-dog is almost a novelty, whilst many of them carry them in their arms or lead them by a ribbon in the streets. The corners are posted with handbills of hospitals for dogs, where the best medical attendance can be had, and dog-medicines and dog-soaps are placarded in all directions. On the boulevards, at night, the dealers in dogs are constantly perambulating with two or three pups in their arms, and ladies will stop and bargain for them on the public thoroughfare. They teach them all manner of tricks, and they are valued according to the education they have received and the intelligence they display. When they travel they take a nurse with them to attend to the wants and comfort of the dog, and these nurses can be seen in the public squares airing and exercising the dogs, and leading them by ribbons. Some idea of the extent of this dog mania may be obtained from the fact that the dog-tax paid into the city treasury last year was four hundred and twenty thousand francs, or nearly one hundred thousand dollars. The men, also, have their dogs, but not to such a great extent as the ladies. The lap-dogs are mostly beautiful little animals, as white as snow, and are kept scrupulously clean, more care being evidently bestowed on them in this respect than many of the children receive from their mothers.

PARIS, August 16, 1873.

YANKEE DOODLE IN PARIS.

The throng of Americans coming to Paris from all parts of the Continent averages two or three hundred per day, and more than half the guests in all the principal hotels are of the same nationality. The L'Athénée has two hundred and ninety-nine of its rooms occupied by Americans, and one occupied by a Russian. At the Grand Hotel, which has six hundred rooms, the proportion is not so great, but nearly all are Americans or English. The itinerant musicians who drop in at the hotel court-yards invariably wind up with the "Star-Spangled Banner" or "Yankee Doodle," and the lady guests strike up these national airs on the piano in the parlor whenever they go in for practice. One little specimen of Young America persists in playing "Yankee Doodle" every morning before the time for us strolling mortals to be getting out of bed. In the dining-room, the reading-room, and all through the passages of the house, the only language spoken is English, and all the waiters speak it fluently. The only persons who speak French are the chambermaids, who, by the way, are all men. They make the beds, sweep the rooms, fill the pitchers, etc., and there is one female in each story who follows after them with a duster, to see that all is right and straightened up as it should be. The females superintend the chambers, but the men do all the work. This is reversing the usual order of things, but it seems to work very satisfactorily here, where men are willing to work for women's wages, and are happy if they can get enough to eat without resorting to laboring work. They probably receive more money from the guests than their wages would be as common laborers.

A GRAND FETE-DAY.

Yesterday was what is called in Paris "Mary's Day," the greatest and most strictly observed religious festival of the year. The stores were more generally closed than on Sunday, and all manner of business was religiously suspended until the evening. Most of the large stores were closed all day, and the American ladies intent on shopping were compelled to take holiday also. For two days past, in anticipation of this festival, all the prominent squares have been occupied by the florists and flower-girls, and all the vacant stores occupied by the display of plants and bouquets. It is customary for the friends of every lady named Mary, all of whom are dedicated to the Virgin in their infancy, to present her with either a bouquet or a blooming plant on the morning of the festival of Mary, and in the evening people carrying home flower-pots were as common as those with bundles of toys on Christmas eve in an American city. The display of flowers was everywhere very elegant, and there is perhaps no other people whose love of flowers is so distinguishing a trait as those of France.

In order to witness the religious observance of the fête, we repaired at an early hour to the Madeleine, where high mass was in progress. The altars were all dressed in flowers, but the side-altar, with a statue of the Virgin and Child, was literally massed with bouquets. At one side of the altar was an iron rack with sharp prongs, on which were burning more than a hundred tallow candles, and others were constantly being added to them by an old lady in attendance. It seems that it is customary for all ladies and children named Mary to bring to the church at which they attend a candle, to be burnt near the altar of the Virgin, and that this old lady was receiving and lighting the offerings as fast as they were handed to her. The music of the services was very fine, and two civilians stood on the steps of the main altar to assist the officiating clergyman in the chants and intonations. We passed the Madeleine and other churches during the morning, and up to one o'clock there was a continuous throng of people passing in and out of them.

The religious observance of the festival closed at one o'clock, and the balance of the day was given up to rejoicing and merry-making. The Champs Elysées was massed with people during the afternoon and evening, and all manner of amusements were in progress. After five o'clock the broad drive to the Bois de Boulogne. through the Arch of Triumph, was thronged with vehicles, it being the ambition of the Parisian to secure a carriage for himself and family and to spend his fête-day in driving to the Bois de Boulogne. The number of these open carriages in Paris is incredible, and they are so cheap, two and a half francs per hour, holding four persons, that they are used by every one. There are omnibuses, but no railways on the streets, and for a party of four the carriages are nearly as cheap as the omnibus, and much more pleasant and desirable, as the drivers seem to know every street in this immense city, and drop you at any point you may name.

It would be impossible to attempt to describe the scene last night on the boulevards. We shall endeavor in another portion of this letter to picture their appearance on ordinary occasions; but on the evening of this fête-day the scene was more bright and brilliant than ever, and the throng of people so great that it was at times impossible to move along the sidewalks. The stores were mostly closed, but the cafés were illuminated with more than ordinary brilliancy. We finally gave up the attempt to promenade, and secured seats at one of the cafés on the Place de l'Opéra, and had a fine view of the moving panorama.

The observance of Mary's Day was, however, so far as the suspension of business was concerned, much more general than it is on Sunday throughout Paris. With the exception of the cafés and cigar-stores, nearly all were closed throughout the day and evening, and all manner of mechanical work was suspended.

THE PARIS BOULEVARDS.

Those of our citizens whose experience of city life is confined to Baltimore, or even those who have made an occasional visit to New York, would be startled if they were to be transported to the Boulevard des Italiens or Capucines, or indeed to be suddenly set down on a warm summer evening anywhere within the extended limits of the city of Paris. Such stirring scenes can be witnessed nowhere else in the world. London is as dull of an evening as Baltimore; the people of Vienna live under the trees after sun-down. All Paris is adrift before the lamps are lit, and thronging towards its great thoroughfares, which are soon blazing with gas-lights for their reception and enjoyment. There are no streets in any other city like these boulevards, which are from house to house one hundred and sixty feet wide, ninety feet being given to the carriage-way, and thirty-five feet on each side for the pavements. Fine rows of trees line the curb-stones, and the carriage-way is mostly asphaltum. Let the reader just imagine this carriage-way so filled with carriages and omnibuses that it is necessary to effect a crossing to wait and watch an opportunity of dodging your way between them, and generally being compelled to stop in the middle to take a fresh start. The pedestrian is expected to get out of the way of the carriages, which never turn aside or hold up for any one. They dash on at full speed; hence it is necessary to keep a sharp look-out to avoid being run down. To look up or down one of the boulevards at night, reminds one of a torch-light procession, every vehicle being required to carry two bright lights. Thus it will be seen that, wide as the carriage-way is, it is none too wide for the rush of vehicles. The moving mass of promenaders on the pavements is also so great that it often becomes necessary to stop and stand aside until there is an opportunity of moving on. Along the curb-stones are lines of chairs for rent, and the thousands of cafés are allowed to occupy about eight or ten feet along their front with their refreshment-tables, where the people sit and rest, and refresh themselves with coffee and ices.

The untraveled reader will imagine that there are two or three of these broad streets in Paris, and that the whole population masses at night on these. This is true with regard to the better classes, who are generally to be found on the Italiens, Capucines, Haussmann, and other central boulevards; but many of the others are equally thronged but not so brilliant. There are in the city of Paris fifty-seven of these wide thoroughfares, called boulevards, running in every direction, and all teeming at night with life and animation. Indeed, the whole city seems to be abroad at night, and every class has its popular localities for congregating in.

But to understand and to properly appreciate the view on these boulevards it must be borne in mind that the houses lining them are nearly all of uniform construction, none less than five stories high, and many of them towering up to six and seven stories, including the mansard roofs. The ground-floors are one continuous line of stores and cafés, with the exception of those of a few private mansions distant from the central portions of the city, but many of these have stores below. On the principal boulevards the first, second, and third stories are generally devoted to business, and at night are all brilliantly lighted.

PARIS UNDERGROUND.

On retiring last evening we were startled by hearing some one, apparently under our window, ranting through portions of Othello. We looked out into the court-yard, but could see nothing but a skylight down where the pavement ought to be. A band of music would occasionally perform some operatic air, and then "the tearing of passion to tatters" would be renewed again, interspersed with milder male and female voices. It continued till nearly eleven o'clock, and we rose at a loss to know what it all meant. This morning, on surveying the building, we found that there was a theatre attached to the Hôtel l'Athénée, and that the skylight down in the yard under our window was the dome over the parquet. Mr. Swinbourne, the English tragedian, was performing Othello in English to an audience nearly all American, which was then being repeated for the ninth time. The theatre, which is about the size of one of our smaller establishments, is down in the bowels of the earth, under the hotel, out of the way of all noise and confusion. It is a very elegant little affair, and quite a fashionable resort for the Parisians. In Vienna we frequently took our meals in a very elegant saloon, considerably larger than the Assembly Rooms, and with quite as high a ceiling, which was down under a row of six-story buildings, the skylight of which protruded a few feet above the pavement of the courtyard; but we were not prepared to find an underground theatre, and that we were sleeping up four flights of stairs, directly over a stage on which Othello was smothering the gentle Desdemona with a pillow. Ground is costly in Paris, and they make the best possible use of it. When you build the new *American* office, be sure to have an Academy of Music down under the press-room, with a sky-parlor box for Mr. Keyser, the pressman, and his engineer and "feeders."

BEAUTIFUL PARIS.

PARIS. August 18, 1873.

It is not an easy matter at this late day to write letters from Paris that will interest and instruct. It is a city which everybody is familiar with, it having been so often described, and its attractions and beauties so vividly spread before the general reader that it would almost seem like undertaking to write something new about Baltimore. We have visited it so often, and ridden and walked through its multifarious thoroughfares until all its crooks and turns are as familiar to us as those of any of our leading American cities. Still there is something about Paris that makes it always appear bright, gay, and sparkling to the visitor. The Parisian does not worship the "dust of ages," or take pride in smoked and begrimed walls, as the Londoner does. If he has anything that is handsome he tries to make it handsomer. He is always rubbing, scrubbing, and polishing old things, or tearing them down to make room for something new and more beautiful. The four handsome clusters of gas-lamps in the centre of the Place de l'Opéra are not only kept as bright and elegant as they were the day they were put up, but the elaborate bronze lampposts are polished with as much regularity as the glasses of the lamps. If the slightest defect is observed in one stone in the street, it is relaid or replaced by a new one; and if a flaw in the asphaltum as large as a man's hand is discovered, a repairing party is at work in a few hours, and the defect removed. Every tenant is held responsible for the cleanliness of the street before his own door, and neither dirt nor rubbish of any kind is permitted. As in public matters, so also in those of private concern. They never allow their houses or store fronts to become dull or dingy. They make them handsome and they keep them handsome. They are always arranging and rearranging the goods in their windows and striving to make them more attractive. All these scores of miles of boulevards are planted with sycamore-trees. When they plant trees they take good care that they shall have a fair chance to grow, and they are all flourishing beautifully. Around each tree an iron grating, extending three feet each way, is inserted in the pavement, in order that its roots may have breathing-room and water. There are hundreds of thousands of these trees all thus planted, and all tended and watered by the city authorities. If one should happen to die, a tree of similar size is brought to take its place, that the uniformity may be unbroken. These trees are the pride of Paris, and are yearly becoming more serviceable as a shade to the broad sidewalks as well as a grand ornament to the boulevards.

Thus it is that the attractions of Paris are always increasing. No rust or decay is permitted, and old things are swept away as having served their day and generation. Antiquity has no worshipers, and is made to yield to the spirit of improvement. New squares, gardens, and fountains are following the march of improvement in the suburbs, and even in those quarters of the city where the poorer classes mostly reside, these pleasure-grounds are being fitted up as elegantly as in the wealthier sections. Paris is not beautiful in spots, but every portion of it abounds in attractions.

THE ABATTOIRS OF PARIS.

These establishments are located on the suburbs of the city, the buildings of which cover sixty-seven acres of land near the fortifications between the Canals de l'Ourcq and St. Denis. The slaughtering of cattle of all descriptions is required by law to be done here, the average per week being two thousand beeves, eight hundred cows, a thousand calves, and ten thousand sheep. There are, also, a good number of horses slaughtered, their meat being sold to the poor, it having been found during the siege to be quite palatable. Worn-out horses are fattened and sold to the butchers, the supply from the carriage and omnibus stalls being very extensive.

The principal entrance to these extensive slaughter-houses is by the Rue de Flandre. It is inclosed by an elegant iron railing, with eleven gates for entrance and exit, and its numerous buildings give it the appearance of an inclosed town. There are now sixty-four pavilions in active operation, some of which are reserved for stalls, in which the cattle awaiting their doom are kept. The others are divided into one hundred and twenty-three places of slaughter, called "échaudoirs."[1] The cleanliness which prevails throughout is admirable. Every échaudoir is provided with abundance of water, and the stone floor is scrupulously scoured every time an animal has been killed, and the foul water runs off into sewers intersecting the grounds in every direction. The ventilation is also excellent, so that, even at this season of the year, there are no foul smells about this extensive establishment. At the entrance to each there is a strong iron ring immovably fixed in the ground. Through this ring the rope is made to pass which has previously been secured to the horns of the animal to be slaughtered. The rope is then drawn tight by means of a pulley, and when the victim's head has been forced down as much as possible, it receives the death-blow with a heavy club. There are also on the premises buildings called *triperies*, where tripe and calves' feet are washed and boiled, melting-houses for tallow, with attics for drying skins, lofts for fodder, etc. Cattle and sheep are kept here at the butcher's expense. The slaughter-men get from one franc to one and a half francs for each animal, besides the entrails, brains, and blood. The butcher-shops in the metropolis, which are daily supplied from the abattoir, number eight hundred and sixty-nine.

WAGES IN PARIS.

From an official inquiry set on foot by the Chamber of Commerce of Paris, it appears that there are employed in the various trades and manufactories 467,311 hands, of whom about 300,000 are men, 120,000 women, and 47,000 children. Of these there are 60,000 males, earning from 50 centimes (10 cents) to 3 francs (60 cents) per day; 211,000 earn from 3¼ to 6 francs (65 cents to $1.20) per day; and 15,000 from 6½ to 20 francs ($1.30 to $4). Of the females, 17,200 earn from 50 centimes (10 cents) to 1 franc 25 centimes (25 to 80 cents); and 700 from 4½ to 10 francs

(90 cents to $2). The wages of children are from 10 cents to 25 cents per day. The shoemakers, carpenters, bricklayers, stonemasons, and painters are among the 211,000 who receive from 65 cents to $1.20 per day. It is not surprising that these mechanics come to the United States whenever they can raise money enough to pay their passages. Our mechanics at home, by denying their own sons the privilege of learning trades, always keep the supply short, so as to provide places for the foreign mechanic whenever he is ready to come. They all deserve leather medals for their philanthropy.

AMERICANS IN PARIS.

The people of Paris are astounded at the American invasion. They have not only filled up all the hotels, but the boarding-houses on Boulevard Haussmann are thronged with them. Those who come to stay over a month or two invariably abandon the hotels and take to the boarding-houses, where they can live much more comfortably and fare better for half the expense. The charge at these houses ranges from eight to twelve francs per day, including finely-furnished chambers and the use of the parlors, pianos, etc., wine at déjeûner and dinner. Many American families are located here permanently, finding the cost of living much cheaper than at home. For three chambers and a private parlor at Madame Feron's, No. 111 Rue Neuve des Mathurins, we pay thirty-six francs per day, which embraces everything, including the very pleasant American company which is usually to be found at these houses. The table is good and the attendance excellent, and we have no doubt that for a prolonged stay much lower rates could be obtained. The papers are filled with advertisements of rooms and apartments to be let to Americans, and every one is finding the importance of speaking English. All the stores are providing themselves with English-speaking clerks. Colored nurses with American children in charge are quite common all over Paris, and the American citizen of African descent walks up and down the boulevards with his yellow kids and ivory-headed whalebone under his arm without being any longer an object of curiosity. American dressmakers are invading the precincts of the famous Worth, and have their establishments in Rue Scribe and Boulevard Haussmann thronged with customers. The American Club-room, the American café, and a number of fancy-goods establishments have been recently started by Americans, and four English newspapers are published in Paris. The American flag is to be seen in various sections of the city, and the carriage-drivers as well as the store-keepers reap a rich harvest. The number of American ladies here is unprecedented, and there is no city in Europe in which they love to linger as they do in Paris.

FEMALE DOCTORS.

The irrepressible American girl is to be found all over Europe, endeavoring to force her way as a student of medicine in the leading universities and hospitals. When she is rebuffed at one point she proceeds to another, and has at last succeeded in getting up a very general discussion of the question. Whenever there is a vote taken on the propriety of admitting females to the universities or the hospitals, the main issue is dodged, as it has just been at the University of Tübingen. It was resolved to admit female students upon the presentation of the proper certificate that they have passed through the classes of a regular grammar-school and have withstood the *abiturient* examination. The conditions imposed are equivalent to a vote of exclusion, as female students are not as yet allowed to attend the grammar-schools. At Vienna the female students who were endeavoring to obtain admission to the lectures were refused in all departments except that of midwifery, which is very generally in the hands of women throughout the Continent. Indeed, it is only within a few years that male doctors have commenced to practice in this department of the profession in the private practice of Paris. Some inferior institutions in Europe have opened their lecture-rooms to females, but this does not satisfy these American female aspirants, and they are endeavoring to force their way where the best education can be had. They meet with many rebuffs, but are earnest and determined. Kate Fields takes up the cudgels for them this week in the *American Register*, published in Paris and London, in reply to the London *Times*, and has certainly the best of the argument. She denies that all medical practitioners are opposed to female doctors, and contends that those who do are governed by the same influence that induces Paddy, the Irish laborer of California, to hate Ah Sin, and declare that Chinese pig-tail has come to take the bread out of his children's mouths; or that one corner grocery does not adore the next corner grocery. When she took to lecturing, all her friends told her that they would rather see her dead. She knew, however, that the prejudice against women lecturers was only temporary, and would cease so soon as woman on the platform ceased to be a novelty. "Every step forward taken by women," she declares, "has been over burning plowshares, and she can always look back to a time when the occupation most abjured by our fastidious friends was of all others the most compromising to womanhood." Miss Fields takes up every objection made by her opponents, and answers them with both ability and logic, quoting from history to show that women lack neither "physical strength" nor "brain-power" necessary for the profession. The strongest point of her argument is probably the following: "I make bold to say, not only are women-doctors to be tolerated, but they are to be heartily welcomed as necessary to their own sex. In many cases it is most unpleasant for women to employ male physicians. Nothing but the knowledge that to them only is the door of science thrown wide open reconciles women to a sometimes revolting necessity. Many a young girl's health has been ruined because of an unconquerable aversion to consult a male physician." She concludes by asking whether, ten years hence, society will draw the line "unfeminine" against women who, having too much pride to hang as burdens about the necks of friends or relatives, take up active business and dare to make as much money as their brothers. The census of England just taken shows that there are one-sixth more females than males in that kingdom, and the same is the case all over Europe, the result of war and emigration; hence it is argued that marriage is no longer woman's chief calling. Girls are advised to look upon marriage as an accident, not as a career, and full opportunity must be given them to seek some opportunity of livelihood by proper training in youth. The three thousand pounds left by John Stuart Mill, in his will, to any university in Great Britain or Ireland that shall be the first to open its degrees to women, have not yet been taken up. The time will come, however, when women will have an equal chance in life; for, as Kate Fields says, "the Deity has created a female, and man cannot get rid of her. The world is wide enough for both sexes. *Place aux dames!*"

HOTELS IN PARIS.

The hotels of Paris have greatly advanced their prices during the past year, which has induced most Americans who have ladies with them to seek quarters at the pensions, or boarding-houses, where they fare much better at one-half the cost. At the Grand Hotel, on the "first floor," which we would call the third floor, the charge for sleeping-accommodations alone is from twelve to twenty-five francs per day. The intermediate floors to the "fourth," which we would call the sixth, are a shade lower, whilst on the "fourth" the charge is from five to twelve francs per day. For a *table-d'hôte* breakfast and dinner, including a very inferior wine, eleven francs are charged. If meals are taken *à la carte* at the hotel, and then not equal to a dinner at an American hotel like the Carrollton, Barnum's, or the St. Clair, including wine, it cannot be accomplished much under twenty-five francs, which would make the average expense not much less than from five to seven dollars per day, according to the location of rooms. They have, however, at the Grand Hotel, partly introduced the American system this year, which is rather moderate for those who like *table-d'hôte* living. Boarders are taken at a fixed price, including apartments, board (wine included), fire, and lighting, at twenty-five francs per day for one person, or for two occupying one room, thirty-five francs. The rooms are, of course, close up under the shingles.

At the *pensions* the charge is from ten to twelve francs per day for everything, with better tables than the hotels furnish, and better rooms and attendance. They are also much pleasanter for ladies, as the boarders are generally Americans or English, the former largely predominating everywhere. It is utterly impossible to get along in Paris without wine, as the conviction is general that water is unhealthy. We supposed this at first to be a trick to induce the purchase of wine, but the idea pervades all classes. Even the chambermaids express astonishment when drinking-water is called for, and insist upon sweetening it with sugar. Ice-water is regarded as positively dangerous without sugar or wine in it.

THE CLEANLINESS OF PARIS.

Paris, September 13, 1873.

The more one sees of Paris, the greater is the astonishment at the wonderful attractions which abound in every direction. The world has much to learn from Paris, although there is much here that it is all the better that the rest of mankind should not attempt to imitate. In the matter of city government, and ornamentation, and cleanliness, and finely-paved streets, and the artistic location of its most elegant buildings so that they may show to the best advantage, the city of Paris carries off the palm. A Parisian would never have located our City Hall down at the opening to "the meadows," or the new Opera-House on Howard Street, or have turned the old Exchange Hotel into a post-office, or located the Carrollton Hotel on Light Street. He never allows speculators in land to fix the location of public edifices, nor "ring-masters" to construct them, but places them just where they will add most to the ornamentation of an already ornamental position. The whole effort has been to make Paris beautiful, and beautiful it is almost everywhere. We drove out to its extreme western suburbs, fully five miles from the Louvre, and found elegant squares, fountains (some of them in the course of erection), and clean, well-paved streets out to its extreme limits. The Paris of to-day has no dirty and offensive districts, and the secret is that it is never allowed to get dirty. The sweepings of a half-mile of any of the streets would not fill a wheelbarrow at any time, and such an instrument as a scraper is not among the tools of the scavenger. Water is only used to boil potatoes (and these are usually fried), wash the streets, and supply the fountains and cascades. For these latter purposes it is most lavishly expended, and hence Paris is always clean and beautiful.

THE BOIS DE BOULOGNE.

The number of public squares and parks in and around Paris exceeds that of any other city in the world, and they are all ornamented with beds of flowers, elaborate fountains, and extensive arrays of fine statuary, whilst the walks and drives are models of good order and neatness. Each tree seems also to be tenderly cared for and watered, and the grass is being constantly dressed and nurtured. So it is with the hundreds of thousands of trees along the boulevards: they were planted for ornament and shade, and care is taken that they fulfill their destiny to the fullest possible extent. The parks of London are kept generally in a slovenly condition in comparison.

The Bois de Boulogne is the principal park of Paris, and is now gradually regaining its old reputation as the most fashionable place of resort for a drive or a walk, where the most splendid equipages and the finest horses of the capital are displayed. It is approached from the city by the Avenue of the Champs Elysées, which is also the favorite promenade of the gay Parisians. The Bois de Boulogne is also distinguished as a favorite place for dueling and suicides, which are still as numerous in Paris as ever. The Avenue de l'Impératrice, three hundred feet wide, commencing at the Arch of Triumph, is the grand thoroughfare through the park, and to the beautiful lakes and cascades by which it is adorned. Here art and taste have conspired to charm the eye with the most picturesque scenery. At the southern extremity of the lakes, opposite the islands, two charming cascades pour their waters, bounding from rock to rock, or gushing from crevices skillfully arranged, into the lake beneath. Winding paths, emerging from the cool fir-groves scattered around, intersect the rich turf which clothes the banks down to the water's edge. On the rocky side of the smaller island is an aviary filled with rare birds, and from the balcony of an elegant kiosk, situated on a promontory which terminates the smaller island, an enchanting view is obtained on a fine summer's day of the gay scene around. The rich equipages enlivening the carriage-road which winds around the lake, the crowds of persons of all ranks enjoying the cool shade on the iron benches provided for their convenience, or sauntering along the gravel-walks, children flocking about in the height of merriment and glee, and the boats flying to and fro with their white canvas awnings shining in the sun, form a maze of bustle and animation most pleasing to the eye. Snug little Swiss cottages may be seen peering here and there from behind the trees, well provided with beer and common wine for the thirsty, or more costly refreshments for those whose inclination may desire them.

There are also several other smaller lakes on the line of the main carriage-road, which makes a circuit of five miles and passes through a variety of attractive scenery. Not far from the head of the first lake is the great race-course of Longchamps, granted by the city to the Jockey Club, where the fall races are now taking place every Sunday afternoon. It incloses one hundred and fifty-three acres.

and is fitted up in the most costly and elaborate manner. The stands accommodate four thousand persons, and chairs for a similar number are distributed about the parterre within the rails. The raceground is laid out in three courses, one of two thousand feet, the second of two thousand five hundred, and the other of three thousand two hundred.

This park, though some miles from the centre, and a considerable distance from the outskirts, of Paris, can be approached by the boats from the Seine, by several lines of omnibuses, or by railroad from the St. Lazare or Porte Maillot stations; hence it is the favorite resort of all classes of the people. To describe it thoroughly would require too much space in a letter, but we must not neglect to mention the Cascade de Longchamps, which is the great central attraction. An artificial mound one hundred and eighty feet in breadth, and forty-two feet high, raises its craggy front above a basin bordered with rocks; a vast sheet of water issuing from a cavern pierced through the body of the mound, falls into the basin from a height of twenty-seven feet, while laterally two minor cascades are seen picturesquely threading their way through various crevices. An intricate rocky passage winds its way under the cascade, leading the visitor through many mock perils, charmingly managed, to the top of the waterfall, where he may enjoy a view of the pretty lake by which it is fed, and which also displays a picturesque island in the centre.

THE JARDIN D'ACCLIMATATION.

This is another of the great attractions of the Bois de Boulogne, being almost as handsome as the Jardin des Plantes, though its collection of animals was greatly reduced during the siege, by the famished Parisians. It is an inclosure of thirty-three acres, belonging to the Société d'Acclimatation, the object of which is to acclimate both plants and animals. It is beautifully laid out in walks, encircling the cages or inclosures where the quadrupeds are kept, and arranged with picturesque little cots, containing the stables. The grounds are intersected by a streamlet, dotted with islands and spanned by rustic bridges. There various aquatic plants are grown, while other rare specimens of the vegetable kingdom abound on the surrounding grass-plats, among which we noticed a collection of California firs. The hot-house is three hundred feet long, and ninety in breadth, with a romantic grotto and rivulet, surrounded with palm-trees and other choice plants from tropical climes. The rivulets and basins swarm with various kinds of fish, and here are also ostriches, ducks, geese and swans from all parts of the world, in endless variety, presenting a scene of agreeable animation. There is also an extensive aquarium, divided into fourteen compartments, occupied by none but the rarest specimens of the piscatorial world. Then there is a vast aviary, swarming with a wonderful collection of rare birds. There are also elephants, bears, and a very good collection of other quadrupeds. In the centre of the garden is a large orchestral canopy, and chairs for a large audience, concerts being given here two afternoons in the week, by the finest bands in Paris. The admission is one franc, but only a half-franc on Sundays and holidays.

THE MARKETS OF PARIS.

We visited at an early hour yesterday morning the great central market of Paris, which presents a most novel scene to the stranger, being so different from those to which he is accustomed. The markets are called Halles, and there are in the city twenty-two for wholesale transactions, fifty-seven for retail dealings, and one central cattle-market, where the slaughtered meat is sold by auction, either the whole animal, or quartered, from whence the butcher-stores throughout the city obtain their supplies. It was to this great central market that we repaired yesterday morning, it combining all the peculiarities of the other markets, both wholesale and retail.

The Central Halles cover a space of ground about as large as that occupied by the Camden Street Depot of the Baltimore and Ohio Railroad, the streets passing through it, but being covered by glass roofs, making the whole *one* building, mainly of iron and glass. It is, however, divided into ten distinct *halles*, or markets. This market is new, and cost for its construction alone twelve million of francs, over and above the cost of two hundred and forty-nine houses pulled down to make room for it, which amounted to twenty-seven millions of francs more, or in all about eight millions of dollars. There are retail pavilions in it for the sale of meat, butter and cheese, fowls and game, and vegetables, and also pavilions for the sale of meat, butter, and fish by wholesale. Underneath this immense structure is a cellar, the vaulting of brick resting upon iron groins, supported by four hundred and thirty cast-iron pillars, forming a curious perspective. Light is admitted through glass bull's-eyes, and there are numerous iron cages rented to dealers for storing their produce. There are immense wired cages for poultry, and a stone tank divided into compartments for the convenience of fishmongers. But the most singular part of this underground portion of the market-house is the parallel lines of tramways extending from these cellars through a tunnel, which passes under the Boulevard Sebastopol, and connects with the Railroad de Ceinture, nearly a mile distant. This railroad encircles the city, and connects with all other roads, so that the produce for this great market is all brought by this underground tunnel direct into the cellar.

The structure above-ground is very imposing. The iron columns or pillars, numbering three hundred, upon which the roof rests, are each thirty-three feet high, and are connected by dwarf walls of brick about ten feet high. The rest of the space up to the arches is closed with blinds of ground-glass plate. The roofing is of zinc, with large skylights over the carriage-ways, thus giving abundance of light and ventilation, whilst hydrants are interspersed for the use of the dealers. It is altogether a mammoth institution, and the amount of business transacted here daily is very large.

SCENE AT THE MARKET.

When we reached the market-house everything was in full blast, wholesale and retail. Instead of stalls in the retail markets, each dealer is provided with an iron cage about ten feet square, and some only half this size, in which they transact their business. The fronts are provided with folding iron doors, so that they can be thrown open, or closed up at night and locked. This contrivance makes ventilation perfect, and keeps everything secure. They are in rows close together, with passage-ways about twelve feet wide between them. One section is for meats, another for cheese, eggs, and butter, another for poultry and game, another for vegetables, and another for flour, feed, and grain. On the opposite side of each of these pavilions is another for the sale of each of these articles by wholesale, and at least fifty auctioneers were busy selling, with clerks and cashiers to note the sales and receive the money. In the first wholesale department we entered, the sale of butter and cheese was progressing. The butter was in lumps of about fifty pounds each, and a hundred or more of small dealers, mostly old women, were crowding around each of the auctioneers, all armed with an iron probe, with which they punctured the rolls and tasted them as they were moved along a table. There were piles of these large lumps inclosed in linen cloths strewn upon the pavements to the number of several hundred, and the porters were carrying them off to the wagons outside as fast as they were sold and paid for. It was an animated scene, the customers being a greasy-looking set of fellows, in blue blouses, but with glib and oily tongues, making themselves heard over the general din. The wholesale meat market was stocked with whole sheep, whole hogs, and quarters of beef, —all hung up on stationary shambles, extending in lines across the building. A half-dozen auctioneers were passing along these lines, and selling piece by piece to a throng of customers, each followed by a clerk noting down the sales. There was some horse-meat also, which could only be distinguished by the experienced eye from the fact that the flesh was a darker red, and the fat yellow instead of white, as is the case with good beef.

MARKET FOR OLD CLOTHES.

This is called the Marché du Vieux Linge. It is a market for old clothes and stuffs, shoes and tools, and is a very extensive affair. It is about seven hundred feet long by two hundred feet broad, built in iron pavilions, and contains *two thousand four hundred* places for dealers, each of about thirteen square feet, and all those stalls are occupied, from which some idea can be obtained of the scene here presented. This market was built as a speculation, the city granting the contractor the right to build it and receive the rents for fifty years. He is to pay the city two hundred thousand francs per annum, and the whole property is to revert to the city at the expiration of the specified period. It cost the contractor three million five hundred thousand francs. The stalls set up for the dealers are so elegant, and the articles offered for sale so cleverly " renovated," that the visitor can scarcely believe himself to be in an " old clothes" mart. It has been a very successful speculation, and the poor man can here procure a very respectable outfit for a very small outlay. These dealers are constantly on the look-out for the contents of rubbish-rooms, old clothes, and all the odds and ends that accumulate in an easy-living household. The space occupied by this structure is two entire blocks, the street passing through it being roofed over with iron, glass, and zinc. It is very elegant, and is built on the model of the Grand Central Market, entirely of iron. The roof is about forty feet high, with a greater elevation in the centre, where there is an immense open gallery, reached by two flights of iron stairs. Seeing that there was a crowd of people up there, we ascended, and found a door-keeper, who required one sou admission. This proved to be a place for the sale of old clothes too far gone for renovation, and the articles were piled up in lines along the floor, through which the purchasers, to the number of probably a thousand, were circulating. Both buyer and seller pay one sou admission, which defrays the expense of this branch of the establishment. Musty-looking old shoes by the cart-load were here, shocking old hats, and all manner of women's apparel. The dealers were doing an extensive business, and during our ramble we were frequently invited to purchase some threadbare garment, from which it may be judged how shabby the traveler gets in his outward appearance by the time he reaches Paris. The goods displayed in the two thousand four hundred stalls below looked as bright and new, almost, as the display in the windows on the boulevards, though many of them were slightly out of fashion.

PARISIAN LOCAL ITEMS.

At the celebrated dry-goods establishment Au Bon Marché, which is extensively patronized by Americans, a new feature has been introduced this season. It having been noticed that American gentlemen frequently get impatient whilst their wives and daughters are shopping, and sometimes hurry them off before they have obtained all they want, a well-fitted-up billiard-saloon has been provided for their amusement whilst the purchases are being made. It seems to answer the purpose well, as the gentlemen are always easily to be found when it is necessary for them to come up to the captain's office and foot the bill.

An American lady tells us that she went to a hair-dresser's establishment this morning to get her hair shampooed, and, asking the cost, she received the answer that it would be three francs. After the operation was finished she was presented with a bill for nine francs, and upon demurring was told that three of the additional francs were for putting her hair up again, two others for the liquid used, and the fourth for the use of the combs and brush. Can any of our Yankee shampooers come up to this sharp practice?

We stopped in this morning at a horse-meat butcher's shop to look at the meat. There were nice-looking sirloin steaks, spare-rib and sirloin roasts, knuckle-joints for soup, and genuine "salt horse" in abundance. We could not have told it from beef, except that the meat was a darker red. The gentleman whom we accompanied assured us that he had eaten it as an experiment, and was of the opinion that it was more tender, as a general thing, than ordinary beef. "But," he added, "I expect you have frequently dined off of it since you have been in Paris, especially if you have taken any meals at the restaurants." Well, perhaps we have, but "where ignorance is bliss 'tis folly to be wise."

The Commune, during their possession of Paris, destroyed, among other things, all the official records of births and marriages. As most of them were family men and women without marriage, or unconscious of their own parentage, the object was to place all on a level of "equality" in this respect. The work of restoring the records is now in progress, as all who are not recorded are regarded in the eye of the law as illegitimate. It has made brisk work for the lawyers.

The Parisians have a singular way of signalizing events in their history by the naming of streets. One of the magnificent boulevards branching off from the Grand Opera-House was named Boulevard 2d December, the day of the Napoleon coup-d'état in 1851. The name is now changed to the Boulevard 4th September, the day of the dethronement of the Emperor and the proclamation of the Republic. Should there be another empire proclaimed, the name will doubtless be changed again to suit the date of its occurrence.

THE "CHATEAU ROUGE."

London has its "Argyle Hall" and "Cremorne Gardens," Vienna has its "Sperle" and "Alhambra," but they are low and disorderly places, which are seldom visited even by respectable gentlemen. They are vicious imitations of the Paris gardens, such as the "Jardin Mabille" and the "Elysée Montmartre," the

"Château Rouge" and the "Closerie des Lilas." In these places the license of the dance is not always confined to the limits of propriety, though there is nothing to be seen at any of them below the level of the artistic dancing on the stage, or what is called the "leg drama." In summer the Parisians resort to similar establishments at the villages of Asnières, Enghien, Lecaux, St. Cloud, Rambouillet, and Montmorency. We have visited the "Jardin Mabille," which is the best place in Paris to meet Americans, and English too, both ladies and gentlemen, as but few fail to spend an evening there during their sojourn in the metropolis. Last evening your correspondent was induced to accompany a young Baltimorean, whose curiosity was not satisfied with the Mabille, over to the Latin Quarter, on a tour of observation at the "Château Rouge." He had been reading Mark Twain's description of the grisettes, and wished to see them in the midst of their evening enjoyments. Mark says that after seeing them he felt sorry for the students, and no longer envied them their felicity. We can truly say that if the effeminate, spindle-shanked, and half-made-up specimens of the genus *homo* who were dancing at the "Rouge" last night were students, the grisettes should have come in for a full share of his pity. The girls were nearly all extremely young, full of life and vivacity, neatly but plainly dressed, and, as a general thing, rather good-looking. The men, on the contrary, although good dancers and mostly young, were, in both form and feature, decidedly repulsive.

The dance at the "Château Rouge" was conducted with as much propriety as at the "Mabille Garden," but was much more exciting. The best female dancers at the Mabille are evidently paid for their services, and but few others appear on the floor; but at the "Rouge" they all joined in the dance, and each tried to excel the other in the *abandon* with which they flew through its giddy mazes. The style of dancing is altogether Spanish, none of the ordinary tame cotillion figures being permitted. The music is rapid, and the dancers take two steps to every note, presenting a scene of "rapid speed" not usually seen in the ball-room. The spectators formed rings around the best dancers, who appeared to be known, and we, being too modest to press forward, had mostly to be contented with what could be seen over the heads of a crowd of people who were between us and the dancers. Every moment a score of neat ladies' boots, with well-turned ankles encased in striped stockings, could be seen flying around the heads of the male dancers, who vainly attempted to get their boots as high. Whether there was any intended viciousness in these kicks we were not informed, though we saw a cigar fly out of the mouth of a spectator on the toe of a lady's boot, and a gentleman's hat sent ballooning up among the chandeliers. Such a jolly set of people, numbering not less than three thousand, nearly half of them females, we have never seen assembled together before. Shouts of laughter and applause greeted any extraordinary feats of agility, and when the music stopped all joined in a grand promenade out from under the dancing-pavilion into the garden, the trees of which were illuminated with innumerable colored lamps, while thousands of gas-jets blazed from upright chandeliers throughout the walks, along which hundreds of refreshment-tables were stationed. At the rear, the water poured down over the rocks of a cascade fountain, and at the sides a series of little shady nooks were filled with parties partaking of wine and ices.

When the music struck up again, we secured a more eligible position, closer to the dancers, and we saw—well, we will let Mark Twain tell what we saw and heard: "Shouts, laughter, furious music, a bewildering chaos of darting and intermingling forms, stormy jerking and rustling of gay dresses, bobbing heads, flying arms, lightning flashes of white and striped stocking calves, and dainty slippers, in the air, and then a grand final rush, riot, a terrific hubbub, and a wild stampede! Nothing like it has been seen on earth since trembling Tam O'Shanter saw the devil and the witches at their orgies that stormy night in Alloway's old haunted kirk."

It was a scene of the most vigorous and earnest dancing that human feet and limbs could possibly be trained to. So also in the waltzes. They flew around so rapidly that at a short distance the twirling couples bewildered the eye, and seemed like tops spinning in the air. There was nothing of the "poetry of motion" about this dancing, but rather the "prose of locomotion," the highest rate of speed being the object to be attained. Still, we did not see anything as shocking to delicate susceptibilities as the famous dansense performances at our most fashionable theatres. These dancers undoubtedly enjoyed the dance, whilst the professionals go through it as part of a laborious duty, and we don't think that any of the latter were able to throw their heels as high as the grisettes of the Latin Quarter. The best of order was observed, and during the promenades there was but little to distinguish the company from an ordinary assemblage of well-dressed people. There were a great many respectable French ladies present as spectators, and an abundance of English and American gentlemen, but no ladies of either of these Anglo-Saxon nationalities. At the Mabille Garden, however, the English and American ladies outnumbered the gentlemen, as this is one of the places in Paris which the ladies all persist in seeing "just once." Among the latter we recognized the family of a Northern bishop, and any number of "fathers and mothers in Israel," with their daughters. There is no use in any one coming to Europe without seeing the people in all their modes and phases of life, and to see Paris without visiting the Mabille would be like going to Rome and not visiting St. Peter's. The stranger, finding himself a stranger in a strange land, feels at liberty to come and go to places that he feels bound to shun at home.

THE GRISETTE.

It is a common remark among strangers in France that about every third man wears a uniform of some kind, and such is almost the case here in Paris. Nearly all of these uniformed men are forbidden by law to marry, and they belong to a class who have never been taught to entertain such an idea as pertaining to their future existence. They have always found it difficult to get food for themselves, and hence have never entertained such a preposterous undertaking as marrying and supporting a family. These men have sisters who have always recognized themselves as belonging to a class who are never to know the relations of husband and wife. Such a thought never enters the head of a girl or boy belonging to the poorer classes of Paris. Sometimes they succeed in drawing themselves out of their unnatural state of existence, and aspire to higher things, but the great mass of them have for generations found that the chief aim of life was bread and wine. They have the natural passions of ordinary men and women, and hence the grisette. They are not taught, even by their spiritual counselors, that there is any sin in the life they lead, and are as punctual in their church attendance as any class in Paris. Nor are they regarded as degraded, unless they fall still lower and become professional courtesans. They are considered as fulfilling their destiny, and love and are beloved as other mortals. Sometimes these ties are permanent, but in the generality of cases they are merely for a time, and when broken a new one is formed. Thus they pass through life, and their children, of whom they furnish the state about eighteen thousand per annum, are sometimes kept and maintained by themselves, but oftener passed over to the orphan-asylums, just as most of their mothers were passed over in their early infancy. The grisette, it will thus be seen, is a feature of Parisian society that is regarded as inevitable, and, being inevitable, those who raise themselves out of its slough are not deemed to have been tainted or tarnished in character. Those who pass through life as grisettes are not regarded as "fallen angels," but as women who are fulfilling their sad and unfortunate destiny, and whose chances for heaven are quite as good as those whose lots are cast in pleasanter ways. So long as youth lasts they live a merry life, and when this departs they become waiting-maids. They are the unfortunate victims of kingcraft, which requires standing armies, and draws the youth of the country away from the ordinary pursuits of life and happiness.

"IT'S NAUGHTY, BUT IT'S NICE."

An American lady, who was chidden by an over-prudish friend for having joined a party of American ladies and gentlemen to spend an evening at the Mabille Gardens, responded, "Well, I admit it was naughty, but then it was so nice." She contended that she had never spent at any place of amusement a more agreeable evening, and had not seen half as much to shock her sense of propriety as could be seen on the boards of our leading theatres during a ballet season. The garden itself, independent of the scenes enacted, is one of the most brilliant spectacles ever presented to the human vision. The number of gas-jets is said to exceed fifty thousand, which, mingled with the foliage of the trees and flowers, and artistically arranged in and around the dancing-circle, almost blinds the eye at times with its brilliancy. Then there are grottoes and arbors and alcoves, refreshment-saloons, and booths for various little games interspersed, all adding to the gay and festive scene. That portion of the garden intended for promenades is only sufficiently lighted to give effect to the illusion produced by some ingenious painter, by which the groves seem to extend indefinitely in the distance, though really not more than a hundred yards in extent. The trees, the grass, the flowers, the fountains, and the bushes, each and all throw forth their blaze of light and contribute to the general effect. A row of thirty iron arches spans the upper end of the garden, each almost twenty-five feet high, and both columns and arch are one blaze of light. The columns appear in the distance as if fluted with fire, and the arches and pillars are formed of numerous rows of gas-jets, and when viewed from the circle, with the intervening fountains and large frosted globes suspended from every available point, present a scene of enchantment surpassing the genius of Mr. Getz to present in scenic illusion.

Whilst the adjuncts to the grand central attraction of the garden are like the visions of a fairy-tale, the dancing-circle eclipses everything else in its brilliant arrangement and the artistic use of gas. It is about two hundred and fifty feet in diameter, with an elegant music-temple in the centre, not quite so large as the pagoda in Druid Hill, but capable of seating a band of fifty musicians, the best that Paris can produce. An immense chandelier is suspended in the centre, with eighty globes, and between each of the ten columns three large globes are suspended. The temple, being constructed of iron, emits gas-jets at all points. Half-way between the temple and the outer circle are arranged, equidistant, twelve large palm-trees, or at least iron representations of the palm, about thirty feet high, and from their broad leaves are suspended innumerable plum-shaped globes, serving as chandeliers. The outer edge of the dancing-arena is encircled with twenty iron arches with double rows of gas-jets, whilst from each arch three mammoth globe lights are suspended. The combination is most charming to the eye in every direction, and each jet has evidently been placed and arranged with a view to its scenic effect from all other portions of the garden.

THE MABILLE AUDIENCE.

The audience consists of all classes, so far as standing in society may designate them, but in appearance and dress they nearly all deport themselves as ladies and gentlemen, excepting of course the most reckless of the dancers. The price of admission, five francs for a gentleman and one for a lady accompanying him, makes it somewhat select on the male side, and keeps away disorderly characters. However, the fully-equipped gendarmes, with drawn swords, standing like statues at various points in the garden, are significant notifications that order must be preserved, and it is preserved with the strictest decorum. Nearly all strangers visiting Paris, both ladies and gentlemen, spend at least one evening at the Mabille Garden, and even staid old English and American mothers and fathers, with their daughters, can be seen nightly enjoying the scene. All desire to go, and when opportunity offers the ladies especially are sure to avail themselves of it. They think they will go without letting any of their acquaintances know of the contemplated indiscretion, but when there they are sure to meet an acquaintance at every turn, and by glancing around among the alcoves are apt to find the very ones from whom they were most desirous of concealing their presence, endeavoring to dodge their own vision. Many amusing scenes of acquaintances meeting nightly occur, and, indeed, if you desire to find out who are in Paris, here is the place to meet them.

THE MABILLE DANCERS.

The Gardens are opened at eight o'clock in the evening, but it is nine before dancing really commences. The first comers are generally strangers, who think they will come early, view the scene, and retire before the sinners make their appearance. They next become interested in the promenaders, who at nine o'clock throng out towards the circle with a suddenness that almost startles the beholder, and in a few minutes it is difficult to work one's way through the broad thoroughfares. The majority of the Cyprians behave themselves with the dignity of matrons, and, with few exceptions, are modestly arrayed, mingling with the promenaders until the dancing commences. After the performance of several operatic airs, the band strikes up a gallopade, and immediately rings are formed in the circle around two or three of the finest female dancers. Partners are secured, and soon they are spinning around like teetotums, with an exposure of finely-formed limbs and an agility that are seldom equaled on the stage. There are, of course, some professional dancers, both male and female, employed by the establishment, who lead off in these furious demonstrations, and the men frequently in the midst of the dance throw their heels over their partners' heads. The females are equally agile, and when too far from the circle to see them the spectator can perceive their neat boots and striped stockings flying around the heads of the throng by whom they are encompassed. Although they wear long dresses, they are appareled like the ballet-girls in all respects, including flesh-colored tights and short pantalets. Saturday night is the gala-night of the week, and it is on these occasions that strangers mostly visit the Mabille. From nine o'clock to midnight, when the gendarmes put a stop to the dancing, and the musicians retire, there is no cessation of this scene of wild abandon and unrestrained hilarity. To all outward appearance they seem to be full of the enjoyment of the occasion, and merry peals of laughter are resounding from all quarters.

THE PARIS OPERA-HOUSE.

To describe the new Paris Opera-House, which has been ten years in the course of construction, so that your readers might have some idea of its wonderful magnificence, is so utterly impossible that we will only endeavor to give a general idea of its outward appearance. It is finished on the outside, but three years of work have not yet completed the interior, and two years more are required for its ornamentation. There is no better way of conveying to an American an idea of anything that he has not seen than to tell him the cost of it. Well, this new opera-house has cost forty million francs, or about eight million dollars in gold, including the square of ground on which it stands. It is a government institution, and was intended as one of the crowning glories of the Napoleonic empire. Who will first occupy the magnificent retiring-rooms constructed for the Emperor and Empress it would be difficult now to say.

The opera-house occupies an open space, from which radiate the Boulevards des Capucines and Italiens, Rues Scribe, Auber, Halévy, and Neuve des Mathurins, like the spokes of a wheel. The area it occupies has a front of four hundred and three feet and a depth of four hundred and sixty-seven. It fronts on the Place de l'Opéra, the width of which must be about six hundred feet in one direction, and one thousand in the other, being the junction of all these great thoroughfares. To stand in the centre of this "place" and look at the front of the building, with its groups, statues, and busts of exquisite execution, and the towering dome, crowned by a group of bronze statuary, puts one out of conceit of the old masters of both statuary and architecture. The streets that encircle the building are all not less than one hundred and fifty feet in width, and a fine view of it can be obtained from any of the great thoroughfares. But it is not the front only that is ornamented with statuary and busts, but the sides, and even the rear, whilst the sculpture of all parts of the building is most elaborate. The side views are even more satisfactory, and give a better idea of its immensity, than the front, as the lateral projections with carriage-ways under arched porticoes, by which vehicles will reach the interior to the level of the first row of boxes, are among the most attractive portions of the building.

HEALTH OF PARIS.

Whilst the cholera is at Vienna, Berlin, and other parts of Northern and Southern Germany, and has put in an appearance among the old castles in Genoa, here in Paris the best possible health prevails. If the cleanliness of a city and all manner of municipal precautions are of any avail in changing the course of this ravaging monster's travels, he will not be able to enter the gates of Paris. People are compelled to live clean and keep themselves clean, whether their inclinations tend that way or not. There are no dirty sections of Paris, the narrow streets being as scrupulously cared for by the authorities as the broad thoroughfares, whilst the houses and their tenants come in for more rigid inspection and supervision. The health of the city is in charge of the Conseil de Salubrité, composed of twenty members, all physicians, surgeons, or chemists, who are especially charged with the sanitary regulations, including the cleanliness of streets, markets, sewers, etc. There is also a Comité de Salubrité Publique in each arrondissement connected with the council. The sewers that run for scores of miles under every street of the city are also cleansed and purified to such an extent that parties of ladies and gentlemen pass through them in boats, as being among the underground curiosities of Paris. More than ordinary care is now being taken, and houses and premises are being rigidly inspected. The large main sewers, of which there are seven, are cleansed by means of four good-sized steamboats, provided with drop-planks in front, whereby such a head of water is obtained as to drive all the sediment, stones included, to the distance of three hundred feet out into the Seine. A large portion of the foul water is now clarified by chemical agents, and the sediment sold for manure at a profit. It takes sixteen days to cleanse the whole extent of the sewers. The aggregate length of all the sewers now built is one million eight hundred thousand feet.

THE CHAMPS ÉLYSÉES ON SUNDAY.

Sunday was a bright and beautiful day, and the scene on the Champs Elysées during the afternoon was viewed with great interest by the thousands of strangers now in the city. To witness this display of Parisian life, a carriage-drive gives but a poor idea of its peculiarities. To view it properly, it is necessary to join the people in their holiday games and amusements, and to ramble with them through the splendid gardens, groves, and ornamental shrubbery and fountains with which this pleasure-ground of the people is adorned. It is a beautiful panoramic scene from a carriage driven along the grand avenue which passes through it, especially at night, when it is so brilliantly illuminated; but, having frequently viewed it in this way, both by day and night, we undertook a pedestrian investigation of its attractions on Sunday afternoon. As we passed from Avenue Marigny, it seemed as if we were entering the precincts of a grand mass-meeting of all the children of Paris, who were here by thousands, the younger of them in charge of parents or nurses, but the vast majority taking care of themselves. It was at times difficult to thread our way through them. All manner of contrivances for their amusement were in progress, the most popular of which appeared to be Punch and Judy shows, the little stages being fitted up with scenery and curtains, and the automatic performers made to hold conversations and to crack jokes of a local character, which drew forth shouts of laughter from old and young. There were not less than a dozen of these little theatres in progress, around each of which there were several hundred spectators, mostly children, who were occupying the seats at ten centimes (about two cents) each. The performances lasted about half an hour, when the chairs were cleared, and the play resumed again so soon as a sufficient audience was seated. The standing spectators paid nothing, and these always outnumbered those occupying the chairs. Under the groves were toy- and gingerbread-stalls, and other attractions for the rising generation, whilst jugglers and itinerant tumblers were attracting a willing and ever-changing throng of spectators. A dozen or more revolving-horse machines, with children astride of wooden ponies, were in motion, and little temples with scales for ascertaining the weight of young humanity were doing a successful business. There are also various concert-gardens and cafés scattered among the trees on either side, where open-air concerts were in progress to large audiences. The avenue for driving and promenading, which is a mile and a quarter long, and fully two hundred feet in width, was thronged with vehicles, whilst the lively spectacle was being enjoyed by thousands of persons seated on the iron chairs with which the sidewalks are lined. These chairs are rented for two or three sous the hour, they being owned by a company which pays twelve thousand francs per annum to the city for the privilege. The city also receives fifty thousand francs per annum for rents from the Punch and Judy shows. A number of little carriages, each holding six to nine children, drawn by six goats in harness, were doing a good business, the boys occupying the drivers' seats and plying the whip with great dexterity. As night set in, all the cafés were brilliantly illuminated, and bands of music in the concert-gardens gave additional animation to the scene. The circus-building was also illuminated, and the doors thrown open for a grand equestrian performance, with all the usual stale jokes and clap-trap performances which prove so attractive to Young America.

The avenue through the Champs Elysées is the grand thoroughfare to the great park of Paris, the Bois de Boulogne, with the Place de la Concorde at one end of it and the Arch of Triumph at the other. Indeed, the Louvre and Tuileries Gardens, the Place du Carrousel, the Place de la Concorde in the Champs Elysées, and the Bois de Boulogne, are all connected, forming one direct line of pleasure-grounds from the heart of Paris out to the fortifications, a distance of six or seven miles. The boulevards and streets have, however, of late years greatly encroached on the

Champs Elysées, leaving but a narrow strip of its former dimensions.

THE PLACE DE LA CONCORDE.

On all the public buildings of France the words "Liberty, Equality, and Fraternity" are emblazoned in large and deeply-cut letters, which Horace Greeley would term a "flaunting lie." So the great square in the heart of the city is called the "Place de la Concorde," upon which there has been more human blood spilt, and more scenes of horror and confusion, than upon any other similar space of ground under the canopy of heaven. It is, however, a majestic square, and its adornments are very grand. In the centre stands the famous Obelisk of Luxor, a monolith that was brought from Thebes by Napoleon, it having been part of the grand temple erected fifteen hundred and fifty years before the birth of Christ. It has also two of the finest fountains in Europe, and various specimens of elegant statuary. It forms a beautiful link between the Tuileries and the Champs Elysées. On the north are two palaces, between which the Rue Royale opens a view of the Madeleine; to the south are the Pont de la Concorde and the Legislative Palace, behind which is seen towering the gilded dome of the Invalides, under which repose the remains of Napoleon. The following are some of the scenes of blood which have transpired in this "Place de la Concorde" during the past two hundred years:

In 1770, during the rejoicings in honor of the marriage of Louis XVI., whilst the fire-works were being discharged, the people took a panic, and one thousand two hundred persons were trampled to death, whilst two thousand were badly wounded. More than two thousand eight hundred persons were executed in this square by the guillotine, including Louis XVI., Charlotte Corday, Marie Antoinette, Danton, Robespierre, and Dumas, all during the eighteen months succeeding January 21, 1793. The first disturbance which ushered in the revolution of 1848 took place here. It was here also that a desperate conflict took place only two years ago between the Communists and the Versailles troops, during which the earth was soaked with blood. The "Place de la Discorde" would be a more appropriate name.

OLD CURIOSITY-SHOPS.

There must be an immense demand in Paris for ancient things, such as are usually consigned to the rubbish-room in a well-regulated American household. There is scarcely a square throughout the whole length and breadth of Paris that has not its old curiosity-shop,—just such places as Dickens chose for the scene of one of his sweetest stories. How it is possible for any one to desire any of the articles in these masses of rubbish it is difficult to conceive, but they are daily ransacked by the English antiquarians, and many of them are doubtless manufactured to meet the demand. Old china of past generations, old stained and defaced engravings, ancient-looking paintings, all cracked and defaced, some of them like Mark Twain's Virgins, "with fly-blisters on their breasts," form the staple commodities of these establishments. Then there are old chairs and tables, some of them with three legs, just as they were left by Julius Cæsar or Mark Antony; heathen gods and goddesses, old Roman lamps, and other odds and ends, all covered with dust and cobwebs to blind the eyes of these modern collectors. On Boulevard Haussmann we passed this afternoon four of these establishments, all adjoining each other, and in the narrow streets they are so numerous as to strike the stranger with wonder. There are enough of them to set up an opposition to the great museum of antiquities at Munich, through which we wandered and wondered a few weeks since.

BUSINESS-WOMEN.

There are very few establishments in Paris, wholesale or retail, in which women do not occupy most of the important positions of trust and responsibility. In a great many of the largest and most successful establishments the wife is the principal business-manager, and to her all matters of importance are referred. An American gentleman who has been exploring the wholesale establishments assures me that this is more generally the case than in those of a retail character. When purchasing goods, all important questions were answered by the female clerks or saleswomen, the males evidently holding subordinate positions. In many cases the wife was called upon to answer questions or make agreements when the husband was present, indicating that she was the brains of the establishment. There can be no doubt that the average Frenchwoman is superior in intellect to the average Frenchman, as she is superior to him in physical development and address. Passing the little stores at night, the wife is seen at the desk, pen in hand, keeping the books, and thousands of the smaller of the Paris stores are kept by women. They have great business capacity, energy, and enterprise, and take more than their full share in supplying the means for the maintenance of the household. A Frenchman remarked the other day that he believed there were as many wives in Paris who support their husbands as there are husbands who support their wives. She almost invariably manages to live free of house-rent by renting a flat of rooms and sub-renting enough of them to pay the rent for the whole. The American ladies who visit Europe and squander so much money which they had no part in earning, generally return better satisfied with their positions in life, and convinced that their destiny has been more fortunate than that of most of the sisterhood of creation.

SOCIAL QUESTIONS.

There is nothing that we take so much interest in investigating, whilst roaming through these European cities, as the great social questions which assume such different shapes. We are bad enough at home, but we have not yet reached the deplorable condition of these great centres of European civilization. We have "social evils," but they are recognized as evils. Here and over a great portion of the Continent these evils in a more aggravated shape are recognized as necessary to the form of government, and no effort is made to reform or remedy them. In order that those of your citizens who profess to have a preference for the monarchial form of government may know some of the very essentials of its existence, and the degradation it brings upon a great portion of the people, we have in this correspondence touched upon many subjects that are by many persons regarded as "open secrets," only to be hinted at, but not discussed or described. As we do not belong to this school of modern philosophers, we shall endeavor in this letter to present your readers with an accurate statement in regard to the French law of marriage, and the evils which spring from its enforcement here in Paris, together with its aggravation by that other necessity of all monarchial governments, "a standing army."

MATRIMONIAL AGENCIES.

The matrimonial agencies of Paris do a thriving business. They are located in all sections of the city, and are of different classes, according to the wealth and standing of the families of the parties they deal with,—young men who are looking for a wife with a good dowry, the money consideration being the main incentive, and parents who have marriageable daughters, being the principal customers. The agents, when they effect a marriage, stipulate that they shall receive five per cent. of the dowry, and generally manage also to get a good retaining-fee from both parties. The larger establishments are in correspondence with similar agencies on all parts of the Continent, and have become a necessity to parents who are looking out for eligible wives for their sons and responsible husbands for their daughters. The successful tradesman who has accumulated a fortune desires his daughters to marry in a higher circle than that in which he associates; hence the necessity of an agent to make the necessary advances. Then elaborate papers must be prepared and signed before the marriage is consummated, and unless the dowry is paid down at the stipulated time the engagement is off. To manage all these preliminaries requires practical knowledge and experience which few parties in private life could be expected to possess. The agency of Madame St. Just only does openly what hundreds of others have for ages been doing secretly, and she has at once risen to the head of the profession. She is one of those business geniuses who believe in advertising, and she is, of course, pushing aside all the old fogies who have transacted their business as if secrecy was necessary to all their movements. Madame St. Just says the French law of marriage, and the national custom, render matrimonial agencies a necessity, and in a recent trial the courts have sustained the position she has taken. No one under twenty-five years of age, either son or daughter, can marry without the consent of his or her parents, or, if the parents are dead, without the consent of the grandparents, if any are living. If none of them are living, applicants must substantiate the fact by bringing certificates of their death and burial. Thus it will be seen that parents make all the arrangements for marriage, and, as they do not know who are the eligible parties in the matrimonial market, they must apply to those who make it a business to keep a record, with the pedigree and pecuniary standing or prospects, of all the young men and girls who are similarly eligible. If John Smith should have settled on his daughter a dowry of twenty thousand francs, he has a money interest in securing for her a husband similarly endowed, and he wants the guarantee of a responsible agent that there is no false pretense being practiced upon him. How would he be able to ascertain that Tom Brown, who applied for the hand of Miss Smith, was all that he represented himself to be, and whether his father was responsible for the twenty thousand francs which he had promised to give his son on the morning of his marriage, or how would he know that there were twenty or thirty young men of good family and good money-standing who are anxious to secure a wife with the twenty-thousand-franc charm possessed by Miss Smith, if there were not an agent to apply to who kept a record of all such young aspirants for matrimony? Or how would the parents of these young men know that there was such an eligible party as Miss Smith in existence, if they had not applied to Madame St. Just for the information?

THE FRENCH MARRIAGE-LAWS.

Young men over twenty-five and young women over twenty-one years of age can marry without the consent of their parents, but still they have many difficulties to encounter before they can become united. Indeed, the obstructions to marriage are so great that it is not to be wondered at that there are twenty thousand illegitimate births in Paris per annum. To marry, according to French law, publication of the marriage must be twice made by the mayor of the commune in which each of the parties resides, with an interval of eight days between each publication. A preliminary civil service is then celebrated by the mayor of the commune in which one of the parties has lived for six months. The parties must produce the certificate of their birth or baptism, or, if not to be had, a declaration of seven persons made before the juge de paix of the date and place of birth of the party, and the consent of their parents properly authenticated; and if their parents are dead, certificates of their burial, and the consent of the grandmother and grandfather, if living. If agencies are necessary for parents to dispose of their children, how much more necessary are they to enable a man over twenty-five to find out where the girls are with good dowries! He can well afford to give the agent five per cent. of the dowry, and save time and make money by so doing. And how would it be possible to wade through such intricate legal arrangements without each party having a legal adviser at their elbow to watch the other contracting party and see that no trickery or rascality is being practiced?

These matrimonial agents, of course, have nothing to do with any marriage-contracts in which the heart has any lot or part in deciding the destiny of the parties. Sometimes children are plighted by their parents to each other at a tender age, and are brought up with the tacit understanding that they are to be married at the proper time. In these cases, love has, of course, some chance to play his part, and matrimonial agents are unnecessary. Nothing ever interferes with the consummation of such marriages except a reverse in business, or some other cause which may prevent the bride's parents from meeting their contract as to the amount of dower. If this is not forthcoming, hearts must go to the dogs, as this is a money consideration for which no prudent father will accept any "promise to pay." The money must be paid down in hard cash to the satisfaction of the legal advisers of the family before the ceremony is allowed to proceed. The father of the groom regards a promise made before marriage as of the same character as the promise of a politician before election-day. The latter are sometimes trusted and always suspected, but the French father never trusts in any promises that are to be fulfilled after marriage. If the dowry is not forthcoming, the son quietly submits to the decision of his parents, pulls off his kid gloves and rolls them up in tissue-paper so that they may not be soiled, and to have them in readiness for use whenever ma and pa may call upon him to be ready to meet some other young lady whose paternal treasury is in a more flourishing condition. If he intended to make any bridal presents, he gathers these up, looks at the bouquet in his button-hole, which won't keep for another occasion, with sadness as so much money lost, and follows his parents home, stopping on the way to witness some one of the ever-recurring fêtes, and to take a cream at one of the boulevard cafés.

OMITTING THE CEREMONY.

With all these obstructions to overcome, it is scarcely to be wondered at that so many young French people "omit the ceremony," especially when the heart has something to do with the matter. To carry out all the provisions of the law, and to be married in due form, is also a very expensive undertaking, which neither party may have the means to meet. The mayors and other officials all receive fees, and it requires both time and money to get all the certificates that are required properly signed, and sealed, and attested by the official authorities. There are also preliminary Church ceremonies to go through with, which combine to make matrimony not only a very serious matter, but one that is very troublesome and very expensive. It must be a bold young man who would undertake to go through them without a heavy money consideration, and if there is any heart in the matter, and no money, they have neither the time, money, nor patience to conform to the provisions of the law. Where there is heart in the matter, and parents refuse their consent, they often "jump the ceremony," and, if love holds out, they have the ceremony performed after they attain legal age, which legitimatizes the children, provided they were, before the marriage, recognized by the father in an authentic manner, as in the register of births, or by declaration before a notary, or even in the marriage-act itself. If love does not hold out, they separate, and the wife becomes a grisette of the Latin Quarter, or a dancing temptress at the Mabille Garden or the Château Rouge, her children going to the Foundling Hospital. Whilst living together, the parents tempt their son with offers of beauty and dowry to abandon her, and generally succeed, though sometimes love and attachment are too strong to yield to the tempter.

SOCIAL DEGRADATIONS.

Where the legal obstructions and the expenses of the marriage ceremony are so great, there is little or no social degradation accompanying the total disregard of it. To condemn many who "omit the ceremony," would be to crush human instincts; for these associations are probably the only ones in France that the heart has much lot or part in before their consummation. Every man and woman feels that the parties have done precisely as he or she would have done under all the circumstances. If they continue to live together in good faith, and subsequently marry as a means of legitimatizing their children, they are more entitled to respect than if they had been lawfully married, or rather sold for a price by their parents. Although there is no opportunity for love before marriage in all these money-marriages, it does not follow that love does not come after marriage. Indeed, the advocates of the French matrimonial law contend that happy unions are more likely to follow these business transactions than if the parties had already gone through the courting process, with all its lovers' quarrels and its close intimacies. They also contend that young people are incapable of judging for themselves, and that they have no right to bring into their circle parties who may be objectionable to the heads of their respective families. They do not look to the evils resulting from these matrimonial obstructions among the poorer classes of the community, nor do they at the same time put any mark of degradation upon them.

ANOTHER KIND OF AGENCY.

These agencies being a necessity under the French law governing marriages, they have of course given rise to another class of agencies, equally numerous, which contemplate association at the will of the parties without marriage. They are not conducted so openly as to matrimonial agency, and the dark side of the contract is kept out of sight. A young man who has rented a room, desiring a companion of the opposite sex to take care of his clothing, make his coffee for him in the morning, and tuck him in at night, and, in fact, to be his servant, applies to these agencies; or a girl desiring to be thus provided for applies for a place, just as a servant-girl in America goes and records her name at an intelligence-office. To properly appreciate this condition of affairs, it must be remembered that here in Paris there are thirty to forty thousand soldiers, who are prohibited under any circumstances from marrying during the four years of their service; that there are fifty thousand young men who have not the means of marrying or paying the expenses of the ceremony, and never will be able to accomplish either; and that there are a still larger number who are awaiting the decision of father and mother as to their marital destiny. These young people, especially those of the poorer classes, have been raised without the remotest thought or expectation of ever being married. Their mothers and fathers before them were never married, and they have been raised as waifs, with few family ties and influences. They see the friends and associates of their infancy taking this anomalous position in life, and they fall into it also, without a thought that they are doing otherwise than what the good Lord intended them to do. Still, this is a country in which the Church and the State are united, and the Church makes no effort to remedy this great social evil. These men and women attend church with more regularity than those who have had the sanction and ceremonies of the Church, and have no reason to believe that they are not leading blameless lives; at least, they are never told to the contrary. The Church undoubtedly winks at the evil, probably having come to the conclusion that the necessity for standing armies, and the enforcement of the matrimonial laws, render the grisette a necessary evil, and that it would evince a lack of patriotism on the part of the priesthood if they were to attempt to have the laws of God respected and enforced among the poorer classes. It may be regarded as an open question whether, in view of the condition of society that exists in Paris, these establishments are not quite as necessary as the matrimonial agency.

ENGLISH AND AMERICAN TRAVELERS.

Our English cousins from across the Channel who are traveling on the Continent have just vented their grievances against American tourists in a very able article in the *Saturday Review*. They say that the Americans are demoralizing hotel-keepers, servants, beggars, and the whole host of people with whom they come in contact, to such an extent that the plain English traveler, with limited means, is invariably snubbed and given poor quarters and attention wherever Americans are abundant. Americans are charged with coming to Europe to run hastily over the Continent, limited in time, but unlimited in means, and that they demand the best rooms, the best attendance, are lavish in their fees to servants, and never dispute the landlords' bills. This is all very true; but Brother Bull must remember that most Americans don't understand the language, and could not dispute the bills if they were so disposed, as it would require something more than linguistic knowledge to read and understand any part of most of the bills except the figures at the end of the lines, and the grand total. We remember having submitted a bill which we paid at Dresden to a good German scholar, and he could not decipher one charge in a dozen on the long list of items covering two foolscap pages. How was it possible for an American to dispute such a bill, especially if he had no words at command to vent his indignation, and only ten minutes left to reach the depot and catch the departing train when he received his bill? Then, again, to the American tourist "time is money," and he would rather part with his money than waste time in quarreling over a few florins or lose his temper when he is on a pleasure-trip. Then, as to the servants, the American feels a commiseration for these poor devils, who receive no wages from the landlord. He charges heavily in the bills for "service," but puts it all in his own pocket. The American feels, with respect to these servants, that he is doing a charitable act when he makes them happy with a few florins and pays them for service to himself and family for which they would otherwise go unpaid. It is a part of his enjoyment of travel to do a little good as he goes along through the Old World. But there is no place in Europe where the American is so systematically fleeced as in London. This is the experience of every American that we have met with. In Paris the charges are high, but not so high as in London, and here the American gets good food and good attendance, neither of which can be had in London. The London *Times*, whilst denouncing the extortions of Vienna, ought to look to the condition of affairs at its own doors, which are equally bad. Good beds, without bugs, can be had in Paris and Vienna, but we have never been able to find them in London. And as to the begging of servants, London is ahead of the Continent. If a servant in a London hotel is asked the simplest question, he expects to be paid for his answer, and everybody about the building is watching and waiting for an opportunity to put in his claim. Americans who travel in Europe are used to good living and good attendance when they travel at home, and they are willing to pay something extra for the best they can get when away from home.

AMENITIES OF TRAVEL.

The *Saturday Review* is correct when it says that the American and Englishman do not assimilate when traveling. Although in the same section of a car or on the same boat on one of the lakes, they seldom exchange a word, and never unless the American breaks the ice. Their answers to questions are in monosyllables, and the questioner feels as if he were being snubbed for having asked them. After one or two attempts of this kind, the American feels more disposed to attempt to commence conversation by signs and motions with a Turk than to make an effort to open any social intercourse with the Englishman who may be sitting on the other side of him. The fact is that John Bull is a surly and suspicious character. He thinks that every man who approaches him without an introduction has some evil intentions, and at once becomes so watchful that he is as dumb as an oyster. In a good deal of experience in Continental traveling we have never known an Englishman to commence or invite a conversation, although we have met with some who have ultimately proved very pleasant and agreeable traveling companions. But this money-question is the one that is invariably predominant in their minds. They always pant to know how it is that so many Americans are able to bring their whole families to Europe and spend money so lavishly; how it is possible for us to go on so rapidly in the payment of our national debt, etc. The natural and only answers that can be given to these questions they set down as American gasconade, American boasting and exaggeration. It thus often happens that what might otherwise have been a pleasant traveling acquaintance ends with ill-feeling, and the American resolves in future to stand aloof from all intercourse with Englishmen. During five months' travel, we have exchanged words with but one Englishman, and he was introduced to us by a Hungarian.

DUVAL'S "BOUCHERIE."

We never pass this magnificent establishment, right in the heart of the city, within a stone's throw of the Madeleine, on the corner of one of the most central of the boulevards, without conjuring up the ghosts of Colonel Mabe Turner, Sterling Thomas, Marcus Wolfe, Harry Kimberly, and a host of the departed Baltimore butchers, who years ago fought so energetically to induce the City Council to prevent the sale of meat from the provision stores. We remember that we differed with them as to the propriety of their proposed action, and we think they all lived to admit that they were wrong. But we would like them to be here, in spirit at least, to take a stroll through the boulevards, and to stand with us, as we do almost daily, and view the internal arrangements of this "boucherie," and the stirring scene always in progress within its precincts. The establishment fronts about one hundred feet on Rue Neuve des Mathurins, and about sixty feet on the Boulevard Tronchet. There is but one door for entrance and exit, but nearly the entire of its combined front is of iron bars, making it virtually open to the street in warm weather, though there are inside sashes which can be closed in winter. Directly opposite the entrance is an elegant white-marble inclosure, behind which sit two clerks, one a very handsome and elegantly-dressed lady, *who handles all the money*, and the other a spruce young Frenchman, who makes the entries. There is another smaller elaborately-ornamented desk at the left side of the door, at which another clerk takes note of all the cards that are passed up to be settled. Between these two desks there is a variegated-marble fountain, in the basin of which tripe and calves' heads are kept for sale. The walls of the "boucherie" are faced with white marble, and all the tables are of white marble, with ornamental iron legs finely gilded. On the racks on the walls the cattle are suspended in quarters, and are dressed with all the care that our butchers sometimes bestow on show-beef. We counted yesterday morning thirty quarters of beef, fifteen calves, and forty sheep, hanging up whole, besides the cut meat that was on the blocks and tables. The salesmen in their neat white dresses—fully twenty in number—were waiting on their customers, and all kept busy. The Parisian never buys his meat until he is ready to cook it: hence the necessity of these establishments, which are to be found, to the number of nine hundred, in all sections of the city, though we have seen none that will compare in extent with Duval's "Boucherie." Everything is kept scrupulously sweet and clean. The hooks upon which the meat is suspended are of polished steel, and are always kept polished. The floors are sprinkled with clean sawdust, and bear the evidence of being daily scrubbed, and, what is most singular, even in this August weather scarcely a fly could be seen within its precincts. The strangers in the city invariably stop as they pass, and regard it as an appetizing curiosity, keeping in remembrance the numerous unsavory establishments of a somewhat similar character at home. There does not appear to be a market anywhere in Paris in which meat is sold, though there are poultry-markets, flower-markets, fruit-markets, grape-markets, and vegetable-markets in abundance. The butcher transacts his business at home or in rented shops,—which is much more convenient to the people, and probably equally profitable to himself. He buys his cattle, but has nothing to do with its killing or dressing for the market. We have something to learn from Paris in this respect before Baltimore gets rid of the droves of cattle passing through the streets, and the nauseous smells in the vicinity of slaughterhouses.

The window-sills of this "boucherie," and indeed of nearly all similar establishments, are always ornamented with flowers and rare exotics in full bloom. In the pork department, across the ceilings are iron racks, upon which hams and tongues are suspended, the hooks of which are kept clean and bright. There are rooms in the rear in which the meat is cut up, and in which a reserve supply is kept to be brought forward when desired. Calves are seldom slaughtered until they are five or six months old, and the veal of Paris is of a very superior quality.

HORSE-BUTCHERIES.

In some sections of Paris the butcheries keep for sale horse-meat, which is sold at about one-half the price of beef, and is extensively used by the poor. When cut up and hanging on the shambles, it is difficult for the inexperienced to tell it from beef, and when tolerably young it is said by those who use it to be equally tender and palatable. It is preferred to the meat of old cows and bulls, with which our army was so extensively fed by some of the contractors during "the late unpleasantness." The abattoir or place of slaughter for horses is at the village of Les Vertes, where about twenty thousand horses are slaughtered per annum, and the meat sent to Paris. Before the late siege, horses were worked to death; but now when they cease to be active they are sold to the butchers, who fatten and kill them. A dead horse is worth nothing, but a live horse has his price, although he may be good for nothing else but the tender mercy of the butcher. Horses in Paris have heavy loads to draw, and if used in omnibuses or carriages must be able to travel fast. When incompetent to meet either of these requirements, a horse soon finds his way to the village of Les Vertes.

A NEW CLASS OF EMIGRANTS.

A throng of emigrants passed through Paris yesterday on their way to America, which is but the commencement of a more extended emigration of the same character. They consisted of fifty nuns and Sisters of Charity, from the old departments of Haut-Rhin and Bas-Rhin. There is undoubtedly a superabundance of these good people in all parts of France, and they can supply the world with all they want of them, without suffering in the least on account of their absence. An immense number of priests, of the Jesuit Order, who have been expelled from Germany, are also taking passage for America. It is hard to say what the Old World would do with all its supernumeraries if it had not America to ship them off to. We have always imagined priests and soldiers to be the pests of Europe, eating up the substance of the people and producing nothing. It is to be hoped that these emigrants will try and make themselves useful in America.

EXEMPTION FROM FIRES.

The great fires we are constantly having in the United States give to Europeans a very poor idea of the construction of our great cities. The outcry against the mansard roofs, as the cause of these great conflagrations, is amusing to the people of Paris, where almost every house is constructed with that appendage, and none but the public buildings have iron superstructures to them. Fires in Paris are always confined to the building in which they originate, and if they commence in the lower part of the building they seldom reach the mansard roofs. The fact is, these houses are not built to be burned, but to stand until time and the spirit of improvement call for their demolition. In the more modern buildings iron is substituted for wood, inside and outside, and it takes a long time for a fire to get under way to such an extent that it cannot be extinguished with buckets. Even the lattice window-shutters are now made of iron, and they are so simple in their construction that they are cheaper than the ordinary wooden shutters. They are of one solid piece of sheet-iron, and the lattice portion of an entire window is made by machinery at the rate of one per minute, by being run under a roller, which cuts and presses them into shape. In the whole city of Paris there is but one steam fire-engine, and it is so seldom required that it is periodically put in motion, to be sure that it is always in order.

We have now been four weeks in Paris, and there has not been in that time even an alarm of fire, and we see no notices in the papers of any conflagrations. When it is borne in mind that the population is more than six times as large as that of Baltimore, some idea may be formed of the general exemption. The houses here are packed more closely together than they are with us, and extend some twenty or thirty feet on an average higher up in the air than ours do. There are also from six to a dozen or more families in every house, which of itself would seem to render them more liable to accidental combustion. The stairs and balusters are required to be constructed of stone and iron, and the lower floors are generally arched and laid in cement. The law is peremptory as to the manner of construction, but, instead of attempting to evade the law, builders contrive in every way to make their buildings more thoroughly fire-proof. Board-yards and packing-box factories are never allowed to be in contiguity to thickly-settled neighborhoods, and hence when such tinder-boxes take fire they burn out without damaging any one but themselves.

The firemen of Paris, called "sapeurs pompiers," consisting of a regiment of two thousand men, are organized on a military footing, and under the orders of the War Department, but in case of fire they obey the orders of the Prefect of Police. A portion are on duty every evening at the theatres. They are efficient as soldiers no less than as active firemen, and are carefully drilled and trained in gymnastics. Medals are annually awarded to such as have distinguished themselves by their exertions and good conduct. The annual cost of the force is five hundred and seventy-five thousand three hundred and ninety francs, or about one hundred and twenty thousand dollars.

The incendiary fires of the Commune in no case spread farther than the structures in which the flames originated. The Communists did their best to destroy all the central portion of Paris, and with any American city would have succeeded. They had no combustible buildings to work with, no tinder-boxes in the heart of blocks, and the flames were generally extinguished as rapidly as they were ignited, by the residents of the neighborhoods.

A MYSTERIOUS WORK OF ART.

There is now exhibiting in Paris one of the most startling works of genius and art that we have ever witnessed. It is a diorama of the siege of Paris, and all Paris is running wild to view it. There is some species of optical illusion in connection with it, that no one seems able to understand. Although a painting, it so closely resembles nature that on suddenly entering the hall the spectator is bewildered, and invariably complains of dizziness as his eye scans the intervening scenes and the distant horizon presented to view. Of course, as we could not understand, we cannot describe, and we scarcely expect the reader to believe that it was difficult to realize that we were not standing on a lofty eminence between the lines of the contending armies, viewing the progress of the siege. The building in which the diorama is exhibited is circular, and about three hundred feet in diameter, with a glass dome. On entering it the visitor passes along a rather dark passage to what seems the centre of the building, and then proceeds up a circular series of stone steps, about forty in number, and finds himself on a circular platform on the top of a veritable hill of earth, strewn with cannon-balls and shell, the object of the artist being to place the spectator in the Fort of Issy, surrounded on every side by the incidents of the siege, with the city of Paris, and its monuments, domes, and steeples, in the distance. By close examination it could be discovered that the nearer earthworks of the picture, and even some of the cannon, for a distance of fifty or sixty feet from the edge of the platform, were veritable earth, and undoubted cannon, and real willow gabions and sand-bags; but the exact spot where the substantials ended and the canvas began was not so easily detected. The reader must take our word for it that, as we stood on the platform, representing an elevated position on one of the bastions of Fort Issy, it appeared to the mortal vision of all of us just as if we were there in reality in the midst of the siege. We could scarcely believe we were inside of a building, as nature was so closely imitated that it seemed as if the vision embraced every tree and hillock up to Fortress Mont Valérien, eight or ten miles distant. The horizon was perfect all around the circle, and there was nothing to indicate that we were not out in the open air, except a circular canvas, suspended as if from the clouds, high up over our heads, and nothing visible anywhere to indicate that we were in reality inside of a building, viewing a painting. The whole seems to be a piece of legerdemain in art that has never been attempted before. When we came out of the building we involuntarily turned around and measured its size with our eyes, in a vain attempt to unravel its mystery.

HOW PARIS IS PAINTED.

It would astonish some of our old house-painters of Baltimore if they could witness the manner in which the painters of Paris climb over the fronts of these six- and seven-story houses and paint them from roof to door-sill without the use of ladder, scaffold, or any other wooden contrivance, either for themselves or their paint-pots. One man, without assistance of any kind, can paint the entire front of one of these tall houses in two or three days. Directly opposite our quarters, a six-story building, fronting about eighty feet, is undergoing a complete renovation, and the painting of the entire walls has been accomplished by two youths, apparently not over nineteen years of age. They are each provided with a rope about an inch in diameter, extending from the apex of the roof to the pavement, on which knots, one foot apart, are made throughout its entire length. By means of an apparatus with straps, clamps, and hooks, to which is appended a board on which they sit, and stirrups to rest the feet in, which are strapped to their legs, they move up and down the rope with great rapidity and apparent ease. They move the clamps from knot to knot, and without changing the position of the rope are enabled to paint about six feet on either side of them. Their smaller brushes are stuck in little loops appended to the seat, and the paint-pot is suspended by a smaller rope, on which it is fastened by a spring of some kind, and is raised or lowered with ease as they may desire. Long practice has given them great agility, and they move up or down, and pirouette and oscillate along the front, with a great deal more ease than if they were on ladders. They use brushes for most of their painting nearly double the size of those used in America, and make rapid progress with their work. House-painting in Paris is a very extensive business, as a periodical renovation of the houses is rendered imperative by law, no one being allowed to disfigure a neighborhood by presenting stained and darkened walls. The houses being all built of a soft cream-colored sandstone, many of the finer structures, instead of being painted, are re-dressed by the stonecutter, and come out, after undergoing the process of scraping and scrubbing, as if fresh from the quarry. In alluding to the amount of work these lads perform in a day, it should be understood that they commence work at six o'clock in the morning and stop at seven o'clock in the evening, twelve hours being a day's work among the mechanics in Paris.

GOVERNMENT OF PARIS.

It may be of interest to our City Fathers to know in what way the means for carrying on the expensive city government of Paris are obtained. Everything that is brought into Paris in the shape of food for sale must pay an *octroi*, or entrance-duty, at the gates of the city, or, if by boats, at the wharf before it is landed. The receipts from this source last year amounted to 102,286,000 francs, or $20,448,000 ; market-dues, $2,000,000 ; weights and measures, $21,020 ; supply of water, $1,028,000 ; slaughter-houses, $600,000 ; rents of stands on the public ways, $90,060 ; dues on burials, $140,000 ; sales of lands in cemeteries, $139,000 ; taxes for paving, lighting, etc., $2,100,000 ; trade-licenses, $3,500,000 ; dog-tax, $90,000 ; sale of night-soil, $132,000 : total receipts, $39,556,410.

Among the items of expenditure are, interest of debt and sinking-fund, $9,214,000 ; expenses of collections, salaries, etc., $1,689,000 ; primary institutions, $1,100,000 ; public worship, $36,000 ; national guard and military service, $576,300 ; repairs of public buildings, $346,000 ; assistance to the poor, including hospitals, $4,469,200 ; promenades and works of art, $653,340 ; public schools, $123,200 ; public festivals, $152,000 ; the police department, $3,124,000 ; new public works, $4,924,000 ; lighting streets, $783,200 : total expenses, $39,416,000.

It will thus be seen that, notwithstanding the tribulations through which Paris has passed, she spent last year nearly $5,000,000 on new public improvements, whilst the receipts exceeded the whole expenses of the city by nearly $150,000. Poor Baltimore, with its "rings" and political bunkers, spends literally nothing on public improvements, and runs deeper in debt every year. The city government of Paris is a model for the world, and if we must continue to keep the incompetents in control, do send them over here to learn something.

BUSINESS OF PARIS.

The stranger visiting Paris is astonished at the vast number of stores and places of business which line every street, even the narrow thoroughfares in the old portions of the city. Every house, almost, has a store in its lower story, and thousands of them are occupied for business purposes up to the second and third stories. On the new boulevards many of these stores are empty, and for rent, but they are all expected to be occupied sooner or later. The wholesale establishments are generally back in court-yards, and can only be found by those who know where to look for them. We spent a day among them with Mr. Samuel Child, and in almost every case they were located back from the streets, and completely out of sight. By the official record we see that the whole number of business-establishments in the city is set down at 101,171. Of this number there are 3199 jewelry-stores; 28,806 in which clothing and material for clothing are sold; 7391 furniture, 2836 textile fabrics, and 29,069 establishments in which food, groceries, and all manner of goods for the inner man are provided. The number of hands employed in these establishments is set down at 417,311. The sales of the industrial establishments are estimated at 3,379,000,000 francs, or $675,980,000, per annum. If England can be called "a nation of shop-keepers," it would seem that France is in a fair way to rival her. There are about 1000 manufactories of haberdashery; 141 of paper-hangings; the shawl-trade counts 752 looms; the number of ladies in dress-making establishments is 879; stay-makers, 653; hat-stores, 644; upholsterers, 519; of looking-glasses, 120; bronze and gilt work, 450; and pastry-cook establishments, 622. The sales of this latter trade net twenty-one millions of francs per annum, and restaurants one hundred and four millions. The rag-collectors, or *chiffonniers*, of Paris, number 22,000, and realize from one and a half to two francs per day. The number of bakeries in Paris is 960, employing 4500 men. In 1863 the price of bread was two sous for a pound loaf; it is now four sous. In 1863 the average price of meat was twelve to fifteen sous per pound; it is now twenty-two to thirty sous. The total number of persons of independent fortune, or engaged in liberal pursuits, is 400,000.

PARIS, September 10, 1873.

THE FETE OF ST. CLOUD.

The fête of St. Cloud commenced on Sunday last, and continued for three weeks. We went out during the afternoon to see it. It is held at the town of St. Cloud, which is rapidly rising from its ashes, having been totally destroyed, with the magnificent palace, during the siege. The Prussians having obtained possession, the guns of Mont Valérien were turned upon it, and the palace set fire to by the shells. The town, after being half destroyed by the French shells, was set fire to by the Prussians, and nothing left but the blackened walls. The palace, which had been the favorite residence of Napoleon, is still a mass of ruins, but the greater portion of the town has since been rebuilt, and the new Cathedral of St. Cloud, which was in the course of erection, has been completed, and here the services of the fête were held. We reached the upper part of the town by railroad, and the whole character of the fête was a surprise to us, in view of the fact that it is proclaimed that a great religious revival is in progress in France. This fête is a Church festival, under the direction of the clergy, and lasts for three whole weeks, commencing every morning with services in the cathedral.

CHARACTER OF THE FETE.

What we expected to see on our visit to St. Cloud was a mass of people assembled to witness the playing of the great fountains, which, next to those at Versailles, are the finest in France. Having landed at the depot, we walked on through the town, stopping occasionally to look at the ruins still standing. The town is located on the side of a hill, descending all the way towards the banks of the Seine. The streets were filled with people, and we followed the crowd until we reached the cathedral, which is not far from the entrance to the park. Here the visitors first entered and made their devotions and moved on. It was too much crowded for mere spectators to venture upon entering, and we passed on towards the park. We would like, if it were possible, to photograph for your readers the scene that was presented to our view. The gates open on a wide avenue of chestnut-trees, nearly a mile in length, running parallel with the river. Either side of this avenue was closely lined with stalls and booths, and packed with people, throughout its entire length, whilst flags and streamers and parti-colored lamps were everywhere suspended for the grand illumination that was to take place at night. The booths had displayed all manner of fancy articles, cakes, and candies, not for sale, but to be gambled for by the drawing of numbers, turning of wheels, or firing of air-guns at glass balls suspended on the top of jets of water over little fountains. The number and variety of the games of chance in this portion of the park exceeded anything we have ever witnessed, many of which we could not understand the mode of operating. The simple manner of buying what you wanted seemed to be entirely ignored. This portion of the exhibition was nearly one mile in length, and the avenue, more than one hundred feet in width, densely packed with people.

After passing slowly through this scene to the immense cascade fountain, located about the centre of the avenue, the character of the exhibition commenced to change, and the woods on either side of the road were densely packed with other attractions. First came fully fifty large tents with revolving horses, not such small affairs as we sometimes have for children, but immense establishments, capable of sending on a flying circuit fifty persons at a time. And they were all fully employed, with grown men and women mounted on the backs of the wooden horses. They were elegantly ornamented, with looking-glasses flying around on the centre-boards, and flags and streamers so closely packed together that but a small passage was left between them for the spectators to pass. Beyond these were revolving wheels, with boxes attached, carrying men and women thirty feet up in the air, and down and up in rapid succession, circular railways, upon which car-loads of men and women were spinning like tops, and other contrivances too numerous to mention. Coming as we did to witness a religious fête, all this seemed strange and startling, and we looked on in amazement, but we must admit that everybody was happy and cheerful, and was fully intent upon making everybody else happy.

A LIVELY SCENE.

After extricating ourselves from this scene of revolving animation, we turned to gaze upon it *en masse*, and as a moving panorama we have seen nothing so animated, unless it was the machinery department of the Vienna Exposition. Here, however, the people were revolving with the wheels, and the flags were revolving, and tents were spinning like tops, and everything was in rotary motion. As we moved farther on, the scene changed, and we were almost deafened by horns, trumpets, drums, bands, cymbals, hand-organs and hurdy-gurdies, all playing different tunes, and each endeavoring to drown the sound of the other. Immense canvas tents filled the woods on either side, covered with paintings representing fat women, dwarfs, strong men lifting weights, giants and giantesses, women with beards, circuses, théâtres comiques, théâtres olympiques, etc. They were all, to the number of about forty, just opening for the afternoon performance, and had their horses, performers, bands of music, dancing-girls, clowns, ponies, strong men, and claqueurs out on platforms in front to induce the people to enter. On some of the platforms girls in semi-nude apparel were dancing, knights in armor glistening in the sun, and the claqueurs were shouting at the top of their voices descriptions of the wonderful performances that were about to commence. The exhibition of the performers was to give some idea of the performance, just as the exhibitor of the fat woman paraded the petticoat she wore, that the width of the waistband might be seen. All the intervening space between the tents was massed with men, women, and children, soldiers, sisters of charity, and priests, and some of the latter entered the tents to witness the performance. We have been at horse-races, cattle-shows, Schützenfests, and Mabille gardens, but we have never witnessed anything to equal this bright Sunday afternoon demonstration in honor of St. Cloud. The people were, however, enjoying the occasion with all the zest of school-boys on a Fourth of July frolic. On returning from this portion of the park, without having reached its end, we found a mass of people pouring in which rendered locomotion almost impossible. The boats were landing thousands of visitors from Paris, the railroads were bringing in all their trains could carry, and the splendid stone bridge across the Seine was literally crowded with pedestrians coming to witness the illumination and take part in the feast after nightfall. There could not, at this time, have been less than one hundred thousand people in the park, and they were still pouring in from every quarter. We had previously visited Versailles, explored its gardens and galleries of paintings, and were too wearied with sight-seeing to remain for the illumination, but doubt not there was a gay time after nightfall. There were also, we must not omit to mention, a half-dozen dancing-establishments, placards announcing that grand balls would commence at eight o'clock in the evening. From all this we should judge that St.

Cloud must have been a merry fellow. A large number of pilgrims, from different parts of France, are going daily to St. Cloud.

PLAYING OF THE FOUNTAINS.

We went to St. Cloud to see the fountains play, and the grand cascade. The cascade is divided into La Haute Cascade and La Basse Cascade: at the summit of the first is a group of statuary representing the Seine and Marne, each reposing on the urns from which water issues. Upon an elevated flight of steps are placed urns and tablets, from which water falls into basins situated one above another, the last supplying, by means of an aqueduct, the lower cascade. The Basse Cascade is in the shape of a horse-shoe, and is remarkable for the abundance and rapid descent of its waters, which fall in sheets, from one basin to another, into a basin two hundred and sixty-one feet in length by ninety-three in its greatest breadth, along which are twelve *jets d'eau*. The grand *jet d'eau*, known by the name of the *Jet Géant*, is to the left of the cascades; it rises with immense force to the height of one hundred and forty feet from the centre of a basin, and throws up five thousand gallons per minute. It is undoubtedly a majestic spectacle when in full play, and, having secured some chairs, we enjoyed the scene for nearly an hour before our departure. We should judge the highest point of the cascade to be nearly one hundred feet, but it is impossible to describe it so as to be understood by the reader.

We returned to Paris by one of the steamboats on the Seine, having a fine view of the surroundings of Paris and the numerous elegant stone bridges by which the river is spanned, most of which have the letter N emblazoned on them, signifying their erection during the reign of Napoleon, and all are ornamented with statuary and bas-reliefs.

MORE SUNDAY AMUSEMENTS.

On this same Sunday afternoon, in honor of the fête of St. Cloud, we presume, the first grand fall races took place at Longchamps, the race-ground of the Bois de Boulogne. On our return to Paris the Champs Elysées was thronged with carriages and pedestrians, as far as the eye could reach, returning from the races, full reports of which appeared in the papers of Monday morning. *Galignani* says the attendance was not as good as usual, as the fashionable world is still at the seaside and watering-places, "and the fête of St. Cloud formed a rival attraction for pleasure-seekers of the multitude." To the stranger coming from England or America these scenes are rather startling, especially when accompanied by long details in the papers of great religious revivals, pilgrimages, etc.

The Punch and Judy shows, concert-gardens, etc., in the Champs Elysées were in full blast during the afternoon and evening, and at night all the theatres and opera-houses, to the number of eighteen, were crowded with visitors, whilst the usual scene of life and gayety was to be witnessed on the boulevards.

AMERICANS EUROPEANIZED.

"When I was home I was one of the pillars of the church, but here in Paris I can hardly be regarded as a brick," was the remark of an American lady, when discussing the tendency to almost wholly disregard the Sabbath in France. "Yes," remarked another, "when I first came to Paris the playing of operatic airs on Sunday shocked me, but now I find myself occasionally doing the same thing without a thought as to its impropriety." Americans residing in Paris any length of time soon get over their antipathy to the Sunday operas, Sunday concerts, and Sunday amusements of all descriptions. All their staid notions disappear, and they learn to do as the Parisians do, and if a favorite opera is to be performed on Sunday evening they do not let that prevent their attendance. "When I first came to Paris I resolved I would not visit the Mabille Gardens, but when I found that so many nice people went there I thought I would like to go also," remarked another lady. "Well, I have been there also," was the reply, "and I did not see anything so very bad; but perhaps it was not a *good* night."

The last census of Paris gives a total of thirty thousand Americans permanently residing in Paris; of these nearly twenty thousand are from Louisiana, five thousand from Virginia, three thousand from other Southern States, and only two thousand from the North and West. The Southerners have located here during and since the war, and have made it their permanent home. There are, in addition to this, fully ten thousand Americans here temporarily, some of them for the purpose of educating their children, but most of them are tourists. With all this population, the great majority of whom are Protestants, there is a very light attendance, not exceeding four or five hundred, at the Methodist and Episcopal churches, and most of these are tourists, who have not been here long enough to learn that church-going is not fashionable in Paris. It is customary on Sunday morning to take a cup of coffee in bed, then a morning nap until ten or eleven o'clock, get dressed for breakfast by twelve o'clock, and take a drive in the Champs Elysées or to the Bois de Boulogne in the afternoon. It is a tempting habit, and very few fail ultimately to fall into it. The American Protestant churches here are mainly supported by the tourists, who give liberally. The English government supports its churches by contributions equal to all the amount received from worshipers, but has given notice that after the expiration of two years all aid will be withdrawn from them.

BOARDING-SCHOOL FRENCH.

Mark Twain, in his "Innocents Abroad," makes many apt hits on the experience of visitors to France who have previously become proficient in what is known as "boarding-school French." He says, in his quaint way, that the Frenchman is great on pronunciation, but a very bad speller. The American is very apt to pronounce a word as it is spelled, and if he does so he might as well talk Greek to a Frenchman and expect to be understood. The slightest deviation from the proper pronunciation renders your words unintelligible, and hence the novice gives up in despair of success, and finally writes the word he is trying to pronounce, and submits it for inspection. We vainly endeavored to tell a coachee the other day to drive to Rue Vantemill, pronouncing it as it is spelt, and every other way that we conceived it possible to torture the word into articulate sound, but all to no effect. He shook his head and shrugged his shoulders, and gave other indications that he did not know of any such thoroughfare. In despair we drew out a card and wrote upon it "Vantemill," when his eyes glistened and a broad grin suffused his countenance as he exclaimed, with a sharp, quick pronunciation, "*Oui, oui, Vont-e-meel.*" So also with Rue *Scribe;* we pronounced it every imaginable way, but it was not until in despair we accidentally hit upon *Screbe,* pronounced sharp from irritation, that we were understandable. The word *Jête* must be pronounced *fest* to be understood, and any deviation from the French pronunciation of the commonest word is totally non-understandable. At dinner, surrounded by twenty Americans, mostly ladies, and all of them fortified with "boarding-school French," their linguistic experience of the day is truly ludicrous. They expected to be able "to get along with the language," but find that pronunciation is of much more importance than the spelling. Thus it is that those who learn to talk the language here before they learn to read or spell it make the most rapid progress, and ultimately master all its peculiarities of pronunciation. Among our guests is a young American girl of sixteen, who, with her mother, has spent five years in Europe, and speaks French, Italian, Spanish, and German fluently and correctly. She mastered French in three months, having been placed at a boarding-school, with sixty scholars, not one of whom could speak a word of English. So also with German, Italian, and Spanish, she lived and associated with those who knew no other language.

AMERICAN FOOD TROUBLES.

Nearly all the American families residing in Paris soon break away from the boarding-houses, hire a suite of furnished rooms, employ servants, and go regularly to housekeeping. They endure French cooking and French living until they can stand it no longer, and then start off "on their own hook." During the five weeks we have been at a French pension two families have already left and gone to housekeeping, and a third is now preparing to follow their example. They are here for the education of their children, and, proposing to remain a couple of years, soon discovered that it would be impossible to endure French living. Still, this house has the reputation of keeping the best table in Paris, but the manner of serving the dishes is so unreasonable that the enjoyment of the food is destroyed. Think of serving roast beef without potatoes or vegetables, and, when it is masticated, having peas or beans, that would have been so delightful to eat with it, served separately. Then the desserts are always a mélange of some kind, so mixed that it is impossible to tell what you are eating, and would puzzle an Andrews or Coleman and Rogers to analyze them. A lady remarked at the table to-day that she ate everything mechanically, without a thought as to what it was, contenting herself with the reflection that she would relish home food better when she got there. "Well, mother," responded a sharp-witted daughter at her side, who had probably been reading Mark Twain, "you can't expect to enjoy sweet potatoes and hot corn, with Michael Angelo and Worth the dressmaker, all at one time."

Breakfast is served in the rooms to each boarder as soon as it is called for, consisting of coffee and bread and butter. At twelve o'clock a lunch is served, of three or four separate courses, generally fried eggs, then beefsteak, or veal-cutlet, and fruit, after all of which is disposed of, coffee is served. Dinner is ready at six o'clock, requiring an hour and a half to dispose of it, each article being served separately and the plates changed, the vegetables invariably following the meat, but never with it. The food is all good enough, and much more abundant than at the hotel *table-d'hôte*, and would be very palatable if not served up in this nonsensical way. There is also an abundance of wine at both lunch and dinner. "How I long to get home to enjoy a good square meal!" is the constant exclamation of the American wanderer. We must not neglect to add that the parties who have gone to housekeeping since our sojourn here reported progress, and are delighted with their experience, viz.: muffins, waffles, or flannel-cakes for breakfast, with beefsteak and ham and eggs; dinner at two o'clock, with roast chicken and boiled ham, potatoes, peas, and Baltimore pearl hominy, all spread out on the table at once, to the horror of the French cooks and servants; supper at eight o'clock, with coffee, cold chicken, and hot rolls from the Boston Bakery, on Boulevard Malesherbes. They are seriously contemplating buckwheat-cakes and pumpkin-pie. The only boarding-house in Paris which serves meals in American style is Madame Dejon's, No. 29 Rue Caumartin, but her table has become so popular that more than a hundred Americans from the Grand and other hotels in the vicinity dine there daily. They have literally turned this once quiet boarding-house into a refectory, much to the discomfort of the home-guests. We should not wonder if some of these American ladies who have just started housekeeping on a small scale should ultimately develop into American boarding-housekeepers, and revolutionize the mode of eating in all these establishments. To an American it seems contrary to reason and common sense to be eating peas or beans as a separate dish, and meats without vegetables. Their guests are all Americans or English, and the sooner the revolution is commenced the better.

FRENCH SUICIDES.

Another of those eminently French suicides took place in Paris on Saturday night, which for a few moments occasioned some excitement, but with the removal of the body the matter was thought no more of than if a candle had been snuffed out. A young man named Jules Huttin, a non-commissioned officer of the Ninth Chasseurs, committed suicide at Hill's Restaurant, on the Boulevard des Capucines. He had come to the city with a woman of loose character, and had for some days been living a rollicking life. On the evening of his death he came to the restaurant with his companion, and called for a luxurious supper, with the most costly wines, and they ate, drank, and were merry for about two hours, when he quietly stepped out on the veranda overlooking the boulevard, and blew his brains out with a pistol. He is said to have been a young man of excellent family and good education, but, having spent all his money, and having come to the city without leave of absence, he killed himself rather than face the disgrace of returning to his corps. On the same evening a young woman at Versailles committed suicide by jumping from the balcony on the fifth story of the house in which she lived; and of the seven bodies exposed at La Morgue this morning, five of them were supposed to have committed suicide.

MENDING THEIR MANNERS.

The large number of American ladies in Paris is having the effect of checking the offensive manners of young Frenchmen to unprotected ladies on the streets. A year ago a lady of youth and personal attractions was sure to be accosted if she attempted to go out alone, and persistently followed by these young street-loungers. Two or three of them have, in the mean time, been punished for their offensive conduct to American ladies, which has had the effect of very generally remedying the evil complained of. On the boulevards, and in the neighborhood of all the large hotels, American ladies move about shopping or promenading, singly or in couples, with perfect immunity, and are as respectfully treated as if on Baltimore Street or Broadway. We record this gratifying improvement with pleasure, and in behalf of the ladies return thanks to those who have taught them better manners. The police are also very watchful, and are doing their best to render the streets of Paris as safe to the unprotected lady as those of any other city. The young French ladies, who never venture on the streets without a gentleman friend or a duenna, are astonished at the bravery of American ladies in venturing abroad alone, and persist that it would not be safe for young French ladies to follow their example. If their fathers and brothers would knock a few of these scamps down, it would soon give them immunity also. But the fact that respectable ladies do not venture on the streets leads to the inference that those who do are not respectable, and they are regarded as such. A Frenchman, however, can tell an American lady at a glance, and, knowing that she refuses to pay any attention to French customs, gives her a wide berth.

PARIS, September 19, 1873.

THE FINANCIAL PANIC.

If there had been an earthquake on Rue Scribe and the Boulevard des Italiens, it could not have created more consternation among the Americans who usually congregate in that neighborhood, than was visible on Friday morning when the bulletin-board of the *American Register* announced the failure and suspension of Jay Cooke & Co., and Clarke & Co., of Philadelphia. There was a general rush to the banking-houses of those who held letters of credit from these firms, and groups and knots of excited men and women were assembled in every direction. Those who held letters from the old Peabody house of Morgan & Co., or Brown Brothers, or McKim & Co., were congratulating themselves on their good judgment, and the unfortunates were foraging around to find friends who could loan them sufficient money to take them home. The Philadelphians especially are the greatest sufferers, most of whom seem to have done business with the house of Jay Cooke & Co. The banks all refused to pay any more money out on the letters of credit of either of these houses, though Messrs. Monroe & Co. offered to cash the drafts of all responsible parties. A similar course was pursued by other leading bankers; but there are still many here who will find it difficult to raise funds. Fortunately for the sufferers, most of their letters of credit were very nearly "played out," they being just closing up their European trip and preparing to start for home.

The failure has not, however, had the effect of injuring the credit of American tourists, which stands very high in Paris. The bankers are cashing their drafts on our principal cities with reckless liberality. We were present at Monroe's when a gentleman stepped in and introduced himself, stating that he desired a draft on America for two hundred pounds discounted. The answer was, "Certainly," without requiring him to produce any other proof than his own word that he was the party he represented himself to be. He drew up the draft, and in a few minutes departed with the money. So also with shop-keepers, tradesmen, and even dressmakers. On hearing of the trouble that some of their customers were in with regard to their letters of credit, they have very generally proffered the acceptance of drafts for the amount of their bills.

NO "RINGS" IN PARIS.

The city of Paris has a costly municipal government, which hesitates at no expense to make the city beautiful, clean, and healthy, but it has no "rings" to manipulate the public funds. It has something to show for every outlay, and the people have the satisfaction of knowing that every dollar levied on them is economically spent. There is something tangible to show for it, as is the case with a giraffe just purchased for five thousand francs, to replace the one eaten up by the Commune. Public functionaries in Paris never grow rich off their small salaries, and, as they are poorly paid, there is no scramble for their places. Twelve hundred francs (about two hundred and twenty dollars) is almost the highest salary paid to any municipal officer, and there is such a system of checks and balances that fraud or unfair dealing is wholly impossible. A police-officer receives from twelve hundred to fifteen hundred francs per annum, or from two hundred to three hundred dollars. The highest salary under the government is to the head of the Police Department, which is twelve thousand francs, or about two thousand four hundred dollars. This is the most important office under the city government. There are twenty-two mayors, one for each arrondissement or ward of the city, whose principal functions relate to births, marriages, and deaths, and one Prefect of the Seine, whose functions correspond very much with those of our own mayors, he having authority over all parts of the city. In connection with the Mont de Piété, or city pawnbroker establishment, there are three hundred officers, whose combined salaries amount to five hundred and one thousand two hundred francs, being an average of about three hundred and thirty-three dollars each. Some receive more than this amount, and some less. The yearly average of money that passes through the hands of these three hundred officers is nearly eight million dollars: so that it will be seen the positions they hold are equal in responsibility to any under our city government.

THE MONT DE PIÉTÉ.

This is one of the most important and extensive establishments connected with the city government of Paris. It is a municipal pawnbroker establishment for the relief and protection of the poor, and, indeed, of all classes who may by either poverty or misfortune be compelled to borrow money on their personal effects. That the extent of this establishment may be understood, it is only necessary to state that it has two principal offices in opposite sections of the city, twenty auxiliary offices in different wards or arrondissements, and has three hundred officers connected with it. The average number of articles pledged daily is three thousand, but no pledges are received from any one unless they are known to be householders, or produce a passport or papers *en règle*, showing who they are, and that the property they offer is their own. The privilege of loaning money on deposits is enjoyed exclusively by this establishment; hence thieves have but little opportunity of disposing of their plunder. Out of two millions of articles pledged per annum, the average number delivered to the police on suspicion of theft is three hundred and ninety-one, representing loans to the amount of eight thousand nine hundred francs. Thus this establishment, instead of encouraging theft, leads to detection, punishment, and the restoration of stolen goods.

The Mont de Piété is under the authority of the Minister of the Interior and the Prefect of the Seine, and is managed by a Director, appointed by the former. It has a Council or Board of Managers, consisting of three members of the City Council, three citizens of Paris, and three members of the Council of Public Assistance. The number of officers employed in its management is over three hundred, and they are kept busy for twelve or fourteen hours per day. Everything that is brought to be pledged is carefully appraised, and the amount loaned is four-fifths of the value of gold and silver articles, and two-thirds of the value of other effects, provided no loan at the two central offices exceeds ten thousand francs, and at the branch establishments five hundred francs. From this it will be seen it is not used entirely by the extremely poor, but all classes at times avail themselves of its advantages to enable them to ride over temporary difficulties.

The establishment is conducted with money borrowed on its own credit, and it requires a capital of about thirty million francs, for the use of which it pays about four per cent. The interest to the public upon pledges used to be twelve per cent., but it is now reduced to nine per cent., or one-half per cent. for fifteen days, being the shortest term for which it can be lent. After the lapse of the first month, the interest must be paid entire, even if the loan last but a few days. The pledges of the previous day are brought every morning to the central establishments or the two storehouses, and it would be difficult to find in the whole of Paris a scene of more stirring business activity. The system with which the whole business is managed is wonderful, there being one department where borrowers are enabled to refund by installments the sums advanced: even one franc is received.

Whilst the work of redeeming pledges is constantly in progress in one part of the establishment, another is crowded with men, women, and children with bundles to offer for small advances, which continues from nine o'clock in the morning until four o'clock in the afternoon. In another section an auction is daily held for the sale of forfeited pledges, which have not been redeemed within the time specified. After a year, or rather fourteen months, the effects, if the duplicate be not renewed by paying the interest due upon it, are thus sold, and the auction-room is a scene for a painter. Here all the old-clothes establishments in the city are represented, and at times the bidding is very lively, nothing being sold and no bids received for a less sum than the amount advanced.

ETIQUETTE OF THE STREETS.

American ladies visiting Paris are apt to be much annoyed until they learn the etiquette of the streets. In the first place, a respectable young lady in Paris seldom appears on the streets in anything but a plain black dress, unless when with a male escort or a duenna. If in a white or light dress her character is liable to be mistaken, especially if she should be young and interesting. If she is without escort she must, to maintain her character, push straight forward, without looking to the right or to the left. If she should stop to take a look at the fine displays in the store-windows, for which Paris is so famous, she must not be surprised if some of the young men who lounge around the cafés walk up to her, nudge her elbow, and enter into conversation. It is the practice of the demi-monde to thus stop when a gentleman is approaching whose attention they desire to attract, and the masculines of loose morals choose to regard any one who may stop to look at the gorgeous array of diamonds in a window as having invited their attention.

So also in riding. A lady seated alone in a carriage, either on the street or in the Bois de Boulogne, is regarded as reserving the seat beside her for any chance gentleman whom she may attract. Thus ladies who have no male companion either take their servant with them when they ride, or borrow a neighbor's child, if they have none of their own. To ride alone would be to invite insult or offensive attention.

The same is the rule in London, and almost throughout Europe. Females of the most respectable classes seldom walk the streets. In London you seldom see what we would call at home a well-dressed lady walking in the streets. Those who seem, and undoubtedly are, reputable are arrayed in plain suits of black, evidently intending and desiring to shun rather than court observation. A finely-dressed female on the streets of London is regarded as a woman of loose character if she have no escort with her, and even then she must carry a very demure face, and her escort must not put on any foppish airs if he does not desire to compromise the character of his companion. But a black dress and a fast walk, as if in a great hurry, will insure for a lady alone in the street entire freedom from improper attentions or insult.

LOVE OF FLOWERS.

The Frenchwoman must have her daily supply of flowers, even if she is compelled to stint her table to obtain them. When she purchases the substantials for her breakfast she is sure to take home with her a bouquet of flowers. One will scarcely pass a window in an inhabited house where, from the basement to the pens erected upon the roofs, six and seven stories from the ground, there is not a display of flower-pots. Having during a former visit to Paris secured quarters high up in the Louvre, we could look down upon the upper stories of the neighboring houses, in each room of which there appeared to be a separate family. The men seemed mostly to be tailors, and at daybreak in the morning would be plying their needles whilst the women were preparing for breakfast and arranging their bouquets for the table. The cultivation of flowers in all the palace-gardens and squares, and even by the street-sides in the Champs Elysées, is carried to perfection. The Luxembourg Garden presents the finest display of flowers cultivated in the open air we have ever seen, and it is thronged every evening with admiring visitors. So also at the Jardin des Plantes. The latter will always be found crowded with visitors, the flowers attracting more attention than the great exhibition of the cattle of the field, the birds of the air, the beasts of the jungle, and the fish of the sea, here collected and open free to the inspection of the public.

CONSTRUCTION OF HOUSES.

The houses on the boulevards, and in all the new portions of Paris, are required to be five stories high, and of uniform appearance. They are in their interior arrangements different from the houses of almost any other city, being constructed with the special view of accommodating a great number of families. On the fourth and fifth stories there is an iron balcony extending across the front, and, if the house is on the corner of a street, around the entire building. This balcony is used for communicating with the different rooms, by which the space for passage-way inside is saved. We were in one of these houses to-day, to visit a very respectable family occupying the fifth story, which is considered one of the best, as the tenants have the use of the roof. It was a corner-house, with stores underneath, the upper floors being occupied by not less than six families. A porteress has charge of the door, and one winding stairway, which is neatly carpeted and as clean as that of most private houses, is used in common by all the tenants. We were assured that there was little or no intercourse between the tenants, and that there were several families in the house our friends had never seen, and did not even know their names.

PARIS ITEMS.

The nurse-girls of Paris who are to be seen in Palais Royal and in the garden of the Tuileries of an afternoon, keep the little boys and girls in their charge out of mischief by having red or blue ribbons tied around their waists, holding the end in their hands. They are never allowed to go farther in advance of their nurse than the limit of the ribbon, which is about four feet long. They do not appear at all restive under the constraint, and have evidently been raised under leading-strings. The nurse-girls in "Franklin Square" would have a merry time of it if they were to attempt to constrain Young America in this way.

"ALL ROADS LEAD TO PARIS."

"All roads lead to Paris," from all parts of the Continent. The tourist, when traveling in Italy, Switzerland, or Germany, can turn westward from any point, and in ten to fifteen hours find himself in the gay and brilliant thoroughfares of Paris. It is easy to get to Paris, but very hard to get away again, as most of the Americans now congregating here find, especially if there are ladies among them. There is no place for the lady tourist like Paris, its attractions being so novel and varied, and its stores so brilliant and extensive in their display of all manner of fabrics. There are delightful excursions to be made in every direction, palaces to visit, drives in the city and out of the city, its daylight scenes and its gas-light displays. All that is gay, attractive, and beautiful in the other great cities of the Continent are here concentrated in one, affording never-failing scenes of interest to the stranger. There are no people in the world so proud of their city as the Parisians, and the marching of a German army through its broad avenues must have been a terrible infliction upon their national pride. They are not only proud of the appearance of the city, but the true Parisian really seems anxious to maintain its general character for fair dealing with strangers in contradistinction to the rapacity and knavery displayed in so many other cities.

SHOP-KEEPERS OF PARIS.

The shop-keepers of Paris have the art of making the most of their wares, and spare no labor to give to their windows and show-cases a new and attractive appearance every morning. This is not only the case with the most brilliant and costly goods, but even with those of trifling value. If the stranger expects on the morrow to recognize a store by any thing he may have seen in the window to-day, he will be greatly mistaken. Even the arrangement of the goods will be found to be different, an effort being made to render them more attractive than on yesterday. They also add to the brilliancy of their establishments by the extensive use of mirrors inserted in the sides of their windows, which multiply and magnify the stock and make a small store appear large and commodious. There is scarcely a show-window in Paris that is not provided with side-glasses, so placed as to give the appearance of double the width which they really have. At night they have outside their windows a number of very brilliant reflectors, casting a glare of light upon the tastefully-arranged articles. This is especially the case in the colonnades of Palais Royal, a favorite resort for strangers in Paris.

With the exception of the few large stores, such as Au Bon Marché, the Louvre, the La Paix, and Petit St. Thomas, which sell everything, the stores of Paris consist mostly of establishments for the sale of special articles. There are lace stores, silk stores, cloth stores, mourning goods, and even doll-baby stores, where nothing else can be had. Of general retail dry-goods stores, such as are so abundant with us, there are very few. They make a specialty of some given article, and it is useless to look elsewhere for them. In the large establishments there is a fixed price marked on all articles, from which they will in no case deviate. An American who goes into a store where the prices are not fixed, must expect to pay one-third more than the regular prices, as there are few who will not take some unfair advantage of the stranger.

The dressmakers, who persist in furnishing the material for their dresses, charge heavy prices, very nearly as much as a dress would cost at home. An American lady told me yesterday that she had just paid fifteen hundred francs, or three hundred dollars in gold, for a silk dress. She was of opinion that Miss Sallie Johnson would have turned out as fine a dress for less money. Silks and velvets are sold at the stores for about two-thirds of the price demanded for them at home, whilst it is contended that the quality obtainable here is superior to that which is exported.

FRUITS OF FRANCE.

The people of France appear to care very little for any fruit except grapes, which are for sale on the streets in great quantities at a half-franc, or ten cents, per pound. Peaches are not raised to any considerable extent, and are sold at three to five cents each. Good pears cannot be had for less than four or five for a franc. They are very fine in appearance, but do not have the rich flavor that our fruit has, and seem to be bought nearly altogether by strangers, the Parisians evidently caring but little for them. Cantaloupes are very large, and have all the aroma of our melon, but yet are very insipid to the taste. They are eaten here with sugar; but very few are brought to market.

The only vegetables which the Parisian seems to care about are cabbage, potatoes, beans, peas, cauliflower, and lettuce: at least no other kind is ever seen at the hotels or cafés, and very little of these. Cabbage is served with fresh meat, and lettuce with chicken, the latter being scalded or soaked in oil. When peas or beans are served at the *table-d'hôte* you are expected to eat them by themselves. Potatoes are only served with fish. When called for at a restaurant, potatoes are served to you fried, but they have evidently been previously boiled, mashed, and then baked, and thus puffed up after the manner of a doughnut. They look like sliced potatoes, but they have gone through some mysterious process which renders them no longer potatoes.

THE MADELEINE.

We paid a visit on Sunday morning to the Madeleine, the most chaste and magnificent of all the modern churches of Europe. The fury of the Commune was spent upon its outer walls and fluted columns and shrubbery, but they did not succeed in making their way to the interior, which presents the same solemn and grand aspect that it did twelve years ago, with its white marble altars and central group of statuary representing the Magdalen borne to heaven on the wings of angels. A large congregation was assembled at the time of our visit, and the regular Sunday morning services in progress. Of the thirty-two massive columns that surround the structure there are but few that do not bear bullet-marks, whilst the walls and many of the statues of saints in the thirty-two niches in the walls were also considerably damaged, but have since been repaired. They appear at some places to have discharged whole volleys of musketry at the solid stone walls, which left their mark but did but little damage. The statues of St. Anne, St. Theresa, St. Agnes, and St. Elizabeth were considerably damaged, that of St. Theresa having had a large bullet-hole directly over the left breast. The work of renovating and removing all evidences of the popular insanity has, however, now been completed.

PARISIAN DRESSMAKERS AND TAILORS.

The fashionable dressmakers of Paris, like our best tailors, will not make dresses unless they furnish the goods themselves. They keep on hand large stocks of silks, satins, and velvets, and tell their customers at what price they will furnish a dress from the piece selected, with trimmings and all complete. They are most particular with regard to fitting their customers, requiring them to make three visits before delivering their work,— the first to be measured, the second to be fitted, and the third to try the dress on and have made any alterations that may be desired. The best tailors of Paris are equally careful with regard to gentlemen's clothing; their customers must be measured, afterwards fitted, and then they must see the coat and vest on before they are willing to deliver them. This is perhaps the reason why Paris tailors have such a high reputation the world over for making well-fitting suits.

HOW IS IT?

The estimation in which America and Americans are now held by both Frenchmen and Englishmen is a matter of pride to all who have visited Europe this year. The number of Americans, and their lavish expenditure of money, together with the anomaly of a nation paying off its debt, perfectly bewilder them. They are constantly asking for explanations, which can only be given at the expense of their own national pride. We tell them we have no standing armies of a million of men to clothe, feed, and pay, while those who are under arms here would be, with us, producers; that we have no immense navy and no royalty to sustain at the expense of the people—no one to hold in subjection—and no palaces to construct and maintain. In reply to inquiries from Englishmen how it was possible for so many Americans to be traveling over Europe with their families, and making extensive purchases of rich and costly goods, the only answer that could be given was that when an American accumulates money he desires that himself and family shall enjoy it, whilst an Englishman hoards it up that he may vie with the aristocracy in having a country-house and a city-house, or marry some of his daughters to a bankrupt nobleman. They often admit that it is so, and take no offense at the only response that can truthfully be given to their inquiries.

"AU BON MARCHÉ."

We spent several hours to-day at Au Bon Marché, the greatest of the three large dry-goods establishments of Paris. A more stirring scene of business activity it would be impossible to find anywhere. At all times during the day the whole building is surrounded with carriages waiting for parties inside making purchases, and the interior is so thronged that it is at times difficult to move about. The number of cashiers and bookkeepers at their desks was thirty-three, and the clerks and salesmen, male and female, exceed three hundred. The most active and probably the most important of these employés we found to be a colored man, who speaks fluently French, Italian, German, and English. He is called hither and thither to sell to all nationalities, or to interpret for the other salesmen, who understand no language but French. In this establishment there are departments for everything that can be called for, from the richest and rarest to the most ordinary goods. The price is marked upon every article, and no amount of purchase can induce the striking off of a franc from the bill. The department for coarse goods was equally thronged by the poorer classes with those for finer and more costly goods. There was a large representation of American ladies, but very few English. There is a refreshment saloon for lady customers, where wine and cake and ice-water are spread for them, and retiring-rooms fitted up in most magnificent style. At one end of the building, on the third floor, is the dressmaking establishment, where about two hundred ladies are employed in cutting, fitting, and making dresses to order, whilst thousands of ready-made dresses of every material are ready for sale, even those made of the richest velvets, satins, and silks. The throng of purchasers passing in and out was very large, whilst the cashiers were kept busy in settling accounts. The stables of this establishment have over forty horses, and twenty elegant carriages for the delivery of goods, which can be seen flying through the city at all hours during the day.

Some idea of the purchases made by Americans may be judged from the fact that Madame François, one of the principal dressmakers, stated to-day that she had just completed twenty-seven silk dresses for one lady from Chicago, "the city," she added, "that was burnt up." An American gentleman at Drexel's banking establishment this morning remarked that his wife had just called upon him for twenty thousand francs to pay for the purchases she had made yesterday!

SCARCITY OF WATER.

"You must not drink water," is the constant cry of the hotel-keepers in Paris, and the addition of ice to it, we are assured, makes it rank poison. It is pretty much the same all over the Continent, water being regarded as of no manner of importance except for fountains, cascades, and to drive water-wheels. If at dinner you tell the waiter that you do not wish any wine, he looks at you aghast, and repeats the question two or three times to be sure that he has properly understood you. He reports the fact to the head-waiter, and he, confident that the stupid fellow has misunderstood, comes himself to inquire, "What kind of wine will monsieur have?"

Then the wine furnished at the hotels is so horrible in quality that it is not fit to be drunk. They evidently export all their best wines, and keep the common kinds for home consumption. The prices are also exorbitant, and it is evidently the large profit that the hotel-keeper makes which occasions so much anxiety that all his guests shall have large wine-bills, and that all shall dine at table-d'hôte, where it would be rank heresy for any one to fail to call for wine. When water is called for it is brought so warm as not to be drinkable, and it requires a half-hour's notice to obtain a few small lumps of ice to cool it. In Italy and Switzerland we made a practice of carrying a cup in order to obtain a drink of cool fresh water occasionally from the springs and fountains. If water is called for in a store or private house, they bring the sugar-dish with it, the idea being that water is unhealthy without being mixed with something else.

HOT BREAD.

The next most deleterious article to cold water, in the estimation of a Frenchman, is bread that is eaten before it is twelve hours out of the oven. It is then nearly all crust, and requires the best of masticators to chew it. Most elderly French men and women have their teeth worn down to stumps, probably from long service on the very hard bread universally eaten by rich and poor. Those who expect to find superior cakes in the confectionery stores will be greatly mistaken, as they all seem to be made out of greasy pie-crust. Nothing can be more beautiful than the display of cakes and condiments in the stores, but to an American fond of home-made cakes they are both unpalatable and unwholesome. If an ice-cream is called for they serve with it a tasteless kind of wafer-cake so thin as to be curled up in little rolls, and so brittle that it will break to pieces with the slightest pressure. This is the only cake that can be had in the ice-cream saloons. The cost of a small wineglass of ice-cream is twenty cents, and it is much inferior in quality to our American cream. Ice-water is served with it, the ice being frozen in a decanter by chemical process. This may possibly be costly, and adds to the price of the cream.

"GET OUT OF THE WAY."

The people of Paris have been educated to keep out of the way of all carriages and vehicles passing on the streets. In the narrower streets most of the pedestrians walk along the carriage-way, the pavements being too narrow to accommodate more than half of them. The streets are paved with asphaltum, and the carriages move along almost noiselessly, with great rapidity, and the gait of the horses is never checked for any one, even if the throng on the street should be women and children. The drivers will halloo, but never check their speed, and you must run or jump to save yourself from being run over. Reckless driving is the rule here, and, in fact, all over the Continent.

PARISIAN STREET-CRIES.

The street-cries of Paris commence at daybreak in the morning, and continue pretty steadily throughout the day. Hundreds of women and girls with hand-carts are always passing through the streets, selling vegetables, fruits, and flowers, and crying their wares. There is an abundance of fruit and meat shops, and the retail vending of such articles seems to be all done in this way. The family supplies, including charcoal to cook with, are purchased at the curb-stone, and during the summer season breakfast is about the only meal eaten at home by those who are able to get out of doors. The cafés are numerous in all parts of the city, where a substantial dinner can be obtained for from one franc to five or ten, according to the taste and purse of the customer. Everything eatable is much cheaper here than in London, and is better cooked and better served.

PARISIAN LOCAL ITEMS.

The Garden of the Luxembourg Palace is a regular baby-show every afternoon and evening. We do not think it would be an exaggeration to assert that several thousand children, from six months to four years of age, can be seen here every afternoon with their nurses.

The glove-makers have at last exterminated all the rats in the sewers, which were formerly so numerous as to be beyond computation. The manufacture of ladies' kid gloves from the skins of these animals made the demand so great that but few are now to be found anywhere in the city.

Carriage-driving, like everything else, is systematized in Paris. The driver is compelled by law to hand you a printed card with the list of charges. For four persons the charge is two and a half francs per hour, or about fifty cents. Four hours' drive to-day, visiting points of interest, cost ten francs. What would our Baltimore hackmen think of that?

There are no street-railways in Paris, and they are hardly needed. The smooth asphaltum pavements that are being laid everywhere enable the broad-wheeled omnibuses, with about forty passengers, inside and outside, drawn by two horses, to move along as easy as railroad cars. There is one line of omnibuses, resembling our city cars, that seat forty-six persons each, inside and on top. Three horses draw them with great rapidity, and they seem always to be full.

CITY OF MARSEILLES.

MARSEILLES, July 7, 1873.

It is not a very easy matter to get away from Paris, especially if there are ladies in your party. This is generally the case with all who stop in Paris on the way to Italy, whilst a great many find the attractions so great that they prefer spending all their time there rather than ramble over the Continent. However, we broke away on the morning of the 6th, and, after eighteen hours' ride, reached Marseilles on Sunday morning at six o'clock.

PARIS TO MARSEILLES.

The route through the southern portion of France has many attractions, passing as we did numerous large cities, including Lyons and Dijon, and the famous region where the grapes employed in making Burgundy wine are grown. Notwithstanding the ravages of recent war, and the destruction of numerous bridges, we found the country most bright and beautiful. Scarcely a foot of ground for the whole distance has not been cultivated to its fullest capacity. Fields of waving grain, meadows redolent with new-mown hay, and miles of vineyards, with the tall poplar, almost the only timber, except cherry- and pear-trees, interspersed with thriving towns and villages, made up the landscape presented from Paris to Marseilles, a distance of nearly six hundred miles. The people appeared gay and happy, and it was difficult to conceive that this whole country had been recently overrun by a hostile army. What a happy thing would it have been had there been industry and energy sufficient in our Southern States to have so rapidly recovered from the effects of the ravages of war! No one could possibly suppose that the country through which we passed had been disturbed by foreign occupation, were it not for the numerous bridges now being rapidly reconstructed. This destruction of bridges in time of war is one of the follies of a past age: as armies now carry their bridges with them, their destruction really causes little or no detention.

SUNDAY IN MARSEILLES.

Sunday in Marseilles is the gayest and brightest day in the week, and there is no day upon which the stranger can see the people and the city to so much advantage. It is a day upon which the whole population are out-of-doors, and intermixed with them are natives of many parts of the inhabited globe, dressed in their native costumes. Turks, Arabs, Algerines, Greeks, Italians, Egyptians, Spaniards, and on this occasion, we must add, a few plain Americans, were encountered in the thronged streets and squares. It must be remembered that the population of Marseilles is equal to that of Baltimore, over three hundred thousand, and that on Sunday no one stays at home that can possibly get out-of-doors.

Marseilles is famous for its fine drives, extending through the southern section of the city and out to the banks of the Mediterranean. The principal avenue is about two hundred feet wide, with three rows of immense sycamore-trees on each side, forming a perfect arch and shade over the main drive. At the end of these drives, which are probably four miles in length, bounded on either side by elegant mansions, or, as they are here called, châteaux, is a magnificent public garden or park, with fountains, cascades, grottoes, and an extensive race-course. The whole park, embracing five or six hundred acres, bordering on the Mediterranean, is adorned with beds of flowers, arranged in the most artistic style of floriculture. Between the walls of the garden and the Mediterranean there is a broad turnpike, along which bathing-houses are erected, where thousands of persons in bathing-dresses, male and female, enjoy themselves in the ocean. Among the bathers here we noticed about one hundred Algerine boys, from twelve to sixteen years of age, in charge of Catholic priests, by whom they are being Christianized and educated.

PUBLIC GARDENS OF MARSEILLES.

The public gardens of Marseilles, attached to the Palace Beauchamp, situated in the heart of the city, are unsurpassed in beauty and cultivation by anything that beautiful Paris can boast of. It would be impossible to attempt a description of the mammoth fountain and cascades by which you approach the entrance to the gardens. The sculpture, statuary, and ornamentations of this fountain and cascades must have cost at least a million of dollars. The water first bursts out in an immense volume from a central arch at the base of a group of statuary about one hundred feet above the entrance to the garden, and falls down over seven beautifully arranged cascades, until it reaches a small circular lake in front of the entrance gate. The fountain itself is on the summit of this rising ground, and is located in the centre of a grand colonnade, extending about one hundred feet on either side, with wings, which consist of two fine marble buildings in which are a museum of curiosities and a gallery of paintings. In the front basin of the fountain are four more than life-size bulls, as if struggling to escape from the water, which falls upon their backs, and pouring over on to a rocky bed in front of them. However, it is impossible to convey to the reader any adequate idea of the vastness of this work of art, further than to say that its front is not less than five hundred feet in length, and that it presents a spectacle of grandeur exceeding anything we have ever beheld. The ascent for pedestrians is by circular walks on either side interspersed and bordered with beds of flowers; and there are also two flights of circular stairs by which the level of the fall of water is approached, and the entrance to the museum and the upper garden reached. Placards everywhere remind the people that this attractive place is their property, and they are all called upon to act as a police for the preservation of its beauty and adornments. In the garden there are a number of living animals, including two immense giraffes.

SCENE ON THE STREETS.

It will not do to say that Sunday is not observed in Marseilles, as all the churches were open, and a large majority of the stores closed. But in some sections of the city the stores were all open, and mechanics were at work at their trades, the same as on weekdays. In the old portions of the city, which resemble an Italian town, the houses being seven and eight stories high, and the streets only about twenty feet in width, there was more activity in business matters than on a weekday. The streets were literally jammed, so that it was almost impossible to get through them. Every house was a store of some kind, and all doing a thriving business. The cafés were open in all sections of the city, and their number beyond computation. The brilliant display of these establishments, decorated as they are with flowers and plants, is scarcely surpassed by the most attractive of those in Paris.

There are markets in Marseilles entirely for the sale of flowers, the love of which is proverbial throughout France. These were all in full blast on Sunday, and the young girls in attendance were kept busy in preparing bouquets for the crowds of customers. They stood in the centre of an elevated circular stand, around which were arranged flowers of all descriptions, and the rapidity with which they formed them into graceful bouquets was truly astonishing.

At six o'clock on Sunday evening a grand concert is regularly given by the military bands of the regiments at the public square in the heart of the city. There could not have been an audience present of less than fifteen thousand men, women, and children. The majority of these were seated on chairs rented at a sou an hour to those who may desire them. The music we found to be truly grand, the two bands in attendance each comprising about forty performers.

Among the shipping in the harbor with their flags displayed, we were gratified to observe two flying the "Stars and Stripes."

The number of soldiers in the streets we found to be greater than at Paris, indicating that a very large military force is stationed here. They are mostly young men ranging from eighteen to twenty-two years, probably a portion of the recent conscription.

Sunday is the only day upon which beggars are allowed to ply their vocation in Marseilles, and the number on the streets to-day was very large, particularly of children, including some Italian boys and girls, singing and dragging after them, as a means of exciting sympathy and extracting pennies, the younger members of their families.

LAW AND ORDER.

Marseilles boasts of the devotion of its people to law and order, and points to its escape from the ravages of the Commune, as an instance of the manner in which the people united for the protection of their beautiful city. The Communists rallied strongly here, joined by the refuse of all nations, but were suppressed before they had time to do any damage. Every Frenchman conscientiously believes that the leaders of the Communists received from Prussia three millions of dollars to inaugurate the work of destruction, and that the motive was revenge for the sullen manner in which the Germans were received on entering Paris.

In Paris, as well as throughout France, every palace and public building now has carved on its walls, "The property of the people," as well as those rallying-cries of the revolution of 1830, "Liberty, Equality, and Fraternity." Here in Marseilles these inscriptions are regarded as meaning something, and were it not for the Napoleonic nightmare of military glory, which every Frenchman considers necessary to the existence of his nation, the people of Marseilles would make first-class republicans.

SCENE AT THE BOURSE.

The Chamber of Commerce or Bourse of Marseilles is a large and elegant building, having been completed about ten years ago. It is built of sandstone, and is ornamented with bas-reliefs and statuary emblematic of commerce. The hall of the Bourse is very large, capable of holding three thousand persons, and has neither desks nor seats of any kind in it. The principal dealers have positions at which they are always to be found during business hours, when to the uninitiated a scene of confusion ensues that is only approached by that of the Gold Room at New York. The hall we found crowded to its utmost capacity, so that it was difficult to pass through it, whilst a similar throng of excited people were on the outside, where what we would call the curb-stone brokers were assembled, filling the area between the hall and the railing on all sides. An estimate of five thousand persons inside and outside the hall, all talking at once, and some of them at the top of their voices, would not be an exaggeration of the scene presented at the Bourse. We are assured that such is but the ordinary scene during dull times, and that when the market is excited it is almost impossible for a stranger to get near the building.

THE PORT OF MARSEILLES.

Marseilles was founded by the Greeks six hundred years before Christ, and was conquered by Julius Cæsar in the year 48 B.C. The positions occupied by the Temples of Diana, Apollo, and Neptune are pointed out, on which churches and cathedrals are now erected. It was here that, in 1792, the Marseillaise Hymn was written, which subsequently became the battle-hymn of the Republican armies. Since 1850 the harbor of Marseilles has been extended to four times its former size, notwithstanding which there is still a demand for increased accommodation. Since 1853 the Basin de la Jolliet has been added to the ancient port, and is now the starting-point of most of the Mediterranean steamers. Several other basins have since been added, and it is now proposed to add two new docks and an entrance-harbor, which will render Marseilles one of the finest seaports in the world. Nearly twenty thousand vessels, of an aggregate burden of two million tons, enter and quit Marseilles annually.

FRUITS OF FRANCE.

There is very fine fruit in this section of France, but not in that abundance which we find it at home. The quality of the fruit indicates that it can be extensively grown, while the price asked for it plainly shows that it is only cultivated as a luxury. Peaches are to be had at the fruit-stores, large and luscious, at five for a franc. Apricots are much larger than with us, and in much greater abundance and cheaper than the peaches, the former being fifteen sous and the latter two francs per pound. Greengages, green figs, and plums are large and luxurious, but still scarce and high. The only fruit that seems to be in abundance is cherries, and these are large and of fine flavor, both sweet and sour. As in Paris, all manner of vegetables and fruit are hawked about the streets by women and girls and sold at the curb-stone. Markets, as places in which the head of the family can purchase meat, vegetables, and fruits, are fast going into disuse in both England and France. The green-grocer alone attends the markets and buys by the wholesale, and those who huckster on the streets are his rivals in business. Thus it is that an Englishman or a Frenchman visiting Baltimore considers our market-houses so great a curiosity.

TABLE-D'HÔTE.

There appears to be more demand for all manner of salads here than for fruits. At the *table-d'hôte* everything is served up with some description of salad, saturated with oil, and it is really difficult to tell exactly what you are eating. You must have confidence to enjoy your dinner, or shut your eyes and go it blind. The salads are of various kinds, some of them strongly resembling four-leaved clover, as insisted upon by one of the ladies of our party,—so we eat it for good luck. When we call for ice-water for dinner we are looked upon with astonishment, as wine is the only beverage which the Frenchman considers proper to imbibe whilst eating. A quart-bottle of claret stands by the side of each plate, which most of them manage to empty during the hour and a quarter it requires to dispose of the numerous courses. If slow eating is conducive to health, Frenchmen ought to be very healthy. The manner of serving the dinner is said to be on gastronomic principles, the courses being so arranged as to be most conducive to digestion and to avoid astonishing the stomach by any violent changes in the matter to be deposited therein. We presume it is on the same principle as adopted by some of our scientific farmers in arranging the compost-heap.

TRIP ON THE MEDITERRANEAN.

We sail to-morrow morning in the steamer Roi Jérôme for Naples, and anticipate a very pleasant trip. We stop six hours at Genoa, six hours at Leghorn, and a few hours at Civita Vecchia, on the route, which is ample time to look over these unimportant places. We will be due at Naples on Sunday, the 13th.

ITALY.
GENOA.

STEAMER ROI JEROME,
BAY OF GENOA, July 12.

On the morning of the 10th of July we embarked on board the steamer Roi Jérôme for Naples, anticipating a pleasant journey. We found the decks of the vessel wet and disagreeable, the cabin had a shocking odor, and we were almost tempted to return to the shore. A number of slouchy-looking Italian men and women were coming on board, and the second officer, whom we supposed at the time to be captain, received us as if we were intruders upon his domain, disputed our right to the state-rooms which our tickets called for, and acted as if he was determined to make us as uncomfortable as possible. We had paid our passage, about five hundred francs, for the trip, and were out in the stream, with our trunks in the hold, where this most disagreeable officer persisted in storing them. In a short time, however, the captain, Lotta, made his appearance, and proved to be the very reverse of his surly subordinate. The whole aspect of affairs was instantly changed, our baggage arranged and stowed to suit our convenience, and we had to deal with a polished Italian gentleman, who seemed intent on securing the comfort of all on board. The rough passengers were all sent forward, the cabin ventilated, and by the time we had cleared the harbor of Marseilles our anticipations of a pleasant journey were renewed. The table proved to be excellently supplied with provisions and fruit, and we came to the conclusion, despite a little nausea which the short, quick waves of the Mediterranean imposed upon one of our party, that (wind and weather permitting) the trip would be a most gratifying one.

THE MEDITERRANEAN.

There is something peculiar about the motion of the waves of the Mediterranean. Before we had fully cleared the harbor of Marseilles several of the passengers were sick, and by the time we were five miles out, with the exception of our Neptune-proof party, but one of whom succumbed for a few moments, nearly all on board were affected. Still, the sea was as calm as the Chesapeake Bay, and the motion of the vessel so slight as to be scarcely perceptible to one who has had much sea-going experience. When seasickness once commences, it is almost impossible to shake it off, and we rather imagine that it is the rock-bound harbor of Marseilles and the eddy among its crags which cause a nausea on starting, for which the sea itself is not responsible. During our four days' trip along shore it has certainly behaved gently. The weather has been bright and beautiful, and we have not at all suffered from the heat.

Passing down the Mediterranean, we kept very close to the Italian coast, affording a fine view. The appearance is that of barren mountains, with occasional towns and fishermen's huts at their base. The railroads pass along these shores, and have of course carried great changes south of it within a few years. The three most interesting points on the Mediterranean, as connected with past history, are the Château d'If, where Mirabeau and the other state prisoners were confined, on a barren rock near Marseilles; the island of Elba, the prison of Napoleon; and the island of Sainte-Marguerite, known in history in connection with the Man with the Iron Mask.

THE CITY OF PALACES.

At daylight on Thursday morning, after a run of twenty hours, we dropped anchor in the harbor of Genoa, in full view of that city of palaces, as well as one of the most prosperous commercial ports on the Italian coast of the Mediterranean. It has a population of nearly one hundred and fifty thousand, and is situated on the slopes of a mountain over five hundred feet high, from the top of which frown fortresses of considerable dimensions, mounting heavy guns, having a clear range of the whole bay. Looming up in the rear of the city are the Apennine Mountains, which during a portion of the year are covered with snow. The view of the city from the harbor, and the harbor itself, are very fine; and, the captain having informed us that he would not sail until seven o'clock in the evening, we all made arrangements for spending the day on shore.

To enter a strange city in this way is certainly to fall into the hands of the Philistines, and we had to run the gauntlet in all shapes. We were plucked a little, but had the satisfaction of getting the worth of our money pretty generally. The railroad connecting Genoa with Marseilles, extending along the shores of the Mediterranean to Rome, Leghorn, and Naples, as well as connecting with Florence and all the interior of Italy, has greatly improved Genoa during the past few years. In commerce the harbor presented a thriving appearance, there being at least a dozen steamships loading or unloading, whilst a forest of masts of sailing-vessels loomed up in all directions. We took an omnibus upon landing, and coursed around the whole water-front of the city, which, like all Italian waterfronts, was crowded with carts, wagons, and donkeys. There being but four streets in Genoa on which wagons can be used, they are of course almost impassable for pedestrians. We met with two or three of the old palaces, most of which have been put to the much better use of trade, but our ride proved a rough and by no means an attractive one. Returning, we stopped at the railroad depot, and, having obtained some fruit and refreshments, engaged a cab to take us around to view the most prominent scenes and sights in the city. We found the ascents to the different levels to have been overcome with much skill, and whilst coursing through the beautiful streets we soon obtained an elevation from which we could look down upon the tall housetops bordering the harbor. We found the interior of the city much more beautiful than we had anticipated, adorned with fountains, public squares, and monuments, and presenting the finest views imaginable in all directions. The palaces are certainly most magnificent structures, and, considering that they were erected in past ages, some of them are still in excellent condition, and still in the possession of the families whose ancestors constructed them at a time when Genoa was a republic. Many are now used as hotels, others as cafés, and others as public buildings. Between these loftily-situated streets and piazzas a complete labyrinth of narrow streets and lanes, scarcely ten feet wide, occupied by seven- and eight-story houses, descends to the harbor.

It was here that Columbus was born, and it was to the Genoese government that he first made application for aid to sail on his voyage of discovery. A magnificent monument to his memory, near the railroad depot, was erected in 1862. It rests on a pedestal adorned with ships' prows. At the feet of the statue of Columbus, which rests on an anchor, kneels a female figure representing America. The monument, which is entirely of white marble, is surrounded by allegorical figures, representing Religion, Geography, Force, and Wisdom. Between these are reliefs of scenes from the history of Columbus, and the inscription of dedication. Opposite the monument is the Palace of Columbus, bearing the inscription "Cristoforo Colombo, Genoese, scopre l'America." There is also another statue of Columbus on the main street of the harbor.

The palaces of Genoa are certainly very grand structures. The entrances to the court-yards of some of them are fully forty feet high, and have over them the coat-of-arms of the families to which they belonged. The former opulence of the city is still evidenced by these numerous and magnificent emblems of the greatness of a by-gone age. The streets are paved with slabs of marble, but many of them are so narrow, steep, and tortuous, as to be inaccessible to carriages.

We of course visited the cathedral and the churches, all of which are rich in decorations, statuary, and paintings. The Capuchin Church of L'Annunziata, erected in 1487, with a most unsightly exterior, is the most sumptuous church in Genoa. The nave and aisles are supported by twelve columns of white marble, inlaid with red. The vault and dome are richly decorated with gilding, and frescoes by the old masters, representing scenes in Scripture history. The colors in these works of art are as bright as if just executed, and the paintings and decorations of the church are of the same rich description.

THE PEOPLE OF GENOA.

The people of Genoa are distinguished for their energy and industry, and our hasty drive through the city showed us as much activity as could be witnessed in the most stirring American city. The women are especially graceful and attractive in their appearance, dress, and carriage. The only head-covering worn by them is a white veil, which is very gracefully thrown over the head, and allowed to flow loosely over the shoulders, fastened at the crown of the head with a silver arrow.

At the Exchange or Bourse of Genoa there was a denser throng of business men than could be seen in Baltimore, and all seemed to be intent on trade and money-making. The sailors of Genoa are said to be superior to any on the Mediterranean, and have long retained their supremacy in this respect.

LEGHORN AND PISA.

STEAMER ROI JEROME, CIVITA VECCHIA, Saturday, July 18.

We closed our last letter in the Bay of Genoa, after having visited its old palaces and penetrated into the more modern and beautiful sections of that mountain-side city. At daybreak next morning we were at anchor in the harbor of Leghorn, the city from whence come the fine straw bonnets which the ladies of Christendom formerly delighted to wear. Most of the passage from Genoa was made while we were asleep, though we had a fine view of the harbor as we passed out about dusk, and also of the gloomy, rock-bound island of Elba, the old prison-house of Napoleon, and of its neighbor, the island of Corsica, on which he was born, and also the island of Sardinia.

THE CITY OF LEGHORN.

On landing at Leghorn we first felt the July heat of an Italian sun. Being accompanied on shore by Captain Lotta, we were relieved from the annoying process of chaffering with boatmen, drivers, and custodians, and were enabled to stand and look coolly on while he disposed of them by paying Italian prices for American travelers. These fellows evidently regarded it as a regular swindle, depriving them of their lawful rights of plunder. We had but little opportunity of seeing Leghorn, except as we landed at the quay and drove through the town, but it seemed to have nothing of the appearances of commercial prosperity that distinguished Genoa. It is a very clean and well-built city, with finely-paved streets, the blocks being about fifteen inches by thirty, and laid diagonally. It has a population of one hundred thousand, and the people have a reputation for thrift and industry. The public and private buildings are useful but not ornamental, and its palazzo is ornamented with some fine statues of the former Grand Dukes, before Leghorn became a part of the domain of Victor Emmanuel. Close to the harbor is an ancient statue erected two hundred and eighty years ago, in honor of Ferdinand I., with four figures of Turkish slaves in bronze chained to the four corners of the pedestal, and looking with terror upon their conqueror.

ROAD TO PISA.

We took carriages at Leghorn for the railroad depot, and on the route stopped at the water reservoir of Leghorn, in a solid stone building, to which the water from several fine springs in the mountains is conducted. The reservoir covers about an acre, and the water is thirty feet deep, but so clear that several stone inscriptions upon the bottom can be distinctly read. All the fountains in the city are supplied from this reservoir. On returning to our carriages we were beset by a crowd of beggars. There could not have been less than twenty of them, men, women, and children, some blind and lame, but all wearing countenances indicating wretchedness and distress. As we distributed among them all the change in our possession, the trembling eagerness with which the outstretched hand clutched the coin satisfied us that, although laziness may be at the root of the evil, necessity was the controlling motive.

We found a large and spacious depot, well arranged, and cars far superior to those on the English roads. The distance from Leghorn to Pisa is about ten miles, passing through a fine agricultural region in which there were fields of corn in tassel, and abundance of grapes. We observed quite a number of women working in the fields, and on one occasion a canal-boat being drawn by two women who were regularly yoked to the rope and seemed to be following their ordinary daily avocation. In Tuscany, however, everybody is expected to work, and although there are a few beggars, one scarcely ever sees even an idle child, the children being employed in making the famous Leghorn hats and bonnets.

PISA AND ITS ATTRACTIONS.

No one visits Italy without stopping a few hours at Pisa, and the passing trains between Florence and Leghorn always drop and take up returning passengers at this point. On passing out of the depot we were surrounded by a score of carriage-drivers, each of whom protested that he was the most honorable man in Pisa. These men, on the other hand, have the reputation of being the most dishonest scamps in creation. We referred them to Captain Lotta, and they soon discovered that nothing but Italian prices must be expected for our party. A drive of about twenty minutes through the town brought us to the cathedral, with its Leaning Tower, Baptistery, and the Campo Santo, all of which were commenced in the years 1000 and 1100, during a period when Pisa was supreme over Corsica, Sardinia, Palermo, and the Balearic Islands.

The cathedral is two hundred and ninety-two feet in length, with nave and double aisles, intercepted by a transept with aisles, and surmounted by an elliptical dome over the centre. The exterior is very fine, but the interior exceeds in artistic and costly ornamentation any cathedral we have ever entered. In statuary, paintings, mosaics, carvings, basso-relievos, by the greatest of ancient artists, it is profuse, and has several specimens of sculpture by Michael Angelo. The interior is supported by sixty-eight columns, many of which are of Greek and Roman origin, having been captured by the Pisans in war. The twelve altars were also designed by Michael Angelo. One of the chapels contains an altar cased in chased silver-work, with gold ornamentation, the gift of Cosmo III. The silver is said to have alone cost, independent of the work, one hundred and eighty thousand dollars.

The Baptistery is a singular building, of white marble, rising to a dome from the ground one hundred and seventy-nine feet high. The font, altar, and pulpit are of white marble, exquisitely carved, almost resembling lace. The great attraction of this structure is its wonderful echo, a deep-chested custodian being in attendance, who sounds several notes, the echo continuing to reverberate for nearly a minute, returning with all the sweetness of an organ, and finally dying off in a whisper.

THE LEANING TOWER

Is a world-wide curiosity. We ascended it and stood upon the iron balustrade, twenty feet above the bell-gallery, and had an extended view of the Apennine Mountains, and the great Valley of the Arno stretching out towards Florence, and the broad blue expanse of the Mediterranean to the west. The tower contains six bells, the heaviest one of them, weighing six tons, being suspended upon the side opposite to the overhanging side of the tower, which is twelve feet out of the perpendicular. Discussions have frequently arisen as to whether this peculiarity was intentional or accidental. The most probable solution is that the foundation settled during the progress of the structure, and that, to remedy the defect as much as possible, an attempt was made to give a vertical position to the upper portion. It has been built seven hundred years, and many of the columns which have shown evidences of decay have been removed and new ones inserted in their places, especially on the leaning side.

THE CAMPO SANTO.

The Campo Santo, or burial-ground, immediately adjoins the Baptistery. Archbishop Waldo, in 1188, after the loss of the Holy Land, had conveyed hither fifty-three ship-loads of earth from Mount Calvary, in order that the dead might repose in holy ground. It is surrounded by a heavy stone wall forty-three feet high, and is roofed towards the centre on the inside, where there is an open court-yard. The walls on the inside are covered with frescoes by eminent painters, representing various scenes in Scripture history, as well as imaginary scenes of the torments of hell. There is a beautiful monument of the singer Angelica Catalani, and a bust of Count Camillo Cavour. This is undoubtedly the most interesting of the four Pisan curiosities, if time could be given to examine it. It is said that the difference between the present time and formerly is this: formerly the dead were required to pay a fee on entering, but, as they never left it, of course nothing more could be demanded of them; and so now the living enter free, but are compelled to pay well before they are allowed to depart!

CIVITA VECCHIA.

Having finished Pisa, we drove through the town back to the depot, and in less than an hour were on board the Roi Jérôme, steaming towards Civita Vecchia, which we reached at daybreak on Saturday morning. Having a remembrance that fleas, beggars, and lazzaroni were its main attractions some twelve years ago, we did not go ashore, but could plainly perceive that it has vastly improved since it passed from the dominion of the pope to that of Victor Emmanuel. A large and powerful fort has been built to protect the harbor, which is regarded as the gate to Rome, and, from the number of new buildings being constructed, the city must have considerably increased in population.

FLEAS AND BEGGARS.

These are the two most annoying impediments to the enjoyment of travel in Italy. They both approach you in swarms, and it is useless to attempt to dodge or avoid them. You must calmly submit, or beat a retreat. The fleas come upon you unawares, and make their approaches to chosen portions of your body, reaching the least vulnerable position before giving notice of their presence. They are most severe upon the ladies, who, in traveling, have few opportunities to expel and punish the invader. The pleasure of visiting strange scenes, and examining curiosities of nature and art, with a score of fleas tugging at your very vitals, is undoubtedly greatly marred. We are, however, assured that we will soon get used to them. The beggars are much easier disposed of, but it can only be done by giving them what they require, otherwise they will cling to you with all the tenacity of their fellow-nuisances. The fleas are equally rapacious with the natives, as it is a common scene to see them catching them on their children or one another. They have a mode of killing them much more expeditious than is adopted by strangers, which is said to be giving them a peculiar twist which breaks their backs. This morning a boatman dropped his oars just under our cabin-window, pulled off his stocking, and in a moment committed to watery graves three of these pests. He had evidently disabled their jumping capacity by some invisible process. The poor beggars are such God-forsaken-looking creatures, and seem so intent, as if starvation would be the result of failure, that we do not know whether it is not a real pleasure to give them temporary relief. Then they are satisfied with such a trifle, and shower such blessings upon you, that they almost convince you that you have done a good action, even if you feel in your heart that you have only encouraged vice and laziness.

TRAVEL ON THE MEDITERRANEAN.

We have had a very pleasant journey upon the Roi Jérôme. With the exception of a few passengers who left us at Genoa, there have been but two other passengers, and Captain Lotta has exerted himself to the utmost for our comfort and enjoyment. The weather has been delightful during our four days' trip, and the ocean as calm and smooth as could possibly be expected or desired, with a bright sun by day and a brilliant moon by night. An awning spread over the deck has enabled us to live in the open air, and notwithstanding the heat reported to us at home, here in sunny Italy we have not been for a moment uncomfortable up to the middle of July. Within a few hours we will be in sight of Vesuvius, and at eleven o'clock to-night will drop anchor in the beautiful Bay of Naples.

ITALIAN COOKING.

Our table has been spread, most of the time on deck, with all the luxuries of the Mediterranean, a fresh variety having been daily procured at Genoa, Leghorn, and Civita Vecchia. Still, we cannot say that Italian dainties and Italian cooking are to our taste. At breakfast, for instance, the first course was three varieties of shell-fish, served in the shell (none of them larger than an English walnut), with wine and bread and butter. Neither of these shell-fish were to our tastes palatable. The second course consisted of fried veal and toast, evidently fried in olive oil, and seasoned with some native herb. The third course was boiled lobster, dressed with native herbs. The fourth course was mutton-chops with fried potatoes. The fifth course was two kinds of cheese. The sixth course consisted of pears, plums, ripe figs, and green filberts. The seventh course was a cup of strong hot coffee. It was evidently a good breakfast for those who like it, but did not suit us as well as the breakfast served by our friend Colonel Coleman. On arising in the morning a cup of hot coffee is served to each passenger who desires it. Breakfast is served at ten o'clock in the morning, and dinner at six o'clock in the evening. Breakfast and dinner are very much alike, and we are assured that no one is considered in good health who does not dispose of a pint-bottle of wine at each meal.

CITY OF NAPLES.

VESUVIUS TRANQUIL AND VESUVIUS IN ERUPTION.

CITY OF NAPLES, July, 1873.

Leaving Civita Vecchia on Saturday afternoon, we found ourselves when we awoke on Sunday morning anchored in the harbor of Naples, with Mount Vesuvius looming up to our right, enveloped in a cloud of mist, except its pinnacle, which protruded above the dense fog which had settled on its sides. A lazily-moving stream of smoke, such as might be seen arising from a cottage chimney, was floating off from the mouth of the crater. Every vestige of the recent great eruption has apparently disappeared. After the smaller eruption in 1858 the lava continued to run in a small stream for nearly two years, but the old mountain seems to have completely exhausted itself for a time in its grand effort of 1871.

OUR LANDING EFFECTED.

About seven o'clock on Sunday morning we disembarked, and found that we had less difficulty than anticipated with boatmen, custom-house officials, carriage-drivers, and especially the usual crowd of volunteers, each one of whom seizes a piece of baggage and insists upon carrying it to your carriage. We disposed of the latter by giving a franc to the most prominent, with gesticulations to share it, leaving them to fight out the question of division among themselves, which they were warmly engaged in when we succeeded in getting our carriage in motion. The boatman and carriage-driver were satisfied with about one-half of Baltimore prices, which we tendered them, and subsequently found upon looking over the tariff of charges that we had paid about double legal rates! The price for a carriage holding four persons is thirty cents an hour for the first hour, and twenty cents for each subsequent hour. The fact is that those who complain of extortion in Europe forget what the charges of travel are at home. Here the waiter or attendant receives little or no salary, and expects a trifle from the guests. He is satisfied with a few pennies, and only dissatisfied if he receives nothing.

OUR LOCATION IN NAPLES.

The season for visitors at Naples is over, and most of the hotels are entirely empty of guests. We finally located ourselves at the Palace of Prince Caramanico, now the Grand United States Hotel. It contains most of the heavy gilded furniture of its palatial days, fronts on the bay, and with Vesuvius on its left commands a fine view of the Villa Nazionale and the Villa Reale. We found upon inquiry that we were the only guests in the extensive house, and that we could have a choice of rooms, with dinner at the *table-d'hôte*, for ten francs each per day. Our other meals are to be furnished to order or picked up wherever we may happen to be in our wanderings. We must not omit to add that we have at this price the use also of an elegant parlor, furnished in all the grandeur of gilt and velvet, fronting on the bay, adjoining our chambers, in which we are now writing. This certainly does not look like extortion, and we did not chaffer or dispute the prices. We have the advantage here of ordering what we want cooked in the way we want it, and have just disposed of a breakfast, *à l'Américaine*, which suited us all better than anything we have eaten since we have left home.

NAPLES ON SUNDAY.

There is little difference apparent here between Sunday and weekdays. As we drove from the custom-house before seven o'clock this morning through the lower part of the city, all the stores and shops were open, the market in full operation, the vehicles of trade in motion, and mechanics at work at their avocations. The streets were thronged with donkeys almost covered up with loads of vegetables; women with hand-wagons crying their fruits; whilst priests, monks, and barefooted friars were intermixed among wandering musicians with bagpipes and dancing-boys. Some persons appeared, however, to be intent on properly observing the day, being arrayed in their best attire, and were moving towards the churches, having first visited the market to purchase bouquets to lay at the shrine of the Virgin. The better classes were also moving towards the churches in carriages, each bearing a bouquet, and apparently intent on the religious duties of the day.

SCENES FROM OUR WINDOWS.

During the last hour a half-dozen singing, dancing, and musical geniuses, all in rags and tatters, and apparently with their skins unwashed for a month of Sundays, have followed in succession under our windows, a half-franc thrown to the first of the callers having apparently brought the whole crowd in pursuit of us. It was truly amusing to witness the wild enthusiasm of the party at so large a sum of money, equal to our ten-cent piece, they having gone on dancing and singing with renewed vigor and earnestness. The practice here is to throw them a small copper coin equal to about one-fourth of a cent.

In front of the Villa Reale, or public square, extending about half a mile on the bay, long stagings and bath-houses have been erected, and the scene from our windows is equal to that at Cape May. There must be many thousands of boys and men floundering and swimming in the water. It is to be hoped that the dingy, dirty-looking men and boys still on the streets will also avail themselves of this free bathing, and, as cleanliness is akin to godliness, they could not better observe the Sabbath day. Among the lower classes of this immense city, nearly double the size of Baltimore, filthiness is the rule and cleanliness the exception.

A WALK ON THE TOLEDO.

About twelve o'clock, desiring to see something of Sunday in the heart of the city, a portion of our party started for a walk, and moved towards the Toledo through the long net-work of narrow streets, too steep, if not too narrow, for a carriage to penetrate, with houses six to seven stories in height, in which the working classes reside. We found them alive with people of all classes, some at work mending shoes or tailoring, all the stores open, the street-hucksters busy plying their vocation, wandering tinners mending pans and kettles, and intermixed with them was a throng of well-dressed people returning from church. The only guide we had in reaching the Strada Toledo out of this intricate line of long and steep ascending or rapidly descending thoroughfares was an occasional glimpse of Vesuvius on one side, or of the Castle of St. Elmo looming up in almost equal grandeur on the other side. We finally struck the Chiaja, and were soon in the moving mass of humanity on the Toledo. This is the main retail thoroughfare of Naples, and one of the few streets of the city through which vehicles can be driven. It is not as broad as Baltimore Street, but it is paved with blocks of granite, and the street forms as good a footpath as the sidewalk, which is kept scrupulously clean. The stores here were generally closed, with the exception of tobacco-stores, cafés, restaurants, and "lira stores" (a lira is twenty cents), which correspond with our "dollar-stores," the goods being of about the same quality and kind. They were thronged with purchasers, and were doing a brisk business. The "money-changers'" stalls upon the corners were open, and the vendors of lemonade were at every corner furnishing this cooling drink for the people, which appears to be a favorite beverage.

It was evident from our observations during this walk that the people of Naples enjoy the largest liberty as to the observance of Sunday, though it is apparent that the only stores that are closed are those that would not be likely to do much business on Sunday if they were open. A great many hat-stores were open, and some glove-stores, with a few jewelry-establishments. A volunteer military company, with a full band, also passed along the Toledo just as the people were leaving the churches.

THE NEAPOLITAN LADIES.

The better classes of the ladies of Naples never walk on the streets, except to and from the church on Sunday; the only promenade they enjoy being on their house-tops, where plants are cultivated and vines trailed upon arbors. Consequently, we had an excellent opportunity to see a large number of them during our walk to-day. We do not know when we have seen so many well-dressed ladies. They were dressed with exquisite taste, in light gossamer materials, all gaudy intermixture of colors being avoided, and we particularly noticed that not a single trailing dress was visible. Trails are worn here only in-doors, or whilst riding; never on the streets, except by the lower classes and by those who make no claims to respectability. The younger ladies here are undoubtedly handsome, most of them brunettes, though we passed many decided blondes. They wear very little jewelry on the streets except diamonds, and, although this is the great depot for coral jewelry, there was not a single set visible. It would be difficult to meet with finer-dressed gentlemen than were accompanying the ladies, and their children were arrayed in the same cool and light material as their mothers and sisters wore.

AN EVENING DRIVE.

Desirous of seeing as much as possible of the people of Naples on Sunday, we started in the afternoon for a drive, and soon found ourselves on the Chinja in a double line of carriages, one passing up and the other down in regular review, in which were all the finest establishments in Naples, including a good many that were anything else but fine. They moved steadily on, presenting a democratic equality quite unexpected in this old capital of the defunct Bourbon dynasty.

The display of liveried footmen and finely-dressed ladies was very large, whilst all the young bloods of the city were out with their fast horses. The fashionable drive appears to be a circle of the city formed by the Strada Toledo, the Chiaja, and the Palazzo, by which a course of a mile is obtained on the line of the bay. Most of the streets are so narrow, and the throng of pedestrians so great, constantly pressing on the carriage-ways, that the scene presented was quite exciting. Later in the evening, after the more stately carriages had withdrawn, the young bloods of all degrees took possession of the drive, and the crack of whips and the yells of the drivers indicated some spirited contests on the Chiaja in front of our hotel. All classes able to procure vehicles took part in this review, which we learn is repeated every Sunday afternoon, weather permitting.

NEAPOLITAN SCRAPS.

The scenes we witnessed to-day all indicated that the people of Naples are bent on enjoying life and seem to be a good-hearted and kindly-disposed people. The number of street-beggars is in a great measure the fault of the people, as an appeal is seldom made to them in vain. The sums they give are small, but they toss them coppers as they walk or ride past them, especially on Sundays, without waiting for an appeal.

The number of priests, monks, and friars on the streets is very great. They are in a variety of dresses, and we observed many riding in carriages on the grand promenade this afternoon. A very black man, apparently about thirty years of age, passed us arrayed in a monk's dress of thick, heavy, brown serge, with a rope around his waist, and bareheaded, with sandals on his feet. He was walking with a brother of the same order.

The weather here is warm, but not what we would call oppressive at home. Our rooms are within fifty feet of the bay, and we have a delightful breeze all day, whilst at night we sleep very comfortably with closed windows. If it were not for the fleas, which are very annoying to the ladies, our sojourn would be very pleasant. There is but one of the party, and he an inveterate smoker, whom they seem to shun. If they happen to alight upon him they soon jump off again, without making any depredations. This will be comforting to smokers who propose to visit Italy.

The tramp of companies and regiments of soldiers is constant, and the police of the city wear military uniforms, carrying a sword in daytime, and both rifle and sword at night. There is evidently great military activity throughout Italy, and the drilling of recruits was going on as we passed through both Genoa and Leghorn. Sunday in Naples is regarded as a holiday, and we learn that all who are required to work upon that day are entitled to demand increased pay, the same as on all other holidays.

CITY OF NAPLES, July, 1873.

HAPPINESS OF THE PEOPLE.

Naples is full of life and animation. It is stirring, bright and beautiful on its principal thoroughfares, and even the denizens of its narrow alleys, with their tall houses, seem to think that they are in a paradise of bliss. The variety of smells that pervade these cracks of the city (which are not more than twelve feet wide, six of which are taken up by the women and children, who mostly live on the streets) may possibly be calculated to conduce to a happy state of mind. They look happy, talk happy, and are a jovial people, in all grades of life, from the lazzaroni to the prince. It is difficult to conceive what makes some of them happy, but that they are gloriously happy no one who has spent a few days in Naples will undertake to dispute. In these contracted quarters one-half of the day is spent by the females in catching and killing fleas off themselves or their children, and whilst engaged in this delectable pursuit they will go on laughing and talking as if it were the most delightful employment that could possibly be undertaken. To be sure, we are here in the season of the year in which these pests are most numerous and active, but the old residents have become so accustomed to them that they scarcely notice them, and go through the operation of catching and killing without apparently knowing that they are engaged in what would be regarded as a terrible infliction by the rest of mankind. Our waiter to-day assured us that we were suffering from mosquito-bites, and actually professed not to know what a flea was. An American lady told me this morning that she had caught and killed thirty-four on her own person before dinner; and as to bites, it was difficult to find where they were not. Hence we propose to make our stay in Naples very short, and shall soon leave for Rome, though in doing so we may probably be getting out of the frying-pan into the fire.

VISIT TO THE MUSEUM.

We spent most of to-day in the Museum of Pompeiian Curiosities, which are very interesting, but would be more so if there was a properly-prepared catalogue of the various articles for the use of visitors, who are necessarily compelled to make a hasty examination. The collection of articles taken from the ruins of Pompeii embraces everything in art that is excellent and wonderful, including both statuary and paintings, their two thousand years of interment in scoria and ashes having failed to mar their beauty or dim their colors. Some of the paintings taken from the walls of the houses are very lascivious, and some of them decidedly vulgar, but they are executed in a style of art and coloring that can scarcely be equaled at the present day. The statuary and busts are in the highest style of art, most of the latter being evidently likenesses of the prominent men and women of the city of Pompeii. The collection of finger-rings, bracelets, necklaces, and ornaments for the hair is very extensive, all of pure gold, and the engraved seals and cornelians are finely executed. Then there are wheat, corn, and even loaves of bread found in an oven, black but in good shape, and every variety of pots and kettles that were used for culinary purposes. A large number of artists were engaged in making copies of the paintings, whilst others were making drawings of scroll-work and metal tables and urns, to have them reproduced, the models being superior to anything of the present age.

Admission to the museum was formerly free, but the custodians managed to get two or three fees out of each visitor. Now the price of admission is one franc, and visitors are admonished to give the custodians nothing, and the custodians are commanded to receive nothing, under pain of dismissal.

SHOPPING IN NAPLES.

We spent our time yesterday in a general exploration of the city, whilst the ladies were engaged in the genial and pleasing occupation of shopping. They returned well versed in the value of kid gloves, coral jewelry, lava, amethysts, and cameos. They found these articles all astonishingly cheap. The finest gauntlet kids were but two and a half francs per pair, or about fifty cents, and ordinary party kids with three buttons, of all colors, from thirty to forty cents per pair. Gentlemen's black kids of the finest quality were but forty cents per pair. The ornamental goods were correspondingly low. A set of medium light coral jewelry, breastpin and ear-rings, such as would cost from seventy-five dollars to one hundred dollars at home, could be had here at from twenty dollars to forty dollars, although prices have greatly advanced within the past few years. A very elegant and elaborate set of coral, consisting of breastpin, ear-rings, bracelet and necklace, was purchased for ninety dollars. So also as to amethysts. Diamonds were found to be surprisingly low, compared with prices at home, both for solitaires and clusters. The ladies of our party tested thoroughly the question as to whether they were being charged exorbitant prices, that is to say, prices in advance of what would be charged native purchasers, and found that charges were fixed, and that the dealers would not deviate one franc, even in articles valued at from fourteen to fifteen hundred francs. All they asked was that the ladies would come back again if not suited elsewhere, with the assurance that nobody in Naples could or would sell goods cheaper than they had offered them. On thoroughly searching the city it was found that such was the case. Hence the conclusion is that the dealers of Naples do not take advantage of strangers, but have fixed prices for their goods, from which they cannot be induced to deviate.

WON'T GO HOME TILL MORNING.

The streets of Naples show as much life and activity in daytime as those of Paris, and with the exception of one hour during the night, from half-past two to half-past three, the same moving panorama is to be witnessed. Carriages and vehicles are running all night, and the merry peals of laughter and cracking of whips during the small hours show that their occupants are seeking pleasure and enjoyment. When one class goes to bed the other gets up, and the clatter of donkeys, with an occasional bray, and the loud shouts of the drivers, keep up a perpetual din until the break of day, when the cries of the vendors of vegetables and fruits are added to the din. An hour later, and all the garrisons of the city, including the awkward squads, are marched down to the solid stone pavement lining the sea-wall of the bay, and here they are drilled until breakfast-time, their steady tramp as they march and countermarch directly under our windows being not in the least calculated to soothe to balmy sleep. The signs of a military government are everywhere visible, even the police being well-drilled men, armed with swords in daytime and a rifle by night. They are mostly very young men, but move about with a soldierly bearing that could only be acquired from active service.

When a stranger drops suddenly into an Italian community where all the active pursuits of life are in full progress, he imagines from the violent gesticulations and loud emphatic language that a general quarrel is in progress. Nothing could, however, do them more injustice than such an opinion. It is only their emphatic and earnest manner of expression that gives ground for the impression. Certain it is that a more orderly city than Naples we have not recently visited. The incident of two boys fighting in the street quickly brought around them a crowd of gentlemen to separate and pacify them.

FRUITS OF NAPLES.

There is evidently an abundance of fruits of excellent quality in the neighborhood of Naples, and, although the season is just commencing, they can be obtained from the fruit-stands at very reasonable prices. Good pears cost ten cents a dozen, and quite large and luscious peaches, equal to those at home, cost twenty-five cents per dozen. At Marseilles we were charged for six peaches furnished at breakfast the enormous price of fifteen francs,—about three dollars in our money. Plums and greengages are very cheap and abundant, and of unusual size. The green figs are very large, but are not as palatable as those of Georgia and South Carolina. Most of the sale of fruits and vegetables by retail, as in Paris, is done by street-peddlers, principally women. It seems like home to get where fruit is again plenty. There are also cantaloupes in the markets, looking very much like those of America, though not so palatable. The plums and greengages are of the largest size, and are entirely free from worms. Cherries are about the size of our damsons, and very firm and luxurious. Peas, beans, lettuce, radishes, and all the garden vegetables grow to perfection here, and cucumbers attain fully twelve inches in length.

HOW THE BABIES ARE NURSED.

The ladies are terribly shocked at the apparent cruel treatment of babies, though, as far as we can observe, they are about as happy as most babies of other countries. They are apparently strapped to boards, and wound up in sheets and bandages, so as to look like little mummies. Their limbs, and indeed their whole bodies, from chin to toes, are covered up and pinned, leaving only their arms loose, and in some cases these seem to come in for a share of the general wrapping. Whether the object is to make them grow straight and erect, or to keep the fleas from getting access to their tender bodies, it is difficult to say, but the practice seems to be universal with all classes. How they are kept clean under such treatment is the question to be solved; but most of the people here seem to have a different idea of cleanliness from the rest of mankind. Among the lower classes the babies, so soon as they can walk, are apparently turned loose to take care of themselves. In passing through the narrow streets, numbers of them can be seen toddling about with no one to look after them, their skin so grimed with dirt and filth that one can scarcely determine their original color. Other infants were in charge of children of slightly advanced age. By the time children reach eight years, they are put at work driving donkeys, carrying water, etc. The only attention the parents seem to give to the children, or at least all that we have yet discovered, is an occasional examination of their little bodies. the operation being interspersed by an occasional picking off of something which receives a mysterious twist between the thumb and forefinger and is then cast upon the ground.

It seems to us that a Yankee baby would not stand such treatment as these Neapolitan brothers and sisters bear with equanimity and apparent satisfaction. Perhaps they have the best of it—who knows?

THE FAITHFUL DONKEY.

What would Naples do without its donkeys? This is a question that intrudes itself every time we look out of the window or perambulate its streets. The little donkey is not much larger than a Newfoundland dog, but he is all muscle, and exhibits much strength and endurance. He can carry on his back as much as an ordinary horse, and then take on top of his load both his master and mistress, and, if necessary, the children of the household. He seems never to be overloaded. No matter how much he is beaten, he maintains his spirits and good nature, and will bray as loud as an elephant at every donkey acquaintance that may pass him. Every household has its donkey, and no household would know how to get along in the world without its donkey. Every youngster of good family has his donkey for saddle-purposes, and every huckster has his donkey for doing all the carrying that he may require. We see almost as many donkeys as men on the streets; hence we ask, what would Naples do without its donkeys?

NAPLES, July, 1873.

We will now proceed to narrate our visit to Pompeii, which, like Mount Vesuvius, far exceeded our anticipations in all its characteristics. We expected to meet with nothing in Pompeii that would astonish or particularly interest us; but it soon became evident that in grandeur and magnificence the buried city rivaled that of Rome, which was contemporaneously destroyed by the violence of man.

We took an early breakfast, and our party, comprising six, started at eight o'clock in a large carriage, which we had engaged for three and a half piastres for the entire day, it being the standing rule of all travelers to offer just half the price charged, though sometimes it is prudent to persist on paying only about one-fourth of the original demand. We proceeded at a brisk pace around the head of the bay, passing through the suburbs of Naples, the towns of Pasagno, Portici, Resina, Favorita, Torre del Greco, Rossi, and Torre dell' Annunziata, to the gates of Pompeii, in the rear of Vesuvius, a distance of fourteen miles, which was accomplished in about two hours.

The whole of this route through these towns, most of them being situated on the base and sides of Vesuvius, was like passing through a continuous street of Naples, paved all the way, and all connecting with each other so closely that without a previous study of the locality the change of corporate limits could not be discerned. The road coasts the eastern shore of the bay to the right, with Vesuvius to the left: but it is so completely shut out from the sea by the dead walls of the numerous villas, overgrown palace-gardens, and large unornamented houses, which stretch in an almost unbroken line as far as Torre dell' Annunziata, that it has more the character of a long, uninteresting, dusty street than of a high post-road. The crowds of villagers were interesting to look upon, as well as the wine-shops, macaroni-establishments, and other quaint spectacles to the eye of a stranger.

EXCAVATIONS OF POMPEII.

When we entered the Herculaneum Gate the first sight that met our view was perhaps a hundred boys, from twelve to fifteen years of age, each with baskets of earth upon his shoulders, marching out of the streets of Pompeii. They were engaged in the excavations now progressing under direction of government,—sixty thousand lire, or about twelve thousand dollars, being appropriated annually for the purpose. Some of the discoveries recently made are very interesting, and are being collected in a museum built on the ruins, which we first entered. Here are the fossilized remains of four of the victims of Pompeii, just as they fell in their struggle with death. There are two, supposed to be a mother and daughter, their limbs entwined, both lying on their faces, the daughter's head leaning on her arm, and both having rings on their fingers. A third is that of a large man, believed to have been an African, who was found with a lamp in his hand and a bag of money strapped to his waist, and is supposed to have been intent upon plunder when he lost his life. In this museum are also to be found the bones of horses and other domestic animals, as well as the various metal cooking and household utensils, earthenware jars, and glass bottles, which have recently been excavated.

HOW POMPEII WAS DESTROYED.

Pliny the Younger, who was a resident of Pompeii at the time of its destruction, gives an interesting account in his well-known letters to Tacitus, describing the death of his uncle, the elder Pliny, distinguished as a naturalist. He speaks of a cloud of vapor as having been seen over Vesuvius on the afternoon of the 24th of August in the year 79, which he likens in form to a pine-tree, ascending to a vast height and spreading out its branches. There had been for many days before some shocks of an earthquake, which were not unusual, but they were so particularly violent that night that they not only shook everything, but seemed to threaten total destruction. In the morning the light was exceedingly faint and languid, the buildings all tottered, and the people resolved to quit the town. Having got to a considerable distance, they stood still in the midst of a most dangerous and dreadful scene. The chariots were so agitated backwards and forwards, though upon the most level ground, that they could not be kept steady even by supporting them with large stones. The sea seemed to roll back upon itself, and to be driven from its banks by the convulsive motion of the earth, leaving several sea-animals on the shore. On the other side a black and dreadful cloud, bursting with an igneous serpentine vapor, darted out a long train of fire, resembling flashes of lightning, but much larger. Soon after the cloud seemed to descend and cover the whole ocean. Immediately after, darkness overspread them, not like that of a cloudy night or when there is no moon, but of a room when it is shut up and all the lights are extinct. Nothing was to be heard but the shrieks of women, the screams of children, and the cries of men; some calling for their children, others for their parents, and others for their husbands, and only distinguishing each other by their voices; one lamenting his own fate, another that of his family; some wishing to die from the very fear of dying; some lifting their hands to the gods, but the greater part imagining that the last and eternal night was come which was to destroy the gods and the world together. At length a glimmering light appeared, which they imagined to be rather the forerunner of an approaching burst of flames, as in truth it was, than the return of day. The fire, however, fell at a distance, and they were again immersed in thick darkness, with a heavy shower of ashes raining upon them, which they were obliged to shake off, otherwise they would have been crushed and buried in the heap. At last this dreadful darkness was dissipated by degrees, like a cloud of smoke; the real day returned, and even the sun appeared, though as under a partial eclipse. Every object which presented itself to their weakened eyes was covered over with white ashes, as with a deep snow. The mountain afterwards threw out deluges of heated water, charged with the dry light ashes which were suspended in the air. This water, as it reached the soil, carried with it in its course the cinders which had fallen, and thus deluged Pompeii with a soft pasty volcanic mud or alluvium, which penetrated into places where neither scoria nor ashes could have reached, and thus completed the work of destruction.

This is the substance of the description given by an eye-witness, and is most valuable as affording reliable evidence of the character of the eruption. This eruption also overwhelmed Herculaneum with lava, some of the ruins of which have been discovered about a mile distant. On account of the difficulty of excavating the lava, but one subterranean excavation has been made, exhibiting the interior of two or three houses and temples.

STREETS OF POMPEII.

Having entered the area of the excavated ruins, we were greatly surprised to find them in so excellent a state of preservation. We found ourselves walking through long paved streets, just as they were when thronged with inhabitants eighteen centuries ago, with the ruins of rows of houses on both sides, closely built up in every direction. The streets are extremely narrow, and it is clear that not more than one vehicle could pass at a time in any but the principal thoroughfares. They are paved with irregular blocks of lava, closely fitted together, and bordered by a narrow pavement and curbstone, elevated a foot or more above the carriage-way. The streets are about twelve feet wide, and even the principal thoroughfares are not more than twenty feet in width. Elevated stepping-stones, like those now used in Baltimore, are frequently seen in the middle of the streets for the convenience of foot-passengers in time of rain. Stones for mounting horses are also found at the side of the pavements, and rings are found in the curbs opposite the principal houses and shops, for fastening the halter. Of the streets that have been excavated, five may be considered as the principal thoroughfares of the city. The sidewalks are of bricks, and occasionally stuccoed.

DECORATIONS OF THE HOUSES.

The private houses are generally small and low, and deficient in all that would be considered comfort at the present day, though it is evident that the whole space within the walls of the city, which are two miles in circumference, was closely occupied by buildings. The ground-floors of the larger houses were generally occupied as shops. The walls and roof were often decorated with great splendor, and the pavement was always of marble or mosaics. In the centre of the space occupied by the smallest houses there is nearly always to be found a sort of courtyard for garden and flowers. The rooms generally would be considered as closets at the present day, the walls of which are covered with rich frescoes and paintings, most of them in excellent preservation, and all evincing a state of gross immorality beyond any thing that can be conceived in the present age. No houses have, however, yet been discovered which can be regarded as having been the dwellings of the poor; and it remains to be proved by further excavations whether the lower orders were located in a separate quarter of the city, or whether Pompeii was really free from any pauper population.

SHOPS AND THEATRES.

The shops were very small, and when first excavated many of them had the names of their owners written over them, mostly in red paint; others had signs to denote the trade that was carried on in them. Thus, a goat indicated a milk-shop or dairy; two men carrying a large jug indicated a wine-shop; two men fighting indicated a gladiatorial school; a man whipping a boy hoisted on another's back indicated a school-master; and checkers denoted the door-post of the publican. The houses of bad repute were evidently marked by the authorities with an indelicate carved figure on the curb-stone, probably in order that no one should enter them without a knowledge of their character.

The wine-shops seem to have been very numerous, and the marble counters, in which were built up large earthenware jars, each capable of holding nearly as much as a barrel, are still standing in good condition. These counters, with openings through their tops through which to dip up the wine, are generally square, with an open space in the middle, in which the vendor stood to supply his customers. There are two undoubted restaurants or cook-shops, where articles were cooked and sold across the counter. There is also a barber's shop, with a stone block in the centre, on which the Pompeians sat to be shaved.

The theatres and amphitheatres are on a most extensive scale, and are in an excellent state of preservation, though none of them are equal to the Coliseum at Rome. The interior of the great amphitheatre was capable of seating ten thousand persons. The part now excavated is about one-fourth of the city, and contains two forums, nine temples, two basilicas, three piazzas, an amphitheatre, two theatres, a prison, several baths, nearly one hundred houses and shops, several villas, a considerable portion of the walls, seven gates, and about a dozen tombs. The tombs are outside of the walls, and are on a scale of great magnificence, the vaults under them having receptacles for urns to hold the ashes of the dead, the mode of burial among the Pompeians having been to burn the bodies and deposit the ashes in funeral urns.

The walls of the city are built of large blocks of lava, evincing fine workmanship. The upper courses, however, have been frequently broken and rudely repaired, showing the effect of breaches, probably from the battering-rams of the enemy. The towers were square, and apparently have been of great height, having doubtless been overthrown by the earthquakes that preceded the destruction and burial of the city.

VILLA OF DIOMEDE.

The villa of Diomede, immediately outside of the walls, judging from the ruins left, must have been a splendid establishment, decorated in the highest style of art, and embellished with statuary, paintings, fountain, bathing-room, and garden. Beneath the portico, and below the level of the gardens, was the wine-cellar, a long archway, not less than one hundred feet in length, in as perfect a state as when last occupied by its owner. A long row of wine-jars, each about four feet high, now stands in this vault, incrusted in lava against the wall. On the night of the eruption the owner of this splendid mansion appears to have lost the love of kindred in the eagerness to save life, for his skeleton was found, with that of an attendant, near the garden gate, the one still holding in his bony grasp the key of the villa, the other carrying a purse containing one hundred gold and silver coins, and some silver vases. While he was thus endeavoring to escape to the sea-shore, the members of his family, whom he had abandoned to their fate, took refuge in the wine-cellar, where seventeen of their skeletons were found near the door, as if they had endeavored to retrace their steps after finding that the place afforded no sufficient shelter from the fiery tempest. From the gold bracelets on the necks and arms of nearly all these skeletons, it would appear that they were mostly females. Two were the skeletons of children, whose skulls still retained some portions of beautiful blonde hair. After they had perished, probably from suffocation, the floor of the cellar was inundated with a fine alluvium, which hardened on the bodies and took casts, not only of their forms, but even of the most delicate texture of the linen they wore, and of the jewels which adorned their persons. One cast of a young girl, part of which we saw in the museum, with her skull, possessed exceeding elegance of form; the neck and breast especially were perfect models of female beauty.

"How sadly echoing to the stranger's tread
These walls respond, like voices from the dead!"

We also examined the spot where the skeletons of a mother and three children were found, all closely folded in each other's arms, which were decked with gold ornaments, elaborately worked, and enriched with pendent pearls of great value.

OTHER RUINS.

The ruins of a tavern are quite interesting. It has numerous apartments in the rear, which served probably as drinking-rooms, as one of the walls contained announcements of the public festivals of the day. The shop itself contained a furnace, steps for displaying the glasses, and a marble counter which still exhibits the stains of the liquor and the marks of the glasses! The figure of Mercury was painted on various parts of the house, and some of the walls are covered with proper names, scratched by the customers upon the plastering, which covered other names of previous scribblers.

The house of the surgeon was found well supplied with surgical instruments, of forty different varieties. The public bake-house was also examined with great interest. It has four stone mills in it. The oven stands in a perfect condition still, and is precisely after the fashion of the ovens of bakers of the present day. It had, when opened, fuel in it, apparently just ready for lighting.

HOUSE OF SALLUST.

The house of Sallust was no doubt one of the most magnificent of the private residences within the walls. It seems to have had attached to it a real prototype of the Oriental harem, every part of it being most elaborately decorated. In the adjoining room was found the skeleton of a young female, supposed to be that of the fair being who was enshrined in this retreat with so much privacy and magnificence. She had four rings on one of her fingers, set with engraved stones; fine gold bracelets, two ear-rings, and thirty-two pieces of money were lying near her. Close at hand were found the skeletons of three other females, supposed to have been her slaves.

The public baths are very fine and still in an excellent state of preservation. One has a vaulted ceiling, richly painted red and blue, with a cold-water basin of white marble in the centre, twelve feet ten inches in diameter and two feet nine inches deep. The warm bath is entered from the disrobing-room, and nearly corresponds with it in size. There is also a vapor bath, the walls and chambers being constructed hollow, so as to allow the steam to circulate freely from the furnaces. The women's baths are at the other side of the furnaces, and are arranged and decorated in the same manner as those for the men. No less than five hundred stone lamps were found in one corridor of this establishment.

THE FORUM.

The Forum is a spacious and imposing spot, surrounded by the Temple of Jupiter, the Temple of Venus, and the Senate Chamber. It was ornamented on three sides by a broad colonnade of Grecian-Doric architecture. The Senate Chamber, or Basilica, was two hundred and twenty feet long and eighty feet broad, and in a vault under its stairway, used for prisoners during the progress of trial, were found two skeletons with their ankles manacled. The Pantheon had also evidently been a most elegant structure, it having been used as a residence for the Augustales, as well as for religious purposes.

The ruins of the House of Venus and Mars are distinguished for a famous well of pure water, said to possess great mineral qualities, one hundred and twenty feet deep, not at all affected by the changes it has undergone.

TEMPLE OF ISIS.

That which attracted our attention most was the famous Temple of Isis. The court presents all the arrangements for that worship. In one end is the sacred well of lustral purification, to which there was a descent by steps. Near it is the altar, on which were found the burnt bones of human victims who had just been sacrificed. In a niche in the wall was a figure of Harpocrates, with his fingers on his lips to enjoin silence upon the worshipers in regard to the mysteries they might witness. In another part was a figure of Isis, in purple drapery, partly gilt, holding a bronze sistrum and a key. In one of the rooms a skeleton was found holding a sacrificial axe, with which he had cut through two walls in the vain attempt to escape from destruction, but perished before he could penetrate the third. The subterranean passage and secret stairs by which the priest could obtain access to the interior of the altar and deliver the oracles as if they proceeded from the statue of Isis herself, we examined with great interest.

RUINS OF THE BARRACKS.

The barracks near the gate were undoubtedly the great headquarters of the Pompeian troops. In the guard-room were found four skeletons with their legs fastened in iron stocks; in the sleeping-apartments, numerous helmets of bronze and iron, with bolts, lances, swords, leather belts, etc. In the rooms of the officers above were found helmets of various kinds, some of the most exquisite workmanship, with swords, and various articles of female dress and ornament of the richest kind, proving that the families of the officers lived in the barracks with them. Among the personal ornaments found were two necklaces of massive gold, one of which was set with twelve emeralds, several gold rings, ear-rings, and bracelets containing precious stones, gilt pins for the hair, and chests of fine linen and cloths of gold. One of these upper rooms contained eighteen skeletons of men, women, and children. The total number of skeletons found in the barracks was sixty-three, a remarkable proof of the discipline of the Roman soldier, who knew that it was his duty to die at his post, and whose death in this instance was shared by those who were dearer to him than life itself.

RELICS FROM THE RUINS.

But we have not time to carry the reader further through these interesting ruins, which abound everywhere in evidences of the highest interest in architecture, arts, sculpture, and painting, thousands of the first specimens of which are to be found in the Museo Borbonico, in Naples, contained in about one hundred rooms, which occupied a whole day in giving to them only a cursory examination. The marble and bronze statuary exhibits a very high state of art, whilst statues of the heathen goddesses are remarkable for their historical interest. This museum has always been regarded as the most interesting in the world, as remarked by an English writer in a work on the subject, for here we find the furniture, the ornaments, the gods, the statues, the busts, the utensils, the paintings, of a great people, whose city was overthrown and buried under thick ashes almost two thousand years ago; their books, their musical instruments, even their bread and their baked fruits, in their pristine form, only blackened by the action of fire, are to be seen. In contemplating these, we retrace with a sort of fascination all their habits and customs, looking with double interest on such as assimilate with those of our own day, thus in idea connecting ourselves with them; and we dwell upon the varied objects presented to our view, all of which are curious and many beautiful, with sensations so lively, so real, that we feel as if the people all lived, still were among us.

ASCENT OF VESUVIUS—VIEW OF THE MOUNTAIN BY NIGHT.

NAPLES, July, 1873.

Having finished our examination of Pompeii about four o'clock, we passed out of the Herculaneum Gate, and were met by one of the Vesuvius guides, who proposed that we should make the ascent of the mountain, which we finally concluded to undertake, although considerably fatigued by the excursions of the day. We will therefore, whilst the awful grandeur of the scene and the incidents of our excursion are fresh on the mind, endeavor to give some idea of this really indescribable and most interesting event of our wanderings in foreign lands.

ASCENT OF VESUVIUS.

We think it may be safely asserted that no one who has not ascended Mount Vesuvius can have the faintest idea of this wondrous mountain. Looking at it from Naples, reading all the numerous works and descriptions that have been published, viewing it in engravings and paintings, or even standing near its base and scanning its mighty proportions, impress the mind with but a comparatively insignificant estimation of the reality.

Thus it was that, standing at the gates of Pompeii, we readily assented to the proposition of a guide to make the ascent, and, having bargained with him for horses and his services, we were soon in the saddle and prepared to start. A mountaineer accompanied each of the six horses, holding on to their tails with one hand and goading them on with heavy sticks which they carried in the other. We had only engaged the services of one guide, and were rather surprised to find seven men with us, but concluded that they were accompanying us to attend to the horses.

We moved along at a brisk gallop through the vineyards and villages on the side of the mountain for fully an hour, the air redolent with orange-blossoms. Throngs of Italian villagers flocked out to see us pass, attracted by the yelling and screaming of the guides, with which they accompanied every stroke of their sticks on the backs of the horses. The ascent is now seldom made from the Pompeii side, which is the opposite to that which faces Naples, and our appearance among these quiet villagers at this late hour in the evening appeared to be quite an event. We, however, desired to see the mountain at night, and, having only a faint conception of the reality of the undertaking, determined to push on to its accomplishment, though at the end of the first hour's ride we felt some forebodings of a rather unpleasant adventure.

After riding an hour and a half, the distance being not less than eight miles, and the roads rather circuitous, we passed beyond the bounds of cultivation, and emerged on the barren desert of black ashes and lava that intervenes between the cone and the habitations of the villagers. The speed of the horses was now checked to a rapid walk by the deepness of the ashes, which was like walking in snow a foot deep, but the men still goaded the beasts on and on up the base of the cone. The roughness of the road, and the irregular gait of the horses, added to the fatigues of the early part of the day, had rendered those of us who were unaccustomed to this species of locomotion in bad condition for the labors yet to be performed.

VIEW FROM THE BASE OF THE CONE.

When leaving Pompeii, with Vesuvius looming up immediately before us, we had no conception of the distance we really were from its summit. It seemed at the farthest not more than three miles, but after nearly two hours' hard riding we had only reached the base of the cone. True, the road we came was not direct, but it was evident that we had traveled fully five miles in a direct line, and were far from the accomplishment of our purpose. On looking upward, after dismounting from our horses, we were fully impressed with the magnitude of the undertaking, whilst a look in the direction over which we had traveled showed the immense altitude we had already attained. The sun was just setting, and the scene was most magnificent. On the right was spread out before us the beautiful bay of Naples, with the bleak mountains of the island of Capri looming up from its bosom, and the villages of Castellamare, Torre dell' Annunziata, and Sorrento, lining its eastern shores. Directly in front of us were the ruins of Pompeii, and the villages and vineyards through which we had passed like so many John Gilpins an hour before. To our left were the towns of Ottajano, Palma, and Somma, with a host of intervening villages, on all of which the setting sun was shedding its brightest rays, imparting a brilliant and glowing aspect to the whole landscape. On the extreme right we gained a slight view of Naples, but it was dimmed by an immense thunder-cloud, which was then pouring out torrents of rain, whilst all was bright and beautiful in other quarters of the heavens. Immediately at our feet, and still throwing out strong fumes of sulphur and covering the ashes all around us with particles of brimstone, was the long-extinct crater that destroyed Pompeii and Herculaneum eighteen hundred years ago. It has been filled up long since with lava from the great craters above, but still has a vent for its hidden fires through this immense mass of ashes and scoria. Whilst viewing the scene before us, it was necessary to breathe through our handkerchiefs to escape the stifling atmosphere by which we were surrounded.

ASCENT OF THE CONE.

Having arrived at the foot of the cone, the immense ascent yet to overcome, at least one mile up a steep bank of black ashes, resembling coarse sand, seemed a feat that we were scarcely competent to accomplish. It now became apparent why six men had accompanied us, holding on to the tails of our horses. They now each drew forth ropes with nooses at the ends, and proposed to draw us up to the top of the crater for twelve carlini each. We refused their proposition on account of its enormity, and started off, declaring our ability to do without their aid, when they commenced to lessen their demand, and we finally, when almost worn down, accepted their proposition at five carlini each (about forty cents). Fifty minutes of hard climbing, considerably assisted by the ropes of our guides, and by taking several rests on lumps of lava encountered by the way, enabled us to reach the summit of the mountain, so fatigued that some minutes' rest, occupied in viewing the magnificence of the scene spread before us at every point of the compass, was necessary before approaching the crater. The mass of lava on which we were sitting, although only slightly warm to the touch, we found, by the insertion of a stick in a fissure at our feet, to be resting on a bed of molten fire. As soon as the stick was inserted to the depth of not over ten inches, a bright flame followed it up, the same as if it had been inserted in a coal-fire. We lit our cigars thus from the fire of the mountain, and then proceeded several hundred yards over a level but rugged plain of lava full of deep cracks and chasms glowing with fire, towards the smaller of the two craters on its summit.

THE CRATERS.

We almost despair of being able to convey to the reader any adequate idea of the scene which now engaged our attention. We walked on amid fumes of sulphur and heated air, for about fifty paces, when we reached the edge of the crater, from the far side of which a heavy volume of smoke was arising. On the side towards us we could look down about one hundred and fifty feet, beyond which the view was dimmed by the smoke. It was like looking down a deep precipice, the wall of that side of the crater being as smooth and horizontal as if built of stone. After viewing the scene for a few minutes we hurled down some large pieces of lava, which we could hear striking in their descent several seconds after they had disappeared from the line of vision. Immediately after a dense volume of smoke would arise, filling the whole crater, evidently caused by the contact of these pieces of rock with the molten lava at its extreme depth. This crater is about a half-mile in circumference, though its extent is not discernible from either side, on account of the volume of smoke constantly pouring out of it.

About one hundred yards to the right we reached the largest crater, which, at its last measurement, was ascertained to be two miles in circumference, though the mountain is undergoing such changes from the effect of the volcanic action below, sometimes upheaving its summit, and at other times enlarging or diminishing the area of the craters, that the precise measurement is not known at the present time.

Owing to the dense clouds of smoke rising, we could not obtain a full view of the awful depth, from which flashes of fire, visible through the vapor, became more and more distinct as the sun receded and darkness set in. We threw a large piece of lava into this crater also, which was instantly succeeded by a dense volume of black smoke, heavily charged with ashes, rising immediately in our faces, and involving us for a moment in almost utter darkness, compelling us to make a hasty retreat, the smoke following us with a rapidity that convinced us we were tampering with too mighty an engine of destruction to be trifled with.

A NIGHT SCENE.

Night having now fully set in, the awful grandeur of the scene was momentarily increased. Through the fissures in the beds of lava under our feet the molten fire was everywhere visible, whilst the gleams of light from the raging element at the bottom of the craters were reflected on the vapors rising above, having the appearance of emitting smoke and flame. Occasionally there were flashes resembling lightning, occasioned by the ignition of the gases constantly arising from its extreme depth. The elevation at which we were standing is four thousand feet above the level of the ocean, and with the moon brightly shining, and the surroundings that we have attempted to describe, some faint idea of the reality may possibly be formed by those who may read this description.

LAVA AND ASHES.

The streams of lava and stones and ashes that have in years past been vomited forth from this mountain have caused the ocean to recede fully a mile from its ancient shore-line as defined in the days of Pompeii, whilst on the inland side there is no doubt that the whole surface of the earth is now thirty to fifty feet above the level of the streets of that unfortunate city, all being one mass of lava and cinders. The eruption of 1871 threw out a stream of lava half a mile in breadth and eighteen to thirty feet deep, which in eight days reached a distance of nine miles from the point of issue. It swept through the richest vineyards, destroyed hundreds of acres of cultivated lands, and injured or destroyed about eight hundred houses. During a similar eruption in 1834, several persons were killed whilst venturing on the mountain, among whom was Charles Carroll Bayard, a midshipman from on board the United States frigate Independence, whose monument we saw in the Protestant burying-ground. Some idea may also be had of the amount of ashes thrown out by these eruptions by viewing the ruins of Pompeii, which city was so thoroughly buried by ashes alone that its site was unknown for seventeen hundred years. During the eruption of 1707, the crater ejected over Naples, across the broad bay intervening, a shower of ashes of such density that the rays of the sun were intercepted and the city was involved in darkness like that of midnight. It was impossible to recognize either persons or objects in the streets, and those who ventured abroad without torches were obliged to return home. Every part of the city resounded with the shrieks of women and children. The magistrates and clergy carried the relics of St. Januarius in procession to Porta Capuana, and all the churches were crowded with people who desired to spend a night of so much terror in devotion and supplication. The city and suburbs were covered with ashes to the depth of nearly three feet. It would probably be no exaggeration to say that one slight eruption of a few days' duration would furnish material sufficient to fill up the basin at Baltimore, from Light Street to Fort McHenry, according to the plan of Dr. Buckler, without the use of pick or spade.

THE DESCENT.

It being now past eight o'clock, we concluded that it was time to commence our descent. Most fortunately, the moon was shining brightly. We approached the edge of the cone, each of us having hold of the arm of one of the guides, and commenced to move slowly down the steep declivity. We had made but a few steps before the steepness forced us to move with more rapidity, and we flew down through the deep black ashes, planting our heels in it, and sliding along with a rapidity that astonished us. The whole descent to where our horses were stationed was not less than a mile, which was accomplished in less than five minutes, where we arrived in a fume of perspiration and breathless from exertion. We have often laughed at the humorous lithographs in the windows representing the way this descent is accomplished, and thought they were exaggerations, but we are now prepared to vouch for the truthfulness and accuracy of the representation. When females are of the party the scene must be still more ludicrous, as they are sometimes carried up by the guides, but must always make their own descent. Crinoline must be a troublesome article in such an adventure.

Our horses had remained where we left them on the bleak desert, each tied by a rope to a lump of lava, and after a few moments' rest we were again in our saddles, and a rapid drive through villages, vineyards, and cottages brought us in an hour and a half to the town of Torre dell' Annunziata, where we had directed our carriage to proceed and wait for us. Here we settled with our guides, and, as usual with all Italians we have yet encountered, although paying them twenty-five per cent. more than the price agreed upon, all were dissatisfied, and grumbled, begged, and growled until we jumped into our carriage and left them jabbering away in Italian, pretending to be in a state of tremendous excitement. A drive of an hour and a half brought us to our hotel in Naples, sore and weary, but highly delighted with our trip. We were soon wrapped too soundly in slumber to dream either of craters or chasms.

We omitted to mention that on our way down the mountain we stopped at one of the villages and procured several bottles of wine, which, in our exhausted condition, seemed to be the most delicious beverage that mortal ever partook of. As we drove off, a general quarrel broke out between several of our guides and the villagers, the former demanding part of the proceeds of the sale for bringing the fish to their net. Such a clatter of tongues, male and female, could scarcely be heard anywhere else than in Italy.

VESUVIUS IN ERUPTION.

Our first visit to Vesuvius was in the year 1859, when it was in partial eruption, with rather a steady stream of lava flowing from the side of the mountain at the base of the cone. As it was a most interesting spectacle, we here insert the account then given, in a letter to the *American*, of

THE FLOWING LAVA.

On a Saturday afternoon, being desirous of closely viewing the stream of lava which we had watched for several nights from our hotel-window as it flowed down the side of the mountain, looking like a torrent of fire; we joined a party who were about making the ascent from the Naples side. We intended to stop at the Hermitage, but on reaching that point concluded to keep on to the crater, and view the lava after night had set in, on our return.

We took horses at Resina, situated at the base of the mountain, at a quarter before three o'clock, and after a steady ride of three hours and a half over the fields of lava of former years, each of which was pointed out by our guide as we passed them, reached the base of the cone at a quarter-past six o'clock, when we commenced the ascent on foot. The ascent of the cone is at an angle of about fifty degrees, and its base is about seven miles in circumference. The time required to ascend, including two stoppages to rest of three or four minutes each, was fifty minutes, the ascent from the level where we left our horses being nearly one mile. It thus required nearly five hours to make the ascent on the Naples side, as we were compelled, on account of the lava having crossed the new carriage-road, to take the old horse-track, about two miles of which winds through a deep gorge in the old lava just wide enough to afford a footing for our horses in single file.

SCENE ON THE SUMMIT.

On reaching the summit our guide was in ecstasies, on account of the aspect of the craters, and assured us that we were most fortunate to have ascended at such a time. We, however, felt anything but gratified, and commenced to beat a hasty retreat, anticipating a general eruption. Large masses of rock were crumbling and falling into the crater from its sides, causing a noise like heavy thunder, and as each mass fell clouds of black smoke would arise, almost shutting out the light of day, mingled with gases and vapors, flying up a thousand feet over our heads, with a hissing noise like the escape of steam from a boiler. The situation was terrific, but our guide assured us there was no danger, and finally persuaded us to approach through the clouds of sulphurous smoke and look down into the awful chasm that yawned at our feet, from which came terrific reports of subterranean thunder, which was declared by an English traveler who accompanied us to remind him of the Rev. Mr. Spurgeon's vivid description of the "gates of hell." The rocks were still crumbling and falling, and flashes of flame filled the whole area of the crater, at times rendering the scene most emphatically diabolical. The commotion at the bottom of the crater evidently had a decided effect on the whole top of the cone, which is nearly level, and about five miles in circumference, though when viewed from Naples it has the appearance of terminating in a point. It caused the sulphurous fumes to pour forth with increased volume from the cracks and crevices in the broken lava on which we were walking, looking into which, scarcely a foot under our feet, we could see the molten fire which sent up a brisk flame whenever we inserted the ends of our walking-staffs.

We remained on the top of the mountain, roasting eggs in the crevices of the hardened lava, and partaking of wine and refreshments, until eight o'clock, when, night having fully set in, we commenced our descent. It was an amusing scene to see some twenty or thirty persons slipping, sliding, and sometimes losing their foothold, rolling in the deep ashes that form the sides of the cone, all going down with a rapidity which accomplished in five minutes a distance that had taken us nearly an hour to ascend. At the foot of the cone our horses were waiting, and an hour's ride down through the dark heaps of lava, twisted and piled up in every conceivable shape, made to appear more desolate and dreary in the gloom of night, over which a horse unaccustomed to the track would have broken his own neck as well as that of his rider, brought us to the "Hermitage," where we dismounted to view the running lava breaking out from the side of the mountain a few hundred yards above this resting-place.

A STARTLING ADVENTURE.

Our horses were taken around about two miles below to meet us, and we started on foot over the fields of newly-formed lava, the surface of which had cooled, but through the cracks and chasms under our feet the stream of molten lava from the mountain could be distinctly seen moving slowly down, whilst at some points it passed up over the surface in a stream about a yard wide and thirty feet in length, and then disappeared again under the hard incrustation that had formed beyond. We stopped at one of these openings, and our guide, with the end of his staff, drew out some particles of the molten lava and pressed copper coins into it, which we preserved as mementos of our visit. A silver coin insorted in the lava immediately melted, so great was its heat.

Having had only a distant view of this flowing lava, we thought that it was only some fifteen feet thick, and the surface only a few hundred feet wide. Our surprise can, therefore, be imagined when we found the stream from a half to three-quarters of a mile in width, and two miles in length, and its thickness varying from thirty to two hundred feet, according to the inequalities of the surface. It had filled up and leveled mountain-gorges half a mile in width and from one hundred to two hundred feet in depth, and was gradually advancing in this great bulk about thirty feet every twenty-four hours.

A FIERY EXPERIENCE.

We followed our guide about two miles over the surface of this field of lava, whilst under our feet the molten stream was flowing downward, amid a heated atmosphere in which it was difficult to exist, though there was an absence of the sulphurous smell that had almost stifled us at the crater. As we approached the terminus of the stream the heat became gradually more intense, so much so that we protested against proceeding any farther, and some of our party actually started back in horror at the scene before us. So great was the heat that our shoes and clothing were almost ready to ignite, whilst the temperature of the atmosphere was momentarily increasing in intensity, so that it became difficult to breathe. We were surrounded on every side by openings in the hardened and rugged lava, through which the stream of molten fire was passing down to the terminus of the stream with increased velocity. We rated the guide soundly for leading us into such a dangerous and fearful locality, whilst he persisted that there was nothing to fear, and that it was the only route that he could take, urging us to follow him through it as rapidly as possible, and we would be off the lava in a few minutes. Not wishing to retrace our steps over such difficulties as our curiosity had already brought us into, we mustered up courage to follow, the heat being too intense for debate. On we went in Indian file, following our guide over the rough and heated surface, at times with a stream of fire on each side of us, jumping from one rough and darkened surface to another, and avoiding as best we could the chasms of fire that opened on every side. The end of the stream was really like a precipice of fire, fully thirty feet high, the fiery streams of molten lava oozing through from all parts of its hardened surface. Down this precipice we were compelled to descend, stepping carefully to avoid touching the red-hot lava oozing out of every crevice on the surface. In a few minutes we had the gratification of once more standing on the solid rock of the mountain-side, whilst the head of the stream was immediately before us, moving steadily on into a deep mountain-gorge, in which a flourishing vineyard was gradually being swallowed up and buried a hundred feet under the advancing wall of fire.

As we stood here and looked back over the path by which we had descended, we more fully appreciated the dangers we had encountered. We could distinctly perceive the moving mass of undercurrent through the crevices, and I am sure that not one of us would have retraced his steps for any amount of money.

At the terminus of the lava-stream we found our horses waiting for us, they having been taken around from the Hermitage; and, after a few moments spent in taking another look at the grand and impressive scene, we remounted and proceeded to Resina, which we reached at eleven o'clock, after an hour's ride, having consumed more than eight hours in our excursion on the mountain. Here our carriage was waiting for us, and an hour's ride brought us to our hotel in Naples, in good condition for a sound night's sleep, though some of us were disturbed by dreams of no very pleasing character.

CHARACTER OF THE LAVA-FLOW.

In order that the reader may better understand the characteristics of this flow of lava, it may be proper to state that when the mouths of the large crater are so narrowed by accumulated matter as to be unequal to the discharge of the lava collected in their central channels, lateral openings are formed, which, being nearer the source of heat, discharge the lava in a state of much greater liquidity than from the great craters. These lava-currents have heretofore ceased to flow in twenty or thirty days, but the present one has flowed slowly but steadily for nearly a year. The cohesion of a lava-current, which exceeds that of any other substance known, causes it to move slowly in the form of a tall ridge until it enters a mountain-gorge, which it fills up and passes on, occasionally diverging to the right or left, and spreading over immense surfaces, but not exceeding twenty to thirty feet in thickness when it passes over a level or descending plain. The surface gradually loses its fluid state as it becomes cooled by the external air, cracks into innumerable heavy fragments, and this scoria, being a bad conductor of heat, enables the central portion of the mass to retain its fluid state, whilst at the same time it renders it possible to cross the current as it flows. Thus it was that we were enabled to perform this excursion over the flowing lava. It is a trip, however, that we would not fancy taking a second time.

CASTLE OF ST. ELMO.

We took a drive this evening to visit the Castle of St. Elmo, and the Carthusian monastery connected with it, which loom up almost from the heart of the city. They are erected on the top of a mountain which rises almost abruptly amidst the surrounding houses to the height of nearly one thousand feet. The view from the balcony of San Martino is of surpassing beauty, and is regarded as unrivaled, on account of the combination of natural attractions and historical associations. The eye embraces in one view the whole city of Naples, with the head of the bay, and Mounts Vesuvius and Somma in the distance. On the right it follows the curve of the Bay of Naples to the Bays of Baiæ and Miseno, with Nisita, Pozzuoli, and the distant islands; on the left it sweeps along the shore of Portici, Resina, Torre del Greco, and Torre dell' Annunziata at the base of Vesuvius. In another direction we see Capodimonte and the rich plains of the Neapolitan Campagna, whilst in the distance may be recognized Monte Triafale, backed by the chain of the Apennines, along which, as they advance towards the sea, may be distinguished the mountains of Gragnano, Vico, Sorrento, and Massa. The monastery was the place of refuge of the Pope during his exile from Rome in the year 1849. The Castle of St. Elmo stands immediately in front of it, from which, down under the city, a subterranean passage leads to the palace. On the top of the ridge, not far from the monastery, is the tomb of Virgil.

THE EXAGGERATIONS OF ITALY.

The observant traveler cannot fail to come to the conclusion that there is no country in the world which has reaped so much benefit from systematic exaggeration as Italy. Its "magnificent skies," its "beautiful women," its "glorious climate," and its "indescribable landscapes" are nearly all to a considerable extent fictions of the imagination. English men, who are accustomed to look at the sky through a fog or a haze of smoke, write home of the wondrous beauty of an Italian sky; and artists, whose business it is to exaggerate and embellish, labor to invest this region of fine marble and ancient models of art with all the romance possible. But of all the descriptions with regard to Italy, that is most erroneous which claims beauty of form or feature, grace or dignity of carriage, or any one of those characteristics which the rest of the world consider as essential to female beauty, for its women. The number of decidedly homely women in Italy is in reality unparalleled. Its old women are shriveled up like Macbeth's witches; the middle-aged women are wrinkled and shapeless; and the young women have lost all traces of girlhood at twenty. The female children are bright and handsome, but at eighteen you seldom see a youthful countenance. They have fine hair, sharp black eyes, and, when animated by mirth or conversation, expressive features; but when in repose they have an angry and forbidding aspect. Some of them would make goodlooking men if they had whiskers; but there is an entire absence of that female modesty and sweetness which in America are regarded as essential to female beauty.

In clear weather the sky is undoubtedly beautiful, but not more so than in America. The sunsets are fine, and the rays of the moon reflected from the blue waters of the Mediterranean will at times attract the attention by their brilliancy, and are wonderful in the befogged eyes of the English traveler; but seen through "American spectacles" there is nothing novel or unusual in the scene. They admire these beauties of nature here as they do at home, but all who come here expecting to find a brighter sunshine, a more brilliant sky, or a moonlight more lovely than they have been accustomed to at home, will be sure to be disappointed.

The mountain scenery is very fine, owing principally to the excessive verdure, and the cultivation and habitation of their rocky ledges, but the level portions of the country are the most dreary imaginable. The twenty-four miles between Salerno and Pœstum are as uninteresting as a journey on an American prairie. The hundred and seventy miles between Rome and Naples have a few fine spots; but the plains are desert wastes, very inattractive to the eye, and the people the most dirty and squalid in appearance that the civilized world can produce. The towns through which we passed, with but few exceptions, were noticeable only for their filth and stench, their beggars and their fleas. Nowhere in Southern Italy have we seen the neat country-houses, the clean and tidy children, or any of those evidences of rural comfort and happiness which are so usual among the agriculturists on our side of the Atlantic. Indeed, we had almost said that a woman or child with a clean face or clean clothing might be regarded as a curiosity outside of the cities of Rome and Naples, and even there they were rarities among those who labor in any way for a livelihood. Cleanliness, in brief, is not here regarded as akin to godliness, as those who are habitually the most dirty seem to be the most strictly observant of religious duties, crowds of whom are to be found kneeling in the churches at all hours of the day.

There is but little strong liquor drunk in Italy, and we have not seen a drunken man, or the drinking of anything stronger than wine. There are wine-shops in abundance, but no regular taverns with bars. The respectable portion of the population assemble in the coffee-houses, and smoke and drink wine and coffee in the evening, but are all very abstemious. The lower classes have also places of similar resort, where they eat macaroni and boiled snails, and drink poor wine; but necessity compels moderation even in this light refreshment.

Among the articles we saw for sale at one of the markets yesterday morning was a two-bushel-basket full of stumps of cigars, which are bought by the poorer classes for smoking-tobacco. Boys are engaged hunting around the streets night and day for these " old soldiers," and at night they carry lamps with them to assist their vision.

LIQUEFACTION OF THE BLOOD OF SAN GENNARO.

The present lack of religious demonstrations in Naples is in striking contrast with the constant street ceremonials which were in progress during our visit some twelve years ago, when we witnessed the following scene, as described in a letter to the *Baltimore American* at the time.

Learning that the semi-annual miracle of the liquefaction of the blood of San Gennaro was to take place on Saturday, being the last day of the octave of the demonstration, we repaired at an early hour in the morning to the Church of Santa Restituta. The crowd was so great that it was with difficulty we could gain an entrance. This ceremony of liquefaction is the greatest religious festival in the kingdom, and such is the importance attached to it by the ardent Neapolitans that all the conquerors of the city have considered it a necessary piece of state policy to respect it.

Before proceeding to give an account of the ceremony, we will explain what is meant by the liquefaction. In the right aisle of the Church of Santa Restituta is the Chapel of San Gennaro, in which are preserved two phials said to contain the blood of the saint. The ceremony of liquefaction takes place twice in a year, and is each time repeated for eight successive days. The tradition of the church represents that when St. Gennaro, or Januarius, as the name is sometimes given, was exposed to be devoured by lions in the amphitheatre of Pozzuoli, the animals prostrated themselves before him and became tame. This miracle is said to have converted so many to Christianity that Dracontius ordered the saint to be decapitated, which sentence was executed at Solfatara in the year 305. The body was buried at Pozzuoli until the time of Constantine, when it was removed to Naples and deposited in the Church of San Gennaro. At the time of this removal a woman who is said to have collected the blood with a sponge at the period of the martyrdom, took it in two bottles to St. Severus, the bishop, in whose hands it is said to have immediately melted. The iron tabernacle which contains the phials is secured by two bolts, one key being kept by the municipal authorities, and the other by the archbishop, and is only opened in the presence of the people.

The ceremony of the liquefaction commenced on Saturday in the Church of Santa Chiara, from whence after mass an immense procession, with bands of music, bishops, priests, and soldiers, bearing crucifixes, banners, and candles, proceeded with the phials of blood to the cathedral. This procession was three-quarters of a mile long. In the line were soldiers bearing large silver statues of saints, and the whole scene was one of the most imposing spectacles we ever witnessed.

At the cathedral, some time before the ceremonies commenced, a number of old women of the lower orders, who claim

14

to be the descendants of Saint Januarius, collected around the balustrade of the altar, exhibiting the most wild and uncontrollable excitement. Some of these women were very old, with countenances shriveled and wrinkled beyond anything in the form of humanity. Immediately after the first mass was finished they commenced a fearful howl, repeating to the full extent of their lungs, in a hoarse and croaking voice, Paternosters, Aves, and Credos. When the saint delays the liquefaction too long, they even claim the right and often do heap imprecations with all the fervency that usually accompanies their prayers.

The relics were exposed in one of the side-chapels, called the Chapel of St. Gennaro, which was magnificently decorated, the altar being brilliant with gold ornaments, diamonds, and precious stones. The face of the altar is of massive silver, ornamented with statues in bas-relief, representing the history of Cardinal Caraffa's bringing back the head of the saint to Naples. All the dukes and princes were present in the robes of royalty; and soldiers, with muskets and bayonets, were scattered throughout the immense edifice, their plumes waving over the heads of the people in every direction. The saint's head, with a rich mitre upon it, fixed on the statue of the saint, having an archbishop's mantle about the shoulders, and a rich collar of diamonds, and cross around the neck, was the first sight that attracted our attention. The bottles containing the blood, one of which appeared like pitch, clotted and hard in the glass, were then shown to the people, and turned upside down to prove that the blood in them was hard and solid. They were then placed at the side of the altar. One appeared like a smelling-bottle, and only had a mere stain of blood, whilst the other was larger, and seemed to hold enough to fill a wineglass. They were shown to the persons admitted within the balustrade, among whom were a considerable number of English Protestants. After being placed on the altar a glass case was put over them, through which they could be seen by all present.

A series of masses was then commenced, at the conclusion of each of which the old women renewed their fearful and unearthly howling, whilst the drums and trumpets joined in the discordant blast, until it was difficult to imagine such a horrible clamor to be intended for Christian worship. These women seemed almost frantic with religious fervor, as also did the priests and a large portion of the people present, cries, screams, and sobbing pervading every part of the edifice. These masses were continued from nine o'clock in the morning until five o'clock in the afternoon, without cessation, except for another procession in the afternoon, during which thirty-five large solid silver statues of saints and martyrs were carried by the soldiers. At the conclusion of the procession the masses were again resumed with all the accompaniments of excitement and clamor that prevailed in the morning, without the desired liquefaction of the blood taking place. At five o'clock the glass was again removed from the bottles, and the blood in the larger one was found to be as limpid as water, and was shown to the people amid the greatest rejoicing, the beating of drums, the clapping of hands, and the blasts of trumpets. The old women were perfectly wild with excitement, and many of them fell down exhausted, while the roar of cannon from the Castle of Elmo announced to the people outside that the miracle was consummated.

Wherever there was any number of English or Americans in the cathedral during the ceremony, soldiers were stationed near them, with special instructions to allow no one to molest them. This rather surprised us, but on inquiry it was ascertained that on several occasions, when the liquefaction had not taken place as soon as was anticipated, the ignorant portion of the people had attacked the Protestants, under the belief that the presence of heretics had prevented the accomplishment of the miracle. If the liquefaction takes place soon, it is regarded as an evidence of happiness and prosperity to the country; and if it is retarded, as indicative of trouble and evil to be anticipated.

This *miracle* the Protestant spectators contend to be a piece of legerdemain,— that the bottles contain colored wax, to which heat is applied through the marble altar-table on which they are placed during the progress of the masses.

THE DEAD OF NAPLES.

We spent an afternoon in visiting the great cemetery of Naples, in which the rich man and the poor man both find their last resting-places. The graves of the rich are distinguished by magnificent monuments, and a large number have miniature family chapels erected over the remains of the dead, giving the cemetery at a distance the appearance of a beautiful country village. The poor, however, are buried in as heathenish a manner as was ever practiced. There are three hundred and sixty-five vaults, each about twenty feet square, for the reception of the bodies of the poor. There is a chapel connected with these vaults, to which the dead poor are brought, where they are stripped of their clothing. At sunset they are brought out of the chapel, then stripped of every vestige of clothing, men, women, and children, the average being about thirty per day. The round slab fitting in the circular opening to the vault in use for the day is taken off, and the bodies dragged by the limbs to the aperture and thrown in head-foremost. They are lowered down by the heels, and swung backward and forward until a sufficient impetus is given to the body to make it fall into the corners of the vaults, where it strikes with a dull thud. We saw thirty-three bodies thus summarily disposed of, the clothing from which was bundled up and carried off. Twelve months from this day this same vault will be opened again to receive a new deposit and more lime, and so on for every successive year, there being one vault for each day in the year. The custodian in attendance offered, for one carlino, to raise the stone from one of the vaults used the week previous, that we might look in upon the horrid and brutal spectacle,—a favor which we decisively declined. These vaults, it is said, when opened on the second day after the bodies have been deposited in them, exhibit swarms of rats and other vermin devouring the flesh from the bones of the dead.

THE FISHERMEN OF NAPLES.

From daybreak in the morning until eight o'clock, the Bay of Naples is literally covered with fishermen's boats, engaged in casting and drawing in their nets. We counted this morning over one hundred in front of our hotel. The fish they catch are small, and the number very limited, though the nets they put out are never less than a hundred feet in length. At eight o'clock they all disappear, but are again in their posts at sunset. They are an industrious, jolly set of men, but occasionally when the nets of one party get entangled with those of another the noise they make sounds very much like hard swearing. They are the lineal descendants of Masaniello, live on fish and macaroni, and carry themselves with the same careless ease and grace.

PÆSTUM AND ITS RUINS—ITALIAN SCENERY, ETC.

NAPLES, July, 1873.

The excursions around Naples are of the most attractive character, not only affording an opportunity to view the antiquities with which the country abounds, but to see the mode of living and the agricultural advancement of the Italian peasantry. There is no part of Italy that affords an equal opportunity to judge of the claims of Italian scenery to the high encomiums which have been heaped upon it.

EXCURSION TO AMALFI.

On Thursday morning we started on a trip to Amalfi, which it had been arranged to visit in combination with Salerno and Pæstum, the latter renowned over the world for its magnificent ruins. Taking the cars on the Naples and Salerno Railroad, we arrived at La Cava, a flourishing town of thirteen thousand souls, and, proceeding to the Hotel de Londres, engaged a carriage to carry us direct to Amalfi.

The railroad from Naples to La Cava passes mostly over a level plain along the sea-shore, abounding in towns and villages, and mountains on the left of the road, including Vesuvius, which are cultivated in grapes, oranges, and lemons up as high as man can obtain a foothold. The line of villages along this road comprises a population of over one hundred thousand souls. Most of those nearest Naples are liable at any moment to be swept into non-existence by an eruption or an earthquake; but their proximity to the sea, the capital, and the rich lands that flank Vesuvius on all sides, must always attract a large population, notwithstanding its dangerous proximity. There is no land in Italy of equal fertility to the slopes of Vesuvius, the ashes and scoria, after a few years' exposure to the atmosphere, becoming decomposed, and forming a dark, friable soil that is susceptible of the highest cultivation. The people seem to have no fears; they have been reared among the terrors of Vesuvius, and—

"Where they dwell
Their fathers dwelt and died, and shall awake;
That love which binds Helvetia's mountaineer
'Mid rocks and Alpine snows, glows in lava here."

ITALIAN SCENERY.

On leaving La Cava we proceeded at a rapid rate for about two miles, when the turning of a precipitous point brought us directly on to the shores of the Mediterranean, along which we proceeded for fifteen miles, over a turnpike road that has few equals in the world, considering the difficulties under which it has been constructed and the substantial and scientific manner in which it has been engineered. A few years back there was no access to Amalfi except by pack-mules, as was the case with all the numerous towns and villages on the coast. The only site for a turnpike was along the slopes of the mountains which project into the sea; and here it has been hewn out of the solid rock, the bed of the road running from fifty to three hundred feet above the level of the sea, according as the projections of the mountain-gorges may have rendered it necessary. Throughout its entire length it is walled up with solid masonry on the sea-side, varying from ten to fifty feet in height, and forming a wall to the road about three feet above its bed. The mountains, which rise very precipitously from the sea, vary in height from seven hundred to one thousand feet, their bases projecting at times far out into the sea, and around these projections the road winds to such an extent that, though Amalfi is not more than seven miles from Sorrento in an air-line, the road is more than fifteen miles long.

MOUNTAIN SCENERY.

The attractions of a visit to Amalfi consist mainly in the magnificence of the mountain scenery along the entire route. The mountains tower five thousand feet overhead, and, although the ascent is so steep that they appear to the eye unapproachable, their sides are dotted with white stone cottages, and the ledges almost to their extreme summits are luxuriant with orange- and lemon-groves and vineyards. Thus you have on one side the blue waves of the Mediterranean, and on the other, and sometimes down below the bed of the road, most varied and attractive scenery, beautified with great skill and labor, and really startling the stranger at every turn by its varied attractions. The villages of the fishermen, some of them with several hundred inhabitants, dot every gorge in the mountain, every spot of land being brought into the richest cultivation around them.

THE CITY OF AMALFI.

Amalfi, encircled and crowned by mountains, is at the mouth of a deep gorge, from which a torrent dashes into the ocean, driving numerous paper-mills, factories, etc., in its precipitous course through the town. Its churches, towers, and arcaded houses, grouped together in picturesque irregularity, are backed by precipices one thousand feet in height, of wild magnificence, justifying probably the assertion "that in no other nook of the earth's surface can the eye of man look upon a scene of more glorious natural beauties." On the extreme top of these precipices are located monasteries and churches, whilst the slopes of the contiguous mountains are terraced and cultivated as lemon-groves, the terraces being walled up in regular succession to an immense height. Every promontory on the road to Amalfi is made picturesque by the ruins of a martello tower, at intervals of a quarter to a third of a mile apart; every cove and beach is occupied by the boats and nets of fishermen, every ledge is covered with houses and vineyards, and every broader crag with a town. The town of Pasitano, perched on a pinnacle of rock, seven hundred feet above the ocean, is one of the most striking objects of the trip. After partaking of an excellent dinner, we returned in the cool of the evening to Sorrento, gladly availing ourselves of a second opportunity to view this most singular and picturesque region of country.

The people along the route seemed to be the most happy and prosperous that we have yet met with in Italy. There were but few soldiers to be seen, who are in such abundance everywhere else—very few beggars, and an absence of the disposition to defraud and extort in their dealings with strangers that is a distinguishing trait in other parts of Italy. The females looked healthy, and are handsomer than the peasantry we have met with elsewhere, presenting, with their skirts barely reaching their knees, with neither stockings nor shoes, and loose bodices, a very novel appearance, especially to the eyes of some of our bachelor companions.

THE RUINS OF PÆSTUM.

Returning from Amalfi, we stopped for the night in the city of Salerno, a prosperous town on the Mediterranean, at the mouth of the Bay of Naples, with a population of thirty thousand souls. We spent a pleasant evening and night, and at seven o'clock on Friday morning started in a carriage for Pœstum, the distance being twenty-four miles, which was accomplished in less than three hours, so excellent are the roads and so rapid the driving in all parts of Italy. The road, however, passes for the greater part of the way through a barren and unhealthy country. Of all the excursions from Naples, there is none presenting such historical interest as a visit to the ruins of Pæstum, which are well-preserved monuments of antiquity, exceeding in interest any to be found in Italy. Indeed, a journey to Southern Italy is not considered complete unless Pæstum has been visited.

The ruins of Pæstum date back to four hundred years before Christ. The walls of the city, part of which are still standing, are nearly three miles in circumference, and in many places twelve feet high. The arch of the eastern gateway, nearly fifty feet high, stands entire.

THE TEMPLES OF PÆSTUM.

The three magnificent temples stand as a record of the taste and architectural skill of the Grecians. The Temple of Neptune, the middle one of the three, one hundred and ninety-five feet long and seventy-eight feet broad, with its massive columns and entablature, stands now as firmly on its foundations as when first erected, nearly two thousand three hundred years ago, and appears as if it would stand for many ages yet, notwithstanding the rocking of earthquakes to which it has so often been subjected. Solidity, combined with simplicity and grace, distinguishes it from the other buildings. Not a single column is wanting, and the entablature and pediments are nearly entire.

The Basilica, the second of these ancient temples, has fifty columns, nine in the fronts, and sixteen in the flanks, exclusive of the angles. The interior is divided into two parts by a range of columns parallel to the sides, of which only three remain. This division leads to the supposition that it was a temple probably dedicated to two divinities. Its length is one hundred and seventy-nine feet, its breadth eighty feet, height of columns twenty-one feet.

The Temple of Vesta is the smallest, and is nearest to the Salerno Gate. It has thirty-four columns, of which six are in the front, and nine in each flank, exclusive of the angles. It is one hundred and seven feet in length, and forty-seven in breadth.

"On entering the ruins of Pæstum," says an English writer, "I felt all the religion of the place; I stood on the sacred ground; I stood amazed at the long obscurity of its mighty ruins. Taking in view their immemorial antiquity, their astonishing preservation, their grandeur, their bold columnar elevation, at once massive and open, their severe simplicity of design,—taking, I say, all this into view, I do not hesitate to pronounce them the most impressive monuments that I ever beheld on earth."

As you approach them from Salerno, passing over a wide expanse of level and dreary country, their huge dusky proportions can be seen two miles distant. Standing alone amidst their mountain wilderness, without a vestige nigh of any power that could have reared them, they look absolutely supernatural. Their grandeur, their gloom, their majesty—there is nothing like them to be seen on this wide earth.

We had prepared to partake of the lunch we had brought with us in the Temple of Neptune, but it commenced raining, and compelled us to retreat to the carriage. At three o'clock we started for La Cava, and arrived there at five o'clock in time to take the cars for Naples, thus, in an excursion of two days, visiting both Amalfi and Pæstum.

NAPLES, July, 1873.
STREET-SCENES IN NAPLES.

The Strada de Toledo is the principal street of Naples, and presents a medley of strange sights, which surprise all who pass for the first time through its tumultuous confusion. Here is to be seen a miscellaneous throng of people whose life is spent in the open air and chiefly upon the streets. The scribe is seen busily inditing letters at a table on the street-corners for the many persons who can neither read nor write; by his side is a lemonade pagoda, and half the thoroughfare is occupied by the chestnut-roaster and the sausage-vendor, with their pans and dishes, frying their commodities over charcoal fires,—all combining to present a scene that has no equal elsewhere. The crowd on the Toledo is moving hither and thither without order or regularity, rolling up and down with its eddies and whirlpools, so that the stranger is lost in its confusion. In the midst of this vast concourse of horses, donkeys, and all grades of humanity, you are jostled against a money-changer's table, and tumbled over the bench of a shoemaker at work on the curb-stone, find yourself mixed up among the pots of a macaroni-stall, and escape behind the stench-emitting basket of a lazzarone. The street-noises are unparalleled. The people are shouting at the top of their voices, the innumerable donkeys are braying and screeching, the drivers are cracking their whips and scolding each other, and confusion is worse confounded by the occasional movement of soldiers and horsemen through the thronged thoroughfare, or the approach of a Church procession, when every one within seeing or hearing distance is expected to kneel down in the street.

Fortunately, carriage-riding in Naples is very cheap, provided you know how to manage the drivers. They are like this fraternity elsewhere, apt to take advantage of strangers. An Italian will ride from any one portion of the city to another for two carlini, about sixteen cents, and pays no more if there are two or three in company than he would for one. His whole family, to the number of six, in a double carriage, will be conveyed five miles for three carlini. It is therefore cheaper to ride than to walk, and a drive through the Toledo at the slow pace that a crowded thoroughfare renders necessary is rather interesting and amusing. Notwithstanding all this medley of sights and sounds, the Toledo is a great street. The topography of the city is such that it is necessary to drive through its whole length in order to reach any other section of the city, and it must of course be necessarily thronged. Tunnels and openings and graded pavements have been made through the mountain-spurs that thus divide the city, which now greatly relieve it.

Another of the great features of Naples is its donkeys. They may be numbered by tens of thousands. Every family seems to have its donkey, using him as a kind of errand-boy, in carrying home marketing, bundles, packages, coal, and supplies of water, all of which for drinking-purposes has to be either bought or brought from one of the distant fountains. The strength and power of endurance of the useful animals are wonderful. The majority of them are about the size of a six-months-old calf, and we have seen them carrying loads on their pack-saddles sufficient for a horse, with a full-grown man perched upon the top of the load. Tall, heavy men, with their feet within two inches of the ground, may be seen riding them with saddles, trotting briskly along, in all sections of the city, and their shrill and screeching bray may be heard at all hours.

Oranges and lemons are almost as cheap here as potatoes in Baltimore. We can get them at a carlino a dozen, being at the rate of about three for two cents, but, as double price is generally charged a stranger for everything, probably an Italian buys them at a much lower rate. They grow in the open air in all the yards of the city, on trees as large as our peach-trees, which are so loaded with fruit that it is necessary to support their branches by an arbor.

The "chain-gang" so often read of in romances and flash stories is a reality here to an extent that is really surprising. Those condemned to it wear red jackets and black skull-caps, and have a heavy chain, each link about six inches in length, extending from an iron girdle around the waist to an iron collar around the left ankle, and sometimes they are chained together in couples. They seem to be used principally as pack-horses for the military, and may be seen drawing wagons through the streets at all hours, each wagon under military guard with fixed bayonets.

THE CITY OF ROME.

ROME, July 19, 1873.

Here we are at last in the Holy City, after nine hours' travel in the cars from Naples, neither suffering from heat nor dust on the route.

The railroad-route from Naples to Rome is not by the old Appian Way, but through an entirely new section of country, with the Alps looming up to the right and the Apennines to the left. We passed the mountain-towns of Caserta, Capua, San Germano, Velletri, and Albano, the latter near Rome. All these cities are quite large, but are located either on the tops of mountains or high up their sides. The sites of all Italian towns have been chosen with an eye to their capacity for defense, and each have their fortifications, and most of them are walled cities. They are so much alike that when one is visited there is no necessity for exploring farther among their narrow courts and steep thoroughfares. The whole country through which we passed, bordering on the Pontine Marshes, was in the highest state of cultivation, the principal crops being Indian corn and the grape. Not a foot of land appeared to have escaped cultivation, showing a decided improvement since we last passed through this country. The railroad and Victor Emmanuel have done much for this section of Italy, and certainly on God's green earth there existed no section of country in which there was more room for improvement than this.

THE ITALIANS AND THE PRIESTS.

We have hitherto refrained from making any comment upon matters connected with religious affairs in Naples and along the line of the Mediterranean. It is, however, evident everywhere that the Roman Catholic clergy are no longer the rulers of Italy, and that were it not for the fear that they may possibly, by some shrewd management of the Jesuits, be able to regain their power, they would scarcely be tolerated. They are extremely humble, and scores of monks can be seen on the streets of Naples and Rome begging for pennies. The men scowl upon them, but the women sympathize with them, and aid them whenever they can. The shop-windows are filled with caricatures of the Pope and cardinals, which the people seem to enjoy very much. One labeled "Progress" has a priest on horseback with his face towards the tail, by which appendage he is endeavoring to drive the animal. Another is Victor Emmanuel and the Pope walking arm-in-arm in Rome, with words signifying that he is taking the sick man out for an airing. The Italian papers, also, in speaking of the probable early death of the Pope, and the election of his successor, contend that the new Pope shall be of the same politics as Bismark.

During our former visit to Naples, twelve years ago, Church ceremonials and processions on the street were encountered at every turn. Everybody in sight was compelled to kneel. Now there is little of the kind to be seen, and the attendance at the churches is not only very light, but consists nearly altogether of women and old men. Whilst in a store at Naples a few days since, a mendicant priest, a man young enough and strong enough to work for his living, came in to beg. He was greeted by the storekeeper as a lazy vagabond, and ordered to go about his business in a manner more vigorous than polite. To hear a Neapolitan thus address a priest startled us, but we were assured that they are no longer in favor, and are regarded as the leeches who have sucked the life-blood of the people. Their number in Naples, including monks and friars, is very great, certainly not less than ten to fifteen thousand, and it is evident that many of them could be spared without detriment to the Church. Here in Rome, with a population not one-fourth that of Naples, the number is said to exceed twenty thousand; and if the female religieuses be included, the number must be over thirty thousand,—verily a large army of non-productives for so small a city. We observe a new caricature on the walls of the city to-day, which is attracting crowds of spectators, who seem to enjoy it very much. It is a number of females swimming in a lake, and they have got among them an old priest, whom they are busily engaged in ducking, whilst one of them has a large stone raised over the head of the priest, ready to hurl it upon him. An old man, whom we do not recognize, is perched up in the branches of a tree, and has two cords under the arms of one of the leading assailants. It is probably intended for Bismark. Another old priest is being dragged into the water by some of the Amazons. What it all means we are unable to determine, but the people seemed to understand and enjoy it.

ITALIAN ANNOYANCES.

There is nothing which the traveler in Italy has more cause to dread than the vexations and continual succession of petty annoyances which he is doomed to encounter upon leaving a city or arriving at a new one. A clerical friend, the Rev. Mr. Barrett, of Jackson, Illinois, whom we met at the Naples depot, insists that it all grows out of pure cussedness, and a determination to do everything just the way in which nobody else would think of doing it. He says if they walk with a cane they persist in carrying the ferrule in their hand and the head on the ground. When you apply for a ticket you must have the exact change required, or expect none from the ticket-seller. The moment you reach the depot at least a dozen men rush at you, all in official garb, each one of whom will seize a separate article, one a shawl, one a cane, one an umbrella, and one a carpet-sack, and, if there is not enough to go around, the balance will run ahead to open the doors and make themselves as annoying as possible. When you secure your ticket, and have your baggage weighed and registered, each one of these dozen semi-officials rushes at you for a *proboi*, and if you give them a *grano* each they will want six, or if you give them one they will want two. On arriving at Rome we fought the whole gang off, carried our bundles to the omnibus, and escaped without much annoyance. They snatched our baggage several times, and we had to show fight to recover it, and they evidently thought we were regular Yankee guerillas. At Naples we paid the hotel-keeper for carrying us to the depot. On arriving there the omnibus-man demanded the fare, and said that the hotel-keeper denied having received it. We paid a second time, and in a few moments after we detected the same man endeavoring to obtain from another of the party pay again, making, if he had obtained it, three payments for carrying us to the cars.

FIRST DAY IN ROME.

We found the weather was quite warm here, and in the sun excessively hot, but still not too warm to ride about and view the painting-galleries in the palaces of Rome. We visited the Palace Doria, the Palace Borghese, and the Palace Farnese, stopping on the way to look in at that grand old heathen temple, the Pantheon. There are some few paintings in these princely galleries, but the great majority of them would not be given wall-room in such a collection as that of William T. Walters, Esq., of Baltimore. The Pantheon, from the fact of its having been built before the birth of Christ as a temple to the heathen gods, gives it a historic interest that always attracts to its halls every visitor to Rome. It is now used as a Catholic church, and the niches in the walls, built for statues of Jupiter, Mars, etc., are now occupied by those of the apostles.

We spent the afternoon in the Vatican palace, the home of the Pope, in which he persists in regarding himself as a prisoner. The paintings and statuary in these galleries are all of the highest order, and are so numerous as to require several hours even merely to stroll by them. Among the statuary the Apollo Belvedere and the Laocoön claim pre-eminence. The frescoes and paintings, principally by Raphael, Perugino, and Murillo, are considered their masterpieces. Scores of artists are always at work in these galleries, making copies of the great masters. Since the occupation of Rome by Victor Emmanuel, the Pope has charged two francs admission to the Vatican.

WATER AND WINE.

An American traveling in Italy in summer will find greater difficulty in obtaining a cool glass of water than anything else. If he drinks water at his meals he is regarded as a lunatic, and if he calls for ice-water and should succeed in obtaining it, he will find it in his bill when he comes to settle. Water is regarded as unhealthy, and is as costly in this country as wine, provided you desire to have it cool and palatable. You are expected to drink wine for breakfast, wine for dinner, and wine for supper. From one to two bottles of wine per day is regarded as essential to health, and even the beggar in the street must have his modicum of wine. They have a great reverence for fountains, and like to look at cascades, or bold jets of the crystal fluid, but when it has performed this function the Italian regards it as having served its purpose. Latterly, in Naples, the institution of bath-houses all around the bay by Victor Emmanuel has induced the Italians to regard water as valuable for purposes of ablution, and thousands of them are all the time luxuriating in their salt-baths. It is to be hoped that this will induce them to have more respect for water. His next movement for the elevation of Italy should be the introduction of soap by the encouragement of its manufacture. It is a singular fact that among the lower classes, and in the agricultural regions, the use of soap is almost unknown, and the article is regarded as a luxury only to be enjoyed by the rich. If the traveler does not carry a supply with him he will never find any in the hotels, and will often be unable to procure it at any price.

THE ENGLISH LANGUAGE.

In every Italian city a majority of the hotels now have American names, the object being to attract American travelers, under the supposition that they will find English spoken. So also with the cafés; but it is almost universally a fraud. In a café to-day we asked a waiter if he could speak English. The answer was, "we, we." We then told him to bring some sugar. He returned in a few moments with a wineglass full of toothpicks. We then asked him in French to bring us sucre, but the fellow could speak nothing but Italian, and he brought a pot of mustard. The stores all over Europe have a notice in their windows that English is spoken, and in nine cases out of ten they cannot understand you, nor can you understand them. They send for some neighbor who knows a few words of English, but you have generally to work your way through by signs and motions and the few words you may have picked up in your travels.

VISIT TO ST. PETER'S.

We devoted Sunday to a visit to St. Peter's, and spent about three hours in viewing its vast interior and magnificent decorations. It is a good place in which to spend a hot day, as you are never too warm within its walls, and a cool draught of air is always sweeping through its broad and lofty interior. Everybody has an idea that this church is immense in size, but their conceptions of its magnitude always fall short of the reality. Let those who desire to conceive its real size draw a cross and set down as the length of its upright six hundred and thirteen feet. Then put down as the length of the arms of the cross four hundred and forty-six and a half feet. Over the centre of this cross is the great dome, the interior diameter of which is one hundred and thirty-nine feet, and the exterior one hundred and ninety-five and a half. The front of the cathedral is three hundred and seventy-nine feet long and one hundred and forty-eight and a half feet in height. The height of the dome from the pavement to the base of the lantern is four hundred and five feet, and to the top of the cross four hundred and forty-eight feet, or more than double the height of our Washington Monument. There are five doors in the front which admit to the vestibule, which is itself much larger than any ordinary church. This vestibule is three hundred and sixty-eight feet long, sixty-six feet high, and fifty feet wide. It is of this great structure that the poet exclaimed,—

"Enter! its grandeur overwhelms thee not;
And why? it is not lessened, but thy mind,
Expanded by the genius of the spot,
Has grown colossal, and can only find
A fit abode wherein appear enshrined
Thy hopes of immortality."

Whatever idea may thus be learned as to its interior, its ornamentation is beyond conception. The whole of its vast walls, railings, columns, corridors, vestibules, arches, massive piers, and numerous altars, are glittering with gold, and ornamented and decorated with statuary, paintings, bas-reliefs, and rich and rare gems and mottoes. The tombs and monuments of nearly all the Popes are here, and of many kings. The high altar, directly under the dome, and over the tomb of St. Peter, with its bronze canopy, is too magnificent to attempt a description. This alone is estimated to have cost nearly nine millions of dollars. The number of altars in this vast structure cannot be less than thirty, and service is said to be perpetual within the walls of St. Peter's, so that any one stepping in, night or day, can always find the service of mass in progress. Whilst we were there, mass was being said constantly: the moment it ceased at one altar, a bell announced its commencement at another. There were about one hundred persons kneeling at each of the altars whilst the masses were in progress.

The Italian soldiers, now in possession of the city, throng St. Peter's, as well as all the prominent places of interest. Most of them were probably never in Rome before. They are a fine-looking set of men, both soldierly and gentlemanly in their deportment, and finely uniformed.

The open court in front of St. Peter's, with its massive colonnades, surmounted by statuary, is worthy of so immense a structure, though it is too large for the front of the building, and gives to the stranger a wrong impression as to its vastness. The colonnades inclose a space of seven hundred and eighty-seven feet in diameter, and are connected with the façade, or front of the church, by two galleries two hundred and ninety-six feet in length. The façade is three hundred and seventy-nine feet long, and one hundred and forty-eight and one-half feet high. The doors are approached by a flight of stone steps, the whole length of the cathedral. What is most to be admired about St. Peter's, inside and out, is that it is always kept clean, bright, and beautiful. The cost of keeping it clean and in good repair is said to be over fifty thousand dollars per annum.

THE DOME OF ST. PETER'S.

We spent an hour on the roof and in ascending the dome of St. Peter's Cathedral. The ascent to the summit is the only means by which a proper idea can be formed of the immensity of the structure, and it then presents one of the most extraordinary spectacles in the world. A broad, paved, spiral ascent, without steps, leads to the roof by so gentle a rise that a horse might mount it. On the walls are tablets recording the names of members of the reigning houses of Europe who have accomplished the ascent, including that of the Prince of Wales, who passed up in 1869. The roof is so immense that it requires a half-hour to walk round it, and the workmen who are constantly employed in repairing it and keeping it in order have houses here, in which they live with their families. Almost all the roof is of brick, set in Roman cement as hard and solid as a rock. A long series of passages and staircases carried us from the roof to the different stages of the dome, winding between its double walls and opening on the internal galleries. From the upper of these galleries, looking down on the altar and floor of the cathedral below, at a height of about four hundred feet, the people scarcely look like human beings, and the mosaics of the dome, which look from below like finely-executed paintings, are found to be coarsely executed in the only style which could produce such an effect at such a distance. The staircases from this point lead directly to the top of the interior dome. Another flight of about thirty steps carried us up into the ball at the base of the cross, which from the front of the building looks not larger than a bomb-shell, but we found it to be capable of easily holding eighteen persons. Six were in it at the time we entered, but the heat was so oppressive that we were soon compelled to retreat.

The view from the balcony below the ball is one of the finest in Europe. The whole of Rome is spread out like a map in the foreground, bounded on one side by the Mediterranean and on the other by the chain of the Apennines.

MIRACULOUS RELICS.

Whilst viewing the churches and cloisters of Rome, many miraculous things were pointed out by our guide which rather startled our credulity. In the cloister of St. John Lateran, an altar-table of white marble, about two inches thick, with a small hole through it, and a round yellow spot on the marble upright which sustained it, we were assured came there by a miracle. A priest who did not believe that the wafer was the real body of Christ was officiating at the altar, and, laying down the wafer, it passed immediately through the stone, and the yellow spot underneath was where it struck in its descent. Then we were shown a long flight of steps, covered with wood, about twelve feet broad, and rising about thirty feet, which we were assured were the identical steps, brought from Pilate's house at Jerusalem, which Christ passed down on his way to be crucified. No good Catholic, we were informed, would pass up or down these steps except on his knees. Then pieces of the veritable cross were in possession, and the place was pointed out to us in which the veritable heads of St. Peter and St. Paul are kept,—all of which may be so; but we also heard of several pieces of the veritable cross in San Domingo, and have heard of parts of St. Peter and St. Paul being in so many places, that we are rather inclined to agree with Mark Twain, that there must be several ship-loads of this sacred material scattered over the world, and that the bones of the saints have been much scattered.

Another great relic is deposited in a small chapel underneath the high altar of Santa Maria Maggiore. It professes to be the boards of the manger in which the Saviour lay after his birth. A solemn ceremony and procession on Christmas Eve commemorate this subject. Five boards of the manger compose the cradle in which the Saviour was deposited at his nativity. An urn of silver and crystal incloses these relics, on the top of which is the figure of the holy child. At St. Peter's the handkerchief which lay over the face of Christ, and the spear with which his side was pierced, are only exhibited from the high balcony during Holy Week. The chain by which St. Peter was manacled is also kept in one of the churches. We also saw one of these chains at Cologne.

There is some reason to believe that the Jerusalem steps are genuine, or at least that there is a very plausible reason given that they are the veritable steps over which Christ passed in going to and from the trial-chamber in Pilate's house. Baedeker says that they were brought to Rome three hundred years after the death of Christ, having been taken from Pilate's house, and were those that led to the trial-chamber. They are of white marble; but as they became so greatly worn by the crowds of Christian worshipers who sought the opportunity of going over them on their knees, it was deemed advisable to cover them with boards, in which condition they now are, presenting the appearance of a board staircase. On Sunday thousands of peasants were crawling over these stairs all day, and applying for indulgences, which a notice over the door announced would be granted for "the living or the dead,"—price, five francs. This rather staggered our faith in the exhibition.

DOWN AMONG THE ANCIENTS.

There is nothing so destructive of the sentiment of romance which envelops the ruins of the ancient Romans as to wander over the hot bricks and cement during a heated term like the present. The explanations and orations of your guide, in such horrible English that it is necessary to repeat it three times to know what he really did say, adds to the torment, and a day's work done leaves a vivid remembrance of the labor and annoyance, and very little gratification. To leave Rome without seeing everything worth seeing would be regarded by Mrs. Grundy as having no sentiment of appreciation for the wonderful in ruins or the grand in art. After seeing Pompeii, a city extinguished like a flash in the midst of its glory, the scattered remnants of ancient Rome, incomplete and broken, become tame and uninteresting, especially as the photographist has made the world familiar with every broken column and ragged wall, and has given us the Coliseum in all its glory and magnificence. Even the statuary of the ancients, or at least all of it that has merit, has been photographed over the world; and to wade among so many miles of stone men and women—as our clerical friend styles them—as is required to ferret out what is world-renowned, becomes a little irksome, to say the least of it. So also with the great galleries of paintings: most of them are mere trash and rubbish, and one feels a kind of inward conviction that, whatever may be their merit, they will not bear a second visit by those who do not make paintings a hobby and ancient paintings a worship. We confess to the weakness of admiring modern art, and to believing that the lauded mellowness of coloring by the ancients is more the effect of age on their productions than of superior touch and skill. So also with statuary. The productions of Powers and other modern artists are equal to those of the ancients. It is a matter of wonder that the old heathens should have become so expert in the art, and that they really reached perfection, but we have seen but few specimens that are superior to the productions of the sculptors of the present generation. Then the latter are bright and beautiful, while those of the ancients are stained and begrimed with the rust of ages. Michael Angelo would probably never have been deemed to have had any merit as a sculptor if he had not secretly buried one of his productions, previously taking off and concealing an arm. After it had time to become earth-stained he caused it to be found, and it was hailed as the most wonderful of all the recovered statuary of the ancients. When the excitement was at its height he produced the missing arm, bright and beautiful, and claimed the work as his own production. If it had not been for this trick, which caused all the critics to commit themselves in admiration of this wonderful piece of statuary, Michael Angelo might have struggled in vain for the eminence he afterwards achieved.

MENDICANT PRIESTS.

We have before alluded to the fact that both here and at Naples mendicant priests and friars are to be met at every turn, begging for pennies. They are certainly the most woebegone-looking creatures possible to conceive, and many of them are both dirty and ragged. We were assured yesterday by an Italian gentleman that their destitution is real, and that there is a determination upon the part of the people to break up and disperse them. In times past they ruled and tyrannized over the people of Rome without mercy, and now they have no pity for them. The women secretly aid them, but they seldom approach a man, unless he is a stranger, for aid. It is a singular thing to find such evidences of joy among Roman Catholics over the overthrow and humiliation of the Pope. But the fact is, it is the cardinals, and not the Pope, against whom the feeling is entertained. The Pope, like Queen Victoria, is beloved by all the people, but the tyranny of the clergy under his rule had become so offensive that the relief afforded them by Victor Emmanuel is a source of constant rejoicing. This feeling is shown by their kindness to the Italian troops, who are certainly well-disciplined and well-behaved soldiers, and withal a remarkably fine-looking body of men.

Both in Rome and Naples the number of street-beggars has greatly decreased. Indeed, we doubt if there are more beggars to be met with now in the streets of Rome than on the streets of Baltimore. Those who are still plying their old vocation are nearly all cripples, or else young children. It is true this may be an unpropitious season for beggars in Rome, but there are very few of them now to be met with except around the church-doors, and these are old crones, who are beyond the age for regeneration or improvement.

IMPROVEMENTS OF ROME.

On entering the city by railroad from Naples, and passing the gates leading towards the Appian Way, among the ruins of the arches of the aqueduct which supplied ancient Rome with water, we were astonished to observe the change, even in this remote section of the Holy City, which had taken place since our visit twelve years ago. There was then no railroad, and we traveled from Naples in diligences along the Appian Way, through the Pontine Marshes, stopping at all the towns along the shores of the Mediterranean, where the famous brigands even at that time made their haunts. We had scarcely passed inside of the walls of Rome when there loomed up before us the new railroad depot, which is one of the most magnificent and handsomely-adorned buildings of the kind that we have yet met with on either side of the Atlantic. It is constructed of stone, extensively ornamented with abundance of statues and bas-reliefs, and is fully six hundred feet in length. In driving down towards the centre of the city we were surprised to find rows of elegant new residences going up on every side, old palaces being renovated and almost reconstructed, and new palaces being built. Indeed, from the present appearances, so great is the change that fortunes have probably been made here in speculating in corner-lots and suburban property. This all grows out of the fact that Rome is now the capital of Italy. Of course all the nobility of Italy must have palaces in Rome, and many of the old palaces have been sold to them at good prices. We also found the hotel-keepers filled with magnificent expectations, all of whom are making efforts to improve and enlarge their establishments.

THE PROTESTANT BURYING-GROUND.

This is one of the most beautiful spots in the environs of Rome, and is well taken care of, the whole interior being ornamented with flowers and shrubbery. It has a high stone wall round it, with a gate-keeper and gardeners always in attendance. There are a large number of very fine monuments, principally of Englishmen who have died in Rome, having come here for the recovery of their health, with a few Americans. Most travelers visit it with melancholy interest. The silence and the seclusion of the spot, and the inscriptions in our mother-tongue, beneath the bright skies of the Eternal City, appeal irresistibly to the heart. Here lie the remains of Shelley, the poet, and his friend John Keats.

THE ROMAN PALACES.

The Pope and the Roman nobles have the most magnificent palaces and villas in the world, in all of which there are extensive galleries of paintings and statuary. Some of these private establishments exceed those of the Pope in their attractions, several of which we visited to-day. The number of these palaces in Rome is seventy-five.

The Pope's summer palace, in which he resides during such portion of the year as the Vatican is rendered unhealthy by the malaria, is a very grand affair. The floors are of mosaic, the walls are covered with paintings and tapestry, and the vaulted ceilings present a succession of grand scriptural paintings in fresco by the best artists of the past century. We passed through about thirty spacious rooms and halls, including the chamber, library, and throne-room of the Pope, the halls and ante-rooms of the Noble Guard and the Swiss Guard, in all of which were numerous fine specimens of statuary. Here, as in all the public buildings and palaces, a number of artists were engaged in making copies of some of the great paintings of the old masters.

The palace of the Borghese family, in the heart of the city, is a grand affair, whilst their villa, immediately outside of the walls, exceeds anything of a private character we have yet met with in Europe. The grounds of their villa are four miles in circumference, and, being always open to the public, supersede the necessity of a public park for the citizens of Rome. It is rich in every variety of park-scenery, diversified by groves of ilex and laurel, by clumps of stone-pine, and by long avenues of cypresses, which supply the landscape artists with endless combinations for their pencils. The grounds are well laid out, and interspersed with numerous gushing fountains in every direction, in all manner of fanciful design and rich sculpture. On the highest point of the grounds stands the villa, a noble building of great extent, the statuary- and painting-galleries of which are open to the public every Saturday afternoon. On the first floor there are two saloons, each sixty feet long and fifty feet high, painted in fresco by artists of the last century, and seven smaller rooms, all of which are filled with statuary, including several fine statues of Venus, Apollo, Diana, Ceres, Mercury, Sappho, and Hercules. The number of works of art in these eight rooms cannot amount to less than five hundred. On the second floor there is also a suite of six rooms, some filled with statuary and others with paintings. The Venus for which the Princess Borghese, the sister of Napoleon, sat to Canova, is also preserved here. She was regarded as the handsomest woman of her time. This is the statue in reference to which the anecdote is told of a lady friend asking the princess how it was possible she could sit in such a nude condition for her statue. Her reply was characteristic of the woman: "Oh, I did not mind it; there was a warm fire in the room."

The city palace of the Borghese family has also an immense gallery of paintings, which is open to the public, filling twelve large rooms, with ceilings almost thirty feet high, vaulted and frescoed in the highest style of art. Some of the paintings in this collection have a world-wide renown, among which are Raphael's magnificent painting of the Entombment of Christ, the Chase of Diana, by Domenichino, the Return of the Prodigal Son, by Guercino, the Three Graces, by Titian, Sacred and Profane Love, by Titian, the Entombment, by Vandyke, etc.

The Barberini Palace also contains a small collection of paintings, among which we noticed the celebrated portrait of Beatrice Cenci, taken by Guido on the night before her execution; and Raphael's Fornarina. There is an extensive library here also, of sixty thousand volumes, and a great collection of ancient manuscripts.

The Corsini Palace has also a fine suite of rooms filled with paintings and statuary, and a library consisting of thirteen thousand manuscripts and sixty thousand printed volumes.

DOWN AMONG THE DEAD MEN.

We have visited several of the monasteries. That of the Capuchins, adjoining the church of Santa Maria della Concezione, was very interesting. The church is celebrated for the picture of the archangel Michael, by Guido. Over the entrance-door is also the cartoon, by Giotto of St. Peter Walking on the Water.

We were received by a Capuchin friar, in his long heavy brown cloth robe and cowl, with rope around his waist, and conducted behind the altar and through the cloisters, from whence we passed into the basement of the church, where a sight met our view for which we were wholly unprepared. It appears that whenever a monk or friar of this order dies he is buried in one of the four vaulted chambers under the church, each one of which has ten graves, with a small cross at the head and the name of its occupant on a card. There is thus room for forty graves, and for the last two hundred years, after these graves were all filled, it has been the custom of the order to take up the body in the oldest grave to make room for a new occupant of the receptacle. By this means there have accumulated the bones of more than a thousand monks, which are piled up in the most fantastic manner around the walls, displaying considerable architectural taste in their arrangement. In one vault the leg- and thigh-bones are thus arranged, in another the skulls, in another the arm-bones, and in another the shoulder-blades are the principal features. They are so arranged as to leave niches and arches in the piles, and in these niches and arches in each vault are seven full skeletons, their arms crossed, and arrayed in black robes, with cords around the waists, three of them reclining and four standing upright. Some of these ghastly skulls are covered with dried flesh, from which long beards are flowing. The ceilings are also decorated with rib-bones and pieces of vertebræ, so skillfully arranged in flowers and quaint figures that at first glance they look like stucco-work. In the centre of each vault, and also in the passage-way adjoining them, are candelabra made of human bones suspended by bones from the ceiling.

The whole range of these cells are on a level with the ground, each having a large grated window, and the bright rays of the sun were shining upon the ghastly spectacle at the time we passed through them. The price of admission for a party is one franc, and the receipts are a source of considerable income to the Church. Since the overthrow of the Papal government this foolish interment has been stopped, and the Capuchins who hereafter die are compelled to take their chance of being found when wanted among the rest of humanity in out-of-door cemeteries. The bone-exhibition is allowed to continue, and an enterprising daguerreotypist was engaged in taking views of each of the six chambers into which the cemetery is divided. They will make ghastly pictures.

BROTHER, WE MUST ALL DIE.

Our next visit was to the Carthusian monastery attached to the magnificent church of Santa Maria degli Angeli, which was originally the great hall of the Baths of Diocletian, built two thousand years ago, but was altered into a church and monastery by Michael Angelo. Eight of the immense granite columns of the baths, which are in one solid piece, forty-five feet high and sixteen feet in circumference, stand in their positions, to which others in imitation have been added. It is one of the finest churches in Rome, and the order of Carthusian monks, to which it belongs, are all Roman nobles.

The monastery cloisters are very fine, and the four long corridors, supported by one hundred columns of travertine, form a hollow square, arranged as a finely-cultivated garden, in the centre of which is a fountain, presenting quite an attractive scene. The monks or friars of this order wear no hats or caps, have long flowing beards, and wear gowns and cowls of white flannel, with a heavy cord tied round their waists. The great rule of this order is silence, they never speaking to one another, except the salutation of, "Brother, we must all die;" to which the one addressed replies, "I know it, brother." This is said to be the only intercourse they have; though the several we met in the cloisters were stout, hearty-looking fellows, with good-natured countenances, and talked very freely to us.

The stable and barn of the monastery was formerly part of Diocletian's Baths also, which were supposed to be over a mile in circumference, the ruins of which show their arched ceilings from fifty to sixty feet high. These old Romans were great sticklers for cleanliness, judging from the extent of the ruins of their bathing-establishments.

THE CHURCHES OF ROME.

There are over three hundred churches in Rome, independent of the seven basilicas or cathedrals, and many of them are of a character that must surprise the visitor at their great extent and the magnificence of their appointments.

The new cathedral of St. Paul is a mile and a quarter outside the gates of the city, and is grand beyond the power of description. With the exception of the great dome, its interior is as magnificent as that of St. Peter's, and the richness of its altars and pillars exceeds it. It abounds in alabaster, malachite, black and yellow marble, green basalt, porphyry, and every variety of rich and rare marble in its altars, pillars, walls, and floors, whilst its ceilings are of white and gilt stucco, its walls filled with fine paintings, and likenesses in mosaic of some two hundred saints. Nothing can exceed the richness of the whole edifice. The roof of the nave is a magnificent specimen of modern carved wood-work and gilding, having the armorial bearings of the present pontiff in the centre. The effect of the four ranges of granite columns, eighty in number, is unparalleled. They are after the Corinthian order, the capitals and bases being of white marble; in addition to which there are two more colossal than the rest, supporting the arch over the high altar, which were presented by the Emperor of Austria, all of them being in solid blocks forty and fifty feet high. The total length of the structure is two hundred and ninety-six feet; the length of the nave, three hundred and six feet; the width of the nave and side-aisles, two hundred and twenty-two feet; and the width of the transept, two hundred and fifty feet. Under the high altar is the tomb, which the tradition of the Church from the earliest times had pointed out as the burial-place of St. Paul, whose body, on the same authority, is inclosed in an urn on which is engraved the name of the apostle. Like the tomb of St. Peter, in St. Peter's Cathedral, one hundred lamps are kept burning around it night and day.

The cathedrals of the Lateran and of Santa Maria Maggiore, both of which we visited, are also very grand, and abound in fine paintings, statuary, mosaics, and a variety of ornamental marbles of every color, presenting a richness beyond all power of description.

We also visited San Pietro in Vincoli, in which the colossal statue of Moses, by Michael Angelo, is the great feature of attraction, though the other specimens of sculpture and paintings are very fine. Here also is kept, as a sacred relic, what is said to be the chain with which St. Peter was bound whilst a prisoner in Rome.

HOTELS OF ROME.

There is much need of improvement in the hotels of Rome, but we must in all truth and candor add that they are far superior to those of London, both in accommodations and attendance, and their *table-d'hôte* is better, both in quality and character of cooking. We are stopping at the Hôtel d'Angleterre, which is said to be the best in Rome in all respects, being intended for John Bull's especial accommodation, who, you know, is an inveterate grumbler. With two or three occasional exceptions, we are the only guests (this being the dull season), and are probably receiving more than ordinary attention. In this country they furnish you good beds, but make no effort to keep the house clean; and though you may, by dint of close watching and constant slaughter, keep your rooms clear of fleas, every time a lady goes to the dining-room or passes through the halls she is sure to gather up a score of them. Before they can have acceptable hotels for foreigners, the keepers of these hotels must have a better appreciation of the annoyance of these terrible pests, and of the necessity of not only sweeping their marble and cement floors, but of making another use of water besides squirting it through the pipes of a fountain. They sweep the floors with a sprawling straw broom, put together something like our scavengers' brooms, and never think of such a thing as mopping up the floors with water. Our party have killed so many fleas since they have been here that we should not wonder if the house has a better reputation in this respect in future.

The general cost of living in a Roman hotel is but little more than three dollars per day, and those who choose to take their meals at the restaurants can reduce their expenses to about two dollars and a half. For a family, or a large party visiting Rome, it is always better to seek furnished apartments, which are to be had in all sections of the city, and take meals in the cafés. There is generally an old lady in charge of the rooms, who keeps everything clean, and will furnish coffee, bread and butter, and eggs for breakfast, if desired, at a very moderate charge. Those who know Rome always seek these quarters in preference to the hotels. Our bill for a party of four, for four days at Rome, was one hundred and fifty-three francs, or about thirty-one dollars, though we took two or three meals at restaurants, which would make it about forty dollars, or just two dollars and a half each per day. The charges were so light that it seemed hard to compel the landlord to strike off nineteen francs for the inevitable errors of addition and charges for articles that we had not called for. An Italian hotel-bill, with its numerous items, is a curiosity, and as it is never delivered to you until the moment you are about starting, very few are able to decipher and correct them.

SUNDAY IN ROME.

There is evidently no Sunday-law in Rome. Everybody here seems to do as they think proper, but a vast majority of the people strictly observe the day, and nine-tenths of the stores are kept closed. Those that are open are restaurants, cafés, tobacco-stores, fruit-stores, and drinking-houses. Every place for the sale of eatables or drinkables is in full blast, and we encountered some few, but a very few, mechanics at work at their trades. The streets were thronged all day with well-dressed people, but the churches into which we dropped had but few attendants, and those were principally old men and women of the lower classes. A great many of these, although clean and well dressed, held out their hands to us for alms, leading to the supposition that this was the main object of their attendance. There were a great many soldiers on the streets, all in full uniform, wearing white cotton gloves, and looking extremely well. The police wear a military dress, carry a sword at their sides, and with coats buttoned up to the throat, and yellow cord and tassel gracefully looped over the breast, carry themselves erect and soldierly. They are all young men, apparently under twenty-five years of age, and have evidently seen military service. The numbers of each regiment are in gilt figures on their stand-up collars, and they also wear white gloves.

PROMENADE ON THE CORSO.

After dinner this (Sunday) evening we started for a promenade on the Corso, which is the fashionable thoroughfare of Rome. The throng was so great that both pavement and street were well filled with pedestrians, ladies and gentlemen, and the officers of the various Italian regiments stationed in Rome. The latter were in their elegant undress uniforms, and presented as trig and smart appearance as our holiday soldiers do when on parade. Their dresses appeared as if just from the tailor-shop, and were remarkable for style and excellent fit. On their breasts were various medals, and they were evidently set upon attracting the attention of the ladies by their fine military appearance and bearing. They all carried side-arms, and wore fancy military caps, and could be seen along the whole line of the Corso.

The Corso was so thronged with pedestrians that the carriages, with a fine display of the fashionables of Rome, could scarcely get along. Our party were recognized as Americans, and were duly inspected, especially by the Roman ladies.

The newsboys throughout the afternoon were busily crying and selling a Sunday paper, which was bought up by the people with great avidity. There are several papers now published here daily, and the newsboys, or rather newsmen, are becoming quite an institution. Twelve years ago there was but one paper published, once a week, in Rome, and it contained nothing but official decrees and Church notices; and although the Italian war was then in progress, it was not allowed even to allude to it. The London *Times* was then not permitted to come through the post-office, and could only be had by smuggling it through by private conveyance. The Rome of the present day is a cradle of liberty compared to what it was then, and there is no mistaking the fact that all Rome, outside of the Pope, the cardinals, and the priesthood, is happy and hopeful. It does one good to see the Italian flag flying from the Castle of St. Angelo, which was for so many years the prison-house of all liberal Italians who had the manhood to entertain and express sentiments favorable to human liberty.

ROMAN LADIES.

There was quite a display of the beauty of Rome on the Corso on Sunday afternoon, and they were regarded by our female critics as quite womanly-looking women, exhibiting more force of character in their presence and bearing than the other sex. There were a few blondes among them, but most of them were dark-eyed brunettes. They dress with great taste, in plain colors, in full European or American costume, including fancy overskirts, hats and feathers, but exhibit very little jewelry.

GARIBALDI AND SAVONAROLA.

While taking a drive on Pincian Hill, our guide, with a quiet chuckle, pointed out to us among the marble busts of distinguished Italians lining the drives, that of Garibaldi, a name that two years ago dared not be mentioned in Rome. It had just been placed here by order of the Italian government, to the great joy of the people. A few moments after we called upon the driver to stop in front of another beautiful bust, with a kind and benevolent countenance, and a wealth of waving hair extending down to the shoulders. Beneath it was engraved the name of Savonarola, the first of Italian patriots, a Dominican priest, who was burned at the stake in Florence, in 1498, on account of what was then deemed by the Pope to be heretical teaching and writing. This bust had also been placed in this position of honor by the Italian government since the redemption of Rome. Savonarola had previously been excommunicated for preaching against the celibacy of the clergy, and for this forfeited his life. The people of Florence and Rome, although earnest Catholics, still honor his memory, and that his bust should be placed among Italy's most honored sons, on Pincian Hill, is a subject of great rejoicing.

CLEANLINESS OF THE CITY.

The streets of Rome are kept very clean, and none of those sharp and disgusting odors greet the olfactory organs at every turn, as was formerly the case. Every paving-stone in the city is carefully swept during the night, and the dust carted off before breakfast-time in the morning. The streets are also watered, and in the early morning it would be difficult to find any city, except Paris, cleaner than the Rome of the present day. The old Jew quarter, into which the Papal government crowded these people, is also broken up, and they have scattered over the city, seeking residences where their inclination may suggest. This was formerly a terribly filthy section; now it is as cleanly as any other, the number of residents being not more than one-fourth what it was.

CITY OF FLORENCE.

FLORENCE, July, 1873.

We left Rome at nine o'clock on Monday morning, and were at our hotel in Florence at seven o'clock the same evening, the distance being about two hundred and fifty miles. The weather was intensely hot. Being boxed up in one of those close cars, with nothing to eat and a very little to drink except an occasional tumbler of water, secured, at a penny a glass, through the car-window, was anything but pleasant.

ROME TO FLORENCE.

The road from Rome to Florence is a marvel of engineering, and has been constructed under difficulties that one would have supposed likely to stagger the *effete* Italians. It crosses a portion of the Apennine Mountains at a grade of about one hundred and fifty feet to the mile, and at one point of the road we counted twenty stone bridges erected over mountain-streams in less than ten miles. Then the tunnels are innumerable, varying in length from one hundred yards to over a mile. They are constructed in enduring masonry, and the equipments of the road, including depots and water-stations, are of a very superior character.

The country through which the road

passed, especially the first part of it, being what was formerly known as a portion of the patrimony of St. Peter, is very sterile, being mostly mountainous. Every spot, however, is closely cultivated; even the mountain-sides, as far up as the olive-tree can be made to grow, are covered with this fruit of commerce.

There are a great many towns and cities along the road between Rome and Florence, all of them during the first half of the route being located either on the tops of mountains or high up on their sides. Their mud-colored walls, red-tiled roofs, with scarcely a green tree to relieve the eye, basking on the mountain-side in the hot sun, give them a most forbidding aspect. They look as if one house was piled against another, and as if there was no room for locomotion within their limits. Every town has its immense fortifications, citadel, and castle, covering more ground and costing more money than the town itself. As we get towards Tuscany, however, the folly of building cities on the tops of mountains is abandoned, and we find them located on the plain, with cottages and farmhouses evincing a superior class of people to those of Southern Italy.

FLORENCE BY GAS-LIGHT.

We reached Florence in time to take a stroll through its streets and view the city by gas-light. The streets all through the heart of the city were literally thronged with promenaders, and the stores and cafés brilliant with gas-jets. Such a shining scene would never be seen in an American city except on the eve of some national holiday. The cafés are all immense establishments, some of them old palaces, and they were thronged to the curb-stones with parties eating and drinking. Newsboys were circulating everywhere, selling the evening papers, and vendors of fruit doing a brisk business. This continued up to twelve o'clock, when the city suddenly became quiet, and all street-scenes and noises ceased. With the stroke of the bell, stores and cafés were closed, and the doings of the day brought to an end.

THE CAPITAL OF ITALY.

Florence has been awarded the title by Byron of "the fairest city of the earth." It was, up to last year, since 1865, the capital of the kingdom of Italy, and Victor Emmanuel here resided at the Pitti Palace, which was formerly called the Palace of the Grand Duke. At the commencement of the present year the king and court removed to Rome, which is now the capital of the nation, thus accomplishing what has been the great purpose of Italian unity, the blotting out forever of what were called the States of the Church.

Florence is situated in the rich valley of the Arno, surrounded by beauties of nature and art. It is revered as the birthplace of Dante, Petrarch, Boccaccio, Galileo, Michael Angelo, Leonardo da Vinci, Benvenuto Cellini, and Andrea del Sarto. Beautiful gardens, adorned with statues, vases, fountains, and other decorations, as well as the open squares or piazzas, continually attract the eye of the visitor, and the palaces, which are very numerous, each containing rare paintings and sculpture, form the principal objects of interest in this delightful city, which is the pride of Italy. The Arno passes through the city, and is crossed by six bridges, but as it becomes at times as unruly as our Jones's Falls at home, they have nearly all at times been swept away.

THE UFFIZI GALLERY.

We visited this morning the Uffizi Gallery, the paintings in which are reputed to be the richest and most varied in the world, with the exception of the Royal Gallery at Madrid, although not as extensive as many others. The Tribune, a small circular chamber, not only contains the chefs-d'œuvre of this gallery but of the world, both in painting and statuary. Among the sculpture are the world-renowned Venus de Medici, which was found in the portico of Octavia at Rome, the Apollino, or young Apollo, the Dancing Faun, the Wrestlers, and the Antonio, a slave whetting his knife. These were all recovered from the ruins of Rome, and are the products of heathen sculptors. The Titian Venus alluded to by Byron is here, with several of the productions of Michael Angelo.

It required several hours to pass rapidly through these galleries, where we encountered not less than fifty artists, male and female, making copies from the great masters. This, however, is the case to some extent in all the galleries of Italy. The business of copying these famous paintings has become quite an extensive one, and many of the copyists have become so expert as to command large prices for their work.

FAIREST CITY OF THE EARTH.

If in Byron's time Florence could be called the fairest city of the earth, it is certainly much more entitled to the title now. A drive through it last evening disclosed vast improvements that have taken place during the past ten years. Its occupation as the Italian capital necessitated the building of large numbers of elegant palaces and public buildings, and the people manifested great anxiety to render their city worthy of the honor. At eight o'clock in the morning it would be impossible for Mrs. Partington, with her finest broom, to gather a shovelful of dirt from any square in the city. It is smoothly paved, like all Italian cities, with slabs of stone about two and a half feet long by eighteen inches broad. These are grooved with the chisel, and occasionally roughened as they become smooth by wear. Its streets are mostly broad, its public squares numerous and beautiful, and its people are evidently very industrious. You never see a beggar on the streets, unless blind or crippled.

The population of Florence has also largely increased during the past ten years, as it now numbers two hundred thousand, and is steadily increasing. The cost of living is very low, and there are a large number of old English retired merchants and business-men who have settled here to live out the balance of their days. Their means are, in most cases, not sufficient to secure for themselves and families the same comforts in England that can be had here at one-half the cost. Although everything is still cheap, it is not so cheap as it was in former years, when a furnished house, with horse and carriage, could be had for five hundred dollars per annum.

THE FLORENCE POLICE.

We have before noticed the fact that the Italian police, both in Naples and Rome, are distinguished for their military bearing. Those of Florence excel in this as well as every other characteristic. They are tall, well-formed men, and their uniform is really elegant. They wear a well-fitting blue swallow-tailed coat, buttoned up to the throat with silver buttons; standing collar, and their number in silver letters on the right collar. On the ends of the skirts of their coats there are several sprays of silver flowering, and across the back of the waist two rows of silver buttons, each eight in number, are displayed. The cap is something of what we would call a chapeau, turned up at the front, on which is a rosette of white, red, and blue, with a silver crown in the centre. To make the military status of the figure complete, they wear long swords at their sides, and white cotton gloves. Every man appears to be standing on his dignity, and to be fully aware of his personal importance.

VISIT TO THE PITTI PALACE.

This was last year the residence of King Victor Emmanuel, but its chief attraction now is the collection of paintings, which number about five hundred, and which to our uncultivated taste are more attractive than those contained in the Uffizi. We spent several hours in examining the paintings and statuary, and especially a mosaic table, about seven feet long, which cost over two hundred thousand dollars, and nearly fifteen years were taken in completing it at the government manufactory.

The Boboli Gardens adjoin the palace, and have a world-wide reputation for the beauty of their adornments and culture. They abound in grottoes, fountains, roses sculpture, and magnificent terraces, from some of which a fine view of the whole city of Florence can be had.

THE MUSEO NATURALE.

This famous establishment also adjoins the Pitti Palace, and is free to all visitors, being sustained by the government. A sight more interesting and instructive it is difficult anywhere to meet. In addition to the well-arranged halls filled with minerals and plants, many departments are devoted to wax models of the human body, as well as of a great number of animals. Here science has laid bare the whole machinery of the human system, colored to resemble nature so closely that it is difficult to conceive that it is not flesh and blood laid out to the view. Every separate part of the human form, bodies, legs, hearts, lungs, etc., are displayed upon cushions, some under glass; whole forms, the size of life, both male and female, lie exposed on white beds, opened from the throat downward, and all the internal organism laid bare. Youth and old age are here as if asleep, with the life-warm coloring of flesh, veins, and skin.

THE CASCINE.

The Druid Hill Park of the Florentines is the Cascine, on the peninsula formed by the junction of the Arno and the Mignone. This is decidedly the most charming drive and promenade in Italy. It derives its name from the dairy-houses of the late grand duke, which are situated near the centre of the drive, and which supply Florence with its purest milk and butter. From the Leghorn Railroad station, immediately outside the Porta al Prato, the bank of the Arno is laid out as a beautiful walk and drive, overshadowed by magnificent trees for the space of two miles. About midway of the grounds there is a large circular plateau. Here, several afternoons in the week, the bands perform, and here the fashionables of Florence make their calls. For the space of two or three hours, from four to seven, all Florence—that is, all Florence that pretends to be anybody—attends this fashionable exchange in all manner of equipages, in number varying from five hundred to one thousand, and they are not excelled in style or richness by any city except Paris. Around the music-stands the carriages congregate; gentlemen descend and visit their lady friends and present them with bouquets, which the flower-girls have in abundance for the occasion. They talk, gossip, and flirt or promenade along the river-bank, where seats beneath shady groves supply the wants of solitaires as well as lovers. Fashionable society of Florence cares not where you live, what you eat, or what you wear, so long as you make your appearance at the opera and drive your turn-out on the Cascine, both of which are cheap enough. For ninety dollars per month a splendid turn-out can be hired, with two horses, coachman, and footman, an open carriage for driving in the Cascine, and a close carriage for the opera. A box at the opera, holding four to eight persons, will cost four to five dollars per night. Is it any wonder that there should be a demand for cottages in Florence, with its delightful climate, abundance of fruits, and cheap living?

BURIAL OF THE POOR.

There is a religious order in Florence which sprang into existence many years since, during the prevalence of the cholera. It undertook to superintend the funeral rites and burial of all persons who had neither friends nor money who died in the city. The members wear black frocks, covering the entire person, leaving only two holes for the eyes, and present a most ghostly appearance, and when seen at night, each with a flaming torch, carrying a hand-barrow covered with a black canopy, beneath which is the body, the scene is a most impressive one. Yesterday afternoon, whilst viewing the baptistery, three of these processions passed, conveying some one departed to their last repose. Each procession included about a dozen members of the order, arrayed in their strange dresses, with a cross and rosary at their sides. These burial societies are supported by public subscription. The pious work of these societies includes also the nursing and attending of the sick poor. As these processions pass, the people invariably raise their hats.

FLORENCE TO BOLOGNA.

We left Florence yesterday morning, and in the evening were in sight of Venice. The railroad from Florence strikes directly towards the Apennine Mountains, through a level plain of about twenty miles of rich land, every inch of which is under cultivation in Indian corn, grapes, hemp, and grass.

The soil of Northern Italy is much richer than that of Southern Italy, and all manner of fruits more abundant and luscious. The market at Florence exhibited a greater variety of fruit than we have ever seen at one time in the Baltimore market. Apples, pears, peaches, strawberries, raspberries, plums, prunes, grapes, apricots, cherries, figs, greengages, cantaloupes, watermelons, and several fruits which we never met with before, were displayed upon one stand. Every description of fruit, except the melons, were very large, and the cherries of all kinds fully double the size of ours, and free from worms.

A GREAT RAILROAD.

After passing through about twenty miles of valley-land, the road commenced to ascend the Apennine Mountains at a very heavy grade, passing over bridges and through tunnels more numerous than we had ever before encountered in railroad engineering. The road from Florence to Bologna is eighty-two miles, and the distance across the mountain is about forty miles, nearly the whole being over viaducts or through tunnels. One of these tunnels is a mile and three-fourths in length, whilst others are short, some only a few hundred yards. It is only an occasional glimpse of the magnificent scenery of the Apennines, through which we are passing, that can be obtained, as the train flies in and out of the tunnels at one point of the ascent as often as thirteen times. The view, however, is sufficient to show that the mountain is largely inhabited, and that every available spot of ground is cultivated to its fullest capacity. The mountain-sides are terraced, and agriculture prosecuted under difficulties that would not be undertaken in a less densely populated country. The whole of the road is constructed with the most solid masonry. Tunnels, bridges, viaducts, and stations all display triumphs of engineering such as have never been accomplished in any quarter of the world before.

The view of Florence and the great valley of the Arno from the first mountain station is regarded as one of the most interesting in Europe. Every eminence is studded with villas; the country, rich in vineyards and olive-groves, seems literally a land of oil and wine. Cultivation appears in its highest perfection; the Etruscan fortress of Fiesole rises magnificently over the opposite bank of the Mignone; and Florence, with its domes, campaniles, and embattled towers, bursts upon the view.

BOLOGNA TO VENICE.

We only stopped one hour at Bologna, and the sun was too hot at mid-day to permit of an extended view of the city. Bologna has about ninety thousand inhabitants, and was until recently under the dominion of the Pope, being the most important province of the Holy See.

About twenty miles before reaching Venice we pass the ancient town of Padua, which is the oldest city in Northern Italy, and seems from the railroad to be almost a congregation of churches, with steeples, campaniles, etc. It has a population of about sixty thousand, and has the appearance of being a thriving city.

APPROACH TO VENICE.

A short time after passing Padua the city of Venice loomed up in the distance, looking to the eye like a city rising from the sea, with towers, steeples, domes, and turrets of white marble gleaming in the sun. All our preconceived ideas of Venice seemed to fall short of the reality. The various islands with their groups of houses appear as if they were floating upon the water.

In my next I will endeavor to convey to your readers some idea of Venice.

VENICE.

CITY OF VENICE, July 6, 1873.

THE QUEEN OF THE ADRIATIC.

Here we are once again in the city of Venice, after less than a year's absence. Being in close proximity to her Majesty of the Adriatic, we could not forego the pleasure of again witnessing a Sunday scene on the Piazza of St. Mark, enjoying another sail in the gay gondola, and a ramble among the palaces of this city of venerable memories.

Venice is an odd place, and it takes some little time to understand and unravel its peculiarities. Only think of having your front door open on the water, without a foot of earth to stand upon. Think of being taken from the depot in a boat, and rowed around from one hotel to another to ascertain whether you can find rooms. The traveler seeks novelties, and it is just here that he will find them to perfection. Lord Byron went into such ecstasies over Venice that the whole world has ever since desired to see it. The first thought that strikes you is the singular taste which induced a polished and educated people to select so damp a site for a city. It has been represented as a delightful place to reside in. At first, no doubt, the novelty gratifies and pleases, but it is too monotonous to be a favorite residence for any length of time. The streets being so extremely narrow and tortuous, and the knowledge that you are dependent upon boats for locomotion, and the want of rural beauty, soon weary one of the scene.

ACROSS THE ADRIATIC.

We embarked at Trieste at ten o'clock last evening, on the steamer Milano, and expected to have very few passengers, but were surprised to find on board about four times as many as the vessel could accommodate, except with standing-room. They were mostly tourists, German, French, and English, and fully one-third were ladies. The run across requiring but six hours, and as the moon came out clear and bright shortly after we started, it was no great hardship to keep on deck, especially as it was too hot to find comfort in the cabin. John Bull grumbled, but the majority of the passengers even sympathized with two omnibus-loads of passengers that reached the wharf just after we had cast loose our moorings, and thus lost the opportunity of spending a Sunday in Venice. After our companion had gotten through his ecstasies over "the blue Adriatic" and "the silver rays of the moon," we disposed ourselves as best we could for a sitting nap, and at break of day the "Queen of the Adriatic" appeared in the dim distance before us, though neither brighter nor younger than when we last saw her. In a short time we commenced to enter among the outer islands, on which some very fine country-villas have been erected, and were soon at quarantine, but were only detained long enough to enable the officer to collect his fee. At five o'clock in the morning, tho "gay gondolier," about whom so much exaggerated prose and poetry have been written, had us in his solemn craft, and in a few minutes landed us on the steps of the Hotel Bauer. Amid the scramble of these "gay gondoliers" at the side of the steamer for passengers, they did not seem more loving or lovely than that class of American citizens engaged in the conveying of passengers and baggage to and from depots and hotels; and they were arrayed in very similar apparel, probably second-hand when it was new, their figures being surmounted by broad-brimmed straw hats, very yellow and dirty. When one of these vehicles struck harshly against its neighbor, the tone of the exclamation from the "gay gondolier," and the subsequent exchange of compliments, sounded to our inexperienced ears very much like the loving phrases we have heard exchanged at our railroad depots when Jehu was similarly provoked.

GONDOLAS AND GONDOLIERS.

The gondolas and gondoliers, of which there are about four thousand licensed, the same as we license public hacks, do not come up to the expectation of the stranger who has read of them in romances and poems. The gondolas are about thirty feet in length, with high iron prows, and are, by a law of the city dating three hundred years back, all painted black having in their centre a black cabin something like the body of a hearse, either painted or covered with black cloth, into which four persons can with difficulty be crowded. Instead of being gay and bright and beautiful, as we had supposed, they are a gloomy and deathly-looking craft, about thirty feet in length, but with two gondoliers can be made to move through the water with great rapidity. The gondolier stands up when propelling his boat, and if there is but one he uses but one oar, but guides his vessel through the intricacies of the canals without grazing the sharp angles which he is required to turn, or even checking his speed. A gondola is sometimes met belonging to private parties, who keep them the same as we do carriages. These have gayer fittings, and the gondolier will be arrayed probably in white, with pink sashes; but the common gondolier of Venice is about as plain in apparel and general get-up as one of our ferrymen. They are very active men, and are about as sharp in getting more than the law allows out of their passengers, especially if they happen to be strangers, as some of our hackmen are. The Grand Canal is always lined with them, moving about with passengers, and they can make short cuts by passing through the small canals, on which a goodly number are always running.

STROLL THROUGH THE CITY.

We started about nine o'clock for a stroll around the Square of St. Mark and some of the contiguous streets. Everything appeared to be precisely as we left it one year ago, except the scaffolding on one side of the Cathedral of St. Mark indicated the repairing of its ancient walls. The stores made precisely the same display under the arcades; the pet pigeons of the city were billing and cooing on the piazza; the fruit-shops were all as well supplied with the varieties for which Italy is famous; the same men, women, and children appeared to be "cheaping around" among the provision stores for their Sunday dinners; and an old sexagenarian whom we saw daily a year ago sitting in the door of a poultry shop picking chickens was still engaged at the same artistical work.

It seems strange that in building the city all these small canals were not filled up, and the whole joined into one solid island. The probability, on the contrary, is that many of the canals were made to accommodate the taste of the people, who had been literally born on the water, and must have it at their doors, so as to come and go in their boats. This seems more reasonable than to suppose that in the small space occupied by the city there should have originally been one hundred and fourteen little islands. The sides of the canals are almost invariably the walls of the houses, and they appear to have secured excellent foundations.

Although there are old palaces scattered through the city on the other canals, all the men of great wealth and distinction have their palaces on the Grand Canal. The gondolier, on passing through, recites to you the names of each, with the character of their owners, all of which you care as little about as what was the color of the hair of those who built them. But they go on in a kind of monotonous song, from which can be gathered the names of Foscari, Mocenigo, Pisani, Barbarigo, etc.

THE STREETS OF VENICE.

The streets of Venice are so narrow that with us they would be called lanes and alleys, the generality of them being not more than six to twelve feet wide from house to house. They form the most incomprehensible net-work imaginable,—a labyrinth from which the stranger will find it difficult to extricate himself if he should venture abroad without a guide. The whole city can be traversed without recourse to the water, but it would require a walk of a quarter of a mile to go from one house fronting on the Grand Canal to another five doors off. These lanes are all paved with broad slabs of stone, and are kept very clean. It must be remembered that there are no horses in Venice, and no streets to use them in. We have only seen one here, and it was in a boat going down the Grand Canal. Where he came from, or where he was going to, or what he was intended for, it would be difficult to say. We are credibly informed that there are many persons who have never seen a horse, unless they were the four bronze horses in front of the Cathedral of St. Mark. In the whole city of Venice, with the exception of a botanical garden on one of the outer islands, and a park upon another, there is scarcely a tree or a particle of foliage to be found, except in flower-pots.

We took a very extended walk this morning, and, although we have had no difficulty in finding our way in the vicinity of St. Mark's, we no sooner penetrated into the interior towards the Rialto bridge than we found ourselves involved in a puzzle. We started for the Rialto, and just at the moment when we had concluded that we had gotten back to near the point we started from, turned a corner and the bridge was before us. After finishing our examination, we turned to walk back, and in about ten minutes found ourselves at the bridge again. Three times we came out at the same point, and the fourth time, after innumerable twists and turns, found ourselves in the rear of St. Mark's, when we had been striking for our hotel, about a quarter of a mile distant. The difficulty is that one must follow the streets wherever they lead. One is continually puzzled to know whether he should turn to the right or left when a cross-street is reached. We, however, found in our wanderings quite a number of open squares, one of them about as large as Monument Square, all paved smoothly with broad blocks of granite, and generally having a well in the centre. Some of the streets also widen at certain points for a short distance, and these are lined with a better class of stores. All the streets, however, over twelve feet in width, are occupied by stores, many of them making quite a fine display of jewelry, dry-goods, and fancy wares, but the great majority are devoted to the sale of eatables of one kind or another. The poultry stores, of which there are a great number, keep teacups full of the blood of fowls for sale, the Venice physicians ordering the drinking of blood, instead of using iron, for the benefit of the blood. The patients stop and drink this strange dose, all coagulated as it is, and move on, satisfied that they have received new life from the dose.

PUBLIC GARDEN.

Venice has one public garden, for which she is indebted to Bonaparte. When he held the city, in 1807, he demolished four churches, cloisters, and whole streets of houses, and filled up several canals and diverted others. On this site he laid out a beautiful garden, which is the only breathing-spot, except the Piazza of St. Mark and the quay, for the city of Venice. There are in the garden a coffee-house, a riding-school, a place for shooting at the mark with pistols, and for other popular amusements. The avenues of the garden serve for promenades, and, it being located on the open bay, it is generally reached by gondolas, but with equal facility on foot. The view from the artificial height near the pavilion overlooks the mirror of the lagoons, with their many small islands in the distance, everywhere lifting their churches, cloisters, and slender towers into the air. In addition to all this entrancing variety of land and water views, a gleam of the open Adriatic is caught through the entrance of the port.

CHURCHES AND BELLS.

The number of churches, all of them large and imposing in their architectural features, and bearing evidence of great antiquity, are met at every turn, all of them open with services progressing at all hours. We, however, discovered one, quite an elegant old establishment, its front abounding with pillars, statues of saints, and bas-reliefs, which had been given up to trade. It was occupied as a second-hand furniture establishment, with a sprinkling of old clothes. From the list of churches we found that there are just one hundred Catholic churches in Venice. There are also one Evangelical church. one synagogue, and one Greek Catholic church. The services of the English Church take place every Sunday, at the dwelling of the Consul. The ringing of bells, of which there appears to be a great superabundance, is not equaled by Rome. In the Square of St. Mark there are no less than five clocks, with large bells, that all strike the hours and quarters about the same time. One of them, over the City Hall, has two full-sized bronze statues, one of which strikes the hours on the bell with a sledge-hammer, and the other strikes the quarters. The bell is suspended so that the figures stand out by its side, and their movements have a very natural appearance.

VENICE, July 8, 1873.
NOT A FINISHED CITY.

It takes some time to explore Venice, both by land and water; and the excursions we have made, on foot and by gondola, during the past two days, have shown us that there are evidences of revival and improvement everywhere. Even the dust of ages is being scrubbed off of the walls of the Doge's palace, and the Cathedral of St. Mark is undergoing ablution and renovation. Whilst taking an airing this evening on the Grand Canal, we observed several new and handsome white marble buildings, which have taken the place of old specimens of antiquity, and that many old palaces which were last year gloomy and desolate are now bustling places of business. An intelligent citizen assured us this evening that at no time within the last fifty years has the future of Venice been more promising, and that it is undergoing a gradual and healthy improvement in every branch of trade and commerce.

A GONDOLA-RIDE.

We spent the evening yesterday in exploring the water-thoroughfares of the city. As we moved along up the Grand Canal, which is about as wide as Broadway, with its compact line of buildings on each side, nearly all four to five stories in height, including many large and elegant public buildings and venerable palaces, the appearance was that of a city temporarily flooded. That it was in its natural condition, no one who was brought here blindfolded and set afloat in a gondola, without knowing where he was, could possibly believe. The signs of merchants and business-men were over the elegant doorways, and boats and barges were about the doors just as they would be in Marsh Market Space if Jones's Falls should again make a Venice of that region, whilst the city authorities are exerting themselves with so much energy and perseverance to discover "how not to do it."

After proceeding nearly a mile up the Grand Canal, and passing under the massive but elegant stone arch of the Rialto bridge, we turned off through one of the small canals, not more than eight feet in width, with the walls of two immense palaces towering over our heads on each side. It seemed like going in a boat through a side-alley; but the gondolier handled his oar with such skill that we neither grazed nor touched the walls, and were soon moving along through the wider interior channels, among houses and stores with their iron-grated windows. Every moment other parties in gondolas, including many ladies, passed us, turning corners, angles, and curves, but never coming in collision or touching each other. We passed under hundreds of arched bridges, all of them light and graceful stone or marble structures, excepting a few made of iron. The level of the water being only about two feet below the level of the streets, it is necessary that all the bridges should be raised arches, so that the gondolier, who invariably stands in his vessel, should be able to pass under them without changing his position. Men and boys, some of the latter being small children, were swimming and diving from the doors and bridges, and mothers and sisters were looking on from the doors and windows. It was altogether a novel scene, such as can be seen nowhere except in Venice. Mothers and fathers could be seen with their small children afloat on boards, teaching them to swim, having ropes tied to the boards. We finally emerged from this net-work of canals into the Grand Canal, a short distance above the Doge's palace and the Bridge of Sighs. Here ocean-steamers and vessels of all classes were discharging or taking on cargoes, and there were all the evidences of active commercial prosperity. A steamer for Liverpool was just taking her departure, and one of the Austrian Lloyds' steamers about to depart for Trieste. Steamboats crowded with people were coming and going from the outer islands, of which there are six or seven, too distant to be connected by bridges with the main portion of the city, one of which is a favorite resort of the people, and occupied principally with gardens for the sale of refreshments. After an hour spent in rowing about near the entrance to the harbor, we returned to our hotel, well pleased with our evening's ride.

There are three or four of these interior canals that are nearly twenty feet in width, and one in the neighborhood of the Ghetto, or Jews' quarter, is over thirty feet wide, while many others range from twelve to twenty feet. The fronts of the buildings on the interior canals are very rough, and give evidence of the work of age in their decayed bricks. Repairs of many of these are in progress, which seems to be a matter of necessity in most cases. As the gondola glides through these water-ways, surrounded by tall and dismal brick walls with grated windows, the scene is novel, but not picturesque, though it is somewhat relieved when the bridges are passed. The lower stories, there being no cellars, are always used for that purpose, and the altitude of the second-story windows forbids the sight of any portion of the family department. A fair face can occasionally be seen from the balcony above, or the prattle of children and the sound of song and merriment are heard, but they seem out of place in such surroundings. Some glances we have obtained of the interior of these houses satisfy us that they must not be judged from outside appearance.

VENETIAN NEWSBOYS.

One year ago there were no daily newspapers published in Venice, but there are now three quite prosperous daily journals. Their rivalry has led to the introduction of those sure marks of commercial and industrial prosperity, the newsboys. These youngsters, a year ago, aspired to nothing beyond the sale of matches and shell bracelets, and made their appeals to the strangers with a whine, or the exhibition of their rags, to induce a purchase by exciting sympathy. Now they strut about as independent and unabashed as the American newsboy, shouting, *La Gazzetta, La Stampa*, etc., as if they had suddenly become an important class in the community. Instead of the whining plaint of their match-days, they are full of spirit and wit, and crack jokes with the purchaser. They have even become importers of foreign goods, and have on sale, for their English, American, and German customers,

Galignani's Messenger, the *American Register*, the *Swiss Times*, and the *Neue Freie Presse*. There is also that other sure evidence of a growing city, the bootblack, who has stationed himself on the corners of all the principal thoroughfares. Venice has its telegraph and cable, and is in momentary communication with all the outside world. After its thousand years of war and strife to maintain its supremacy, it is now reaping the fruits of peace under the banner of "united Italy," free at last from Austrian rule. The Venetian detests the name of Austria, and involuntarily scowls if he is asked if he can speak the German language.

THE VENICE BOURSE.

The Stock Board of Venice is located in the National Library building, on the Piazzetta of St. Mark, and will compare favorably in all its appointments with even the new quarters of a similar organization in an American city with which we are familiar. It occupies all the rooms surrounding a beautiful court-yard, in the centre of which is a fountain, and a little temple, on the top of which is a beautiful statue of Apollo. Gold here commands a premium of twelve per cent. at the present time. Speculating in gold is, however, unlawful, it being regarded as calculated to depreciate the paper money of the country and thus injure its financial standing. In the passage-way of this building are two colossal statues in threatening attitude, probably intended to represent the "bulls" and the "bears," though, as business had not commenced when we entered, all present were as quiet as lambs. Two colossal statues of women at another entrance were suggestive of Woodhull and Claflin. The rooms on the four sides of the court have evidently been recently renovated, as even the walls and the caps of the niches of Italian marble seemed entirely new, as did all the furniture and appointments. In various parts of the vestibule quite handsome bulletin-boards, each giving quotations at London, Paris, Vienna, Trieste, etc., were suspended. The floors are laid in white marble, and the rooms all open on the court-yard. An elegant doorway, with marble steps, opens on one of the canals, at which the gondolas land the bankers and money-kings of Venice, whose places of business are generally on the Grand Canal, at some distance from the Bourse. The money-men of Europe generally hide themselves away in some remote corner of the cities, and do not even have out a sign. They evidently know that those who want them must find them, and that money never fears competition. The kings and princes of the Bourse are becoming a more important element in Europe than the kings and princes "born in the purple," and their reign is more enduring. The leading bankers everywhere appeared to be Israelites.

THE GAY GONDOLIER.

After a few days' experience with the gondolier, we are compelled to recognize him as a jovial, good-natured fellow, who does his best to amuse and interest the traveler, and is satisfied with a moderate recognition of his services. The prices are regulated by law, and a party of four is charged, for a gondola with one rower, for the first hour one franc (about twenty cents), and for every subsequent hour a half-franc. If there are two gondoliers, double the price is the legal charge. Strangers usually pay them more than the law prescribes: hence they labor to please and accommodate. An American especially considers the charge as shamefully cheap, and cheerfully disregards its provisions. There are thousands of gondolas always in motion for business or pleasure, and quite a number are kept by private families, which can be seen emerging from the small canals into the Grand Canal as soon as the sun gets behind the lofty houses. These private establishments are compelled to have their craft black, as prescribed by law, but they are usually richly ornamented with plated standards and handsome awnings and cushions. The greatest points of display, however, are the dress of the gondolier and the skill with which he handles the oar. Some of the gondolas present quite a gay appearance when filled with handsome and well-dressed ladies and children. The dress of the private gondoliers is usually white, trimmed with blue, green, or yellow, wearing rich silk sashes of the same color, and a straw hat with flowing ribbon. The dress of all the gondoliers is prescribed by law, but most of the public water Jehus totally disregard its provisions, and seem to select their wearing-apparel from the second-hand-clothes stores.

An innovation has recently been made in the introduction of "omnibus-gondolas," carrying from six to a dozen persons, with three or four gondoliers. The price on these is about five cents per hour for each person. To the outer islands, which are from one to two miles from St. Mark's, at which the bathing-establishments and refreshment-saloons are located, small steamers run hourly, the fare being only about two cents, or ten centimes.

A FIRE-PROOF CITY.

Venice is essentially a fire-proof city from necessity, as there is no room in its narrow streets for the passage of an engine larger than a wheelbarrow, and no water-supply, except such as can be baled with buckets from the canals. The founders and builders of Venice were "wise in their day and generation" when they decreed that as few combustible materials as practicable should be used in the construction of their houses, and that wood should nowhere be used where it was possible to employ stone. With our inflammable houses, Venice would not have existed twelve hundred days instead of twelve hundred years. They decreed that there must be no such thing as "fires," because their plan permitted of no opportunity for extinguishment. The narrowness of the streets, with inflammable houses, would necessarily involve the whole city. There are, of course, fires at times, but they are extinguished with the primitive "machine" called a bucket, and very seldom extend beyond the room in which they originate. Fire-insurance companies are not deemed of much account in Venice, a fact which it would be well for insurance solicitors to remember.

VENICE AS IT IS.

Every one has heard of Venice, and nearly every one has formed some idea from what they have read of the character and peculiarities of this strange old city. Thus it is that every one who comes here for the first time finds that their previously formed ideas are wrong, and that Venice is an entirely different city from that which they expected to find. There is no city in the world which the tourist approaches with more curiosity than he does Venice, and there is probably no city which the great untraveled public more generally desire an opportunity to inspect. We will, therefore, during our present visit, undertake the rather difficult task of endeavoring to make our readers see exactly what we see, and to know Venice as it is, rather than as they imagined it to be. In order to do this it will be necessary to compile a brief sketch of the history of Venice, and how it happened that this city in the sea rose to such greatness and importance.

HISTORY OF VENICE.

When the Roman Empire was destroyed in the sixth century, about twelve hundred years ago, by the barbarians, the inhabitants of Padova, Albino, and Aquileja, on the Italian coast, calling themselves Venetians, had their cities also destroyed by the same hordes. The inhabitants of these towns took refuge in the islands of the lagoons on which Venice now stands, and formed a republic. They soon commenced an active trade with the East, and engaged extensively in commerce. In the year 697 they felt the want of a united government, and elected their first Doge, or President, Pauluccio Anafesto. It was not, however, until the year 819 that Doge Angelo Participazio transported the seat of government from Malamocco to Rialto, near the site of the famous Rialto bridge, and commenced to join the little islands by bridges, thus laying the foundation of the present city. In spite of civil wars, the power of Venice in the following centuries grew rapidly, and her greatness atoned for the stern political cruelties during the epoch of the crusades. In 1204, the Venetian republic, under Doge Henry Dandolo, conquered Constantinople, aided by the French crusaders, which led to the division of the Oriental Empire, and gave to Venice the shores of the Adriatic, and many islands, among which was Candia. During the next hundred years the Venetians kept up bloody wars against the Genoese, and it was not until 1352 that they obtained a complete triumph over their Genoese rivals. During the twelve years preceding 1380 the Italians and Hungarians carried on a fierce war against Venice, and it was finally blockaded by the Genoese for a whole year, when Venice was compelled to surrender unconditionally. When peace was declared, Venice lost all her possessions on the continent, after having been compelled to yield Dalmatia to the King of Hungary. In spite of these disasters, Venice continued to war against her oppressors for the next forty years, and in 1421 reconquered the whole Dalmatian coast, from the Po to Corfu.

Towards the end of the fifteenth century the glory of Venice reached its utmost height, and her population exceeded two hundred thousand souls. She was the centre of the commerce of the world, and was admired and respected by all Europe. Her fall began in the sixteenth century, by the discovery of the new way to India *via* the Cape of Good Hope, when nearly all her commerce passed into the hands of the Portuguese. She continued steadily to decline, until she received her greatest blow from the ascendency which the Turks obtained in Europe and Asia, and between the years 1509 and 1540 lost all her possessions. It was then that Venice lost her importance in history. She remained neutral in the great wars which succeeded, and her power became less and less. At the beginning of the French Revolution she opposed the opinions of the socialists, but when the French were victorious in their wars, Venice tried to maintain a neutral position, declining the alliance of Bonaparte. This irritated him, and he broke the negotiations and occupied the city on the 16th of May, 1797. Under the French government the city became poorer and poorer, and the Venetian population was finally reduced to ninety-six thousand souls. In subsequent wars Venice was given to Austria, and then to Italy, and finally, in 1814, passed again to the possession of Austria.

In 1848 Venice revolted from the Austrians, and proclaimed a republic; but after a heroic defense, and a siege of fifteen months, suffering famine and the other misfortunes of a siege, and the ravages of cholera in its most malignant form, she was compelled to capitulate again to the Austrians. The war of 1859, broken by the peace of Villafranca, left Venice to the Austrians, but the one of 1866 gave her to the kingdom of Italy, in consequence of the united votes of the people, which took place in October of the same year. The city is again prospering under the Italian government, and the people appear to be happy. Perfect religious freedom is enjoyed, and Venice now hopes to go on improving and prospering under the reign of peace.

THE ISLANDS AND CANALS.

Before proceeding further, it will be necessary to convey to the reader some idea of the character of the territory upon which Venice is built. In the first place, it must be borne in mind that the city is built upon one hundred and fourteen little islands, the streams running between them, with the exception of the Grand Canal, being seldom more than twenty feet in width. The tide from the sea rises and falls and flows through these canals, which are to the number of three hundred and forty-one, keeping the water always pure and healthy. Indeed, many of the lateral canals are scarcely more than twelve feet in width. Out of these canals the houses all rise abruptly, and their principal front and entrance always faces the canal, visitors stepping from the boat on to the door-sill. The houses of Venice have no yards, side-alleys, or any vacant ground connected with them. One end is on a canal, and the other on a narrow lane, or perhaps backed up solid against a neighbor's house. The city is "finished," because there is scarcely room left large enough to erect a lime-shed, except on the distant outlying islands. It is compact and solid, with the exception of some small squares or court-yards left near the churches.

THE STREETS OF VENICE.

Those who suppose that Venice cannot be thoroughly explored by the pedestrian without resort to the gondolas and the canals are equally mistaken. It is provided with bridges, most of them very elegant little structures, of white marble or iron, to the enormous number of *three hundred and seventy-eight*. They are all arched bridges, springing up to the centre, so as to afford free passage under them for the gondolas. There is no street, or rather lane or alley, in Venice, which leads to a canal, that is not provided with a bridge, so that those who know how to find their way can make as much speed from point to point as if using a gondola. Both the streets and canals, with the exception of the Grand Canal, are so crooked that one hundred yards ahead can seldom be seen on either; indeed, fifty yards would be nearer the mark. They both turn and twist with equal facility, and it would require a long time for any one to become thoroughly familiar with them. The canals all intersect each other, and thus it becomes necessary to lay out the streets so as to meet the turnings of the canals.

THE PIAZZA OF ST. MARK.

The great central attraction of Venice is St. Mark's Square, and, although it presents an irregular quadrangle, it is undoubtedly the finest square in all the world for the elegant magnificence of surrounding structures. Across the east end of the square the Cathedral of St. Mark stands out as the most prominent feature, with its three domes and numerous steeples. In the left corner of the square, facing the cathedral, stands the Campanile, or bell-tower, which rises to the height of three hundred feet, its base being thirty-eight feet wide, and its width at the top thirty-five feet. The base of this tower is very beautiful, and is finely ornamented with sculpture and statuary. On the south side of the square are the old City Hall and Clock Tower, on the west the Doge's palace, and on the north side the new City Hall and one side of the Old Library. These buildings all, with the exception of the cathedral, stand together in close order and constitute the outlines of the square. The lower story of all forms a continuous colonnade, similar to that around the interior of the Palais Royal at Paris, and like it, also, this story is occupied by stores and cafés on the three sides of the square. The entire square is paved with smooth blocks of granite interspersed with iron pillars, bearing clusters of gasjets, whilst another line of illumination extends along the entire fronts. The buildings fronting the square are all of white marble, four stories high, and adorned with an abundance of statuary. The entire length of the square is five hundred and forty feet, and the width two hundred and forty-six feet, whilst the Piazzetta leading past the palace of the Doges and the Old Library, which is really a portion of the square, is three hundred and eleven feet long by one hundred and forty-six in width, extending down to the water's edge, at the mouth of the Grand Canal.

Directly in front of the cathedral, at the distance of about fifty feet, there stand three flag-staffs, each about one hundred feet in height, the lower part to the height of about ten feet being encased in elaborately ornamented bronze bases. From these three staffs there were suspended on Sunday three immense Italian national flags, each not less than thirty feet in length, which were raised at the commencement and lowered at the termination of the cathedral services for the day.

On the Piazzetta, immediately facing the Grand Canal, are two majestic pillars of Oriental granite, not less in diameter than those before the Pantheon at Rome. These grand columns were brought to Venice in the year 1127 by Doge Michael, who found them lying on an island in the Grecian Archipelago, on his return from the Holy Land. There were originally three of them, but one was lost overboard in debarkation. They lay for forty-four years on their sides, after their arrival, no one being found to undertake the putting of them up. In the year 1371, a man named Niccolò undertook to put them on the bases prepared for them. He was called "barattier" (a man who cheats in gaming), and exacted for his services the privilege of keeping a gaming-table between them. This was allowed for nearly two hundred years, but the permission was rescinded in the year 1529, and the wooden shops were broken up.

On the top of one of these ancient pillars, which doubtless antedate the birth of Christ, is the famous winged lion of St. Mark's Church, which was carried to Paris by Napoleon, and on the other the stone statue of St. Theodore, the ancient spiritual protector of Venice, before he was deposed by St. Mark.

ST. MARK'S ON SUNDAY.

Sunday was an excessively warm day, even in the shade, but in the rays of the sun it was almost beyond human endurance. Whilst strolling through the city, we stopped on every bridge to catch a breath of cool air as it swept up these water-thoroughfares from the Adriatic. Those of the inhabitants whose dwellings faced on the canal could get along very well, but the denizens of the narrow streets had a hard time of it. Many of these streets are so narrow that we found on trial that we could stand in the middle and lay the palms of our hands upon both walls. The people were protruding their heads from the windows of their tall four-story houses, and anxiously waiting for the setting sun and their evening promenade and music in the Square of St. Mark. As early as six o'clock in the evening they commenced to pour in, all classes commingling, and by eight o'clock this vast space, as well as what is called the Piazzetta, or Little Square, running towards the Grand Canal, were thronged to their utmost capacity. Soon after a fine military band took position in the centre of the square, and the grand promenade commenced, whilst thousands were partaking of ice-cream and lemonade, seated at the cafés on the side of the square. The music was kept up until nearly eleven o'clock, when the people slowly, and apparently with great reluctance, commenced to retire to their homes. Along the front of the Doge's palace, and near the Bridge of Sighs, the throng of people remained enjoying the cool air from the sea until after midnight.

No such scene as this Sunday evening gathering in the Square of St. Mark can be seen anywhere else in Europe, the whole space being brilliantly illuminated by hundreds of gas-jets. Of course all the strangers in the city were here also, and the number at this warm season is truly surprising.

During our afternoon stroll we found the interior canals swarming with boys and men swimming, all wearing swimming-clothes, as required by law. They were diving out of their front doors and windows, and off the bridges, like so many amphibious animals, whilst the gondolas were flying along and gliding past them, mostly with parties of ladies taking their evening airing. Tourists, both ladies and gentlemen, traveling in Europe, become familiarized with the sight of half-nude men and boys, and are generally thankful when it is no worse.

THE CRIES OF VENICE.

The street-cries of Venice are very numerous, and the voices of the vendors ring with a peculiar shrillness through the quiet streets. There being neither carts, horses, nor vehicles of any kind in the city, it has none of the usual noises of other communities, but the gondoliers, as they glide along under our window, give out their cries with an earnestness that is at times quite startling. Among others are men carrying demijohns of water, with lime-juice, which they sell at two centimes, or less than half a cent, a glass. Others sell candied fruits, and various articles not usually found in the stores. The cries of these people are of course in Italian, a language peculiarly fitted for shrill but smooth flowing notes.

THE VENICE CANALS.

The Grand Canal winds through the city of Venice, being traced on the map in the shape of the letter S. It varies somewhat, but is probably about one hundred and twenty-five feet in width for most of its length. It has but two bridges across it, the Rialto and the Ponte di Ferro, the first being of stone, and the latter a modern iron structure. The main canal is not navigable for vessels drawing more than six feet of water, except at its immediate mouth. All the commercial business of the city was formerly kept at deep water along the city front east of the Doge's palace, which is in reality the open sea, and the Grand Canal was the favorite location for the palaces of the great men of the nation. Now, however, these old palaces are for the main part given up to business, or are used as hotels. We are now writing in an old palace, and much of the gilded furniture of its day of greatness is scattered through the house. Barges and lighters now pass up the Grand Canal, and load and unload at the doors of what were formerly palaces. In all the other canals nothing larger than a gondola is allowed to enter. Many of these are of course devoted to the business of carrying, and do the work of our carts and wagons.

STORES OF VENICE.

The jewelry and fancy stores which surround the extensive Piazza of St. Mark will compare favorably for their fine display and their stocks of valuable goods with those of Vienna. So also in many of the stores in its narrow thoroughfares leading from the Piazza. All the fine mosaics of Italy, including the Florentine, Roman, and Byzantine, as well as corals and diamonds, can be purchased in Venice as cheap as anywhere else in Europe, provided the purchaser will bear in mind that the first price named is always fully one-third more than they will be willing to sell at. The best plan is to select what you want, ascertain the price, and then offer one-third less. You will then be told that if you pay in gold you can have them at this "ruinous rate." Put on your hat and propose to leave, and Italian paper money, which is twenty-two per cent. below gold, will be accepted. They make it a rule never to allow a purchaser to leave their establishments. In some of these narrow thoroughfares, where more than three persons would find it difficult to walk abreast, there are also many very fine dry-goods establishments, grocery and furniture stores, but the majority of them are for the sale of provisions and fruits, coffee, or confectionery, or are beer-saloons. There are here, as elsewhere on the Continent, very few places where intoxicating liquors can be had,—no gin-palaces or rum-shops. Indeed, beer and wine are not drunk to any great extent in public, and beer can only be had at the restaurants where meals are furnished. The principal thoroughfares were thronged on Sunday with people of all classes, and many ladies were passing and repassing on their way to and from church with veils over their heads, a lady never going to church in Venice with a bonnet on. On their way home they would stop to do their shopping, and then move on.

FEEDING THE PIGEONS.

The pigeons of Venice, of which there are thousands, have not only the freedom of the city, but are fed at two o'clock every afternoon in the Square of St. Mark at the public expense. They are the pets of the people, and to injure or throw a stone at one of them would cause the perpetrator to be sent to the guard-house. They not only make their nests among the statuary and the ornamental portions of St. Mark's Cathedral and the eaves of the elegant structures surrounding the square, but the windows of the lofts of these buildings are left open and free access is given to them. Thus they have multiplied to many thousands, and have scattered all over the city, making their nests among the statuary of all the old churches.

At two o'clock yesterday afternoon we repaired to the square to witness the process of feeding. At the moment the bronze man on the town-clock struck the first blow announcing two o'clock, they came in by thousands, and swept up the square towards the window from which they are daily fed, and hundreds of them even entered the room. The man who does the feeding was entirely hidden from view, and the scramble of the birds indicated that the strongest fared best. A few minutes before the window was opened a boy placed a little paper of corn in the hands of one of our party. On throwing some of it on the pavement, the pigeons literally swarmed over us, and partook of the food from our hands.

As to the meaning of this care for the pigeons, there is no settled theory. It is said by some that on one occasion during the Venetian wars, whilst Admiral Dandolo was besieging Candia, at the commencement of the thirteenth century, a carrier-pigeon brought him important information from the islands. It has been a custom for centuries thus to feed them, and the old chroniclers differ as to its origin. One says that on Palm-Sunday it was the custom to loose pigeons, many of which repaired for shelter to St. Mark's, and, multiplying with time, they remained around the square as the best place for obtaining food. The practice of maintaining pigeons at public expense is very general in Russia and Persia, as well as among the Arabs, and the custom might easily have been carried thither by Venetian merchants. Other authors assert that, although the city is credited with feeding the pigeons, they are in reality fed and cared for by the liberality of an old lady, who left a large amount to be expended for this purpose. The stained and blackened condition of the marble structures on this square is in a great measure due to the pigeons.

VENICE, July 10, 1873.

THE SURROUNDINGS OF VENICE.

The population of Venice is now one hundred and thirty-seven thousand, it having largely increased and improved since it passed out of the hands of Austria and became a part of the dominion of Italy under Victor Emmanuel. It is only separated from the mainland of Italy by a swamp or lagoon, the depth of the water between the nearest of the islands and the shore being only from two to five or six feet, mainly covered with reeds and water-plants. The outer of the islands, comprising Venice, has a bridge nearly two miles in length (twelve thousand feet) and thirty feet in breadth, which crosses the lagoon over which the Lombardo-Venetian Railroad run their cars to the depot in Venice. This bridge is formed of two large earthworks, one in Venice and the other on the mainland, five expansions, of which a large one is in the middle, as well as two hundred and twenty-two arches, with one hundred and eighty isolated and thirty-six united pillars of Italian marble. The traveler arriving at Venice from Italy or France is thus landed in the city. On the seaward side of the one hundred and fourteen little islands which comprise the heart of Venice there are about twenty other islands, too distant to be united by bridges, which also constitute part of Venice. The principal of these islands are called Giudecca, San Giorgio Maggiore, San Servilio, San Lazzaro, San Vecchio, Lido, San Andrea, La Certosa, Santa Elena, San Clemente, La Grazia, San Spirito, Poveglia, Malamocco, Sotto Marino, San Michele, Murano, Mazzorbo, Burano, and Tonello.

La Giudecca is divided from the city by a broad canal, and is itself subdivided by seven small canals, bridged as are those of Venice, and is really eight small islands. It has three thousand inhabitants, and two of the finest and largest churches of the city are located here, as well as a number of the most elegant palaces, it having been the favorite resort of the nobility. On this island are the brick-yards which furnish Venice. The greatest Church festival of the year takes place at the Church del Redentore, on which occasion it is united to the mainland by two temporary bridges of boats. The principal festivities of the day usually take place in the evening, on the water, when a multitude of gondolas, all decorated with flowers and colored lamps, pass and repass from shore to shore. The people feast and sing, and every hour swells the mirth of a naturally joyous race, the festivities lasting until the dawn of day.

San Giorgio Maggiore is opposite the Doge's palace, a separate island, on which is now located the custom-house, though it was until the year 1806 in the possession of the Benedictine monks. The finest church in the city, that of San Giorgio, is on this island, facing the mouth of the Grand Canal. Another of these islands, San Servilio, is occupied by an insane asylum and a hospital for chronic diseases. San Lazzaro is used as a hospital for the leprous. San Vecchio, at the mouth of the harbor, contains the lazaretto. Lido is the fortification, and has on it extensive facilities for sea-bathing. Other of these islands have on them the navy-yards, powder-mills and magazines, barracks for troops, etc. Others are cultivated as kitchen-gardens, from which a supply of vegetables is obtained for the city, and others are used for sea-bathing and summer resorts, which are reached from the Piazzetta hourly by steamers. All of these islands are within a mile from St. Mark's, and most of them are not five hundred yards distant from what may be regarded as the mainland of Venice. They all have some population, ranging from a few hundred to a few thousand, but are only accessible by water.

Chioggia, which consists of ten small islands, with a population of thirty thousand, mostly fishermen and sailors, is a second Venice. It is connected with the Lido of Brondolo by means of a bridge two thousand five hundred feet long, on fifty-three piers, and is thus accessible from the mainland on foot. San Michele is the burial-place of all the Catholics of Venice. The burial-place of the Protestants is now at the eastern end of this island. The island of Murano has a population of five thousand, whose principal means of livelihood is the manufacture of glass, etc. The mirrors and glass-ware of Bohemia, France, and England have so excelled them that the manufacture of mirrors has been abandoned, and a specialty is now made of the manufacture of glass beads. There are at Murano a fine cathedral and several famous churches.

ST. MARK'S CATHEDRAL.

This great central attraction of Venice no one would expect to find, with its adjoining spacious square, in a city of such peculiar characteristics. The cathedral stands at the head of the square, with a front of one hundred and fifty-six feet. It is divided into five arches, and has five entrances. Its length is two hundred and forty-one feet, and the width at the cross one hundred and eighty-eight feet. The style of architecture is Byzantine. It was built some six hundred years ago, and the columns that have been used, from their varied styles and colors, are believed to have been taken from the most ancient edifices of Greece, and from the destroyed cities of Erachea and Altino. Standing in the centre of the square and looking at it, three domes and about a dozen small steeples are visible rising above its roof. The five lofty arches over the doorways each form a half-dome, the ceilings of which are ornamented with mosaic representations of the embarkation of the body of St. Mark in Alexandria and its debarkation at Venice, with other incidents connected with the life of this patron saint of Venice. The central arch has a plain blue field, with stars, executed in mosaic. Over the doorway in the centre are the four famous bronze horses, which once ornamented Nero's triumphal arch. They were stolen by Constantine the Great, and carried to Constantinople, just one thousand years ago. When the crusaders took Constantinople, in 1205, the horses were brought to Venice by one Marino Zeno, and placed in their present position. When Napoleon I. took Venice, in the year 1797, they were again stolen and sent to Paris. In 1815 the Emperor Francis the First caused them to be sent back to Venice, where they were replaced in their former and present position. They are thus historical horses, and, although not rampant, are fine specimens of the animal, and, by the way, the only horses in Venice.

INTERIOR OF THE CATHEDRAL.

The interior of the cathedral is wonderful for the richness and profusion of its Oriental marble, and for its carvings, both of the ancient and middle ages and its bronzes and mosaics, from the tenth to the eighteenth century. Even the form and style of this ancient church are taken from the Church of the Mother of God, in Constantinople. The interiors of the large and small domes are also brilliant with mosaics, as also the hundreds of niches in the walls, each representing some event in Scripture history. The interior is one mass of mosaics, executed from the cartoons of the greatest painters of past ages. Everything in the interior is on a grand scale. The high altar is especially imposing. The tabernacle and the semicircular arches are supported by four columns of Greek marble, covered all over with bas-reliefs, a work of the fourteenth century. There are six small marble figures upon the frame of the tribune. Behind the altar, sustained by marble bases, is the famous golden altar-piece. It is a wonderful and very rich piece of workmanship, studded with pearls and precious stones, measuring eleven feet in breadth and five and a half feet in height. It has the form of a rectangle, divided into two larger horizontal divisions and subdivided into eighty-three smaller ones. The value of the metal and precious stones, not counting the workmanship, is calculated at three millions of pounds sterling. Indeed, there is no better evidence of the great wealth of Venice in past ages than this Cathedral of St. Mark. Church-builders in those days went foraging around the world for pillars and columns and bas-reliefs, and St. Mark's is a museum of remote antiquity as well as of the middle ages. The Museum of St. Mark has many ancient relics, most of which are truly interesting. We regretted, however, to see among them a golden shrine in a silver gilt case, containing, as was indicated, "the blood which issued from an *image* of the cross at Bernit in the year 320."

The Campanile, or bell-tower, stands in front of the left side of the cathedral, and has a highly ornamental base. The first two hundred feet above the base is of brick, and was erected some eight hundred years ago. Above this is a spire, making the whole height of the tower three hundred feet. The width of the tower at the base is thirty-eight feet. In former times there was a scaffold on the side about one hundred and fifty feet from the ground, from which there was an iron cage hanging, in which condemned priests were confined. Bread and water were lowered to them by a string. This shameful punishment was totally abolished in the year 1750, at least so we are informed by the chronicler of Venice, and the platform and cage were removed. The tower contains a clock and a fine chime of bells, and can be ascended, by those who have ambition in that way, as far as the bells.

THE FEMALE WATER-CARRIERS.

Venice is poorly supplied with water for drinking and cooking purposes. The entire supply is from wells, the water being obtained by lowering buckets with a rope. The supply being very small, the wells are only opened at certain hours during the day, after which they are closed and locked by the authorities. During the time they are opened it is necessary that every one should procure a supply sufficient to last until they are open again. This has led to the employment of female water-carriers, who have with them ropes and two copper buckets. The two buckets being filled, they suspend them on the ends of a hickory rod, curved to fit the shoulders, and during the times the wells are open they can be seen flying in every direction with their buckets, furnishing their customers with their supply. Among them are many very handsome girls, and they seem, notwithstanding their heavy labor, a light-hearted and jovial class.

THE GHETTO, OR JEWS' QUARTER.

Entering a gondola this afternoon, we requested to be taken to the Ghetto, or Jews' quarter of the city, and were landed near the mouth of a large canal, which intersects with the Grand Canal near the Academy of Fine Arts. We had scarcely landed when we were taken charge of by two men and a throng of barefooted and almost bare-backed boys, who led us into a covered court, when they informed us this was the entrance to the famous Ghetto. Here was pointed out to us a marble tablet, which was inserted there centuries ago, forbidding any converted Jew from ever passing or entering that quarter of the city. So soon as we entered the court-yard, a crowd of old women, men, and boys surrounded us, begging for money. We scattered around some change among a few of the oldest of them, which brought a new supply of supplicants, from whom we escaped by entering one of the synagogues near the entrance, which was fitted up in the most costly manner, in strange contrast to the squalid poverty by which it was surrounded. From thence we passed down through the street, the houses on either side of which were eight stories high, and finally entered a broad court-yard, at one end of which was a building devoted to manufacturing rugs and carpets, established to give employment to the poor of that quarter. Here men, women, and boys were at work. This court extends down to a canal, over which is an iron bridge, which, before the French occupation in 1808, had a gate that was closed by the authorities at sundown, and there was a similar gate at the entrance of the quarter. It appears that Bonaparte suspended this cruel edict, and gave them the same liberty as other citizens, which is recorded on a block of marble at the foot of a flag-staff in the centre of the court-yard, alongside of which is a larger tablet recording the granting of liberty and equality by Victor Emmanuel in 1858. On returning, the crowd of beggars had been reinforced, and our voluntary guides had increased to a half-dozen. We then entered another synagogue, much handsomer than the first, which had been built by a bequest of ninety thousand florins by some wealthy Hebrew. After paying our guides, and emptying our purses among the poor destitute creatures, we were followed to the gondola by another throng of anxious supplicants, and felt that we had a safe deliverance when it glided out into the stream.

We give the account of this visit precisely as it occurred, and hope that it may have the effect of calling the attention of some of our wealthy Israelites to the relief of these poor people. They have got synagogues enough; what they want is bread and meat, or work wherewith to obtain the means of securing it. The whole number of Jews in Venice is less than four thousand, and they have eleven synagogues, but no bread at the Ghetto. The wealthy Israelites of Venice are, it appears, Germans, who have no sympathy or affiliation with the Italian Jews who occupy the Ghetto. There was no mistaking the fact that these people were in want. There were among them old men and women who seemed to be tottering to the grave, whose anxious countenances betokened that they were really suffering for food.

THE BRIDGE OF SIGHS.

There is nothing which the stranger visiting Venice looks to with more interest than the Bridge of Sighs, which Lord Byron has made famous in the fourth canto of Childe Harold. As some of our readers have not seen photographs of it, we will endeavor to make them see it as we saw it. Let them suppose that the Baltimore Court-House is the Doge's palace, and that the St. Clair Hotel is the prison of Venice, whilst Court-House Lane is a canal. Having mastered this idea of location, let them imagine a beautiful covered white marble arched bridge, springing from the second-story window of the hotel over to the wall of Judge Dobbin's court-room. This bridge is open sculptured work, highly ornamented. It is closed at the top and sides, the light entering through this open-work. The court-house being in the Doge's palace, this bridge was used to convey prisoners back and forth for trial. The interior of the bridge is divided into two passages, each with its own means of ingress and egress, and entirely independent of one another. By these passages, thus connecting the prison and the palace, the accused were brought before their judges without causing public disturbance, it being thirty-three feet above the canal. The name, the "Bridge of Sighs," is one of those expressive appellations so common in Italy, and, it is asserted, has no reference to the administrative system of the old republic. It was built at the end of the sixteenth century, and the chroniclers of Venice protest that it was never used except for criminal prisoners and common offenders, awaiting their generally merited fate. Hence Byron is accused of using a poetical license unwarranted by the facts in his reference to the structure. A bridge crosses the canal just below, and another just above, the Doge's palace, from which a fine view of the Bridge of Sighs can be obtained, whilst the gondoliers generally take their customers through the canal under it. It has been immortalized by Byron in the fourth canto of Childe Harold, thus:

"I stood in Venice, on the Bridge of Sighs,
A palace and a prison on each hand;
I saw from out the waves her structures rise
As from the stroke of some enchanter's wand.
A thousand years their cloudy wings expand
Around me, and a dying glory smiles
O'er the far times when many a subject-land
Looked to the winged islands' marble piles,
Where Venice sat in state, throned on her hundred isles."

A REMARKABLE CITY.

The stranger who has never visited Venice is apt to regard it as a city of ruins, a great city that has gone to decay. But a few days' sojourn will satisfy him that Venice is still a great and remarkable city. Its palaces and churches are old, but they are built of enduring stone that will last forever. They are stained with the dust of ages, but stand as firm on their watery foundations as if built but yesterday, and most of them, as specimens of architecture, will compare favorably with the best productions of the present day. Some of the old palaces on the Grand Canal show that they were built regardless of expense, and the churches were reared apparently as specimens of the architectural rivalry which prevailed at the time of their construction. Expense appears to have been no consideration, and we find few churches at the present day in the construction of which there has been such lavish expenditure. If it were not for the pride of antiquity which prevails in all these old countries, and that the stains and cobwebs of age are regarded as adding to the attractions of architecture, Venice might, with a little rubbing and scrubbing, be made a very beautiful city. In order that the reader may fully understand this, it will be necessary to give some idea of the character of these buildings.

THE CHURCHES OF VENICE.

In what we have described as the heart of Venice there are precisely one hundred Catholic churches, besides the great Cathedral of St. Mark. Each and all of these churches have in front of them a small court-yard, most of them not more than from sixty to one hundred feet square, in the centre of which is a well. These court-yards are mainly to allow a full view of the architecture of the front of the buildings, and of the statuary with which they are so extensively ornamented. There are no plain churches, and no two of them that resemble one another in their style or ornamentation. There are more churches here than at Rome, and the ornamentation and embellishment of them are more elaborate and expensive. It would be difficult to say why they are so numerous, or how they are all maintained. In one section of the city there are six of these large churches within five minutes' walk, and several of them so close that even in this closely-packed city the spires of most of them can be seen from one stand-point. They are the Churches of San Andrea, the Visitation, Gesuiti, the Holy Spirit, Santa Eufemia, and the Redeemer. The most of them were built about three hundred years ago, the present generation or their predecessors having had nothing in this line left for them to do. To build a church in Venice at the present day would be the supreme of folly. We find service generally progressing in them, and seldom more than a dozen old persons present and participating.

The interiors of all these churches are

well supplied with paintings and statuary, and some of their altars are rich in rare stones and sparkling gems. It may seem singular how foundations could be obtained for these massive buildings, many of which border on the canals; but this may be explained by an account of the building of the Church of Our Lady, which says, "The foundation-stone was laid in 1631, and one million two hundred thousand piles were used to make its foundations." An account of the construction of the Rialto bridge says that "it rests upon twelve thousand piles of elm."

But, independent of these one hundred churches in the heart of the city, there are fully forty more on the outer islands, most of which will vie in architectural grandeur with the best of them. Indeed, several of the finest churches of Venice are on these islands. There are also numerous monasteries and nunneries, but most of them have their large establishments on the contiguous islands.

The number of priests connected with the churches of Venice exceeds one thousand, being about one for every twenty inhabitants. We notice this fact, that if there is a scarcity of them in any part of the world, it would be an act of charity to relieve suffering Venice.

THE VENETIAN PALACES.

The whole number of old palaces reaches nearly one hundred and fifty in all the islands, of which one hundred and three are mostly on the Grand Canal and in the central part of the city. They are called by the names of their founders, and many of them are still in the possession of and occupied by their impoverished descendants. Some of them have old painting-galleries, museums of antiquities, etc., which are exhibited for a small fee to the curious. Many of the others stand in silent grandeur, apparently empty; whilst others are converted into storehouses or made use of as public buildings. From a list of these palaces I extract the following curious note appended to the account of Palazzo Giustiniani: "The Giustiniani family is said to have descended from Justinian, Emperor of Constantinople. This noble family was, in the year 1160, near being extinguished, all the males having died in the battle against Emanuel Comneno. In order to maintain it, one Niccolò Giustiniani was taken out of a monastery, and, having been absolved from the vow of chastity, married the daughter of Doge Vitalmichiel II., and, after having had offspring, and thus secured the succession, re-entered the cloister." So it will be seen that Père Hyacinthe is not the first married priest who has had an offspring christened. It also appears that the title of nobility in old Venice was a merchantable commodity, and that the price to be paid for it was one hundred thousand ducats. Quite a number of the founders of these palaces are recorded as having thus purchased their honors, having contributed to the state one hundred thousand ducats when they were "elevated to the Venetian nobility." In our day the having a bank-account of a few hundred thousand ducats gives a man all the eminence in social life that he may desire.

THE RIALTO BRIDGE.

Every one who has perused the old Italian romances has heard of the Rialto, the famous stone bridge of Venice, which has been also invested by Byron with a romantic interest. It is a massive stone structure, spanning the Grand Canal, being neither suggestive of poetry nor romance. Considering that it was built three hundred years ago, and is still as ponderous and solid as it was when the last stone was laid, it is well worthy of inspection as a sample of the durable work of that age. It is about one hundred feet long, consisting of a single arch, and seventy feet broad. There being no vehicles or horses in Venice, it is simply for pedestrians, and is divided into three parts, the centre having the greatest breadth, and is lined with stores or booths built of stone along its entire length. These booths are in reality a part of the bridge, there being clear footways on each side as well as between them in the centre of the bridge, its great width furnishing ample room. The height of the arch above the water is twenty-two feet, and to the top of the balustrade about thirty-two feet. It is in reality a bridge with houses on it, and is always thronged with pedestrians passing and repassing or stopping at the booths. The Rialto always presents a lively aspect, especially in the morning, as the approaches to it on both sides of the canal are used as a market-place for the sale of vegetables and fruits. As we passed under it in a gondola yesterday we were startled by seeing several swimmers jump from the balustrade into the water, a crowd being assembled on the banks of the canal to witness the feat. The abutments of the arch are built out in the water about fifteen feet from the edge of the canal on either side, and the rise to the bridge is made by a succession of about one dozen long and massive stone steps built into the abutments.

VENICE BY GAS-LIGHT.

Last evening we made a general round through the Grand Canal, to see Venice by gas-light. The gondolier, as we moved slowly along the Grand Canal, called out the names of the palaces we were passing, most of which seemed to be deserted. They were broad and massive stone and marble buildings from four to five stories in height, stained and blackened by the hand of time. We passed in our trip of two miles nearly fifty of these structures, none of which had been erected less than three hundred years. The impression constantly forced upon us in this trip was that we were sailing through the streets of a flooded city, and the vision of Harrison Street on several memorable occasions when Jones's Falls was not in an amiable mood rose to the imagination. Many of the gondolas exhibited lights, whilst the lights from the houses and the city gas-lamps tended to give life and animation to the scene. At most of the openings of the streets the splash made by the boys who were diving into the canal and swimming could be heard. It may fairly be presumed that in so finely a watered city the children take to water like young ducks.

Returning from our trip about nine o'clock in the evening, our gondolier brought us back through the narrow canals, passing through the heart of the city, and under dozens of bridges, over which the people were moving to and fro. The houses all loomed up five stories above us, in which could be heard the sound of pianos, and, with the exception of the openings where the bridges crossed, it was one unbroken line of stone and mortar. We passed a large number of gondoliers in this part of our excursion, and it seemed strange that in so narrow a channel there were no collisions. The shouts of a gondolier on turning a corner are peculiar, and most necessary in such darkness, viz., *gia è*, a boat ahead; *preme*, pass to the right; *sta li*, pass to the left, etc.

THE LADIES OF VENICE.

The better class of ladies of Venice dress with considerable taste, mostly in light gossamer material, and in the evening a large number are visiting the stores, or reclining with their children and friends in their gondolas on the Grand Canal.

The great evening resort is an island called Toledo, to the left of the city, on which bath-houses are in successful operation, and sea-bathing is enjoyed to its fullest extent. Two steamers make hourly trips to Toledo during the afternoon. On the streets the ladies are remarkable for their grace and dignity of carriage, and our female critics pronounce them decidedly handsome. The water-girls and the flower-girls are also a feature of Venice. The former supply customers with water carried in copper buckets from the artesian wells. What is singular, most of the former are decidedly good-looking, and always wear a cheerful countenance and seem overflowing with vivacity. The flower-girls are handsome and modest in deportment, and all do a thriving business.

THEATRES OF VENICE.

Venice has no less than seven theatres, all of them quite fine establishments, though not so large as with us. The theatre La Fenice is one of the most elegant little establishments conceivable. It is quite aged, having been in use more than a hundred years. Four of them are now open, and giving nightly performances to crowded houses.

We must not omit to mention that in our wanderings yesterday we found that Venice has a very elegant botanical garden, covering five or six acres of ground, whose beautiful and interesting avenues are but little visited. What here more particularly attracts northern visitors is the growth of small European shrubs to a great height. The plants are mostly exotics, and between the avenues of the trees the vacant ground is devoted to various scientific objects. The number of the different species of plants is more than seven thousand. There is the greatest collection of cacti in the garden to be found anywhere in the world, some of them from fourteen to twenty-four feet high.

Venice also has an academy of fine arts, containing over seven hundred fine paintings, mostly of the Venetian school. These paintings are principally those that have been brought hither after the demolition and devotion of churches to other objects. These have been enlarged by considerable gifts and purchases, until it is now a richly-stocked gallery, filling twenty separate halls.

VENICE FICTIONS.

The guides here point out the old palace now occupied as the New York Hotel as having been the veritable house of Desdemona, from whence she eloped with the tawny Moor. The house of the Moor is also said to be still standing, as well as that of Iago. The same entertaining gondoliers point out the residence of Shylock, who was so terribly hard on the Merchant of Venice. As these characters are all fictitious, it is about as well that the fiction should continue. At Verona they go so far towards verifying the truth of Shakspeare's Romeo and Juliet as to point out the balcony on which the fair Juliet listened to the wooing of Romeo, and, to make the matter more certain, carry their visitors to the grave of Juliet.

LOVE OF MUSIC.

In the evening, whilst floating quietly down the canals of Venice, the ear is frequently startled by the sounds of most skillfully-executed music on the piano, accompanied at times by female voices of great volume and sweetness. The sounds would come from the window of a building, the outside appearance of which would be suggestive of anything but refinement. Occasionally, from a balcony high up on these bleak and desolate-looking walls, ladies would be sitting, warbling operatic airs, and the sound of merriment and song amid the stillness of the night, undisturbed by the rattling of wheels and the clatter of hoofs or the ordinary street noises, was peculiarly distinct and pleasing. So also in strolling through the narrowest of the streets, there seemed to be a piano in every house, and, judging from the sounds, were being manipulated by skillful hands. The gondoliers of the Grand Canal, all of whom have good voices, are frequently heard at night warbling Italian melodies, whilst many musical associations go about at night serenading. On the three evenings of the week when the military bands appear on the Piazza of St. Mark, the whole population turn out, and the attendance usually ranges from ten to fifteen thousand. Aquatic parties also frequently charter one of the small steamers, and with a band of music. accompanied by voices, cruise about in front of the Doge's palace and along the city front.

GOOD-BY, VENICE.

We leave Venice to-night, after spending several days very pleasantly within its water-bound walls. Whether we have succeeded in giving our readers any idea of what Venice really is, we shall probably never know, but we hope that all will have a better appreciation of the place than heretofore. We would, however, advise all to see Venice for themselves, when opportunity serves.

VERONA AND ITS ROMANCE.

VERONA, ITALY, July 28, 1873.

We left Venice, the city of extensive water-privileges, yesterday afternoon, and although we had no dust to shake from our feet, we did endeavor to leave behind as many of the animated atoms as possible which had so greatly annoyed us during our sojourn. It was there that the Merchant of Venice coined his wealth, and the remorseless Shylock demanded his pound of flesh, and there that the gentle Jessica slipped out the front door and glided off with her lover in his gay gondola. Well, whatever may be said of the others, we think she did right, especially if she was compelled to live in the Ghetto, the Jews' quarter, which was undoubtedly a good place to run from.

ROMEO AND JULIET.

We reached Verona, the reputed home of Shakspeare's Two Gentlemen of Verona, as we all know it to have been the native town of the gentle Juliet and her loving Romeo. Here are the tombs of the Capulets and Montagues, and in the garden of the Orfanotrofio is the tomb of Juliet. It, however, does but little justice to her memory, and the government proposes to erect a more suitable monument to the fair heroine, over whose trials and tribulations and sad death the world will con inue to shed tears until the end of time. It has been proven by a strict inquiry into the history of Verona that all the circumstances, characters, and incidents of the story were faithfully retained by Shakspeare in writing his great play, and that Juliet was indeed most beautiful, fully warranting the exclamation of Romeo, when, looking up to her balcony, the counterpart of which every house in town seems to be provided with, he exclaimed:

"But, soft! what light through yonder window
  breaks?
It is the east, and Juliet is the sun!
Arise, fair sun, and kill the envious moon,
Who is already sick and pale with grief
That thou her maid art far more fair than she. . .
Two of the fairest stars in all the heaven,
Having some business, do entreat her eyes
To twinkle in their spheres till they return.

"What if her eyes were there, they in her head?
The brightness of her cheek would shame those stars,
As daylight doth a lamp; her eye in heaven
Would through the airy region stream so bright,
That birds would sing, and think it were not night."

The narrow but lofty house of Juliet's parents, in the street of San Sebastiano, now a tavern, still bears the hat over the entrance to the court, which was the distinctive emblem in the armorial bearings of the family, and the memorable veranda under which Romeo poured into the willing ear of Juliet his passion, and the balustrade over which the lovely Juliet plighted her troth, are still preserved. Verona appears to have been famous for its development of the tender passion, for here it was that the Roman poet Catullus, eighty-six years before the birth of Christ, in speaking of his Lesbia and how many of her kisses would satisfy him, declared "that he desired as many as there were grains of sand in the desert of Libya and stars in the heavens." What wonder, then, that such a town should have produced a Romeo and a Juliet fifteen hundred years after?

THE CITY OF VERONA.

Verona has a population of about seventy thousand. The rapid-running river Adige flows directly through the town, the flow of the current being sufficient to drive the wheels of large numbers of floating grist-mills anchored in the stream. It is distinguished as one of the most industrious cities of Italy, its people being largely engaged in the weaving of silk, linen, and woolen fabrics. The climate is healthy, but a little keen in winter, on account of its near approach to the Alps.

ROMAN AMPHITHEATRE.

We were surprised to find in Verona so many and such perfect specimens of old Roman architecture. One of the most important objects of interest which first attracts the attention of the stranger, and is the great glory of Verona, are the ruins of the old Roman amphitheatre, which stands in the centre of the city. It is almost equal in size, and in a far better state of preservation, than the Coliseum at Rome, being regarded as the finest specimen now in existence of Roman architecture. It presents a most imposing appearance, the interior having suffered but little, owing to the great care that has been taken to preserve it, though most of the outer circle of the arches were nearly all destroyed by an earthquake some six hundred years ago. The height of the building when perfect exceeded one hundred and twenty feet. It is elliptical in form, the extreme length of its diameters to the outer walls being five hundred and ten and five hundred and twelve feet. The corridors, stairs, and stone seats are in a remarkable state of preservation. There are forty successive tiers of granite seats, each row being eighteen inches high and the same in breadth, the whole number being equal to the accommodation of twenty-five thousand persons. There is no authentic information as to the founders of this great work, though it is supposed to have been built between the reigns of Titus and Trajan. It was used for the exhibition of shows and sports in the middle ages, and sometimes as an arena for judicial combats. A wooden theatre is now erected in the arena, and the arches of the old building are rented out for stores by the city.

There are various other monuments of antiquity in Verona deserving of notice, in a fine state of preservation. The ancient double gallery, composed of marble, built under Gallienus, in memory of whom it is named, stands surviving the abrasion of the weather, its walls now, after sixteen hundred years of exposure, being as perfect as if erected yesterday.

The fortifications of Verona are most extensive, and surround the whole city, as well as frown from the top of every hill. They are attributed to Charlemagne. The locality has been the scene of many severe battles in both ancient and modern times, and the city has been alternately in the possession of the Austrians, French, and Italians. Like all the rest of Italy, it has vastly improved under the reign of Victor Emmanuel.

CHURCHES AND CATHEDRALS.

We have visited most of the old churches and cathedrals of Italy, but have alluded to but very few of them in these letters. They are interesting as showing how the people have been starved and impoverished to build and ornament vast structures, most of which were neither needed for the worship of God nor the service of man. Most of them are in a dilapidated condition, which gives promise that the age for such needless expenditure has nearly passed. But few of them have been constructed within the past three hundred years, with the exception of St. Paul's outside the walls of Rome, which has been restored since its destruction by fire, in 1823, on a scale of grandeur that when completed promises to eclipse St. Peter's. It is located a mile and a half outside of the walls of Rome, in the midst of a sparsely-settled country, and is only attended by a few strolling peasants. Once a year it is visited by the Pope in great state, and the balance of the year is devoted to making preparations for the great occasion by the colony of clergymen who are here quartered. This church has cost more money than all the churches of Baltimore combined, including the cathedral, one altar and chapel alone in it having cost ten millions of dollars. The money for its construction and ornamentation has been charged to the "Peter's pence" fund. It is an attempt to re-establish the magnificent folly of an age that is past and gone, and which, now that Rome belongs to free Italy, will never return. It may be deemed heretical to say so, but it seems to us that they have been erected and ornamented more for the glory of their founders than the worship of God, and that the same amount of labor and treasure expended in the education and improvement of the people would have been more acceptable and praiseworthy.

THE ALPS.

We are making haste to get under the shadow of the Alps, and hence make a brief stay at Verona, intending to stop at Milan to-night.

MILAN.

THE FINEST CITY IN ITALY.

MILAN, July 29, 1873.

We arrived here last evening after a warm ride from Verona, passing through a most beautiful and interesting country on our route. The numerous towns and cities we found as usual extensively fortified, and the view from the cars was most picturesque and attractive. Along the road from Brescia to Mantua, a distance of fifteen miles, we passed the field upon which the battle of Solferino was fought, which is as level as one of our Western prairies. We also had a fine view of the magnificent Lake of Garda, which is thirty-seven miles in length, and at one point fourteen miles in width, having a depth in some places of one thousand feet. The greater part of this fine sheet of water lies within the kingdom of Italy, the northern extremity only belonging to Austria.

The whole distance from Verona to Milan, one hundred miles, presents a scene of the most luxuriant vegetation to be found anywhere in the world, and the cultivation of the soil is most thorough and systematic. A great deal of it is irrigated from the Mincio, a rapid-running stream of clear and sparkling water. The grape, corn, and grasses are the principal products.

CITY OF MILAN.

As we progress northward, the appearances of Italian cities undergo a change, and, instead of the narrow streets of Southern Italy, we have at Milan broad, well-ventilated thoroughfares, and evidently a higher state of civilization and progress among the people. Milan is undoubtedly one of the very finest cities in Italy, and indeed there are few cities in any country that can excel it in appearance and attractiveness. Like most ancient cities, it is very irregularly laid out, but it is one of the most interesting in Europe, full of activity and wealth. It has some noble thoroughfares, and is rapidly improving, the buildings going up in its suburbs being of a very superior class to the old sections of the city. It is a walled city, but the interior side of the wall is laid out with gardens and planted with trees, an arrangement which surrounds the whole city with a park.

MILAN ON SUNDAY.

Sunday in Milan is a good day to see the city and its people. As is the case in all Catholic countries, the day is observed both as a day of worship and of pleasure-seeking. Before twelve o'clock everybody is intent on their religious duties, and after that hour the pursuit of recreation and pleasure is the universal rule. The thousands of cafés were in full blast, each surrounded by as many customers as could be furnished with seats and tables to partake of their refreshments. Gentlemen with their wives and families could be seen everywhere in festive gatherings, partaking of creams, lemonade, and in some cases beer and wine. Carriages were driving to and fro thronged with ladies and children, and the omnibuses were packed to their utmost capacity. The public grounds around the city were filled with people, and here the cafés were supplying them with refreshments. Good order and quiet were, however, observable everywhere until midnight, when there was a simultaneous outbreak of noisy revelers all over the city, and for an hour or more the singing of songs, with stirring choruses, resounded in every direction.

CATHEDRAL OF MILAN.

Every stranger who comes to Milan of course desires to see the world-renowned cathedral, the dome and spires of which are the first things visible in approaching from any direction. It certainly is a most wonderful structure, and if its architects desired to leave a building that will never be excelled in its ornamentation, they have, very likely, been successful. It is a perfect forest of marble pinnacles, with life-size statues peeping out from every niche in its walls. Wherever you cast your eye on any part of the exterior walls, your gaze is returned by a throng of those "stone men and women" who, Father Barrett protests, are the main production of Italy. The number of these statues is variously estimated by different authors, but they are certainly so numerous that it would be folly to attempt to count them. Dr. S. I. Prime, author of "Travels in Europe and the East," affirms that there are already seven thousand, and places for three thousand more. Murray says four thousand four hundred, which is probably more nearly correct. The central tower and spire is especially beautiful, and, surrounded as it is by a throng of smaller spires, each surmounted by a statue, presents a combination of rare elegance almost impossible to describe. Then the wilderness of tracery in beautiful white marble which surrounds the roof, delicately marked against the sky, gives to the whole structure, large and massive as it is, the appearance of being as light and fragile as if the first gust of heavy wind might be expected to topple it over. The entire length of the cathedral, which is in the form of a Latin cross, is four hundred and ninety feet, breadth one hundred and eighty feet, height to top of the statue three hundred and fifty-four feet, length of the transept two hundred and eighty-four feet, and height of the nave one hundred and fifty-two feet. As a monument of ornamental architecture it will probably stand forever unrivaled, as the taste of the present age does not run in the same direction. The interior of the cathedral is still more grand and imposing than the exterior. Its double aisles and clustered pillars, its lofty arches, the lustre of its walls, its numberless niches filled with noble figures, and its monuments, combine to give a grandeur and solidity to its appearance much more effective than the exterior view. It was commenced over five hundred years ago, and was nearly a century in the course of construction. The scene in the interior, with the morning sun shining through its magnificent stained windows, is most strikingly beautiful. From the roof, looking down on the fine marble tracery and the forest of spires, a better idea is obtained of the vastness of the structure than from any other point. The Alps, with Mont Blanc in the distance, are distinctly visible from this elevated position.

THE STREETS OF MILAN.

All the cities of Europe are considerably ahead of the United States in the paving of streets, but we think that Milan is the best-paved city in Europe. There are no curb-stones, and no gutters, even in streets as broad as say Baltimore Street, all being smooth, from house to house, with a slight depression in the centre, where there are openings, narrow slits, in the stone carriage-way, to allow the rain to pass off into the sewers underneath. The drainage from the houses passes directly into the sewers by pipes, and there is nothing to provide for in the drainage of the streets except rain. The foot-paths next to the houses are about six feet in width, of smooth granite. There are also two lines of granite for the wheels of vehicles to run upon in the centre of the street, by which means an omnibus with two horses can draw as many passengers as a street-railway car, rendering the latter unnecessary in a city so perfectly level as Milan. The balance of the street is paved with small round stones, which are laid in cement, and form an excellent pavement, smooth and solid. The smooth granite blocks, which form the whole bed of the streets in Naples, Florence, and Rome, are very hard upon the horses, almost one-half of which wear leather caps on their knees to protect the knee-joint from damage in case of falling, as they are apt to do if moving with any speed. The pavements of Milan afford excellent footing for the horse, even better than our rough pavements, whilst the wheels glide over them with but little resistance. It is wonderful where so many stones of the right size can be obtained, but they appear as if having been through a sieve, and all rejected that exceed the standard size. If the pavements are crowded, as is constantly the case, people readily step upon them to pass, without the slightest inconvenience. The streets are carefully swept and washed at night, and at daylight there is not a particle of dust or dirt to be seen. This is the case not only in the better parts of the city, but like cleanliness is observable everywhere. Men also go about all day with small handcarts and brooms, carefully sweeping and sprinkling to prevent dust.

THE LADIES OF MILAN.

By visiting the cathedral and the churches at an early hour in the morning we have had a good opportunity to see the ladies of Milan in their simple and elegant attire, the only covering for their heads being light gossamer veils. The younger females are quite handsome, but they evidently lose their beauty at an early period. A handsome elderly or middle-aged lady is seldom seen in Italy, and those that are very old become wrinkled and sallow to an extent that is not seen in any other country. The children, with their large, dark, and piercing eyes, are very handsome, and full of brightness and vivacity. The younger ladies wear their dresses very low in the neck in front, but high up on the shoulders. They have very small feet, and take care to show them.

SHOPPING IN MILAN.

The storekeepers of Milan are very sharp at a bargain, and charge foreigners enormous prices for everything they may purchase. They will, however, on being pushed, readily strike off one-third from the asking price, even though at first they may have told you that they had but one price.

The stores are very elegant, but not as numerous as those of Naples. The Galleria Vittorio Emanuele forms the central point for the traffic of Milan, and is being largely extended and beautified. It is an immense arcade, roofed in with glass, the roof having at the central point of the cross which it forms an elevation of one hundred and eighty feet. The lower story is devoted to fancy and jewelry stores, of which there are fully one hundred and fifty. The building is adorned with twenty-four statues of famous Italians. It is lighted in the evening by two thousand gas-jets, independent of the light from the stores, and presents a gay scene. There are several large cafés in this great establishment for the sale of ices and confectionery, in front of which seats and tables are arranged. The avenues are fifty feet wide, the flooring being of finely-executed mosaics of different colors. There are other arcades in different sections of the city, but none equal to this. The rays of the sun are so fierce here that ladies who are out shopping naturally seek these shaded stores in preference to those upon the open streets.

A VOYAGE ON LAKE COMO.

THE BEAUTIES OF THE LAKE AND ITS SURROUNDINGS.

COLICO, ITALY, July 30, 1873.

We left Milan at nine o'clock this morning, anxious to get to a cooler climate, and at four o'clock reached Colico, at the head of Lake Como, the point of departure for the diligence through the Splügen Pass of the Alps, which are here looming up before us nine thousand feet in mid-air, capped with snow, rapidly melting under the rays of the summer sun.

FAREWELL TO ITALY.

We are by no means sorry that our tour in Italy is completed. There is no country in Europe more replete with interest and instruction to the tourist, but the modern Italians are not a pleasant people to dwell among. They make great claims to refinement and progress in science and the arts, but by so doing they only invite more attention to the degeneracy which has brought them down from the high position attained by their masters. Sydney Smith summed up his experience in Italy by asserting that whilst the old Italians were all Jupiters, the present race were all *jew-peters*. But, adepts as they now are in all their little schemes to take advantage of strangers, they have greatly improved for the better during the past few years. Both the country and its people have improved, and there is every reason to hope that the efforts of Victor Emmanuel to regenerate Italy will be successful. The only drawbacks seem to be the soldiers and the priests. Every fifth man you meet is a soldier, and every twentieth man a priest or a friar. The latter may be all very good people, but there are too many non-producers in the country. The people do not evince any excess of piety on account of this great excess of ecclesiastics, and it is very evident that most of them are better fitted to work in the vineyards on the hills than in the vineyard of the Lord. The soldiers are everywhere, and we must say they are the best-disciplined and the finest-uniformed men of the fighting order that we have yet met with.

FROM MILAN TO COMO.

The railway from Milan to Como traverses a fertile plain, luxuriantly clothed with vineyards, mulberry plantations, and fields of corn, intersected by numerous canals and cuttings for purposes of navigation. The route also passes numerous country residences, and the towns of Monza, Lecco, Bellaggio, Seregno, Canzo, and Camerlata. The old towers, fortresses, and cathedrals, towering up over the luxuriant verdure of the fields, render the view very picturesque. The trains stop at Camerlata, and a diligence conveys passengers to the town of Como, which has over twenty thousand inhabitants. Here was the birthplace of the elder Pliny, and of the experimental philosopher Volta. It consists of but two or three streets, and is about a mile and a half in length, having all the usual peculiarities of Italian towns. The only attraction about it is the old cathedral, which was commenced in 1396 and completed in 1521, said to be one of the best structures in North Italy. Indeed, there are very few churches in Italy that are less than three hundred years old. There are extensive silk-weaving factories at Como.

THE LAKE OF COMO.

We were driven in the diligence direct to the wharf, and soon found ourselves with a number of passengers, some of whom were Americans, on board the steamer Unione, on the famous Lake Como. Everybody who has seen the play of the Lady of Lyons has had impressed upon their mind the idea that Lake Como is the Paradise of Europe; and, whatever it may be as a place of residence, it is certainly magnificent to the eye. The views from every part of this lovely sheet of water constantly charm and startle the beholder. Bulwer makes Claude Melnotte speak of Como, in describing to Pauline his fictitious palace, as "A deep vale, shut out by Alpine hills from the wide world, margined by fruits of gold and whispering myrtles, glassing softer skies, cloudless save with rare and ricate shadows," and his palace "as lifting to eternal heaven its marbled walls from out a glassy bower of coolest foliage musical with birds."

The scene from the deck of the steamer on Lake Como is sublime. The lake is so closely shut in by the surrounding mountains that it is difficult to discover the outlet. On turning the quay of Como, and passing the first promontory, the great beauty of the lake is brought to view, and during the whole trip to Colico, requiring some four hours, the scene is one of almost unbroken beauty and grandeur. Those who speak of the scenery of Lake George or the Hudson as equally picturesque as Lake Como have certainly never seen the latter, especially at this season of the year, when its mountain-sides are clothed with verdure, and many of their tops, seven thousand feet high in the air, are glistening with perpetual snow.

For the first ten or fifteen miles after leaving Como, numerous bright and gay villas of the Milanese aristocracy, surrounded by luxuriant gardens and vineyards, are scattered along the hillsides of the lake, and there are also many hamlets and villages far up the mountainsides. In the forests beyond, the brilliant green of the chestnut and walnut contrasts strongly with the grayish tints of the olive, which to the unaccustomed eye bears a strong resemblance to the willow. The mountain-peaks rise mostly to the height of over seven thousand feet above the surface of the lake, the depth of which, at some points, is over two thousand feet, the water being as clear and beautifully blue as the Bay of Naples. The lake winds and turns among the mountains, and at no time can one see more than half a mile ahead of the boat. Along the lake-shores are a large number of palaces of the royal and aristocratic families of Italy, and various hotels for summer resorts, at which a large number of passengers stop to spend a few days, to escape from the heat of Milan.

The mountain-sides for the whole distance of thirty miles, from Como to Colico, are largely inhabited, and every spot of land is under cultivation. The mountain-sides are terraced, and mostly planted with grapes up to the elevation of over a thousand feet. To the eye, the houses and even villages high up on the precipitous sides of these mountains look as if they would topple over into the lake. The churches and monasteries on the sides of the mountains are very numerous, and can always be recognized by their steeples and belfries. At one point nine could be counted, and not more than two or three hundred cottages within two miles of them. When about half-way up the lake the atmosphere rapidly changed as the snow-clad mountains loomed in the distance. At first shawls and thicker coats were in requisition, but before we reached Colico overcoats, waterproofs, and every sort of wrap we could command, were necessary to comfort,—a rapid change in temperature, when it is remembered that when we left Milan in the morning the thermometer was at ninety. The same evening at Colico, with winter clothing, a fire would have been decidedly comfortable.

BEAUTIES OF THE LAKE.

Lake Como cannot be so described as to do justice to its varied attractions. Its width is not more than three or four miles, and the shore on each side is always visible from the deck of the steamer. The private villas are painted in bright colors, gleaming amid gardens and groves of lemon-, orange-, and citron-trees. Every establishment of any pretension has its fountain, and all have solid granite walls built up out of the water, with water-gates supplied with steps for landing and embarkation. The little steamer Unione glided from side to side of the lake, stopping at the villages, and landing or taking off passengers, giving us full opportunity to view all points of interest. Byron's description of the lake is certainly by no means exaggerated:

"Sublime, but neither bleak nor bare
Nor misty are the mountains there—
Softly sublime—profusely fair;
Up to their summits clothed in green,
And fruitful as the vales between,
They lightly rise,
And scale the skies,
And groves and gardens still abound;
For where no shoot
Could else take root,
The peaks are shelved and terraced round.
Earthward appear, in mingled growth,
The mulberry and maize; above
The trellis'd vine extends to both
The leafy shade they love.
Looks out the white-wall'd cottage here,
The lowly chapel rises near;
Far down the foot must roam to reach
The lovely lake and bending beach;
While chestnut green and olive gray
Checker the steep and winding way."

But, notwithstanding all these romantic surroundings, the people here have a practical turn of mind. The streams which come down from the snow-clad mountains in the rear are availed of for milling-purposes, and there are numerous manufacturing villages on their banks, most of them being for the manufacture of silk. On the eastern shore of the lake a turnpike, with walled bank, frequently tunneling its way through the mountain-spurs, extends the whole distance from Como to Colico, connecting with the Splügen Pass across the Alps. We reached Colico at four o'clock. and, having secured a pretty good dinner, prepared to take our departure in the diligence which leaves at half-past eight o'clock for Chur, in Switzerland, crossing the Alps at Splügen Pass.

SWITZERLAND.

CHUR, SWITZERLAND, August 1, 1873.

CROSSING THE ALPS.

We arrived here last evening at five o'clock, having been for twenty hours, since half-past eight o'clock on Tuesday night, confined to a diligence crossing the Alps in the midst of a furious storm of thunder, lightning, and rain, which by no means added to the pleasures of the trip. The whole distance from Milan, consuming over thirty-two hours, was made without rest, a pretty severe ordeal for the ladies of the party, especially when the numerous incidents of this stormy night are taken into consideration. To cross the Alps has never been an accomplishment of which we were very ambitious, being always inclined to dodge them by taking to the Mediterranean or passing under them at Mont Cenis, and we shall certainly never undertake to cross them again during a thunder-storm.

A FEARFUL NIGHT ON THE ALPS.

Starting at nine o'clock, we moved off into impenetrable darkness, amid a rapidly-falling rain, which, as we progressed up the foot-hills of the mountain, increased to a storm, accompanied with lightning and thunder, that echoed and re-echoed among the mountains like the explosion of a thousand pieces of artillery. Suddenly the diligence stopped, and a not very prepossessing countenance, with lantern in hand, opened the door and told us we must all alight. At least this was all we could make out of his mixture of German and Italian. We obeyed orders, and found that the torrent coming down from the mountain had swept away the bed of the road for a long distance, and that some planks had been laid on the rocks for the passengers to cross. The water was still rushing down in great volume, but we were enabled to get over with dry feet, and then the vehicle was somehow dragged over the chasm, bouncing and jumping in a way that would not have made its occupancy at the time very pleasant. We were soon in and off again, and in two hours reached Chiavenna, a town of about three thousand inhabitants, at the foot of the chief ascent. On the route the roaring of the swollen mountain-streams was equal in sound to that of Niagara, and, although we could not see, indicated close proximity to a cataract of rushing water.

At Chiavenna, at midnight, we were again invited to get out and take seats in another diligence, a portion of the passengers in which had left to cross by another route. We were all crowded in, with scarcely room to move our limbs, compelled to carry both baskets and bundles in our laps, and soon the lumbering vehicle was crawling slowly up the mountain-ascent. The road was smooth, as all Italian turnpikes are, and must have been constructed at immense cost, being mostly walled to the height of five to ten feet, and having many stone bridges thrown across the mountain-streams. Where the ascent is very rapid it is accomplished by a succession of zigzag roads, and at break of day we could count six or seven road-beds in sight from below, over which we had passed in our winding course. At some points of the road we passed through tunnels cut through the solid rock, and on all sides of us were beds of snow filling the ravines, where it had accumulated during the past winter, and thus far resisted the warmth of the summer sun. The atmosphere was cold and chilly, and the rain continued to pour down in torrents, causing numerous cataracts of water, tearing and roaring down the mountain-sides, the peaks of which towered thousands of feet above our heads.

STORM ON THE ALPS.

It was truly a grand spectacle; but it requires energy and enthusiasm to make the enjoyment counterbalance the annoyances and fatigue of Alpine journeying. We had not gone far after daybreak before the diligence was stopped by information that the road a short distance ahead of us was washed out by a cataract, and it would be impossible to pass. In a few minutes we reached the point of the disaster, and found a mountain-stream of great volume pouring down, bringing with it boulders and rocks, and had already washed out the bed of the road to the depth of about six feet. The rain was still falling in torrents, and the volume of the stream momentarily enlarging. To get the diligence over this break was an impossibility; but in the course of a half-hour another arrived on the opposite side of the breach, when it was determined to change passengers. Some boards were fixed across the chasm, and the men were compelled to find their way over as best they could, though the diligence-men did their best to aid the ladies, in some cases lifting them bodily. We finally all got seated and ready for moving on again, pretty well soaked with rain and splashed with mud. Among the passengers with whom we exchanged vehicles were a number of ladies and children.

ACROSS THE SPLUGEN PASS.

At eight o'clock we reached the highest point of the Splügen, and were much pleased to see the mountain-streams reversing their course. There was, however, no cessation in the rain, and the roaring and dashing torrents were still sweeping madly past us. Every mountain-peak that we passed had a miniature cataract pouring down from crag to crag, all tending to swell the rush of water below. We of course moved down the mountain at a much more rapid rate than we ascended, and at ten o'clock, after passing at Piannaco a miniature waterfall of nearly eight hundred feet, reached the town of Splügen, near the source of the Rhine, where it is simply an insignificant mountain-stream, now swollen considerably, and tumbling in wild confusion in its steep descent over its rocky bed.

At Splügen we were among the Swiss, and found a capital hotel, where we obtained the best breakfast we had partaken of for three weeks, and enjoyed it with an appetite sharpened by our night's travel. The cooking of everything in olive oil, which is the practice in Italy, is not very palatable to Americans, especially as the aforesaid oil, in most places, is quite rancid; and to get where good butter was substituted was quite a treat. Then the cleanliness of everything about gave assurance that we would not take back to the diligence any more fleas than we had brought across the mountains with us in our clothing. This was quite a comforting reflection, especially to the ladies, who do not expect to be whole again in flesh for a week to come.

THE VIA MALA.

After leaving Splügen the turnpike follows close to the banks of the Rhine, with towering and almost perpendicular mountains on either side. In fact, at various points of the road the Rhine winds its way through upright walls of rock from twelve to thirty feet apart, and six hundred feet below the turnpike. The river, now swollen and enlarged in volume by the torrents coming down from the mountains, presented a wild rushing avalanche of muddy water of a deep chocolate color. Even when coursing along over the rocks, with a hundred feet of channel, it dashed its spray high in the air, and when forced through these narrow chasms roared so wildly as almost to make the rocks tremble with its force. These narrow chasms are called by the Swiss the Via Mala. Thousands of tourists are attracted here to view the Rhine forcing its way through these rocky gorges. The chasms at some points are a half-mile in length, and the scene is a grand one where this mighty torrent breaks away again into a wider bed and sweeps on, only again to be forced and compressed through what might almost be considered a crevice in the rocks. The heavy rain still falling and numerous mountain-torrents pouring into the river rendered the scene as we viewed it impressively grand. The storm was the greatest one that had occurred for years, bringing down from the mountains rocks weighing in some instances a half-ton, and sweeping away a turnpike and its bridges that had stood undisturbed amid the raging of the elements for forty years or more.

MORE DISASTERS.

At several points on the route the turnpike was found to be badly washed by the mountain-streams, but we were enabled to drag along through them until we arrived near the village of Andrea, when we were again stopped by a stream that had not only torn away the stone turnpike bridge, but had piled up on either side of the road-bed about ten feet of mud and rock, the former of the consistency of very soft mortar, as a number of the passengers found upon venturing to walk over it to view the stream of mud and rock still pouring down from the mountain and losing itself in the rushing waters of the wild and turbulent Rhine. Here we found a number of men belonging to the diligence-company at work making preparations to carry the passengers and baggage across the chasm, which was finally accomplished by laying new boards over the mud and over the bed of the torrent rapidly subsiding, as the rain had ceased to fall for about an hour. The ladies of course got their skirts muddy and their feet wet again, but after the experiences of the night they had learned to regard this as a slight matter, and we were soon off once more on our way through the magnificent valley of the Rhine, with its towering mountains, some of them rising six thousand feet above us, and all with their sides and foot-hills terraced and cultivated wherever vegetation could be made to take root.

HEAD OF THE RHINE.

It was interesting, as we coursed our way along the banks of the Rhine, to notice its gradual increase in volume, swollen by various tributaries, and as it was on this occasion by thousands of mountain-torrents. Long before we reached Chur it had increased from an insignificant stream to a wide and rushing river, hurled along with wonderful impetuosity. At Chur its bed is half a mile in width, and its current indicates that it is still rapidly and madly coursing its way down towards the falls, where it takes a tumble over one hundred feet, and thenceforth becomes a quiet, respectable, staid, and navigable river, distinguished throughout its course for the magnificence of its scenery and the beauty of the castles and palaces on its banks, as well as the verdure and superior cultivation of the bordering land.

Switzerland is a land of mountains and lakes, a land of valleys teeming with vegetation, a land of glaciers, torrents, and waterfalls. It is a famous summer resort for the whole world, and now here at Chur all the hotels, at least a dozen in number, are thronged with strangers, and every train brings a new supply. This is the point from which excursions are made to view the famous Via Mala, and as we came down the turnpike yesterday we passed scores of tourists, with their guide-books and glasses in hand. There were also a considerable number visible at all the hotels on the route, and this morning we witnessed the departure of a half-dozen more loaded diligences, with ladies and gentlemen of all nationalities.

ATTRACTIONS OF SWITZERLAND.

The whole of Switzerland is not as large as the State of New York. The Alps divide it from Germany on the east, and Italy on the south and southwest. It is a glorious little republic, situated in the very heart of Europe, and the love of the people for independence, and their intense affection for their native land, have taught the surrounding monarchies that they cannot bring it into subjection. The great charm of Switzerland, next to its natural scenery, is the air of well-being, the neatness, the sense of propriety imprinted on the people, their dwellings, and their plots of land. They generally own their homesteads, and are always building, repairing, altering, or improving something about their tenements. In the agricultural regions everybody works, men, women, and children, and even the cows have their allotted task, whilst the land is cultivated almost entirely by hand- or garden-labor. The female, although not exempt from out-door work, undertakes the thinking and managing departments in the family affairs, and the husband is but the executive officer. The wife is, in fact, very remarkably superior in manners, habits, tact, and intelligence to the husband in almost every family in the middle and lower classes of Switzerland.

The hotels of Switzerland are the best in Europe, and some travelers go so far as to assert that they are the best in the world. They are neat and clean and comfortable, and the food is prepared in a plain but substantial manner, which is peculiarly palatable to those who have been sojourning in Italy or France and eating they scarcely know what. You see snails in market in Italy and imagine that the *pâtés* have one or two coiled up in their depths. The meat is first boiled to make your soup, and then served up as roast meat. Of all things detestable to spend an hour over is an Italian *table-d'hôte*, with its incomprehensible succession of dishes and its scarcity of everything that is palatable. They feed one hundred persons at a dollar per head off of ten dollars' worth of provisions, and then boil the bones and whatever is left to make the soup for the next meal. With this kind of feed it does not cost us as much to live as it does at home, but we imagine that our hotel-keepers would soon become millionaires if they could economize food as it is done in an Italian hotel.

ZURICH, SWITZERLAND, August 2, 1873.

We remained over a day longer than we anticipated in the Swiss town of Coire (pronounced Chur), in order to enjoy the delicious climate, view the town and its surroundings, and visit the famous springs of Pfäffers, at the village of Ragatz, about fifteen miles distant, which is regarded as one of the most singular spots in Europe.

THE TOWN OF COIRE.

Coire is situated on the river Plessur, which a short distance below empties into the Rhine. It is the capital of the Grisons, and contains about seven thousand inhabitants. It owes its importance to the trade of the Splügen and Bernardin Passes of the Alps, which have attracted to it all the railroads of Switzerland whose termini are here. All travel across the Alps by either of these passes concentrates at Coire, and a half-dozen diligences leave here daily with excursionists and travelers. Those who desire to see all that is beautiful and wonderful in the Alps without crossing them come here to make an excursion to Splügen, which can be reached by diligence in about four hours. A seat on the top of the diligence gives a fine view of the whole country, as well as of the roaring Rhine on its passage through the Via Mala.

THE SPRINGS OF PFAFFERS.

The scenery around Ragatz is wild and romantic. Here, too, a mountain-stream comes tearing down the clefts of a rock like the Via Mala, and were it not so near the Via Mala it would be considered a great wonder. The rush of water is as great, the roar as loud, but the width of the cleft through which the river is forced is much narrower, though equally as deep from the surface. There were large numbers of visitors arriving on every train to view the springs and the scenery, and at least one hundred carriages with visitors from neighboring resorts arrived during our stay.

As we approach the village of Ragatz the precipitous sides of the foot-hills beyond are seen to have a break or divide in the middle, forming a deep ravine, through which the Tamina River flows, or rather seethes and surges between a narrow cleft in the rocks with an impetuosity equal to that of the Rhine among the Alps. A carriage-road so narrow that turn-out places have been made at certain points, and which barely admits of a carriage- and foot-way, has been constructed high up on one side of this ravine, at great expense. The sides of this cañon rise precipitously to a height of six hundred to eight hundred feet, in some places overhanging the path and shutting out a view of the lofty mountains which hem it in. Trees here and there hang over the edge of the cliffs as if just ready to fall and close the gorge with their own wrecks. It seems sometimes almost as if the walls of the rocky cliffs had met in front and swallowed the intruding road which crept within its jaws; but over embankments and grooves, in the sheer upright rocks, and cuts not large or long enough to deserve the name of tunnels, the road dodges as it were the difficulties and works its tortuous way along for two and a half miles to the Bath House and Hôtel Pfäffers, which extend across the entire width of the ravine.

It is through this house that you enter the great gorge, which might rather be termed a crack in the mountain. The sides here are but a few feet apart, rising perpendicularly from the foaming waters far below and almost meeting overhead, so far above you that you cannot distinguish the exact outlines of the overhanging cliffs, from the edges of which small rivulets drop their tiny streams to mingle with the noisy torrent below. The only path through this part is a wooden balcony fastened or suspended to the rock on one side, with the rushing river far below and a glimmering light overhead. Following this fragile pathway, with umbrella raised, for six or eight hundred feet, you come to the source of the Hot Springs in a chamber cut into the solid rock, whence a steam continually issues, and where, by the aid of a lamp, you see the hot water pouring into a large tank, from which it is conveyed in wooden pipes to the bath-house for use. The temperature of the water is 100° Fahrenheit. It is remarkably pure, but tasteless.

Returning, you note the crowd of visitors, for this is no unusual day, who fill the route. During our brief visit of two or three hours there must have been three hundred visitors, of whom two hundred walked to and from the railroad station. In one procession were twelve carriages, each with its driver walking and cracking his whip to give warning to pedestrians of his approaching team. It was curious to note the difference in the several nationalities who there made a display of their good or bad breeding. The Germans invariably bowed and often removed the hat, the French said a sparkling "Bon-jour," but the Americans and English passed on without a sign, unless, indeed, the turn of the head for one last look after passing generally distinguished the American from his English cousin.

THE SWISS RAILROADS.

We left Coire this morning by railroad for Zurich, which is about one hundred miles distant. On entering the cars we found them, for the first time in Europe, constructed on the American plan, except that they have a partition at one end for ladies who are traveling alone. They have conductors the same as our roads, who pass through the cars and collect the tickets. They carry a silver whistle, with which they signal to the engineer to go ahead; he responds with the steam-whistle, and the train moves off. There are three classes and three rates of fare, the only difference in the cars being that the higher rates have better upholstering than the lower rates.

BEAUTY OF SWITZERLAND.

The country which we passed, although very mountainous, was through a broad valley, and most of the mountains being of very gradual ascent were cultivated to their very summits. The vegetation is very luxuriant, and the cottages and farm-houses bright and beautiful, with all the evidences around them of thrift and industry. We passed a large number of ruins of old castles, with their towers and battlements, which are left standing as a reminder of the days when they were the strongholds of a tyranny now passed away forever. There are no palaces in Switzerland except those reared by industry, the homes of men who have carved out their own fortunes by the sweat of the brow. Royalty has no home here, and the people have allowed everything that pertained to it to go to ruin. Well would it be if some of their neighbors would follow their example. There are no soldiers of any account here, no standing army, very few fortifications, no extensive garrisons or military structures. The people are all producers, and the country is prosperous. Every man is, however, accustomed to arms, and ready to do battle for his country at a moment's notice.

The great mass of the people through the section of Switzerland we are now traverisng are Protestants, though in the rural and mountainous districts the majority are Catholics. It is estimated that three-fifths of the whole population of the country are Protestants, and two-fifths Catholics.

ON "FAIR ZURICH'S WATERS."

This, if we remember right, was the title of a sentimental love-song, or it may have been "By the Margin of Fair Zurich's Waters," which the young ladies of America a long time ago delighted to sing to their admirers. Well, here we are on Lake Zurich, and a fairer or more beautiful sheet of water it would be difficult to find anywhere. On reaching Rupperschwyl on the railroad, which is at the head of navigation of the lake, we left the cars and took passage on the steamboat St. Gothard for Zurich, in order to view the scenery on the route. On both sides of the lake there are large and stirring towns, the houses presenting a neat appearance with their white walls and green shutters. Here there are numerous manufacturing villages, the silk-mills being run by the mountain-streams, and many of them by steam. The distance to Zurich on the lake is about twenty miles, but, as the boat stopped for passengers at many of the towns, first on one side and then on the other, the distance run was fully thirty miles. The lake is five miles wide at its broadest point, but the general average width is only about three miles.

The mountains bordering Lake Zurich are not more than fifteen hundred feet high, and are not as bleak and bold as those around Lake Como. Their ascent is so gradual that they are cultivated mostly to their tops, the dark green of the mulberry-trees and the lighter shade of the newly-mown fields presenting a charming contrast. The neat cottages and farmhouses, all pure white, present from the lake a most attractive picture. Lake Como is for the most part adorned with gay villas and hotels for the accommodation of pleasure-seekers, with summer palaces for royal retirement; but Lake Zurich presents everywhere a scene of busy life and of industry. Steamers were plying upon it, towing rafts and lighters, whilst other gay and handsome crafts were conveying passengers to and fro. We passed before reaching Zurich probably thirty towns, ranging from two thousand to ten thousand inhabitants, the buildings generally being from four to five stories, all painted white, with the never-failing green shutters. The red-tiled roofs of Italy give way here to slate and cedar shingles, and we can almost imagine that we are passing the towns on one of our Western rivers, even the German names on the houses which greet our vision as we stop at the wharves serving to increase the illusion.

As we approach Zurich the mountains become less elevated, and towns and cottages and manufacturing establishments more numerous. Gay villas and country-seats of the solid men of Zurich are also interspersed among the cottages, some of which have their towers and parapets in imitation of the olden time when Switzerland was an appendage of Austria, and before she had secured and maintained her independence from royalty and kingcraft. Perhaps some of them are the remnants of those days, now in possession of the sturdy republicans who have labored to prove to the nations of Europe the capacity of man for self-government.

Most of the manufactories on the banks of Lake Zurich are for silk and velvets, for the hills are covered with mulberry-trees. The large buildings standing high up on the hills, all of them white, checkered with black, are the cocooneries, where the worms are fed that supply those immense establishments with the raw material. As we approach Zurich, towards the easternmost end of the lake, the grape is also largely cultivated, at some points scarcely anything else appearing in the fields. Although Zurich has three times the number of inhabitants that Como has, it has not one-third the number of churches. What there are of them are bright and beautiful and new, with steeples and clocks, and have the merit of having been erected by the present generation, instead of having come as heirlooms from remote ancestors.

ZURICH, SWITZERLAND, August 4, 1873.

THE CITY OF ZURICH.

The city of Zurich is situated at the northern extremity of the lake, the river Limmat passing through it. This is a stream of considerable volume, and its waters are so clear that the pebbles can be seen at a depth of some twelve or fifteen feet. The population of Zurich, including the suburbs, is about forty-six thousand, and its location on the banks of the lake is one of surpassing beauty. The hills which surround it are green to the summit, gemmed with lovely villages and beautiful villas, whilst the snow-capped towers of the Alpine region fill up southward the distant view. Turning as it were their swords into pruning-hooks, the ramparts which formerly surrounded Zurich have been changed into delightful promenades and flower-gardens, the scene from which about sunset is perfectly enchanting.

The inhabitants of Zurich are distinguished for their spirit and enterprise, and the numerous institutions for the cultivation of learning in the town have given it the name of the literary capital of Protestant Switzerland. They are quite puritanical, however, in their notions, so much so that there are no theatres allowed here, and to give a private ball special permission must be asked of the authorities.

THE PEOPLE OF ZURICH.

There is probably less intoxicating liquor or even beer consumed in Zurich than in any city of its size in the world. Taverns or drinking-houses are very scarce, and these are confined mostly to the sale of beer and wine. Drunkenness is said to be almost unknown, and many other vices that prosper elsewhere have no existence here. There are no corner loungers, everybody appearing to have something to do and being intent upon doing it. We have not in three days met a beggar, or any of the usual sharpers who dog the steps of strangers in other cities on the Continent.

The streets of the city are elegantly paved and are kept scrupulously clean. The stone blocks used for paving are all precisely one size, cut for the purpose, being about four by two and a half inches upon the surface.

The drives around Zurich are neither very extensive nor attractive, and the chief source of amusement therefore is sailing and boating on the lakes. A great many ladies can be seen every evening out with their friends handling the oars as gracefully as a Spanish lady would her fan. The boys all have their neat little boats with oar-blades tipped with crimson, and take great pride in keeping them bright and beautiful.

We have already mentioned that the dogs and cows are made to work here. We saw to-day quite a number of cows drawing wagons. They were very large white animals, and one of them had evidently brought her milk with her from the country, for a woman was milking her as she stood with the yoke around her neck. The dogs also work, and appear as happy and contented as our useless curs. The hand-carts have generally a dog yoked on one side, whilst a woman will be pulling on the other. Thus woman and dog walk side by side, each performing their share of the labor. They appear to be fond of each other, and kind and sociable. When the mistress leaves her wagon the dog guards it, and it would generally be hazardous for any one to interfere with it until she returns.

SIGHTS OF ZURICH.

Zurich has quite a number of popular institutions. There are here a university, which was established in 1833, a polytechnic school, in a magnificent building recently erected a deaf and dumb institution, and one for the blind, an institution for medicine and surgery, and various educational institutions for the poor. It is noted as being the place where the Reformation first broke out in Switzerland; and the cathedral in which Zuinglius, the great Reformer, first denounced the errors of the Church of Rome in 1519, is still standing. The town library is a large and spacious edifice, containing some fifty-five thousand volumes and a large collection of antiquities. Among the curiosities in the arsenal is exhibited what is claimed to be the identical bow with which William Tell is said to have shot the apple from his son's head; though historians generally contend that Tell and his bow and apple are chiefly fictions of Schiller. The battle-axe, sword, and coat of mail of Zuinglius, which are also exhibited, are doubtless genuine.

The promenades in and about Zurich are numerous and delightful. The Höhe, or High Promenade, is one of the principal, and is reached by winding stairs, overlooking the whole city. A beautiful avenue of old linden-trees surrounds them, and from the seats here provided the lake and surrounding country are spread out like a map. A monument is here erected to Hans Georg Nägeli, the celebrated composer.

EUROPE AND AMERICA.

To make a rapid tour of Europe is undoubtedly very pleasant. It is pleasant to notice the habits and manners of the people, and it is pleasant to look upon scenes and views often read of but never fully comprehended. But how any American can prefer life in Europe to a residence in his own country we have never been able to comprehend. Switzerland, is pleasing to the American because the government is not upheld by the bayonet, because the people are free and independent, and for the reason that "liberty, equality, and fraternity" are not here unmeaning words, as they are in France. It is pleasant to be in Switzerland, because the people are happy and contented and proud of their country and its institutions. It is interesting to view its mountain-peaks, clad in never-melting snow, and to sail on its beautiful lakes and scan its vine-clad hills. But, with all its exemptions from the evils which afflict nearly all other European countries, we can discover no attractions for an American that would counterbalance the blessings and advantages of life at home.

Italy has its attractions which may warrant a prolonged visit, but there is nothing in the country, the people, or the climate that could induce a permanent residence. The study of painting or sculpture or vocalism induces a great many Americans to remain for some time in Rome or Florence, but it would be difficult to find a more unhappy set of men and women than these same American artists. Even Mr. Powers, who had been tied to Italy for half a lifetime, always sorrowed over the necessity which had prevented him until almost the close of his life from making that visit to his beloved Cincinnati.

Of all the states of Europe, Switzerland is the only one in which the American can feel fully at home, provided he understands the language. Paris will do for a season, but the American can find no attractions in London. The worship of blood and the toadyism to the scions of aristocracy, however infamous they may be in all their private relations, are sickening to the American. There is a freedom and manliness among the Swiss that are not to be found in any monarchial government. Their pride of nationality has something more than mere military glory to rest upon, whilst they reverence and worship brain rather than blood. The American can here educate his children and engraft them in the languages better than at home, but still it seems to us that America is a better place both to live in and to die in than any European country. That many millions of Germans are of the same opinion is evidenced by the number who have already emigrated, and by the hundreds of thousands of those who are looking forward with hope to the time when they can move off with their families for the same destination. Of all the Germans the Swiss alone seldom emigrate, being happy, contented, and prosperous at home.

SUNDAY IN ZURICH.

Sunday in Zurich is more strictly observed than in any European city we have yet visited. The stores, with the exception of bakeries and tobacco-shops, are all closed, and every manner of business suspended. The whole population is out in Sunday attire, and the beautiful promenades that surround the city are thronged during the afternoon and evening with ladies, gentlemen, and children. The churches, both Protestant and Catholic, are all well attended in the morning. American ideas of the German or Swiss, both as regards social characteristics and customs, are generally formed from the appearance of the throngs of emigrants constantly passing through Baltimore and other cities. It will, therefore, be a matter of surprise to many to learn that in the city of Zurich the people, both male and female, dress precisely as American citizens. The ladies have their over-skirts looped up, and wear waterfalls, and bonnets, and ribbons, and laces, lockets, chains, and jewelry, just as American ladies. Fewer of the class of Germans we meet coming from the ships are to be seen here than in Baltimore. We passed a number of emigrants yesterday walking Indian file, probably making their way to a seaport to emigrate. There is, in fact, but little here in the appearance of the city, its houses, or its people to distinguish it from an American city, except that the streets are kept cleaner and are better paved. The ladies look strong and hearty, and appear to know nothing of any exclusive claim of the sex to constitutional weakness. They generally have fresh, rosy cheeks, and the majority of them are blondes, though they do not appear to be aware that such is the fashionable complexion on the other side of the ocean. The children on the streets are neat and tidy, but no effort seems to be made to array them prematurely in the style of men and women. They look well and comfortable, clean and happy, as everything does "by the margin of fair Zurich's waters."

THE HOUSES IN ZURICH.

Very few of the private residences in Zurich have front doors on the street. They have side-yards, with a high iron gate in front, and the main entrance is on the side of the house, inside the gate. This is also the case with the banks and a great many wholesale business houses, which are not only shut in after this manner, but which have no signs up, and no indication of their business. Many of the stores, and especially the bakers' shops, are without front doors to their establishments. In the centre of their front windows there is a sash on hinges, and a bell to pull. You pull the bell, and some one comes to the opening to serve you with what you may want. Others that have doors and a fine display in their windows keep them locked, and you must ring the bell to obtain admission. It is evidently not a very stirring town for retail trade, but what they have for sale is of extra quality. The confectionery establishments are equal to any in our large cities,

17

and much better than we have met with either in France or Italy. The houses are generally four or five stories high, built of stone and rough-cast white, with green shutters.

The public buildings are constructed of blue sandstone, and most of them very elegant and elaborate in their architecture. The railroad depot is a grand structure of blue stone, adorned with statuary and sculpture, and the main building is much larger than our "Camden Station." It has along its entire front, which is about five hundred feet, a high colonnade formed of heavy stone pillars. The waiting-rooms for passengers are elegantly fitted up.

EINSIEDELN, August, 1873.

THE BLACK VIRGIN OF SWITZERLAND.

It would not do for us to leave Zurich without visiting Einsiedeln, a few miles from Richterswyl, on the lake, where the "Black Virgin of Switzerland" draws many thousands of Roman Catholic pilgrims every year to her shrine. In former years the number of pilgrims was estimated at two hundred thousand annually, but of late the number has somewhat declined. Next to Notre Dame de Lorette, of Italy, Einsiedeln is more visited by pilgrims than any other place in the world.

THE SWISS MECCA.

The route to Einsiedeln for an hour and a half was over the Lake of Zurich, now graced by the visible presence of the grand Alpine peaks, which had been hitherto shrouded with clouds. The great Rhone glacier was plainly distinguished from the white caps of the mountain-summits, being different in shape and shade of whiteness.

At Richterswyl we left the boat and mounted on top of a diligence for a ride of nine miles over a mountain to this place, the Mecca of German and Swiss Catholics. The scenery was finer and the views over the lake district far more extensive than can be obtained in the vicinity of Zurich. The scattered houses were large and picturesque in appearance, lighted with immense numbers of windows, before which could be seen small looms in operation on every variety of stuff which consists of "woof and warp," —here a silk of glossy blackness, next an ingrain carpet, then plaids and stripes, each with its industrious weaver, and these operatives invariably men.

While our diligence waited at the wharf for its full complement of passengers, our attention was directed to the stream of carriages and pedestrians which constantly came to the landing-place; when once started, this concourse in no wise lessened. Most were of the laboring classes, and fully half were women, presenting every variety of dress and feature. Many walked devoutly along, repeating their prayers in an audible voice, and all were staid and solemn. Those who could pay but a scant price for a ride had bargained for a half-starved steed and driver, and several times we counted fifteen able-bodied persons drawn by a skeleton horse.

Seven hundred and eighty-five houses, besides the buildings of the abbey and monastery, constitute the town of Einsiedeln, with a population of eight thousand devoted to the entertainment of pilgrims, and to traffic in prayer-books, beads, images, and candles. The rows of little shops and booths, and the display of cheap gewgaws, which are considered religious (made so by a colored print of the Virgin or of some saint), will surpass belief. From the rear window of the hotel we can count over fifty, and this not at the abbey front. The saleswomen, who speak half a dozen languages, are weaving the beads with silver wire, while they artfully shake their precious stock in trade, making the shop alive with the tinkling of the beads and the swaying back and forth of the pendent clusters. Some articles are curiously wrought and dyed, some are odorous with gums of the tropics, but most are of gay colors in glass and bone. Everywhere is displayed the crucifix. We passed an immense crucifix on the street on entering the town, and found the principal ornament of the dining-room of this really elegant hotel to be a crucifix, where one usually finds a mirror!

So extensive is the traffic in toys and relics here offered that in one publishing-office in the village fourteen lithographic presses, sixty bookbinders, and one hundred and fifty children (the latter engaged in illumination) are constantly employed.

THE ABBEY OF EINSIEDELN.

The abbey building is surrounded by a high wall, decorated with statues and immense gateways, which gives to the establishment an appearance of great extent. The cathedral, clearly defined by its two slender towers, occupies the central part, and is one hundred and seventeen feet in width. The present building dates from 1704, but the abbey was founded by Charlemagne. The title of the abbot has been Prince of Einsiedeln since the year 1274. This title was conferred in consequence of the great riches and influence of this order. At present there are from eighty to one hundred monks in the abbey. They teach the village schools, which are considered superior to others, and manage their large farm with skill and economy. Their horses are remarkably fine, and their cattle also. The number of services which are held every day in the cathedral, and the time they must necessarily devote to the confessional, would make their life a busy one.

THE BLACK VIRGIN.

The interior of the cathedral is decorated with modern pictures, statuary, and elaborate gilded ceilings. In the nave, isolated from the rest of the church, stands the Chapel of the Virgin, of black marble, adorned with panels wrought in bas-relief. The lower part is sadly disfigured by the rubbish of melted wax and tallow. Each devotee lights from one to a dozen tapers, and with a bit of the melted candle they are made to adhere to the costly polished exterior. Through a grating you can see in the interior an image of the Virgin in black marble, the eyes and lips painted, and the statue dressed in a gold-embroidered brocade of dingy, uncertain color. The height of this statue is not over two feet. It is placed above an altar, and the head of the Virgin and the cross in front glisten with precious stones, while the entire altar is lit up with reflected rays from the sapphires and emeralds. The golden swinging lamp, which always is lighted, was the gift of Queen Hortense, and is an art treasure in itself.

The great candelabrum in the midst of the cathedral was the gift of Napoleon I. The Hohenzollern princes have also made valuable presents here, especially in the last few years. The paintings given by them, representing Bible scenes, have portraits of the Hohenzollern family introduced. The excuse for this is found in the tradition that Saint Meinrad, from whose sanctity all this wealth has grown, was one of their ancestors.

THE VESPER CHANTS.

There are six great organs among the arches and pillars and recesses of the cathedral, and in the rear of the great altar there is a screen, formed of rows of black marble pillars, which conceal from the worshipers the monks who chant the vesper service. Upon several of the side-altars are effigies, life-size, of the saints to whom they are dedicated; some are nearly skeletons and almost nude, others have swords and plenty of gilt trappings. All are in recumbent postures.

FOUNTAIN OF THE VIRGIN.

In the large sloping court which fronts the cathedral stands the famous fountain of the Virgin, with its fourteen jets of water, surmounted by a bronze image. The legend says that St. Meinrad saw the Saviour, when He came to consecrate the abbey, drink from one of these jets; but, as it is uncertain which, pilgrims avoid the possibility of mistake by religiously drinking from each in succession.

"Begging is forbidden in this church, under pain of corporeal punishment," was an inscription in former times; but it is now changed to a fine of five francs for the first offense, and twenty for the second. We were hugely amused with the novelty of the idea, but in that district it may be less incongruous to fine beggars than elsewhere, for nowhere can a more thrifty, industrious, and prosperous community be found. There are no beggars in Switzerland.

INDIVIDUAL PRAYER.

The distinguishing feature of this cathedral service is its avowed approval of individual, spontaneous prayer. The pilgrims, who come from every nation on the globe, either singly or in groups, attracted together by some common sympathy, make the rounds of the altars, and each in his own dialect and his own chosen words audibly utters his petitions. A young couple walked hand in hand near us, uttering thanksgivings and pouring forth their grateful emotions, who may have vowed that their wedding tour should be to "Our Lady of the Hermits."

LAMENTATIONS OF THE PILGRIMS.

But more impressive than all besides is the earnestness of the congregation gathered here. The lame, the halt, the blind, have brought here their heavy burdens, and the desolate and the sorrow-stricken have come here for comfort. There was no indifferent worshiper in the church. The number present at vespers was not less than three hundred, and few if any of these were residents of the village; and this is only a repetition of the daily scene that has been enacting here for hundreds of years. Many aged, decrepit women prayed till their souls seemed to light up their faces with their inmost thoughts.

One young man habited in army blue, but with a crutch and missing leg, prostrated himself before the Virgin's chapel, and there, with covered face and trembling hands, he still lay when the audience slowly withdrew. At times the church resounds with beseeching prayers, the groans and lamentations of the pilgrims; but never has this noise or confusion been found to detract from the solemn emotions or the reverential tone of those who partake in its services.

SCENE AT THE CONFESSIONALS.

Passing from the cathedral to the confessionals, which are in as many languages as at St. Peter's in Rome, we found throngs waiting their turn. The room is exceedingly chaste, and all the pictures are drawn from the history of the Prodigal Son.

When the usual vesper service was ended, eighteen monks slowly walked through the cathedral to the Chapel of the Virgin; the iron gratings were opened; they entered, and, kneeling, sang a wailing, broken-hearted lamentation, which was echoed again and again through the vaulted ceiling, and, as their tones softened and mingled, more than once the echoes gave back their notes in pure soprano voices, mingling with the clear and powerful tenors and bassos. Hearing this, one could understand how superstition and credulity might find here fresh miracles every day, and "Notre Dame des Érémites" might receive her two hundred thousand annual visitors in the years to come as she has done in the years gone past.

Apart from these religious interests, the town is well located for a summer sojourn. There are six lines of diligences departing from it every day, and by another summer they will be served by the railroad, which is more than half completed at this time. It has been known most favorably in England, and many English families spend the entire season there.

LAKE LUCERNE, SWITZERLAND,
TOWN OF FLUELEN, August 8, 1873.

The great drawback to travel upon the lakes of Switzerland is the certainty of rain, no matter how promising the weather may be when you take your departure for an excursion on their placid waters. It is certain to come at some time during the day, more especially at such times as you especially desire to view some of the grandest scenery.

TRIP TO FLUELEN.

We left Lucerne yesterday morning for a trip to Fluelen, intending to return in the afternoon in time to ascend Mount Righi and remain on its summit until morning to witness the rising of the sun and obtain the three-hundred-mile view which is said to be obtainable from its six thousand feet of elevation. We had scarcely been an hour on the lake, however, before the inevitable rain commenced to fall, and finally settled into a steady storm, inducing us to go ashore at Fluelen and take up our quarters for the night at the William Tell Hotel, that being the most inviting in appearance of the several hotels of which that town mainly consists.

LAKE LUCERNE.

The Lake of Lucerne is said to be the most beautiful of all the lakes of Switzerland. If the guide-books had described it as the grandest there would have been no disputing the fact, but for beauty the Lake of Zurich is far superior. The mountains are more steep and imposing on Lucerne, towering up in awful grandeur six to seven thousand feet above the level of the lake, and looking as if they might topple over upon you at any moment, or that the cottages, hamlets, and summer resorts high up on their sides might with a slight gust of wind lose their hold upon the rocks. Most of the mountains are covered with cedar-trees, except where too precipitous for the roots to hold, whilst there is an occasional clearing and a cottage at points where, as you look at it from the deck of the steamer, it looks as if inaccessible for any two-legged creature not provided with wings. Still, you can see the smoke curling up from their chimneys three and four thousand feet above what would be considered a foothold for ordinary mortals. At several points on the lake we could see, high up on the mountain-sides, large hotels, four or five hundred feet front, with flags waving from their steeples, and all the evidences of being occupied to their full capacity.

THE TOWN OF FLUELEN.

The width of the lake is not more than a mile to a mile and a half, and so abrupt are its windings and turnings among the mountains that at no time can the eye discern its course half a mile ahead.

The boat appears all the time as if shut up in a basin of water with no outlet, and as if steering direct for the rocks. Every mountain is precipitous, many of them so much so as to be uninhabitable, except in an occasional gorge, and in each of these is sure to be found a town with its array of hotels. We have spent the past night in one of these towns, the mountain in its upward course standing erect not more than twenty feet from the back window. Still there are, somewhere in the mountain behind or beyond, inaccessible to the eye, several large hotels; at least we should judge so from the fact that whenever a boat arrives at the wharf five capacious hotel omnibuses make their appearance and carry off nearly all the passengers. Then the diligences are all the time going to and coming from more distant points in the mountains, rendering the little town of Fluelen, consisting of four hotels, a church, and about fifty houses, a place of great importance on the lake.

Suffice it to say that the mountains of Lake Lucerne are abrupt, perpendicular, grand. There are none of them less than three thousand feet in height, and most of them are six thousand, and, with their snowy summits reflected in the glassy water, they present a scene of nature both grand and sublime.

We left Fluelen at eleven o'clock for Vitznau, where the railroad station for ascending Mount Righi is located. The morning was bright and beautiful, but before we had been a half-hour afloat the inevitable rain-storm came sweeping down upon us from the mountains.

TOWNS AND VILLAGES.

In passing down the lake our boat stopped at a dozen or more towns, and at each discharged more than half of its passengers and took on board as many more. The boat was crowded when we started, and it continued equally full throughout the trip, returning back from the head of the lake with a full complement. The passengers were principally English and Americans, with some Germans and a few French. They were taking the circuit of the lake, passing from one town to another, and stopping at each for a few days to visit the points of interest in the vicinity. At every town on the lake there are several lines of diligences running daily through the mountains to other towns and notable places in the interior; and to make the round of the lake and visit them all would require a whole summer.

At every town at which the steamer stopped the whole water front was occupied by hotels. Their balconies were crowded with guests, and a large number were at the wharves to meet the boat. We also passed upon the lake a half-dozen other steamers, each well filled with passengers, all bearing the mark of being strangers in a strange land. They had their alpenstocks in hand, glasses strapped over their shoulders, and a red-covered guide-book protruding from their pockets. Each boat-load seemed to be a counterpart of ours, and all were on the same mission of spying out the beauties of the land.

HONORS TO WILLIAM TELL.

The borders of Lake Lucerne were the scene of the exploits of William Tell, the hero of Switzerland. A short distance from Brunnen, on the eastern bank of the lake, on a perpendicular rock which rises from the water, is an inscription in immense gilded letters: "Au chantre de Tell." Farther on we arrive at a small ledge, covered with verdure and chestnut-trees. It was here, according to tradition, that Fürst, Stauffacher, and Melchthal, accompanied by confederates from three of the cantons, met on the night of the 7th of November, 1307, for the purpose of taking a solemn oath to deliver their country from the tyranny of their Austrian oppressors. According to tradition, on the same spot where the three conspirators took the oath three springs of water spouted up, over which a small hut has been erected. Six miles farther on we arrive at Tell's Chapel, the Mecca of all Switzerland. It is on a small plateau bathed by the waters of the lake. The end towards the water is without a wall, and the entire interior of the chapel and the altar are visible to the passengers on passing boats. It was erected in 1388, thirty-one years after the death of William Tell, to whose memory it was consecrated, we are told, in the presence of one hundred and fourteen persons who knew him personally. It is located in a wild and romantic glen, on the very place where, according to tradition, Tell leaped on shore from the boat in which Gessler was conveying him to prison. Every Sunday after Easter a procession of boats, richly decorated, proceeds slowly to this chapel, where, after mass is celebrated, a patriotic sermon is preached to the worshiping pilgrims.

Farther on, the town of Fluelen was

pointed out to us as the place where Tell shot the apple from his son's head. The spot where he stood is marked by a fountain and a statue of Tell, presented by the Shooting Society of Zurich. Close by, another fountain marks the spot where Gessler hung his hat to be worshiped, and where the son of Tell was bound with the apple on his head, preparatory to the shot which gave freedom to Switzerland.

MOUNT RIGHI.

MOUNT RIGHI, SWITZERLAND, August 9, 1873.

We closed our last letter at Vitzuen, at the foot of Mount Righi, and are now writing at the hotel within a few hundred feet of the summit, having spread out before us one of the grandest views possible for mortal to behold.

THE ASCENT OF MOUNT RIGHI.

At four o'clock we took our seats in an open car holding fifty-four persons, with a locomotive behind and the car in advance. The ascent being six thousand feet, the track is laid at an angle of about thirty degrees, rising about one foot in three. In order that the locomotive should be on a level, the rear wheels are considerably larger than the fore wheels, and cogs in the centre of the track hold the train, a cog-wheel working in them. The motion is slow but steady, and the view of the surrounding lakes and mountains as we gradually rise higher and higher becomes more and more grand and imposing. The time required for the ascent to the first hotel, which is about four thousand five hundred feet, is just one hour. After rising about five hundred feet more we are at our present location; but the Hotel Righi Culm is still five hundred feet higher, and it required thirty minutes' climbing to reach our present stopping-place, over a rugged road slippery from the rain.

CHANGE OF CLIMATE.

The climate as we ascended became gradually colder, and shawls and overcoats were in requisition. Although there is no snow on Righi, it catches the breeze from the higher snow-clad mountains, and is as winterish as Baltimore in January. The cold is damp and penetrating, and the heaviest of winter clothing can alone insure comfort. After reaching our destination another inevitable rain-storm blew over the mountain, although a bright, warm sunshine had been brightening every object only five minutes previously. The prospect had been grand, but now the dense clouds that "lowered down upon our house" and all out-doors shut out the view in every direction, and the rain poured down in torrents. We had hoped to view the setting sun from the pinnacle of the mountain, but had to content ourselves with the hope of seeing his majesty rise in the morning.

THE MOUNTAIN HOTELS.

There are at least six hotels on the mountain, one of them as large as Congress Hall at Cape May. The first one we reached, the Kalbad Hotel, is probably the largest, as it is evidently the most fashionable, and can be attained without climbing. It has a front of six hundred feet, is five stories high, and has a balcony about forty feet in width along the whole front. As we passed it, a military band of about thirty performers was playing upon the balcony, whilst the guests were promenading, presenting a gay and brilliant scene. The hotel can accommodate one thousand guests, and it was said to be full. The more elevated house at which we are stopping, the Hotel Staffel, is also well filled, as we could only obtain rooms in the fifth story. The third house, on the tip-top of the mountain, which is said to be the largest of all, the Righi Culm Hotel, is filled with gentlemen, there being very few ladies so high up. There are also two other hotels of immense proportions high up on the other slopes of the mountain within sight. It is customary for tourists to spend a day or two at each of these hotels, so as to view the scenery from the various points, all of which have their peculiar beauties, and it is estimated that during the months of July and August there are never less than from fifteen hundred to two thousand persons at the different hotels on Righi. The number who ascend the mountain every day during the season, either by railroad, horseback, in chairs, or as pedestrians, is from five to six hundred, though the most of them return the same day.

A NIGHT ON RIGHI.

Well, we have spent a night on the top of Righi, and it has been one of the stormiest that we have encountered since our memorable night in the diligence on the Alps. We were comfortably quartered, with abundance of blankets and cider-down quilts for a top-covering, but the whistling of the wind and the rattling of the rain against the windows and on the roof admonished us that there would be no sunrise visible for Righi's guests in the morning. When daylight came, the temptation to lie still rather than go out into the cold and cloud-laden atmosphere was irresistible. The Alpine horn which summons visitors to witness the rising sun was silent, and a peep through the window gave proof that it was impossible for any one to see beyond their noses.

At a later hour in the morning, however, the fog cleared away, and the sun shone out occasionally. The driving clouds disappeared, only to return again with sprinkling rain, but still we had ample opportunity to obtain a view of the magnificent landscape spread before us. To the north we have the Lake of Zug, the Black Forest filling up the horizon; to the south, the high Bernese Alps and the Lakes of Alpnach and Sarnen; to the west, the Lake of Sempach, and the winding Reuss, looking like a blue thread; while around the base of Righi, Lakes Lucerne and Zug seem to infold the mountain with their lovely waters of blue and green. When the mist would occasionally unfurl, all the glorious panorama of mountain, plain, and silver lake became revealed.

The lakes over which we have just passed to reach Righi were bordered by towering mountains, none of them probably less than two thousand feet high, but in looking down on them they appear like meadows, level with the lakes and rivers which flow through them. Righi appears to be the only mountain anywhere near you: everything else appears to the eye flat as a prairie. The section of country embraced in the view from Righi's elevated summit is said to extend over three hundred miles. The city of Zurich, some sixty miles distant, can be seen distinctly, and with a glass its prominent buildings recognized. Lucerne, some twenty miles off, appears as if we could almost throw a stone into its streets, and, independent of the magnificence of sunrise, the midday scene is very grand.

THE SUNRISE SCENE.

We did not see the sun set or the sun rise, sights which are seldom seen from Righi; but, in order that your readers may know what the sight is, we give Baedeker's description:

"A faint streak in the east, which pales by degrees the lightness of the stars, is the precursor of the birth of day. This insensibly changes to a band of gold in the extreme horizon; each lofty peak is in succession tinged with a roseate blush; the shadows between the Righi and the horizon gradually melt away; forests, lakes, villages, towns, reveal themselves; all is at first gray and cold, until at length the sun suddenly bursts from behind the mountains in all his majesty, flooding the superb landscape with light and warmth."

Among the most picturesque points of the magnificent scene, which embraces three hundred miles, are the Lakes of Zug and Lucerne, which last branches off in so many directions as almost to bewilder the eye. They approach so close to the foot of the Righi that it seems as if a stone might be thrown into them. Eleven other small lakes are also visible.

For a quarter of an hour before and after sunrise the view is clearest; at a later hour the mists rise and condense into clouds, frequently concealing a great part of the landscape. The chamois-hunter, in Schiller's play of Tell, aptly observes,—

"Through the parting clouds only
The earth can be seen.—
Far down 'neath the vapor,
The meadows of green."

But the mists themselves have a peculiar charm, rising suddenly from the depth of the valleys, veiling the Culm, and struggling against the powerful rays of the sun. The different effects of light and shade, varying so often in the course of the day, are a source of constant admiration to the spectator. At a very early hour the Bernese Alps are seen to the best advantage, and in the evening those to the east of the Bristonstrit.

DESCENT OF RIGHI.

We left the summit of Righi about ten o'clock in the morning, the rain pouring down, and a thick cloud of fog shutting out the view in all directions. Sending the ladies to the station in chairs, we slid down the mountain through the mud, and found at the station about a hundred passengers waiting around a hot stove for the cars. The train soon arrived on its upward trip, bringing us many ladies and gentlemen as there were waiting to embark. Travelers in Switzerland never seem to mind the rain. They are mostly Germans with their families, who come to the Alps to rough it, no one being expected to make a display of dress. There are, however, a good many Americans and English now on the mountain, with some Russians and French. Every grade of society is here represented, and at times all the languages of Europe contrive to produce a very Babel of incongruous sounds. When we reached the station at the foot of the mountain, two more steamboats were just landing their passengers, and there was a rush and struggle for tickets, many fearing that they would not be able to obtain seats for the ascent. The rain was still pouring down; but nothing seems to deter these Alpine travelers.

The descent was made in an hour and a quarter, requiring the same time as the ascent. At one part of the road there is a tunnel of about three hundred feet to pass through, and an iron trestle-work over a chasm, very much like the Cheat River Viaduct, except that if we should happen to get off the track the fall would be about one thousand feet. The difference, however, would not be much in the result. Never having ascended a mountain before unless it was because there was no other way to get on the other side of it, we cannot say that our experience on Mount Righi was very satisfactory.

BERNE, SWITZERLAND, August 10, 1872.
THE BERNESE ALPS.

As we approached Berne last evening we obtained our first view of the Bernese Alps, looming up in the far distance like great mountains of ice. They looked very much like the icebergs we encountered off Newfoundland, the rays of the setting sun tinging their turreted pinnacles. They are said to be nearly fifty miles distant; but their immense height, from twelve to thirteen thousand feet, more than double the height of Righi, makes them tower high above the lesser mountains in the vicinity.

On reaching Berne we repaired to the terrace of Federal Hall, to witness the sun setting on the snow-clad peaks of the Bernese Oberland, which are visible from every open space around the city. Nothing can surpass in sublimity the aspect of these mountains at sunset in fine weather, especially when the western horizon is partly veiled with thin clouds. Long after the shadows of evening have fallen upon the valleys, and the lingering rays of the evening sun have faded from the snowy peaks themselves, the mountains begin to glow from their base upwards, as if illuminated by a bright internal fire. This is one of the principal attractions of Berne.

BERNE AND ITS BEARS.

Berne is a quaint old town, being rapidly modernized by its active and energetic population, which now exceeds thirty thousand. The city is built upon a peninsula formed by the windings of the beautiful river Aar, which flows rapidly, furnishing an abundance of water-power for various mills, many of which are driven by the mere force of its current. Of all the cities of Switzerland, Berne most closely adheres to its traditions and its ancient peculiarities. Fountains are as numerous here as in Rome, and their adornments are quaint and very singular. The most striking is the Fountain of the Ogre, in the Corn Hall Square, which is surmounted by a grotesque traditional figure in the act of devouring a child, while a dozen others, chubby and jolly-looking urchins, doomed to the same fate, protrude from his pockets and girdle; beneath is a troop of armed bears. The bear is the heraldic emblem of Berne, which signifies bruin in German, and is a constantly-recurring subject. On a neighboring public building bruin appears equipped with shield, banner, and helmet. Two gigantic bears, tolerably executed in granite, keep guard over the pillars of the upper gate, others support a shield in the pediment of the Corn Hall, and a whole troupe of automatic bears go through a performance at the clock-tower every hour in the day. At three minutes before the close of the hour a wooden cock gives the signal by clapping his wings and crowing; one minute later a half-dozen automatic bears dance around a seated figure with crown and sceptre; the cock then repeats its signal, and when the hour strikes, the seated figure, an old man with a beard, turns an hour-glass and counts the hour by raising his sceptre and opening his mouth, while the bear on his right inclines his head; a grotesque figure strikes the hour on a bell with a hammer, and the cock concludes the performance by flapping his wings and crowing for the third time. All strangers visit the clock-tower, and the people take great pride in it.

We passed it twice at the striking-hour, and there was quite a throng of tourists waiting for the performance. But this peculiarity in regard to bears, although traditional and emblazoned in stone, is still religiously preserved by the people. The ancient Egyptians had not a greater veneration for the ibis, or the modern Venetians for the pigeon, than the Bernese have for the bear. A bears' den, with four venerable animals and their cubs in state, is kept in the city at the public expense, according to immemorial usage, and great is the amusement they afford by their cumbrous gambols. They are under the special protection of the law, which forbids the public from making them any offerings except bread or fruit, so great is the solicitude for their health. On the night of the 3d of March, 1861, an English officer fell into one of the public dens, and was torn to pieces by the male bear, after a long and desperate struggle. The den is a circular basin of stone, about one hundred and fifty feet in diameter, the walls about twenty feet high, on a level with the street, surrounded by an iron railing. It is divided in the centre by a stone wall, on either side of which are a pair of old bears, with their young, looking as if they might be one hundred years old. They each are provided with fountains for ablution and dens for shelter, and the floor of the inclosure is laid with smooth stone. In the centre of each partition is a tall cedar-tree for climbing. When the sun is shining, the bears climb on these poles, and afford great amusement for the children. In our stroll through the city we found bronze bears and stone bears in abundance, one on the top of a fountain being armed *cap-à-pie*, with his vizor down, sword buckled at his side, and carrying a banner aloft. Even the cake-shops have gingerbread bears.

BERNESE WOMEN.

At an early hour this morning the scavengers were at work with scrapers and brooms all over the city, and carts were gathering up the dirt. The strangest part of the matter was that the whole business was being conducted by females, most of them old, but some of them decidedly young and pretty. They were not only handling the broom and wielding the scraper, but were actually drawing the hand-carts containing the garbage. The work was being done well, as a matter of course, and they all seemed to be merry and happy. We have no doubt that they have had their municipal contest over this matter, and the women have triumphed in claiming their exclusive right to the use of the broom.

The markets seem to be in the entire control of the women, as we did not see a man in any of them engaged in vending either meat or vegetables. A number of women were also to be seen in different sections of the city sawing firewood with horse and saw. One we observed was at work alongside of her mother, and was young and beautiful both in form and feature. She worked as if it was her daily occupation, and seemed contented and happy. There can be no doubt of the fact that the women have their rights in Switzerland,—that is to say, the right to labor and share the burdens of active life.

The countrywomen attending market wear two silver chains with silver rosettes; one rosette is fastened over each breast, and passing loosely under the arm connects with others fastened over the shoulder-blades. The poorer classes have the same ornaments made of steel, and the still wealthier have them of gold, with precious stones in the rosettes. They all have the appearance of being strong-minded and energetic, and capable of taking care of themselves, notwithstanding the laborious occupations they pursue. The mother is looked upon as the head of the family.

INTERLAKEN, SWITZERLAND, August 11, 1873.

If we could shut out the mountainous surroundings of Interlaken, we might have imagined ourselves last night roving among the hotels at Saratoga, and looking in at the same class of stores that temptingly array their goods around that famous resort during the season. There was also the usual round of entertainments in progress in the parlors, and the same crowd of "dead-heads" outside, peeping in at the windows or listening to the performance. At the Victoria a traveling magician was bringing doves and vases of fish from under a shawl, and at the Scheurzanhoffen a band of strolling Swiss vocalists was giving a concert. A little farther on, a fine band was performing at the extensive Café Kursaal, where ices and cakes were being served to about a thousand visitors by a band of Swiss damsels arrayed in their picturesque costume.

The hotels at Interlaken are on a grand scale, and are more numerous than at any of our watering-places at home. The town of Interlaken is located in the valley of the river Aar, which connects Lake Thun with Lake Brienz, and hence boats by both lakes bring passengers from different points of Switzerland. Every nation and every tongue are here represented. Fully one-half of my fellow-passengers were Americans, and we are assured that there cannot be less than one thousand now here. They considerably outnumber the English, though, as usual, the Germans are more strongly represented than any other nationality.

ATTRACTIONS OF INTERLAKEN.

The Falls of Staubbach, which are the steepest and highest in Europe, disappoint the visitor at first view. They are variously estimated at from eight hundred to eleven hundred feet in height; but the quantity of water is so small that it does not impress one with any degree of sublimity. The water is precipitated from such an immense height that it is broken into spray, resembling dust, long before its arrival at the bottom; hence its name. Byron, in his "Manfred," compares its appearance to the tail of the white horse. When illuminated at night, the effect is very beautiful and attracts a large number of visitors.

On the route to Lauterbrunnen the castle of Unspunnen is passed, the supposed residence of Lord Byron's "Manfred." The Baron of Unspunnen, who was the last male descendant of his race, had an only daughter, lovely as—well, as they make them,—who had captivated the heart of a noble knight, a dependant and kinsman of the baron's greatest enemy, Berchtold of Zähringen. "The youthful lover, knowing his case was desperate, scaled the outer walls in the dead of night and carried off the beauteous maiden whilst her unsuspicious parent lay indulging in the arms of Morpheus. For years the outraged father followed up his wrongs with fire and sword, and ruinous were the results between the conflicting parties. At last one morning the knight, his bride, and infant son, appeared alone and unarmed at the stronghold of the baron. Such confidence could have but one result: the father was overcome, he pardoned his son and daughter, took his grandchild to his heart, and immediately gave orders to kill the fatted calf and celebrate the day with feasting, rejoicing, and games."

The Cave of St. Beatus is also located on the Lake of Thun. According to tradition, this fabulous saint took a notion to take up his residence in this cave, which was at the time occupied by a dragon. He gave orders to the quadruped to "stand not upon the order of his going, but to go at once," and he took up his bed and went. The principal steamer on the lake is named the St. Beatus, and the people generally believe in the legend. The cave is visited by pilgrims as well as by tourists.

THE LAKE OF BRIENZ.

The sun having put in an early appearance this morning, giving promise of the first bright and dry day that we have experienced in Switzerland, we determined to make an excursion to the Falls of Giesbach, which are regarded as one of the greatest attractions of Interlaken. The Aar River, which connects the Lakes of Brienz and Thun, flows directly under the windows of our hotel, having a fall of twenty-three feet between the two lakes, the Brienz emptying into the Thun. The Giesbach Mountain is on Lake Brienz, about six miles from Interlaken, and a fine steamer which communicates with the various towns on the lake was preparing to start when we reached her wharf on the river Aar.

At the appointed hour we steamed out into the lake, which is regarded by some persons as the most beautiful of the lakes of Switzerland, although its whole length is but seven and a half miles. The width of Lake Brienz is about two and a quarter miles, whilst its depth varies from five hundred to two thousand feet. Its banks are surrounded by lofty wooded mountains and rocks, the outcroppings of which would indicate that they are either white marble or limestone. They tower up so perpendicularly from the lake that there is very little cultivation except close down to the water's edge, where a few small towns are located, which are the termini of various passes through the mountains, and are mostly peopled by those connected with the diligences. There are, however, numerous hotels in the gorges, where tourists who spend the summer here stop for a day or two for change of scene and to explore the mountains. To the southeast in the background is the snow-clad mountain of Sussen, and to the left the Trifterhorn. The view of the magnificent mountain scenery from the steamer is very imposing, there being a solemnity in moving along under the shadow of these towering rocks on the quiet waters of the lake.

THE GIESBACH FALLS.

In a half-hour we were directly under the shadow of Mount Giesbach, and could hear the roar of the great cataract, and see the water come tearing out through an opening in the rocks to join the waters of the lake. A wharf and landing have been erected by the hotel company, and a few minutes after passing in front of the lower cascades of the Falls we were landed, with about two hundred other passengers who had come to spend the day at this romantic spot. The hotel and restaurant are in a gorge of the mountain, at an elevation of about four hundred feet, from which a grand view is had of the seven upper cascades. To reach this point required considerable climbing through zigzag paths cut in the rocks, and the whole cavalcade was soon in motion, men, women, and children, with their alpenstocks and guide-books. They consisted of Germans, English, and Americans, the first-named nationality predominating in numbers. The Swiss say that these Germans are the contractors in the late war, who have become suddenly rich, and that they are for the first time bringing their families to Switzerland. They look upon them as a kind of shoddy aristocracy, similar to those who filled the fashionable summer resorts of America, sparkling with diamonds, for a year or two after the close of our war.

THE CASCADES OF GIESBACH.

The restaurant was finally reached, and most of the visitors contented themselves with sitting here to enjoy the view under the cool shade of the trees, and partake of refreshments. The scene which here opens to the view is very grand. Seven cascades, each from one hundred and fifty to two hundred feet fall, come pouring down the mountain directly towards you, the volume of water spreading over a surface of about twenty feet, accompanied by a roar almost as loud but not so ponderous as that of Niagara. This is said to be the finest cataract, or rather cascade, in Europe; and all the adjuncts of scenery harmonize so well that the attractions are greatly enhanced. The mountain, for a mile on each side of the falls, although very precipitous, is densely covered with tall cedar-trees, only here and there the white rock cropping out among the trees and looking like a marble wall streaked with weather-stains. The opening in this mass of dense foliage, through which the cataracts come pouring from ledge to ledge, leaping over rocky chasms and tumbling over precipice after precipice, presents one of the most picturesque scenes that it has been our good fortune to view; and no one who visits Switzerland ought to fail to take the trip to the Giesbach.

ASCENT OF THE GIESBACH.

The Giesbach was inaccessible until 1848, when a schoolmaster named Keholi constructed a path, for the use of which he exacted a small toll from visitors. The steamboat company in 1854 bought his right and erected a fine hotel here, since which it has become one of the most delightful and popular resorts in Switzerland. The pathway up to the cascades has been improved, and, having some four hours to remain for the next boat, we determined to ascend and explore the mountain-torrent. Not more than a dozen visitors, among whom were several ladies, followed our example, and we were soon moving along under the shade of the trees, in our zigzag course up the sides of the mountain. The path winds along the edge of the cascades, and at the foot of each cascade a bridge is erected, on which visitors stop to view the rushing of the water as it comes pouring over the rocky ledge more than a hundred feet above, throwing off a spray that renders an umbrella necessary for the preservation of a dry coat. The path skirts both sides of the stream as far as the second bridge, and then to the upper fall there is a path on the right bank only. There is no bridge over the second fall, but the visitors can pass behind it by means of a grotto which connects the banks of the stream.

As we reached the upper falls, nearly one thousand feet above the plateau, at the restaurant, the mid-day sun was shining down over the cataracts, the spray from which formed a succession of rainbows of the richest imaginable tints. The view from this elevated point of the roaring water and the surrounding landscape is very picturesque and imposing, the richness of the foliage and the emerald verdure of the mountain-sides investing the scene with a peculiar charm. On reaching the summit of the upper falls, the cataract appears as if issuing from a gloomy ravine in the rock, struggling to force its way through a narrow crevice, reminding one of the roaring waters of the Rhine when driven through the Via Mala. It comes out of the mountain-side about two hundred feet below its summit, and is supposed to have its origin from the melting of the snow on the great mountains in its rear, some of which reach the elevation of twelve thousand to thirteen thousand feet.

The ascent to the upper cataract occupied nearly one hour, and, as we slowly ascended, a full opportunity was afforded of a more critical examination of the several cataracts as seen from the pathway on the right side of the ascent. The rocks immediately under the several falls have been worn out by the water into hollow basins from ten to twenty feet in depth. Into these pools the torrent descends, and comes bubbling and boiling up to flow on a few feet before taking another leap of a hundred or more feet off the precipitous ledges of the protruding rocks. The seven leaps bring it down to the restaurant plateau, and from this point, an elevation of about four hundred feet, it struggles and roars among the rocks, and finally takes a leap into the calm waters of the lake.

INTERLAKEN ATTRACTIONS.

Located as Interlaken is on a tract of land only a few miles in length, hemmed in by immense mountains on the north and south, and by the heads of Lakes Brienz and Thun on the east and west, its principal attraction appears to be that it is a good place with abundance of accommodations for the tourist to rest after hard travel through the mountains. It formerly had a great reputation for cheapness, which brought immense colonies of English here to spend the summer; but the construction of large and fashionable hotels has made it one of the most expensive. The town consists principally of one main street, on which the hotels are located, about a mile in length, which presents about as gay a scene in the evenings as it is possible to conceive. The Jungfrau Mountain, capped with eternal snow, looms up in front of the hotels, being seen between the ridges of the nearer mountains, and seeming to be only a few miles distant, but in reality being about twenty miles to the north of us.

The principal hotels, numbering about twenty, are very perfect in all their appointments, each being surrounded by gardens laden with flowers, brilliant with their variegated bloom, while all have fountains and pools of water in front. Their dining-rooms, parlors, and chambers are all elegantly fitted up, and the bedding is far superior to that of the hotels of our summer resorts. Balconies, window-shades, and lace curtains render most of the rooms comfortable for a prolonged residence, and the tables are well furnished with the best of provisions.

The waiters at the hotels are all smart Swiss girls arrayed in the peculiar and picturesque costume of the villagers, and they perform their duties very acceptably.

BLUE-BEARD'S CASTLE.

The Castle of Unspunnen, the ruins of which are near Interlaken, is claimed by tradition to have been the home of the famous Blue-beard of the story-books. Every nook and corner of Switzerland has its traditions, and they are all implicitly believed by the peasantry. They will tell you anecdotes of Blue-beard and of the wives he buried alive to give place to more favored ones, and of the huge dog which guarded the treasures hidden in the ruins. The dungeon is still seen in which authentic history asserts that fifty brave warriors from Hasli, after their defeat before Unspunnen, spent four years of misery and suffering from 1330 to 1334. The old count was, according to all accounts, a terrible old fellow.

SUNDAY AT INTERLAKEN.

Sunday at Interlaken is religiously observed in the morning by both the inhabitants and strangers. The stores were mostly closed, and everything quiet around the hotels. A number of country-people were strolling through the village, and the churches were all well attended. There are a Catholic church, a Scotch Presbyterian church, and an English Episcopal church, all located in one building, an old convent, which was disbanded many years since. The doors of the Catholic and Episcopal churches are alongside of each other, each designated by a tin sign, whilst the Scotch church is in another wing of the building. They all seem to get along smoothly together, though—to avoid difficulty, we suppose—, one has service at nine in the morning, another at ten, and the third at eleven o'clock. The English church was largely attended, many being unable to gain admittance. In the afternoon the scene was different, all the stores being open, and people making purchases. The Kursaal, with its restaurant, billiard-halls, and band of music, was in full blast, and Sunday seemed to be done with after two o'clock in the afternoon.

INTERLAKEN, SWITZERLAND, August 13, 1873.

We have spent three days very pleasantly at this great international summer resort, where are gathered the pleasure-seekers of every country of Europe, and not a few of their American cousins. The attractions of Interlaken are various. There are also crowds of consumptives here, and those afflicted with throat- and chest-diseases, to avail themselves of the climate, and the once famous "whey cure." The main portion of the visitors are, however, those who have a mania for climbing mountains, who start off every morning on some new route, with alpenstock in hand, to ascend the mountaintracks. Artists and sketchers, male and female, are also here in abundance, and in every direction we meet them with portfolio and pencil in hand. There is little or no dressing, and none of the frivolities of fashionable life that unfortunately pervade our summer resorts.

The guide-books give a list of fifty different mountain and lake excursions, each of which would require not less than a day to accomplish. There are also ruins of old castles to visit, towers perched upon rocks, and abandoned monasteries. The guide-books detail enough of these excursions, most of which have to be made on foot, to occupy a whole summer. The mountain cascades and waterfalls are also a great attraction to tourists, many of them leaping off precipices one thousand feet high, and becoming, before they reach the ground, scattered in minute particles of spray, which the breeze blows into fantastic and ever-varying forms, whilst the rays of the sun falling upon them create a succession of beautiful rainbows.

THE JUNGFRAU.

The Jungfrau Mountain, covered with an eternal shroud of snow, is visible from nearly all parts of Interlaken in all its majesty. The two peaks called the Silberhorn and the Schneehorn tower above the immense fields of snow. The proportions are so gigantic that the traveler is bewildered in his vain attempts to compute them; distance is annihilated by their vastness. The summits and higher peaks—twelve thousand two hundred and eighty-seven feet above the sea—are covered with snow of dazzling whiteness, whilst the lower and less precipitous slopes also present a boundless expanse of snow and glaciers. The loftiest summit, which is farther south, is not visible from Interlaken. The view when the setting sun gilds the lofty peaks is most brilliant. The base of the mountain is precipitous, and the avalanches from the accumulation of snow and ice on the upper parts of the mountain come down with amazing velocity. The influence of the summer's sun detaches immense masses, the fragments as they fall resembling rushing cataracts, often accompanied by a noise like thunder. The awful stillness which generally pervades these desolate regions is interrupted by the echoing thunders of the falling glaciers. These apparently insignificant white cascades, when viewed from a distance, often contain hundreds of tons of ice, capable of sweeping away forests and whole villages, should any unfortunately be encountered in their course. Happily, however, they fall in uninhabited districts, and are seldom fatal in their effects. What is called the drift avalanche only takes place in winter, after an unusually heavy fall of snow, large fields of which become detached by the wind from heights where they have accumulated. These increase in their progress to an enormous extent, and are precipitated with overwhelming force into the valleys beneath. The current of air which accompanies these snow-torrents, as they may aptly be called, is said to be capable of uprooting forest-trees. The Jungfrau has been frequently ascended, and in 1863 by a lady, but never without risk of life. The mania among people to ascend these snow-mountains is incomprehensible: they might reach a greater height in a balloon with not one-half the risk.

A FLOWER-GARDEN.

Switzerland is a perfect flower-garden. Notwithstanding its cold climate and rather sterile soil, all manner of vegetation is as profuse as in the tropical regions. All of our garden-flowers thrive in the open air, and bloom with a profusion that cannot be equaled in Maryland. They are mostly in pots; though we have seen many fine beds of all varieties. Every hotel and almost every house in Interlaken is surrounded and almost imbedded in flowers. The bloom is more profuse, and the plants attain a more vigorous growth, and seem to require little or no attention. The climate is always moist, which may be the cause of their vigorous growth.

THE CITY OF GENEVA.

GENEVA, August 15, 1873.

We left Interlaken on Tuesday morning on a steamer on the Lake of Thun, and, as usual, the rain commenced to fall before we had been ten minutes afloat. In an hour and a half we were at the town of Thun, at the head of the lake, and were carried from thence by rail in an hour back to the ancient city of Berne, in which we spent a day *en route* to Interlaken. Having an hour to spare, we took a turn through the town, looked again at its live bears, its bronze bears, its stone bears, wooden bears, and gingerbread bears, and soon after took the train for Lausanne, near the head of Lake Geneva.

THE CITY OF LAUSANNE.

We spent the evening and night at Lausanne at the Gibbon House, which was the site of the residence of the great historian Gibbon. In the garden are the trees which he planted, and under the shade of which he wrote his "History of the Decline and Fall of the Roman Empire." The view of the lake from the summer-house at the back of the hotel is grand and romantic. Here oft sat Voltaire, as well as Gibbon, to watch "clear, placid Leman." Lausanne is now, as in the days of Gibbon, distinguished for its good society, and is considered a most desirable place of residence. It has a population of about twenty-five thousand, and, like all the cities of Switzerland, shows evidence of progress and prosperity. The private residences around the city and in the vicinity of the lake are very elegant, and most of them are surrounded by gardens brilliant with foliage and flowers. They are said to be the private residences and châteaux of some of the wealthiest citizens of Europe, who spend their summers here to enjoy the healthy and balmy atmosphere. It was this that Cooper, the great American novelist, declared to be "the noblest of all earthly regions." Kemble, the great tragedian, died at his villa about two miles from Lausanne, and his tomb is in the cemetery of Pierre de Plain.

LAKE OF GENEVA.

We left Lausanne on Wednesday morning for Geneva, on one of the fine steamers which daily traverse the lake. This is the most extensive of all the Swiss lakes, its breadth being at some points from seven to ten miles, and it is the only lake of Switzerland on which sailing-vessels are seen. All the others are so hedged in by mountains and wind around so continually through mountain-gorges, causing a change of wind almost every mile, that sails are perfectly useless. Its banks are lined with towns and cities of considerable size, and, there being very few steep mountains, it is a vast region for the cultivation of the grape. The climate is a great deal warmer than in any other portion of Switzerland, notwithstanding its close proximity to Mont Blanc and many of the highest snow-clad mountains.

The weather was bright and clear, and our three hours' run on this beautiful lake, before reaching Geneva, was both pleasant to the eye and enjoyable. For the first time in Europe we were sailing on a lake without an accompanying storm. The Lake of Geneva is in reality a portion of the river Rhone, the mouth of which can be seen from the railroad just before reaching Lausanne. Flowing into such a vast lake, it is navigable to Geneva, and is one of the finest rivers in Europe.

CITY OF GENEVA.

When seen from the lake, Geneva presents an attractive appearance, the river Rhone passing from the lake directly through the city. It is about five hundred feet wide, and rushes with such force as to drive the wheel of the water-works, located near one of the bridges, which supplies the fountains of the city with water. It is so clear that the pebbles can be seen at its bottom, whilst the fish are visible as they fly along in the rapid current.

It would be difficult to find a more beautiful night-scene than the quay and the bridges of Geneva present, with the thousands of lamps that are reflected from the blue waters of the Rhone on both sides of the river. Here all the hotels are located, and here the citizens spend their evenings in promenading and loitering in the cafés to listen to the singing of strolling vocalists. The stores on Rue du Rhône and Rue Centrale, as well as on the quay, on both sides of the river, make a tempting display of their goods. The principal productions of Geneva seem to be watches and musical boxes, the number of watches manufactured in a year being over one hundred thousand, and of musical boxes almost as many. The population is about fifty thousand.

MONT BLANC.

Mont Blanc, the monarch of European mountains, can be distinctly seen from the quay on the right bank of the river, where seats are arranged for those who desire to sit and watch the rays of the setting sun silver its snowy peaks. On a clear evening the view is grand beyond description, and many travelers content themselves with this glimpse rather than undergo the exposure and fatigue of traveling in those icy regions. The glacier domain of Switzerland extends from Mont Blanc to the Oertler, the entire area thus occupied being computed at nine hundred square miles. The waters from the melting of the snow of these regions form the lakes of Switzerland and the two greatest rivers of Europe, the Rhine and the Rhone.

To make the ascent of Mont Blanc requires two days from Chamouni, and the expense is nearly one hundred and fifty dollars. The ascent is never undertaken with less than six guides, each of whom charges one hundred francs for his services; and little enough for these poor fellows who peril their lives on account of the extra pay to gratify a most unworthy curiosity. With Horace Bénoit de Saussure, who was the first scientific man who made the ascent, it was a different matter: he penetrated all its mysteries, and reported the same to the world. Three ladies only have as yet accomplished the feat: Mlle. Paradis, Mlle. d'Angeville, and Mrs. Hamilton, an English lady. The two latter ladies, when at the summit, had themselves lifted over the shoulders of the guides, that they might be able to say they had risen to a greater height than any of their predecessors. De Saussure, who, after twenty-seven years of longing and fruitless endeavor, reached the summit in August, 1837, says the desire to make the ascent had become with him a kind of disease. He says, "The arrival on the summit did not give me immediately all the pleasure which might have been expected, because the length of the struggle, and the sense of the trouble which it cost me to reach it, seemed as it were to have irritated me, and it was with a kind of wrath I trampled the snow upon its highest point. Besides, I feared that I might not be able to make the observations which I desired, so greatly was I troubled by the rarity of the atmosphere and the difficulty I felt in breathing and in working at this height. We all suffered from fever. I scarcely believed my own eyes; I seemed to myself to be dreaming when I saw beneath my feet the terrific majestic peaks, the acute summits of Midi, Argentière, and Le Géant, the very base of which it had been to me so difficult and hazardous to climb. I understood their connection and their form, and at one single glance was able to clear up the uncertainty which years of labor alone could not have done.

"When any adventurous traveler undertakes the ascent of Mont Blanc, numerous spectators take up their station on the sides of the Breven, from which the progress of the party, as soon as it has emerged upon the snow-line, may be traced the whole way to the summit. Great is the excitement in Chamouni when they are seen returning in the evening across the plain towards the inn. Here they come,—the men who have been up Mont Blanc! Surely earth seems like velvet; they walk not like common men; honor and glory await them; twelve of them get five-and-twenty shillings each, and the thirteenth has his name painted on a board by the side of De Saussure. He has periled his life a score of times within the last forty-eight hours, but it is over now. He has been at the top of Europe, has stood like a fly on the cold tip of the earth's nose, and is perfectly justified in writing a book. They almost all do. That is one of the reasons why they go up."

The skin of most people peels off after the ascent, their eyes become weak, and they suffer more or less in health. How any person can desire to go through the fatigue of making the ascent, when they can risk their life in a balloon for half the expense, we cannot understand.

BURDENS FOR THE BACK.

Every people have their peculiar way of doing things, different from those of their neighbors. In Jamaica the practice is to carry everything, light or heavy, on the top of the head, where it is sure to be balanced, even if it should be an empty bottle. In Venice all manner of burdens are balanced at the ends of poles and carried over the shoulder. In Switzerland the practice is to carry everything, even a bucket of water, on the back. Buckets, tubs, and contrivances of all imaginable kinds are made to fit the human back, with straps to go over the shoulders. If a woman should happen to carry one of her children, a sight not often seen, she is sure to make it straddle her back, with its arms around her neck. Even the milkmen carry their churns on their backs, and the school-boys their books in knapsacks. At Geneva this morning we saw a mother with her three sons, with a basket strapped on the back of each. In one she deposited the fruit, in another the vegetables, and in the third the meat. This was making good use of the boys, who seemed accustomed to the vocation.

Geneva, August 17, 1873.

ROAMING AMERICANS.

The hotels of the city are all overrun with Americans to-day, they having come in like an avalanche from all quarters. The streets, the stores, the watch and music-box factories are all thronged with Americans, representing two-thirds of the States of the Union. They are here with their wives, their daughters, and their sons, and Geneva is profiting greatly by their expenditures. The sons are getting watches and chains, and the daughters jewelry, diamonds, and music-boxes. Everywhere on the street parties are moving along with that free and careless manner peculiar to Americans, and during a three-hours stroll in the business section of the city, English appeared to be the only language spoken. There are also a goodly number of English here, but the Americans far outnumber them. The main retail business of the city comes from the Americans and English, and there are but few stores in which the language is not spoken fluently.

MUSIC-BOXES.

The extent to which this business is carried on in Geneva is a matter of surprise to Americans, and the magnificence of some of the instruments turned out exceeds anything that most persons have any idea of. We were shown an instrument this morning which played thirty-six tunes, with flute, bell, drum, and castanet accompaniments. The cost of it complete was seven thousand francs, or about fourteen hundred dollars, the purchaser to have the privilege of naming twelve airs to be arranged on two of the cylinders that were blank. These instruments range in price from five francs to seven thousand. There are musical chairs, which play when you sit down upon them, musical decanters, which strike up a merry air, such as "The Flowing Bowl," when you pour anything out of them, musical snuff-boxes, musical flower-pots, and musical toys of all descriptions. The fourteen-hundred-dollar instrument had volume of sound sufficient for a church, and would occupy as much space in a parlor as an ordinary piano, though it might be taken for an old-style sideboard.

HOTEL MISTAKES.

Most of the hotels have the American and English flags suspended from their balconies, the object being to attract the tourists who swarm through Switzerland during the summer. There are plenty of Germans here, but most of them go to the boarding-houses, and they are not considered as profitable or desirable guests as the English and Americans. They are apt to take their meals at the cafés rather than at the hotels, and to take good care that their bills have no mistakes in them. A bill for two or three days' board consists of at least twenty items, and it is never given to you until the moment that you are about departing to catch the train. Ten chances to one neither the American nor the Englishman can read anything but the figures and the sum total. He glances hastily over it, pulls out his purse and pays it, not liking to acknowledge his ignorance. We have had occasion to encounter a number of bills, duly settled and receipted, in all of which there proved to be a variety of charges that, in the language of a New Yorker, "hadn't oughter be there." The German detects these mistakes at a glance and corrects them. When rooms are scarce they reserve them for American or English travelers, and are always full to German or Swiss applicants.

THE PETS OF THE PEOPLE.

The city authorities have placed in the river, near the bridges, a large number of white swans, having houses for them on Voltaire's Island, which is connected by a short suspension-bridge with the Bridge des Alpes. These Geneva swans are honored by the people, who throw them bread and crackers as they swim about the bridge, and take delight in watching their gambols in the water. The rapid current will sometimes sweep them some distance down the stream, when they will rise and fly, or rather skim along on the surface, back to the bridge. They have little platforms for their accommodation anchored in the stream, and they are undoubtedly quite an ornament to the city, whilst they are the pets of the people.

GASTRONOMY IN EUROPE.

The Americans in Europe, or at least most of those with whom we have conversed, complain constantly of their inability to get good and palatable food, even at the best of the European hotels. They find, after struggling to get their food properly cooked, that they are compelled to resign themselves to the table-d'hôte, and to eat whatever is given to them, whether they like it or not, or know what it is that they are called upon to digest. If anything comes along that they recognize, such as a chicken, they find it cut up in infinitesimally small particles, about fifty to a chicken, of which they are expected to take but one. In fear of depriving their neighbor, they take the first piece that their fork lights upon, and generally find themselves incapable of scraping a thimbleful of meat from their share of the pullet. Next comes some green spinach, which they are expected to eat by itself, and be thankful. This is followed by some veal, which appears to have done duty in soup before it was roasted, flavored with onions. A dish of potatoes comes along, which they think they recognize as Christian food, but they find that these have been cut up and fried with onions. As everybody does not like onions, would it not be well for all cooks to cook them separately, and allow those who like them to make the mixture? An artichoke comes next, of which all must take a few leaves and suck them. But previous to all this there are about three spoonfuls of very thin soup, and then some fish, generally about the size of a minnow, cut in two, as an intimation to the guest that a half of a fish is his share. Then comes some salad, with another chicken, cut up so as to give an atom to each of the forty guests to make chicken-salad out of. This is succeeded by a spoonful of pudding, a thimbleful of ice-cream, some grapes, and a cake about the size of an American half-dollar, so far as our memory of that coin serves. After every mouthful plate and knife and fork are changed. Those who get through with this very unsatisfactory dinner in an hour and twenty minutes, as we did to-day, may think themselves very fortunate. "Life is too short" for such waste of time.

The American who leaves home during summer must expect to be deprived of all the blessings that summer brings to him at home. He may pick up a hard peach or flavorless pear occasionally, and pay seven francs for five peaches, as we did at Marseilles; or if he can stand the climate and fleas of Italy, he may find some palatable fruit there; but he must forego all hopes of peaches and cream, watermelons, cantaloupes, and even hotcorn must be to him as a thing of the past. He gets no good bread after he passes the capes; and as to griddle-cakes of any kind, we very much doubt if they know what a griddle is in Europe. At Liverpool we called for the famous English muffins, and were furnished with cold and clammy half-cooked dough.

France used to be distinguished for the sweetness of its bread, but we have found it as hard and tasteless as it is possible to make bread. If an American has the dyspepsia, and desires to be where his food will not tempt him to overload his stomach, Europe is the place for him; but if he thinks that good living is essential to enjoyment, he had better stay at home.

THE CITY OF LONDON.

LONDON, September 28, 1873.

We left Paris on Monday for Havre, the principal seaport of France on the Atlantic, which we found greatly improved since our visit some fourteen years ago. The English language is almost as much spoken at Havre as the French, and the line of steamers connecting with Southampton is composed of English vessels, officered by Englishmen. When we reached the wharf, the same burly Englishman who accosted us years ago urged us again to enter his hotel and take "a good old-fashioned English dinner." After dinner, which was not very "good," we strolled over the city, the streets being thronged with promenaders and brilliant with gas-lights, as is the case in all French cities. The main streets were lined with very elegant stores, and the market-house we found well supplied with grapes and pears, the latter being the best we had tasted in Europe.

CROSSING THE CHANNEL.

The Channel between Havre and Southampton is very wide, requiring nine hours to cross, whilst from Calais the trip is made in less than two hours. If people get sick between Dover and Calais, it may naturally be supposed that they get very sick between Havre and Southampton, a fact which we can bear ample testimony to. Having secured our sleeping-places on the steamer, which were mere open bunks erected in the cabins, we concluded it would be better to retire early, before the passengers by the midnight train arrived, at which hour the steamer was to take her departure. We were aroused about half-past eleven o'clock by a noisy crowd of men and women, some quarreling with the officers of the boat because all the sleeping-places were disposed of, whilst others were drinking beer and voraciously eating cold meat and bread, supplied to them by the steward. In a few moments the boat left the wharf, when the scolding and grumbling at once changed to groaning and moaning, and urgent calls for basins, which were handed around in profusion, many taking them into their bunks and hugging them to their bosoms as if they were life-preservers against the perils of the ocean. In all our experience we never witnessed a more rapid transformation. If these people had all taken emetics the effect could not have been more simultaneous. As they had just loaded their stomachs with porter and beer, we will leave the reader to imagine the details of the scene and the vile effluvia that pervaded the closely-packed cabin. The motion of the vessel was really very slight, and it was difficult to imagine what there was to affect any one's stomach; but as everybody expects to be sick in "crossing the Channel," they seem to make haste to meet their destiny. At early dawn we gladly escaped to the deck from the sickly hole in which we had spent the night. Here there was fresh air, but the surroundings were scarcely more inviting. All the benches on deck were occupied by men and women, with the inevitable basin, and it was difficult to walk about, on account of the slippery condition in which the sufferers had managed to convert it during the night.

There is not a river-steamer out of the port of Baltimore having such poor accommodations as these Channel steamers, and none that would not be shunned as nuisances if kept half so vile and filthy. There is a project for tunneling the Channel, and the sooner it is accomplished the better, as the present means of crossing is disgraceful to both England and France. If people have to be sick, we rather think it could be accomplished more satisfactorily to themselves, as well as to their fellow-travelers, in a private state-room, than in an open cabin.

AN AGREEABLE SENSATION.

After five months' sojourn among people speaking foreign languages, we acknowledge having experienced a decidedly pleasurable sensation on Tuesday morning when we reached the wharf at Southampton, and were greeted in broad English by a Jehu, with the salutation, "Will yer 'onor 'ave a coach, sir?" and to hear our English traveling companions giving directions for the careful handling of their "'at-boxes." Every Englishman travels with a ponderous sole-leather hat-box, which seems to be the object of his most sedulous care and consideration. You may smash his trunk or tread upon his favorite corn with impunity, provided you handle his "'at-box" carefully. Then to hear the porters lauding their hotels in an understandable language, and the newsboys crying, "Times! News! Chronicle! Standard!"—"Great Financial Bust-up in America!" "Latest from the Thames Mystery!" etc., was quite refreshing. We made haste to secure a supply of London papers, and enjoyed the felicity of reading fresh news again on the morning of its publication. In short, we were gratified to get back to Old England, which, notwithstanding all its drawbacks, is the only land in Europe, except Switzerland, where there is any real semblance of "liberty, fraternity, and equality."

"UP TO LUNNEN TOWN."

A run of two hours and a half through the green fields of Merry England brought us to Waterloo Bridge, on the Surrey side of the Thames, in the heart of London. The last few miles of the road is on an arched viaduct, passing over the tops of most of the houses, and broad enough for four tracks. Some of the roads enter the city by tunnels, but most of them are on these elevated tracks, which are undoubtedly better than tunnels, where room can be had for their construction. It was an unusually bright and sunny day for London, but the inevitable cloud of smoke and haze had settled down over the city, causing a gloomy sensation, especially to one coming direct from bright and sunny Paris.

London is undoubtedly a grand old city, but all who desire to enjoy it should do so before going to the Continent. After returning hither from the Continent, its atmosphere and aspect are oppressive, especially in the heart of the city. The suburbs and surroundings are picturesque and beautiful, but its vast business centre appears gloomy and sombre in the extreme. The brightest and most ornamental as well as most cleanly and attractive portion of Paris is its business centre, but the very contrary is the case in London. The greater portion of the buildings are nearly coal black, or streaked and stained, whilst the mud and dirt in the streets partakes largely of soot, and is trod upon the pavements by the throngs of pedestrians, so that ladies never think of indulging in the luxury of trailing skirts. The humid state of the atmosphere keeps the streets always damp, so that watering is unnecessary, and dust a novelty. Indeed, the city has the appearance from this cause of being much dirtier than it really is. The crookedness of its thoroughfares is not equaled by any other city in the world. It seems to have been built hap-hazard, without a plan, and never to have been improved or straightened, or its old original thoroughfares widened. There are but three broad streets in the business centre of the city—the Strand, Regent Street, and Oxford Street—and these are not much more than half as broad, and not half as long, as any one of the numerous boulevards of Paris. Its heavy and gloomy architecture, and the smoked and stained walls of what otherwise would be very elegant public structures and churches, its whity-brown brick, streaked and stained and innocent of paint, its winding, turning, and twisting streets, are all in strong contrast with those of Paris, or with almost any of the Continental cities. Around the parks and in the outskirts there are many very elegant private residences and straight and broad streets, but none, with the exception of those occupied by the nobility, will compare in elegance with the numerous private residences of the merchant-princes of America, or such, for example, as those of Robert McLean, George Small, John W. Garrett, J. Stricker Jenkins, or any of the mansions surrounding or in the vicinity of Mount Vernon or Eutaw Place.

LONDON AND PARIS.

We have spent the greater part of the past two days in walking and strolling over the city. Having mastered its plan, such as it is, we have occasionally crossed diagonally through the narrow thoroughfares from one point to another, and, although the weather was clear and dry, we do not think any portion of Baltimore could present such an uninviting appearance. Narrow and dirty pavements, dirty streets, and dirty front doors and steps were the rule, and cleanliness the exception. Indeed, it was often necessary to move along with care to prevent defilement and bad smells, whilst ragged and dirty children were the only embellishments of the scene. In Paris, the police arrest any one who appears on the street ragged and dirty, and, go where you will, neither dirty nor ragged men, women, or children are to be seen. There everybody is compelled to keep their pavements and the street in front of their houses clean, but in London everybody has the privilege of making as untidy an appearance as they may like. This species of liberty the Englishman certainly enjoys to his heart's content.

DRUNKARDS AND BEGGARS.

During nearly five months' sojourn in Prussia, Austria, Italy, and France, we never saw or encountered any one laboring under the effect of intoxicating liquors, not even sufficiently exhilarated to be noisy. But during a two hours' walk in the streets of London, within a half-mile of Trafalgar Square, about four o'clock in the afternoon, we passed more than a dozen reeling drunkards, and, in one case, two drunken women, each trying to help the other home. The "gin-mills" and rummeries and "corner groceries" were as numerous as in some of our narrow thoroughfares, and both men and women could be seen at the counters imbibing, and engaged in noisy controversy. If such was the aspect of affairs in the middle of the day, it is not difficult to imagine what it must be after nightfall. We also encountered beggars and solicitors for alms under various pretenses every few minutes, and dirty and ragged children innumerable. These beggars dart at every carriage that stops, and solicit a penny for opening the door. Indeed, Italy cannot now compare with London for the number and pertinacity of its beggars, and for the woe-begone aspect with which they make their solicitations. In Paris any one caught in the act of begging is at once arrested, whilst in London they swarm about with impunity. They beg or steal, as the opportunity may offer, and are arrayed in such rags and tatters as to be positively offensive.

HOW TO SEE A CITY.

There is no way in which a city can be seen by the stranger so thoroughly as by walking over it, and getting occasionally on the top of an omnibus, all of these vehicles in London being what might be called double-deckers. There are some passenger railways above ground, and a good many under ground, but the omnibus is still the great vehicle for travel in all parts of London. We have thus spent several days in roaming over London, which seems like a dozen large cities that have grown into each other. If you turn off from such fashionable thoroughfares as Regent Street, Oxford Street, Pall Mall, or the Strand, in a few minutes narrow streets are encountered, with their gin-shops and poverty-stricken tenements, whilst a few squares farther will bring you to a fashionable neighborhood, with its public squares and terraces, and so on ad infinitum through the length and breadth of the city. There are but few straight streets in any direction, the city presenting a labyrinth through which it would be difficult to thread your way without a map in hand. London is certainly sadly in need of a Napoleon to open boulevards through its length and breadth. Then the naming of the streets is on a system most perplexing. The name of a street is frequently changed every few squares. That London is a congregation of towns that have finally grown into each other is palpable from the fact that there are within its limits thirty-seven King Streets, thirty-five Charles Streets, and twenty-nine John Streets.

THE STORES OF LONDON.

The reader will probably be surprised to learn that in the whole of London we saw no retail dry-goods store as large as that of Hamilton, Easter & Sons in Baltimore, and only one about the size of that of Mr. Neal. There are thousands upon thousands of stores, but they are, with a few exceptions, small. There are silk stores, hose stores, lace stores, poplin stores, cloth stores, linen stores, but those with a general assortment of dry goods or any other kind of goods are very limited. Many of them make a splendid display in their windows, but if you go inside their shelves will be found comparatively empty, the window seeming to be the chief receptacle of their meagre stocks, even when the signs over the doors indicate that they have the patronage of Her Majesty the Queen and His Royal Highness the Prince of Wales. The stores of London will not compare with those of Paris in any respect, and it is very difficult for the stranger to find what he may be wanting after the most diligent search. Even the book stores are cut up in the same way. There are scientific book stores, poetical book stores, and separate stores for school-books, novels, and other literary productions. But this lack of generality is observable in everything; consequently retail business is on a small scale compared with such establishments in American cities. There is not in the whole of London a gentlemen's furnishing establishment the stock of which would be sufficient to decorate the windows of one of our large establishments on Baltimore Street. As to household goods, the establishment of Samuel Childs & Co., on Charles Street, or of Messrs. Hopkins, on Baltimore Street, contains more goods than forty of the largest stores of the kind in London. If a half-dozen shirts are called for, some samples are shown, and the balance is promised to be furnished next day. The fact is that the whole visible stock of a majority of the stores could be packed into a furniture-wagon and carted off at twenty minutes' notice. The jewelry store of Frodsham, the great watchmaker on the Strand, is about as large as the space between the counter of The American office and the front door, and does not contain as many goods as are daily exhibited in the show-windows alone of the store of Messrs. Canfield & Co., A. E. Warner, Larmour & Co., or Webb's on Baltimore Street. There are numbers of arcades, the stores of which are eight or ten feet deep, nearly everything being in the windows or arranged on tables at the doors.

THE PUBLIC PARKS.

The great glory of London is its public parks, which are numerous and very extensive, and, being located in the very heart of the city, are easily approached from almost any direction. They are seven in number, and are not inaptly termed the lungs of London. They are chiefly at the west end, but St. James's Park, the Green Park, Hyde Park, and Kensington Gardens lie so close to each other that one may walk from Charing Cross, the very heart of the metropolis, to Bayswater, a distance of three miles, without scarcely taking one's feet off the sod. These three parks, embracing over six hundred acres, inclose London on its west side, whilst Regent's Park lies to the northwest, Victoria and Finsbury Parks to the northeast, and Battersea Park, a beautifully-kept flower-garden, cricket-grounds, etc., on the Thames, opposite Chelsea, is to the southwest. In all these parks there are one thousand nine hundred and twenty-six acres, and they are all inside of the city of London. Each of them has extensive cricket-grounds, where the boys of the metropolis throng on Saturday afternoon with bat and ball to play the national game. They are inclosed with iron railings, and during the season are thronged with gay equipages. Everybody of distinction being, however, out of town at the present time, we found the turn-outs at Hyde Park very plain and limited.

THE LONDON NEWSPAPERS.

A close reading of the London newspapers for a week past causes much astonishment at the lack of enterprise evinced by them, even including the great *Times*. We do not think the dispatches from America for the entire week exceeded twenty-five lines, and most of this was market-reports. From Europe the readers of *The American* will find from a column to a column and a half of foreign news daily, whilst the great *Times* contents itself with two or three lines from our side of the Atlantic. Its domestic dispatches are equally as meagre, and some days literally amount to nothing. There are seldom less than four or five columns of telegraphic news in our leading newspapers, and sometimes it extends to double that, which is equal to the amount contained in a whole week's issue of the *Times*. The domestic correspondence in the London papers is also very meagre, and it would be difficult to find more dull and spiritless journals anywhere. Their main attraction to the Englishman is their editorials and local news and letters from the people, especially during this season of the year, when Parliament is not in session.

SERVICE AT WESTMINSTER.

We attended service on Sunday morning at Westminster Abbey, and found it filled to overflowing with an immense congregation, mostly made up of strangers in the city, who make it a rule to always attend one Sunday service at the abbey. The morning service consumed precisely one hour and thirty minutes, it requiring about double the time that is deemed necessary in the old-fashioned Episcopal churches at home. The organ and the fine voices of the choristers combined to make the service sound very similar to the services at St. Peter's in Rome, fully equaling it in its volume and its fine musical execution. The intoning of the Litany and the Creed, as well as of other portions of the service, was more decided than we had ever before heard it in an Episcopal church. The sermon was preached by Dean Stanley, but although we were seated within what would be considered good hearing-distance in almost any other building, his articulation was entirely drowned by the reverberation of his voice among the vaulted columns of the spacious structure. The only words that reached us during the entire delivery, occupying nearly an hour, were "the Church of England," which, being repeated so often, indicated that it was a church-establishment sermon; hence we comforted ourselves with the conviction that we had probably heard sufficient of it. The dissensions in the Church of England are certainly doing great damage to the cause of religion.

UNDERGROUND RAILWAYS.

The underground railways of London are of the most extensive character, fourteen miles of which are now complete and in running order. The enterprise proposes, when completed, to finish an inner circle and an outer circle, through which the cars will continue to run round and round all day, stopping at the numerous stations on the route to take in and discharge passengers. Most of the stations are open to the daylight, but there are some entirely underground and lit with gas. The number of passengers carried over this road last year was forty millions, and there has been a large increase this year. The cars are driven by steam, the locomotives being of a peculiar construction, which enables them to consume their own smoke. They carry six to eight cars, with first, second, and third-class compartments, and move along at the rate of about fifteen miles per hour, including stoppages at the stations. Almost any point in the city can be reached in thirty minutes, even to a distance that would require a couple of hours to go in a cab or an omnibus. These cars are well lighted with gas, and there is not the least inconvenience to passengers from smoke, dust, or gas. Nothing escapes from the locomotive but a small amount of steam. There are numerous openings or vestibules along the route, besides the large and spacious stations, which are fitted up with every convenience for the accommodation of passengers waiting for the trains, one of which passes every few minutes, some of them passing off into branch tunnels leading to widely different stations. The old Thames Tunnel has been utilized by the underground roads, and now trains are constantly flying through it to stations on either side of the river. After being so many years a mere engineering curiosity, it has at last been made serviceable in relieving the streets and bridges of the metropolis from the great rush of travel. This road passes under streets, sewers, gas- and water-pipes, and houses, without incommoding any one or making the slightest noise above ground. Indeed, a stranger in London would scarcely know of its existence were he not to follow the throng of people who are constantly passing in and out of the stations. It is a great relief to the streets, which are still thronged with omnibuses, carriages, and pedestrians. The street-railways are also being extended in some parts of the city above ground, but still meet with much opposition, organized by the powerful omnibus companies.

RAMBLES IN LONDON.

Our first afternoon in London was devoted to the parks, and there were not many better turn-outs than can be seen in our own Druid Hill on a fair day. There were powdered footmen dressed in gaudy liveries, but neither horseflesh, vehicles, nor occupants struck us as particularly excellent or attractive. It is the fashion to disfigure the horses by "banging" their tails, which has been copied by even the cab-horses, destroying all grace and beauty in the animals.

We spent the evening at Madame Tussaud's Wax-Works, and found the spacious halls, as usual, crowded with visitors. From ten o'clock in the morning until ten o'clock at night there is a constant throng of visitors at this popular resort, and no American ever stops in London without paying it a visit. The figures are so perfect in expression of countenance, likeness, and dress of the distinguished personages represented, that the effect is peculiarly pleasing. The whole royal family are here in court dress; but the group that attracted most attention was that of Abraham Lincoln, General Grant, and Andrew Johnson. The latter is a good likeness, but the other two are poor, yet still sufficiently correct to be recognized. Among these wax figures are those of all the great statesmen, kings, and murderers of the past generation, as well as the infant children of the Prince of Wales. If a visitor happens to take a seat on one of the ottomans interspersed among the "figgers" it is sometimes difficult for a moment to decide which is which. Mrs. Jarley is certainly distanced by Madame Tussaud.

THE TOWER OF LONDON.

Having a couple of days to spend in London, we visited this ancient historical pile on Saturday morning, and found as usual a great crowd of visitors, including many Americans. The warders, twelve in number, in the ancient dress worn by their predecessors three centuries ago, were all busy, each having a party of from twenty to thirty with them passing through the tower. In some portions of the building we would pass two or three of these parties, and at times had to stop in our progress to let them pass. The warder as he progresses describes everything briefly, and points out all the prominent matters of historical interest. We passed through the Bloody Tower, the Bell Tower, the Beauchamp, Devereux, Flint, Bowyer, Brick, Jewel, Constable, Broad Arrow, Salt, and Record Towers, all of which have their separate histories and traditions. The Bloody Tower is the traditionary scene of the murder of the royal children, the two sons of Edward IV., in 1483. The Bell Tower was Queen Elizabeth's prison when incarcerated here. The Beauchamp Tower was the prison of Lady Jane Grey and her husband, Lord Guilford Dudley, as well as of a host of other distinguished prisoners who suffered martyrdom during the bloody eras. Immediately in front of the tower is an inclosure about twenty feet square, where the scaffold was erected upon which Lady Jane Grey and Anne Boleyn and a number of other female prisoners were executed. The White Tower was the prison of Sir Walter Raleigh, and here is exhibited the veritable block upon which he was beheaded. The inscriptions cut in the stone walls in all these towers by the prisoners are most curious and interesting, and are religiously preserved. That attributed to Lady Jane Grey was traced on the wall with a pin, as follows:

"To mortals' common fate thy mind resign:
My lot to-day, to-morrow may be thine."

The horse-armory is very interesting, containing as it does specimens of armor and of weapons of almost every age of English history, commencing as far back as the year 1422. The various implements of warfare and torture for so many centuries are most curious, and are arranged with artistic skill. The most interesting, especially to the ladies, is the Jewel Tower, containing a large iron cage, about twelve feet square, in which are exhibited all the crown jewels and royal regalia.

This is a splendid sight, and we presume the whole collection is worth probably not less than twenty millions of dollars, judging by the value of the crown of Queen Victoria, which the custodian assures us cost nearly one million of dollars. The great Koh-i-noor diamond is also among this collection, and is the property of the Queen. It is about as large as an English walnut.

The crown of her Majesty Queen Victoria is a cap of purple velvet, inclosed in hoops of silver, surrounded by a ball and cross, all of which are resplendent with diamonds. In the centre of the cross is the "inestimable sapphire," and in front of the crown is the heart-shaped ruby said to have been worn by the Black Prince.

THE CRYSTAL PALACE.

We spent the afternoon and evening at the Crystal Palace, which was fortunately a gala-day at that celebrated resort of citizens and strangers. Vocal and instrumental concerts, with Santley as one of the singers, performances on the great organ, the playing of the immense fountains, and a grand illumination at night of the extensive gardens and grounds, were among the attractions of the day. The number of visitors could not have been less than six thousand, and as the price of admission, about $1.50, was three times larger than usual, the audience was very select. The scene from the terrace in the evening, when the fountains were throwing up their hundreds of streams of water, bands of music performing, glee-clubs singing, and thousands of lanterns blazing among the foliage and beds of flowers, amid all which the gay throng of visitors were promenading, was grand beyond description.

The beds of flowers and general floricultural embellishments of these grounds, embracing several hundred acres, are certainly unsurpassed in artistic arrangement. No carriages are admitted into the inclosure, its broad and smooth avenues being entirely reserved for pedestrians. On some days, when admission and railroad-fare are low, there have been fifty thousand persons in attendance.

THE ZOOLOGICAL GARDEN.

We spent a few hours at the famous Zoological Garden of London, which is located in the centre of Regent Park, and were much disappointed in the extent of its collection of animals. It is a beautiful flower-garden, covering about twenty acres, and has a few very fine lions and tigers, but the whole establishment scarcely contains more curiosities in the animal kingdom than Forepaugh's traveling menagerie. There are numerous monkeys, but even these are all of the smaller species, two small elephants, a couple of dromedaries, and a small collection of birds. There are several varieties of bears, a zebra, and a fine specimen of the American elk and deer. The collection of seals is very good, and the huge basin in which they are kept was constantly surrounded by a throng of spectators viewing the antics of two very tame creatures, which would come out of the water at the sound of the whistle of their keeper, and climb upon two chairs placed on a platform for their accommodation. The old one would kiss and fondle his keeper the same as a dog, and even climb into his lap. The two elephants were carrying about a dozen children on their backs, and walking leisurely around among the people. The Paris Zoological Garden is far more extensive and elegant, and the number and variety of the animals on exhibition double that of the royal establishment of London.

THE AMERICAN ABROAD.

Every American who has traveled through Europe this year has felt, in his daily intercourse with the people, that our country never before stood so high in their estimation. That we should be paying off our national debt is a thing that no European can understand, and especially that whilst doing so we should show such evidence of national and individual prosperity. The presence of so many thousands of Americans in Europe, and their lavish expenditure, startle them still more. Many Englishmen whom we encountered taking a summer trip in Switzerland were full of curiosity as to all these matters, and asked as many questions as could have been propounded by the most inquisitive Yankee. There is, however, a very sore feeling in England about the result of the Alabama claims negotiations.

Our little party are very plainly dressed, and very plain-looking people, arrayed precisely as other people are here in London, and moving along modestly and quietly on the thoroughfares. Still, by some kind of intuition, even the children in the streets recognize us as Americans, and many stop to stare at us and turn to look after us. We frequently hear the exclamation "Americans" from old and young, and imagine that there is good feeling and respect in the recognition. The cab-drivers all know an American, and rush to secure him; the bootblacks are equally pertinacious, and the shopkeepers evince evident gratification when an American enters their doors. Prices advance wherever they go, and, as they generally spend their money like princes, the world is filled with wonder as to how they manage to get so much of it. The possession of money, and its liberal expenditure by those who are supposed to have earned it, is a novelty in Europe, and the American is the only traveler who does not keep a tight watch upon his purse-strings. They try to account for it by supposing that living is so costly in America that our countrymen save money by spending their summer vacations in Europe, or that they stint themselves at home to come over here and make a splurge. That the American is more of an enigma at the present time in Europe than ever before, is very perceptible, and that John Bull is more at a loss than heretofore to fathom his American cousin is evinced by all classes.

LONDON LOCAL ITEMS.

The newsboys of London have none of the manly characteristics of those of America. They follow and whine after passers-by as if they were a set of beggars, and are generally most ragged and forlorn-looking specimens of the rising generation. The business appears to be overdone, and they are probably too numerous to prosper.

Advertising on the walls and fences is extensively followed by the London papers, especially the *News* and the *Telegraph*, both by hand-bills and elaborately-painted signs, the latter with lettering from twelve to eighteen inches in size. Wherever there is room, or liberty can be obtained to put up one of these signs, it is availed of, and we have passed not less than a thousand of them proclaiming that the *News* is of "world-wide circulation," and that the *Telegraph* has the "largest circulation of any newspaper in the world." *Punch*, and all the weekly papers, follow the same system of advertising.

On returning from the Crystal Palace on Saturday, we passed in the suburbs a large factory for the preparation of "Dog Cake and Poultry Food," by some patent process, "delivered to customers without extra charge."

The cooks and waiting-maids are holding meetings and making speeches in favor of higher wages, fewer hours of labor, and are stipulating for better temper on the part of their lady employers. One speaker urges that the society keep a book of record as to the character of mistresses, for the guidance of members in making engagements.

Asphaltum pavements are being extensively laid in the business sections of London, and some wooden pavements. The streets for miles in the neighborhood of St. Paul's and the Bank of England are laid in white asphaltum, and are very beautiful. They have been in constant use for two years, and, notwithstanding the immense throng of vehicles, are as perfect as if just laid. They are very slippery for the horses, especially if driven fast, but that is generally impossible in most parts of London.

Street railroads, or, as they call them here, "tramways," are being extensively laid on the Surrey side of the Thames, and a number of them are already in operation. The cars are the same as ours, except that they have seats upon the top. The interiors of the cars are almost exclusively occupied by ladies, the gentlemen preferring the top-seats, where they can enjoy their pipes. They do not allow more to get in them than there are seats for, though they can seat forty-eight. In this respect they certainly differ from our cars. The city being very level, this number can be drawn with ease by two horses.

SUNDAY IN LONDON.

Sunday is a very quiet day in London, and the weather being fine to-day the attendance at the churches seems to be very large. Everybody on the streets is in Sunday apparel; the omnibuses and cars are crowded, and the Thames steamers are thronged with passengers. Being located at Charing Cross Hotel, within a stone's throw of St. Ann's and Trafalgar Squares, and in close proximity to Victoria Tower, we were aroused this morning by the sweetest chime of bells in the world, which are rung with artistic skill. The boys were, however, on the streets selling the Sunday papers and boxes of matches as usual, but we judge they are not allowed to cry their wares on Sunday, as they move about in dignified silence.

WESTMINSTER ABBEY.

We spent a few hours to-day among the chapels, cloisters, and tombs of Westminster Abbey, viewing the tombs of Milton, Shakspeare, Dickens, Addison, Sheridan, Beaumont, Spenser, Campbell, Southey, and other distinguished poets and writers. These attract more attention than the tombs of kings and queens, being of men distinguished for their great intellect rather than the accident of birth, and unstained by the crimes which mar the characters of so many of those who lie in close proximity to them.

In this venerable structure all the coronations have taken place since the days of Edward the Confessor. Here it is

"Where royal heads receive the sacred gold ;
It gives them crowns, and does their ashes keep—
There made like gods, like mortals there they sleep."

The abbey is of Gothic design, built in the form of a cross, and is four hundred feet long by two hundred feet wide. It was originally founded in 658, the first building being destroyed by the Danes, and afterwards rebuilt in 958, nearly one thousand years ago.

MR. SPURGEON IN THE PULPIT.

On Sunday morning we moved towards the Tabernacle of the Rev. Mr. Spurgeon. We reached the front of the immense structure at about twenty minutes of eleven o'clock, and found several hundred persons waiting at the front doors, which were not yet opened. The pewholders and those holding tickets had previously been admitted at a side-door. A moment after our arrival the front doors were opened, and a rush was made to secure an entrance, the rule being to admit only as many as the vacant seats can accommodate. We had scarcely got inside of the sill when the doors were closed again, and at the same moment Mr. Spurgeon advanced to the front of his platform and gave out a hymn, which was sung by the whole congregation, rising. The services usually commence as soon as the house is full, and then the doors are closed.

The vast tabernacle has two tiers of galleries going entirely around the interior, and the front of the first tier is the point from which Mr. Spurgeon holds forth, so that he has at least two thousand of his auditors behind him. This was probably necessary to enable his voice to be heard in all parts, which is accomplished with remarkable effect and distinctness.

Mr. Spurgeon, in his mode of conducting the services, is energetic and earnest. He is a man of remarkably ungraceful appearance, short and thick-set, with high shoulders and short neck. His head is round and face full, having his hair parted in the middle, and short, thick, brown whiskers circling his face, both chin and upper lip being closely shaven. At first sight the impression is one of disappointment, as it would seem impossible to expect anything original or impressive from so ordinary and material a looking man. He rushed into his pulpit duties as if he was in a hurry to get through with them, not waiting for the hundreds of persons to obtain seats who had just crowded themselves into the aisles and vestibules. Three hymns were given out and sung before the sermon, two extempore prayers delivered, and a chapter of the Bible read, the speaker commenting upon each verse as he progressed, making a practical application and explaining and expounding its meaning. This was a most pleasing part of the service, replete with something that the hearer would remember after leaving the church. The entire services occupied two hours, the only time Mr. Spurgeon sat down being whilst the three hymns were being sung, after he had read them to his congregation. Among the striking expressions in his prayers were the following: "May the words given us to utter to-day be like burning arrows to the hearts of our hearers." "The breath in our nostrils is Thy gift." "O God, put our tears into Thy bottle and preserve them." He frequently alluded in the most impressive manner to the spread of idolatry over the land, and seemed to refer to the growth of High Church doctrines as tending to the worship of idols. He took his text from the eighteenth chapter and fourteenth verse of the First Book of Kings, declaring at the outset that what he would have to say this morning would not be addressed to the sinner, but to those who professed to be regenerate, and who would with him approach the communion-table in the afternoon. He wanted no profession without daily practice, exclaiming, "Let us have no profession, or make it perfect and true: there is no sin that Jesus loves, consequently there is no sin that Jesus spares." So long as there was a single sin clung to, there was no regeneration. There were "little sins and big sins," and it was these little sins that were most dangerous to the professing Christian, leading, as they would, to a total disregard of Christian duty. Among these little sins he alluded to bad temper in the family or place of business, little acts of unkindness to our fellow-men, lack of patience, uncharitableness, and unkindness to servants and dependants. He at times became very eloquent and impressive, and told his hearers that they were deluding themselves if they imagined their hearts were regenerate so long as they clung to these little sins. They could not be Christians and practice the couplet of Hudibras,—

"Compound for sins they are inclined to,
By damning those they have no mind to."

At the close of the sermon, which lasted about fifty minutes, the congregation were dismissed without any collection, but the rattling of money called our attention to the fact that permanent boxes were located in all parts of the church, into which the congregation dropped their contributions as they passed out. The fact that Mr. Spurgeon has been preaching for nearly twenty years to congregations numbering eight to ten thousand, and that it requires a ticket to insure a seat in so large a church every Sunday morning and evening, in good or bad weather, is a sufficient refutation of those who persist in regarding him as sensational. That he has built up the largest congregation in London, with most extensive charitable organizations, is sufficient evidence that his popularity and usefulness depend on something more tangible than mere superficial oratory. He speaks without a note of any kind, and at times, leaning upon the Bible, seems as if holding a conversation with his hearers. His fluency is wonderful, and the originality of thought and expression seems as if entirely suggested at the moment of utterance, without any previous forethought or preparation.

MR. SPURGEON'S PECULIARITIES.

The following sketch of a sermon we heard Mr. Spurgeon preach on a former visit to London will better illustrate his peculiar style, and the reason why he attracts such never-failing crowds of listeners.

The services commenced with reading a hymn, showing him to be a beautiful and impressive reader, with a voice attuned and capable of the most distinct and impressive enunciation. After the hymn was sung by the congregation, he opened the Testament and commenced reading portions of the twenty-second chapter of St. Luke, relative to Peter's denial of Christ, commenting upon them as he proceeded, in a conversational manner, applying the course of Peter to many professed followers of Christ at the present day. When alluding to Christ's exclamation to Peter, "Simon! Simon! behold, Satan hath desired to have you, that he may sift you as wheat!" he exclaimed, "Ah, brethren, it is well we should all be sifted at times, *even if the* devil *do hold the sieve.* It will do us good, even as it did Peter good, and prepare us for that true repentance and conversion which many of us need." These quaint expressions occurred all through his remarks, but they seemed to flow from him so naturally as to add to the impressiveness of his language rather than to mar it. He occupied about fifteen minutes in this portion of the services, and, after the singing of another hymn, he took for his text the sixty-second verse of the same chapter:—" And Peter went out and wept bitterly."

The subject he proposed to expound to his hearers was True Penitence, and he would use the case of Peter to illustrate—first, its cause; second, its object; third, its nature; fourth, its signs; fifth, the place for repentance; and sixth, its effect. He took up each of these divisions of his subject separately, his manner being that of a person in careless conversation with one or two friends. Most of his time he leaned down with his elbows on the Bible, but occasionally rose as he fired up with his subject with startling energy and thrilling effect. Still, it appeared so entirely natural that no one could possibly accuse him of any studied effort. In fact, his style and language rather impress one with the feeling that he speaks without preparation, and without caring whether he pleases or displeases his hearers.

When speaking of the nature of true repentance and the tears of Peter, considering that he was speaking to his own congregation in his own church, he fully illustrated this independence of style. As to the tears of a man, he placed great value on them, especially if he was a strong-minded man like Peter, full of power, energy, and determination. But there were some persons whose tears flowed at trifles—even at reading a sickly and sentimental story; there were silly women who were always crying; and he knew some persons *whose tears are not worth a farthing a quart.* Some who applied to him for admission to church-membership did not know what true repentance was, and some already in the fold ought to be sifted. Instead of being prompt in doing good, they were dissentious, and quarrel over matters that have nothing to do with the saving of souls or the advancement of the kingdom of God on earth. He wanted to hear nothing of these dissensions and divisions, but hoped that all present who believed in Christ and were truly penitent would meet him at the communion-table without regard to sectarianism of any kind.

At another point in his discourse he said he had no confidence in those who were always praying in public and weeping in public, any more than he had in those who *jump into religion at a spring*. He was always afraid of them; he feared there was a want of deep-toned feeling. Peter, when he wept, went out from the company he was in; he wanted to be in private; and so every one who is truly repentant seeks privacy for prayer and tears. Speaking of the bitterness of true repentance, he said it was like *breaking the teeth up with gravel-stones*, it was crushing out the *infernal impudence* and selfishness from the heart of man.

These of course are only a few disjointed sentences, which were intermixed with eloquent and at times most mild and sweetly-spoken language. His easy and graceful conversational manner is undoubtedly the great secret of his success, whilst his earnest and impressive style must always carry with it a conviction of deep-toned piety. Several times during his discourse he repudiated sectarianism, and declared that it had nothing to do with true religion,—that men were wasting their energies and throwing dissensions into the kingdom of Christ on earth by the discussion and propagation of views and doctrines that were not essential to salvation, and therefore of no importance.

COVENT GARDEN MARKET.

Before the sun has pierced the heavy London smoke, and while the main part of its citizens are enjoying their last morning nap, Covent Garden Market is in its glory. The space it covers is similar in shape and size to Hanover Market, but a little smaller. No wagon or cart drawn by horses has any access to it, and the building and square are filled only with vegetables, fruits, and flowers. The compactness with which these are stored is a novelty, there being no dividing-line between the baskets of different owners, and the pathways left for purchasers are seldom more than two feet wide. These are intersected by others a little wider, through which run the handtrucks to carry off purchases. The sales at this market are almost exclusively to dealers, and families are supplied, as in New York, from small green-groceries. Except the dealers in cabbage, no single huckster occupied more than two yards square, and the majority not more than one. Everything was in stout circular baskets with upright sides, holding about half a bushel, and piled on top of each other to such a height above your head that to the stranger it seemed unsafe. Green peas, and much finer ones than grow in our State, are sold already shelled. A knot of women, miserably clad, gaunt and brown-faced, stowed so close together that they cannot move their arms, are busy shelling the peas, while the master salutes each passer-by with the never-varying invitation, "Have a pea?"

There were tomatoes, peaches, plums, cherries, and strawberries, all looking ripe and fresh, the latter as large as English walnuts, but at prices which alone prove their scarcity. Tomatoes the size of an egg were four shillings a dozen. Peaches, small and yellow, were six shillings and sixpence the half-dozen. These fruits were neatly packed in boxes filled with fine raw cotton.

We stopped in admiration before a stand of cut pansies. The size, freshness, depth, and brilliancy of color were wonderful. Fully a dozen flowers were in each bunch. Putting out our hand to purchase a bunch, "Twelvepence a dozen," said the market-woman. "We want but one bunch." "Never sell except a dozen," was the rejoinder, and she turned to bestow her smiles upon a couple of poor girls behind us, who were eagerly counting the number of stems in a bunch, with an eye to a fresh division of flowers before selling again on the streets. The calceolarias, fuchsias, and geraniums have a much more brilliant bloom than with us, or else the cool moist air of England preserves the flowers, so that the first are still bright when the latest are opening. When the pots are set in rows on the pavement the green leaves are entirely hidden, and the florist's stand seems to be only a mass of gorgeous tinted flowers. Still, to an untrained eye the exotics are less beautiful than the flowers of the field. The pastures are red with the scarlet poppies, the fields of grain are gay with them, and they peep out from between the stones and from the hawthorn hedges, while the least wind gives them a nodding motion, which adds to their grace and beauty. The crimson foxglove, too, grows in the forest, with a spike of flowers twice the length it attains in our gardens. These flowers and numerous others are offered for sale in bunches which show no artistic skill of arrangement, each kind of flower forming a nosegay by itself, yet the effect is there.

The buds overhang the full-blown flowers; the cone-shaped bunch is never ungraceful; and it was a pleasure to see on the street-corners how rapidly the retail traders in bouquets disposed of their sixpenny stock and darted back for a fresh supply. As we passed out we gave a look at the enormous gooseberries, each one of which would suffice for a small tart, and such lemons as never cross the Atlantic, so that we pardon the Englishman who called Baltimore lemons "only limes," and begin to doubt if we have ever seen such perfection of fruit before.

The quantity of fruit provided is very scant for the number to be fed. But the English heart is very liberal in pies; beef, pork, mutton, lobster, ham, jellies, jam, dried fruits, all are served on the table in pies. Ask for a plate of cake with ice-cream, and they bring an assortment of little pies. The desserts served at dinner are always pies of some sort. Frequently they are made more attractive by a French name, but the pastry, more or less bad, is never wanting.

ENGLISH HOTELS.

Four days' experience in English hotels has encouraged an anxiety to get out of them as soon as possible. No wonder the Englishman when traveling is given to grumbling and the loss of temper, when he has to put up with such accommodations and miserable attendance as are received here. Nobody about the hotels is supposed to know anything, and take no trouble to inform themselves as to local knowledge that every citizen ought to possess. At table there is about one waiter to every twenty guests, and if you can get through with an ordinary dinner in an hour and a half you are very fortunate. If you call for a glass of ice-water it is put in your bill, as it is an article only made to order. The elevators, or "lifters," as they call them, only run from the bottom floor, and everybody is required to walk down-stairs. As to the departure of trains, no one knows anything, and you are referred to the depot-officer. The bills presented you upon your departure are a mass of items of which you know nothing, including 1s. 6d. per day for attendance. You are notified that servants are not allowed to receive gratuities, but if you ask one of them the simplest question their hands are extended for a shilling.

As to the expense, in addition to the trouble of giving a written order for everything you want at table, it averages about four dollars per day, provided you call for about one-half of what would be furnished you at any one of our leading hotels. Indeed, going to dinner soon becomes a positive nuisance to be dreaded, rather than a source of pleasure.

EXCURSION ON THE THAMES.

One of the most interesting sights in London is to take one of the steamboats on the Thames, which passes directly through the heart of the city for about fifteen miles. There are several hundred small steamers moving day and night, stopping a moment to land and take off passengers at every bridge, and they are always crowded to their fullest capacity, each boat carrying from one hundred and fifty to two hundred passengers. For tenpence one can travel the whole distance. These boats serve the purpose of omnibuses to carry citizens from one part of the city to another, greatly relieving the crowded thoroughfares. It is indeed a highway of the metropolis, and displays in a more complete manner than any other what London really is, both in extent and character.

Starting from the Westminster Bridge, we had a good view of the Houses of Parliament, starting almost at the water's edge, with their immense towers rising three hundred and fifty feet in the smoky atmosphere, the tops of them seeming as if half enveloped in clouds. The Westminster Bridge is a splendid specimen of architecture, built at a cost of one million dollars, with seven broad arches. As we descend the stream, Hungerford Suspension Bridge, starting on the Middlesex shore from the Italian-looking Hungerford Market, next hangs its thread-like chains across the widest portion of the Thames. Then we approach the Adelphi Terrace, in the centre of which lived and died the famous David Garrick. Then is seen Waterloo Bridge, built at a cost of about five million dollars, with its nine arches, the centre one having a span of one hundred and twenty feet, crowded, as are all the bridges, at all times, with carriages, vehicles, and pedestrians. The magnificent water-front of the Somerset House, so famous in English history, rises from a terrace immediately below this bridge, and extends four hundred feet along the river. Still farther down on the same shore, the pleasant Temple Gardens are seen on the left, green and flourishing amid the surrounding blackness of the city. Blackfriars Bridge, over which is visible the stately dome of

St. Paul's, is next passed; then comes the densest portion of the city, with its crowd of spires, especially on the left bank. Southwark Bridge, with its centre span of two hundred and forty feet, built of iron, is next passed, and we approach London Bridge, the last of the metropolitan bridges, with its living tide of humanity, and its five massive granite arches, dividing the city into what is called "above" and "below" bridge. "Above" bridge, the traffic of the river consists of coal-barges, the bright-colored and picturesque barges laden with straw, and small steamers darting about with railroad speed.

Immediately after passing under the arches of London Bridge the scene is changed, and we emerge on a vast estuary crowded with vessels as far as the eye can reach, whilst to the left of the river are St. Catherine's Docks, and those of the East India Company, filled with immense vessels, and extending for a mile along the shore. All the great commercial buildings of London lie on the left bank of the Thames below the bridge. Next we pass the famous Billingsgate fishmarket, and then the Coal Exchange, and approach the Tower of London, the great massive structure, with its irregular buildings, and famous Traitor's Gate, through which so many of the noblest men in England, in times long past, entered never to return again. Shortly after leaving the Tower we pass over the Thames Tunnel, the last land connection between the two banks of the river.

Greenwich, the great English hospital for worn-out men in the naval service, is next reached on the right bank, with the Isle of Dogs on the left, and the East India Company's docks in the background, the forests of masts rising from it presenting an impenetrable mass to the eye.

Below Greenwich the banks of the river are remarkable for their pastoral beauty, passing down from Woolwich Arsenal to Gravesend, and present a very pleasing continuation to the trip through the metropolis. At Twickenham we pass Pope's Grotto, and Strawberry Hill, the sham castle of Horace Walpole. Below Richmond extends Kew Park, once famous as the farm where George III. used to play gentleman-farmer, and places of historical interest line its banks on both sides.

The trip up the Thames to Chelsea, a distance of about five miles from Westminster Bridge, is also very interesting, passing Vauxhall Bridge, and several other fine structures, whilst the banks of the river continue all the way up lined with buildings.

THE HOUSES OF PARLIAMENT.

Near Westminster Bridge, and nearly by the side of Westminster Abbey, are the Houses of Parliament, a grand Gothic structure, covering eight acres of ground. It may be called grand in its appearance, but is neither a handsome nor attractive structure. It is built of a reddish sandstone blackened by the smoke of London. It has a river-front of nine hundred feet, raised upon a terrace of Aberdeen granite, and seems to spring almost out of the murky waters of the Thames. It has three towers, the Victoria being the largest, and a richly decorated belfry spire, rising to the height of three hundred and twenty feet. Various other subordinate towers, by their picturesque forms and positions, add materially to the effect of the whole building. Being Gothic, it is of course without pillars, but its walls are everywhere ornamented with statues and elaborate carving.

The outside, when examined in detail, —and it can only be seen by piecemeal,— has a very disjointed appearance, and, except from the river, looks like anything but one continuous building. As a whole there is neither symmetry nor beauty about it, and it reminds one somewhat of the Smithsonian Institute in Washington, which has been styled "a convention of pepper-boxes." After entering a dreary, barn-like hall, called Westminster Hall, lighted by an immense stained-glass window at the extreme end, with a Gothic roof, you pass into a series of narrow passage-ways and small chambers which lead into the House of Lords, everything appearing narrow and contracted, and lighted from above. The largest rooms that we encountered were the cloak-rooms; and on entering the House of Lords this condensation of space strikes one who has been used to the Hall of the American Congress as most remarkable. This chamber is a room forty-five feet wide, with ceiling of the same height, and about seventy feet long, with a narrow iron-railed gallery around it. About one-third of the length is taken up with a magnificent throne at one end, from which her Majesty delivers her annual message, and by the seats for the presiding officers at the other end. No expense has been spared to make this the most splendid chamber in the world, but the architect, we think, failed in his purpose.

Indeed, the decorations have been so profusely piled together, and the hall is so small, that it is a difficult matter to examine any one of them. The extreme height of the ceiling makes the chamber appear much smaller than it really is. The lords sit like boys in a country school-house, on long and broad benches, with backs covered with purple morocco and stuffed, one rising above the other, whilst the Lord Chancellor sits on a crimson sack, called the "woolsack." The lords have no desks nor anything to hoist their heels upon like our members of Congress, unless it be on the shoulders of the noble lords sitting in long rows on the benches before them. The hall is said to be unhealthy; and we should think it was when so closely packed with aristocratic humanity, and the only air to be breathed coming in from the surface of the Thames. The House of Commons is precisely of the same size, one hundred feet long, forty-five feet wide, and forty-five feet high. It is also gaudily decorated with paintings and statues, but is not much larger, and not half so comfortable, as that occupied by the House of Delegates at Annapolis. We admit the extreme verdancy that induced us, after walking through, to ask the attendant for what purpose it was used. It has six rows of high-backed benches on each side, extending nearly the whole length of the hall, rising like the seats in a circus, one above the other, so that the feet of one member are necessarily somewhat near the coat-tail of the member before him. And this is the great House of Parliament of England!

ENGLISH LADIES' PECULIARITIES.

We have some very critical companions with us,—connoisseurs in all the belongings and attractions of the gentler sex,—who are constantly calling attention to matters that might otherwise escape observation. They have already come to the conclusion that the English ladies are unlovely about the feet. The foot is long, broad, and flat, the instep low, and the ankle devoid of gracefulness. The palpable defect of the English ladies in this respect, no matter how lovely they may be in form, feature, and carriage, is rendered more prominent by the lack of artificial skill on the part of the shoemakers of her Majesty's dominions. Among the English ladies whom we have met in our travels, the fact was freely admitted, not only that American ladies excelled in their pedal attractions, but that American shoemakers knew how to adorn them to the best possible advantage. English shoes may be good for service, but they are undoubtedly less ornamental than useful, either in the fit or the decoration of the human foot. To be sure they have not much to encourage them to aim at artistical effect in that direction, as their lady customers have no ambition to rival each other in any claim of superior excellence. All their feet seem to be of the same ungraceful shape, of the same length and breadth and flatness. What chance is there for the ambitious son of Crispin to distinguish himself in his profession, when the same last would suit nearly all his customers, and where it is scarcely deemed necessary for any one to get measured for a pair of shoes? However, the English girl makes up in her bright and beautiful complexion for her defects in foot and ankle. Perhaps it is due to the fact that she takes more exercise and delights in a freer use of her feet than her American sisters.

At the organ-concert at Liverpool, our attention was called to the immense waterfalls worn by the English girls. They commence high up on the top of the head, and extend not only to the neck, but far down between the shoulders, being at least two sizes larger than the largest we have ever seen on our side of the Atlantic. Anything more unnatural in appearance or unbecoming it would be impossible to conceive. They are gathered up in a knot, and look as solid as if they were bags stuffed with bran, or blown-up bladders covered with something resembling the human hair. Otherwise the ladies were dressed with taste and neatness, but their heads were actually deformed by this unnatural appendage.

PECULIARITIES OF ENGLISHMEN.

The Englishman dresses well, and generally looks as if he had just come out of a bandbox. He still clings to his stove-pipe hat, and although he may travel in a felt hat or a Scotch cap, would as soon think of leaving home without a change of linen as without a hat-box. There are great loads of luggage constantly arriving at our hotel, and the ponderous leather hat-case, with its brass lock and key, accompanies every trunk, and at the depot the most earnest words of caution which one hears about luggage are generally an exhortation to some porter to "be careful with me 'at-box." So also you can scarcely meet an Englishman traveling who will not recount to you how and where he lost his hat-box, with the additional fact that it contained also some other valuables, from which it may be presumed that the thieves have discovered that the practice of carrying something more valuable than a *tile* has induced the introduction of such formidable sole-leather brass-locked boxes. We shocked a gentleman by assuring him that hat-boxes had gone into disuse in America, and that a pile of baggage such as stood before us, festooned with hat-boxes, would create a decided sensation at any of our railroad-stations. On his expressing surprise that a gentleman would undertake to travel without his hat, we explained to him that provision was made in our railroad-cars for gentlemen to hang up their hats, and that whilst in the car they could draw from their pocket a cap to ride in. "Well," he replied, "we are behind the age in railroad-conveniences; but you see how '*dem* ridiculous' it would be for us to attempt to travel without a hat-box in our cars. They are thrown in among the trunks, and must necessarily be heavy and strong to stand the crush and protect their contents."

ENGLISH ODDITIES.

The other evening, whilst partaking of a "chop" in one of the London chop-houses, we heard a gentleman near us call for "a 'alf-go" of brandy, and, turning to the bill of fare, we found a regular entry of rates, as follows:

"A go" of brandy, . . One shilling.
"A half-go" of brandy, . Sixpence.
"A go" of whisky, . . Sixpence.
"A half-go" of whisky, . Threepence.

The same rate of measurement was also given for wine and gin. We suppose from the variation of price that a whole "go" must be a sufficiency to make an ordinary man drunk, as some persons require more for a "go" than others do.

SCOTLAND.

THE CITY OF EDINBURGH.

RAPID TRAVELING.

We left London at nine o'clock on a fine June morning, and, after a most delightful railroad journey of eleven hours, were snugly quartered in the Royal Hotel of Edinburgh. The distance being four hundred and ten miles, we calculated that it would require at least twenty hours to accomplish it, and were altogether unprepared for such a rate of speed. The first eighty-two and a half miles were run in precisely two hours, being forty-one and a quarter miles per hour, though on some parts of the route, after we passed the borders of Scotland, in order to make up the time lost on the ascent of the hills, we ran *fifty miles* an hour. Only eleven hours were consumed in the whole trip, and one hour of this was lost in stopping for dinner, and at various stations, so that the average time for the whole distance was forty-one miles per hour. This is rather ahead of railroad travel in America; and it may not be amiss to remark here that whilst a visit to Europe is sure to make a man return a better American and more attached to his own institutions than when he left home, yet he is very apt to have some of his vanity abstracted, especially as to rapid traveling.

SCENES ON THE ROUTE.

The scenery through the North of England is very fine, and the agricultural appearance of the country cannot fail to attract the attention of the tourist. There is no waste land; all is cultivated even down to the side of the track; whilst the well-trimmed hedges add to the beauty of the scene. We passed within sight of Manchester, with its numerous factories, and dense smoke pouring from hundreds of tall chimneys, and the waters of the Irwell, the Irk, and the Medlock flowing through its centre, combining to make it the metropolis of manufactures.

We arrived at Carlisle about five o'clock in the afternoon, a border town of England, three hundred miles from London, and soon after crossed the border into Scotland, having a full view of the famous Gretna Green, the resort of runaway matches in the "days of auld lang syne." It is a beautiful green level, with a little church on the banks of a creek that divides the two countries. After crossing the line and passing over the Cheviot Hills, there was not only a most marked change in the climate, but the country became barren and dreary, and that which was cultivated seemed to be chilled by the atmosphere.

THE CITY OF EDINBURGH.

On approaching Edinburgh, the first point that strikes the eye is the top of an immense hill, known as "Arthur's Seat," towering above the roofs of its tall and massive houses, in the distance having the appearance and form of a monster lion sitting at his ease. Its summit is eight hundred and twenty-two feet above the level of the sea. It derives its name, as every student of history knows, from the fact that tradition designates it as the spot from which King Arthur looked down upon the scene of his victory over the Saxons. Immediately at the foot of this mountain is the famous Palace of Holyrood, the home of Mary Queen of Scots, which is frequently visited by Queen Victoria, when she may be seen every morning ascending to the top of Seaton's Hill.

We reached our quarters in Edinburgh precisely at eight o'clock in the evening, and after supper started for a walk, it being still bright daylight, although the clock had already struck nine. We continued our perambulations until ten o'clock, and then it was only just dark, daylight lasting in this latitude, at this season of the year, from half-past two in the morning until ten o'clock at night, there being only four and a half hours' partial darkness. At Inverness, in Scotland, there is said to be no darkness at all at the present season, the twilight of the evening continuing until daylight in the morning.

MONUMENT TO WALTER SCOTT.

Edinburgh is a grand old city, filled with massive public buildings, of elegant architecture, and it is renowned for its monuments and charitable institutions, evincing a patriotism and public spirit among its people which but few cities in Europe can boast of. The monument to Sir Walter Scott, which looms up in the square directly opposite the window at which we are writing, had no equal in London for grandeur and beauty of design before the erection of the great monument to Prince Albert. Indeed, that city of monuments, Paris, has nothing to compare with it in the way of monuments, so far as architectural beauty is concerned. It is built on a pediment of marble, about thirty feet each way, the lower portion of it being a double-flanked open arch, under which is the statue of Sir Walter Scott and his favorite dog Maida, in gray Carrara marble. It is a picturesque structure in the shape of an open spire, two hundred feet in height. Some idea of its ornamental character may be formed from the fact that it has fifty-four niches reserved for statues of different impersonations in Sir Walter Scott's works. The four lower statues are, Prince Charles (from Waverley) drawing his sword, Meg Merrilies, the Lady of the Lake stepping from her boat, and the Last Minstrel. This monument was erected by subscription, at a cost of seventy-five thousand dollars. There are also statues and monuments in Edinburgh to Burns, Charles II., the Duke of Wellington, Duncan Forbes, the Duke of York, George IV., James Watt, Lord Melville, Jeffrey, Boyle, Blair, Dundas, Pitt, Queen Victoria, David Dickinson, Dugald Stewart, Nelson, and Professor Playfair.

NELSON'S MONUMENT.

Nelson's Monument is a grand affair, standing on Calton Hill, directly at the head of the city, but resembles more a light-house than a monument, or, as has been wittily remarked by an English writer, it looks like a Dutch skipper's spyglass partly opened. It is a massive brown-stone tower, one hundred and four feet in height, from the top of which a magnificent view of the city and surrounding country is obtained, having the Grampian Hills in the distance, on which young Norval's "father fed his flocks," and the Frith of Forth, whilst the whole harbor of Leith, with the bay, opens up to the eye of the spectator. Near the Nelson Monument is what is called the National Monument, which was commenced in 1822, and designed to commemorate the gallant achievements of the Scotchmen who fell in the battle of Waterloo. It was intended to be a model of the Parthenon of Athens, but has never been completed, for want of funds. Lord Melville's column, surmounted by his statue, stands in the centre of the town, and is about one hundred and twenty feet high. The monument to Burns also stands near the Nelson Monument, and is quite an elegant affair, forming a small temple, surrounded by about twenty marble pillars.

The population of Edinburgh is over two hundred thousand, and the city is full of attractions. In the old portions of the city the lowest of the houses are five stories, and some go as high as eleven and twelve stories, built of gray sandstone. In the new portions, which comprise all the business sections and the residences of the wealthier classes, the streets are broad, and the houses of most elegant construction, some of them displaying architectural merit of the highest order. The public buildings, which are quite numerous, are truly elegant, and the churches are very fine.

CHARITABLE INSTITUTIONS.

There are probably more charitable institutions, and of a higher grade, than in any other city of a similar population in the world. George Heriot's Orphans' Asylum, with its two hundred scholars, which we visited to-day, is almost as extensive an establishment as that of Girard in Philadelphia, especially as it has six or seven adjunct free schools, with over one thousand scholars, all supported by the fund left by this worthy Scotchman. Then there is Donaldson's Hospital, a similar institution, which gives instruction, clothing, and maintenance to one hundred and fifty boys, and a like number of girls, including ninety deaf and dumb of both sexes, with all the necessary apartments for teachers and servants. James Donaldson was a printer of Edinburgh, who died in 1830, leaving $1,050,000 for this institution. Then there is John Watson's Foundling Hospital, George Watson's Asylum for the daughters of decayed merchants, and the Merchant Maiden Hospital, for the education of the daughters and grand-daughters of insolvent or deceased merchants. There is also Gillespie's Hospital, founded by the celebrated snuff-merchant of that name, for the reception of about forty-five men and women of forty-five years and upwards, which also has a free school attached to it for the education of about two hundred boys. Then there are a National Gallery and five extensive museums all worthy of a visit.

EDINBURGH NOTABLES.

We must not omit to mention a most interesting spot visited to-day, the house of David Deans, the home of Jeanie Deans, celebrated in Scott's novel of "The Heart of Midlothian," which stands at the foot of Arthur's Seat. We also saw the house of Burke, the famous murderer of Edinburgh, who, it will be remembered, forty years or more ago killed, according to his own confession, nineteen persons, and sold their bodies to the doctors for dissection. Afterwards, when visiting the Museum of the College of Surgeons, we stood face to face with the skeleton of the old rascal, which stands erect in one of the cases.

The house in which the renowned John Knox, the great Reformer, was born, was also visited, as well as that in which he died, which is said to be the oldest in that section of the city. Here, it is said, he wrote a part, if not the whole, of his "History of the Reformation." An inscription on the door runs thus: "Love God above all, and your neighbor as yourself."

THE PALACE OF HOLYROOD.

The greatest attraction in the city of Edinburgh is the Palace of Holyrood, from its connection with the sufferings and persecutions of that beautiful but unfortunate woman, Mary Queen of Scots. Here is not only the room she occupied, but the bed she slept upon, the chairs, tables, work-stands, and even the work-basket she used, together with some specimens of needle-work executed by her own hands during her imprisonment. Here also is the Presence Chamber in which Queen Mary had the interview with John Knox which resulted in her conversion; the dressing-room and the small apartment adjoining it, which has a secret stair leading from the chapel to the palace, by which Darnley and his associates entered and assassinated her secretary Rizzio, on the charge that he was an emissary of the pope. This is by far the most interesting portion of the palace, and will ever remain so from its associations with the unfortunate Mary. Rizzio's blood still marks the floor at the head of the stairs, where his body was found with fifty-six wounds. These rooms, in which the fair and unfortunate queen dwelt and spent a good portion of her life, are well calculated to carry back the mind of the spectator to the olden time. Their loneliness and desertion now strongly contrast with the brutal and atrocious murder that was perpetrated within their bounds. The chamber and dressing-room of Lord Darnley are also here, which have in them much of the furniture of the olden time, including a state bed on which Charles I. reposed when a resident of Holyrood.

The chamber of Queen Mary is a room about twenty feet square. The ceiling is of carved oak, and the walls are hung with decayed tapestry illustrative of the mythological tale of the fall of Phaeton. The bed of Queen Mary stands here, the decayed hangings of which are of crimson damask, with green silk fringes and tassels, and the melancholy and faded aspect of the room is in admirable keeping with its tale of sorrow and of crime.

The ruins of the old chapel royal, attached to the palace, in which Queen

Mary and Darnley were married, are also full of historical associations. Within these walls many of the kings and queens of Scotland were crowned; here James II. was married to Mary of Gueldres, and James III. to Margaret of Denmark; this was the scene also of that high ceremonial at which the papal legate presented to James IV., in the name of Pope Julius II., a purple crown, and that richly-ornamented sword which, under the name of the " Sword of State," is still preserved among the regalia of Scotland; and at the eastern extremity of the existing church, under the great window, Mary, in an evil hour, plighted her troth to the foolish and dissipated Darnley.

The southern wing of the palace has been elegantly fitted up for the use of Queen Victoria and the royal family, who make it a stopping-place on their way to the queen's private country-seat in the Highlands of Scotland, where she spends a few weeks every summer.

We also visited the Castle of Edinburgh, and viewed the Scottish crown jewels, with the crown, sceptre, and sword of state. The eastern side of this castle was once a royal residence, and here is shown the room in which James VI., the only son of Mary Queen of Scots, was born, 19th of June, 1566, just three hundred and seven years ago.

We were obliged to forego the pleasure of a visit to "Roslin's lovely glen," with its castle and chapel and romantic scenery, as well as to Abbotsford, and prepared for our departure for Glasgow, en route for Ireland.

DEPARTURE FROM EDINBURGH.

We left Edinburgh at eleven o'clock in the morning, by railroad, en route for Glasgow, a distance of forty-five miles, which was accomplished in less than two hours. The country through which we passed was finely cultivated, and interspersed with neat cottages and all the evidences of industry and prosperity. The cultivation was nearly equal to any we had seen in England, and there were better cottages, and more evidences of genuine home comforts among the tillers of the soil. As we approached Glasgow, the character of the buildings gradually improved, until the whole country was occupied in every direction with beautiful country villas, surrounded with all those evidences of taste, refinement, and wealth which generally characterize rural neighborhoods near the large commercial cities of America.

THE CITY OF GLASGOW.

We reached Glasgow at one o'clock, and, having but little time to spare for sight-seeing, we employed our time to the best possible advantage. Taking seats on the top of the first omnibus (the omnibuses everywhere in Europe have seats on top, and carry more passengers outside than within), we had a fine view of the principal thoroughfares. To say that we were surprised at the extent, business character, and beauty of the city would but feebly express the feeling with which Glasgow inspires every stranger who visits it for the first time. He finds an immense commercial metropolis, with a population of over five hundred thousand souls, bustling with energy and activity, where he expected to find a second- or third-rate port. The main business streets of Glasgow will compare favorably with the most active portions of any of our commercial cities, not even excepting Wall Street or Broadway of New York, at the busiest seasons of the year.

Forty years ago there were scores of towns within the limits of Great Britain that were superior to it in wealth, extent, and population. It has now no superior, if the precincts of Liverpool are excluded, with the exception of London. It is called " the Yankee city of Great Britain," and has a larger population than Edinburgh, Dublin, Liverpool, or Manchester, and combines within itself the commercial and manufacturing advantages possessed by the two last mentioned. Like Manchester, it is a city of tall chimneys and daily increasing manufactures, and, like Liverpool, is a commercial port, trading extensively with every part of the known world, and is distinguished for the industry, perseverance, and intelligence of its inhabitants.

The new portion of the city, which is rapidly spreading northwest of the ancient town, is distinguished for the architectural beauty of its public and private buildings, and the length, breadth, and elegance of its streets, squares, and crescents. The motto upon the city arms is "*Let Glasgow Flourish,*" and it seems to be the determination of her people that she shall continue to flourish and prosper, if it is possible for united energy, perseverance, industry, and frugality to accomplish such a purpose.

When Bailie Nicol Jarvie, and his worthy father the deacon, " praise to his memory," lived in Glasgow, before the American Revolution, it was a great place for the tobacco-trade, but since 1792 cotton and iron have largely engaged the attention of its enterprising population.

The river Clyde passes through the city, and is spanned by some fine stone bridges, five hundred feet long and sixty feet wide. The city is located on a level, four or five miles square, chiefly on the north side of the river. On the south side the great manufacturing districts are principally located. Its port is the open river, lined by noble quays above, and so much improved that first-class ships, which formerly had to stop at Port Glasgow, eighteen miles lower down, can now come up to the city, the river having been deepened so that where it was formerly fordable there is now twenty feet of water. The work of excavation is always progressing, and the earth, taken from the bed of the river by numerous mud-machines, has been used to fill up the marshes and form uniform walled embankments to a distance of ten miles down below the present city limits.

There is a magnificent park on the northern borders of the city, surrounded by private residences that will compare favorably with those of our Mount Vernon Square. Numerous monuments and statues adorn various sections of the city, expressing the national pride and loyalty of its citizens.

TRIP DOWN THE CLYDE.

At five o'clock in the afternoon we embarked on a steam ferry-boat for Greenock, a city of considerable and growing importance, located on the Clyde, twenty miles below Glasgow. But for the stench arising from the waters of the river, which is more offensive than that from the Thames, the trip would have been a most agreeable one. The boat was thronged with passengers, and, as none of them seemed in the least discomfited by this peculiarity of the stream, we came to the conclusion that it is not impossible to become accustomed to anything, however offensive or displeasing to the senses,—even to the odor from our "Basin" at Baltimore. The trip was, however, one of great interest, not only on account of the business activity observable along the banks of the river, but for the fine display of villas and country-seats, with their gardens, groves, and beautiful surroundings.

The river Clyde has become famous all over the world for the manufacture of iron steamers and ships along its shores, the term "Clyde-built" being familiar as a household word. Whilst so many have been constructed to navigate other waters, an immense number are employed in the trade of the river. On our passage down we could not have passed less than thirty or forty small-class iron steamships going towards Glasgow, being regular packets trading with different ports on the coasts of Ireland, Scotland, and England. Notwithstanding the general depression in ship-building, there is still considerable activity in the yards along the Clyde, the number of large-class vessels we passed in the course of construction being not less than one hundred. There were also numerous large-class side-wheel iron steamers lying at the wharves of Glasgow, receiving the finishing touch of the machinist.

THE CITY OF GREENOCK.

We reached the port of Greenock about six o'clock, and, as the steamer for Belfast did not leave until dark, which in this latitude at this season means ten o'clock at night, we availed ourselves of the opportunity to take a bird's-eye view of the city. Greenock is a city of not less than thirty thousand inhabitants, built on the side of a hill, with a fine harbor, in which were floating several large three-deck frigates of war, besides an old hulk used as a receiving-ship. There were also a large number of merchant-vessels and steamers at the wharves; and Greenock may undoubtedly be considered as a prosperous seaport.

IRELAND.

CITY OF BELFAST.

We left Greenock at ten o'clock at night for a short trip on the Atlantic, and reached Belfast, in Ireland, before daylight next morning. Having good berths, we were soon oblivious to the rolling of the sea, and, like the man in the mill, woke up as soon as the machinery had ceased its motion, in the harbor of Belfast.

The train of cars for Dublin not leaving until ten o'clock, we had four or five hours for breakfast and in which to view the city, which we made the best possible use of.

Belfast is the chief seat of the Irish linen-trade, and, though ranking the second port in Ireland, it is the first so far as trade and manufactures are concerned. The tall chimneys and factories for spinning linen and cotton yarn are conspicuous everywhere. Few cities in Europe have progressed so rapidly as that of Belfast, the population having, in the course of thirty years, increased from thirty-three thousand to nearly one hundred and fifty thousand. The general appearance of the town is that of a clean, thrifty business place, with the trade and manufactures of Glasgow or Manchester, but without the smoke and dirt of either. The buildings are good, and many of the streets very regular and wide, especially towards the interior of the town.

The flax-mills naturally attract the visitor's attention. They are situated in all parts of the town. The interminable hum of myriads of spindles, and the subdued sound of the machinery, together with the light and airy appearance of the rooms and quiet and orderly behavior of the hands employed, appear at first sight to be an entirely new feature in Ireland. The first spinning-factory was, however, established in 1806, whilst the mills now number over one hundred, with no less than one million spindles in operation, representing nearly six millions sterling of capital. The firm of Mulhollands employ over one thousand hands.

The population of Belfast is about one hundred and fifty thousand, nearly one-half of whom are Presbyterians, the Roman Catholics being very few. The churches of Belfast are enumerated as follows: Presbyterians, fourteen; Episcopalians, seven; Roman Catholics, three; Unitarians, three; besides chapels for Methodists, Friends, Independents, Covenanters, and other sects, in all more than fifty houses of worship.

The harbor of Belfast is one of the finest in the United Kingdom, and its commerce is improving and increasing as rapidly as its manufactures.

TRIP TO GALWAY.

Before proceeding with our narrative of travel from Belfast to Dublin, we will anticipate somewhat, and give a brief notice of a trip to Galway. N. P. Willis, in recording his visit to Galway, speaks of the universality of red petticoats, and the same brilliant color in most other articles of female dress, which give a foreign aspect to the population, and prepare you somewhat for the completely Italian or Spanish look of the streets. It is a quaint and peculiar city, with antiquities such as can be nowhere else met with in Ireland. The older portion of the city is throughout of Spanish architecture, with wide gateways, broad stairs, and all the fantastic ornaments calculated to carry the imagination back to Granada and Valencia. The monks, the churches, and the convents, also give to the town a complete Roman Catholic appearance, whilst the population of the adjoining country have preserved something of the picturesque national costume of their ancestors. Galway was at one time a port having considerable commercial intercourse with Spain, and many of the grandee merchants located here. The richer merchants of the town also made periodical visits to Spain, and returned with Spanish luxuries and Spanish ideas, and very frequently with Spanish wives. The result was that mansions in the Spanish style arose, and were filled with Spanish furniture, whilst the ladies sported in their dresses the highest colors and light textures of Spain.

This was, however, some three hundred years ago, and the palaces of the merchant-princes are now occupied as stables or drinking-houses. After years of decline, Galway is commencing to revive in business importance, and there is now a prospect of its regaining its ancient standing. It has a population of nearly fifty thousand, and with a fine bay and harbor, and surrounded by a rich agricultural region, there is no reason why it should not emulate Belfast. The principal articles of trade are fish and marble. The government has erected an elegant stone custom-house and post-office, and there is everywhere evidence of fostering aid in the effort to restore the ancient prosperity of the town.

The country in this section of Ireland is poorly cultivated, whilst the adobe and mere mud cabins of the peasantry show the improvident character of the inhabitants.

THE CITY OF DUBLIN.

IRISH WAYSIDE SCENES.

We reached this ancient city, the capital of Ireland, yesterday, after a very pleasing railroad-ride from the city of Belfast, the distance being one hundred and twenty-seven miles, passing through the counties of Antrim, Down, Armagh, Louth, Meath, and Dublin. To say that we were pleased with the general aspect of the country would but poorly express our first impression. If all portions of Ireland presented as many evidences of industry, frugality, and fine cultivation, we imagine that there would be less emigration, and less complaint among the people.

The houses of the farmers are generally of stone, rough-cast, and as white as snow, with beautiful gardens, arbors, and bowers, whilst the surrounding fields are generally small, and divided by hedgerows, neatly trimmed, and presenting as fine a view from the road-side as can be found in either England or Scotland. The trees are much larger, and more like those of America than any we have seen in Europe, and indeed the climate as well as the general aspect of the country so closely resembled "home" that we could scarcely realize that we were traveling through Ireland. The impression produced on the mind by the wholesale emigration from Ireland leads us to look for evidences of squalid misery, a cheerless and barren soil, and a cold inhospitable climate; instead of which we were flying through a country that would compare favorably with any within twenty miles of Baltimore, not only in its natural advantages, but in the general evidences of good husbandry and the thrift and industry of its inhabitants.

We passed on the route the ruins of several old castles and round towers, distinguished in the feudal history of Ireland, with quite a number of thriving towns, cities, and villages. The manufacture of Irish linen is extensively pursued in this section of Ireland, and acres of it we noticed spread out to bleach in the neighborhood of all the towns. We occasionally passed through some of the bog-districts, in which large forces of men were engaged in digging turf and spreading it out to dry in the sun, to be prepared for fuel, whilst others were digging ditches and draining, preparatory to restoring large tracts of waste-land to agricultural purposes.

THE BATTLE OF THE BOYNE.

The river Boyne is crossed near the spot where the celebrated battle was fought between the Prince of Orange and his father-in-law, James II., in which the Irish forces, under the latter, were routed by the English, when their leader fled to France. All historians agree in estimating the character of James as a man without foresight, decision, or even principle. Nevertheless, James sought to throw the blame of the whole defeat on the Irish. On arriving at the Castle of Dublin, history relates that he met the Lady Tyrconnell, a woman of ready wit, to whom he exclaimed, "Your countrymen, the Irish, madam, can run very fast, it must be owned." "In this, as in every other respect, your Majesty surpasses them, for you have won the race," was the apt and ready-witted rebuke which the lady administered to his discomfited Majesty.

We reached Dublin about three o'clock in the afternoon, and were soon tolerably quartered at the Royal Arcade Hotel, College Green, facing the Bank of Ireland, formerly the Irish Parliament-House.

DUBLIN BEAUTIES.

We have spent a couple of days very agreeably in the capital of Ireland, and have been much pleased both with the city and its people. The first thing that strikes the stranger in Dublin as most remarkable is the fine appearance of the men and the marked beauty of the women. In this respect Dublin undoubtedly surpasses any city in the United Kingdom. The men are well formed, solid, substantial, and healthy in appearance, and dress with excellent taste. The ladies are also of fine form and feature, with ruddy countenances, and dress with taste and neatness. Indeed, there is an entire absence here of the stereotyped form and feature that distinguish such a large portion of the natives of the Emerald Isle who come to the United States. We have among us, it is true, many fine specimens of the Irish gentleman, such as are to be seen in Dublin, but an American will meet with more persons in Baltimore or New York whom he can recognize at a glance as Irish than he will meet with in the streets of Dublin.

Dublin has been styled by some travelers the "City of Beggars," but a great change must have taken place in this respect, for we could discover no foundation for the appellation. Every part of the city was explored, and fewer beggars were encountered than in the streets of London, whilst there was a delightful contrast in this respect to Naples or Rome. There has no doubt been a great improvement in the social condition of Ireland within a few years.

THE CAPITAL OF IRELAND.

The city of Dublin is undoubtedly a very beautiful and attractive city, the pride of every Irishman at home or abroad. It is the seat of learning, wealth, and refinement, is full of evidences of a high state of civilization, and is a perpetual monument in refutation of the unfavorable impression which the character of a portion of the emigrants from Ireland has created in America. Here is the home of the true Irish gentleman, with public and private buildings, squares, and parks, some of its streets being unrivaled even by those of London. In proportion to the size of the two cities, Dublin is built in a better style, and architectural skill and good taste are more generally exhibited.

The river Liffey passes through the centre of the city, and is spanned by eight very fine stone bridges, which add considerably to the beauty of the place. The city is located only a mile from the entrance of the river into the fine Bay of Dublin, giving it commercial advantages which, as the surrounding country improves, must add greatly to its wealth and importance. The environs of the city on the south and west are very fine. A lofty range of hills, covered with the villas and country residences of wealthy citizens, surrounded by finely-cultivated gardens extending southwardly to the coast, interspersed with well-cultivated lowlands, presents a beautiful panoramic view from every elevated position in the city. Sackville Street, nearly two hundred feet in width, is spread out to the north, with its noble column to Nelson, its ranges of lofty and elegant buildings, the Ionic portico of the post-office, and its throngs of pedestrians and vehicles presenting a combination of attractions that can scarcely be found elsewhere. Westmoreland Street opens to the south, with the Corinthian portico of Trinity College at its head, and the massive architectural structure occupied by the Bank of Ireland to the right.

The view from this point up the Liffey to the west discloses a series of heavy stone bridges and some suspension foot-bridges that will compare favorably with those of London; the interminable range of lofty buildings, and the massive granite walls which inclose the banks of the river, also give a picturesque aspect to the view. To the east, below Carlisle Bridge, there is presented a forest of masts and funnels of steamers, with lofty warehouses; whilst the majestic front of the custom-house overlooks the stream from the left as it expands towards the bay.

TRINITY COLLEGE.

The public edifices of Dublin are all distinguished for their solid architectural beauties, and are most favorably located for the embellishment of the city. Trinity College, which is in the very heart of the city, has buildings and accommodations superior to those of any institution of learning in Europe, excepting only Oxford and Cambridge. The buildings are all constructed of granite, and are arranged in three separate quadrangles, leaving an open court in the centre, not less than three hundred feet in width, and six or seven hundred feet in length. Attached to the college is a park of twenty-five acres, for the recreation of numerous students.

The library of the college is said to contain over three hundred thousand volumes, arranged in a room two hundred and twenty feet long and over forty feet in breadth. Many valuable manuscripts are also contained in the library, and among these a Latin copy of the Gospels, known as the Book of Kells, attributed to Saint Columba, who lived in the sixth century. The Museum of Natural History is very large, and embraces a most valuable collection, with many curiosities. Among the latter is the harp of Brian Boroinhe, and the old charter-horn of King O'Kavanagh.

PHŒNIX PARK, ETC.

Phœnix Park is the Hyde Park of Dublin, and as the resort of the beauty and *élite* of the metropolis, as well as for its extent, will compare favorably with the latter, whilst St. Stephen's Green, Merion Square, Mountjoy Square, etc., combine to add greatly to the beauty and health of the city. Phœnix Park covers an area of upwards of seventeen hundred and fifty-two acres, and is well shaded with ancient native forest-trees, interspersed with trees of other climes. The whole park is inclosed with a stone wall, and affords such a pleasure-ground as few cities in the world can equal. It is open to all who may choose to ride, drive, or walk through it. Smooth roads traverse it in every direction, and ravines in their native wildness, entangled with furze and hawthorn, and green plots, with walks and blooming flowers, combine to make it a lovely scene. Deer are plentiful, and, as in other public gardens, they are frequently caressed by visitors, being very tame and docile.

In the midst of the park is a quadrangular obelisk, erected at a cost of one hundred thousand dollars, in 1817, by contribution, to testify the esteem of the citizens of Dublin for the Duke of Wellington as a military commander. Here also are the palatial mansions of the Lord Lieutenant and the Chief Secretary of Ireland, an institution for the education of sons of soldiers, and many neat little lodges for the porters and keepers. There is also in the park a Zoological Garden, with a small collection of animals.

THE TOMB OF O'CONNELL.

The stranger in Dublin seldom fails to pay a visit to the tomb of Daniel O'Connell, in the cemetery out Sackville Street, beyond the city limits. This "home of the dead" occupies a space of about nine acres, but, being a level plot of ground, it lacks that picturesque effect which is generally secured in the location of our cemeteries. The attention paid to the graves of deceased friends and relatives is, however, a feature peculiar to Irish cemeteries that cannot fail to attract attention. Widows, mothers, sisters, and daughters may be seen wending their way, with little baskets of fresh flowers, to the graves of their hopes and their loves, and with tearful eyes strewing them over the sod, or hanging the stones and monuments with wreaths and garlands. In winter, wreaths of never-fading flowers are substituted, of yellow, pink, and blue, with a cross of solemn black suspended.

Shortly after entering the gate a fingerboard is observed, with the words, "To the tomb of O'Connell," which leads you to about the centre of the grounds. Above the gate is the word "O'Connell," in gilt letters. Looking through the door, the crimson coffin of the great "agitator" is exposed to view under a canopy. The number of Irishmen who daily visit this tomb is incredible, and it is a touching sight to see many a poor pilgrim, with a crownless hat, raise his shabby "tile" and exclaim, "Poor Dan!" The coffin was strewn with flowers, thrown through the railing by visitors, and it is said that even in the depth of winter the bright camellias and arbutus are brought by the pilgrims from the country to be strewn around his bier.

The remains of Tom Steele are also deposited in this mound, close to those of O'Connell, whose self-denying devotion to the fortunes of the great leader procured for him the sobriquet of "Honest Tom Steele," which is the simple inscription on his vault. Like the inscription of "O rare Ben Jonson!" in Westminster Abbey, it was often used while he lived, and is therefore less like flattery now he is dead.

THE IRISH JINGLE.

One of the peculiar features of Dublin that attracts the stranger's eye on reaching the city is the "jaunting-cars," or "jingles," as they are sometimes called, which take the place of cabs, and with which he must make his first acquaintance in proceeding to his hotel. They are so unlike any other vehicle, with the exception of having round wheels, that it is almost impossible to describe them. They are full with four passengers and the driver, will hold eight very well, and may be considered crowded with twelve. The seats are sideways, and extend in a series of steps over the wheels of the vehicle, whilst the driver is perched up in front. When he has but one passenger he takes a side-seat, to balance the weight on the springs. They are quite pleasant to ride in when one gets used to them, and for a frolic there could be nothing more suitable. A stranger looking at one of these vehicles rushing past with a full load expects to see them slide off in the street at every bound, and rather wonders that they are not "spilled out" at the first corner they turn. They are, however, very safe, and are used by ladies as well as gentlemen. We noticed some very fine vehicles of this sort moving about, evidently used as private family-carriages.

There are a number of fine churches in Dublin, but, having visited so many in Italy, we were rather surfeited with this species of sight-seeing. Like all public buildings in Dublin, their exteriors are very fine in architectural display, and they are said to contain some excellent paintings and statuary.

THE POLICE OF IRELAND.

Wherever you go in England, Ireland, or Scotland, the police are the admiration of the stranger. They seem to be everywhere the same class of men, all dressed in the same uniforms, each of the required height of six feet, drilled to walk erect with a military step, and to maintain an air of respectability and authority that gives character to them in the community. They are dressed in blue swallow-tailed coats, and pants of the same color, the coat being buttoned up to the throat with metal buttons. Their hats are of fur with oil-cloth tops, the number being displayed on the hat-band in silver figures. The fact of their being all of uniform height, and erect, manly carriage, shows that they are picked men, none of them seeming to be over forty years of age or under thirty. They are never seen without white cotton gloves on, or with the slightest evidence of negligence in dress or personal appearance. These officials move about with their cleanly-shaved faces and neat appearance like so many walking statues, always alert in the performance of duty, and when they have occasion to interfere it is with a voice and air of authority that no one would dare to dispute. To the stranger their services are invaluable, as, with the politeness of a Chesterfield, they are always ready to impart whatever information may be required, or direct him to pass on to the next officer, who will point out the locality he is in search of.

This efficient organization grows out of the fact that a police-officer is never removed except for neglect of duty, and is promoted for good conduct. They enter on their duties with this assurance, and regard it as a permanent means of livelihood. They are not liable to removal for any political or personal cause, and each man is held to his good behavior and the faithful performance of duty as essential to the retaining of his position. There is no suspension or other half-way measure for the unfaithful officer,—a prompt discharge following the slightest neglect of the rules laid down for his government. Sometimes they are transferred from one city to another, the police of the whole kingdom being under one government, which is as strict in its discipline and as stringent in its enforcement of rules as if it were a military organization. In fact, it combines all the power of both a civil and military force, and has done away in a great measure with the necessity of a purely military force in large cities.

THE CITY OF CORK.

We arrived at Queenstown, and were soon quartered at Kilmurry's Hotel. With dirty linen and cat-tail beds to sleep upon, we fared poorly in that respect, but the mountain salmon and trout, excellent bread, and genuine Irish welcome, make some recompense for such deficiencies. It is a singular fact that we have had good clean beds everywhere in our journeyings except in Old Ireland, which is so famous for the skill of its washerwomen away from home. It may therefore be presumed that all the good ones have emigrated. The beds are like lying on a mass of soft clay; when one impression is made it is folly to attempt to make another indentation. If you take a position on the side of the bed its contents will all slip from under you, and form a solid heap on the other side as hard as a bank of sand.

THE COVE OF CORK.

The Cove of Cork, or, as it is now called, Queenstown, is undoubtedly a most beautiful spot, resembling an Italian town. Being built on the side of a mountain, the roofs of the houses on the lower tier are about on a level with the cellar-floors of those on the next tier or street above, which are approached by winding streets. It has a southern aspect, and its descent to the harbor prevents its streets from ever being muddy or dirty. The houses, some of them very fine, are all built of stone, and are white rough-cast. A most picturesque view can be obtained from the heights above the magnificent harbor, which is probably the most extensive and commodious in the United Kingdom, being capable of affording shelter to the entire British navy. The harbor, the entrance to which is not a half-mile in width, forms a circular basin, about five miles in diameter. The tops of the lofty hills at the entrance are capped with immense fortresses of great strength. There are also within this immense harbor four small islands, though Queenstown is itself an island, a branch of the river Lee completely surrounding it on its western side. Spike Island is most conspicuous, and is used as a convict-depot, with accommodations for two thousand prisoners, who are employed in various ways. Rocky Island is next, and contains the powder-magazine, which occupies six chambers excavated in the solid rock. It usually contains about ten thousand barrels of gunpowder, besides other species of ammunition. Directly opposite Rocky Island is Hawlboline Island, which contains the ordnance stores, an armory, and a fresh-water tank capable of holding five thousand tuns.

The Cove of Cork is said to be the most healthy spot in the United Kingdom, and is mainly sustained by the throng of invalids and their families who resort here during the summer season, to enjoy the bathing, the bracing atmosphere, and the beautiful scenery with which it is surrounded for many miles. The hills above the town are also covered with hundreds of delightful cottages, with beautiful gardens, many of which are permanently occupied by invalids from England.

THE RIVER LEE.

We proceeded in the steamer at nine o'clock on Friday morning for a trip to Cork, and a visit to Blarney Castle and the Blarney Stone of Old Ireland.

Cork River, or the river Lee, enters into the harbor of Queenstown by a sudden turn of its southern extremity, in which direction the steamer proceeded, and the mouth of the river had scarcely been turned before the scene that was presented to the vision drew forth an exclamation of surprise and admiration. Let the reader imagine that he is viewing the most attractive spot on the North River, where the hills on either side are finely cultivated and clothed with the richest verdure, whilst their sides are dotted with elegant and picturesque mansions. The fields on the hill-sides are generally small, and divided by hedges and thickets, smoothly trimmed, the gardens laid out with artistic skill, and the skirts of the stream down to the water's edge in full cultivation. For fourteen miles, the distance to Cork, the whole route is one perpetual variety of beautiful scenery, and no part is barren or uninteresting. It possesses all the charms of the most romantic landscape, and whilst gazing on one scene the eye is imperceptibly carried by the motion of the steamer to another that exceeds it in beauty and novelty.

THE CITY OF CORK.

As we approached the city of Cork, famous as the home of the most shrewd and witty of the sons of Erin, the villas on the banks of the river became more attractive and picturesque. Monkstown Castle, an elegant ruin, built in 1636, by the wife of John Archdeken, during the absence of her husband whilst serving in the army of Philip of Spain, is visible from the river. She determined to surprise him with a noble residence which he might call his own. She purchased provisions, so the story runs, by wholesale, and retailed them out to the country-people, and upon balancing her accounts it appeared that the retail profit had paid for the castle except fourpence. Hence the common saying that "Monkstown Castle was built for a groat."

Some portions of the city are quite beautiful, with broad streets and elegant houses, whilst others present a squalid and dirty appearance. Distilleries are in abundance, drinking-shops and taverns in excess, and, as an evidence of the destitution and improvidence which prevail among a portion of its inhabitants, we were informed that there are no less than thirty-three licensed pawnbrokers doing a thriving business. The city has about seventy thousand inhabitants, and there are few towns in Ireland that can boast so wide a range of ably-supported benevolent and charitable institutions, including hospitals, infirmaries, loan-societies, and saving-institutions. The insane-asylum is a most extensive and elegant structure. The Queen's College is also a beautiful structure, under the charge of three deans, one an Episcopalian, one a Presbyterian, and one a Catholic.

THE IRISH JAUNTING-CAR.

Our party having secured a number of Irish "jaunting-cars," we soon made a rapid survey of the city of Cork, and were moving at full speed on our way to the famous world-renowned Blarney Castle and its "Blarney Stone." A "jaunting-car" is an indescribable vehicle, peculiarly Irish, but quite a comfortable mode of conveyance. Though very secure, it has when filled with passengers—and the number it will hold is indefinite—quite a rollicking and frolicking appearance. To a spectator unaccustomed to the sight, when flying along the street, a general spilling out of the party might be anticipated at every lurch, as it has no back or sides, and the principal seats are on shelves projecting over the wheels; but it is withal so comfortable and secure that, although a number of our party were ladies, they enjoyed the trip very much. As a matter of course, such a conclave of strangers driving at full speed attracted considerable attention, but we were soon outside of corporate limits, wending our way through a beautiful country, profuse in vegetation, and tolerably well cultivated, where our gay and dashing appearance attracted the farmer from his labor, frightened the horses, startled the children from the mud-puddles they were playing in at the road-sides, and brought out from the farm-houses and whisky-cabins their tenants to see the "wrecked Americans," as we were styled by the car-drivers.

BLARNEY CASTLE.

The road to Blarney Castle, which is located about five miles from the city, has numerous ascents, being so steep at times that it was necessary to relieve the horses by walking; but we finally reached the Lake of Blarney, a beautiful sheet of water a mile in circumference, about a quarter of a mile beyond which the square turret of Blarney Castle could be seen rearing its dreary height. A circuitous drive of about a mile brought us to the farm on which the ruin stands, when we had a specimen of "blarney" from the dame at the gate, that proved her proficiency in this Corkonian accomplishment.

We were soon roaming through the spacious ruins of Blarney Castle, which was built in the year 1449, by Cormack McCarty, Earl of Clancarty, who was first summoned to Parliament as Baron of Blarney, in the year 1458. The castle, as history tells us, was held for James II., and stood out a severe siege against the forces of the Prince of Orange. A battery was finally placed on an elevated position, which compelled them to surrender the castle. The main turret and tower is one hundred and twenty feet, and the stone circular stairway to its extreme height is still in an excellent state of preservation. Its walls, inside and out, are overrun to their extreme height with woodbine and ivy, adding interest and beauty to the ruins.

THE BLARNEY STONE.

Near the top of the wall of this castle is the famous "Blarney Stone." A curious tradition attributes to it the power of endowing whoever kisses it with the sweet, persuasive, wheedling eloquence so perceptible in the language of the people of Cork, and which is generally termed "blarney,"—which has been described by some ill-natured person as "a faculty of deviating from veracity with an unblushing countenance whenever it may be convenient." The stone generally pointed out as the "real stone" is situated on the top of the building, and, besides a sculptured trefoil, bears the date 1703. Croker's favorite song of the "Groves of Blarney" made this stone famous, and it is annually viewed by thousands of tourists, for, as the song says,

"There is a stone there,
That whoever kisses,
Oh! he never misses
To grow eloquent.
Don't hope to hinder him,
Or to bewilder him;
Sure he's a pilgrim
From the blarney stone."

THE GROVES OF BLARNEY.

The grounds around the castle are still very beautiful and romantic, but the beauty has been gradually diminishing, and its walks are choked up with rubbish. Close at hand, however, are the famous "Groves of Blarney :"

"'Tis there's the daisy,
And the sweet carnation,
The blooming pink,
And the rose so fair;
The daffadowndilly,
Likewise the lily,
All flowers that scent
The sweet fragrant air."

These are kept in good condition, and present a wild and pleasing scene, with the Druids' Cave, in which tradition says that sacrificial offerings were made by the last of these ancient people.

AN IRISH RACE.

On our return to Cork our drivers, either excited by blarney whiskey, or having gained new life from a sight of the stone, started off at full speed, and we had a regular Irish race, each endeavoring to pass the other on the road. The younger passengers joined in the sport, and cheered as each successively passed the other, encouraging the drivers by the waving of handkerchiefs and shouts of triumph. It was quite an exciting drive, during which we frightened a priest's horse, and the reverend gentleman was compelled to join in the race, whilst the country-people flocked to the road-side to see what was the commotion. However, as we approached the precincts of Cork we quieted the drivers and checked the horses, marching in as soberly and demurely as if returning from a funeral.

In coming down the river Lee, we passed Blackrock, a bold promontory, on which is erected a beautiful country mansion, from whence it is said William Penn embarked for America. He resided for some years in this vicinity, and was converted to the doctrines of the Friends by hearing a sermon at Cork.

THE ROUND TOWERS OF IRELAND.

During our visit to Cork we passed in sight of some of the round towers of Ireland, many of which we noticed in other parts of the country. The origin and use of these towers seem to be wrapped in impenetrable mystery, and antiquaries differ in their conjectures on the subject. There are about sixty of them remaining in the kingdom, most of them being in a good state of preservation. Their height varies from twenty-five to one hundred and thirty feet, and the only aperture in these strange structures consists of a door at some distance from the ground, all resembling each other in structure, and four small windows also near the top. They are very strongly built, the cement being as hard as that employed in ancient Rome. A few stand on high ground, but most of them are in remote situations, and sometimes in valleys, forbidding the idea that they could have been built for watch-towers.

CITY OF LIVERPOOL.

ASPECT OF LIVERPOOL.

We find Liverpool looking, if possible, more solid, more sombre, and more ponderous than it did twelve years ago. The same mammoth horses, with their elephantine legs and hoofs, seem to be drawing the same heavy loads of merchandise, and the same Irishmen seem to be urging them on. We observe, however, vast improvements in the business centres, in the construction of new and elegant establishments, which have taken the place of the antiquated structures of the past, whilst at every turn there are indications of the flood of wealth which commerce is pouring into its harbor.

CITY OF LIVERPOOL.

Although the greatest commercial city in the world, it does not come up to the anticipations of the stranger in all those stirring, bustling scenes of activity which an American will look for as inseparable from the transactions of so vast a business. On approaching the city from the sea, the whole front presents a series of blank granite walls, tall warehouses, and yawning entrances to dock basins, over the top of which, and apparently in close contact with the chimneys of the houses, the topmasts of vessels can be discerned spread for many miles around. If the tide is low, the granite walls of the docks tower up thirty-five feet from the water, as the fluctuation of the tide here is never less than twenty feet, whilst the spring-tides vary from twenty-nine to thirty-three feet.

The warehouses fronting on the docks are generally of immense proportions, six or seven stories high, without any attempt at architectural display, but of solid and massive appearance, their brick fronts dingy and blackened, or sometimes coated with the dust from the many thousands of barrels of flour which are constantly being conveyed to and from their upper stories. With the exception of the public buildings, no money seems to have been expended in business sections for beautifying the city, strength and utility being the only objects aimed at. In proportion to the size of the city, which has nearly six hundred thousand inhabitants, the retail business seems to be very small, and is certainly not equal to that of Glasgow. In comparison with any of our large American cities, it would rate in this respect as a fourth-rate city, and we doubt if there are more than half as many such establishments as may be found in Baltimore.

STREET SCENES.

The drinking-houses and resorts for sailors along the front of the city, adjoining the docks, are very numerous, and, notwithstanding the vigilance of the police, it is not regarded as safe to visit that section of the city after gas-light. The streets swarm with the most brazen and vicious of a herd of courtesans that the world can produce, whose language and conduct in the streets would not be tolerated even in New York. Although they are numerous in all parts of the city, they seem to be under more rigorous police control elsewhere, and are not allowed to annoy or insult respectable people.

The portions of the city occupied by private residences are very extensive, and though there are not many costly or elegant establishments, the houses are generally of good size, the streets broad and well paved, an air of comfort and neatness being prevalent not always seen in large commercial cities. In 1830 the whole population of Liverpool, including its dependencies, was but two hundred thousand, whilst it has now reached six hundred thousand, and Birkenhead, on the opposite shore of the Mersey, like Brooklyn is to New York, is growing to be an immense city, with great lines of docks for shipping, which promise to rival those of Liverpool.

THE LIVERPOOL DOCKS.

The shipping and trans-shipping of goods being mostly carried on within the walls of the dock-yards, the casual visitor sees nothing but a forest of masts as indicating the vastness of the commerce of Liverpool. Commerce does not show itself here as it does in our American cities, but is confined within prescribed limits and bounds. The cargo of a vessel arriving will often be taken to load another ready to depart, and not hauled and stored and rehauled, as in New York. The docks are all supplied with immense sheds, and many of them with large warehouses, in which goods are temporarily piled away under the control of the custom-house authorities. The immense products of the manufactories of Manchester, only about thirty miles distant, are brought by rail direct to the docks, and immediately placed in the holds of the ships for which they are designed, the American merchants buying direct from the factories, and naming the dock, vessel, and time at which they are to be delivered in Liverpool for transportation to America. Liverpool is thus rather a great mercantile depot than such a magnificent commercial city as an American would expect to find it.

The docks of Liverpool are undoubtedly fine specimens of engineering. Their immense solidity is, however, a matter of necessity, as the rushing tide of the Mersey, even in its calmest moods, would quickly sweep away a structure of less massive character. Each dock has a large basin in front, into which the gates of the dock open, for the entrance or departure of vessels. These gates can only be opened at high tide, and are closed as soon as the water commences to fall, keeping one depth of water always inside the docks, whilst that in the basin fluctuates twenty feet with the tide of the river. The great weight of water, from twenty to thirty feet deep, thus retained inside the docks, as will readily be understood, requires the most massive masonry to retain it within bounds.

The number of docks along the five miles of the city front is thirty-three, and yet the line is steadily being extended by the erection of others, still longer and more massive in their construction. These arrangements for commercial convenience originated with Liverpool, and have since been adopted at most of the tidal ports of Europe. Without them it would be necessary to load and unload vessels by lighters, and the whole river Mersey could scarcely afford anchorage for the shipping that is now floated within these granite walls at high tide, and moored in deep water whilst unloading and receiving cargo for a new voyage. The area of the docks varies from twenty thousand to sixty thousand square yards, their massive gates being mostly opened and closed by steam-power. Each is supplied with a graving-dock, just large enough to hold one first-class ship, into which a ship requiring repair is floated, after which the gate of this inner dock is closed and the water pumped out, thus forming a perfect dry-dock.

ST. GEORGE'S HALL.

The public buildings of Liverpool, although few in number, are very extensive and grand specimens of architecture. The custom-house is an immense white freestone building, surmounted by a cupola and dome; the Exchange and City Hall are also very imposing structures; but the pride and glory of Liverpool is "St. George's Hall," which it seems was built with the determination that it should exceed in size, architectural beauty, and grandeur of design and finish, any other building in the United Kingdom, excepting only the Houses of Parliament at London. It occupies the centre of what seems to be a mound in the very heart of the city, and approach it from any of the numerous streets converging towards St. George's Square, and it looms up before the eye in all its grand prominence. The building is constructed in the Corinthian style of architecture. The eastern façade is four hundred and twenty feet long, and has a columnar projecting centre, with depressed wings. Indeed, the building has really four fronts, each presenting striking architectural features. One end of the building is occupied by the Assize Courts, whilst the other contains concert-rooms, one of which is of immense proportions, fitted up and decorated in a style of magnificence seldom attempted in a hall for such purposes. The interior of this largest hall is one hundred and sixty-seven feet long by seventy-seven in breadth, with an altitude of eighty-two feet.

ST. GEORGE'S ORGAN.

The grand organ in St. George's Hall is claimed to be the largest instrument in the world, costing about sixty thousand dollars. It is thirty-three feet in breadth and forty-two feet in height, and stands in a splendid gallery of a receding semicircular form. We were present at a concert given on this grand instrument by a distinguished organist. The music comprised marches and overtures, and displayed the wonderful power and compass, as well as the sweetness of its tones, with fine effect. Concerts are given on this great organ every Wednesday and Saturday afternoon, when there are large audiences present, the charge for admission being sixpence.

LIFE AT SEA.

EXPERIENCES—JOLLITIES, INTIMACIES, MISERIES, AND SICKNESS—THRILLING EXPERIENCE AMONG ICEBERGS.

We have crossed the Atlantic between America and Europe six times, and our ocean-traveling in other directions has been very extensive, yet we have been so fortunate as never to have encountered a genuine storm, and very little rough weather, at sea. As those who may be contemplating a trip to Europe will like to know something about "Life on the Ocean Wave," we select the following extracts from our journal of observations on various occasions:

FIRST IMPRESSIONS OF THE SEA.

On our first trip across the Atlantic, some years ago, we recorded the following as our first experiences of life at sea:

The weather has been delightful, with a fair wind, and what a sailor would call a "fine rolling sea," but which by us, a sea-sick landsman, has been regarded as a most abominable pitching and tossing, at one moment tumbling us from the right to the left, and at the next jerking us forward and backward, like uninitiated equestrians, unable to catch the motion of a rough-back steed.

We left the harbor of New York at twelve o'clock on Saturday, with a bright sunshine overhead, steamed past Sandy Hook, and before sundown had lost sight of land. The cabin-passengers mustered in full force at dinner and supper, and all partook of their meals with vigorous appetites, each entertaining the hope that, from the first few hours' experience, we were to escape the demands of old Neptune. After promenading the deck until midnight, we retired to our state-rooms, in good condition, and awoke on Sunday morning all right, still fondly imagining that our stomachs were safe. But no sooner had our feet touched the floor than the inward rebellion commenced, and, after a few moments of tumbling backward and forward, unable to catch the motion of the vessel, and receiving sundry bruises on our craniums, alternately against the door and wall of our contracted apartment, we sank down hopeless and prostrate, a few moments serving to obliterate all anticipations of escape from that most prostrating of all the trials and tribulations of the stomach with which poor humanity can be beset. After resisting the temptation to return to our berths prostrate and hopeless, we succeeded, amid the pitching and tossing of the vessel, in finding our way into our clothing, and with combless heads, unwashed faces, and woe-begone countenances, scrambled through the narrow passages beneath deck, and thence, by clinging tenaciously to the balusters of the companion-way, we crawled out into the open air, where we met with throngs of fellow-sufferers. Such a woe-begone collection of humanity it would be difficult to describe. The old "sea-dogs," accustomed to the roll of the waves, with cigars in their mouths, calmly surveyed us and smiled at our calamity, from which they were so happily exempt.

The only sure relief from sea-sickness being to struggle against that feeling of utter prostration which tempts you to dive down into your state-room, and boldly to face the wind and encounter the rolling of the vessel in the open air on the promenade-deck, a score or more of sufferers were soon reeling to and fro around the deck, until they finally sank down exhausted, where they lay wrapped up in shawls and blankets like a tribe of Bedouin Arabs. Any attempt to secure a perpendicular position immediately aggravated the difficulty. The fumes from the kitchen, which occasionally reached us, and the sound of the dinner-bell, were anything but agreeable. Most of the passengers thus remained nearly all day on Sunday, occasionally venturing on an upright position to familiarize themselves with the motion of the vessel. By supper-time, after about fifteen hours of prostration, we had sufficiently recovered to venture to the table, though with fear that we would be compelled to retreat without eating a mouthful. We, however, succeeded in forcing down a few morsels of food, with a cup of tea, and again resumed our positions on the promenade-deck. Here, by keeping in motion until midnight, we began to realize that we had conquered the tyrant who had ruled over us with such a sickening influence since the break of day.

We finally retired, full of hope that our troubles were at an end, and spent quite a comfortable night; though when daylight arrived it was with fear and trembling that we ventured from our berths, in the expectation of a repetition of the sickening visitation of the preceding morning. However, the feat was accomplished in safety, and, as we stood once more erect upon the cabin-floor, we felt that we had "our sea-legs on," to use a nautical phrase, and could encounter the rolling of the vessel without danger of bringing our heads in contact with the timbers. It was indeed a most happy relief to be enabled to walk the undulating deck with head erect, and to march in to breakfast with an appetite sharpened by our long fast.

MISERIES OF THE SEA.

In our notes of a subsequent voyage we find the following recorded under the heading "Miseries of the Sea:"

The Peruvian left Liverpool in a storm, or at least a heavy head-wind, with occasional showers of rain, which drove everybody below deck before we had scarcely passed beyond the gates of Wellington dock. We had on board one hundred and twenty cabin passengers, and nearly two hundred intermediate and steerage passengers, mostly bound to Canada, with a few inevitable Yankees, as our English cousins style us. The weather became, during the night, thick and heavy, with fitful gusts of wind, all of which persisted in coming from the wrong direction. In the morning the weather was what a sailor would term decidedly "dirty," with occasional fogs, so dense that it became necessary to slow down the engine and sound the fog-whistle. It was just such weather as might be regarded as calculated to promote sea-sickness, and there were few on board who were not affected more or less with the preliminary symptoms of the epidemic. One gentleman who was making his thirty-fifth passage failed to respond to the breakfast-bell, and fully ninety of the hundred seats were vacant. Even one of our little party of nauticals who had braved the terrors of the Mediterranean and had twice crossed the Channel temporarily succumbed, and those that ventured below did not linger long over their coffee. The number in attendance at lunch was still more limited, but as we put into the quiet harbor of Queenstown about dinner-time there was quite a good attendance, and hopes were entertained that this brief respite would be of permanent service. We had scarcely returned to the Irish coast, however, before the sea became still more rough, with intermittent rains and a head-wind, which continued until the close of the third day. Suffice it to say that during these three days sickness was almost universal fore and aft, the decks, notwithstanding their dampness, being strewn with sufferers. Those who remained in their state-rooms were reported to be quite ill, and it was not until the fourth day, when the sea became more calm, that they could be prevailed upon to allow themselves to be helped to the deck. Sudden as was the sickness, the recovery was now equally rapid, and every meal showed a larger attendance at the table, until the fifth day, when every seat was reoccupied. A bright sun gave new life to every one, and, although we still had a rolling sea, our heads were adjusted to the motion of the vessel, and our "sea-legs" were fairly on.

It is interesting to note the change among passengers on a steamer when they become accustomed to the rolling and pitching that are inevitable during the greater portion of a passage over the great deep. The rattling and upsetting of the dishes at table as they slide to and fro are at first appalling, but after recovery these mishaps are greeted with shouts of laughter, and even the upsetting of a plate of soup into one's lap is not considered much of a disaster, all being arrayed in clothing that they do not expect to wear again after leaving the ship. The brain no longer swims, nor does the stomach respond to the up-and-down motion of the vessel as she sweeps through the rolling sea. At night the saloon rings with laughter instead of the wails of the sufferers, and those who had deemed it prudent to sit still and hold fast to keep from being thrown from their seats now move about without scarcely noticing the motion of the vessel, to which they have learned to accommodate themselves. Every night the saloon presents a gathering of happy people, the piano responds to the skillful handling of the performers, and song and merriment speed the pleasant hours. Groups will be found engaging in games of whist, and the evening amusements always close with some refreshments, such as anchovy-toast and tea. The deck, which early in the voyage had been strewn with sufferers, is now devoted to promenading, dancing, shuffle-board matches, and all manner of pastimes. The roll of the ship becomes a source of amusement instead of terror, and the days pass with a rapidity that is truly marvelous in comparison with those of the sickly season.

INTIMACIES OF THE SEA.

The scenes on board an ocean-steamer during the first few days of a voyage which commences with rough weather can scarcely be imagined by those who have not witnessed them. The first evening is all gayety and jollity, and the dinner-table is thronged, with all the passengers in their seats. All are in high glee, and full of hope that the morning will disclose a bright sky and a calm sea. The children, of whom there are always a goodly number, gambol around the cabin, and finally settle down on the sofas, drowsy and tired, but delighted with the novelties by which they are surrounded. Parents take them to their state-rooms to dispose of them for the night, intending to return to the saloon for supper, but a few moments below bring on the nausea preceding sea-sickness, and they conclude to retire for the night. Morning comes, and they feel an earnest desire to escape from the close and confined air which they have been breathing, and make a frantic effort to dress. But they are no sooner on their feet than they find themselves flying back and forward like shuttlecocks between the door and the berth, or with their heads in contact with the looking-glass, for the vessel always seems to roll and pitch with more than usual vindictiveness about getting-up time. A nausea that is blinding and bewildering immediately sets in, which causes many to give up the task of dressing as a hopeless one, and they fall back in their berths as limp and nerveless as if they had suddenly been stricken with paralysis. Those who thus yield are seldom seen again for some days, or at least until calmer weather sets in. A great many, however, renew the effort to dress, and finally succeed in reaching the deck, with blankets or rugs. where they coil themselves on benches or the deck, jumping up occasionally and staggering to the side of the vessel. At first it is an amusing sight to those who are exempt, but the suffering gradually becomes so intense, and the prostration so complete, that earnest sympathies are awakened, and the kindness and attention then extended soon break down all formalities and obviate introductions. Those who remain in their state-rooms, confined to a dark and narrow berth, in which it is difficult to turn, become in two or three days so weak and prostrate that they can only reach the deck by being taken up bodily, when they will fall upon the couches prepared for them, pale and prostrate, as if all vitality had forsaken them. Those who refused to succumb have by this time fully recovered, and, like good Samaritans, may be seen exerting themselves in all directions to aid and assist the sufferers. Husbands and wives are at times both prostrate, and their children equally unable to help themselves. It is not to be wondered at, therefore, that before the close of the passage an intimacy and friendship is established between the passengers that could not be attained in a year on dry land.

JOLLITIES OF THE SEA.

There are always a set of jolly fellows on board of every steamer,—fellows who never get sick, and are always getting up some kind of amusement. During the sickly season they have their fun all to themselves, and keep to the smoking-room or hug the smoke-stack. So soon as the sun is out, and their fellow-passengers recover stamina sufficient to enable them to walk the deck, they become valuable adjuncts to the captain in his endeavor to make everybody feel happy and comfortable. Although they do not sing hymns in the smoking-room, they can furnish the bass voices for the music at the Sunday services, and aid in the choruses at the nightly concerts given in the saloon, or sing a comic song by way of diversifying the entertainment. They get up all manner of games upon deck, and are proficient in all the most approved modes of killing time. They arrange for match games at shuffle-board, promenade the decks with the ladies who have no male attendants, and are determined not only to be happy themselves, but to do all in their power to promote the happiness and enjoyment of others. These good fellows are generally merchants or foreign buyers passing to and from Europe on their annual journey for goods, and are never at a loss for anecdotes and incidents with which to enliven the smoking-room in dull or rainy weather. They hunt up among the steerage-passengers some cases worthy of pecuniary aid, making them happy by liberal contributions, or presenting such cases to the consideration of the other passengers. Sometimes their boisterous mirth disturbs the quiet of the night; but then they are privileged characters, and beyond a little scolding from the captain they find nothing to interrupt or mar their jollity. When everything else fails, they make wagers on the number of miles the log will record at noon as having been run during the preceding twenty-four hours, and, when nearing port, on the number of the pilot-boat which will first hail them. A pool of twenty or thirty dollars is thus raised, which will be swept by the one fortunate enough to name the winning figures, the money being generally handed over for some charitable object.

Captain Smith, of the Peruvian, is one of the jovial kind, and devotes every moment of spare time from the duties of the ship to the amusement of his passengers. He has a kind word for every one, and is quite as attentive to the comfort of the steerage and intermediate passengers as to those in the cabin. He sings an excellent song, tells a good story, and, on Sunday evening last, showed that he could not only go through the services of the Church of England, but actually read a good sermon to the cabin and steerage passengers assembled in the saloon, to the number of nearly two hundred.

The smoking-room is throughout the passage the centre of fun and amusement, occasionally varied with discussions on colonial or American politics. It is taken possession of at first by the few who bid defiance to the turmoil of Neptune's vagaries, until they are gradually reinforced by those who a few days before had thought they would never again be enabled to enjoy the fragrant weed. When a smoker is enabled to light his pipe or cigar he is considered cured, and from thenceforth he spends his time in responding to the five invitations per day from the dining-room bell, with an astonishing appetite, takes a few strolls upon the deck, and returns to his smoking. The stories, yarns, songs, and discussions of the jolly fellows who assemble in the smoking-room, often continuing until past midnight, render it an attractive lounging-place also for those who do not take to the weed, who remain until the smoke gets too dense for their sensitive lungs and stomachs.

SUNDAY ON SHIP-BOARD.

Sunday was a bright and beautiful day. The sick had all recovered, and the sea was calm and quiet. Throughout the ship everybody appeared in their best attire. We were now in about mid-ocean, half-way between Liverpool and Halifax, steaming at the rate of three hundred miles per day, the wind being so light as scarcely to create a ripple. After breakfast there was a very general promenade on deck, and at ten o'clock the bell commenced to sound for worship, when all repaired to the saloon, which was soon filled to its utmost capacity by as attentive a congregation as ever assembled in any church at home. An impromptu choir had been organized on the preceding night by Captain Smith and Purser Clarke, assisted by Miss Philpot, a lady passenger of fine musical attainments, and the rehearsal promised that this portion of the service would be well rendered. Among the passengers is the Rev. Mr. Pendleton, of Lexington, Va., formerly known as General Pendleton, of General Lee's staff, during the rebellion. He resigned the pulpit to take up the sword, and at the close of the war was among those who surrendered to General Grant. He then returned to his ministerial duties. The reverend gentleman delivered an excellent sermon, his voice being distinctly heard, notwithstanding the noises of the sea, in all parts of the spacious cabin. After supper the bell again tolled, and the congregation reassembled, when Captain Smith went through the entire Church service, and delivered a brief but excellent address. A collection was taken up for the benefit of the Aged Seamen's Home, of Liverpool. On Monday night a concert was given in the cabin for the benefit of the Asylum for Sailors' Orphans and Widows. The receipts on both these occasions amounted to about twelve pounds, or thirty dollars for each charity.

THE NAUTICAL BELLS.

The landsman traveling on the ocean finds it difficult to understand the mode of keeping the hour which he hears sounded on the bells every thirty minutes. Having obtained an explanation of the bells, we will endeavor to make it plain to the comprehension of the general reader. There are five regular watches of four hours each, making twenty hours, and two watches of two hours each, called the "dog-watch." Commencing at twelve o'clock, the first bell is struck at half-past twelve, and they continue as follows:

REGULAR WATCH.

12½ o'clock	. . .	1 bell.
1 "	. . .	2 bells.
1½ "	. . .	3 "
2 "	. . .	4 "
2½ "	. . .	5 "
3 "	. . .	6 "
3½ "	. . .	7 "
4 "	. . .	8 "

DOG-WATCH.

4½ o'clock	. . .	1 bell.
5 "	. . .	2 bells.
5½ "	. . .	3 "
6 "	. . .	4 "
6½ "	. . .	1 "
7 "	. . .	2 "
7½ "	. . .	3 "
8 "	. . .	4 "

The watch thus goes on for the balance of the twenty-four hours, changing every four hours, from eight to twelve o'clock, from twelve to four, from four to eight, and from eight to twelve, striking eight bells for each regular watch. The "dog-watch" is to relieve the officers from double watches on successive nights.

CABIN AMUSEMENTS.

As we approach our journey's end, joy and gladness seem to pervade the whole ship. The sailors sing their nautical airs with new spirit, and the passengers join in sports and amusements with more than usual zest. Last night the cabin was the scene of general hilarity, songs were given of various nationalities, and stories told with great spirit. A party of young Americans, of whom there are not more than fifteen out of the two hundred and fifty-nine souls on board, concluded the pleasures of the evening by singing the song of "Uncle Sam's Farm," all the passengers joining in the following chorus:

"Come along! come along! make no delay!
Come from every nation, come from every way!
There is room enough for all, and don't be alarmed,
For Uncle Sam is rich enough to give us all a farm."

The English officers flocked around, and seemed greatly amused at the Yankee enthusiasm evinced.

ICEBERGS ON THE OCEAN.

The greatest terror of ocean-travel is the icebergs which are so frequently met with on the coast of Newfoundland during the early summer months. Whilst crossing the ocean in June, 1852, on the steamer Moravian, we had some experience with these monsters, which we noted as follows in our journal of the trip.

ICEBERGS—A GRAND SIGHT.

During all of Wednesday afternoon and night we were enveloped in a dense fog, which required the constant blowing of the steam-whistle and occasional stopping of the steamer for soundings. We also were compelled to slow down to half-speed, Captain Graham being one of those careful men who are determined to keep out of the way of disasters if possible. At ten o'clock in the morning the fog cleared away, and the coast of Newfoundland could be seen in the far distance. The atmosphere was decidedly winterish, although it was the middle of June, the thermometer being down to forty-six degrees. We had previously heard of icebergs being on the coast, and soon descried one about ten miles distant, looming up about fifty feet out of the water, and evidently aground. It was a novel sight to landsmen, and all hands were soon upon deck, whilst all the glasses on board were brought into requisition. Subsequently we passed nearly twenty bergs at different points, all stranded. The winterish atmosphere was attributed to these floating monsters, which annually come down from the coast of Labrador.

At the mouth of the harbor of St. John three large icebergs were stranded, and in entering we were compelled to pass within a hundred yards of them. They looked like immense mountains of pure white polished marble, glistening in the sun, towering up sixty feet above the surface of the waves. The entrance of St. John resembles very much that to the harbor of Havana, only that Moro Castle is wanting on the towering rocks to the left. The passage between these rocks is not more than four hundred yards in width, and on either side of the entrance to this narrow passage stood two immense icebergs, which had stranded here on their passage down the coast. They were nearly opposite each other, that on the right side of the ship being about a hundred yards farthest seaward. The distance from the vessel to either of them as we passed in was not more than fifty feet. After viewing the first one, all hands rushed to the left side of the ship to see the other monster, and just as the ship was full abreast of it a large mass from the top, towering up about fifty feet in the air, and weighing probably one hundred tons, cracked and fell into the sea with a tremendous crash, dashing the waves up against the side of the steamer with great force. The breaking of the ice was accompanied by a noise like a scattering volley of musketry. No sooner had the astonishment at this sight subsided than the huge mountain of ice began to rise in the sea, and slowly commenced to topple over towards the vessel, showing that its depth under water must have been, as the pilot assured us, one hundred and sixty feet, that being the depth at this point. As it toppled over, the water from what appeared to have been a small lake collected upon its broad and extended summit poured over, forming for a moment a grand cascade, as it rushed down the pure white sides of the berg, deeply tinted with green. Not knowing whether the motion of the monster would be rapid or slow, a slight tremor of terror passed over the minds of the passengers, as its motion was towards the vessel, which was gliding along within a few feet of the reeling mountain. In a minute, however, we had passed out of danger, and as we viewed it from the stern of the steamer it quietly settled down again in its own bed, surrounded by the floating masses of crumbling ice that had become detached from it whilst turning over. The ground-swell caused by the passage of our steamer so close to the berg had evidently disturbed its equilibrium, though its fellow-monster stood firm as a rock, throwing off from its summit a steady cascade of green-tinted water, which poured into the sea, showing the melting process it was undergoing from the warm rays of the sun.

On coming out of the harbor two hours afterwards, Captain Graham gave these bergs a wider berth, but fired his parting guns at each of them as he passed, evidently hoping to get up another spectacle for the amusement of his passengers. It was indeed a glorious sight, and one well worth a visit to St. John to witness. The close view we had of these immense icebergs was grand in itself, but to see one turning itself leisurely was a spectacle seldom so closely witnessed even by the denizens of the shores bordering the Arctic current. They, however, resisted all further motion, and returned our gaze with a frozen stolidity, reflecting the rays of a full rising moon as they had previously those of the setting sun. The Newfoundlanders on board said they had never in their lives witnessed so grand a sight, and that in twenty years we could not have entered the harbor under such novel circumstances.

COURSE OF THE ICEBERGS.

The vast number of icebergs which are borne past the shores of Newfoundland during the spring and early summer is almost incredible, and it is believed that all the missing ocean-steamers have met their fate by coming in contact with them. About the end of May of last year, says a writer in the *Canadian Illustrated*, from Signal Hill, an eminence at the mouth of the harbor of St. John, six hundred feet high, sixty icebergs, great and small, were visible to the naked eye. "They were moving slowly southward to their grave in the Gulf Stream. There could not be a more strikingly beautiful object than one of these stately wanderers of the deep, huge and solitary, proudly sailing onwards, regardless alike of wind and tide, yet borne irresistibly along the deep-sea current. The waves that dash in foam against its sides shake not the strength of its crystal walls nor tarnish the sheen of its emerald caves. Sleet, and snow, and storm, and tempest are its congenial elements. Ice-floes come in its way, and are shivered to atoms; storms rage, but it heeds them not. Proudly it flings back the billows from its projecting crags and pinnacles, which gleam like cliffs of chalk or white marble. We might fancy that nothing could avail to destroy such a giant mass, and that it might sail on forever. But all the while the rays of the sun are playing upon its surface and penetrating its substance, and the warm breath of spring is loosening its joints and relaxing its strength. Streams begin to pour down its great sides. Huge crags drop down with sullen plunge into the ocean, awakening the echoes among the neighboring rocks and hills. Large fragments are detached, and float away in independent existence. Presently it becomes top-heavy, loses its equilibrium, and turns upon its side or reels completely over with a thundering crash, making the sea boil into foam, and causing a swell that is perceptible for miles."

DANGERS OF THEIR MOVEMENTS.

Woe to the luckless boat or vessel that may be in too close proximity when the monster makes one of these lunges. At times the berg cannot recover its equilibrium, as ours did at the mouth of St. John harbor, and continues rolling and tumbling like a huge porpoise, dropping fragment after fragment in its uncouth gambols, till the whole mass falls asunder like a wreck. These rolling icebergs, which are peculiarly dangerous, our sealers call "growlers." Or the berg may right itself by a complete immersion, and sail onward, reduced in dimensions and enveloped in mist, until it reaches the warm waters of the Gulf Stream, where it is finally dissolved. Seldom, however, are any icebergs met with farther southward than forty degrees of north latitude. Even now, when the summer warmth is so slight, it is surprising to note how rapidly the smaller bergs that drift into the bays and harbors and get aground dissolve under the influence of the sun's rays. As the summer advances, they become very brittle, and then a slight degree of violence is enough to rupture them. Should a vessel be caught between two bergs or between a floe and a berg in motion, she could no more resist the pressure than a wineglass the effect of a ball discharged from an Armstrong gun.

SIZE AND FORM OF THE BERGS.

The majority of bergs that float past are of no great size, but occasionally they are of vast dimensions. One was reported last year by several captains as half a mile in length. This might seem an exaggeration; but one is reported to have been seen by Ross, in Baffin Bay, the birthplace of the bergs, two miles and a half long, two miles wide, and fifty feet high, nine times as much of its bulk being under the water as above its surface. The weight of this iceberg was estimated at a billion and a half of tons. The visible portion of an iceberg is only about one-ninth part of the real bulk of the whole mass; so that if one be seen a hundred feet high, its lowest point may perhaps be eight hundred feet below the waves. But we are assured that bergs are frequently seen two hundred and three hundred feet above the sea, and these, if their submarine proportions sank to the maximum depth, must have reached the enormous total of two thousand seven hundred feet. The bergs are of all shapes as well as sizes, sometimes rising into pointed spires like steeples, sometimes taking the form of a conical hill, sometimes having domes and pinnacles. They have been seen bearing the forms of old abbeys afloat, with walls and buttresses of marble, and others with a striking resemblance to a crouching lion. The most general form, however, is with one high perpendicular side, the opposite side very low, and the intermediate surface forming a gradual slope. Some have been seen containing prodigious caverns, and some with hollows containing vast accumulations of snow. Their appearance is that of chalk-cliffs, with a glittering surface, and emerald-green fractures. Pools of azure blue water lie upon the surface or fall in cascades from them. From these reservoirs vessels often obtain supplies of water peculiarly sweet and agreeable. They are entirely of fresh water frozen, and when opposite Newfoundland have floated nearly two thousand miles from the place of their formation.

PERILS OF THE ARCTIC STREAM.

The scene presented during a storm by these floating ice-mountains is represented to be peculiarly grand and frightful, and woe to the luckless mariner whose vessel is caught among them. Doubtless the several ocean-steamers that have been lost since the days of the ill-fated steamer President have met their fate from contact with icebergs. That these dangers are not imaginary may be gathered from the results of this season's operations amid our ice-fields. At this date it is known that seventeen sailing-vessels and three large steamers have been wrecked and totally destroyed, and at least fifty seal-hunters have met a watery grave, and twenty or thirty besides were seriously injured. Not for half a century has such a season of peril and destruction of life and shipping been known.

APRIL FOOLS AT SEA.

The officers and crew of our steamer, numbering one hundred and five, are all Englishmen, and hence the old English custom of making April fools was carried out to its fullest extent, especially between midnight and daylight on the morning of the first. The carpenter was roused up from his sleep to stop a leak, and only discovered the trick after he had searched with his lantern in vain. The bar-keeper was aroused and sent with a bottle of brandy to the captain's office, who had been reported as suffering with colic. The surgeon of the ship also arrived simultaneously on the same errand. The chambermaid was called up to attend a lady who was reported to have fallen down the cabin steps. Captain Jeffreys, whom we had picked up at sea on a wrecked vessel, was requested to relieve Captain Petrie on the promenade-deck, who it was said had been taken suddenly ill. Some of the passengers also caught the mania and joined in the fun, one gouty old gentleman having been roused up under the conviction that the vessel had sprung a leak, that the pumps were out of order, and that the sailors were in superstitious dread of sinking because a monkey, which had been brought on board by the crew of the Grey Oak, had jumped overboard. He only discovered the "sell" when he reached the deck and met the monkey chattering on the top of a sea-chest, and heard the men on watch exchange bells with the cry of "all's well."

The game of "hanging the monkey," played on English steamers when the passengers get tired of shuffle-board, being a peculiarly nautical amusement, requiring the rolling of the vessel for its full enjoyment, may need some description to the uninitiated. A rope with a noose at the end of it is suspended from the rigging to the centre of the promenade-deck. One of the players, with his handkerchief twisted and knotted, swings himself by this noose under his arms, the other players being stationed around with handkerchiefs similarly knotted, and as the "monkey swings" each is at liberty to strike him. This sport continues until he succeeds in striking one of his tormentors, when the one struck must take his place, and thus the exhilarating game progresses until all are worn down by its fatigues.

OUR LAST TRIP.

We conclude our volume of travels with the following notes of our return from Europe in the fall of 1873, being the close of the tour which is here recorded.

We left Southampton at ten o'clock on Friday, September 26, 1873, with fine clear weather, and the prospect of a pleasant voyage. In the dock at Southampton, preparing to follow us, were two other steamers of the North German Lloyds, one bound to New York and the other to New Orleans, crowded with German emigrants, including a considerable number of Roman Catholic priests and Sisters of Charity who had been expelled from Germany. To the American, the sight of these throngs of people seeking his favored land, and leaving forever the homes of their childhood, naturally occasioned a flutter of national pride. If all who desire to come to America could procure the means, the number of steamers would have to be increased fourfold. The laboring classes of Europe are yearning to emigrate to America, especially the young and vigorous, and this feeling is increased by the large number of naturalized foreigners who are visiting their native land. Those whom they left in poverty they find still in poverty, and their sons scattered around in the barracks doing military duty. The visit of such persons to Europe with their families on a pleasure-tour among the scenes of their youth is a conclusive proof of the prosperity which they have met with in their adopted country.

HOMEWARD BOUND.

There is an immensity of pleasure in the knowledge, after six months' absence, that we are homeward bound. Every day and every hour is counted, and a reckoning of the miles passed over each day is scrupulously kept, by way of estimating the distance yet remaining. The state of the wind, and the condition of the barometer, also receive hourly attention, and impatience is evinced at the slightest detention. All are anxious to reach home, and especially to escape from "life on the ocean wave," which is much more irksome on the return than on the outward-bound voyage. Next to solitary confinement, there is nothing more wearisome than a homeward trip across the Atlantic, and nothing more trying to patience, nerves, and the stomach. To be rolled and pitched and tossed about for twelve or fourteen days and nights is a trying ordeal even for those who are proof against sea-sickness, but to the great majority it is worse than can be possibly conceived of by those who have not passed through the ordeal. Many ladies who have not strength to brave the deck and seek fresh air lie in their berths during most of this long period, afflicted with perpetual nausea, constantly irritated by the motion of the vessel. During rainy and stormy weather all must keep in the close cabin, holding fast to their seats to prevent being pitched headlong across the table. Reading or writing is next to impossible in such a moving scene, and lounging about and smoking is the only resort to kill time. Two weeks on shore is a very brief space, but on shipboard it seems like two long and weary months. At the time of writing, we have been but five days at sea, and the nine days expected to intervene before our vision shall be greeted with the sight of Cape Henry seems like a "little eternity." The Baltimore is an experienced roller, and at nights it is at times difficult to keep from pitching out of our berths, sleep being next to impossible. At meals, the soup or coffee is constantly spilling into our laps, and the plates are clashing together and dancing all manner of pirouettes on the table, apparently making an effort to jump out of their racks. This stirring scene is very trying to the stomach, too much so at times for some of our companions, who are compelled to jump and run for fresh air and immediate relief. Such is life at sea, with its dreary monotony and many discomforts, which the poets have invested with all manner of romance for the deception of landsmen. Those who follow the sea are always longing for the day to come when they can drop their anchors on shore, and sailors are becoming so scarce that half the crews of the merchant marine are little better than landsmen.

THE STEERAGE PASSENGERS.

Our steerage passengers are, as usual, nearly all victims to sea-sickness. During the first four days of the passage the decks were strewn with men, women, and children, rolled up in blankets, groaning and moaning in reckless abandon, whilst others were leaning over the bulwarks, looking as if contemplating a plunge into the sea as a relief from the misery that was harrowing their very vitals. The few who had escaped the visitation were endeavoring to arouse others to locomotion, as the surest means of recovery. One bright young German, with an accordeon in hand, who started off for a promenade, performing one of Strauss's waltzes, succeeded in getting about twenty young girls to fall in line, keeping them in motion as long as he could obtain recruits. Some would stagger along for a while, and fall back to their blankets in despair, but to those who persisted in resisting the inclination to retreat it proved a better remedy than any the doctor could furnish. To overcome sea-sickness requires nerve, determination, and pluck. It must be fought with vigor, or there is no escape so long as the cause exists.

Among the steerage passengers are several large families, having with them sufficient means for purchasing land and locating in the West. Most of the young girls, of whom there are quite a number, bright German blondes, have been sent for by their betrothed, who have gone on before them, and others by parents who have preceded them to the land of promise. There is one young soldier in Prussian uniform, with a medal decoration on his breast, who has just completed his three years' service and distinguished himself in the Franco-Prussian war. A Jesuit priest is also in the steerage, and a few old fathers and mothers who are going out to spend the remainder of their days with their children, who have long since become American citizens. Among the cabin passengers is a venerable German who has three brothers and a sister in Missouri, and also a married daughter who left him when she was twelve years of age, and who is now the mother of a family of children. His brothers are among the largest of the merchant millers of the West, having taken to the business of their parents in the old country.

HOME AGAIN.

Our journey is nearly over, and we will make the passage in fourteen days from Southampton. The voyage has been a tolerably pleasant one, though we have had an abundance of squally and rainy weather, with light but generally favorable winds. The following is the journal of our run:

	Miles.		Miles.
September 27	236	October 4	247
September 28	246	October 5	256
September 29	275	October 6	276
September 30	263	October 7	276
October 1	252	October 8	280
October 2	268	October 9	199
October 3	246	October 10	180

Total distance 3500

THE OCEAN HIGHWAY.

We give the above run of the Baltimore to show the inexperienced reader that the ocean is virtually a highway, and that navigation has been reduced to such a science that the passenger may feel as if he was traveling on a well-defined road, with its mile-stones and telegraph wires. At noon every day the precise position of the vessel is ascertained, and the number of miles run during the preceding twenty-four hours bulletined by the captain. He can point out upon his map precisely where he is, although surrounded by a vast expanse of water, to which the horizon is the only boundary. The sun seems to come up out of the sea in the morning and retire to its ocean-bed in the evening, and, although fogs and storms may intervene, we keep steadily on our course. Every day one or more ocean-steamers are passed within sight, all pursuing the same track, and, though the vessel may pitch and toss in a most uncomfortable manner, a feeling of safety is assured to all on board.

FINIS.

We are now steaming up the Chesapeake, and will soon be in sight of Fort Carroll. Although our trip has been one of unbroken pleasure and enjoyment, we return home better satisfied than ever that we have the best form of government in the world, and the only country, except perhaps England and Switzerland, in which the citizen is something more than a mere slave. "Liberty, fraternity, and equality" are unmeaning words in most European countries, and are merely used to gull the ignorant and to cover up the designs of ambitious masters. If in this correspondence we have given cause to Americans to feel more attached to their own institutions, by our descriptions of social life under monarchial rule, we shall feel that we have accomplished some good in our day and generation.

We have endeavored to give a fair and truthful statement and description of everything that has passed under our observation likely to interest and instruct the reader. In the haste of writing we have no doubt committed some minor errors, and may at times have formed and expressed opinions too hurriedly; but we have endeavored to treat every subject fairly and candidly, availing ourselves of the most reliable sources of information within our reach. We have striven also to enable the reader to see what we were viewing, and to form correct ideas of life in European countries. How far we have succeeded, the demand which greeted us upon our arrival for the publication of our "Europe viewed through American Spectacles" in book form is some assurance that we have not entirely failed in our purpose.

HINTS TO EUROPEAN TOURISTS.

We have been urged to append to our book of travel a few practical hints to those contemplating a tour of Europe, and also to give such information as we may possess as to the cost of travel. Considerable information on these points will be found in the foregoing pages, which we briefly summarize for the benefit of the inexperienced.

PATIENCE AND GOOD TEMPER.

We have met many Americans in Europe who have failed to take with them a stock of good temper and patient forbearance. They grumble and growl, and find fault with everything and everybody. They thus render themselves unhappy, and fail to enjoy the trip as those of more equable temperament always do. All tourists should go with the determination to take the world as they find it, and have a jolly good time. Although they may discover that Europe has much to learn from America, they will finally come to the conclusion that we have still much to learn from these old countries. The great majority of American tourists enjoy the sights and scenes and life in Europe, and come home wiser and better; but there are still many who fail to make good use of their opportunities.

FIREARMS.

Firearms of all kinds should be locked up carefully and left at home. The European tourist is more apt to shoot himself than to require them to shoot any one else. Leave them at home, by all means.

CLOTHING.

Those who visit Europe to enjoy travel should burden themselves with as little clothing as possible, taking only sufficient for comfort and respectable appearance. One medium-sized trunk is abundant, for the transportion of which pay by weight is required at every depot.

MONEY.

A *circular letter of credit* from a responsible house, like that of Messrs. William McKim & Co., of Baltimore, is sure never to come to grief during the journey. A *very* important consideration.

GUIDES.

Avoid guides as much as possible. Sometimes they are useful for a day or two in Rome; but gentlemen traveling without ladies can do very well without them. Not one of these guides in ten can talk understandable English, and they are sure to swindle their employers in some way before they are done with them.

LANGUAGE.

Tourists who do not deviate from the regular track of travel will find the English language spoken at nearly all the hotels and in most of the principal stores. A little knowledge of French and German is, however, very useful, and will add much to the enjoyment of travel.

GUIDE-BOOKS.

It is almost impossible to travel through Europe without guide-books, and we have no hesitation in recommending those of Baedeker as the most serviceable and reliable. Murray's London and Galignani's Paris are essential for those cities. With these books the tourist will be, in a measure, independent of hotel-keepers, commissionnaires, and guides, and if he possesses the ordinary shrewdness of the roaming American, they will save him ten times their cost in fees and extortions. It costs money to ask questions in Europe.

PASSPORTS.

Passports are no longer a necessity, except in Spain, Turkey, and Egypt. We have made two journeys over the Continent without any, and were never asked for them in any of the various countries through which we passed. They are, however, a convenience in case of meeting with any trouble, and it is well to be provided with one. To obtain a passport it is only necessary to go before a magistrate and take oath that you are a native-born or naturalized citizen of the United States, appending to the oath the age of the applicant, a statement of the stature, forehead, nose, eyes, mouth, chin, hair, and shape of the face. This should be mailed to the State Department at Washington, with stamps sufficient to pay the postage on the passport, which will be forwarded by return of mail without charge of any kind. If traveling with a family, one passport is sufficient, but their names and ages must be furnished the Department.

RAILROAD TRAVEL.

Second-class cars in all parts of Europe are good enough for any one, and the cost is about one-third less than first-class. If traveling at night, it may be well to take first-class tickets, as these cars are seldom crowded, and room can be had to stretch out and take a nap.

HOTELS.

The average hotel charges are much cheaper, in most parts of Europe, than they are in the United States, and the beds and attendance are invariably good, even in second-class establishments. By taking meals in the restaurants the cost is but little more than half the hotel charges, and generally the quality of the food is much better. The *table-d'hôte* dinners at the hotels are, to most Americans, an abomination, and are only submitted to when ladies are of the party. A tourist of moderate wants can live almost anywhere in Europe at three dollars or less per day, *without wine*. When leaving a hotel, it is next to impossible to get the bill until the carriage is at the door ready to start for the depot. There is then no time to examine its long array of items, but there is sure to be an abundance of improper charges. If time is taken to call attention to them, they are stricken off, with all manner of apologies for the *errors* of the stupid clerk.

THE COST OF TRAVEL.

The cost of travel depends altogether on the tourist, and can be made to range all the way from five dollars to ten dollars or more per diem. Three or four young men of abstemious habits can land at Queenstown, visit all the principal cities and sights of Ireland, cross to Glasgow and Edinburgh, then to London, and on to Paris; from thence to Marseilles, and down the Mediterranean on one of the coasting steamers, stopping a day at Genoa, another at Leghorn and Pisa, a few hours at Civita Vecchia, and on to Naples, visiting Vesuvius and Pompeii; thence to Rome, Florence, Venice, Verona, and Milan; thence to Como, and up the lake to Colico; across the Splügen Pass of the Alps into Switzerland, visiting all its lakes and principal cities and summer resorts, as well as climbing some of its mountains; thence to Mannheim, and down the Rhine to Cologne, and back to Paris, London, Liverpool, and home, for one thousand dollars each, or less, if very economical. The time required for such a tour would be about four months; at least we, although not as young and active as we once were, made it, in 1872, in two weeks less than four months, and had abundance of time to see everything that was worth seeing. If parties making such a trip finish up Paris and London before starting for Italy, they can strike off from Cologne to Brussels, and thence to Prague, Dresden, and Berlin, and take steamer at Bremen for home without prolonging their time, increasing their expenses, or passing twice over the same ground.

RAPID TRAVELING.

The tourist can travel as rapidly in Europe as in the United States, the trains everywhere making connections. Most Americans visiting Europe are limited in time. This was our own case during the summer of 1872. Three of our party of four were ladies. We were absent from Paris fifty-seven days, and during that time visited Marseilles, Genoa, Leghorn, Pisa, Civita Vecchia, Naples, Pompeii, Vesuvius, Rome, Florence, Venice, Verona, Milan, Lake Como, crossed the Alps, visited Coire, Zurich, Lucerne, Lake of Zurich, Fluelen, Mount Righi, Einsiedeln, Berne, Interlaken, Lausanne, Geneva, Mont Blanc. Neufchâtel, Baden-Baden, Mannheim, down the Rhine, and Cologne. We saw all that was worth seeing, and much more than most persons who spend a year in their journey. It requires, however, love of travel, and pluck and perseverance, to move so rapidly.

COOK'S TOURS.

During last summer we met several of Cook's continental parties, mostly Americans, and they invariably expressed themselves as well pleased. They were generally those who were limited in time and not overstocked with money. They had one of the Messrs. Cook accompanying them, who shielded them from all the annoyances of travel, took care of their luggage, acted as guide and general purveyor, and protected them from the horde of vultures who make a business of fleecing travelers. They had plenty of companions, and were generally the most jolly of all the tourists we met. The cost to each was undoubtedly less than it would have been if they had been traveling alone, whilst they had nothing to annoy or vex them or ruffle their temper. The party we met at Munich—mostly "Yankee school-teachers"—told us that they paid eight hundred dollars each, and were to be back in New York in one hundred and ten days from their departure.

PUBLISHED BY

J. B. LIPPINCOTT & CO., PHILADELPHIA.

DOROTHY FOX.
By LOUISA PARR, author of "Hero Carthew," etc. With numerous Illustrations. 8vo. Paper cover, 75 cents. Extra cloth, $1.25.
"Such an artist is the author of 'Dorothy Fox,' and we must thank her for a charming novel. The story is dramatically interesting, and the characters are drawn with a firm and graceful hand. The style is fresh and natural, vigorous without vulgarity, simple without mawkishness. Dorothy herself is represented as charming all hearts, and she will charm all readers. . . We wish 'Dorothy Fox' many editions."—*London Times.*
"One of the best novels of the season."—*Philadelphia Press.*
"It is admirably told, and will establish the reputation of the author among novelists."—*Albany Argus.*

JOHN THOMPSON, BLOCKHEAD,
And Companion Portraits. By LOUISA PARR, author of "Dorothy Fox." 12mo. With Frontispiece. Extra cloth. $1.75.
"Extremely well-told stories, interesting in characters and incidents, and pure and wholesome in sentiment."—*Boston Watchman and Reflector.*
"They are quite brilliant narrative sketches, worthy of the reputation established by the writer."—*Philadelphia Inquirer.*

WHY DID HE NOT DIE?
Or, The Child from the Ebräergang. From the German of AD. VON VOLCKHAUSEN. By Mrs. A. L. WISTER, translator of "Old Mam'selle's Secret," "Gold Elsie," etc. 12mo. Fine cloth. $1.75.
"Few recently published novels have received more general perusal and approval than 'Only a Girl;' and 'Why Did He Not Die?' possesses in at least an equal degree all the elements of popularity. From the beginning to the end the interest never flags, and the characters and scenes are drawn with great warmth and power."—*New York Herald.*

THE DAUGHTER OF AN EGYPTIAN KING. An Historical Romance. Translated from the German of GEORGE EBERS by HENRY REED. 12mo. Extra cloth. $1.75.
"It is a wonderful production. There have been ancient novels before now, but none, according to our recollections, so antique as this."—*New York World.*
"The plot is a most interesting one, and in its development we are given an accurate insight into the social and political life of the Egyptians of that time."—*Boston Evening Traveller.*

AT THE ALTAR.
A Romance. From the German of E. WERNER, author of "Hermann," "The Hero of the Pen," etc. By J. S. I.. 12mo. Fine cloth, ornamented. $1.50.
"A vigorous, graphic picture of German life."—*Home Journal.*
"A striking story, well conceived, powerfully written, and finely translated."—*Trade Circular.*

THROWN TOGETHER.
A Story. By FLORENCE MONTGOMERY, author of "Misunderstood," "A Very Simple Story," etc. 12mo. Fine cloth. $1.50.
"The author of 'Misunderstood' has given us another charming story of child-life. This, however, is not a book for children."—*London Athenæum.*
"A delightful story, founded upon the lives of children. There is a thread of gold in it upon which are strung many lovely sentiments. . . One cannot read this book without being better for it, or without a more tender charity being stirred up in his heart."—*Washington Daily Chronicle.*

PEMBERTON;
Or, One Hundred Years Ago. By HENRY PETERSON. 12mo. Extra cloth. $1.75.
"One of the most attractive works of fiction issued this season."—*Philadelphia Evening Bulletin.*

EXPIATION.
By Mrs. J. C. R. DORR, author of "Sybil Huntington," etc. 12mo. Cloth. $1.50.
"A work of absorbing interest."—*Boston Gazette.*
"A story of mystery, and almost tragedy, intensely portrayed."—*Washington Chronicle.*

ERMA'S ENGAGEMENT.
By the author of "Blanche Seymour." 8vo. Paper, 75 cents. Cloth, $1.25.
"Is a thoroughly readable book."—*Appletons' Journal.*
"The style is fresh and entertaining, and the various characters are sketched with great animation."—*Boston Gazette.*

"NOT PRETTY, BUT PRECIOUS,"
And other Short Stories. By Popular Writers. Illustrated. 8vo. Paper cover. 50 cents.
"Deserving of wide-spread and lasting popularity."—*Cincinnati Chronicle.*

*** For sale by all Booksellers, or will be sent by mail, postpaid, upon receipt of the price by the Publishers.

PUBLISHED BY
J. B. LIPPINCOTT & CO., PHILADELPHIA.

THE WORKS OF E. MARLITT.

THE OLD MAM'SELLE'S SECRET. From the German of E. MARLITT, author of "Gold Elsie," etc. By Mrs. A. L. WISTER. 12mo. Cloth. $1.50.

"A more charming story, and one which, having once commenced, it seemed more difficult to leave, we have not met with for many a day."—*The Round Table.*

"Is one of the most intense, concentrated, compact novels of the day. . . . And the work has the minute fidelity of the author of 'The Initials,' the dramatic unity of Reade, and the graphic power of George Eliot."—*Columbus (O.) Journal.*

GOLD ELSIE. From the German of E. MARLITT, author of "The Old Mam'selle's Secret," etc. By Mrs. A. L. WISTER. 12mo. Cloth. $1.50.

"A charming book. It absorbs your attention from the title-page to the end."—*The Home Circle.*
"A charming story charmingly told."—*Baltimore Gazette.*

COUNTESS GISELA. From the German of E. MARLITT, author of "Gold Elsie," etc. By Mrs. A. L. WISTER. 12mo. Cloth. $1.50.

"There is more dramatic power in this than in any of the stories by the same author that we have read."—*N. O. Times.*
"The best work by this author."—*Philadelphia Telegraph.*

THE LITTLE MOORLAND PRINCESS. From the German of E. MARLITT, author of "The Old Mam'selle's Secret," etc. By Mrs. A. L. WISTER. 12mo. Fine cloth. $1.75.

"By far the best foreign romance of the season."—*Philadelphia Press.*
"It is a great luxury to give one's self up to its balmy influence."—*Chicago Evening Journal.*

OVER YONDER. From the German of E. MARLITT, author of "Countess Gisela," etc. With a full-page Illustration. 8vo. Paper cover. 30 cents.

"'Over Yonder' is a charming novelette. The admirers of 'Old Mam'selle's Secret' will give it a glad reception, while those who are ignorant of the merits of this author will find in it a pleasant introduction to the works of a gifted writer."—*Daily Sentinel.*

MAGDALENA. From the German of E. MARLITT, author of "Countess Gisela," etc. And THE LONELY ONES. From the German of PAUL HEYSE. With two Illustrations. 8vo. Paper cover. 35 cents.

"We know of no way in which a leisure hour may be more pleasantly whiled away than by a perusal of either of these tales."—*Indianapolis Sentinel.*

THE WORKS OF WILHELMINE VON HILLERN.

ONLY A GIRL. A Romance. From the German of WILHELMINE VON HILLERN. By Mrs. A. L. WISTER. 12mo. Fine cloth. $2.00.

"This is a charming work, charmingly written, and no one who reads it can lay it down without feeling impressed with the superior talent of its gifted author. As a work of fiction it will compare favorably in style and interest with the best efforts of the most gifted writers of the day, while in the purity of its tone and the sound moral lesson it teaches it is equal, if not superior, to any work of the character that has for years come under our notice."—*Pittsburg Dispatch.*

"Timely, forcible, and possessing far more than ordinary merits."—*Philadelphia North American.*

BY HIS OWN MIGHT. A Romance. Translated from the German of WILHELMINE VON HILLERN, author of "Only a Girl," etc. 12mo. Fine cloth. 1.75.

"The story is well constructed. It is vivacious, intricate, and well sustained. . . . It is one of the best of the many excellent novels from the German issued by this house."—*Phila. Ev. Bulletin.*

A TWOFOLD LIFE. From the German of WILHELMINE VON HILLERN, author of "Only a Girl," etc. 12mo. With Portrait. Fine cloth. $1.75.

"A capital novel, admirably written. None will arise from its perusal without acknowledging the strength and brilliancy of its writer."—*Boston Gazette.*

*** For sale by all Booksellers, or will be sent by mail, postpaid, upon receipt of the price by the Publishers.

PUBLISHED BY

J. B. LIPPINCOTT & CO., PHILADELPHIA.

MUST IT BE?
A Romance. From the German of CARL DETLEF. By MS., translator of "By His Own Might" and "A Twofold Life." Illustrated. 8vo. Paper cover, 75 cents. Fine cloth, $1.25.

"The scene is laid in Russia, and the story is told with great vigor and picturesqueness of style. It has some charming domestic scenes, in addition to a number of intensely dramatic situations. The plot is exceedingly well managed, and the descriptions of Russian character, manners, and scenery are particularly happy. Its striking independence of treatment and its utter freedom from conventionality will prove not the least of its recommendations."—*Boston Globe.*

ARTICLE 47.
A Romance. From the French of ADOLPHE BELOT. By JAMES FURBISH. 8vo. Cloth, $1.25. Paper, 75 cents.

This highly interesting novel, on which the play of the same name is based, is a powerful story of French life, with a plot which absorbs the attention of the reader throughout.

SERGEANT ATKINS.
A Tale of Adventure. Founded on Fact. By an Officer of the United States Army. With Illustrations. 12mo. Extra cloth. $1.75.

"It is the best Indian story, because the truest to life, that we have lately seen."—*Boston Post.*

"Apart from its mere literary merits as a graphic, well-told, and spirited narrative of border experience and Indian warfare, 'Sergeant Atkins' really gives us all the facts of the Florida war which are necessary to a clear understanding of its origin, progress, and character."—*Army and Navy Journal.*

BEECHWOOD.
By Mrs. R. R. SPRINGER. 12mo. Fine cloth. $1.50.

"A book so thoroughly genuine in its utterance of feeling, so good in design and pure in style, is altogether above the average."—*Philadelphia Age.*

WHO WOULD HAVE THOUGHT IT?
A Novel. 12mo. Fine cloth. $1.75.

A bright and attractive romance, with an interesting plot, well sustained throughout.

MARIE DERVILLE.
A Story of a French Boarding-School. From the French of Madame GUIZOT DE WITT, author of "Motherless," etc. By MARY G. WELLS. 12mo. Extra cloth. $1.50.

"It is gracefully written, the moral is unexceptionably pure, the plot is very prettily evolved, and the characters are drawn with delightful naturalness."—*Philadelphia Evening Bulletin.*

UNDER LOCK AND KEY.
A Story. By T. W. SPEIGHT, author of "Brought to Light," "Foolish Margaret," etc. 12mo. Fine cloth. $1.75.

"To all who are fond of exciting situations, mystery, and ingeniously constructed plots, we unhesitatingly recommend this work."—*Boston Globe.*

THE TRUE HISTORY OF JOSHUA DAVIDSON, COMMUNIST. By the author of "A Girl of the Period." 12mo. Extra cloth. $1.50.

The book is a work of remarkable ability, and has made its mark in England, as it will, doubtless, do in this country."—*Boston Eve. Traveller.*

MAN IS LOVE.
An American Story. By ONE WHO KNOWS. 12mo. Fine cloth. $1.75.

"American home-life is faithfully depicted."—*Philadelphia Press.*

VICTOR NORMAN, RECTOR;
Or, Bessy's Husband. A Romance. By Mrs. MARY A. DENISON, author of "What Not?" "Among the Squirrels," "The Lovers' Trials," etc. 12mo. Fine cloth. $1.50.

"A charming story, by a writer who passes from pathos to humor with infinite ease and naturalness."—*Peterson's Magazine.*

THE SCAPEGOAT.
A Novel. By LEO. 12mo. Paper cover, $1.00. Cloth, $1.50.

"The book has a good deal of life and spirit in it."—*Philadelphia Age.*

"It is bold and vigorous in delineation, and equally pronounced and effective in its moral."—*St. Louis Times.*

*** For sale by all Booksellers, or will be sent by mail, postpaid, upon receipt of the price by the Publishers.

PUBLISHED BY

J. B. LIPPINCOTT & CO., PHILADELPHIA.

FERNYHURST COURT.
An Every-day Story. By the author of "Stone Edge," "Lettice Lisle," etc. With numerous Illustrations. 8vo. Paper cover. 60 cents.
"An excellent novel of English society, with many good engravings."—*Philadelphia Press.*
"An excellent story."—*Boston Journal.*

CROSS PURPOSES.
A Christmas Experience in Seven Stages. By T. C. DE LEON. With Illustrations. 16mo. Tinted paper. Extra cloth. $1.25.
"The plot is most skillfully handled, and the style is bright and sparkling."—*New York Commercial Advertiser.*

HIMSELF HIS WORST ENEMY;
Or, Philip, Duke of Wharton's Career. By ALFRED P. BROTHERHEAD. 12mo. Fine cloth. $2.00.
"The story is very entertaining and very well told."—*Boston Post.*
"The author is entitled to high praise for this creditable work."—*Philadelphia Ledger.*

THE STRUGGLE IN FERRARA.
A Story of the Reformation in Italy. By WILLIAM GILBERT, author of "De Profundis," etc. Profusely Illustrated. 8vo. Paper cover, $1.00. Cloth, $1.50.
"Few works of religious fiction compare with this in intensity, reality, and value."—*Philadelphia North American.*

"IT IS THE FASHION."
A Novel. From the German of ADELHEID VON AUER. By the translator of "Over Yonder," "Magdalena," "The Old Countess," etc. 12mo. Fine cloth. $1.50.
"It is one of the most charming books of the times, and is admirable for its practical, wise, and beautiful morality. A more natural and graceful work of its kind we never before read."—*Richmond Dispatch.*
"It is a most excellent book, abounding in pure sentiment and beautiful thought, and written in a style at once lucid, graceful, and epigrammatic."—*New York Evening Mail.*

WHAT WILL THE WORLD SAY?
A Novel of Every-day Life. By OJOS MORENOS. 12mo. Cloth. $1.50.

MARGUERITE KENT.
A Novel. By MARION W. WAYNE. 12mo. Fine cloth. $2.00.
"Is a novel of thought as well as of action, of the inner as well as of the outer life."—*New York Evening Mail.*
"The plot is novel and ingenious."—*Portland Transcript.*

IN EXILE.
A Novel. Translated from the German of W. VON ST. 12mo. Fine cloth. $2.00.
"No more interesting work of fiction has been issued for some time."—*St. Louis Democrat.*
"A feast for heart and imagination."—*Philadelphia Evening Bulletin.*

DEAD MEN'S SHOES.
A Novel. By J. R. HADERMANN, author of "Forgiven at Last." 12mo. Fine cloth. $2.00.
"One of the best novels of the season."—*Philadelphia Press.*
"One of the best novels descriptive of life at the South that has yet been published. The plot is well contrived, the characters well contrasted, and the dialogue crisp and natural."—*Baltimore Gazette.*

ISRAEL MORT, OVERMAN.
A Story of the Mine. By JOHN SAUNDERS, author of "Abel Drake's Wife." Illustrated. 16mo. Fine cloth. $1.25.
"Intensely dramatic. . . . Some of the characters are exquisitely drawn, and show the hand of a master."—*Boston Saturday Evening Gazette.*
"The book takes a strong hold on the reader's attention from the first, and the interest does not flag for a moment."—*Boston Globe.*

IN THE RAPIDS.
A Romance. By GERALD HART. 12mo. Toned Paper. Extra cloth. $1.50.
"Full of tragic interest."—*Cincinnati Gazette.*
"It is, on the whole, remarkably well told, and is particularly notable for its resemblance to those older and, in some respects, better models of composition in which the dialogue is subordinated to the narrative, and the effects are wrought out by the analytical powers of the writer."—*Baltimore Gazette.*

UNDER THE SURFACE.
A Novel. By EMMA M. CONNELLY. 12mo. Fine cloth. $1.50.

⁎* For sale by all Booksellers, or will be sent by mail, postpaid, upon receipt of the price by the Publishers.

POPULAR NOVELS
PUBLISHED BY
J. B. LIPPINCOTT & CO., PHILADELPHIA.

OUIDA'S WORKS.

TRICOTRIN.
The Story of a Waif and Stray. By "OUIDA." With Portrait of the Author from an Engraving on Steel. 12mo. Cloth. $2.00.
"The story is full of vivacity and of thrilling interest."—*Pittsburg Gazette.*
"Tricotrin is a work of absolute power, some truth, and deep interest."—*N. Y. Day Book.*
"The book abounds in beautiful sentiment, expressed in a concentrated, compact style which cannot fail to be attractive, and will be read with pleasure in every household."—*San Fran. Times.*

GRANVILLE DE VIGNE;
Or, Held in Bondage. A Tale of the Day. By "OUIDA." 12mo. Cloth. $2.00.
"This is one of the most powerful and spicy works of fiction which the present century, so prolific in light literature, has produced."

STRATHMORE;
Or, Wrought by His Own Hand. By "OUIDA." 12mo. Cloth. $2.00.
"It is a romance of the intense school, but it is written with more power, fluency, and brilliancy than the works of Miss Braddon and Mrs. Wood, while its scenes and characters are taken from high life."—*Boston Transcript.*

IDALIA.
By "OUIDA," author of "Under Two Flags," etc. 12mo. Cloth. $2.00.
"It is a story of love and hatred, of affection and jealousy, of intrigue and devotion... We think this novel will attain a wide popularity, especially among those whose refined taste enables them to appreciate and enjoy what is truly beautiful in literature."—*Albany Evening Journal.*

UNDER TWO FLAGS.
A Story of the Household and the Desert. By "OUIDA." 12mo. Cloth. $2.00.
"No one will be able to resist its fascination who once begins its perusal."—*Phila. Evening Bulletin.*
"This is probably the most popular work of 'Ouida.' It is enough of itself to establish her fame as one of the most eloquent and graphic writers of fiction now living."—*Chicago Journal of Commerce.*

PUCK.
His Vicissitudes, Adventures, Observations, Conclusions, Friendships, and Philosophies. By "OUIDA." 12mo. Cloth. $2.00.
"Its quaintness will provoke laughter, while the interest in the central character is kept up unabated." It sustains the widely-spread popularity of the author."—*Pittsburg Gazette.*

FOLLE-FARINE.
By "OUIDA," author of "Under Two Flags," etc. 12mo. Cloth. $2.00.
"'Ouida's' pen is a graphic one, and page after page of gorgeous word-painting flow from it in a smooth, melodious rhythm that often has the perfect measure of blank verse, and needs only to be broken into line. There is in it, too, the cloquence of genius."—*Philadelphia Evening Bulletin.*
"This work fully sustains the writer's previous reputation, and may be numbered among the best of her works."—*Troy Times.*

CHANDOS.
By "OUIDA," author of "Strathmore," etc. 12mo. Cloth. $2.00.
"Those who have read these two last-named brilliant works of fiction (Granville de Vigne and Strathmore) will be sure to read *Chandos*. It is characterized by the same gorgeous coloring of style and somewhat exaggerated portraiture of scenes and characters, but it is a story of surprising power and interest."—*Pittsburg Evening Chronicle.*

PASCAREL.
By "OUIDA," author of "Strathmore," "Idalia," "Under Two Flags," "Tricotrin," etc. 12mo. Cloth. $2.00.
"A charming novel, far in advance of 'Ouida's' earlier novels."—*London Athenæum.*
"It is masterly as a romance."—*London Spectator.*

A LEAF IN THE STORM,
And other Novelettes. By "OUIDA." Two Illustrations. 8vo. Paper cover. 50 cents.
"Those who look upon light literature as an art will read these tales with pleasure and satisfaction."—*Baltimore Gazette.*

CECIL CASTLEMAINE'S GAGE,
And other Stories. By "OUIDA." 12mo. Cloth. $1.75.

RANDOLPH GORDON,
And other Stories. By "OUIDA." 12mo. Cloth. $1.75.

BEATRICE BOVILLE,
And other Stories. By "OUIDA." 12mo. Cloth. $1.75.
"The many works already in print by this versatile authoress have established her reputation as a novelist, and these short stories contribute largely to the stock of pleasing narratives and adventures alive to the memory of all who are given to romance and fiction."—*New Haven Journal.*

*** For sale by all Booksellers, or will be sent by mail, postpaid, upon receipt of the price by the Publishers.

CHAMBERS'S BOOK OF DAYS,

A Miscellany of Popular Antiquities in connection with the Calendar.

INCLUDING

ANECDOTE, BIOGRAPHY AND HISTORY, CURIOSITIES OF LITERATURE, AND ODDITIES OF HUMAN LIFE AND CHARACTER.

REVISED UNDER THE SUPERVISION OF ROBERT CHAMBERS.

TWO VOLUMES ROYAL 8vo.

Price per Set: Cloth, $8; *Sheep,* $9.50; *Half Calf, Gilt, Extra,* $12.

THIS WORK CONSISTS OF—

I. *Matters Connected with the Church Calendar.*
II. *Phenomena Connected with the Seasonal Changes.*
III. *Folk-Lore of the United Kingdom:* namely, Popular Notions and Observances connected with Times and Seasons.
IV. *Notable Events, Biographies and Anecdotes Connected with the Days of the Year.*
V. *Articles of Popular Archæology,* of an entertaining character, tending to illustrate the Progress of Civilization, Manners, Literature and Ideas.
VI. *Curious Fugitive Pieces and Inedited Pieces.*

The work is printed in a new, elegant and readable type, and illustrated with an abundance of Wood Engravings.

☞ For sale by Booksellers generally, or sent free of charge on receipt of the price by

J. B. LIPPINCOTT & CO., Publishers,
715 and 717 Market St., Philadelphia.

NOW BEING ISSUED.

ANCIENT CLASSICS

FOR

ENGLISH READERS.

A SERIES OF BI-MONTHLY VOLUMES.

Small 12mo. Fine Cloth. $1 each.

Edited by REV. W. LUCAS COLLINS.

Now Ready.

1. HOMER'S ILIAD.—2. HOMER'S ODYSSEY.—3. HERODOTUS.—4. CÆSAR.—5. VIRGIL.—6. HORACE.—7. ÆSCHYLUS.—8. XENOPHON.—9. CICERO.—10. SOPHOCLES.—11. PLINY.—12. EURIPIDES.—13. JUVENAL.—14. ARISTOPHANES.

OTHER VOLUMES IN PREPARATION.

The aim of the present series will be to explain, sufficiently for general readers, who these great writers were, and what they wrote: to give, wherever possible, some connected outline of the story which they tell, or the facts which they record, checked by the results of modern investigations; to present some of their most striking passages in approved English translations, and to illustrate them generally from modern writers; to serve, in short, as a popular retrospect of the chief literature of Greece and Rome.

"Each successive issue only adds to our appreciation of the learning and skill with which this admirable enterprise of bringing the best classics within easy reach of English readers is conducted."—*New York Independent.*
"One of the most ingenious and successful literary enterprises of the day."—*Every Saturday.*

☞ For sale by all Booksellers, or will be sent by mail, postpaid, on receipt of the price by

J. B. LIPPINCOTT & CO., Publishers,
715 and 717 Market St., Philadelphia.

THE CHEAP EDITION OF

THE ALDINE SERIES

OF THE

BRITISH POETS.

This Series of the British Poets, in 52 volumes, originally projected by the late Mr. Pickering, has long been acknowledged to be the best hitherto published. The present proprietors have subjected the texts, memoirs and notes to a strict revision wherever any improvement was possible, and they now lay this complete and correct edition before the public at such a price and in such a manner as to place it within the reach of all classes.

EACH WORK SOLD SEPARATELY.

Bound in Ornamented Cloth, 75 Cts. per vol.

THE SERIES CONTAINS THE FOLLOWING POETS:

Akenside, 1 vol. Beattie, 1 vol. Burns, 3 vols. Butler, 2 vols. Chaucer, 6 vols. Churchill, 3 vols. Collins, 1 vol. Cowper, 3 vols. Dryden, 5 vols. Falconer, 1 vol. Goldsmith, 1 vol. Gray, 1 vol. Kirke White, 1 vol. Milton, Memoir by Mitford, 3 vols. Parnel, 1 vol. Pope, 3 vols. Prior, 2 vols. Shakespeare, 1 vol. Spenser, 5 vols. Surrey, 1 vol. Swift, 3 vols. Thomson, 2 vols. Wyatt, 1 vol. Young, 2 vols.

☞ For sale by all Booksellers, or will be sent by mail, postpaid, on receipt of the price by

J. B. LIPPINCOTT & CO., Publishers,
715 and 717 Market St., Philadelphia.

NOW COMPLETE.

A NEW AND REVISED EDITION

OF

Chambers's Miscellany

OF

INSTRUCTIVE AND ENTERTAINING TRACTS.

PROFUSELY ILLUSTRATED.

Complete in Twenty 12mo Volumes.

Neatly bound in boards. Only 50 cents per volume.
Two volumes bound in one volume,
fine cloth, $1.25.

This series of volumes covers a wide range of subjects—

FICTION, POETRY, HISTORY,
TRAVEL AND ADVENTURE,
POPULAR SCIENCE, BIOGRAPHY,
THE MECHANIC ARTS—

And a variety of pleasing and instructive topics are successively presented, and are so arranged as to gratify the fancy and suit the comprehension of every class of readers.

EACH VOLUME SOLD SEPARATELY.

☞ For sale by all Booksellers, or will be sent by mail, postpaid, on receipt of the price by

J. B. LIPPINCOTT & CO., Publishers,
715 and 717 Market St., Philadelphia.

Novels and Novelettes
By "OUIDA."

Novels. 12mo. Cloth. Price, $2 each.

TRICOTRIN; with Portrait of the Author from Steel.
CHANDOS.—GRANVILLE DE VIGNE.—STRATHMORE.—PUCK.—UNDER TWO FLAGS.—IDALIA.—FOLLE-FARINE.—PASCAREL.

These Novels are universally acknowledged to be among the most powerful and fascinating works of fiction which the present century, so prolific in light reading, has produced.

Novelettes. 12mo. Cloth. Price, $1.75.

Each of these Volumes contains a Selection of "Ouida's" Popular Tales and Stories.

First Series. CECIL CASTLEMAINE'S GAGE.
Second Series. RANDOLPH GORDON.
Third Series. BEATRICE BOVILLE.
Fourth Series. A LEAF IN THE STORM. Illustrated. 8vo. Paper. 50 cents.

"Ouida's pen is a graphic one, and page after page of gorgeous word-painting flows from it in a smooth, melodious rhythm that often has the perfect measure of blank verse, and needs only to be broken into lines."—*Phila. Eve. Bulletin.*

☞ For sale by all Booksellers, or will be sent by mail, postpaid, on receipt of the price by

J. B. LIPPINCOTT & CO., Publishers,
715 and 717 Market St., Philadelphia.

The most Charming Works of Fiction of the Present Day.

THE WORKS OF E. MARLITT.

After the German, by Mrs. A. L. Wister.
16mo. Extra Cloth. Price, $1.50 each.

THE OLD MAM'SELLE'S SECRET.
"A more charming story, and one which, having once commenced, it seemed more difficult to leave, we have not met with for many a day."—*The Round Table.*

GOLD ELSIE.
"'Gold Elsie' is one of the loveliest heroines ever introduced to the public."—*Boston Advertiser.*

COUNTESS GISELA.
"The author of 'The Old Mam'selle's Secret,' one of the most charming stories ever written, has already won an extended reputation in this country as a faithful delineator of German life, and the present work will doubtless find many delighted readers."—*N. Y. Times.*

THE LITTLE MOORLAND PRINCESS.
12mo. Fine Cloth. Price, $1.75.
"The story is very fresh and charming, and the central figure lovingly and delicately drawn."—*N. Y. Ev. Mail.*

After the German, by Mrs. B. Elgard.

OVER YONDER.
With Frontispiece. 8vo. Paper. 30 cents.

MAGDALENA.
With Two Illustrations. 8vo. Paper. 35 cents.
"Both of these stories are exceedingly clever and entertaining."—*Richmond Enquirer.*

☞ For sale by all Booksellers, or will be sent by mail, postpaid, on receipt of the price by

J. B. LIPPINCOTT & CO., Publishers,
715 and 717 Market St., Philadelphia.

THE "WIDE, WIDE WORLD" SERIES.

THE WORKS OF
THE MISSES WARNER.

THE WIDE, WIDE WORLD. 12mo. Two Steel Plates. 694 pages. Fine Cloth. $1.75.

QUEECHY. 12mo. Two Illustrations. 806 pages. Fine Cloth. $1.75.

THE HILLS OF THE SHATEMUC. 12mo. 516 pages. Fine Cloth. $1.75.

MY BROTHER'S KEEPER. 12mo. 385 pages. Fine Cloth. $1.50.

DOLLARS AND CENTS. 12mo. 515 pages. Fine Cloth. $1.75.

DAISY. Two Volumes. 12mo. 815 pages. Fine Cloth. $1.75 per vol.

SAY AND SEAL. Two Volumes. 12mo. 1013 pages. Fine Cloth. $1.50 per vol.

☞ Complete sets of the above volumes bound in uniform style can be obtained, put up in neat boxes.

The sale of thousands of the above volumes attests their popularity. They are stories of unusual interest, remarkably elevated and natural in tone and sentiment, full of refined and healthy thought, and exhibiting an intimate and accurate knowledge of human nature.

☞ For sale by all Booksellers, or will be sent by mail, postpaid, on receipt of the price by

J. B. LIPPINCOTT & CO., Publishers,
715 and 717 Market St., Philadelphia.

Three Powerful Romances
By WILHELMINE VON HILLERN.

I.
ONLY A GIRL.
FROM THE GERMAN, BY MRS. A. L. WISTER.
12mo. Fine Cloth. $2.
"This is a charming work, charmingly written, and no one who reads it can lay it down without feeling impressed with the superior talent of its gifted author."

II.
BY HIS OWN MIGHT.
From the German, by M. S.
12mo. Fine Cloth. $1.75.
"A story of intense interest, well wrought."—*Boston Commonwealth.*

III.
A TWO-FOLD LIFE.
From the German, by M. S.
12mo. Fine Cloth.

TWO CHARMING NOVELS
BY THE AUTHOR OF "THE INITIALS."

I.—QUITS. By the BARONESS TAUTPHŒUS. 12mo. Fine Cloth. $1.75.

II.—AT ODDS. By the BARONESS TAUTPHŒUS. 12mo. Fine Cloth. $1.75.

☞ For sale by all Booksellers, or will be sent by mail, postpaid, on receipt of the price by

J. B. LIPPINCOTT & CO., Publishers,
715 and 717 Market St., Philadelphia.

"A LIBRARY IN ITSELF."

Chambers's Encyclopædia,

A DICTIONARY OF UNIVERSAL KNOWLEDGE for the PEOPLE.

REVISED EDITION OF 1872.

ILLUSTRATED WITH

NUMEROUS WOOD ENGRAVINGS AND MAPS.

In Ten Volumes Royal Octavo.

BOUND IN VARIOUS STYLES.

The Publishers have the pleasure of announcing that they have recently concluded the revision of CHAMBERS'S ENCYCLOPÆDIA, and that the work is now complete in TEN ROYAL OCTAVO VOLUMES, of over 800 pages each, illustrated with about 4000 engravings and accompanied by FORTY MAPS; the whole, it is believed, forming the most complete work of reference extant.

The design of this work, as explained in the Notice prefixed to the first volume, is that of a *Dictionary of Universal Knowledge for the People*—not a mere collection of elaborate treatises in alphabetical order, but a work to be readily consulted as a *Dictionary* on every subject on which people generally require some distinct information. The editors confidently point to the Ten volumes of which it is composed as forming the most *Comprehensive*—as it certainly is the *Cheapest—Encyclopædia* ever issued in the English language.

☞ Descriptive Circulars mailed on application. Agents Wanted.

J. B. LIPPINCOTT & CO., Publishers,
715 and 717 Market St., Philadelphia.

"No diligent reader will willingly be without a copy."

Lippincott's Pronouncing Dictionary

OF

BIOGRAPHY AND MYTHOLOGY,

CONTAINING

Memoirs of the Eminent Persons of all Ages and Countries, and Accounts of the various subjects of the Norse, Hindoo and Classic Mythologies, with the Pronunciation of their Names in the Different Languages in which they occur.

By J. THOMAS, A.M., M.D.

Complete in One Imp. 8vo Volume of 2348 pages. Bound in Sheep. $15.
Complete in Two Vols. Imperial 8vo. Toned paper. Price per vol.: Fine Cloth, $11; Sheep, $12.

This invaluable work embraces the following peculiar features in an eminent degree:

I. GREAT COMPLETENESS AND CONCISENESS IN THE BIOGRAPHICAL SKETCHES.
II. SUCCINCT BUT COMPREHENSIVE ACCOUNTS OF ALL THE MORE INTERESTING SUBJECTS OF MYTHOLOGY.
III. A LOGICAL SYSTEM OF ORTHOGRAPHY.
IV. THE ACCURATE PRONUNCIATION OF THE NAMES.
V. FULL BIBLIOGRAPHICAL REFERENCES.

"Lippincott's Biographical Dictionary, according to the unanimous opinion of distinguished scholars, is the best work of the kind ever published."—*Phila. Ledger.*

☞ For Sale by all Booksellers. Descriptive Circulars mailed on application.

J. B. LIPPINCOTT & CO., Publishers,
715 and 717 Market St., Philadelphia.

An Indispensable Work in every Library and Family.

LIPPINCOTT'S
PRONOUNCING
Gazetteer of the World,
OR
GEOGRAPHICAL DICTIONARY,

GIVING A

DESCRIPTION OF NEARLY 100,000 PLACES,

WITH THE

CORRECT PRONUNCIATION OF THEIR NAMES,

With an Appendix, containing nearly 10,000 Additional Notices.

EDITED BY

J. THOMAS, M.D., and T. BALDWIN.

Together with a Table of Populations from the Latest Census Returns.

In One Imperial Octavo Volume of 2300 pages. Bound in Sheep. Price $10.

"A work of immense labor, very wisely directed."—PROF. C. A. GOODRICH, *Co-Editor of the New Edition of Webster's "Unabridged Dictionary."*

"I consider it a desideratum alike to the scholar and the man of business, as well as a very valuable contribution to our American literature."—*From* ELIPHALET NOTT, D.D., LL.D., *President of Union College.*

☞ For Sale by Booksellers generally, or will be sent free upon receipt of the price by

J. B. LIPPINCOTT & CO., Publishers,
715 and 717 Market St., Philadelphia.

AN INVALUABLE WORK.

A CRITICAL DICTIONARY
OF
ENGLISH LITERATURE
AND
British and American Authors,

LIVING AND DECEASED,

From the Earliest Accounts to the Latter Half of the Nineteenth Century. Containing over Forty-six Thousand Articles (Authors), with Forty Indexes of Subjects.

By S. AUSTIN ALLIBONE.

Complete in Three Volumes. Imperial 8vo. 3140 pages. Price per vol.: Extra Cloth, $7.50; Library Sheep, $8.50; Half Turkey, $9.50.

OPINIONS OF THE PRESS.

"All things considered, the most remarkable literary work ever executed by one man."—*American Literary Gazette.*
"It may be safely said that it is the most valuable and comprehensive manual of English literature yet compiled."—*N. Y. Evening Post.*
"As a bibliographical work it is simply priceless."—*N. Y. Independent.*
"There is nothing to compare with it in any language."—*N. Y. Observer.*
"We are proud that it is the work of an American. We earnestly recommend every reader, student and teacher, and, we had almost said, every patriotic citizen, to secure a copy of Allibone's Dictionary of Authors."—*Boston Ev. Transcript.*
"As the work of a single man, it is one of the wonders of literary industry. EVERY MAN WHO EVER OWNED AN ENGLISH BOOK, OR EVER MEANS TO OWN ONE, WILL FIND SOMETHING HERE TO HIS PURPOSE."—*Atlantic Monthly.*

☞ For Sale by all Booksellers. Descriptive Circulars mailed on application.

J. B. LIPPINCOTT & CO., Publishers,
715 and 717 Market St., Philadelphia.

www.ingramcontent.com/pod-product-compliance
Lightning Source LLC
Chambersburg PA
CBHW030753230426
43667CB00007B/954